# Autism Spectrum Disorders: Pathogenesis, Diagnosis and Treatment

# Autism Spectrum Disorders: Pathogenesis, Diagnosis and Treatment

Editor: Harison Bailey

MURPHY & MOORE
www.murphy-moorepublishing.com

www.murphy-moorepublishing.com

MURPHY & MOORE

**Cataloging-in-Publication Data**

Autism spectrum disorders : pathogenesis, diagnosis and treatment / edited by Harison Bailey.
p. cm.
Includes bibliographical references and index.
ISBN 978-1-63987-066-0
1. Autism spectrum disorders. 2. Autism spectrum disorders--Pathogenesis. 3. Autism spectrum disorders--Diagnosis.
4. Autism spectrum disorders--Treatment. 5. Developmental disabilities. I. Bailey, Harison.
RC553.A88 A983 2022
616.858 82--dc23



Murphy & Moore Publishing,
1 Rockefeller Plaza,
New York City, NY 10020, USA

ISBN 978-1-63987-066-0 (Hardback)

# Contents

# Preface

I am honored to present to you this unique book which encompasses the most up-to-date data in the field. I was extremely pleased to get this opportunity of editing the work of experts from across the globe. I have also written papers in this field and researched the various aspects revolving around the progress of the discipline. I have tried to unify my knowledge along with that of stalwarts from every corner of the world, to produce a text which not only benefits the readers but also facilitates the growth of the field.

Autism spectrum disorders (ASDs) is a broad term used for a wide range of neurodevelopmental disorders. Individuals that have ASD display restricted and repetitive patterns of interests or behavior, and experience difficulties with social interaction and communication. Many children are not diagnosed with the symptoms of ASD until they are older. The severity of symptoms varies in autism spectrum disorders. Mildly affected people experience some difficulty and are able to function independently. Those who have moderate to severe symptoms need more support in their lives. The exact cause of ASDs is not known but the risk factors may involve genetic conditions, a family history of autism and having an older parent. The objective of this book is to give a general view of the autism spectrum disorders. It provides significant information of this discipline to help develop a good understanding of the pathogenesis and diagnosis of autism spectrum disorders. This book will prove to be immensely beneficial to students and researchers in this field.

Finally, I would like to thank all the contributing authors for their valuable time and contributions. This book would not have been possible without their efforts. I would also like to thank my friends and family for their constant support.

**Editor**

# 1

# GABAergic signaling as therapeutic target for autism spectrum disorders

**Giada Cellot[1] and Enrico Cherubini[1,2]***

[1] Department of Neuroscience, Scuola Internazionale Superiore di Studi Avanzati, Trieste, Italy
[2] European Brain Research Institute, Rome, Italy

**Edited by:**
*Yuri Bozzi, University of Trento, Italy*

**Reviewed by:**
*Yehezkel Ben-Ari, Institut National de la Santé et de la Recherche Médicale, France*
*Laura Cancedda, Istituto Italiano di Tecnologia, Italy*

***Correspondence:**
*Enrico Cherubini, Department of Neuroscience, Scuola Internazionale Superiore di Studi Avanzati (SISSA), Via Bonomea 265, Trieste 34136, Italy
e-mail: cher@sissa.it*

γ-Aminobutyric acid (GABA), the main inhibitory neurotransmitter in the adult brain, early in postnatal life exerts a depolarizing and excitatory action. This depends on accumulation of chloride inside the cell via the cation–chloride importer NKCC1, being the expression of the chloride exporter KCC2 very low at birth. The developmentally regulated expression of KCC2 results in extrusion of chloride with age and a shift of GABA from the depolarizing to the hyperpolarizing direction. The depolarizing action of GABA leads to intracellular calcium rise through voltage-dependent calcium channels and/or *N*-methyl-D-aspartate receptors. GABA-mediated calcium signals regulate a variety of developmental processes from cell proliferation migration, differentiation, synapse maturation, and neuronal wiring. Therefore, it is not surprising that some forms of neuro-developmental disorders such as autism spectrum disorders (ASDs) are associated with alterations of GABAergic signaling and impairment of the excitatory/inhibitory balance in selective neuronal circuits. In this review, we will discuss how changes of $GABA_A$-mediated neurotransmission affect several forms of ASDs including the Fragile X, the Angelman, and Rett syndromes. Then, we will describe various animal models of ASDs with GABAergic dysfunctions, highlighting their behavioral deficits and the possibility to rescue them by targeting selective components of the GABAergic synapse. In particular, we will discuss how in some cases, reverting the polarity of GABA responses from the depolarizing to the hyperpolarizing direction with the diuretic bumetanide, a selective blocker of NKCC1, may have beneficial effects on ASDs, thus opening new therapeutic perspectives for the treatment of these devastating disorders.

**Keywords: autism spectrum disorders, GABA receptors, bumetanide, neuro-developmental disorders, excitatory inhibitory balance**

Autism comprises a heterogeneous group of neuro-developmental disorders known as autism spectrum disorders (ASDs) characterized by deficits in verbal and non-verbal communication, social interaction, restricted interests, and stereotyped behavior (1). The incidence of ASDs (20–60/10000 children) has dramatically increased over the past decades because of the improvement of diagnostic criteria and increased attention of medical community (2). Complications arising from later age pregnancies and from excessive exposure of fetuses with a genetic vulnerable background to environmental factors (i.e., toxic agents) may also contribute to the higher incidence of these disorders in recent years.

In spite different etiologies, ASDs share overlapping symptoms, indicating common deficits in some neuro-developmental pathways. One of these involves the γ-aminobutyric acid $(GABA)_A$-mediated neurotransmission, known to play a crucial role in synaptic tuning and neuronal wiring in late pre and early postnatal days (3). Studies from animal models of ASDs indicate that a dysfunction in GABAergic signaling within particular neuronal circuits may account for most of the clinical symptoms found in autistic patients. The high co-morbidity of ASDs with epilepsy (30% of cases) further confirms this issue (4).

γ-Aminobutyric acid is the main inhibitory neurotransmitter in the adult mammalian brain. It inhibits neuronal firing by activating two different classes of receptors, $GABA_A$ and $GABA_B$. $GABA_A$ receptors are integral ion channels while $GABA_B$ receptors are coupled to ion channels via guanine nucleotide-binding proteins and second messengers. The opening of $GABA_A$ receptors causes a net influx of chloride with consequent membrane hyperpolarization and reduction of cell firing. However, in particular conditions and during brain maturation the intracellular chloride concentration $[Cl^-]_i$ rises in such a way that the opening of anion channels by GABA produces a chloride efflux and a membrane depolarization that through the activation of a persistent non-inactivating sodium conductance (5) may reach the threshold for action potential generation (6, 7). Generally, low $[Cl^-]_i$ facilitates GABA-mediated inhibition, whereas high $[Cl^-]_i$ facilitates GABA-mediated excitation. The mechanisms underlying chloride accumulation inside immature neurons, start to be unveiled with a different efficacy of chloride co-transporters such as NKCC1 and KCC2, which import and export chloride, respectively. Before and immediately after birth, chloride accumulates inside the cell due to a reduced expression of the cation–chloride exporter KCC2. Later in development, the intracellular chloride concentration decreases thanks to the up-regulation of KCC2 (8–10). GABA-induced membrane depolarization facilitates calcium entry via voltage-dependent calcium channels and *N*-methyl-D-aspartate

(NMDA) receptors. Calcium rise leads to the activation of second messengers involved in a variety of developmental processes from cell migration and differentiation to synaptogenesis and circuit formation (11).

How GABA orchestrates these processes has been extensively reported (3, 12–14). GABAergic signals operate with multiple modalities at different developmental stages before glutamatergic ones (15). At the beginning, GABA works as a trophic factor, modulating neuronal migration and maturation (16). GABA receptors are expressed in neuronal progenitors before the establishment of synaptic contacts (17). At this stage, the receptors work as sensors for GABA present in the extracellular space after its release in a calcium- and SNARE-independent way from growth cones and astrocytes (18). The absence of an efficient uptake system enables this neurotransmitter to accumulate in the extracellular space and to reach a concentration sufficient to exert its depolarizing and excitatory effects on distal neurons. Blocking the depolarizing action *in utero* heavily affects migration and circuit formation (11, 19, 20).

At later developmental stages, when synapses are formed, the release of GABA and glutamate, generate a primitive form of network-driven oscillatory events known as giant depolarizing potentials (GDPs). GDPs are characterized by recurrent membrane depolarizations (lasting several hundred of milliseconds) that give rise to bursts of action potentials, separated by quiescent periods. This network activity thought to be the *in vitro* counterpart of "sharp waves" recorded in pups during immobility periods, sleep, and feeding (21), is reminiscent of the "trace discontinue" first described by Dreyfus-Brisac in the electroencephalogram of immature babies and characterized by intermittent bursts separated by periods of virtually complete suppression of activity (22).

In analogy with the synchronized activity generated in the disinhibited hippocampus by $GABA_A$ receptor antagonists (23), GDPs emerge when a sufficient number of cells fire and the excitability of the network attains a certain threshold within a restricted temporal window (24). Although the entire hippocampus possesses the capacity to generate GDPs, for its extensive glutamatergic connections via recurrent collaterals, the CA3 area is particularly well equipped to generate synchronized activity. Furthermore, this area is able to initiate, upon membrane depolarization, intrinsic bursts which, by virtue of their spontaneous discharges and large spike output can drive other neurons to fire (25, 26). Burst firing is facilitated by a persistent slow sodium current (27) and by a tonic $GABA_A$-mediated conductance generated by the activation of extrasynaptic $GABA_A$ receptors by "ambient" GABA whose depolarizing action would bring the membrane to the voltage window for activation of voltage-dependent sodium and calcium channels (28). Intrinsic bursting activity is boosted by the low expression of Kv7.2 and Kv7.3 channels responsible for the non-inactivating, low-threshold M current ($I_M$), which in adulthood controls spike after-depolarization and burst generation (29). The low density of $I_M$ at birth contributes to produce intrinsic bursts that, in comparison with those observed in adults, are more robust, last longer and recur more regularly (25). GDPs-associated calcium transients act as coincident detector signals for enhancing synaptic efficacy at emerging GABAergic (30) and glutamatergic synapses (31). Therefore, this early synchronized activity is fundamental for synaptic wiring and refinement of local neuronal circuits according to the Hebbian rule that "neurons that fire together wire together."

$\gamma$-Aminobutyric acid is released from GABAergic interneurons that constitute a very heterogeneous group of cells, differentially classified according to their morphology, biophysical properties, molecular expression profile, and connectivity (32). These cells, mainly derived from the medial and caudal ganglionic eminences, undergo their final mitosis in these regions prior to their tangential migration into the cortical plate. The migration process, supposed to be calcium dependent, is regulated by a sequence of well-orchestrated processes involving guidance cues, neurotransmitter receptors (NMDA, $GABA_A$ receptors) and voltage-dependent calcium channels (33, 34).

GABAergic interneurons not only exert a powerful control on network excitability but, in spite of their relatively low number (10–15% of the entire neuronal population), are able to synchronize a large number of principal cells giving rise to coherent oscillations, which support different behavioral states of the animals and high cognitive tasks (35).

Altogether, these observations point to GABA as one of the major players in the early assembly and formation of neuronal circuits in the developing brain. Therefore, it is not surprising that dysfunctions of GABAergic circuits have been implicated in various neuro-developmental and psychiatric disorders such as schizophrenia, autism, and epilepsy.

## GABAergic DYSFUNCTIONS IN THE BRAIN OF ASD PATIENTS

The high frequency of epileptiform activity and the altered brain rhythms detected in the EEG of ASDs patients suggest a dysfunction of GABAergic transmission and an imbalance between excitation and inhibition (E/I) in local circuits involved in sensory, mnemonic, social, and emotional processes. However, as summarized in **Table 1**, more direct evidence in favor of a GABAergic dysfunction in ASDs derives from:

a. Genetic observations
b. *In vitro* analysis of post-mortem brain tissues
c. *In vivo* studies on patients affected mainly by idiopathic forms of ASDs.

It is clear from the **Table 1** that most of cases are from juvenile and adult patients. This can be attributed to difficulties in obtained post-mortem material from young children and to perform complex *in vivo* examinations such as positron emission tomography (PET) and single photon emission computed tomography (SPECT) in children of pediatric age. However, we cannot exclude that the same alterations are already present at early stages of development.

### GENETIC OBSERVATIONS

The involvement of $GABA_A$ receptors in ASDs was provided by genetic studies that have revealed submicroscopic abnormalities known as "copy-number variations" in chromosomal loci 15q11–q13, which contains a number of genes encoding for $GABA_A$ receptor subunits (54). These loci can be affected either directly by

**Table 1 | Alterations of GABAergic signaling in patients with idiopathic forms of autism and Rett syndrome.**

| Clinical phenotype | Alterations of GABAergic signaling | Age (years) | Reference |
|---|---|---|---|
| **GENETIC OBSERVATIONS** | | | |
| Idiopathic autism | Linkage disequilibrium in *GABRB3* | 7.6 ± 6.2 | (36, 37) |
| Idiopathic autism | Altered gene expression in interneurons | Not specified | (38) |
| ***IN VITRO* ANALYSIS OF POST-MORTEM BRAIN TISSUES** | | | |
| Idiopathic autism | Reduction in the density of $GABA_A$, $GABA_B$ receptors and benzodiazepine binding sites in the anterior cingulate cortex | 19/43 | (39) |
| Idiopathic autism | Reduction in the density of $GABA_B$ receptors cingulate cortex and fusiform gyrus | 19/43 | (40) |
| Idiopathic autism | Reduction in 3[H]flunitrazepam labeled benzodiazepines binding sites in the hippocampus | 16/22 | (41) |
| Idiopathic autism | Decreased number of GABAergic Purkinje cells in cerebellum | 13/54 | (42) |
| Idiopathic autism | Reduced level of GAD65 and GAD67 in Purkinje cells of cerebellar and parietal cortices | 19/30 | (43) |
| Idiopathic autism | Decreased GAD67 mRNA levels in cerebellar Purkinje cells | 16/30 | (44) |
| Idiopathic autism | Decreased GAD65 mRNA levels in cerebellar dentate nuclei | 16/30 | (45) |
| Idiopathic autism | Increased expression of GABAergic interneurons expressing calcium-binding proteins in the hippocampus | 13/63 | (46) |
| Rett syndrome | Disruption in the inhibitory architecture of the cell mini-columns | 14.4 ± 4 | (47) |
| ***IN VIVO* STUDIES** | | | |
| Idiopathic autism | Reduction of GABA concentration in the frontal lobe | 2/12 | (48) |
| Idiopathic autism | Reduced GABA levels in the perisylvian region of the left hemisphere | 12.4 ± 5.2 | (49) |
| Idiopathic autism | Reduced expression of $GABA_A$ receptors in the superior and medial frontal cortex | 7.3 ± 3.5 | (50) |
| Rett syndrome | Reduced $GABA_A$ receptor density in fronto-temporal cortex | 27/41 | (51) |
| Idiopathic autism | Significant reduction of α5 $GABA_A$ receptor subunits in limbic areas | 34/43 | (52) |
| Rett syndrome | Reduced KCC2/NKCC1 ratio in the cerebrospinal fluid | 0/19 | (53) |

*Numbers refer to mean (usually ± SEM) or range values.*

single point mutations or indirectly by epigenetic factors. Potential gene targets include *GABRB3*, *GABRA5*, and *GABRG3*, encoding for β3, α5, and γ3 subunits containing $GABA_A$ receptors, respectively (36, 37). Systematic changes in $GABA_A$ receptor subunit expression were found in the superior frontal cortex, parietal cortex, and cerebellum of autistic subjects. In addition, autism-related genes have been found to be expressed mainly in GABAergic interneurons (38).

### *IN VITRO* ANALYSIS OF POST-MORTEM BRAIN TISSUES

Post-mortem analysis on brain tissues from ASD patients as well as genetic and *in vivo* studies have largely contributed to unveil the impact of GABAergic signaling in these disorders. Thus, as compared to controls, a significant reduction in the density of $GABA_A$, $GABA_B$ receptors, and benzodiazepine binding sites was detected in the supra and infragranular layers of the anterior cingulate cortex (known to participate in a variety of processes including socio-emotional behavior and other associative functions via prefrontal cortex connectivity) in brain samples from autistic subjects (39, 40). A reduction of $^3$[H]muscimol labeled $GABA_A$ receptors and 3[H]flunitrazepam labeled benzodiazepines binding sites was found also in the hippocampus (41, 55). Neuropathological studies from the cerebellum of individuals with ASDs have demonstrated that GABAergic Purkinje cells are particularly vulnerable since their number appears considerably reduced respect to controls (42, 56, 57). This effect was found to be associated with reduced levels of mRNA encoding for glutamic acid decarboxylase (GAD) 65 and 67, rate limiting enzymes responsible for the conversion of glutamate to GABA (43–45, 58). In contrast with Purkinje cells, enhanced levels of mRNA for GAD67 were found in stellate cells, a subtype of interneuron innervating Purkinje cells (43). Interestingly, pathological studies of brains of individual affected by autism demonstrated an increased expression of GABAergic interneurons expressing calcium-binding proteins such as calbindin-, calretinin-, and parvalbumin in the hippocampal formation (46). Since these interneurons are capable of buffering calcium, the intracellular messenger that controls several transduction pathways, an alteration of calcium signaling may have dramatic consequences on neuronal functions and dynamics.

Abnormalities in micro-columnar organization of prefrontal cortex in brain tissues from autistic individuals, including two with Angelman syndrome, have been also detected (59, 60). The narrower size of mini-columns in autistic patients respect to controls may reflect defects in GABAergic fibers within and between cortical mini-columns due to reductions in the neuropil, which separates adjacent mini-columns (47). This may alter local connectivity and lateral inhibition.

### *IN VIVO* STUDIES ON PATIENTS AFFECTED MAINLY BY IDIOPATHIC FORMS OF ASDs

*In vivo* studies from ASD patients are rather limited due to the difficulty of measuring GABAergic function *in vivo*. Using proton magnetic resonance spectroscopy, Harada et al. (48) reported a reduction of GABA concentration in the frontal lobe of children with ASDs respect to controls. However, in this study ASD patients were sedated with triclofos a compound that, by potentiating GABA action, may have biased the results. Using the same technique, Rojas et al. (49) have reported reduced GABA levels in the perisylvian region of the left hemisphere of autistic patients, further supporting the involvement of GABAergic neurotransmission in ASDs. Using SPECT and $^{123}$I-iomazenil, a selective $GABA_A$-benzodiazepine ligand, a reduced expression of $GABA_A$ receptors in the superior and medial frontal cortex of autistic patients was detected (50). Using the same technique, a reduced $GABA_A$ receptor density was observed in three adult females affected by the Rett syndrome (51). In addition, a pilot study using PET and [$^{11}$C]Ro15-4513 to measure the expression levels of α5 $GABA_A$ receptor subunits (localized mainly to extrasynaptic regions where they mediate tonic inhibition), has demonstrated a significant reduction of these subunits in limbic areas of ASD patients respect to controls (52).

Indirect evidence for deficits of GABAergic transmission in ASDs was provided by a recent magneto-encephalographic study that revealed impaired gamma-band activity in selective brain areas of adults with autism during perceptual visual processing (61). Gamma-band oscillations known to critically depend on negative feedback inhibition of principal cells by GABAergic interneurons, including parvalbumin-positive ones (62), are crucial for integrating multisensory information into a coherent representation (63). Although no data from young ASD patients are available, the possibility that such impairment may result from aberrant pre and perinatal development cannot be excluded.

Although informative, these studies referred mainly to idiopathic forms of ASDs and failed to address whether particular types of autistic syndromes, including monogenic ones were similarly affected. In this perspective, it is worth noting that a significant reduction of the cation–chloride importer KCC2 in the cerebrospinal fluid of Rett syndrome patients as compared to controls, with a consequent reduction in the KCC2/NKCC1 ratio was found (53). In accord with the notion that the methyl-CpG-binding protein 2 (MeCP2), encoded by the X-linked *Mecp2* gene, is highly expressed in GABAergic interneurons where it regulates their function these data suggest that a GABA dysfunction underlies the pathophysiology of the Rett syndrome.

Altogether, these findings indicate that alterations of GABAergic signaling in selective microcircuits of well-defined brain areas exert a fundamental role in the pathogenesis of ASDs.

## GABAergic DYSFUNCTIONS IN ANIMAL MODELS OF ASDs

Over the last decade several animal models of ASDs have been generated, in order to identify the molecular and cellular mechanisms underlying these disorders and to develop new therapeutic tools. To this aim, genetic defects detected in patients with ASDs have been introduced in the genome of mice. Animal models have been produced not only by manipulating candidate genes but also environmental factors or drugs such as valproic acid (VPA), an antiepileptic known to be a risk factor for autism in offspring of mothers treated during pregnancy with this drug (64). In accordance with human observations, animal studies have revealed important dysfunctions in GABAergic signaling occurring at different locations of the GABAergic synapse (**Figure 1**).

**Table 2** summarizes alterations of GABAergic transmission observed in the most commonly used animal models of ASDs.

The *Fragile X* syndrome is a monogenetic disorder caused by mutations of the *FMR1* gene, located in chromosome X (Xq27.3) and encoding for the *Fragile X* mental retardation protein (FMRP), which is involved in the translation of a variety of mRNAs. Gene mutations do not allow the expression of the FMRP protein, determining a phenotype characterized by intellectual disabilities associated with language deficits, hyperactivity, autistic behavior, and seizures (85). Mice lacking the *FMR1* gene (Fmr1 KO mice) show an increased network excitability associated with an E/I imbalance in cortical circuits involving specific types of interneurons (65, 67, 86, 87). Thus, in the somatosensory cortex, the reduced activity of parvalbumin-positive cells (66) may contribute to enhance cell excitability and to affect gamma frequency oscillations, thought to be involved in high cognitive functions (86). The enhanced coupling of group I metabotropic glutamate receptors (mGluR) signaling and cannabinoid receptors mobilization may further enhance suppression of inhibition (88). Other factors contributing to enhance cell excitability include: (i) a reduced expression of $GABA_A$ receptors subunits in the cortex. This may represent an evolutionary conserved hallmark of the *Fragile X* syndrome since similar reduction has been detected in the *Fragile X* fruit fly model (89). (ii) A down regulation of mRNA encoding for GAD65 and GAD67 in presynaptic terminals of the cortex and cerebellum; (iii) a reduction of mRNA encoding for gephyrin, the scaffold molecule responsible for glycine and $GABA_A$ receptor clustering and stabilization at post-synaptic sites; (iv) reduced phasic and tonic $GABA_A$-mediated conductances in the amygdale associated with a down regulation of $GABA_A$ receptor subunits (65, 68, 89); (v) a down regulation of $GABA_A$-mediated tonic inhibition associated with a reduced expression of α5 and δ $GABA_A$ receptors subunits in subicular neurons (69). In contrast, electrophysiological recordings from the striatum of Fmr1 KO mice have revealed a selective increase in basal inhibitory neurotransmission, caused by the enhanced probability of GABA release (90). Overall these data suggest that in this animal model modifications of the GABAergic function are region-specific. Interestingly, a recent study from the hippocampus of mice carrying the *Fragile X* mutation, has revealed the loss of oxytocin-mediated $GABA_A$-mediated inhibition during the delivery process (70). In rats, oxytocin, the maternal hormone involved in delivery, has been shown to cause an abrupt shift of GABA from the depolarizing to the hyperpolarizing direction, thus exerting a neuroprotective and analgesic action on newborns (91). Unlike wild-type animals, the depolarizing action of GABA, apparently caused by the reduced expression of KCC2 with consequent high $[Cl^-]_i$, persists in juvenile life. The

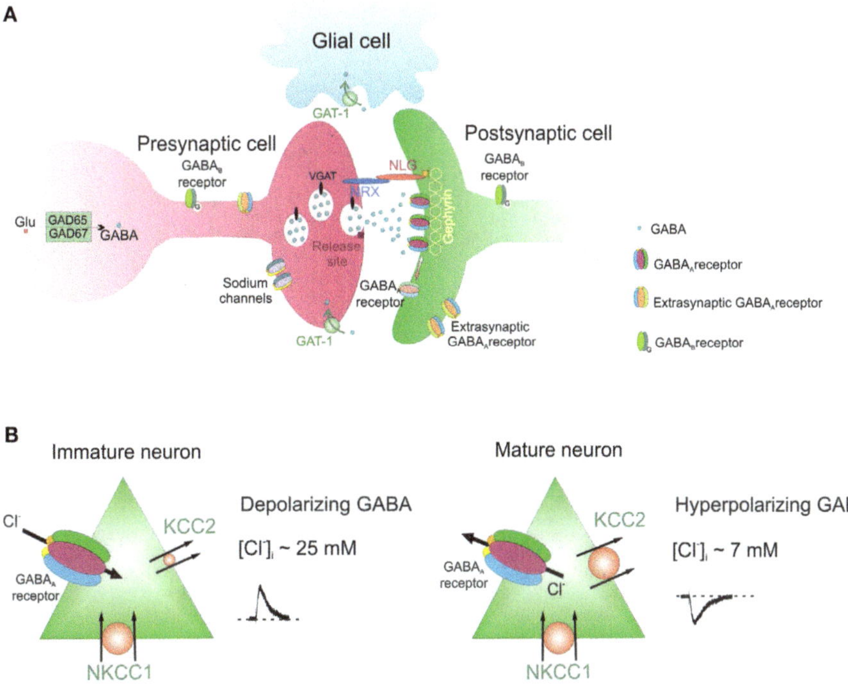


**FIGURE 1 | GABAergic synapse**. **(A)** Pre and post-synaptic sites of the synapse with different components whose functions can be altered in ASDs. **(B)** Direction of GABA action (depolarizing and hyperpolarizing) in immature and mature neurons.

increased excitatory drive to principal cells boosts network activity in the hippocampus, suggesting that an altered E/I balance may be caused not only by a decreased $GABA_A$-mediated inhibition but also by an enhanced $GABA_A$-mediated excitation (70).

Another neuro-developmental disorder showing high co-morbidity with autism is the *Rett syndrome*. This is caused by mutations in the X-linked *Mecp2* gene that codes for the transcriptional factor MeCP2, highly expressed in GABAergic neurons (92). This disorder affects mainly girls who develop normally until the age of 6/18 months. Later, they develop cognitive deficits, loss of speech, motor abnormalities, respiratory dysrhythmias, stereotyped behavior, and seizures leading sometimes to premature death (93). Mice lacking MeCP2 or engineered to express an allele mimicking some mutation present in the *Rett syndrome* exhibit neurological symptoms reminiscent of those found in patients affected by the *Rett syndrome*. Similarly to Fmr1 KO mice, these animals exhibit alterations of the E/I balance (71), associated with a decrease in somatic GABA content and low levels of mRNA encoding for GAD65 and GAD67 in cortical and striatal neurons (75). While in the thalamus, the *Mecp2* gene appears to differentially regulate the development of GABAergic synapses in excitatory and inhibitory neurons (94), in the brain stem, the E/I imbalance is due to the depression of GABAergic transmission originating at both pre- and post-synaptic levels (72). A reduced GABAergic inhibition is present also in the locus coeruleus (73). In the hippocampus of *Mecp2* KO mice, a significant reduction in the quantal size of miniature inhibitory post-synaptic currents (mIPSCs) has been detected. This would account for the impairment of long-term potentiation (LTP) induced at CA3–CA1 synapses by theta burst stimulation (74).

An E/I imbalance has been found also in individuals with *Tuberous sclerosis*, a genetic multisystem disorder characterized by wide spread hamartomas in several organs, including brain, heart, skin, eyes, kidney, lung, and liver (95). Tuberous sclerosis patients exhibit a variety of neurological disorders including mental retardation, autism-like disorders, and epilepsy. The affected genes are *Tsc1* and *Tsc2* encoding hamartin and tuberin, respectively. The hamartin–tuberin complex inhibits the mammalian target of rapamycin pathway that controls cell growth and proliferation (95). Immunocytochemical and western blots experiments have demonstrated that this disorder is associated with a decrease of α1 $GABA_A$ receptor subunits and reduced and enhanced levels of KCC2 and NKCC1, respectively, in tubers. Changes in the expression of KCC2 and NKCC1 account for the excitatory action of GABA revealed with patch clamp in slices from *Tuberous sclerosis* tubers (96). However, electrophysiological data are still preliminary and should be taken with caution since they refer only to experiments from cortical slices obtained from tubers of a single patient. The *Angelman* or the closely related *Prader–Willi* syndromes (depending from which parent the deletion has been inherited), characterized by mental retardation, autistic behavior, and seizures, are determined by the loss of function of the *Ube3a* gene encoding for the a ubiquitin E3 ligase or *Gabrb3*, *Gabra5*, and *Gabrg3* genes, encoding, respectively for β3, α5, and γ3 $GABA_A$ receptor subunits localized in the same chromosome region 15q11–q13. Ube3a-deficient mice exhibit a reduced tonic

**Table 2 | Alterations of GABAergic signaling in animal models of ASDs (E, embryonic day; P, postnatal day).**

| Animal models | Alterations of GABAergic signaling | Age | Reference |
|---|---|---|---|
| Fmr1 KO *(X Fragile)* | Reduced GABA release in the amygdala | P20–30 | (65) |
| | Reduced number of parvalbumin-positive interneurons | Adult | (66) |
| | Altered E/I balance | P14–P30 | (67) |
| | Decreased expression of GAD67 and $GABA_A$ receptor subunits | Adult | (68) |
| | Down regulation of $GABA_A$-mediated tonic inhibition | Adult | (69) |
| | Persistent depolarizing effect of GABA in juvenile animals | E20–P30 | (70) |
| MECP2 KO (Rett syndrome) | Altered E/I balance | P14–P35 | (71) |
| | Depressed GABAergic synaptic transmission | P7 | (72) |
| | | P14–P28 | (73) |
| | | Adult | (74) |
| | Reduced expression of GAD65 and GAD 67 | Adult | (75) |
| Ube3a-deficient mouse (Angelman syndrome) | Reduced $GABA_A$-mediated tonic inhibition | P25–P28 or adult | (76) |
| GABRB3 KO (Angelman syndrome) | Decreased expression of $GABA_A$ receptors | Adult | (77) |
| *Scn1a*$^{+/-}$ mice (Dravet's syndrome) | Altered E/I balance | P21–P30 | (78) |
| NL3$^{R451C}$ KI | Increased GABAergic neurotransmission; increased VGAT and gephyrin expression | P13–P16 | (79) |
| | Increased frequency of GDPs | P4–P35 | (14) |
| | Circuit specific changes in GABAergic signaling in the hippocampus and in the cortex | P21–P35 | (80) |
| | | P9–P15 | (81) |
| | Decreased number of PV$^+$ interneurons | P21–P35 | (82) |
| En2 KO | Reduction of GABAergic markers during development; reduced number of GABAergic interneurons | Adult | (83) |
| VPA model | Decreased $GABA_A$-mediated neurotransmission | P23–P45 | (84) |
| | Persistent depolarizing effect of GABA in juvenile animals | E20–P30 | (70) |

GABA-mediated inhibition in the cerebellum, caused by a GAT-1 dependent decrease of GABA concentration in the extracellular space (76). Moreover, β3-deficient mice, which have a phenotype similar to some forms of *Angelman* syndrome, exhibit a reduced expression of $GABA_A$ receptors in selective brain regions as determined by quantitative autoradiography (77).

The *Dravet's* syndrome is caused by a haploinsufficiency of the *SCN1A* gene encoding for voltage-gated sodium channel $Na_V1.1$. Children affected by this disorder show intractable seizures, cognitive deficit, and autism spectrum behaviors. GABA plays a pivotal role also in this disorder as demonstrated by the reduced activity of $Na_V1.1$ channels in forebrain GABAergic interneurons of *Scn1a*$^{+/-}$ mice. These animals exhibited an E/I imbalance resulting from a decreased frequency of spontaneous inhibitory post-synaptic currents and an increased frequency of spontaneous excitatory post-synaptic currents in the hippocampus and prefrontal cortex. The impairment of GABAergic neurotransmission is associated with behavioral and cognitive deficits similar to those found in patients affected by the *Dravet's* syndrome (78).

Although rare, single mutations of genes encoding for adhesion molecules of the Neuroligin (NL) family found in individuals with autism have been introduced in mice. One of these, the R451C mutation of the *Nlgn3* gene encoding for NL3, has been found in a family with children affected by ASDs (97). NLs are adhesion post-synaptic proteins that, by binding to their presynaptic partners, neurexins, functionally couple the post-synaptic densities with the transmitter release machinery, thus contributing to synapses stabilization (98). Mice carrying the NL3 R451C mutation (NL3$^{R451C}$ knock-in mice) show modifications of GABAergic signaling associated with behavioral deficits reminiscent of those found in autistic children (79, 99). These mice exhibit an increased frequency of mIPSCs in the somatosensory cortex (79) and in the CA3 region of the hippocampus (100) where they contribute to boost GDPs activity. A more detailed analysis of GABAergic microcircuits in the hippocampus has unveiled an increased GABA release at synapses between cholecystokinin (CCK)-positive endocannabinoids-sensitive interneurons and pyramidal cells and a decreased GABA release at synapses between parvalbumin-positive basket cells and principal cells (80). The similar phenotype found at CCK–pyramidal cell synapses in NL3$^{R451C}$ knock in mice and in NL3 KO mice suggests a loss of function consisting in the loss of tonic endocannabinoid signaling at these connections. It is worth noting that NL3$^{R451C}$ knock-in mice present an asymmetric reduction of parvalbumin-positive basket cells across the two hemispheres (82).

Similarly to Földy et al. (80), a reduced probability of GABA release has been found in parvalbumin-positive basket cell–spiny neuron synapses in layer IV somatosensory barrel cortex of juvenile $NL3^{R451C}$ knock in mice. Such deficit determines an alteration of the E/I balance in this cortical layer together with a modification of the temporal window for integration of sensory inputs in principal cells (81). The altered sensory representations may underline deficits in coherent percepts of autistic children.

Mutations in the *En2* gene, coding for the homeobox-containing transcription factor engrailed-2 (EN2), involved in patterning and neuronal differentiation of the midbrain/hindbrain region, have been associated with ASDs. *En2* KO mice have been proposed as a model for ASDs due to their behavioral abnormalities similar to those observed in individuals with ASDs (101). The *En2* gene is also involved in the development or maintenance of GABAergic interneurons as demonstrated by the selective loss of parvalbumin, somatostatin, and neuropeptide Y positive interneurons in the cortex and hippocampus of *En2* KO mice (83). This effect appears to be region-specific since different subpopulations of interneurons are affected in posterior brain areas (102). Deficits in GABAergic neurotransmission account for the higher susceptibility to seizures of En2 KO mice respect to controls (103).

Valproic acid is a histone deacetylase inhibitor, widely used to cure epilepsy and bipolar disorders. VPA is also a potent teratogen since children exposed *in utero* to this drug have a much higher risk of developing an autistic-type behavior than normal children (64). Pups exposed to VPA *in utero* show neuro-developmental abnormalities and behavioral deficits similar to ASDs (104). As in other animal models of ASDs, the autistic phenotype is associated to an altered E/I balance due to a decreased GABAergic signaling, which affects both pre- and post-synaptic sites, leaving the extrasynaptic transmission unaffected (84). Interestingly, like the NL3 model, the VPA model exhibits an asymmetric reduction of parvalbumin-positive cells across the two hemispheres (82). Similarly to *FRM1* KO mice, also in this animal model a loss of oxytocin-mediated $GABA_A$-mediated inhibition occurs during the transition from fetal to postnatal life (70). Also here as in Fmr1 KO mice, the depolarizing action of GABA in the hippocampus persists in juvenile life. The excitatory GABAergic drive to principal cells leads to an increased network activity in a broad spectrum of frequencies including gamma oscillations.

The different animal models mentioned here have in common dysfunctions of GABAergic signaling leading to alterations of the E/I balance in selective brain circuits. These alterations can be rescued by selective tools that regulate $GABA_A$-mediated synaptic transmission.

## THERAPEUTIC INTERVENTIONS TO RESCUE GABAergic DYSFUNCTIONS IN ASDs

**Figure 1** shows a GABAergic synapse with its different constituents.

As summarized in **Figure 1A**, GABA released from a presynaptic terminal binds to post-synaptic $GABA_A$ receptors localized on precise apposition to presynaptic release sites. It binds also to presynaptic and post-synaptic $GABA_A$ and $GABA_B$ receptors [for a review see Ref. (105)]. Post-synaptic $GABA_B$ receptors are localized mainly at perisynaptic sites. Post-synaptic $GABA_A$ receptors are maintained in the right place by gephyrin, a scaffold protein which, by interacting with cytoskeletal anchoring elements, contributes to regulate receptor trafficking in and out of the synapses (106). Before being released in a calcium-dependent way, GABA is synthesized by GAD65 and GAD67 and it is stored in presynaptic vesicles by the vesicular transporter VGAT, which uses the electrochemical gradient for $H^+$ to shuffle and pack GABA into synaptic vesicles (107). The probability of GABA release is under control of presynaptic receptors including $GABA_A$ and $GABA_B$ receptors. Adhesion molecules of the neuroligin–neurexin families ensure the cross-talk between post and presynaptic elements of the synapses (98). The figure also shows that the presynaptic terminal contains sodium channels, since, as already mentioned, a selective mutation of these channels in GABAergic interneurons of the forebrain is responsible for the Dravet's syndrome. After being released, GABA is taken up into nerve terminals and astrocytes by GABA transporters (GATs) localized on presynaptic nerve terminals and astrocytes.

**Figure 1B** shows the direction of chloride fluxes through post-synaptic $GABA_A$ receptors in immature and mature neurons. The influx or efflux of chloride in and out of the cells is mainly dictated by the activity of two developmentally regulated cation–chloride co-transporters, the NKCC1 and KCC2, which pump chloride inside and outside of neurons, respectively (8). Therefore, different components of the synapses can be selectively targeted by agents that can rescue their functions.

Due to the co-morbidity of ASDs with epilepsy, anticonvulsants are widely used for the symptomatic treatment of these disorders (108). Some of these drugs have also an anti-anxiety effect and may indirectly increase $GABA_A$ neurotransmission by promoting the synthesis of GABA or by inhibiting their reuptake or breakdown. Interestingly, treatment with vigabatrin, which blocks GABA catabolism by inhibiting GABA transaminase, is able to control seizures and to improve the autistic behavior of children affected by tuberous sclerosis (109).

$\gamma$-Aminobutyric acid agonists have proved to be effective in normalizing the E/I imbalance in animal models of Autism: they can either directly enhance inhibition or indirectly reduce excitation. Thus, in BTBR mice [an animal model of idiopathic autism, Ref. (110)] or in $Scn1a^{+/-}$ mice [a monogenic model of ASDs, Ref. (78)], in which a reduced $GABA_A$-mediated inhibition occurs, the treatment with low non-sedative, non-anxiolytic doses of benzodiazepines, or clonazepam, known to enhance GABAergic signaling *via* allosteric modulation of post-synaptic $GABA_A$ receptors, leads to an improvement of social and cognitive deficits. Interestingly, in both BTBR and $Scn1a^{+/-}$ mice, the up-regulation of $\alpha 2$ and/or $\alpha 3$ containing $GABA_A$ receptors subunits by L-838,417, a selective positive allosteric modulator of these subunits, which does not induce tolerance, is able to mimic the effects of benzodiazepines, thus providing an attractive tool to enhance GABAergic neurotransmission and to improve behavioral deficits in ASDs (110). Consistent with this view, clinical trials using $\alpha 2/\alpha 3$ selective positive allosteric modulators of $GABA_A$ receptors have been developed with AstraZeneca and the National Institutes of Health (http://clinicaltrials.gov/show/NCT01966679).

Animal models of the Rett syndrome are currently used in translational studies for the preclinical evaluation of new therapeutic trials (111). Genetic studies have provided evidence that neuronal dysfunctions and autistic symptoms can be reversed upon restoration of MeCP2 protein in mice in which the *Mecp2* gene has been silenced using a *lox-Stop-lox* cassette (112, 113), suggesting that in this animal model, the neuronal connectivity is not altered and neurons and glia are not permanently damaged by the *Mecp2* loss. Pharmacological studies have demonstrated amelioration of autistic symptoms with IGF-1 (114) or BDNF (115). However, since most of autistic features of the Rett syndrome can be recapitulated by deleting the *Mecp2* gene in GABA releasing neurons (75), these are expected to be rescued by drugs that enhance GABAergic neurotransmission.

Treatment of Fmr1 KO mice (an animal model of *Fragile X* syndrome), exhibiting an hyper-excitability and a GABAergic dysfunction in the basolateral nucleus of the amygdala, with gaboxadol (THIP), a selective agonist at δ subunits containing perisynaptic or extrasynaptic $GABA_A$ receptors, results in an increased $GABA_A$-mediated tonic conductance and in beneficial effects on learning deficits and behavioral disturbances linked to this disorder. This supports the hypothesis that tonic inhibition is a putative target for the treatment of *Fragile X* syndrome (65, 116). In addition, consistent with the notion that mGluR are important regulators of protein synthesis, which is translationally repressed by the FMR protein, partial inhibition of mGluR5 or inhibition of excessive glutamate release by the $GABA_B$ receptor agonist arbaclofen in *Fmr1* KO mice have led to promising results (117, 118). Although the selective activation of $GABA_B$ receptors with arbaclofen has the potential to improve social function and behavior in patients with Fragile X syndrome (119), its use in clinical trials is still under debate (120).

It is worth mentioning that in some children affected by ASDs, allosteric modulators of $GABA_A$ receptors such as benzodiazepines have a paradoxical effect, increasing anxiety, and aggression (121). Therefore, restoring low $[Cl^-]_i$ and the inhibitory action of GABA, using the selective blocker of the NKCC1 chloride importer bumetanide, may have beneficial effects. In an elegant study, Tyzio et al. (70) have convincingly demonstrated that, treating pregnant VPA rats and *Fragile X* mice shortly before delivery with bumetanide, suppresses in both animal models the excitatory action of GABA and prevents the autistic-like behavior in off springs. Bumetanide may not only reverse GABA action from the depolarizing to the hyperpolarizing direction, but it may also reduce cell excitability by an ephaptic type of mechanism involving regulation of the cell volume and the extracellular space (122). Animal data validate previous findings by the same group, showing amelioration of autistic symptoms in children treated for 3 months with bumetanide (123, 124). Although these studies should be expanded to larger multicenter trials with more restricted inclusion and exclusion criteria and more extended investigations on the dose/response action of the diuretic as well as persistence of action after drug's withdrawal, the significant improvement of the autistic behavior associated with a statistically significant amelioration of childhood autism rating scale (CARS) and clinical global impressions (CGI) scores in the absence of clear side effects make this diuretic a very promising drug to cure ASDs. In a parallel study, bumetanide was shown to improve accuracy in facial emotional labeling and to increase brain activation in areas involved in social and emotional perception (125).

## CONCLUSION

Several lines of evidences suggest that ASDs are neurodevelopmental disorders characterized by a clear E/I imbalance in selective neuronal circuits. Such disequilibrium appears to be mainly related to heterogeneous defects of GABAergic signaling in different brain structures. This has paved the way toward the development of new drugs for the cure of these devastating disorders. In particular, several studies have shown that drugs acting on GABAergic synapses are able to rescue behavioral deficits in animal models of autism and to ameliorate at least some of the symptoms observed in ASD patients.

In order to successfully translate therapeutic approaches from animal to humans, it is necessary to develop animal models of ASDs that faithfully trace the behavioral alterations detected in ASD patients. In addition, the effects of drugs should be validated in humans in large scale clinical trials with accurate controls.

Since ASDs are developmental disorders, the early pharmacological intervention, guaranteed by an early diagnosis, is essential. This means that very young children will receive drugs, whose side effects have to be carefully considered. For instance, many drugs acting on GABAergic synapses can generate addiction or give rise to paradoxical reactions, as brain circuits are still immature and GABA may still exert a depolarizing and excitatory action which can be prolonged at late stages of development. Only accurate studies and the use of well suited animal models can help to design pharmacological tools with minimal risks.

## AUTHOR CONTRIBUTIONS

Giada Cellot and Enrico Cherubini wrote the paper.

## ACKNOWLEDGMENTS

This study was supported by a grant from Telethon (GGP11043) and from Ministero dell'Istruzione, dell'Università e della Ricerca (PRIN 2011) to Enrico Cherubini. The authors are particularly grateful to Dr. R. Pizzarelli who contributed to some of the original work on an animal model of ASDs, as well as all members of the laboratory for useful discussions.

## REFERENCES

1. American Psychiatric Association. *Diagnostic and Statistical Manual of Mental Disorders*. Arlington, VA: American Psychiatric Association (2000).
2. Levy SE, Mandell DS, Schultz R. Autism. *Lancet* (2009) **374**:1627–38. doi:10.1016/S0140-6736(09)61376-3
3. Ben-Ari Y, Woodin MA, Sernagor E, Cancedda L, Vinay L, Rivera C, et al. Refuting the challenges of the developmental shift of polarity of GABA actions: GABA more exciting than ever! *Front Cell Neurosci* (2012) **6**:35. doi:10.3389/fncel.2012.00035
4. Frye RE, Rossignol D, Casanova MF, Brown GL, Martin V, Edelson S, et al. A review of traditional and novel treatments for seizures in autism spectrum disorder: findings from a systematic review and expert panel. *Front Public Health* (2013) **1**:31. doi:10.3389/fpubh.2013.00031
5. Valeeva G, Abdullin A, Tyzio R, Skorinkin A, Nikolski E, Ben-Ari Y, et al. Temporal coding at the immature depolarizing GABAergic synapse. *Front Cell Neurosci* (2010) **14**:4. doi:10.3389/fncel.2010.00017
6. Ben-Ari Y, Cherubini E, Corradetti R, Gaiarsa JL. Giant synaptic potentials in immature rat CA3 hippocampal neurones. *J Physiol* (1989) **416**:303–25.
7. Cherubini E, Gaiarsa JL, Ben-Ari Y. Review GABA: an excitatory transmitter in early postnatal life. *Trends Neurosci* (1991) **14**:515–9. doi:10.1016/0166-2236(91)90003-D
8. Rivera C, Voipio J, Payne JA, Ruusuvuori E, Lahtinen H, Lamsa K, et al. The K+/Cl- co-transporter KCC2 renders GABA hyperpolarizing during neuronal maturation. *Nature* (1999) **397**:251–5. doi:10.1038/16697

9. Yamada J, Okabe A, Toyoda H, Kilb W, Luhmann HJ, Fukuda A. Cl-uptake promoting depolarizing GABA actions in immature rat neocortical neurones is mediated by NKCC1. *J Physiol* (2004) **557**:829–41. doi:10.1113/jphysiol.2004.062471
10. Dzhala VI, Talos DM, Sdrulla DA, Brumback AC, Mathews GC, Benke TA, et al. NKCC1 transporter facilitates seizures in the developing brain. *Nat Med* (2005) **11**:1205–13. doi:10.1038/nm1301
11. Wang DD, Kriegstein AR. Defining the role of GABA in cortical development. *J Physiol* (2009) **587**:1873–9. doi:10.1113/jphysiol.2008.167635
12. Ben-Ari Y, Gaiarsa JL, Tyzio R, Khazipov R. GABA: a pioneer transmitter that excites immature neurons and generates primitive oscillations. *Physiol Rev* (2007) **87**:1215–84. doi:10.1152/physrev.00017.2006
13. Cherubini E, Griguoli M, Safiulina V, Lagostena L. The depolarizing action of GABA controls early network activity in the developing hippocampus. *Mol Neurobiol* (2011) **43**:97–106. doi:10.1007/s12035-010-8147-z
14. Pizzarelli R, Cherubini E. Alterations of GABAergic signaling in autism spectrum disorders. *Neural Plast* (2011) **2011**:297153. doi:10.1155/2011/297153
15. Tyzio R, Represa A, Jorquera I, Ben-Ari Y, Gozlan H, Aniksztejn L. The establishment of GABAergic and glutamatergic synapses on CA1 pyramidal neurons is sequential and correlates with the development of the apical dendrite. *J Neurosci* (1999) **19**:10372–82.
16. Behar TN, Schaffner AE, Scott CA, O'Connell C, Barker JL. Differential response of cortical plate and ventricular zone cells to GABA as a migration stimulus. *J Neurosci* (1998) **18**:6378–87.
17. Nguyen L, Rigo JM, Rocher V, Belachew S, Malgrange B, Rogister B, et al. Neurotransmitters as early signals for central nervous system development. *Cell Tissue Res* (2001) **305**:187–202. doi:10.1007/s004410000343
18. Demarque M, Represa A, Becq H, Khalilov I, Ben-Ari Y, Aniksztejn L. Paracrine intercellular communication by a Ca2+- and SNARE-independent release of GABA and glutamate prior to synapse formation. *Neuron* (2002) **36**:1051–61. doi:10.1016/S0896-6273(02)01053-X
19. Manent JB, Demarque M, Jorquera I, Pellegrino C, Ben-Ari Y, Aniksztejn L, et al. A noncanonical release of GABA and glutamate modulates neuronal migration. *J Neurosci* (2005) **25**:4755–65. doi:10.1523/JNEUROSCI.0553-05.2005
20. Cancedda L, Fiumelli H, Chen K, Poo MM. Excitatory GABA action is essential for morphological maturation of cortical neurons in vivo. *J Neurosci* (2007) **27**:5224–35. doi:10.1523/JNEUROSCI.5169-06.2007
21. Leinekugel X, Khazipov R, Cannon R, Hirase H, Ben-Ari Y, Buzsáki G. Correlated bursts of activity in the neonatal hippocampus in vivo. *Science* (2002) **296**:2049–52. doi:10.1126/science.1071111
22. Stockard-Pope J, Werner SS, Bickford RG. *Atlas of Neonatal Electroencephalography*. New York, NY: Raven Press (1992).
23. De la Prida LM, Huberfeld G, Cohen I, Miles R. Threshold behavior in the initiation of hippocampal population bursts. *Neuron* (2006) **49**:131–42. doi:10.1016/j.neuron.2005.10.034
24. De la Prida L, Sanchez-Andres JV. Heterogeneous populations of cells mediate spontaneous synchronous bursting in the developing hippocampus through a frequency-dependent mechanism. *Neuroscience* (2000) **97**:227–41. doi:10.1016/S0306-4522(00)00029-4
25. Safiulina VF, Zacchi P, Taglialatela M, Yaari Y, Cherubini E. Low expression of Kv7/M channels facilitates intrinsic and network bursting in the developing rat hippocampus. *J Physiol* (2008) **586**:5437–53. doi:10.1113/jphysiol.2008.156257
26. Sipilä ST, Huttu K, Soltesz I, Voipio J, Kaila K. Depolarizing GABA acts on intrinsically bursting pyramidal neurons to drive giant depolarizing potentials in the immature hippocampus. *J Neurosci* (2005) **25**:5280–9. doi:10.1523/JNEUROSCI.0378-05.2005
27. Sipilä ST, Huttu K, Voipio J, Kaila K. Intrinsic bursting of immature CA3 pyramidal neurons and consequent giant depolarizing potentials are driven by a persistent Na+ current and terminated by a slow Ca2+ -activated K+ current. *Eur J Neurosci* (2006) **23**:2330–8. doi:10.1111/j.1460-9568.2006.04757.x
28. Marchionni I, Omrani A, Cherubini E. In the developing rat hippocampus a tonic GABAA-mediated conductance selectively enhances the glutamatergic drive of principal cells. *J Physiol* (2007) **581**:515–28. doi:10.1113/jphysiol.2006.125609
29. Yue C, Yaari Y. KCNQ/M channels control spike after depolarization and burst generation in hippocampal neurons. *J Neurosci* (2004) **24**:4614–24. doi:10.1523/JNEUROSCI.0765-04.2004
30. Kasyanov AM, Safiulina VF, Voronin LL, Cherubini E. GABA-mediated giant depolarizing potentials as coincidence detectors for enhancing synaptic efficacy in the developing hippocampus. *Proc Natl Acad Sci U S A* (2004) **101**:3967–72. doi:10.1073/pnas.0305974101
31. Mohajerani MH, Sivakumaran S, Zacchi P, Aguilera P, Cherubini E. Correlated network activity enhances synaptic efficacy via BDNF and the ERK pathway at immature CA3 CA1 connections in the hippocampus. *Proc Natl Acad Sci U S A* (2007) **104**:13176–81. doi:10.1073/pnas.0704533104
32. Freund TF, Buzsáki G. Interneurons of the hippocampus. *Hippocampus* (1996) **6**:347–470. doi:10.1002/(SICI)1098-1063(1996)6:4<347::AID-HIPO1>3.0.CO;2-I
33. Komuro H, Rakic P. Orchestration of neuronal migration by activity of ion channels, neurotransmitter receptors, and intracellular Ca2+ fluctuations. *J Neurobiol* (1998) **37**:110–30. doi:10.1002/(SICI)1097-4695(199810)37:1<110::AID-NEU9>3.3.CO;2-Q
34. Spitzer NC. Activity-dependent neuronal differentiation prior to synapse formation: the functions of calcium transients. *J Physiol Paris* (2002) **96**:73–80. doi:10.1016/S0928-4257(01)00082-1
35. Klausberger T, Somogyi P. Neuronal diversity and temporal dynamics: the unity of hippocampal circuit operations. *Science* (2008) **321**:53–7. doi:10.1126/science.1149381
36. Cook EH, Courchesne RY, Cox NJ, Lord C, Gonen D, Guter SJ, et al. Linkage-disequilibrium mapping of autistic disorder, with 15q11-13 markers. *Am J Hum Genet* (1998) **62**:1077–83. doi:10.1086/301832
37. Shao Y, Cuccaro ML, Hauser ER, Raiford KL, Menold MM, Wolpert CM, et al. Fine mapping of autistic disorder to chromosome 15q11-q13 by use of phenotypic subtypes. *Am J Hum Genet* (2003) **72**:539–48. doi:10.1086/367846
38. Xu X, Wells AB, O'Brien DR, Nehorai A, Dougherty JD. Cell type-specific expression analysis to identify putative cellular mechanisms for neurogenetic disorders. *J Neurosci* (2014) **34**:1420–31. doi:10.1523/JNEUROSCI.4488-13.2014
39. Oblak A, Gibbs TT, Blatt GJ. Decreased GABAA receptors and benzodiazepine binding sites in the anterior cingulate cortex in autism. *Autism Res* (2009) **2**:205–19. doi:10.1002/aur.88
40. Oblak A, Gibbs T, Blatt GJ. Decreased GABAB receptors in the cingulated cortex and fusiform gyrus in autism. *J Neurochem* (2010) **114**:1414–23. doi:10.1111/j.1471-4159.2010.06858.x
41. Guptill JT, Booker AB, Gibbs TT, Kemper TL, Bauman ML, Blatt GJ. [3H]-flunitrazepam-labeled benzodiazepine binding sites in the hippocampal formation in autism: a multiple concentration autoradiographic study. *J Autism Dev Disord* (2007) **37**:911–20. doi:10.1007/s10803-006-0226-7
42. Whitney ER, Kemper TL, Bauman ML, Rosene DL, Blatt GJ. Cerebellar Purkinje cells are reduced in a subpopulation of autistic brains: a stereological experiment using calbindin-D28k. *Cerebellum* (2008) **7**:406–16. doi:10.1007/s12311-008-0043-y
43. Fatemi SH, Halt AR, Stary JM, Kanodia R, Schulz SC, Realmuto GR. Glutamic acid decarboxylase 65 and 67 kDa proteins are reduced in autistic parietal and cerebellar cortices. *Biol Psychiatry* (2002) **52**:805–10. doi:10.1016/S0006-3223(02)01430-0
44. Yip J, Soghomonian JJ, Blatt GJ. Decreased GAD67 mRNA levels in cerebellar Purkinje cells in autism: pathophysiological implications. *Acta Neuropathol* (2007) **113**:559–68. doi:10.1007/s00401-006-0176-3
45. Yip J, Soghomonian JJ, Blatt GJ. Decreased GAD65 mRNA levels in select subpopulations of neurons in the cerebellar dentate nuclei in autism: an in situ hybridization study. *Autism Res* (2009) **2**:50–9. doi:10.1002/aur.62
46. Lawrence YL, Kemper TL, Bauman ML, Blatt GJ. Parvalbumin, calbindin, and calretinin immunoreactive interneuron density in autism. *Acta Neurol Scand* (2010) **121**:99–108. doi:10.1111/j.1600-0404.2009.01234.x
47. Casanova MF, Buxhoeveden DP, Gomez J. Disruption of the inhibitory architecture of the cell minicolumn: implications for autism. *Neuroscientist* (2003) **9**:496–507. doi:10.1177/1073858403253552
48. Harada M, Taki MM, Nose A, Kubo H, Mori K, Nishitani H, et al. Non-invasive evaluation of the GABAergic/glutamatergic system in autistic patients observed by MEGA-editing proton MR spectroscopy using a clinical 3 Tesla instrument. *J Autism Dev Disord* (2011) **41**:447–54. doi:10.1007/s10803-010-1065-0
49. Rojas DC, Singel D, Steinmetz S, Hepburn S, Brown MS. Decreased left perisylvian GABA concentration in children with autism and unaffected siblings. *Neuroimage* (2014) **86**:28–34. doi:10.1016/j.neuroimage.2013.01.045

50. Mori T, Mori K, Fujii E, Toda Y, Miyazaki M, Harada M, et al. Evaluation of the GABAergic nervous system in autistic brain: (123)I-iomazenil SPECT study. *Brain Dev* (2012) **34**:648–54. doi:10.1016/j.braindev.2011.10.007
51. Yamashita Y, Matsuishi T, Ishibashi M, Kimura A, Onishi Y, Yonekura Y, et al. Decrease in benzodiazepine receptor binding in the brains of adult patients with Rett syndrome. *J Neurol Sci* (1998) **154**:146–50. doi:10.1016/S0022-510X(97)00223-2
52. Mendez MA, Horder J, Myers J, Coghlan S, Stokes P, Erritzoe D, et al. The brain GABA-benzodiazepine receptor alpha-5 subtype in autism spectrum disorder: a pilot [(11)C]Ro15-4513 positron emission tomography study. *Neuropharmacology* (2013) **68**:195–201. doi:10.1016/j.neuropharm.2012.04.008
53. Duarte ST, Armstrong J, Roche A, Ortez C, Pérez A, O'Callaghan Mdel M, et al. Abnormal expression of cerebrospinal fluid cation chloride cotransporters in patients with Rett syndrome. *PLoS One* (2013) **8**:e68851. doi:10.1371/journal.pone.0068851
54. Coghlan S, Horder J, Inkster B, Mendez MA, Murphy DG, Nutt DJ. GABA system dysfunction in autism and related disorders: from synapse to symptoms. *Neurosci Biobehav Rev* (2012) **36**:2044–55. doi:10.1016/j.neubiorev.2012.07.005
55. Blatt GJ, Fitzgerald CM, Guptill JT, Booker AB, Kemper TL, Bauman ML. Density and distribution of hippocampal neurotransmitter receptors in autism: an autoradiographic study. *J Autism Dev Disord* (2001) **31**:537–43. doi:10.1023/A:1013238809666
56. Williams RS, Hauser SL, Purpura DP, DeLong GR, Swisher CN. Autism and mental retardation: neuropathologic studies performed in four retarded persons with autistic behavior. *Arch Neurol* (1980) **37**:749–53. doi:10.1001/archneur.1980.00500610029003
57. Bauman ML, Kemper TL. Histoanatomic observations of the brain in early infantile autism. *Neurology* (1985) **35**:866–74. doi:10.1212/WNL.35.6.866
58. Yip J, Soghomonian JJ, Blatt GJ. Increased GAD67 mRNA levels in cerebellar interneurons in autism: implications for Purkinje cell dysfunction. *J Neurosci Res* (2008) **86**:525–30. doi:10.1002/jnr.21520
59. Casanova MF, Buxhoeveden DP, Switala AE, Roy E. Minicolumnar pathology in autism. *Neurology* (2002) **58**:428–32. doi:10.1212/WNL.58.3.428
60. Casanova MF, Buxhoeveden DP, Switala AE, Roy E. Asperger's syndrome and cortical neuropathology. *J Child Neurol* (2002) **17**:142–5. doi:10.1177/088307380201700211
61. Sun L, Grützner C, Bölte S, Wibral M, Tozman T, Schlitt S, et al. Impaired gamma-band activity during perceptual organization in adults with autism spectrum disorders: evidence for dysfunctional network activity in frontal-posterior cortices. *J Neurosci* (2012) **32**:9563–73. doi:10.1523/JNEUROSCI.1073-12.2012
62. Sohal VS, Zhang F, Yizhar O, Deisseroth K. Parvalbumin neurons and gamma rhythms enhance cortical circuit performance. *Nature* (2009) **459**:698–702. doi:10.1038/nature07991
63. Uhlhaas PJ, Singer W. Neural synchrony in brain disorders: relevance for cognitive dysfunctions and pathophysiology. *Neuron* (2006) **52**:155–68. doi:10.1016/j.neuron.2006.09.020
64. Meador KJ, Loring DW. Risks of in utero exposure to valproate. *JAMA* (2013) **309**(16):1730–1. doi:10.1001/jama.2013.4001
65. Olmos-Serrano JL, Paluszkiewicz SM, Martin BS, Kaufmann WE, Corbin JG, Huntsman MM. Defective GABAergic neurotransmission and pharmacological rescue of neuronal hyperexcitability in the amygdala in a mouse model of Fragile X syndrome. *J Neurosci* (2010) **30**:9929–38. doi:10.1523/JNEUROSCI.1714-10.2010
66. Selby L, Zhang C, Sun QQ. Major defects in neocortical GABAergic inhibitory circuits in mice lacking the Fragile X mental retardation protein. *Neurosci Lett* (2007) **412**:227–32. doi:10.1016/j.neulet.2006.11.062
67. Gibson JR, Bartley AF, Hays SA, Huber KM. Imbalance of neocortical excitation and inhibition and altered UP states reflect network hyperexcitability in the mouse model of Fragile X syndrome. *J Neurophysiol* (2008) **100**:2615–26. doi:10.1152/jn.90752.2008
68. Gantois I, Vandesompele J, Speleman F, Reyniers E, D'Hooge R, Severijnen LA, et al. Expression profiling suggests underexpression of the GABA(A) receptor subunit delta in the Fragile X knockout mouse model. *Neurobiol Dis* (2006) **21**:346–57. doi:10.1016/j.nbd.2005.07.017
69. Curia G, Papouin T, Séguéla P, Avoli M. Downregulation of tonic GABAergic inhibition in a mouse model of Fragile X syndrome. *Cereb Cortex* (2009) **19**:1515–20. doi:10.1093/cercor/bhn159
70. Tyzio R, Nardou R, Ferrari DC, Tsintsadze T, Shahrokhi A, Eftekhari S, et al. Oxytocin-mediated GABA inhibition during delivery attenuates autism pathogenesis in rodent offspring. *Science* (2014) **343**:675–9. doi:10.1126/science.1247190
71. Dani VS, Chang Q, Maffei A, Turrigiano GG, Jaenisch R, Nelson SB. Reduced cortical activity due to a shift in the balance between excitation and inhibition in a mouse model of Rett syndrome. *Proc Natl Acad Sci U S A* (2005) **102**:12560–5. doi:10.1073/pnas.0506071102
72. Medrihan L, Tantalaki E, Aramuni G, Sargsyan V, Dudanova I, Missler M, et al. Early defects of GABAergic synapses in the brain stem of a MeCP2 mouse model of Rett syndrome. *J Neurophysiol* (2008) **99**:112–21. doi:10.1152/jn.00826.2007
73. Jin X, Cui N, Zhong W, Jin XT, Jiang C. GABAergic synaptic inputs of locus coeruleus neurons in wild-type and Mecp2-null mice. *Am J Physiol Cell Physiol* (2013) **304**:844–57. doi:10.1152/ajpcell.00399.2012
74. Zhang L, He J, Jugloff DG, Eubanks JH. The MeCP2-null mouse hippocampus displays altered basal inhibitory rhythms and is prone to hyperexcitability. *Hippocampus* (2008) **18**:294–309. doi:10.1002/hipo.20389
75. Chao HT, Chen H, Samaco RC, Xue M, Chahrour M, Yoo J, et al. Dysfunction in GABA signalling mediates autism-like stereotypies and Rett syndrome phenotypes. *Nature* (2010) **468**:263–9. doi:10.1038/nature09582
76. Egawa K, Kitagawa K, Inoue K, Takayama M, Takayama C, Saitoh S, et al. Decreased tonic inhibition in cerebellar granule cells causes motor dysfunction in a mouse model of Angelman syndrome. *Sci Transl Med* (2012) **4**:163ra157. doi:10.1126/scitranslmed.3004655
77. Sinkkonen ST, Homanics GE, Korpi ER. Mouse models of Angelman syndrome, a neurodevelopmental disorder, display different brain regional GABA(A) receptor alterations. *Neurosci Lett* (2003) **340**:205–8. doi:10.1016/S0304-3940(03)00123-X
78. Han S, Tai C, Westenbroek RE, Yu FH, Cheah CS, Potter GB, et al. Autistic-like behaviour in Scn1a+/- mice and rescue by enhanced GABA-mediated neurotransmission. *Nature* (2012) **489**:385–90. doi:10.1038/nature11356
79. Tabuchi K, Blundell J, Etherton MR, Hammer RE, Liu X, Powell CM, et al. A neuroligin-3 mutation implicated in autism increases inhibitory synaptic transmission in mice. *Science* (2007) **318**:71–6. doi:10.1126/science.1146221
80. Földy C, Malenka RC, Südhof TC. Autism-associated neuroligin-3 mutations commonly disrupt tonic endocannabinoid signaling. *Neuron* (2013) **78**:498–509. doi:10.1016/j.neuron.2013.02.036
81. Cellot G, Cherubini E. Reduced inhibitory gate in the barrel cortex of neuroligin3 $^{R451C}$ knock-in mice, an animal model of autism spectrum disorders. *Physiol Rep* (2014) **2**:e12070. doi:10.14814/phy2.12077
82. Gogolla N, Leblanc JJ, Quast KB, Südhof TC, Fagiolini M, Hensch TK. Common circuit defect of excitatory-inhibitory balance in mouse models of autism. *J Neurodev Disord* (2009) **1**:172–81. doi:10.1007/s11689-009-9023-x
83. Sgadò P, Genovesi S, Kalinovsky A, Zunino G, Macchi F, Allegra M, et al. Loss of GABAergic neurons in the hippocampus and cerebral cortex of engrailed-2 null mutant mice: implications for autism spectrum disorders. *Exp Neurol* (2013) **247**:496–505. doi:10.1016/j.expneurol.2013.01.021
84. Banerjee A, García-Oscos F, Roychowdhury S, Galindo LC, Hall S, Kilgard MP, et al. Impairment of cortical GABAergic synaptic transmission in an environmental rat model of autism. *Int J Neuropsychopharmacol* (2013) **16**:1309–18. doi:10.1017/S1461145712001216
85. Oostra BA, Chiurazzi P. The Fragile X gene and its function. *Clin Genet* (2001) **60**:399–408. doi:10.1034/j.1399-0004.2001.600601.x
86. Paluszkiewicz SM, Martin BS, Huntsman MM. Fragile X syndrome: the GABAergic system and circuit dysfunction. *Dev Neurosci* (2011) **33**:349–64. doi:10.1159/000329420
87. Gonçalves JT, Anstey JE, Golshani P, Portera-Cailliau C. Circuit level defects in the developing neocortex of Fragile X mice. *Nat Neurosci* (2013) **16**:903–9. doi:10.1038/nn.3415
88. Zhang L, Alger BE. Enhanced endocannabinoid signaling elevates neuronal excitability in Fragile X syndrome. *J Neurosci* (2010) **30**:5724–9. doi:10.1523/JNEUROSCI.0795-10.2010

89. D'Hulst C, Heulens I, Brouwer JR, Willemsen R, De Geest N, Reeve SP, et al. Expression of the GABAergic system in animal models for Fragile X syndrome and Fragile X associated tremor/ataxia syndrome (FXTAS). *Brain Res* (2009) **1253**:176–83. doi:10.1016/j.brainres.2008.11.075
90. Centonze D, Rossi S, Mercaldo V, Napoli I, Ciotti MT, De Chiara V, et al. Abnormal striatal GABA transmission in the mouse model for the Fragile X syndrome. *Biol Psychiatry* (2008) **63**:963–73. doi:10.1016/j.biopsych.2007.09.008
91. Tyzio R, Cossart R, Khalilov I, Minlebaev M, Hübner CA, Represa A, et al. Maternal oxytocin triggers a transient inhibitory switch in GABA signaling in the fetal brain during delivery. *Science* (2006) **314**:1788–92. doi:10.1126/science.1133212
92. Akbarian S, Chen RZ, Gribnau J, Rasmussen TP, Fong H, Jaenisch R, et al. Expression pattern of the Rett syndrome gene MeCP2 in primate prefrontal cortex. *Neurobiol Dis* (2001) **8**:784–91. doi:10.1006/nbdi.2001.0420
93. Amir RE, Van den Veyver IB, Wan M, Tran CQ, Francke U, Zoghbi HY. Rett syndrome is caused by mutations in X-linked MECP2, encoding methyl-CpG-binding protein 2. *Nat Genet* (1999) **23**:185–8. doi:10.1038/13810
94. Zhang ZW, Zak JD, Liu H. MeCP2 is required for normal development of GABAergic circuits in the thalamus. *J Neurophysiol* (2010) **103**:2470–81. doi:10.1152/jn.00601.2009
95. Curatolo P, Bombardieri R, Jozwiak S. Tuberous sclerosis. *Lancet* (2008) **372**:657–68. doi:10.1016/S0140-6736(08)61279-9
96. Talos DM, Sun H, Kosaras B, Joseph A, Folkerth RD, Poduri A, et al. Altered inhibition in tuberous sclerosis and type IIb cortical dysplasia. *Ann Neurol* (2012) **71**:539–51. doi:10.1002/ana.22696
97. Jamain S, Quach H, Betancur C, Råstam M, Colineaux C, Gillberg IC, et al. Mutations of the X-linked genes encoding neuroligins NLGN3 and NLGN4 are associated with autism. *Nat Genet* (2003) **34**:27–9. doi:10.1038/ng1136
98. Südhof TC. Neuroligins and neurexins link synaptic function to cognitive disease. *Nature* (2008) **455**:903–11. doi:10.1038/nature07456
99. Etherton M, Földy C, Sharma M, Tabuchi K, Liu X, Shamloo M, et al. Autism-linked neuroligin-3 R451C mutation differentially alters hippocampal and cortical synaptic function. *Proc Natl Acad Sci U S A* (2011) **108**:13764–9. doi:10.1073/pnas.1111093108
100. Pizzarelli R, Cherubini E. Developmental regulation of GABAergic signalling in the hippocampus of neuroligin 3 R451C knock-in mice: an animal model of autism. *Front Cell Neurosci* (2013) **4**(7):85. doi:10.3389/fncel.2013.00085
101. Cheh MA, Millonig JH, Roselli LM, Ming X, Jacobsen E, Kamdar S, et al. En2 knockout mice display neurobehavioral and neurochemical alterations relevant to autism spectrum disorder. *Brain Res* (2006) **1116**:166–76. doi:10.1016/j.brainres.2006.07.086
102. Sudarov A, Joyner AL. Cerebellum morphogenesis: the foliation pattern is orchestrated by multi-cellular anchoring centers. *Neural Dev* (2007) **3**(2):26. doi:10.1186/1749-8104-2-26
103. Tripathi PP, Sgadò P, Scali M, Viaggi C, Casarosa S, Simon HH, et al. Increased susceptibility to kainic acid-induced seizures in engrailed-2 knockout mice. *Neuroscience* (2009) **159**:842–9. doi:10.1016/j.neuroscience.2009.01.007
104. Wagner GC, Reuhl KR, Cheh M, McRae P, Halladay AK. A new neurobehavioral model of autism in mice: pre- and postnatal exposure to sodium valproate. *J Autism Dev Disord* (2006) **36**:779–93. doi:10.1007/s10803-006-0117-y
105. Cherubini E. *Phasic GABA*$_A$-Mediated Inhibition: Jasper's Basic Mechanisms of the Epilepsies. Bethesda, MD: National Center for Biotechnology Information (2012).
106. Kneussel M, Betz H. Receptors, gephyrin and gephyrin-associated proteins: novel insights into the assembly of inhibitory postsynaptic membrane specializations. *J Physiol* (2000) **1**:1–9. doi:10.1111/j.1469-7793.2000.t01-4-00001.x
107. Buddhala C, Hsu CC, Wu JY. A novel mechanism for GABA synthesis and packaging into synaptic vesicles. *Neurochem Int* (2009) **55**:9–12. doi:10.1016/j.neuint.2009.01.020
108. Di Martino A, Tuchman RF. Antiepileptic drugs: affective use in autism spectrum disorders. *Pediatr Neurol* (2001) **25**:199–207. doi:10.1016/S0887-8994(01)00276-4
109. Jambaqué I, Chiron C, Dumas C, Mumford J, Dulac O. Mental and behavioural outcome of infantile epilepsy treated by vigabatrin in tuberous sclerosis patients. *Epilepsy Res* (2000) **38**:151–60. doi:10.1016/S0920-1211(99)00082-0
110. Han S, Tai C, Jones CJ, Scheuer T, Catterall WA. Enhancement of inhibitory neurotransmission by GABAA receptors having α2,3-subunits ameliorates behavioral deficits in a mouse model of autism. *Neuron* (2014) **81**:1282–9. doi:10.1016/j.neuron.2014.01.016
111. Katz DM, Berger-Sweeney JE, Eubanks JH, Justice MJ, Neul JL, Pozzo-Miller L, et al. Preclinical research in Rett syndrome: setting the foundation for translational success. *Dis Model Mech* (2012) **5**:733–45. doi:10.1242/dmm.011007
112. Guy J, Gan J, Selfridge J, Cobb S, Bird A. Reversal of neurological defects in a mouse model of Rett syndrome. *Science* (2007) **315**:1143–7. doi:10.1126/science.1138389
113. Giacometti E, Luikenhuis S, Beard C, Jaenisch R. Partial rescue of MeCP2 deficiency by postnatal activation of MeCP2. *Proc Natl Acad Sci U S A* (2007) **104**:1931–6. doi:10.1073/pnas.0610593104
114. Tropea D, Giacometti E, Wilson NR, Beard C, McCurry C, Fu DD, et al. Partial reversal of Rett syndrome-like symptoms in MeCP2 mutant mice. *Proc Natl Acad Sci U S A* (2009) **106**:2029–34. doi:10.1073/pnas.0812394106
115. Kline DD, Ogier M, Kunze DL, Katz DM. Exogenous brain-derived neurotrophic factor rescues synaptic dysfunction in Mecp2-null mice. *J Neurosci* (2010) **30**:5303–10. doi:10.1523/JNEUROSCI.5503-09.2010
116. Olmos-Serrano JL, Corbin JG, Burns MP. The GABA(A) receptor agonist THIP ameliorates specific behavioral deficits in the mouse model of Fragile X syndrome. *Dev Neurosci* (2011) **33**:395–403. doi:10.1159/000332884
117. Wang LW, Berry-Kravis E, Hagerman RJ. Fragile X: leading the way for targeted treatments in autism. *Neurotherapeutics* (2010) **7**:264–74. doi:10.1016/j.nurt.2010.05.005
118. Zoghbi HY, Bear MF. Synaptic dysfunction in neurodevelopmental disorders associated with autism and intellectual disabilities. *Cold Spring Harb Perspect Biol* (2012) **4**:a009886. doi:10.1101/cshperspect.a009886
119. Berry-Kravis EM, Hessl D, Rathmell B, Zarevics P, Cherubini M, Walton-Bowen K, et al. Effects of STX209 (arbaclofen) on neurobehavioral function in children and adults with Fragile X syndrome: a randomized, controlled, phase 2 trial. *Sci Transl Med* (2012) **4**:152ra127. doi:10.1126/scitranslmed.3004214
120. Oberman LM. mGluR antagonists and GABA agonists as novel pharmacological agents for the treatment of autism spectrum disorders. *Expert Opin Investig Drugs* (2012) **21**(12):1819–25. doi:10.1517/13543784.2012.729819
121. Marrosu F, Marrosu G, Rachel MG, Biggio G. Paradoxical reactions elicited by diazepam in children with classic autism. *Funct Neurol* (1987) **2**:355–61.
122. Hochman DW. The extracellular space and epileptic activity in the adult brain: explaining the antiepileptic effects of furosemide and bumetanide. *Epilepsia* (2012) **1**:18–25. doi:10.1111/j.1528-1167.2012.03471.x
123. Lemonnier E, Ben-Ari Y. The diuretic bumetanide decreases autistic behaviour in five infants treated during 3 months with no side effects. *Acta Paediatr* (2010) **99**:1885–8. doi:10.1111/j.1651-2227.2010.01933.x
124. Lemonnier E, Degrez C, Phelep M, Tyzio R, Josse F, Grandgeorge M, et al. A randomised controlled trial of bumetanide in the treatment of autism in children. *Transl Psychiatry* (2012) **2**:e202. doi:10.1038/tp.2012.124
125. Hadjikhani N, Zürcher NR, Rogier O, Ruest T, Hippolyte L, Ben-Ari Y, et al. Improving emotional face perception in autism with diuretic bumetanide: a proof-of-concept behavioral and functional brain imaging pilot study. *Autism* (2013). doi:10.1177/1362361313514141

2

# Involvement of synaptic genes in the pathogenesis of autism spectrum disorders: the case of synapsins

**_Silvia Giovedí[1†], Anna Corradi[1†], Anna Fassio[1,2] and Fabio Benfenati[1,2*]_**

[1] *Department of Experimental Medicine, University of Genova, Genova, Italy*

[2] *Department of Neuroscience and Brain Technologies, Fondazione Istituto Italiano di Tecnologia, Genova, Italy*

***Edited by:***
*Yuri Bozzi, University of Trento, Italy*

***Reviewed by:***
*A. Kimberley McAllister, University of California, USA*
*Laurie Doering, McMaster University, Canada*

****Correspondence:***
*Fabio Benfenati, Department of Neuroscience and Brain Technologies, Fondazione Istituto Italiano di Tecnologia, Via Morego 30, 16163 Genoa, Italy*
*e-mail: fabio.benfenati@iit.it*

*[†]Silvia Giovedí and Anna Corradi have contributed equally to this work.*

Autism spectrum disorders (ASDs) are heterogeneous neurodevelopmental disorders characterized by deficits in social interaction and social communication, restricted interests, and repetitive behaviors. Many synaptic protein genes are linked to the pathogenesis of ASDs, making them prototypical synaptopathies. An array of mutations in the synapsin (Syn) genes in humans has been recently associated with ASD and epilepsy, diseases that display a frequent comorbidity. Syns are pre-synaptic proteins regulating synaptic vesicle traffic, neurotransmitter release, and short-term synaptic plasticity. In doing so, Syn isoforms control the tone of activity of neural circuits and the balance between excitation and inhibition. As ASD pathogenesis is believed to result from dysfunctions in the balance between excitatory and inhibitory transmissions in neocortical areas, Syns are novel ASD candidate genes. Accordingly, deletion of single Syn genes in mice, in addition to epilepsy, causes core symptoms of ASD by affecting social behavior, social communication, and repetitive behaviors. Thus, Syn knockout mice represent a good experimental model to define synaptic alterations involved in the pathogenesis of ASD and epilepsy.

**Keywords: autism, synaptopathies, synaptic vesicles, synaptic transmission, social behavior, human mutations, knockout mice**

Autism spectrum disorders (ASDs) represent a wide array of neurodevelopmental disorders characterized by restricted interest, defective social interactions, repetitive behaviors, and deficit in language and verbal communication that manifest within the first 3 years of life (1, 2). The complexity of ASD is evident both at the levels of symptoms variability and of causative factors. An important genetic contribution has been observed for ASD, however, the mechanism of inheritance remains largely unknown (1). More than 500 genes have been associated with different forms of autism, but each of them account only for the minority of ASD cases and indeed environmental contributions and other modulating factors, as environment-genetic interplay and epigenetic modifications, are emerging as potential risk factors for ASDs (3).

## INVOLVEMENT OF SYNAPTIC PROTEINS IN THE PATHOGENESIS OF ASDs

Autism spectrum disorders may result from mutations in a large array of genes having roles in various physiological processes such as chromatin remodeling, translation, metabolism, and synaptic functions. In experimental models of ASD, a common breakdown appears to occur at the level of synapse formation and stabilization, as well as of the ability of synapses to be modified by experience through plasticity mechanisms. Synapse dysfunctions are also at the convergence between ASD and other neuropsychiatric disorders with unknown etiology, such as schizophrenia and intellectual disabilities (4). In addition, ASDs frequently occur together with epilepsy and there may be common underlying mechanisms as well as common genetic and environmental risk factors. Synapse maturation and function rely on a vast array of compartmentalized protein–protein interactions that allow fidelity in neurotransmitter release and synaptic vesicle (SV) cycling at the pre-synaptic site and in neurotransmitter receptor localization and signaling at the post-synaptic site. Moreover, synaptic adhesion molecules link and stabilize pre- and post-synaptic sites and control synaptic modification induced by plasticity.

The synaptic theory for autism originally stems from the identification of ASD mutations in the Neuroligin genes [NLGN3 and NLGN4X; (5, 6)] coding for synaptic adhesion molecules expressed at the post-synaptic site. Since then, a growing repertoire of synaptic genes, coding for both pre- and post-synaptic proteins, have been implicated in non-syndromic ASDs: synaptic adhesion molecules [neuroligins, neurexins, cadherins, contactins and contactin-associated protein-like 2, or CNTNAP2; (7–9)], synaptic scaffold proteins [PROSAP/SHANK gene family; (10)], ion channels, and neurotransmitter receptors (11–13). Moreover, mutations in additional synaptic genes, such as the pre-synaptic RIMS3/NIM3 and the post-synaptic IL1RAPL1 and SynGAP1, involved in either SV organization or synapse formation, have been recently associated with ASD cases [(14–17); **Figure 1** and **Table 1**]. The identification of synaptic genes implicated in ASDs is expanding together with the characterization of the respective animal models bearing mutations or deletions in these genes. These models allow a more systematic analysis to study the role of those genes in ASD etiology, to discover the biological mechanisms underlying autistic behaviors and evaluate the efficacy of new potential treatments (18–21).

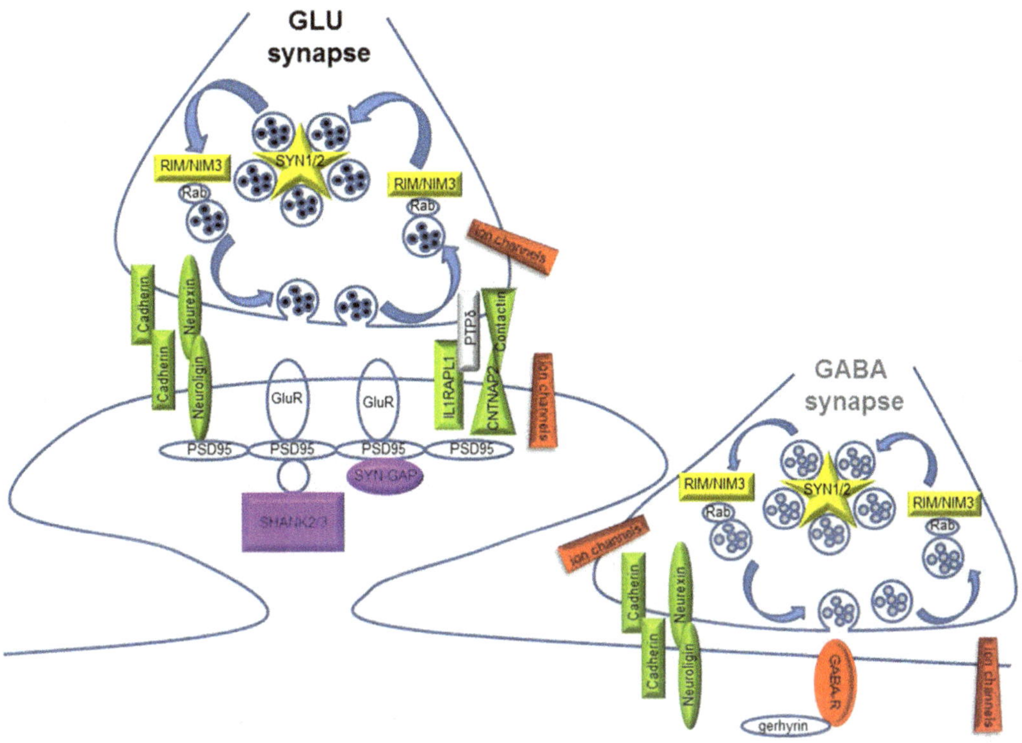


**FIGURE 1 | Schematic diagram illustrating pre- and post-synaptic gene products implicated in ASD.** Glutamate (GLU) and GABA synapses are shown. Different colors code for synaptic function: yellow, synaptic vesicle cycling; green, synapse formation and maintenance; red, neuronal excitability and neurotransmission; violet, glutamate receptors (GluR) signaling/trafficking.

## ASD IS ASSOCIATED WITH DYSFUNCTIONS IN CORTICAL CIRCUITS THAT ALSO PREDISPOSE TO EPILEPSY

Autism spectrum disorder-like phenotypes are observed in a wide variety of neurological and neurodevelopmental disorders, including epilepsy, Rett syndrome, Fragile X Syndrome, Tuberous Sclerosis, or Fetal Anticonvulsant Syndrome, which are characterized by an imbalance of the excitatory/inhibitory tone. This aspect is consistent with the very high prevalence of epilepsy in autistic patients (about 25%) with respect to the average prevalence of 1% in the general population. Characteristic ASD phenotypes are associated with impairments or gains of GABAergic transmission (22–25).

Decreases in the GABA synthesizing enzyme GAD and a reduction in quantal size have been reported in the experimental model of Rett syndrome, the Mecp2 knockout (KO) mice (26). Various impairments in GABAergic function, including deficient GABAergic circuitry, decreased expression of $GABA_A$ receptor subunits (particularly $\alpha5$ and $\gamma$ subunits) and of the tonic GABA current, have been observed in mice lacking FMRP, a recognized experimental model of Fragile X Syndrome (27). The chromosomal region 15q11–q13, which is deleted or duplicated in 1–2% of idiopatic ASD patients, contains a cluster of genes encoding GABA receptor subunits [Gabra5, Gabrb3, and Gabrg3; (11)] and deletion of the Gabrb3 gene in mice, encoding for the $GABA_A$ $\beta3$ receptor subunit, leads to an ASD-like phenotype (28). Moreover, Reeler mice, lacking the protein reelin that is expressed in cortical interneurons, display an ASD phenotype that is associated with a decrease in GABA turnover (29, 30). Mice lacking synapsins (Syns) also display a primary impairment in GABA release dynamics that is associated with an ASD-like phenotype [see below; (31–35)]. Taken together, all these experimental data indicate that GABA systems are major actors in the development and functioning of cortical networks, and that their dysfunction can lead to altered development and/or function of cortical circuits resulting in epilepsy, ASD, or both. Moreover, the role of GABAergic dysfunctions in ASD pathogenesis is complex given the switch between excitatory and inhibitory GABA transmission that occurs during development and the multiple sites of action of GABA in mature neuronal networks, where it acts on predominantly post-synaptic $GABA_A$ receptors, extrasynaptic $GABA_A$ receptors regulating excitability and predominantly pre-synaptic $GABA_B$ receptors modulating glutamate release and short-term plasticity properties of excitatory synapses. Thus, disruption or dysfunction of GABAergic systems may delay critical periods in specific brain regions and perturb $\gamma$-oscillations implicated in high cognitive functions. Given the importance of the excitation/inhibition balance in the activity-dependent formation and plasticity of neocortical networks, we here review on the role of the Syns, a family of pre-synaptic proteins regulating release and plasticity in inhibitory and excitatory synapses, in the etiology of ASDs and the use of Syn KO animals as a model for these complex neuropsychiatric disorders.

**Table 1 | Synaptic genes associated with ASD.**

| Gene | Name | Chromosomal locus | Phenotype | Function |
|---|---|---|---|---|
| SYN1 | Synapsin1 | Xp11.23 | ASD, epilepsy | Synaptic vesicle cycling |
| SYN2 | Synapsin2 | 3p25 | ASD, epilepsy | Synaptic vesicle cycling |
| RIMS3 | Regulating synaptic membrane exocytosis 3 | 1p34.2 | ASD | Synaptic vesicle cycling |
| CACNA1E | Calcium channel, voltage-dependent R type, alpha 1E subunit | 1q25.3 | ASD | Neurotransmission |
| CACNB2 | Calcium channel, accessory beta2 subunit | 10p12 | ASD | Neurotransmission |
| SCN1A | Voltage-regulated sodium channel type 1 | 2q24.3 | Dravet syndrome, ASD | Neuronal excitability |
| SCN2A | Voltage-regulated sodium channel type 2 | 2q24.3 | ASD, epilepsy | Neuronal excitability |
| SCN3A | Voltage-regulated sodium channel type 3 | 2q24 | ASD, epilepsy | Neuronal excitability |
| KCNMA1 | Potassium calcium-activated channel, subfamily M, alpha member 1 | 10q22.3 | ASD | Neuronal excitability |
| KCNMB4 | Potassium calcium-activated channel, subfamily M, beta member 4 | 12q | ASD | Neuronal excitability |
| KCNQ3 | Potassium voltage-gated channel | 8q24 | ASD, epilepsy | Neuronal excitability |
| KCNQ5 | Potassium voltage-gated channel | 6q14 | ASD, epilepsy | Neuronal excitability |
| KCND2 | Potassium voltage-gated channel | 7q31 | ASD, epilepsy | Neuronal excitability |
| NRXN1 | Neurexin1 | 2p16.3 | ASD, schizophrenia | Cell-adhesion |
| NLGN3 | Neuroligin3 | Xq13.1 | ASD | Cell-adhesion |
| NLGN4X | Neuroligin4 | Xp22.32–p22.31 | ASD, intellectual disability | Cell-adhesion |
| CNTNAP2 | Contactin-associated protein-like 2 | 7q35 | ASD, intellectual disability, epilepsy schizophrenia | Cell-adhesion |
| CDH5 | Cadherin 5 | 16q22.1 | ASD | Cell-adhesion |
| CDH8 | Cadherin 8 | 16q22.1 | ASD | Cell-adhesion |
| CDH9 | Cadherin 9 | 5p14 | ASD | Cell-adhesion |
| CDH10 | Cadherin 10 | 5p14.2 | ASD | Cell-adhesion |
| CDH11 | Cadherin 11 | 16q21 | ASD | Cell-adhesion |
| CDH13 | Cadherin 13 | 16q23.3 | ASD | Cell-adhesion |
| CDH15 | Cadherin 15 | 16q24.3 | ASD, intellectual disability | Cell-adhesion |
| PCDHB4 | Protocadherin beta4 | 5q31 | ASD | Cell-adhesion |
| PCDH10 | Protocadherin delta 10 | 4q28.3 | ASD | Cell-adhesion |
| PCDH19 | Protocadherin delta 19 | Xq22.1 | ASD, intellectual disability | Cell-adhesion |
| CNTN4 | Contactin 4 | 3p26.3 | ASD, intellectual disability | Cell-adhesion |
| CNTN5 | Contactin 5 | 11q22.1 | ASD | Cell-adhesion |
| CNTN6 | Contactin 6 | 3p26–p25 | ASD | Cell-adhesion |
| IL1RAPL1 | Interleukin 1 receptor accessory protein-like 1 | Xp22.121.3 | ASD, intellectual disability | Cell-adhesion |
| SHANK1 | SH3 and multiple ankyrin domain protein 1 | 19q13.3 | ASD | Glutamate receptor signaling |
| SHANK2 | SH3 and multiple ankyrin domain protein 2 | 11q13.3 | ASD | Glutamate receptor signaling |
| SHANK3 | SH3 and multiple ankyrin domain protein 3 | 22q13.3 | ASD | Glutamate receptor signaling |
| SYNGAP1 | Synaptic Ras GTPase activating protein 1 | 6p21.3 | ASD | Glutamate receptor signaling |
| GABRG3 | Gamma3 subunit of GABA-A receptor | 15q12 | ASD | Neurotransmission |

## SYNAPSINS

The Syns are a family of abundant neuronal phosphoproteins that participate as regulators in synaptic transmission and plasticity, as well as in neuronal development [see Ref. (36, 37), for review]. The family is composed of 10 homologous proteins: Syn Ia–b, Syn IIa–b, and Syn IIIa–f (38–40), encoded in mammals by alternative splicing of three distinct genes (*SYN1*, *SYN2*, and *SYN3*) mapping on distinct chromosomes (chromosome X, 3, and 22, respectively) in human and mouse. Notably, Syn III is the most precociously expressed isoform that has a role in the early phases of neural development and is downregulated in mature neurons (40). On the other hand, Syn I and Syn II are expressed at low levels at birth and their expression progressively increases along synaptogenesis to reach a stable plateau at 1–2 months of life, approximately the time window epilepsy appears (41).

All Syn isoforms display a domain structure with the $NH_2$-terminal region, highly conserved across isoforms and species, divided in domains A, B, and C, and the COOH-terminal portion, more divergent, composed of different spliced domains [D–I; (38)]. Many of these isoforms share consensus sequences for phosphorylation by several protein kinases, which all contribute to the modulation of Syn function (36). Domain A contains the phosphorylation site for PKA and CaMKI/IV that modulates the reversible association of Syn with SVs. Domain B, less conserved and considered as a link region, contains phosphorylation sites for MAPK/Erk, which also causes the redistribution of Syn from SVs to the cytosol. Domain C, a large central region of about 300 amino acids, mediates the interaction with actin filaments and SVs and promotes SV clustering by inducing Syn homo/hetero-dimerization (42, 43). This domain is phosphorylated by the tyrosine kinase Src (44) and contains residues mediating the binding to ATP (45). The sequences of Syn isoforms at the COOH-terminal region diverge (domain D in Syn Ia and Ib, domain G in Syn IIa and IIb, domain H in Syn IIa, and domain J in Syn IIIa), although they all bear proline-rich regions binding to several SH3-containing proteins (46, 47), and additional phosphorylation sites for CaMKII, MAPK/Erk, and cdk1/5, which affect the biochemical properties of Syn I resulting in a drastic reduction of its binding to both actin and SVs (48, 49). Finally domain E, highly conserved and common to all "*a*" isoforms, modulates Syn targeting to the pre-synaptic terminals and SV trafficking (50–53).

The best-characterized function of Syns is to control SV trafficking and modulate neurotransmitter release at the pre-synaptic terminal. The fine regulation of the balance between the reserve and the readily releasable pool of SVs is strictly controlled by Syn site-specific phosphorylation in response to stimulation, which modulates Syn association with SVs, actin cytoskeleton, and other synaptic proteins, and leaves SVs free to move close to the active zone and undergo fusion. Besides the function of Syns in these pre-docking stages of neurotransmission, recent data, supported by the fact that at least part of Syn do not dissociate from SVs upon fusion, strongly indicate that Syns play a role in the final post-docking stages of exocytosis, including SV priming, fusion, and recycling of the synaptic membrane in the area surrounding the active zone [see Ref. (36), for review].

Beyond the role in synaptic transmission, the various Syn isoforms play an important role in neuronal growth and synaptogenesis. Lack of Syn I or Syn II was shown to impair neurite outgrowth during the first days *in vitro* (54), while downregulation or ablation of Syn III caused an impairment in the development of axons at early stages in culture (55). Moreover, clear-cut structural and physiological defects were observed in the pre-synaptic terminals of Syn KO neurons (56–58), confirming the role of Syn isoforms in the modulation of synapse formation, maintenance, and rearrangement [see Ref. (37), for review].

## SYNAPSIN KO MICE ARE EPILEPTIC

Knockout mice for either Syn gene are viable and fertile, have a normal life expectancy and brains of normal size and gross structure. As Syns are involved in the regulation of the excitability of neuronal networks, it is not surprising that the impairment of Syn function can result in epilepsy. Syn I KO, Syn II KO, Syn I/II double KO, and Syn I/II/III triple KO are all prone to epileptic seizures that appear approximately at 2–3 months of age, and progressively aggravate with aging and the number of Syn genes ablated [(59, 60); see Ref. (61) for review]. The fact that epilepsy does not appear at birth after ablation of Syn I or Syn II genes and that Syn III KO mice are not epileptic can be explained by the specific expression profile of the three Syn genes during development (55, 62). It is therefore likely that mature synapses require physiological levels of both Syn I and Syn II to achieve a stable excitation/inhibition balance during activity, while Syn III seems to be dispensable in this respect. In general, the loss of Syns disrupts the reserve pool of SV and alters release dynamics. However, the pre- and post-docking effects of the Syns differentially affect excitatory and inhibitory neurons. This, together with the selective distribution of the various Syn isoforms in distinct neuronal populations and the non-overlapping functions of Syn isoforms on neurotransmitter release, can result in an imbalance between excitatory and inhibitory synaptic transmission, both under conditions of basal activity and of high-frequency stimulation, potentially leading to epileptogenesis (31, 33, 34).

## SYNAPSIN KO MICE DISPLAY AN ASD-LIKE PHENOTYPE

Although it is not an easy task to translate the complex symptoms of human ASD into mouse behaviors, the study of the phenotype of mice bearing deletions in the genes found to be mutated in ASD patients is fundamental for the understanding of how dysfunction of single components of the synaptic protein network may result in a general functional impairment that generates the disease. Such mouse models of ASDs should display decreased interest toward the environment, impaired sociability, and social interactions/communication, as well as repetitive behaviors.

Synapsin KO mice have generally preserved cognitive functions. A prospective study performed on Syn I and Syn II KO mice revealed that cognitive and emotional performances are not altered before the onset of epilepsy both in terms of spatial memory, object recognition, and emotional memory. Only later on, during aging and in the presence of an overt epileptic phenotype, behavioral deficits in emotional memory in both genotypes and spatial memory in Syn II KO mice emerged with respect to wild type controls, and were associated with neuronal loss and gliosis in the cortex and hippocampus (63). On the other hand, Syn III KO mice that are not epileptic, exhibit only minor alterations in spatial memory, object recognition, fear conditioning, and fear-potentiated startle (40, 64).

When an array of socially directed behaviors (social interaction and novelty, social recognition and social dominance, social transmission of food preference, and social memory) were investigated in Syn I, Syn II, and Syn III KO mice before (2-months old) and after (6-months old) the appearance of epilepsy (in Syn I and Syn II KO mice), it was immediately clear that mice presented various impairments in social behaviors and repetitive behaviors well before the appearance of the epileptic phenotype (65).

Synapsin III mice had the mildest phenotype and showed impairments only in social interactions with an intruder, a decreased social dominance and a decreased social transmission of food preference. Syn I KO mice had an intermediate phenotype and had deficits in social and environmental exploration, social transmission, and an increased social dominance. Finally, Syn II KO had the more severe behavioral phenotype and exhibited significant deficits in virtually all social behaviors tested (with the exception of the social transmission of food preference) together with an increased social dominance and repetitive self-grooming behaviors (**Figure 2**). These data indicate that Syn KO mice represent an interesting animal model for ASDs. The physiopathological importance of this model for the understanding of ASD pathogenesis is underlined by the occurrence of ASD-linked loss-of-function mutations in human SYN genes, as described in the following section.

## MUTATIONS IN THE SYN GENES ARE ASSOCIATED WITH ASD IN HUMANS

Autism spectrum disorder-associated mutations were found in both human SYN1 and SYN2 genes. Mutations in SYN1 were mainly identified in patients affected by both epilepsy and autism, whereas, mutations in SYN2 were observed in cases of ASD without association with epilepsy. The identified mutations are schematized in **Figure 3**. Two SYN1 nonsense mutations, causing truncations at protein level (W356X and Q555X), were identified in two large families with epilepsy with recessive X-linked transmission. In addition to epilepsy, few males carrying the mutations in SYNI also presented learning difficulties, low average IQ and three of them meet criteria for ASD (66, 67). The SYN1 missense mutation A550T was isolated in four patients: two with epilepsy, one with autism, and one with both, whereas, the missense mutation T567A was isolated in two individuals with ASD only. A frameshift (A94fs199X) and two missense (Y236S and G464R) mutations were identified in the SYN2 gene in three males affected by ASD (68). The mutation was transmitted by the non-affected mother. Although this phenomenon was observed only in a limited number of individuals, it is consistent with a recent report on the autosomal SHANK1 gene deletions associated with ASD in males but not females (69). Autosomal sex-limited expression, in addition to the mutation in X-linked genes, may contribute to the increased prevalence of ASD in males with respect to females. The exact mechanism at the basis of the higher penetrance in males remains to be determined.

## EFFECTS OF HUMAN SYN MUTANTS EXPRESSED IN SYN KO NEURONS

To get insight into the molecular mechanisms of the pathogenesis of these diseases, the physiological effects of the SYN genetic variants associated with ASDs or epilepsy (or both) were analyzed *in vitro* by expressing the mutants in primary hippocampal neurons from Syn I KO or Syn II KO mice and their effects on neuronal development, nerve terminal targeting, dynamics of exo-endocytosis, and synaptic transmission were studied and compared with wild type Syn.

For the W356X mutation in Syn I, the presence of a premature stop codon in the human SYNI transcript leads to nonsense-mediated mRNA decay (NMD). The few transcripts escaping NMD process give rise to a mislocalized and non-functional protein (70). On the contrary, the second nonsense mutation (Q555X) in Syn I does not lead to NMD and a truncated form of Syn I is expressed that lacks about a half of the D domain and the COOH-terminal domains E/F. The lack of D domain impairs its binding to SVs, its phosphorylation by CaMKII and MAPK/Erk and its interactions with SH3 domain-containing proteins such as PI3K, Src, endophilin, and intersectin (67). Neurons expressing the Q555X-Syn I showed a transient impairment of axonal outgrowth, but normal dendritic arborization, nerve terminal targeting, and synaptic density (67). However, the exocytosis was impaired and the size of the readily releasable and recycling pools of SVs decreased. Electrophysiological recordings from neurons expressing Q555X-Syn I mutant in Syn I KO background showed that, while the basal

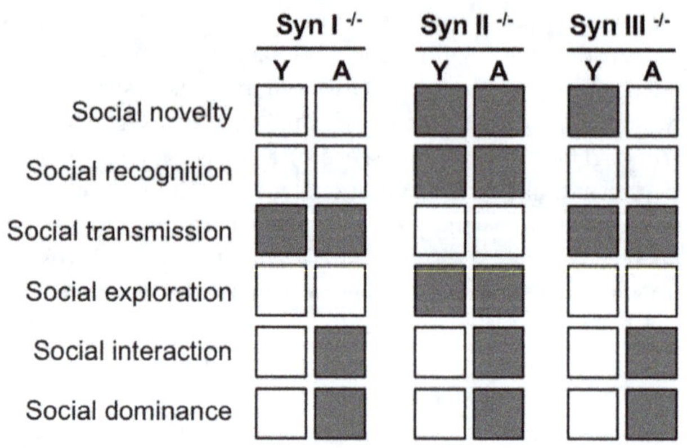


**FIGURE 2 | Summary of the abnormalities in social behavior (gray squares) observed in young (Y, 2-month old) and adult (A, 6-month old) Syn I, Syn II, and Syn III KO mice with respect to the behavior of age-matched controls sharing the same genetic background [data from Ref. (65)].** Adults, but not young, Syn I and Syn II KO mice are epileptic.

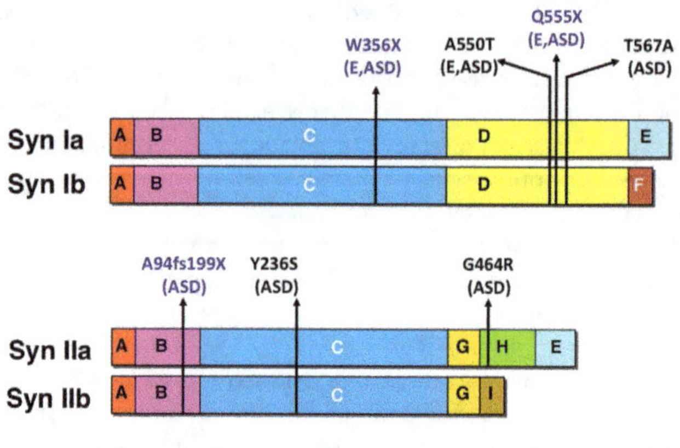


**FIGURE 3 | Human mutations in SYN1 and SYN2 associated with epilepsy and/or ASD.** Nonsense and missense mutations are indicated in blue and black, respectively together with the associated pathology (E, epilepsy; ASD, autism spectrum disorder).

excitatory and inhibitory transmissions were equally depressed by the mutant, a clear imbalance in short-term plasticity was present with excitatory synapses showing markedly increased paired-pulse facilitation and post-tetanic potentiation as well as faster recovery from depression, whereas, inhibitory synapses displaying an enhanced post-tetanic depression and synaptic depression during sustained high-frequency stimulation, as well as a marked slowed-down recovery from depression. This excitatory/inhibitory balance in the temporal domain of short-term synaptic plasticity produced a marked hyperexcitability and enhanced network bursting behavior at network level as demonstrated by multi-electrode array recordings, also underlining the key role of short-term plasticity at excitatory and inhibitory synapses in the regulation of network excitability (71). Two further missense mutations in Syn I (A550T and T567A) located in domain D did not significantly affected phosphorylation, molecular interactions of Syn I, or neuronal development. However, the mutants were not correctly targeted to nerve terminals and, in addition, the dynamics and sizes of the readily releasable and recycling pools of SVs at synaptic terminals were impaired (67).

The Syn II mutants had distinct physiological effects. The A94fs199X-Syn II mutant was not expressed in neurons, probably because fast degradation of the aberrant protein. Both missense mutants Y236S- and G464R-Syn II were correctly expressed in Syn II KO neurons and targeted to nerve terminals. However, both mutants impaired the size of the recycling pool of SVs, leaving the readily releasable pool unaffected. Moreover, the G464R-Syn II mutant also caused an impaired axonal growth and dendritic development of neurons (68). Similar defects in neuronal development and dendritic arborization were found in neurons silenced for the ASD-associated gene CNTNAP2, with a resulting impairment of neural circuit assembly and changes in network activity, possible causes of ASD pathogenesis (72).

Synapsin KO neurons expressing the genetic variants of Syns share common defects in SV pool dynamics. Syn I and Syn II are known to control the density of SVs at the nerve terminal and regulate their availability for release differentially, with Syn I affecting both the readily releasable and recycling pools of SVs, and Syn II only affecting the latter pool. The analysis of the dynamics of exo-endocytosis in neurons expressing genetic variants of Syns reflects these distinct effects. ASD manifestations begin in the second/third year of life, a period of intense refinement, remodeling, and experience-dependent plasticity of synapses. This periods overlaps with developmental expression pattern of Syns. Impairments in SV pool dynamics, associated with defects in short-term plasticity and/or neuronal development, may thereby destabilize the key processes of assembly of neuronal networks and the balance between excitation and inhibition.

## CONCLUDING REMARKS

Synapsins are not essential for synaptic transmission, but play a key role in synaptic homeostasis and plasticity with direct consequences in network activity and excitatory/inhibitory balance. Based on the findings in human and mice, Syn genes may represent a common genetic basis for epilepsy and ASD and, accordingly, Syn KO mice can be considered a potentially interesting animal model for ASD. Similar to what occurs in children with ASDs and epilepsy, ASD-related behaviors in Syn I KO and Syn II KO mice precede the onset of seizures and epilepsy does not significantly affect the expression of the behavioral alterations in adult mice. Moreover, the non-epileptic Syn III KO mice also display some traits of social deficits. These observations lead to the idea that epilepsy and ASD follow distinct and independent pathogenic pathways, although the genetic basis appears to be largely shared by the two diseases. Although the mutations in the Syn genes found thus far account only for a limited number of ASD cases, they map into a "synaptic autism pathway" in which dysfunctions of any of the genes essential for the regulation of synapse formation, excitation/inhibition balance and activity-dependent plasticity can result in a similar ASD phenotype. Despite the inherent redundancy and robustness of mammalian biological systems, a focused dysfunction in one synaptic gene can induce secondary changes in the synaptic machinery impacting on synaptic plasticity, leading to complex dysfunctions at the circuit level associated with the appearance of the pathological phenotype. An example of this potential derangement of a complex machinery by genetic dysfunction of a single component is provided by the numerous and diverse genes implicated in phototransduction whose mutation converges toward the common clinical phenotype of *Retinitis pigmentosa* (73). In addition, it has been proposed that gene alterations and secondary dysfunctions may accumulate non-linearly in complex gene networks implicated in neural computation and higher brain functions, such as those constituting the synaptome (74, 75). In conclusion, although our map of ASD vulnerability genes is rapidly progressing, many challenges remain for the future, particularly concerning the interactions between genetic, epigenetic, and environmental factors to produce the complex ASD clinical manifestations.

## ACKNOWLEDGMENTS

We are grateful to Dr. Paul Greengard (The Rockefeller University, New York, NY, USA) for providing us with the Syn KO mice, for the fruitful discussions and the continuous support and to Dr. Patrick Cossette (Université de Montreal, Montreal, QC, Canada) for the fruitful collaboration on human SYN mutations. This study was supported by research grants from the Italian Ministry of University and Research (PRIN to Fabio Benfenati and Anna Corradi and FIRB 2010 "*Futuro in Ricerca*" to Silvia Giovedí), EU FP7 Integrating Project "*Desire*", Jerome Lejeune Foundation (to Anna Fassio) and Cure Epilepsy "*Advanced Innovator Award*" (to Fabio Benfenati). The support of Telethon-Italy (Grants GGP09134 and GGP033 to Fabio Benfenati) is also acknowledged.

## REFERENCES

1. Abrahams BS, Geschwind DH. Advances in autism genetics: on the threshold of a new neurobiology. *Nat Rev Genet* (2008) **9**:341–55. doi:10.1038/nrg2346
2. Levitt P, Campbell DB. The genetic and neurobiologic compass points toward common signaling dysfunctions in autism spectrum disorders. *J Clin Invest* (2009) **119**:747–54. doi:10.1172/JCI37934
3. Persico AM, Napolioni V. Autism genetics. *Behav Brain Res* (2013) **251**:95–112. doi:10.1016/j.bbr.2013.06.012
4. Pinto D, Delaby E, Merico D, Barbosa M, Merikangas A, Klei L, et al. Convergence of genes and cellular pathways dysregulated in autism spectrum disorders. *Am J Hum Genet* (2014) **294**:677–94. doi:10.1016/j.ajhg.2014.03.018

5. Jamain S, Quach H, Betancur C, Råstam M, Colineaux C, Gillberg IC, et al. Mutations of the X-linked genes encoding neuroligins NLGN3 and NLGN4 are associated with autism. *Nat Genet* (2003) **34**:27–9. doi:10.1038/ng1136
6. Zoghbi HY. Postnatal neurodevelopmental disorders: meeting at the synapse? *Science* (2003) **302**:826–30. doi:10.1126/science.1089071
7. Sudhof TC. Neuroligins and neurexins link synaptic function to cognitive disease. *Nature* (2008) **455**:903–11. doi:10.1038/nature07456
8. Bentacur C, Sakurai T, Buxbaum JD. The emerging role of synaptic cell adhesion pathways in the pathogenesis of autism spectrum disorders. *Trends Neurosci* (2009) **32**:402–12. doi:10.1016/j.tins.2009.04.003
9. Redies C, Hertel N, Hübner CA. Cadherins and neuropsychiatric disorders. *Brain Res* (2012) **1470**:130–44. doi:10.1016/j.brainres.2012.06.020
10. Jiang YH, Ehlers MD. Modeling autism by SHANK gene mutations in mice. *Neuron* (2013) **78**:8–27. doi:10.1016/j.neuron.2013.03.016
11. Shao Y, Cuccaro ML, Hauser ER, Raiford KL, Menold MM, Wolpert CM, et al. Fine mapping of autistic disorder to chromosome 15q11-q13 by use of phenotypic subtypes. *Am J Hum Genet* (2003) **72**:539–48. doi:10.1086/367846
12. Li X, Zou H, Brown WT. Genes associated with autism spectrum disorder. *Brain Res Bull* (2012) **88**:543–52. doi:10.1016/j.brainresbull.2012.05.017
13. Schmunk G, Gargus JJ. Channelopathy pathogenesis in autism spectrum disorders. *Front Genet* (2013) **4**:222. doi:10.3389/fgene.2013.00222
14. Piton A, Michaud JL, Peng H, Aradhya S, Gauthier J, Mottron L, et al. Mutations in the calcium-related gene IL1RAPL1 are associated with autism. *Hum Mol Genet* (2008) **17**:3965–74. doi:10.1093/hmg/ddn300
15. Kumar RA, Sudi J, Babatz TD, Brune CW, Oswald D, Yen M, et al. A de novo 1p34.2 microdeletion identifies the synaptic vesicle gene RIMS3 as a novel candidate for autism. *J Med Genet* (2010) **47**:81–90. doi:10.1136/jmg.2008.065821
16. Hamdan FF, Daoud H, Piton A, Gauthier J, Dobrzeniecka S, Krebs MO, et al. De novo SYNGAP1 mutations in nonsyndromic intellectual disability and autism. *Biol Psychiatry* (2011) **69**:898–901. doi:10.1016/j.biopsych.2010.11.015
17. Berryer MH, Hamdan FF, Klitten LL, Møller RS, Carmant L, Schwartzentruber J, et al. Mutations in SYNGAP1 cause intellectual disability, autism, and a specific form of epilepsy by inducing haploinsufficiency. *Hum Mutat* (2013) **34**:385–94. doi:10.1002/humu.22248
18. Zoghbi HY, Bear MF. Synaptic dysfunction in neurodevelopmental disorders associated with autism and intellectual disabilities. *Cold Spring Harb Perspect Biol* (2012) **4**:a009886. doi:10.1101/cshperspect.a009886
19. Delorne R, Ely E, Toro R, Leboyer M, Gillberg C, Bourgeron T. Progress toward treatments for synaptic defects in autism. *Nat Med* (2013) **6**:685–94. doi:10.1038/nm.3193
20. Banerjee S, Riordan M, Bhat MA. Genetic aspects of autism spectrum disorders: insight from animal models. *Front Cell Neurosci* (2014) **8**:58. doi:10.3389/fncel.2014.00058
21. Kleijer KT, Schmeisser MJ, Krueger DD, Boeckers TM, Scheiffele P, Bourgeron T, et al. Neurobiology of autism gene products: towards pathogenesis and drug targets. *Psychopharmacology (Berl)* (2014) **231**:1037–42. doi:10.1007/s00213-013-3403-3
22. Zoghbi HY. Dysfunction in GABA signalling mediates autism-like stereotypies and Rett syndrome phenotypes. *Nature* (2010) **468**:263–9. doi:10.1038/nature09582
23. Ramamoorthi K, Lin Y. The contribution of GABAergic dysfunction to neurodevelopmental disorders. *Trends Mol Med* (2011) **17**:452–62. doi:10.1016/j.molmed.2011.03.003
24. Pizzarelli R, Cherubini E. Alterations of GABAergic signaling in autism spectrum disorders. *Neural Plast* (2011) **2011**:297153. doi:10.1155/2011/297153
25. Coghlan S, Horder J, Inkster B, Mendez MA, Murphy DG, Nutt DJ. GABA system dysfunction in autism and related disorders: from synapse to symptoms. *Neurosci Biobehav Rev* (2012) **36**:2044–55. doi:10.1016/j.neubiorev.2012.07.005
26. Chao H-T, Chen H, Samaco RC, Xue M, Chahrour M, Yoo J, et al. Dysfunction in GABA signalling mediates autism-like stereotypies and Rett syndrome phenotypes. *Nature* (2010) **468**:263–9. doi:10.1038/nature09582
27. Selby L, Zhang C, Sun QQ. Major defects in neocortical GABAergic inhibitory circuits in mice lacking the fragile X mental retardation protein. *Neurosci Lett* (2007) **412**:227–32. doi:10.1016/j.neulet.2006.11.062
28. DeLorey TM, Sahbaie P, Hashemi E, Homanics GE, Clark JD. Gabrb3 gene deficient mice exhibit impaired social and exploratory behaviors, deficits in non-selective attention and hypoplasia of cerebellar vermal lobules: a potential model of autism spectrum disorder. *Behav Brain Res* (2008) **187**:207–20. doi:10.1016/j.bbr.2007.09.009
29. Bailey A, Luthert P, Dean A, Harding B, Janota I, Montgomery M, et al. A clinicopathological study of autism. *Brain* (1998) **121**:889–905. doi:10.1093/brain/121.5.889
30. Carboni G, Tueting P, Tremolizzo L, Sugaya I, Davis J, Costa E, et al. Enhanced dizocilpine efficacy in heterozygous reeler mice relates to GABA turnover downregulation. *Neuropharmacology* (2004) **46**:1070–81. doi:10.1016/j.neuropharm.2004.02.001
31. Gitler D, Takagishi Y, Feng J, Ren Y, Rodriguiz RM, Wetsel WC, et al. Different presynaptic roles of synapsins at excitatory and inhibitory synapses. *J Neurosci* (2004) **24**:11368–80. doi:10.1523/JNEUROSCI.3795-04.2004
32. Baldelli P, Fassio A, Valtorta F, Benfenati F. Lack of synapsin I reduces the readily releasable pool of synaptic vesicles at central inhibitory synapses. *J Neurosci* (2007) **27**:13520–31. doi:10.1523/JNEUROSCI.3151-07.2007
33. Chiappalone M, Casagrande S, Tedesco M, Valtorta F, Baldelli P, Martinoia S, et al. Opposite changes in glutamatergic and GABAergic transmission underlie the diffuse hyperexcitability of synapsin I-deficient cortical networks. *Cereb Cortex* (2008) **19**:1422–39. doi:10.1093/cercor/bhn182
34. Farisello P, Boido D, Nieus T, Medrihan L, Cesca F, Valtorta F, et al. Synaptic and extrasynaptic origin of the excitation/inhibition imbalance in the hippocampus of synapsin I/II/III knockout mice. *Cereb Cortex* (2013) **23**:581–93. doi:10.1093/cercor/bhs041
35. Medrihan L, Cesca F, Raimondi A, Lignani G, Baldelli P, Benfenati F. Synapsin II desynchronizes neurotransmitter release at inhibitory synapses by interacting with presynaptic calcium channels. *Nat Commun* (2013) **4**:1512. doi:10.1038/ncomms2515
36. Cesca F, Baldelli P, Valtorta F, Benfenati F. The synapsins: key actors of synapse function and plasticity. *Prog Neurobiol* (2010) **91**:313–48. doi:10.1016/j.pneurobio.2010.04.006
37. Fornasiero EF, Bonanomi D, Benfenati F, Valtorta F. The role of synapsins in neuronal development. *Cell Mol Life Sci* (2010) **67**:1383–96. doi:10.1007/s00018-009-0227-8
38. Südhof TC, Czernik AJ, Kao H-T, Takei K, Johnston PA, Horiuchi A, et al. Synapsins: mosaics of shared and individual domains in a family of synaptic vesicle phosphoproteins. *Science* (1989) **245**:1474–80. doi:10.1126/science.2506642
39. Porton B, Kao H-T, Greengard P. Characterization of transcripts from the synapsin III gene locus. *J Neurochem* (1999) **73**:2266–71. doi:10.1046/j.1471-4159.1999.0732266.x
40. Porton B, Wetsel WC, Kao H-T. Synapsin III: role in neuronal plasticity and disease. *Semin Cell Dev Biol* (2011) **22**:416–24. doi:10.1016/j.semcdb.2011.07.007
41. Bogen IL, Jensen V, Hvalby O, Walaas SI. Synapsin-dependent development of glutamatergic synaptic vesicles and presynaptic plasticity in postnatal mouse brain. *Neuroscience* (2009) **158**:231–41. doi:10.1016/j.neuroscience.2008.05.055
42. Benfenati F, Valtorta F, Rossi MC, Onofri F, Sihra T, Greengard P. Interactions of synapsin I with phospholipids: possible role in synaptic vesicle clustering and in the maintenance of bilayer structures. *J Cell Biol* (1993) **123**:1845–55. doi:10.1083/jcb.123.6.1845
43. Hosaka M, Südhof TC. Homo- and heterodimerization of synapsins. *J Biol Chem* (1999) **274**:16747–53. doi:10.1074/jbc.274.24.16747
44. Onofri F, Messa M, Matafora V, Bonanno G, Corradi A, Bachi A, et al. Synapsin phosphorylation by SRC tyrosine kinase enhances SRC activity in synaptic vesicles. *J Biol Chem* (2007) **282**:15754–67. doi:10.1074/jbc.M701051200
45. Esser L, Wang CR, Hosaka M, Smagula CS, Südhof TC, Deisenhofer J. Synapsin I is structurally similar to ATP-utilizing enzymes. *EMBO J* (1998) **17**:977–84. doi:10.1093/emboj/17.4.977
46. Onofri F, Giovedí S, Kao H-T, Valtorta F, Bongiorno Borbone L, De Camilli P, et al. Specificity of the binding of synapsin I to SRC homology 3 domains. *J Biol Chem* (2000) **275**:29857–67. doi:10.1074/jbc.M006018200
47. Giovedí S, Darchen F, Valtorta F, Greengard P, Benfenati F. Synapsin is a novel Rab3 effector protein on small synaptic vesicles. II. Functional effects of the Rab3A-synapsin I interaction. *J Biol Chem* (2004) **279**:43769–79. doi:10.1074/jbc.M404168200
48. Benfenati F, Valtorta F, Rubenstein JL, Gorelick FS, Greengard P, Czernik AJ. Synaptic vesicle-associated $Ca^{2+}$/calmodulin-dependent protein kinase II is a binding protein for synapsin I. *Nature* (1992) **359**:417–20. doi:10.1038/359417a0
49. Verstegen AM, Tagliatti E, Lignani G, Marte A, Stolero T, Atias M, et al. Phosphorylation of synapsin I by cyclin-dependent kinase-5 sets the ratio between the resting and recycling pools of synaptic vesicles at hippocampal synapses. *J Neurosci* (2014) **34**:7266–80. doi:10.1523/JNEUROSCI.3973-13.2014

50. Hilfiker S, Schweizer FE, Kao H-T, Czernik AJ, Greengard P, Augustine GJ. Two sites of action for synapsin domain E in regulating neurotransmitter release. *Nat Neurosci* (1998) **1**:29–35. doi:10.1038/1147
51. Gitler D, Xu Y, Kao H-T, Lin D, Lim S, Feng J, et al. Molecular determinants of synapsin targeting to presynaptic terminals. *J Neurosci* (2004) **224**:3711–20. doi:10.1523/JNEUROSCI.5225-03.2004
52. Fassio A, Merlo D, Mapelli J, Menegon A, Corradi A, Mete M, et al. The synapsin domain E accelerates the exoendocytotic cycle of synaptic vesicles in cerebellar Purkinje cells. *J Cell Sci* (2006) **119**:4257–68. doi:10.1242/jcs.03194
53. Monaldi I, Vassalli M, Bachi A, Giovedí S, Millo E, Valtorta F, et al. The highly conserved synapsin domain E mediates synapsin dimerization and phospholipid vesicle clustering. *Biochem J* (2010) **426**:55–64. doi:10.1042/BJ20090762
54. Chin LS, Li L, Ferreira A, Kosik KS, Greengard P. Impairment of axonal development and of synaptogenesis in hippocampal neurons of synapsin I-deficient mice. *Proc Natl Acad Sci U S A* (1995) **92**:9230–4. doi:10.1073/pnas.92.20.9230
55. Ferreira A, Kao H-T, Feng J, Rapoport M, Greengard P. Synapsin III: developmental expression, subcellular localization, and role in axon formation. *J Neurosci* (2000) **20**:3736–44.
56. Li L, Chin LS, Shupliakov O, Brodin L, Sihra TS, Hvalby O, et al. Impairment of synaptic vesicle clustering and of synaptic transmission, and increased seizure propensity, in synapsin I-deficient mice. *Proc Natl Acad Sci U S A* (1995) **92**:9235–9. doi:10.1073/pnas.92.20.9235
57. Takei Y, Harada A, Takeda S, Kobayashi K, Terada S, Noda T, et al. Synapsin I deficiency results in the structural change in the presynaptic terminals in the murine nervous system. *J Cell Biol* (1995) **131**:1789–800. doi:10.1083/jcb.131.6.1789
58. Rosahl TW, Spillane D, Missler M, Herz J, Selig DK, Wolff JR, et al. Essential functions of synapsins I and II in synaptic vesicle regulation. *Nature* (1995) **375**:488–93. doi:10.1038/375488a0
59. Cambiaghi M, Cursi M, Monzani E, Benfenati F, Comi G, Minicucci F, et al. Temporal evolution of neurophysiological and behavioral features of synapsin I/II/III triple knock-out mice. *Epilepsy Res* (2013) **103**:153–60. doi:10.1016/j.eplepsyres.2012.07.012
60. Etholm L, Bahonjic E, Heggelund P. Sensitive and critical periods in the development of handling induced seizures in mice lacking synapsins: differences between synapsin I and synapsin II knockouts. *Exp Neurol* (2013) **247**:59–65. doi:10.1016/j.expneurol.2013.03.025
61. Fassio A, Raimondi A, Lignani G, Benfenati F, Baldelli P. Synapsins: from synapse to network hyperexcitability and epilepsy. *Semin Cell Dev Biol* (2011) **22**:408–15. doi:10.1016/j.semcdb.2011.07.005
62. Feng J, Chi P, Blanpied TA, Xu Y, Magarinos AM, Ferreira A, et al. Regulation of neurotransmitter release by synapsin III. *J Neurosci* (2002) **22**:4372–80.
63. Corradi A, Zanardi A, Giacomini C, Onofri F, Valtorta F, Zoli M, et al. Synapsin-I- and synapsin-II-null mice display an increased age-dependent cognitive impairment. *J Cell Sci* (2008) **121**:3042–51. doi:10.1242/jcs.035063
64. Porton B, Rodriguiz RM, Phillips LE, Gilbert JW IV, Feng J, Greengard P, et al. Mice lacking synapsin III show abnormalities in explicit memory and conditioned fear. *Genes Brain Behav* (2010) **9**:257–68. doi:10.1111/j.1601-183X.2009.00555.x
65. Greco B, Managò F, Tucci V, Kao H-T, Valtorta F, Benfenati F. Autism-related behavioral abnormalities in synapsin knockout mice. *Behav Brain Res* (2013) **251**:65–74. doi:10.1016/j.bbr.2012.12.015
66. Garcia CC, Blair HJ, Seager M, Coulthard A, Tennant S, Buddles M, et al. Identification of a mutation in synapsin I, a synaptic vesicle protein, in a family with epilepsy. *J Med Genet* (2004) **41**:183–6. doi:10.1136/jmg.2003.013680
67. Fassio A, Patry L, Congia S, Onofri F, Piton A, Gauthier J, et al. SYN1 loss-of-function mutations in autism and partial epilepsy cause impaired synaptic function. *Hum Mol Genet* (2011) **20**:2297–307. doi:10.1093/hmg/ddr122
68. Corradi A, Fadda M, Piton A, Patry L, Marte A, Rossi P, et al. SYN2 is an autism predisposing gene: loss-of-function mutations alter synaptic vesicle cycling and axon outgrowth. *Hum Mol Genet* (2014) **23**:90–103. doi:10.1093/hmg/ddt401
69. Sato D, Lionel AC, Leblond CS, Prasad A, Pinto D, Walker S, et al. Shank1 deletions in males with autism spectrum disorder. *Am J Hum Genet* (2012) **90**:879–87. doi:10.1016/j.ajhg.2012.03.017
70. Giannandrea M, Guarnieri FC, Gehring NH, Monzani E, Benfenati F, Kulozik AE, et al. Nonsense-mediated mRNA decay and loss-of-function of the protein underlie the X-linked epilepsy associated with the W356X mutation in synapsin I. *PLoS One* (2013) **8**:e67724. doi:10.1371/journal.pone.0067724
71. Lignani G, Raimondi A, Ferrea E, Rocchi A, Paonessa F, Cesca F, et al. Epileptogenic Q555X SYN1 mutant triggers imbalances in release dynamics and short-term plasticity. *Hum Mol Genet* (2013) **22**:2186–99. doi:10.1093/hmg/ddt071
72. Anderson GR, Galfin T, Xu W, Aoto J, Malenka RC, Sudhof TC. Candidate autism gene screen identifies critical role for cell-adhesion molecule CASPR2 in dendritic arborization and spine development. *Proc Natl Acad Sci U S A* (2012) **109**:18120–5. doi:10.1073/pnas.1216398109
73. Ferrari S, Di Iorio E, Barbaro V, Ponzin D, Sorrentini FS, Parmeggiani F. *Retinitis pigmentosa*: genes and disease mechanisms. *Curr Genomics* (2011) **12**:238–49. doi:10.2174/138920211795860107
74. Lips ES, Cornelisse LN, Toonen RF, Min JL, Hultman CM, International Schizophrenia Consortium X, et al. Functional gene group analysis identifies synaptic gene groups as risk factor for schizophrenia. *Mol Psychiatry* (2012) **17**:996–1006. doi:10.1038/mp.2011.117
75. Ruano D, Abecasis GR, Glaser B, Lips ES, Cornelisse LN, de Jong AP, et al. Functional gene group analysis reveals a role for synaptic heterotrimeric G proteins in cognitive ability. *Am J Hum Genet* (2010) **12**(86):113–25. doi:10.1016/j.ajhg.2009.12.006

# 3

# GH dysfunction in Engrailed-2 knockout mice, a model for autism spectrum disorders

**Giovanni Provenzano[1‡], Elena Clementi[1‡], Sacha Genovesi[1], Manuela Scali[2,3], Prem Prakash Tripathi[2,3†], Paola Sgadò[1] and Yuri Bozzi[1,2*]**

[1] Laboratory of Molecular Neuropathology, Centre for Integrative Biology (CIBIO), University of Trento, Trento, Italy
[2] Neuroscience Institute, National Research Council (CNR), Pisa, Italy
[3] Laboratory of Neurobiology, Scuola Normale Superiore, Pisa, Italy

**Edited by:**
Roberto Canitano, University Hospital of Siena, Italy

**Reviewed by:**
Munis Dundar, Erciyes University, Turkey
Alessandro Sale, National Research Council (CNR), Italy
Anne Leighton Calof, University of California, Irvine, USA

***Correspondence:**
Yuri Bozzi, Laboratory of Molecular Neuropathology, Centre for Integrative Biology (CIBIO), University of Trento, Via delle Regole 101, Mattarello, Trento 38123, Italy
e-mail: bozzi@science.unitn.it

Insulin-like growth factor 1 (IGF-1) signaling promotes brain development and plasticity. Altered IGF-1 expression has been associated to autism spectrum disorders (ASD). IGF-1 levels were found increased in the blood and decreased in the cerebrospinal fluid of ASD children. Accordingly, IGF-1 treatment can rescue behavioral deficits in mouse models of ASD, and IGF-1 trials have been proposed for ASD children. IGF-1 is mainly synthesized in the liver, and its synthesis is dependent on growth hormone (GH) produced in the pituitary gland. GH also modulates cognitive functions, and altered levels of GH have been detected in ASD patients. Here, we analyzed the expression of GH, IGF-1, their receptors, and regulatory hormones in the neuroendocrine system of adult male mice lacking the homeobox transcription factor Engrailed-2 (*En2*$^{-/-}$ mice). *En2*$^{-/-}$ mice display ASD-like behaviors (social interactions, defective spatial learning, increased seizure susceptibility) accompanied by relevant neuropathological changes (loss of cerebellar and forebrain inhibitory neurons). Recent studies showed that *En2* modulates IGF-1 activity during postnatal cerebellar development. We found that GH mRNA expression was markedly deregulated throughout the neuroendocrine axis in *En2*$^{-/-}$ mice, as compared to wild-type controls. In mutant mice, GH mRNA levels were significantly increased in the pituitary gland, blood, and liver, whereas decreased levels were detected in the hippocampus. These changes were paralleled by decreased levels of GH protein in the hippocampus but not other tissues of *En2*$^{-/-}$ mice. IGF-1 mRNA was significantly up-regulated in the liver and down-regulated in the *En2*$^{-/-}$ hippocampus, but no differences were detected in the levels of IGF-1 protein between the two genotypes. Our data strengthen the notion that altered GH levels in the hippocampus may be involved in learning disabilities associated to ASD.

**Keywords: autism spectrum disorders, hippocampus, pituitary gland, liver, growth hormone, insulin-like growth factor, neuroendocrine axis, mouse model**

## INTRODUCTION

Insulin-like growth factor 1 (IGF-1) is a hormone primarily produced by the liver, which exerts an endocrine action on multiple target tissues. It is also locally produced in tissues, including brain, where it acts in a paracrine/autocrine fashion. Several studies demonstrate that IGF-1 profoundly modulates brain function, both during development and adult life. During development, IGF-1 promotes neuronal survival [reviewed in Ref. (1)] and maturation of cortical and retinal function (2–4), whereas in adult life, it exerts multiple actions ranging from the control of synaptic plasticity to neuroprotection [reviewed in Ref. (1, 5)]. During adulthood, IGF-1 is crucial for both basal and exercise-induced hippocampal neurogenesis (6, 7) and markedly regulates learning and cognition (8).

A link between IGF-1 pathway and autism spectrum disorders (ASD) has been proposed. IGF-1 levels have been found increased in the blood (9) and decreased in the cerebrospinal fluid (10, 11) of ASD children, as compared to healthy individuals. In addition, deregulation of IGF-1 signaling pathway, which involves downstream effectors such as PI3 kinase (PI3K), protein kinase B (AKT), and mammalian target of rapamycin (mTOR), has been shown in syndromic forms of ASD [reviewed in Ref. (12)]. This led to propose that IGF-1 treatment might be beneficial for ASD, and clinical trials have been approved[1]. Indeed, IGF-1 administration is able to rescue ASD-related molecular changes in neurons derived from ASD patients (13) as well as ASD-like behavioral deficits in mouse models (14, 15). Altered levels of other hormones of the IGF-1 pathway have been associated to ASD (9). IGF-1 synthesis in the liver depends on levels of circulating growth hormone (GH) produced in the pituitary gland. GH also modulates cognitive functions (16), and altered GH levels have been detected in ASD patients (17).

Genome-wide association studies identified the transcription factor Engrailed-2 (*En2*) as a candidate gene for ASD (18), and two recent studies confirmed that *En2* expression is altered in the

[1] http://clinicaltrials.gov

cerebellum of ASD patients (19, 20). Mice lacking the homeobox domain of *En2* [$En2^{hd/hd}$ mice; (21); here referred to as $En2^{-/-}$] are considered a suitable animal model to study the neurodevelopmental basis of ASD. $En2^{-/-}$ mice display neuropathological and behavioral changes relevant to ASD. Reduced social interactions, defective spatial learning (22–24), and increased seizure susceptibility (25) accompanied by neuropathological changes relevant to ASD [loss of cerebellar and forebrain inhibitory neurons; (26, 27)] were indeed described in $En2^{-/-}$ mice. In addition, we recently showed that several genes related to ASD are markedly deregulated in the cerebellum and hippocampus of $En2^{-/-}$ mice (28), thus indicating that *En2* mutants are a reliable model to investigate gene expression changes relevant to ASD.

A recent study established an important link between *En2* and the modulation of IGF-1 pathway (29). During postnatal development, *En2* controls proliferation and differentiation of cerebellar granule neuron precursors (GNPs). Notably, in postnatal $En2^{-/-}$ cerebellum, the activity of downstream effectors of IGF-1 is increased, and IGF-1 has a stronger mitogenic effect on GNPs, as compared to WT (29). These results indicate that *En2* negatively regulates IGF-1 signaling during postnatal cerebellar development.

Here, we investigated the relationship between *En2* and GH/IGF-1 pathway in the neuroendocrine system. We analyzed the expression of GH, IGF-1, their receptors, and regulatory hormones in the brain–pituitary–liver axis of adult wild-type (WT) and $En2^{-/-}$ mice. We show that GH levels are lowered in the hippocampus of $En2^{-/-}$ mice, suggesting that this alteration might contribute to learning disabilities in this ASD mouse model.

## MATERIALS AND METHODS

### ANIMALS

Experiments were conducted in conformity with the European Community Directive 2010/63/EU and were approved by the Italian Ministry of Health. Animals were housed in a 12-h light/dark cycle with food and water available *ad libitum*, and all efforts were made to minimize animal suffering during the experiments. The generation of *En2* mutants were originally generated on a mixed 129Sv × C57BL/6 genetic background (21) and then backcrossed at least five times into a C57BL/6 background (27). $En2^{+/+}$ (WT) and $En2^{-/-}$ mice used in this study were obtained by heterozygous mating ($En2^{\pm} \times En2^{\pm}$) and genotyped by PCR as previously described (27). A total of 34 adult (3–5 months old) male mice were used: 6 mice per genotype for quantitative RT-PCR, 5 mice per genotype for enzyme-linked immuno-sorbent assay (ELISA) tests, 3 mice per genotype for immunohistochemistry, and 3 mice per genotype for *in situ* hybridization.

### QUANTITATIVE RT-PCR

Tissues from WT and $En2^{-/-}$ mice ($n = 6$ per genotype) were dissected and frozen in dry ice. Blood samples were centrifuged in an Eppendorf benchtop centrifuge for 15 min at 3,000 rpm to separate serum from cell fraction, and then frozen in dry ice. All samples were stored at −80°C until use. Total RNAs were extracted by Trizol reagent (Invitrogen), treated with DNAse, purified by the RNAeasy Kit (Qiagen), and pooled. cDNAs were synthesized from pooled RNAs (3 μg) by SuperScript VILO cDNA Synthesis Kit (Invitrogen). Quantitative reverse-transcription PCR (RT-PCR) was performed in a C1000 thermal cycler (BioRad) with real-time detection of fluorescence, using the KAPA SYBR FAST master mix reagent (Resnova). Mouse mitochondrial ribosomal protein L41 (Mrpl41) was used as a standard for quantification. Primers (Sigma Genosys, UK) sequences are reported in **Table 1**. Ratios of comparative concentrations of each mRNA with respect to L41 mRNA were then calculated and plotted as the average of three to four independent reactions with technical replicates obtained from each RNA pool. Expression analyses were performed using the CFX3 Manager (BioRad) software.

### BIOINFORMATIC ANALYSIS

Analysis of *En2* binding sites on GH, GHR, mGRF, SST, IGF-1, and IGF-1R gene promoters was performed using the Matinspector web-based search algorithm available from Genomatix Software[2]. The algorithm calculated the similarity between the core motif and overall sequence of the *En2* consensus binding site (matrix ID: V$EN2.01) and the gene promoter sequences of interest. The *En2* matrix was determined based on the Genomatix Matrix Library Version 9.1.

### IMMUNOHISTOCHEMISTRY

Brains from adult WT and $En2^{-/-}$ mice ($n = 3$ per genotype) were used for immunohistochemical characterization of

[2]http://www.Genomatix.de

**Table 1 | Primers used for quantitative RT-PCR experiments.**

| Gene | GenBank no. | Forward primer (5′–3′) | Reverse primer (5′–3′) |
|---|---|---|---|
| En2 | NM_010134.3 | ACTGCACGCGCTATTCTG | ACCTGTTGGTCTGAAACTCAG |
| GH | NM_008117.3 | GCAATGGCTACAGACTCT | AAACAGACTGGACAAGGG |
| GHR | NM_001286370.1 | CGTTCCCCTGAACTGGAGAC | CAGCTTGTCGTTGGCTTTCC |
| IGF-1 class 1 | NM_001111275.1 | AGCGATGGGGAAAATCAGCA | CAGAGCGCCAGGTAGAAGAG |
| IGF-1 class 2 | NM_001111276.1 | CTGATGTCTGGTCCTTCGGG | CACCCTCCATGACGAAACGA |
| IGF-1R | NM_010513.2 | CTGATGTCTGGTCCTTCGGG | CACCCTCCATGACGAAACGA |
| mGRF | NM_010285.2 | AGGATCCAGGAACAAAGGGC | GCAAGATGCTCTCCAGGGTC |
| SST | NM_009215 | AGGACGAGATGAGGCTGG | CAGGAGTTAAGGAAGAGATATGGG |

*Abbreviations are as in the text.*

hypothalamic SST. Brains were fixed by transcardial perfusion with 4% paraformaldehyde followed by 1 h post-fixation, and coronal sections (40 μm thickness) were cut by a vibratome (Leica). Serial sections at level of the hypothalamus were incubated overnight with and anti-SST rabbit polyclonal (Peninsula-Bachem; 1:2000 dilution). Signals were revealed using appropriate secondary antibodies and fluorophores as described (27). Hypothalamic nuclei were identified according to the Allen Brain Atlas[3]. Images were acquired at 10× objective magnification using a Zeiss AxioImager M2 microscope.

### *IN SITU* HYBRIDIZATION

Brains from WT and *En2*$^{-/-}$ mice ($n = 3$ per genotype) were rapidly removed and frozen on dry ice. Coronal cryostat sections (20 μm thick) were fixed in 4% paraformaldehyde. Non-radioactive *in situ* hybridization was performed as previously described (27) using digoxigenin-labeled riboprobes specific for GH [GenBank ID: X02891; (30)], mGRF (31), and IGF-1 (GenBank ID: NM_010512). The IGF-1 cDNA was cloned by PCR from hippocampal cDNA and recognizes both class 1 and class 2 IGF-1 mRNAs. Signal was detected by alkaline phosphatase-conjugated anti-digoxigenin antibody followed by alkaline phosphatase staining. The specificity of the results was confirmed by the use of sense riboprobes (not shown).

### ENZYME-LINKED IMMUNO-SORBENT ASSAY

Blood samples ($n = 5$ per genotype) were collected at the time of animal sacrifice, kept in ice for 30 min, and then centrifuged in an Eppendorf benchtop centrifuge for 15 min at 3,000 rpm to separate serum. Dissected liver and hippocampal tissues ($n = 5$ per genotype) were homogenized in lysis buffer (50 mM Tris–HCl pH 7.5, 1% NP-40, 1% Triton-100, 1 mM PMSF, 10% glycerol, and protease inhibitor cocktail; Sigma-Aldrich). Homogenates were incubated in ice for 30 min, centrifuged at 12,000 rpm for 5 min at 4°C, and supernatants were recovered and stored at −80°C. Protein concentration in serum, liver, and hippocampal samples was determined by BCA method (Pierce). Samples were processed for GH (EZRMGH-45K, Millipore) and IGF-1 (ELM-IGFI; RayBiotech) ELISA according to manufacturers' protocol. All samples were analyzed in duplicate.

### STATISTICAL ANALYSIS

Statistical analysis was performed with SigmaPlot 11.0 and Prism 6 (GraphPad) softwares. Values were expressed as mean ± SEM and quantitative gene expression differences between WT and *En2*$^{-/-}$ mice were assessed by Student's *t*-test, with the level of statistical significance set at $p < 0.05$.

## RESULTS

### EXPRESSION OF *En2* AND IGF-1 SIGNALING GENES IN THE MOUSE BRAIN–PITUITARY–LIVER AXIS

By using quantitative RT-PCR, we first investigated mRNA expression of *En2*, GH, GH receptor (GHR), mGRF, SST, IGF-1, and IGF-1 receptor (IGF-1R) in the neuroendocrine axis of WT adult male mice from our colony. mRNA expression was studied in the hypothalamus, pituitary gland, and liver (the crucial tissues involved in GH and IGF-1 synthesis), as well as hippocampus and blood cell fraction. In agreement with previous findings, we confirmed that *En2* mRNA is expressed in the hypothalamus and hippocampus (23, 25, 27). *En2* mRNA was also expressed at detectable levels in blood, pituitary gland, and liver (**Figure 1A**). As expected, GH mRNA was mainly detected in the pituitary gland, while much lower levels were present in the hippocampus, hypothalamus, liver, and blood (**Figure 1B**). Consistent with the notion that liver is the main target of GH action, we found GHR mRNA predominantly expressed in the liver, and at lower levels in the other tissues analyzed (**Figure 1C**). mRNA expression of mGRF and SST, the two hypothalamic hormones controlling GH synthesis, was mainly detected in the hypothalamus (**Figures 1D,E**). High levels of SST mRNA were also present in the hippocampus, as previously described (27). Two major different transcripts have been described for IGF-1 [class 1 and class 2; (32, 33)]. Both IGF-1 class 1 and class 2 mRNAs were predominantly expressed in the liver (**Figures 1F,G**), as expected (32). Finally, IGF-1R mRNA was mainly expressed in the pituitary gland (the target for IGF-1 negative feedback for GH production) (**Figure 1H**), but also throughout the neuroendocrine axis, consistent with the widespread action of IGF-1 on multiple tissues. These results clearly indicate that our RT-PCR protocol can detect the expression of genes belonging to the GH/IGF-1 pathway in the appropriate tissues throughout the brain–pituitary–liver axis.

### ALTERED GH mRNA EXPRESSION IN THE BRAIN–PITUITARY–LIVER AXIS OF *En2*$^{-/-}$ MICE

Before investigating GH, GHR, mGRF, SST, IGF-1, and IGF-1R mRNA expression in the neuroendocrine axis of *En2*$^{-/-}$ mice, we first verified whether *En2* might directly regulate their transcription. Indeed, bioinformatic analysis revealed that *En2* binding sites are present in the promoters of all these genes (**Table 2**). We next studied GH and GHR mRNA expression in the neuroendocrine axis of WT and *En2*$^{-/-}$ adult mice. We found that GH mRNA expression was markedly deregulated throughout the neuroendocrine axis in *En2*$^{-/-}$ mice. A statistically significant increase of GH mRNA levels was detected in the pituitary gland (+72%, $p < 0.001$), liver (+376%, $p < 0.001$), and blood (+87%, $p < 0.05$) of *En2*$^{-/-}$ mice, as compared to WT littermates (**Figure 2A**). GH mRNA levels were instead significantly lower in the *En2*$^{-/-}$ hypothalamus (−97%, $p < 0.001$) and hippocampus (−98%, $p < 0.001$), as compared to WT (**Figure 2A**). *In situ* hybridization confirmed GH mRNA decrease in the *En2*$^{-/-}$ hippocampus, mainly in the CA3 subfield (**Figure 2C**). No significant differences in GHR mRNA levels were detected between genotypes in the analyzed tissues, with the exception of blood, where a marked increase was detected in mutant mice compared to controls (+312%, $p < 0.05$) (**Figure 2B**).

### ALTERED EXPRESSION OF mGRF AND SST IN THE HYPOTHALAMUS OF *En2*$^{-/-}$ MICE

We then investigated the expression of mGRF (also known as growth hormone releasing hormone, GHRH) and SST, the two hypothalamic hormones regulating GH synthesis, in the

[3]http://www.brain-map.org/

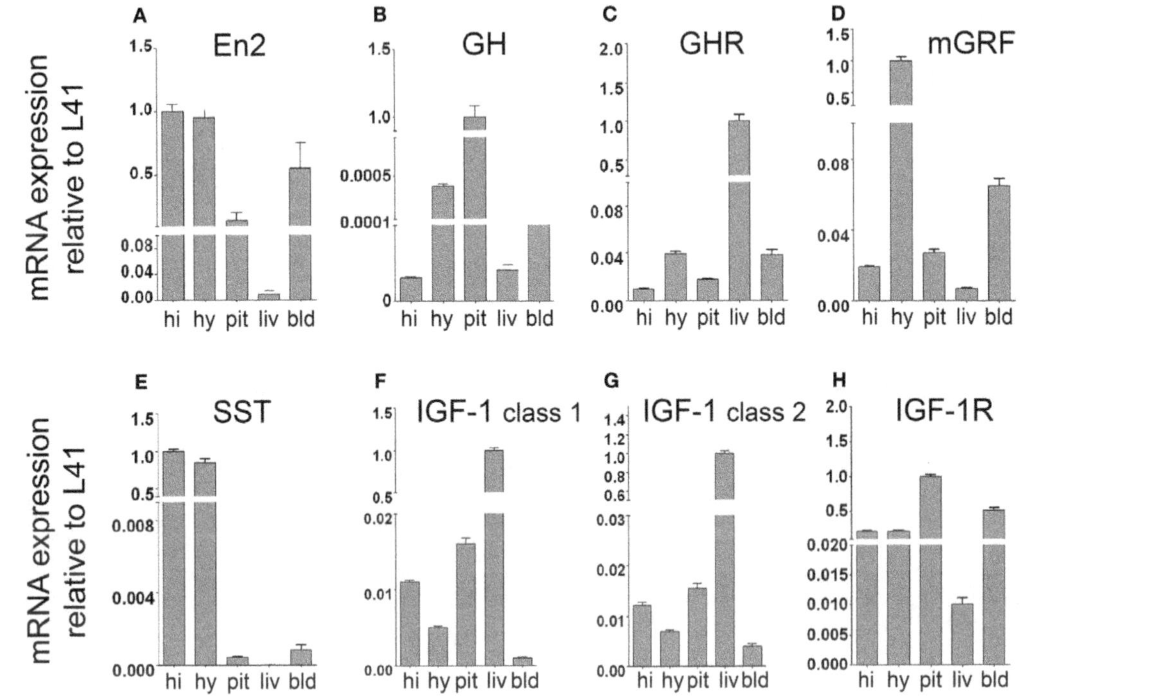


**FIGURE 1 | mRNA expression of *En2* and genes involved in the GH/IGF-1 pathway in the neuroendocrine axis of WT mice.** *En2* **(A)**, GH **(B)**, GHR **(C)**, mGRF **(D)**, SST **(E)**, IGF-1 **(F,G)**, and IGF-1R **(H)** mRNA expression levels in the hippocampus, hypothalamus, pituitary gland, liver, and blood, obtained by quantitative RT-PCR. For each mRNA, relative expression levels (normalized to L41) are reported on a log scale. Two different transcripts (class 1 and class 2) were analyzed for IGF-1. Values are plotted as mean ± SEM of three independent experiments. Abbreviations: hi, hippocampus; hy, hypothalamus; pit, pituitary gland; liv, liver; bld, blood (cell fraction). Other abbreviations are as in the text.

**Table 2 | Presence of *En2* binding sites onto GH, GHR, mGRF, SST, IGF-1, and IGF-1R gene promoters.**

| Gene | Accession no. | Start | End | Strand | Core | Matrix | Sequence |
|---|---|---|---|---|---|---|---|
| GH | GXP_219787 | 534 | 552 | + | 0.752 | 0.73 | agccatgAATAaatgtata |
| GHR | GXP_889069 | 584 | 602 | – | 1 | 0.863 | ccccataAATTaataatcc |
| IGF-1 | GXP_4345839 | 966 | 984 | – | 1 | 0.858 | ttttatgAATTaagccctc |
| IGF-1R | GXP_183481 | 512 | 530 | – | 1 | 0.854 | aacattgAATTagttcttg |
| mGRF | GXP_4357410 | 266 | 284 | – | 1 | 0.797 | ggaaacaAATTgaacaaat |
| SST | GXP_82140 | 62 | 80 | – | 1 | 0.774 | cagaatgAATTtgcaatta |

*The promoter regions of the six genes belonging to the GH/IGF-1 pathway were analyzed for the presence of En2 binding site using the Matinspector program. Core similarity (Core) indicates the match against the nucleotides representing the core motif of the En2 binding site (AATT), where 1 is 100% identity. Matrix similarity (Matrix) is the overall similarity to the En2 binding motif, where 1 is 100% identity. For each sequence, the start/end position respect to ATG is indicated, together with the strand on which they are present. For each promoter, several regions containing the En2 binding site were found; the table reports only those with highest values for core and matrix similarity. Genomatix Promoter database (GXP) accession numbers are given for each gene. Abbreviations are as in the text.*

brain–pituitary–liver axis of WT and *En2*$^{-/-}$ adult mice. As compared to WT controls, a marked increase of mGRF mRNA (+53%, $p < 0.05$; **Figure 3A**) and a significant decrease of SST mRNA (−13%, $p < 0.01$; **Figure 3B**) was found in the *En2*$^{-/-}$ hypothalamus. Significantly higher mRNA levels for the two hormones were also found in blood (mGRF: +125%, $p < 0.05$) and liver (mGRF: +129%, $p < 0.01$; SST: +147%, $p < 0.001$) from *En2*$^{-/-}$ mice (**Figures 3A,B**). According to our previous study (27), lower levels of SST mRNA were found in the *En2*$^{-/-}$ hippocampus, as compared to WT (−10%, $p < 0.05$; **Figure 3B**). *In situ* hybridization and immunohistochemistry experiments, respectively, confirmed the increased expression of mGRF mRNA and decreased levels of SST protein in the dorsomedial/ventromedial paraventricular nuclei of the *En2*$^{-/-}$ hypothalamus, as compared to WT (**Figure 3C**).

### ALTERED IGF-1 mRNA EXPRESSION IN THE BRAIN–PITUITARY–LIVER AXIS OF *En2*$^{-/-}$ MICE

We next analyzed mRNA expression of IGF-1 and its receptor in the brain–pituitary–liver axis of WT and *En2*$^{-/-}$ adult mice.

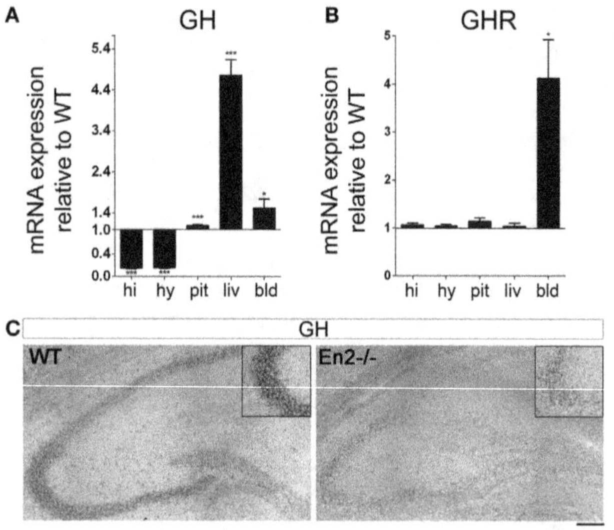

FIGURE 2 | Expression of GH and GH receptor mRNAs in the neuroendocrine axis of WT and *En2*$^{-/-}$ mice. (A) GH mRNA quantitative RT-PCR. (B) GHR quantitative RT-PCR. Values are plotted as each gene/L41 comparative quantitation ratios normalized on the expression of WT (mean ± SEM of three replicates from pools of six animals per genotype; $*p < 0.05$, $***p < 0.001$; Student's *t*-test, *En2*$^{-/-}$ vs. WT).
(C) Representative pictures of GH mRNA *in situ* hybridization on the dorsal hippocampus from WT and *En2*$^{-/-}$ mice. Insets show the CA3 subfield. Scale bar: 200 μm (whole hippocampi) and 125 μm (insets). Abbreviations are as in **Figure 1**.

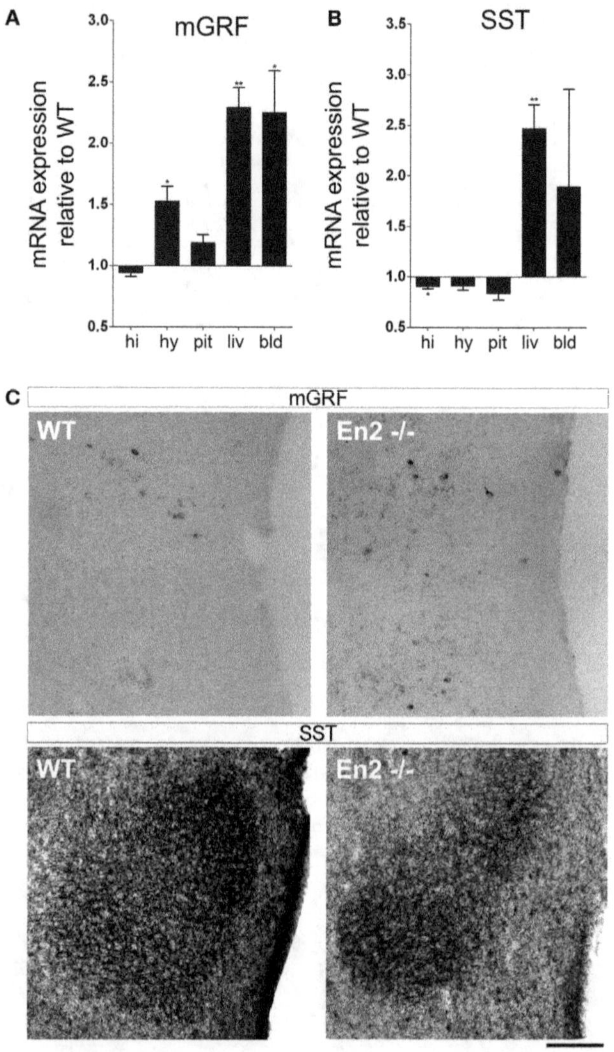

FIGURE 3 | Expression of mGRF and SST mRNAs in the neuroendocrine axis of WT and *En2*$^{-/-}$ mice. (A,B) mRNA expression levels of mGRF (A) and SST (B), obtained by quantitative RT-PCR. Values are plotted as each gene/L41 comparative quantitation ratios normalized on the expression of WT (mean ± SEM of three replicates from pools of six animals per genotype; $*p < 0.05$, $**p < 0.01$; Student's *t*-test, *En2*$^{-/-}$ vs. WT). (C) mGRF *in situ* hybridization and SST immunohistochemistry. Representative pictures show mGRF mRNA and SST protein staining in the dorsomedial and ventromedial paraventricular nuclei of the hypothalamus. Scale bar: 200 μm. Abbreviations are as in **Figure 1**.

IGF-1 mRNA exists in two major forms (class 1 and class 2), class 2 mRNA transcription being directly regulated by GH (33, 34). We found that levels of IGF-1 class 1 mRNA were significantly reduced in the hippocampus but not other tissues of *En2*$^{-/-}$ mice, as compared to WT (−18%, $p < 0.05$ for all comparisons) (**Figure 4A**). In keeping with GH mRNA expression data (**Figure 2**), IGF-1 class 2 mRNA was significantly up-regulated in the liver (+43%, $p < 0.001$) and down-regulated in the hypothalamus (−19%, $p < 0.001$) of *En2*$^{-/-}$ mice, as compared to WT littermates; increased levels of IGF-1 class 2 mRNA were also detected in *En2*$^{-/-}$ pituitary gland (+16%, $p < 0.01$) and blood (+312%, $p < 0.001$) (**Figure 4B**). *In situ* hybridization with a riboprobe specific for both class 1 and class 2 IGF-1 mRNAs confirmed that IGF-1 mRNA levels are decreased in the *En2*$^{-/-}$ hippocampus (**Figure 4D**). Finally, IGF-1R mRNA levels did not differ between genotypes in hypothalamus, hippocampus, and pituitary gland, while a significant increase was found in blood (+84%, $p < 0.01$) and liver (+52%, $p < 0.05$) from *En2*$^{-/-}$ mice compared to WT controls (**Figure 4C**). **Table 3** summarizes mRNA expression data for all the analyzed genes in the brain–pituitary–liver axis of WT and *En2*$^{-/-}$ adult mice.

### REDUCED LEVELS OF GH PROTEIN IN THE *En2*$^{-/-}$ HIPPOCAMPUS

The altered levels of GH and IGF-1 mRNA expression detected in the *En2*$^{-/-}$ neuroendocrine axis prompted us to investigate the levels of these hormones in the hippocampus, serum, and liver of both genotypes. ELISA assays revealed a significant reduction (−54%, $p < 0.05$) of GH protein levels in the hippocampus of *En2*$^{-/-}$ mice, as compared to WT littermates, while no difference was detected in serum samples (**Figure 5A**). Hippocampal, liver, and serum IGF-1 protein levels did not significantly differ between the two genotypes (**Figure 5B**).

## DISCUSSION

### BRIEF SUMMARY OF RESULTS

In this study, we analyzed the expression of GH, IGF-1, their receptors, and regulatory hormones in the brain–pituitary–liver axis of adult *En2*$^{-/-}$ mice, a mouse model for ASD. We found that in mutant mice, GH and IGF-1 mRNA levels were significantly higher in the pituitary gland and liver, respectively, but this increase was not paralleled by higher levels of circulating hormones. In *En2* mutants, GH and IGF-1 mRNA levels were instead significantly down-regulated in the hippocampus, and this reduction was accompanied by a significant decrease of GH but not IGF-1 protein levels.

### *En2* INTERACTS WITH IGF-1 SIGNALING IN THE MOUSE NEUROENDOCRINE AXIS

Our results, schematically summarized in **Figure 6**, indicate that regulatory mechanisms controlling GH and IGF-1 mRNA expression in the neuroendocrine system are altered in *En2*$^{-/-}$ mice. The presence of *En2* mRNA in the hypothalamus–pituitary–liver axis (**Figure 1**) and that of an *En2* binding site in the promoters of GH, IGF-1, and other genes of the pathway (**Table 2**) suggest that *En2* might directly contribute to their transcriptional control. Indeed, recent studies revealed an unprecedented interaction between *En2* and IGF-1 signaling. In the absence of *En2*, IGF-1 has a stronger mitogenic effect on cerebellar GNPs, due the increased activity of downstream effectors of IGF-1 signaling, such as S6 kinase (29). Thus, *En2* appears to negatively regulate IGF-1 signaling during postnatal cerebellar development. Our results strengthen this link between *En2* and IGF-1 signaling, and suggest that a direct transcriptional control of *En2* onto genes belonging to the IGF-1 pathway takes place also in the brain–pituitary–liver axis.

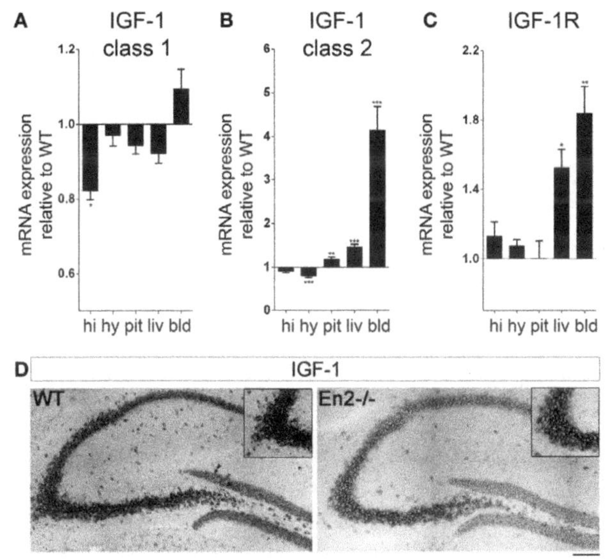


**FIGURE 4 | Expression of IGF-1 and IGF-1R mRNAs in the neuroendocrine axis of WT and *En2*$^{-/-}$ mice. (A,B)** Quantitative RT-PCR for IGF-1 class 1 **(A)** and class 2 **(B)** transcripts. **(C)** IGF-1R quantitative RT-PCR. Values are plotted as each gene/L41 comparative quantitation ratios normalized on the expression of WT (mean ± SEM of three replicates from pools of six animals per genotype; $*p < 0.05$, $**p < 0.01$; $***p < 0.001$; Student's *t*-test, *En2*$^{-/-}$ vs. WT). **(D)** Representative pictures of *in situ* hybridization for IGF-1 mRNA (both transcripts) on the dorsal hippocampus from WT and *En2*$^{-/-}$ mice. Insets show the CA3 subfield. Scale bar: 200 μm (whole hippocampi) and 125 μm (insets). Abbreviations are as in **Figure 1**.

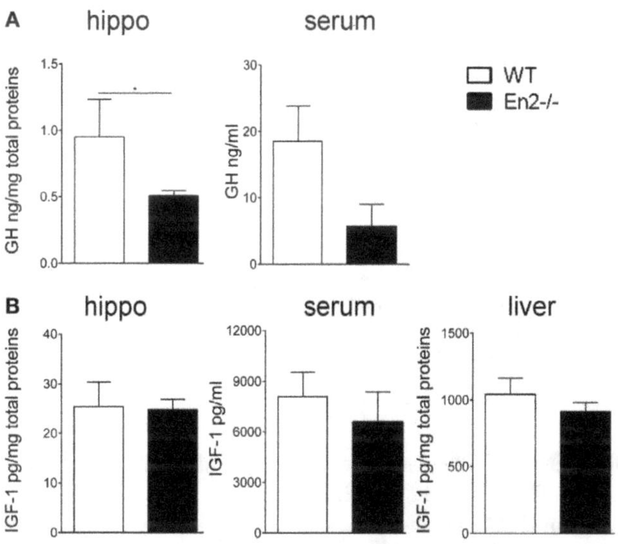


**FIGURE 5 | Levels of GH and IGF-1 hormones in WT and *En2*$^{-/-}$ mice. (A,B)** ELISA quantification of GH **(A)** and IGF-1 **(B)** levels in serum and hippocampal (hippo) and liver protein extracts, as indicated. Values are plotted as mean ± SEM (five animals per genotype, in duplicate; $*p < 0.05$, Student's *t*-test, *En2*$^{-/-}$ vs. WT). Genotypes are as indicated.

**Table 3 | Summary of the expression of *En2*, GH, GHR, mGRF, SST, IGF-1, and IGF-1R mRNAs in the neuroendocrine axis of *En2*$^{-/-}$ mice, as compared to WT**.

| Gene | Hippocampus | Hypothalamus | Pituitary | Liver | Blood |
|---|---|---|---|---|---|
| GH | −98%*** | −97%*** | +72%*** | +376%*** | +87%* |
| GHR | No difference | No difference | No difference | No difference | +312%* |
| mGRF | No difference | +53%* | No difference | +129%** | +125%* |
| SST | −10%* | −13%** | No difference | +147%** | No difference |
| IGF-1 Class 1 | −18%* | No difference | No difference | No difference | No difference |
| IGF-1 Class 2 | No difference | −19%*** | +16%** | +43%*** | +312%*** |
| IGF-1R | No difference | No difference | No difference | +52%* | +84%** |

*Summary of quantitative RT-PCR data. Data are presented as the mean percentage of the decrease/increase of each mRNA in En2*$^{-/-}$ *mice, as compared to WT littermates.*

*Statistical significance:* $*p < 0.05$, $**p < 0.01$, $***p < 0.001$ *(En2*$^{-/-}$ *vs. WT). Abbreviations are as in the text.*

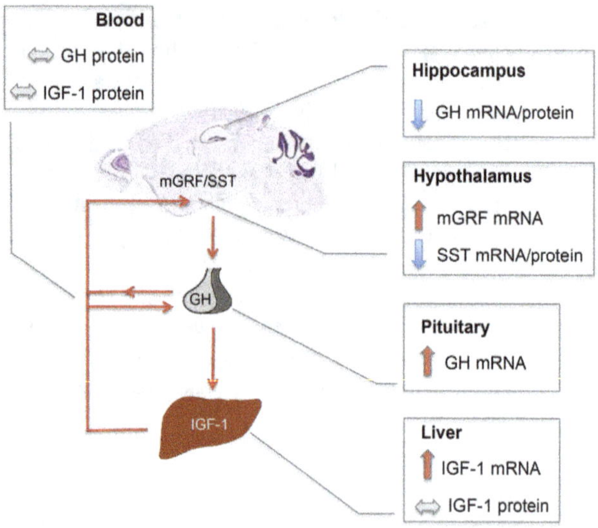


**FIGURE 6 | Schematic summary of SST, mGRF, GH, and IGF-1 expression in the *En2*$^{-/-}$ neuroendocrine axis.** Red and blue arrows, respectively, indicate up- and down-regulations observed in *En2*$^{-/-}$ mice as compared to WT controls. Double-arrowed gray lines indicate comparable levels between WT and *En2*$^{-/-}$ mice. Increased levels of GH and IGF-1 mRNA, respectively observed in *En2*$^{-/-}$ pituitary and liver, are not paralleled by higher levels of circulating hormones, suggesting that a complex post-translational control of GH and IGF-1 synthesis takes place in mutant mice. GH mRNA and protein levels are instead significantly down-regulated in *En2*$^{-/-}$ hippocampus. Arrowed red lines connecting different organs indicate the action of circulating hormones onto their target tissues. The mouse brain sagittal section is a Nissl stain taken from the Allen Mouse Brain Atlas (see text footnote 2). Abbreviations are as in the text.

## DIFFERENTIAL EXPRESSION OF GH AND IGF-1 mRNAs IN THE BRAIN AND PERIPHERAL TISSUES OF *En2*$^{-/-}$ MICE

IGF-1 mRNA exists in two main isoforms, derived from alternative splicing of the two first exons contained in the 5′ untranslated region (5′ UTR) of the mRNA precursor. Class 1 transcripts contain exon 1, whereas class 2 transcripts contain exon 2 (33). Inclusion of exon 1 or exon 2 is mutually exclusive, resulting in different 5′ UTRs of the IGF-1 mRNA containing different leader sequences of the pre-pro-IGF-I peptide. In addition, transcription of class 1 and class 2 mRNAs is differently controlled; class 2 mRNA being directly regulated by GH. It is, however, important to note that both class 1 and class 2 transcripts code for the same IGF-1 mature peptide (33).

In *En2* mutants, we described a differential expression of IGF-1 mRNAs in different tissues of the brain–pituitary–liver axis. A significant increase of IGF-1 class 2 mRNA was detected in liver and blood, whereas IGF-1 class 1 mRNA was significantly decreased in the *En2*$^{-/-}$ hippocampus (**Figure 4**). The negative regulation exerted by *En2* onto IGF-1 signaling in the cerebellum (29), therefore, appears to occur also at a transcriptional level in the hippocampus.

Interestingly, *En2*$^{-/-}$ mice showed increased hypothalamic levels of mGRF and decreased levels of somatostatin (SST), the two hormones controlling GH synthesis. Previous studies from our laboratory already showed that loss of *En2* results in lower levels of SST mRNA and protein in the hippocampus and cerebral cortex. Here, we extended this observation, demonstrating that lower levels of SST are also present in the *En2*$^{-/-}$ hypothalamus; hypothalamic levels of mGRF mRNA were instead increased in mutant mice (**Figure 3**). Deregulation of hypothalamic hormones controlling GH synthesis might result in increased levels of circulating GH and IGF-1 in mutant mice. However, we showed that serum levels of both hormones, as well as IGF-1 levels in liver did not differ between WT and *En2*$^{-/-}$ mice (**Figure 5**). Indeed, behavioral studies did not reveal gross weight and growth abnormalities in *En2* mutants (23), suggesting that differences in GH and IGF-1 mRNA levels might be blunted at the protein level, via multiple post-transcriptional control mechanisms. Indeed, a tight dependence of IGF-1 translation via several miRNA binding site in the 3′ UTR of the transcripts has been described (33, 35).

## FUNCTIONAL CONSEQUENCES OF REDUCED GH LEVELS IN THE *En2*$^{-/-}$ HIPPOCAMPUS

The decreased expression of GH mRNA and protein observed in the *En2*$^{-/-}$ hippocampus might contribute to learning deficits observed in *En2* mutants. Indeed, *En2*$^{-/-}$ mice show impaired learning in hippocampal-dependent tasks, such as the Morris water maze and contextual fear conditioning (22, 23). Profound effects on cognitive function have been demonstrated for GH. GH-deficient spontaneous dwarf rats display marked deficits in hippocampus-dependent spatial learning and memory, accompanied by an imbalance in hippocampal glutamatergic/GABAergic synapses and neurogenesis (36). Chronic stress, which is known to affect hippocampal function, also reduces hippocampal GH levels (37). Restoration of normal GH levels in the hippocampus (obtained via viral-mediated gene transfer) is able to reverse stress-dependent behavioral impairment, as tested by hippocampus-dependent tasks (contextual fear conditioning) (37). Taken together, these results indicate that reduced levels of hippocampal GH detected in *En2*$^{-/-}$ mice might contribute to hippocampal dysfunction observed in these mutants.

## CONCLUSION

To our knowledge, this is the first demonstration that brain GH levels are reduced in a mouse model of ASD. Considering the important role of GH on cognitive functions, our data strengthen the notion that reduced expression of GH in the hippocampus may be implicated in learning disabilities associated to ASD.

## AUTHOR CONTRIBUTIONS

Giovanni Provenzano and Elena Clementi equally contributed to this study. Giovanni Provenzano designed and performed experiments, analyzed data and wrote the paper. Elena Clementi designed and performed experiments, analyzed data. Sacha Genovesi, Manuela Scali, Prem Prakash Tripathi, and Paola Sgadò performed experiments. Yuri Bozzi provided funding, conceived the study, analyzed data and wrote the paper.

## ACKNOWLEDGMENTS

We are grateful to the technical/administrative staff of the Centre for Integrative Biology (University of Trento). We thank

Prof. Emiliana Borrelli (University of California, Irvine, CA, USA) for the kind gift of GH and mGRF cDNAs. This work was funded by grants from the Italian Ministry of University and Research (PRIN 2008 grant 200894SYW2_002 and PRIN 2010-11 grant 2010N8PBAA_002) and the University of Trento (CIBIO start-up) to Yuri Bozzi. Paola Sgadò is supported by Provincia Autonoma di Trento (Italy) under the Marie Curie-People cofunding action of the European Community.

## REFERENCES

1. Llorens-Martín M, Torres-Alemán I, Trejo JL. Mechanisms mediating brain plasticity: IGF1 and adult hippocampal neurogenesis. *Neuroscientist* (2009) **15**:134–48. doi:10.1177/1073858408331371
2. Sale A, Cenni MC, Ciucci F, Putignano E, Chierzi S, Maffei L. Maternal enrichment during pregnancy accelerates retinal development of the fetus. *PLoS One* (2007) **2**:e1160. doi:10.1371/journal.pone.0001160
3. Sale A, Berardi N, Maffei L. Enrich the environment to empower the brain. *Trends Neurosci* (2009) **32**:233–9. doi:10.1016/j.tins.2008.12.004
4. Guzzetta A, Baldini S, Bancale A, Baroncelli L, Ciucci F, Ghirri P, et al. Massage accelerates brain development and the maturation of visual function. *J Neurosci* (2009) **29**:6042–51. doi:10.1523/JNEUROSCI.5548-08.2009
5. Torres-Aleman I. Toward a comprehensive neurobiology of IGF-I. *Dev Neurobiol* (2010) **70**:384–96. doi:10.1002/dneu.20778
6. Trejo JL, Llorens-Martín MV, Torres-Alemán I. The effects of exercise on spatial learning and anxiety-like behavior are mediated by an IGF-I-dependent mechanism related to hippocampal neurogenesis. *Mol Cell Neurosci* (2008) **37**:402–11. doi:10.1016/j.mcn.2007.10.016
7. Llorens-Martín M, Torres-Alemán I, Trejo JL. Exercise modulates insulin-like growth factor 1-dependent and -independent effects on adult hippocampal neurogenesis and behaviour. *Mol Cell Neurosci* (2010) **44**:109–17. doi:10.1016/j.mcn.2010.02.006
8. Trejo JL, Piriz J, Llorens-Martín MV, Fernandez AM, Bolós M, LeRoith D, et al. Central actions of liver-derived insulin-like growth factor I underlying its pro-cognitive effects. *Mol Psychiatry* (2007) **12**:1118–28. doi:10.1038/sj.mp.4002076
9. Mills JL, Hediger ML, Molloy CA, Chrousos GP, Manning-Courtney P, Yu KF, et al. Elevated levels of growth-related hormones in autism and autism spectrum disorder. *Clin Endocrinol* (2007) **67**:230–7. doi:10.1111/j.1365-2265.2007.02868.x
10. Vanhala R, Turpeinen U, Riikonen R. Low levels of insulin-like growth factor-I in cerebrospinal fluid in children with autism. *Dev Med Child Neurol* (2001) **43**:614–6. doi:10.1017/S0012162201001116
11. Riikonen R, Makkonen I, Vanhala R, Turpeinen U, Kuikka J, Kokki H. Cerebrospinal fluid insulin-like growth factors IGF-1 and IGF-2 in infantile autism. *Dev Med Child Neurol* (2006) **48**:751–5. doi:10.1017/S0012162206001605
12. Chen J, Alberts I, Li X. Dysregulation of the IGF-I/PI3K/AKT/mTOR signaling pathway in autism spectrum disorders. *Int J Dev Neurosci* (2014) **35C**:35–41. doi:10.1016/j.ijdevneu.2014.03.006
13. Shcheglovitov A, Shcheglovitova O, Yazawa M, Portmann T, Shu R, Sebastiano V, et al. SHANK3 and IGF1 restore synaptic deficits in neurons from 22q13 deletion syndrome patients. *Nature* (2013) **503**:267–71. doi:10.1038/nature12618
14. Tropea D, Giacometti E, Wilson NR, Beard C, McCurry C, Fu DD, et al. Partial reversal of Rett Syndrome-like symptoms in MeCP2 mutant mice. *Proc Natl Acad Sci U S A* (2009) **106**:2029–34. doi:10.1073/pnas.0812394106
15. Bozdagi O, Tavassoli T, Buxbaum JD. Insulin-like growth factor-1 rescues synaptic and motor deficits in a mouse model of autism and developmental delay. *Mol Autism* (2013) **4**:9. doi:10.1186/2040-2392-4-9
16. Nyberg F, Hallberg M. Growth hormone and cognitive function. *Nat Rev Endocrinol* (2013) **9**:357–65. doi:10.1038/nrendo.2013.78
17. Iwata K, Matsuzaki H, Miyachi T, Shimmura C, Suda S, Tsuchiya KJ, et al. Investigation of the serum levels of anterior pituitary hormones in male children with autism. *Mol Autism* (2011) **2**:16. doi:10.1186/2040-2392-2-16
18. Benayed R, Choi J, Matteson PG, Gharani N, Kamdar S, Brzustowicz LM, et al. Autism-associated haplotype affects the regulation of the homeobox gene, ENGRAILED 2. *Biol Psychiatry* (2009) **66**:911–7. doi:10.1016/j.biopsych.2009.05.027
19. James SJ, Shpyleva S, Melnyk S, Pavliv O, Pogribny IP. Complex epigenetic regulation of Engrailed-2 (EN-2) homeobox gene in the autism cerebellum. *Transl Psychiatry* (2013) **3**:e232. doi:10.1038/tp.2013.8
20. Choi J, Ababon MR, Soliman M, Lin Y, Brzustowicz LM, Matteson PG, et al. Autism associated gene, Engrailed 2, and flanking gene levels are altered in post-mortem cerebellum. *PLoS One* (2014) **9**:e87208. doi:10.1371/journal.pone.0087208
21. Joyner AL, Herrup K, Auerbach BA, Davis CA, Rossant J. Subtle cerebellar phenotype in mice homozygous for a targeted deletion of the En-2 homeobox. *Science* (1991) **251**:1239–43. doi:10.1126/science.1672471
22. Cheh MA, Millonig JH, Roselli LM, Ming X, Jacobsen E, Kamdar S, et al. En2 knockout mice display neurobehavioral and neurochemical alterations relevant to autism spectrum disorder. *Brain Res* (2006) **1116**:166–76. doi:10.1016/j.brainres.2006.07.086
23. Brielmaier J, Matteson PG, Silvermanm JL, Senerth JM, Kelly S, Genestine M, et al. Autism-relevant social abnormalities and cognitive deficits in Engrailed-2 knockout mice. *PLoS One* (2012) **7**:e40914. doi:10.1371/journal.pone.0040914
24. Brielmaier J, Senerth JM, Silverman JL, Matteson PG, Millonig JH, DiCicco-Bloom E, et al. Chronic desipramine treatment rescues depression-related, social and cognitive deficits in Engrailed-2 knockout mice. *Genes Brain Behav* (2014) **13**:286–98. doi:10.1111/gbb.12115
25. Tripathi PP, Sgadò P, Scali M, Viaggi C, Casarosa S, Simon HH, et al. Increased susceptibility to kainic acid-induced seizures in Engrailed-2 knockout mice. *Neuroscience* (2009) **159**:842–9. doi:10.1016/j.neuroscience.2009.01.007
26. Kuemerle B, Zanjani H, Joyner A, Herrup K. Pattern deformities and cell loss in Engrailed-2 mutant mice suggest two separate patterning events during cerebellar development. *J Neurosci* (1997) **17**:7881–9.
27. Sgadò P, Genovesi S, Kalinovsky A, Zunino G, Macchi F, Allegra M, et al. Loss of GABAergic neurons in the hippocampus and cerebral cortex of Engrailed-2 null mutant mice: implications for autism spectrum disorders. *Exp Neurol* (2013) **247**:496–505. doi:10.1016/j.expneurol.2013.01.021
28. Sgadò P, Provenzano G, Dassi E, Adami V, Zunino G, Genovesi S, et al. Transcriptome profiling in Engrailed-2 mutant mice reveals common molecular pathways associated with autism spectrum disorders. *Mol Autism* (2013) **4**:51. doi:10.1186/2040-2392-4-51
29. Rossman IT, Lin L, Morgan KM, Digiovine M, Van Buskirk EK, Kamdar S, et al. Engrailed 2 modulates cerebellar granule neuron precursor proliferation, differentiation and insulin-like growth factor 1 signaling during postnatal development. *Mol Autism* (2014) **5**:9. doi:10.1186/2040-2392-5-9
30. Saiardi A, Bozzi Y, Baik JH, Borrelli E. Antiproliferative role of dopamine: loss of D2 receptors causes hormonal dysfunction and pituitary hyperplasia. *Neuron* (1997) **19**:115–26. doi:10.1016/S0896-6273(00)80352-9
31. Park OK, Gugneja S, Mayo KE. Gonadotropin-releasing hormone gene expression during the rat estrous cycle: effects of pentobarbital and ovarian steroids. *Endocrinology* (1990) **127**:365–72. doi:10.1210/endo-127-1-365
32. Rotwein P. Two insulin-like growth factor I messenger RNAs are expressed in human liver. *Proc Natl Acad Sci U S A* (1986) **83**:77–81. doi:10.1073/pnas.83.1.77
33. Oberbauer AM. The regulation of IGF-1 gene transcription and splicing during development and aging. *Front Endocrinol* (2013) **4**:39. doi:10.3389/fendo.2013.00039
34. Mathews LS, Norstedt G, Palmiter RD. Regulation of insulin-like growth factor I gene expression by growth hormone. *Proc Natl Acad Sci U S A* (1986) **83**:9343–7. doi:10.1073/pnas.83.24.9343
35. Xie X, Lu J, Kulbokas E, Golub TR, Mootha V, Lindblad-Toh K, et al. Systematic discovery of regulatory motifs in human promoters and 3' UTRs by comparison of several mammals. *Nature* (2005) **434**:338–45. doi:10.1038/nature03441
36. Li E, Kim DH, Cai M, Lee S, Kim Y, Lim E, et al. Hippocampus-dependent spatial learning and memory are impaired in growth hormone-deficient spontaneous dwarf rats. *Endocr J* (2011) **58**:257–67. doi:10.1507/endocrj.K11E-006
37. Vander Weele CM, Saenz C, Yao J, Correia SS, Goosens KA. Restoration of hippocampal growth hormone reverses stress-induced hippocampal impairment. *Front Behav Neurosci* (2013) **7**:66. doi:10.3389/fnbeh.2013.00066

4

# Region specific up-regulation of oxytocin receptors in the opioid *Oprm1*$^{-/-}$ mouse model of autism

**Valentina Gigliucci[1], Marianna Leonzino[1,2], Marta Busnelli[1,2], Alessandra Luchetti[3], Viola Stella Palladino[3], Francesca R. D'Amato[3,4] and Bice Chini[1,2]***

[1] Institute of Neuroscience, National Research Council, Milan, Italy
[2] Dipartimento di Biotecnologie e Medicina Traslazionale, Università degli Studi di Milano, Milan, Italy
[3] Institute of Cellular Biology and Neurobiology, National Research Council, Rome, Italy
[4] IRCCS Santa Lucia Foundation, Rome, Italy

**Edited by:**
Yuri Bozzi, University of Trento, Italy

**Reviewed by:**
Valery Grinevich, German Cancer Research Center (DKFZ) and University of Heidelberg, Germany
Valentina Colonnello, Albert Ludwigs University of Freiburg, Germany

***Correspondence:**
Bice Chini, Institute of Neuroscience, CNR, via Vanvitelli 32, Milano 20129, Italy
e-mail: b.chini@in.cnr.it

Autism spectrum disorders (ASDs) are characterized by impaired communication, social impairments, and restricted and repetitive behaviors and interests. Recently, altered motivation and reward processes have been suggested to participate in the physiopathology of ASDs, and μ-opioid receptors (MORs) have been investigated in relation to social reward due to their involvement in the neural circuitry of reward. Mice lacking a functional MOR gene (*Oprm1*$^{-/-}$ mice) display abnormal social behavior and major autistic-like core symptoms, making them an animal model of autism. The oxytocin (OXT) system is a key regulator of social behavior and co-operates with the opioidergic system in the modulation of social behavior. To better understand the opioid-OXT interplay in the central nervous system, we first determined the expression of the oxytocin receptor (OXTR) in the brain of WT C57BL6/J mice by quantitative autoradiography; we then evaluated OXTR regional alterations in *Oprm1*$^{-/-}$ mice. Moreover, we tested these mice in a paradigm of social behavior, the male–female social interaction test, and analyzed the effects of acute intranasal OXT treatment on their performance. In autoradiography, *Oprm1*$^{-/-}$ mice selectively displayed increased OXTR expression in the Medial Anterior Olfactory Nucleus, the Central and Medial Amygdaloid nuclei, and the Nucleus Accumbens. Our behavioral results confirmed that *Oprm1*$^{-/-}$ male mice displayed social impairments, as indicated by reduced ultrasonic calls, and that these were rescued by a single intranasal administration of OXT. Taken together, our results provide evidence of an interaction between OXT and opioids in socially relevant brain areas and in the modulation of social behavior. Moreover, they suggest that the oxytocinergic system may act as a compensative mechanism to bypass and/or restore alterations in circuits linked to impaired social behavior.

**Keywords: oxytocin receptor, μ-opioid receptor, brain autoradiography, social behavior, autism, *Oprm1*$^{-/-}$ mice, ultrasonic vocalizations**

## INTRODUCTION

Autism spectrum disorders (ASDs) are characterized by a triad of symptoms that includes impaired communication, social impairments, and restricted and repetitive behaviors and interests (1). The prevailing hypothesis regarding the physiopathology of ASDs identifies the area of social cognition as a primary deficit. In particular, it focuses on the impaired capabilities of affected people to attribute mental states to others (and oneself) in order to explain and predict behavior (i.e., the theory of mind hypothesis proposed by Baron-Cohen and colleagues (2, 3). However, altered affectivity is evident in autistic children (4) and, as recently proposed by Chevallier and others (5), motivation and reward processes might also participate to the physiopathology of ASDs. Reward circuitry dysfunctions might lead to deficits in social seeking and maintenance, resulting in reduced social capabilities and interests, and if appearing early in life, in social learning. Deficit in social cognition will thus be a consequence, rather than a cause, of impaired social behavior. Excessive brain opiate activity has been proposed in the past as a neurochemical feature in autism (6) and due to their involvement in the neural circuitry of reward, μ-opioid receptors (MORs) have also been investigated in relation to social reward, emotion, and social behavior (7–9), and represent a key target to understand the neurobiological basis of social reward dysfunction in humans and animals.

In humans, MOR activation in specific brain regions such as the amygdala, the periaqueductal gray, and the subgenual cingulated cortex is believed to be protective or adaptive in relation to social rejection. In fact, positron emission tomography (PET) scanning showed that social rejection, exemplified by a paradigm in which the test subject shows interest toward another individual who does not return it, could increase the binding of endogenous opioids to MOR in these areas, where greater binding also seemed to correlate to better resiliency. In a contest of social acceptance, MOR activation in the ventral striatum was shown to correlate with desire for social interaction (10). In a similar study, the G variant of the A118G polymorphism of the MOR-encoding gene (OPRM1) correlated with a greater sensitivity to social rejection, reflected in a higher activation of specific brain regions, such as the dorsal anterior cingulate cortex and the anterior insula. Genetic variations in the OPRM1 gene can also influence individuals' ability to engage in social interactions. People carrying the G allele of the A118G polymorphism of the OPRM1 gene seem to experience a greater pleasure during social situations and they tend to engage in affectionate relationships more easily in comparison with people carrying the more common A variant of the gene (11). A crucial role of MOR in partner preference has also been established by studies in prairie and mountain voles. In the monogamous prairie vole, dorsal striatal MOR has been proved fundamental for the development of partner preference, which leads to the establishment of pair bonding, although pharmacological disruption of MOR signaling did not consistently alter the pattern of mating behaviors (9, 12).

In species where individuals develop selective affective bonds during their life, such as sheep or primates, MOR signaling has been implicated in the modulation of the mother–infant attachment: in infant rhesus macaques the genetic variant C77G of the MOR gene, which increases its affinity for β-endorphin (13), has been associated with increased attachment to the mother and stronger protest response and distress during separation (14). At the same time, the maternal attachment toward the offspring seems to be subjected to MOR effects. Higham and colleagues (15) evidenced that free-ranging macaque females carrying at least one copy of the minor allele (G) of the OPRM1 gene were more possessive toward their infants than mothers homozygous for the C allele. Mouse pups where the MOR gene (*Oprm1*) has been permanently disrupted (*Oprm1*$^{-/-}$ mice) produce fewer ultrasound vocalizations (USVs) in response to isolation from the mother when compared to wild type mice, to indicate that lack of MOR may induce resilience to isolation (16). Moreover, it is possible that the lack of MOR prevents the establishment of an association between maternal stimuli and feelings of reward, as transgenic mice do not show a marked preference for a familiar environment over an unfamiliar one (16). Later on in their life, these mice display reduced interest for interaction with other mice of the same sex and age (17) and they appear indifferent to ultrasounds emitted by mice of the opposite sex (18). A recent extensive behavioral characterization of *Oprm1*$^{-/-}$ mice confirmed that these animals display major autistic-like core symptoms and elegantly provided key neuroanatomical and neurofunctional correlates (19). In particular, *Oprm1*$^{-/-}$ mice display abnormal social behavior, as evidenced by a decreased time in close social contact and increased self-grooming in the direct social interaction test, reduced sociability, and social novelty recognition in the three chamber test, accompanied by increased aggression, and impaired ability in building a nest. These mice also display increased perseverative and stereotyped behaviors such as increased rearing, grooming, circling, and head shaking associated with behavioral inflexibility, as evidenced by deficient pattern of exploration in a Y-maze test. Concerning the neurobiological substrates of such phenotype, of particular interest is the observation of changes in oxytocin (OXT) gene expression in specific areas of the brain: OXT transcripts were found to be reduced in the Nucleus accumbens (NAcc) but not in the Caudate–putamen (CPu) and Central amygdala (CeA) (19).

Together with the opioid system, the OXT system is a key regulator of all the aspects of social behavior, including those involved in reproduction and care of the offspring (20). In humans, OXT facilitates the processing of social information, improves cognitive emphatic abilities and increases interpersonal trust (21). As originally put forward by Modahl (22), a deficit in the OXT system linked to an altered opioid regulation may underline the social deficits in autism. Evidence of opioid–OXT interactions is indeed well established. Endogenous opioids are involved in the modulation of OXT release into the brain and the periphery via mu- and kappa-receptors expressed on OXT-secreting neurons (23–26). Even though the opioidergic modulation of OXT release may account for many shared effects, the interplay of these two systems does not probably end with that. A social motivation circuitry in which OXT, vasopressin, endogenous opioids, and catecholamines were hypothesized to participate in a wide variety of affiliative behaviors was proposed more than 15 years ago (27) and has been more recently integrated into a network of neurobiological mechanisms, which include neuronal, neurotransmitters, and hormone systems whose alterations could underline the social impairment observed in autism (28).

To contribute to unravel the critical interactions between the opioid and OXT systems in the brain, we first reviewed the literature on oxytocin receptor (OXTR) and MOR distributions in the mouse brain. As shown in **Table 1**, we found an overlapped receptors' expression in several regions involved in social behavior.

This observation suggests that OXTR and MOR may reciprocally modulate each other even at the cellular and/or molecular level. To investigate, if alterations in MOR expression might induce changes in the OXTergic system we decided to evaluate the expression and distribution of OXTRs in the brain of *Oprm1*$^{-/-}$ mice.

Oxytocin receptors represent the pharmacological target of OXT, and OXT administration has been proposed as a potential treatment of social deficits in autistic patients (35). In particular, intranasal OXT administration is believed to circumvent the poor blood–brain barrier (BBB) permeability of this peptide. Even if the direct passage of intranasal OXT into the brain is still matter of debate (36, 37) acute and chronic intranasal OXT administration have been shown to exert behavioral effects in rodents (34, 38, 39). Even if it cannot be excluded that some of the behavioral effects of OXT are mediated via peripheral mechanisms, intranasal OXT administration in awake animals represents at present the most convenient and reproducible method to assess the therapeutic effects of this peptide on social behavior. We thus tested *Oprm1*$^{-/-}$ mice in a paradigm of social behavior and analyzed the effect of intranasal OXT treatment on their behavioral performances.

## MATERIALS AND METHODS

### ANIMALS AND HOUSING CONDITIONS

*Oprm1*$^{+/+}$ (WT) and *Oprm1*$^{-/-}$ mice were used in this study. *Oprm1*$^{-/-}$ mice were generated by disruption of exon 2 in the *Oprm1* gene as described elsewhere (40). The homozygotic parents (*Oprm1*$^{+/+}$ and *Oprm1*$^{-/-}$) were derived from heterozygous breeding pairs that were fully backcrossed on a C57BL6/J genetic background. The two homozygous lines were maintained separately. Animals were weaned when 28-day-old and maintained

**Table 1 | MOR and OXTR expression levels in mouse brain as reported in the literature.**

| Brain region | MOR | Reference | OXTR | Reference |
|---|---|---|---|---|
| Olfactory bulb | + | (29–31) | +++ | (32) |
| Anterior olfactory nucleus | ++ | (31) | +++ | (32–34) |
| Lateral Septum | +/++ | (29–31) | +++ | (32, 34) |
| Bed nucleus of the stria terminalis | ++ | (29–31) | +/+++ | (32) |
| Amygdala | | | | |
| Basolateral (comprising BLA and BLP) | ++/+ | (29–31) | ++ | (33) |
| Medial | ++++ | (29–31) | ++ | (32) |
| Central | ++++ | (31) | ++/+++ | (32, 33) |
| Cortical amygdaloid area | ++ | (31) | +++/++++ | (32, 33) |
| Amygdalohippocampal area | + | (31) | ++/+++ | (33) |
| Hippocampus | + | (29–31) | ++ | (32–34) |
| Caudate–putamen | ++/+++ | (29–31) | + | (32) |
| Nucleus accumbens | ++++/++ | (29–31) | +/++++ | (32–34) |
| Paraventricular thalamic nucleus | +++ | (31) | ++ | (32, 33) |
| Habenula | ++++ | (29–31) | N.D. | |

in same sex/genotype groups of four to five subjects in transparent high-temperature polysulfone cages (27 cm × 21 cm × 14 cm) with water and food available *ad libitum* (2018 Teklad Global 18% Protein Rodent Diet, Harlan, Lyon, France). Room temperature (21 ± 1°C) and a 12:12 h light–dark cycle (lights on at 1900 h) were kept constant.

Two different groups of adult WT and *Oprm1*$^{-/-}$ male mice (3–4 months old) were used: the first group (4 WT and 3 *Oprm1*$^{-/-}$ mice, one subject per litter) was used for autoradiography and histological examination; the second group of males (18 WT from 6 litters and 17 *Oprm1*$^{-/-}$ mice from 7 litters) underwent intranasal OXT treatment; USVs and behavior during exposure to a female partner were observed shortly after. The genotype of all animals used in this study was controlled by PCR at the end of the experiment, according to already described procedures (40). Every animal procedure used was in strict accordance with standard ethical guidelines (European Community Guidelines on the Care and Use of Laboratory Animals 2010/63/EU) and the Italian legislation on animal experimentation (D.Lvo 116/92).

### OXTR AUTORADIOGRAPHY

Naïve WT and *Oprm1*$^{-/-}$ mice were sacrificed by cervical dislocation, the brains quickly removed and immediately frozen by immersion in cold isopentane at −25°C and subsequent storage at −80° C.

Coronal brain sections (14 μm) were sliced with a cryostat, thaw-mounted on microscope slides pre-coated with chrome-alum–gelatin and kept at −80°C until further use.

Oxytocin receptor autoradiography was performed as described in Huang et al. (34). Briefly, sections were fixed with 0.2% paraformaldehyde in 0.1 M phosphate-buffered saline (pH 7.4) and rinsed twice with 0.1% bovine serum albumin in 50 mM Tris-HCl buffer (pH 7.4). OXT binding sites were detected by incubation (1 h at room temperature in a humid chamber) with the radioiodinated OXTR antagonist ornithine vasotocin analog ([$^{125}$I]-OVTA, specific activity 2200 Ci/mmol; Perkin Elmer, MA, USA) at 0.02 nM in a medium containing 50 mM Tris-HCl, 0.025% bacitracin, 5 mM $MgCl_2$, and 0.1% bovine serum albumin. Sections immediately adjacent to the ones used for [$^{125}$I]-OVTA binding were used to determine non-specific binding by addition of 2 μM OXT to the incubation solution.

At the end of binding, the unbound excess of ligand was washed out by two rinses in ice-cold incubation medium and a final rinse in cold distilled water. The slides were quickly dried under a stream of cool air and exposed to Biomax MR Films (Kodak) in an autoradiographic cassette for 72 h. The final autoradiograms were digitalized by grayscale high-resolution scanning (600 × 600 dpi) and analysis of the optical binding density of the brain regions of interest (ROIs) was carried out using the ImageJ 1.47v software (NIH, USA). ROIs were identified by comparison with a reference mouse brain atlas (41) and manually delineated with the ROI manager tool of the software. Specific densitometric gray intensity was calculated by subtraction of the gray level of the respective section treated for non-specific binding. For each animal, the final gray intensities of each brain region were calculated by averaging two [for anterior olfactory nucleus (AON), LS, AHiPM, BLP, and PMCo] or three (for OB, NAcc, CPu, Hipp CA3, PV, Hb, BLA, MeA, and CeA) sections at different coronal planes from bregma. The regions of a limited rostro-caudal extension [medial AON (AONm) and BNST] were analyzed on a single coronal plane from bregma. Brain regions were selected on the basis of co-expression of OXTR and MOR receptors at medium-high level as resulting from a review of the data currently available in the literature and summarized in **Table 1**. Even though in literature neither OXTR nor MOR expressions in the hippocampus are reported to be high, we also included the CA3 field of this region in our analysis because it appeared intensely labeled in WT mice. Binding specificity was ensured by comparison with the adjacent sections incubated with an excess of OXT in order to displace any OVTA specifically bound to the OXTRs.

Autoradiographic $^{125}$I microscales (Amersham International, UK) also were exposed for 72 h and a reference standard curve was generated. Levels of gray intensity were then converted to nanocurie per milligram tissue equivalent by interpolation with the standard curve.

In order to increase accuracy in identifying the brain regions within each brain section, the slides labeled for non-specific binding and the slides labeled for total binding were further colored with Nissl staining and acetylcholinesterase (AChE) staining, respectively (see below).

## HISTOLOGICAL STAINING

### *Nissl staining*

The non-specific binding labeled slides were treated for Nissl staining. They were defatted by immersion in deionized water (2 min) followed by subsequent immersions in increasing concentrations of ethanol (EtOH 70% v/v, 95% v/v, and 100%, 2 min each). Sections were then rehydrated by 30 s immersions in decreasing concentrations of ethanol (EtOH 100%, 95% v/v, and 70% v/v) and after a final dip in deionized water they were left for 6 h in cresyl violet solution (0.1% cresyl violet, 0.65% sodium acetate trihydrate in 0.5% acetic acid, pH 3.3). Differentiation was obtained by two consecutive changes (3 s each) of deionized water, EtOH 70% (v/v) and EtOH 95% (v/v), and final dehydration was achieved by two changes (10 s each) in EtOH 100%. Sections were finally cleared by immersion in xylene and coverslips were mounted onto the slides with permanent mounting medium (Entellan®, Merck-Millipore, Germany) and left to dry overnight under a fume hood.

### *Acetylcholinesterase staining*

The slides labeled for total binding in autoradiography were processed for AChE staining following the protocol described by Franklin and Paxinos (41). All the reagents used in this procedure were obtained from Sigma Aldrich (Italy) with the exception of the mounting medium. Sections were immersed over night at room temperature in an incubation solution (50 mM sodium acetate, 4 mM copper sulfate, 16 mM glycine, 4 mM S-acetylthiocholine iodide, 10 nM ethopropazine, and pH 5.0 with HCl 1 N) and developed the following day by incubation for 10 min at room temperature in a solution containing 1% sodium sulfide (pH 7.5 with glacial acetic acid). The colored precipitate from the reaction was fixed to the sections by an overnight incubation with formalin 10%. Finally, the slides were left to dry under a fume hood, dehydrated by subsequent immersions in ethanol 100% and xylene 100%, coverslipped with permanent mounting medium (Entellan®, Merck-Millipore, Germany) and left to dry overnight under a fume hood.

For both histological protocols, dried slides were digitalized at high resolution and the obtained images were used as guidance for the identification of brain regions within the sections.

## BEHAVIORAL EFFECTS OF OXT INTRANASAL ADMINISTRATION

### *Oxytocin intranasal administration*

Adult males were gently handled during the 4 days before testing to progressively habituate to the intranasal administration protocol. The first-day they were simply handled, the second-day they were firmly kept, the third-day they were firmly kept in supine position with their back supported by the palm of the manipulator's hand, and the fourth-day a drop of saline was introduced in each nostril. After the last manipulation, they were isolated in clean cages for 24 h, treated with OXT or saline and their vocalizations and behavior were recorded.

Oxytocin (Sigma Aldrich, Italy) was dissolved in saline (0.9% NaCl) to a concentration of 0.6 mg/10 ml. A total volume of 5 µl of the OXT solution was administered intranasally by gently placing drops in each nostril, that were taken in when the mice reflexively inhaled (600 ng OXT/mouse). The dosage of OXT was based on data from the literature (34, 38, 39). Control mice received an equal volume of saline (Veh). A 20-µl Eppendorf pipette with gel-loading tips was used for administration. Administration was rapid ($<15$ s) and handling was consistent across treatment groups.

### *Male–female social interaction test*

Adult WT and *Oprm1*$^{-/-}$ males were isolated for 24 h in clean cages. A total of 17 *Oprm1*$^{-/-}$ (8 OXT and 9 Veh) and 18 WT (9 OXT and 9 Veh) males was used as subjects and an equivalent number of females of the two genotypes were used as partners. Each animal was used only once and administered with OXT or saline. The estrous cycle of the female partners was not considered, as irrelevant on USV quantitative performance during the first minutes of interaction in sexual naïve males facing unfamiliar females (42–44). Five minutes after the male's intranasal drug/saline administration, a female of the same genotype was introduced into the male's home cage and left for 5 min. The delay of only 5 min was chosen according to previous studies analyzing the behavioral effects of OXT after intranasal administration (34, 39). *Oprm1*$^{-/-}$ males were exposed to *Oprm1*$^{-/-}$ females and WT males to WT females. The cage was placed in front of a video-camera and under a microphone for the recording and subsequent analysis of behavior and ultrasonic vocalizations. The videos were analyzed with the Observer software (Noldus Technology, The Netherlands) and the following males' behaviors were considered for the statistical analysis: locomotion, exploration (sniffing, rearing, digging, and climbing), social investigation (following, sniffing nose, body, and ano-genital region of the partner), and self-grooming. Ultrasonic vocalizations were recorded using an UltraSoundGate Condenser Microphone (CM16, Avisoft Bioacoustics, Berlin, Germany) lowered 5 cm above the top of the cage, and analyzed by SasLab Pro (version 4.40; Avisoft Bioacoustics). Details concerning USVs recording and analysis can be found in previous papers (17, 45). According to previous literature, USVs recorded during the first minutes of male–female social interaction, are considered to be mainly uttered by the male (46).

## STATISTICAL ANALYSIS

In autoradiography, we quantified the intensity of the binding signal in *Oprm1*$^{-/-}$ mice and compared it with the binding showed by WT mice. Average nanocurie per milligram of tissue equivalents were compared by Student's $t$-test with GraphPad Prism 5.0 (GraphPad Software, USA). Results were deemed statistically significant when $p < 0.05$. The effect of the genotype and treatment on behavioral measures was first analyzed by multiple analysis of variance (MANOVA) followed by univariate ANOVAs and, in cases of significance ($p < 0.05$), Tukey HSD *post hoc* tests.

## RESULTS

### QUANTITATIVE ANALYSIS OF OXTR DISTRIBUTION IN WT MICE BRAIN

To analyze the pattern of OXTR distribution in *Oprm1*$^{-/-}$ mice, we first analyzed [$^{125}$I]-OVTA binding data in WT mice on which *Oprm1*$^{-/-}$ animals are backcrossed. **Figure 1** shows representative autoradiographic sections for the selected area and associated Nissl staining of adjacent slices; the reported distances from bregma of the different coronal planes are deduced from a reference mouse brain atlas (41).

The use of a commercial $^{125}$I microscales standard allowed us to quantify the levels of [$^{125}$I]-OVTA binding in the brain of our mice. Quantification of OXTR expression in several areas of the brain in WT mice is reported in **Figure 2.** In WT mice, we found the highest levels of OXTR (here in the text reported as mean nanocurie per milligram tissue equivalent $\pm$ SD) in the olfactory bulb (OB, 0.91 $\pm$ 0.25), the AON (0.88 $\pm$ 0.22), and in some posterior nuclei of the amygdala, specifically the amygdalohippocampal area (AHiPM, 0.94 $\pm$ 0.16), the posteromedial cortical amygdaloid area (PMCo, 1.06 $\pm$ 0.16), and the posterior part of the basolateral amygdaloid nucleus (BLP, 0.87 $\pm$ 0.16). Medium level of OVTA binding was detected in lateral septum (LS, 0.41 $\pm$ 0.06), the bed nucleus of the stria terminalis (BNST, 0.34 $\pm$ 0.06), the CA3 field of the hippocampus (Hipp CA3, 0.30 $\pm$ 0.06), the paraventricular thalamic nucleus (PV, 0.32 $\pm$ 0.06), and in the medial amygdaloid nucleus (MeA, 0.26 $\pm$ 0.04). In the other anterior nuclei of the amygdala analyzed, the CeA nucleus (0.16 $\pm$ 0.05) and the anterior part of the basolateral amygdaloid nucleus (BLA, 0.18 $\pm$ 0.04), and in the NAcc (0.10 $\pm$ 0.04) OXTR expression was rather low. Interestingly, Dölen et al. (33) report the basolateral nucleus of the amygdala as a whole to display "average" OXTR expression, however, from observation during analysis we noticed a clear difference in OXTR expression between the anterior and the posterior parts of this nucleus, therefore, we deemed it more appropriate to analyze the two subregions separately, distinguishing them into BLA and BLP. Finally, we found minimal expression of OXTR in the CPu (0.02 $\pm$ 0.02) and the habenula (Hb, 0.04 $\pm$ 0.02) of WT mice. Overall, the expression and the distribution of OXTR in the brains of WT mice, at least in relation to the regions analyzed, is consistent with what has been previously reported (see **Table 1**).

The regions with the lowest OXTR binding signal (CPu and Hb) presented a 20-fold lower signal compared to the regions with the highest OXTR expression such as the PMCo. The NAcc also showed a very low level of OXTR expression, being it around a tenth of the PMCo's OXTR expression. All the remaining regions, such as the anterior nuclei of the amygdala, the LS, the BNST, and

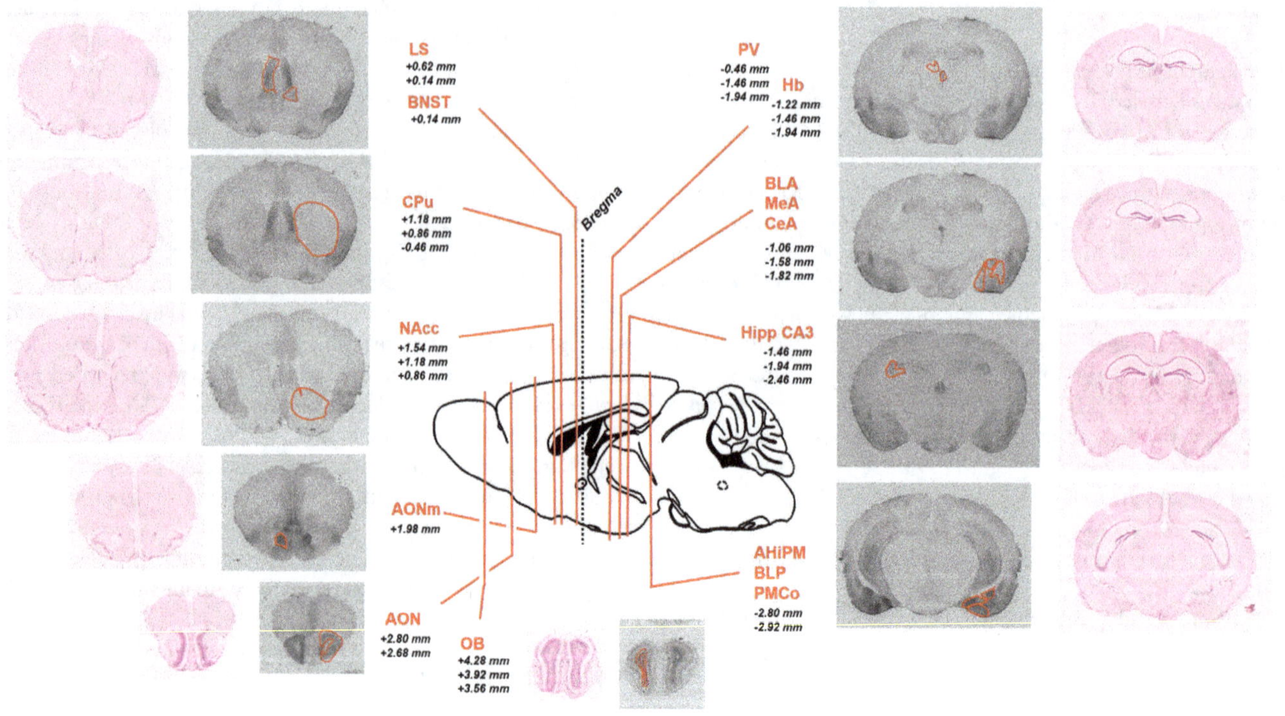


**FIGURE 1 | Schematic representation of the brain regions of interest analyzed in the study**. Representative sections of autoradiographic labeling of OXTR with [$^{125}$I]-OVTA 20 pM are displayed in grayscale, flanked by corresponding Nissl stained sections. Red contours outline the regions of interest analyzed. A sagittal schematic representation of a mouse brain is reported in the central panel. Lines indicate the antero-posterior localization of the coronal sections taken into account, defined by the reported distances (millimeter) from bregma (according to the Franklin and Paxinos (41) mouse brain atlas). AHiPM, amygdalohippocampal area, posteromedial part; AON, anterior olfactory nucleus; AONm, anterior olfactory nucleus, medial part; BLA, basolateral amygdaloid nucleus, anterior part; BLP, basolateral amygdaloid nucleus, posterior part; BNST, bed nucleus of the stria terminalis; CeA, central amygdaloid nucleus; CPu, caudate–putamen; Hb, habenular nucleus; Hipp CA3, hippocampus, field CA3; LS, lateral septum; MeA, medial amygdaloid nucleus; NAcc, nucleus accumbens; OB, olfactory bulb; PMCo, posteromedial cortical amygdaloid area.

the PV, showed instead an average OXTR expression, comprised between one-fifth and one-half of the PMCo's levels.

### ABSENCE OF MOR INDUCES SPECIFIC INCREASES OF OXTR EXPRESSION IN THE AONm, IN THE ANTERIOR AMYGDALOID NUCLEI AND IN NACCS

In order to reveal possible interaction(s) between MOR and OXTR, we looked for alterations in oxytocinergic binding levels in the brains of *Oprm1*$^{-/-}$ mice.

Our data indicate that the expression of OXTR did not differ significantly between WT and *Oprm1*$^{-/-}$ mice in the OB {*t*-test; [$t(4) = 0.139$, $p = 0.897$, n.s.]}, AON {coronal planes corresponding to its central part; *t*-test; [$t(5) = 0.577$, $p = 0.589$, n.s.]}, CPu {*t*-test; [$t(4) = 1.238$, $p = 0.284$, n.s.]}, LS {*t*-test; [$t(5) = 0.046$, $p = 0.965$, n.s.]}, BNST {*t*-test; [$t(5) = 0.315$, $p = 0.766$, n.s.]}, Hipp CA3 {*t*-test; [$t(5) = 0.160$, $p = 0.880$, n.s.]}, PV {*t*-test; [$t(5) = 1.269$, $p = 0.260$, n.s.]}, and Hb {*t*-test; [$t(5) = 0.219$, $p = 0.835$, n.s.]} (**Figure 3A**). Similarly, the posterior nuclei of the amygdala (AHiPM, BLP, and PMCo), did not present alterations in OXTR expression linked to the lack of MOR {*t*-test; [$t(5) = 1.891$, $p = 0.117$, n.s.], [$t(5) = 1.442$, $p = 0.209$, n.s.], and [$t(5) = 1.087$, $p = 0.327$, n.s.], respectively} (**Figure 3B**).

On the contrary, in the anterior nuclei of the amygdala, and in particularly in the CeA and MeA, the absence of MOR led to an up-regulation of OXTR {*t*-test; [$t(5) = 3.102$, $p < 0.05$] and [$t(5) = 4.299$, $p < 0.01$], respectively, **Figure 3C**}. A trend ($p = 0.07$) toward an increase in OXTR was also found in the anterior basolateral amygdala (**Figure 3C**).

Another region in which we found an up-regulation of OXTR is the AONm in the posterior part of AON {*t*-test; [$t(7) = 3.590$, $p < 0.01$]} (**Figure 4A**). Because discriminating between the AON and NAcc is particularly tricky in this area of the brain, we performed AChE staining on the same slices processed for autoradiography. AChE selectively labels the NAcc and the olfactory tubercle but not the AON, thus allowing unambiguous identification of the two structures. **Figures 4C,D** show examples of brain sections labeled with [$^{125}$I]-OVTA and AChE. In the blow-ups of the merged images it is evident that the strong autoradiographic signal observed in this area does not overlap with the AChE staining, but it is adjacent to it. This allowed us to assign the strong specific [$^{125}$I]-OVTA labeling of this region to the AONm. Given

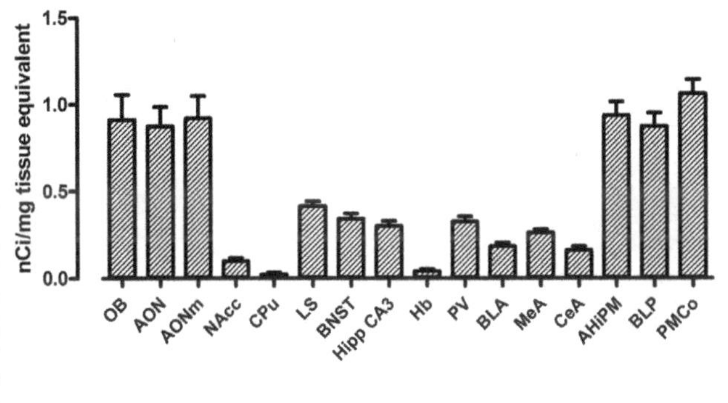


**FIGURE 2 | Regional distribution and quantification of OXTR in WT mice.** Average regional expression of OXTR defined by [$^{125}$I]-OVTA binding in WT mice. For each animal, final levels of OXTR expression were calculated averaging data obtained from the different coronal planes analyzed within the same region of interest. Each bar represents data expressed as mean and SEM of four animals.

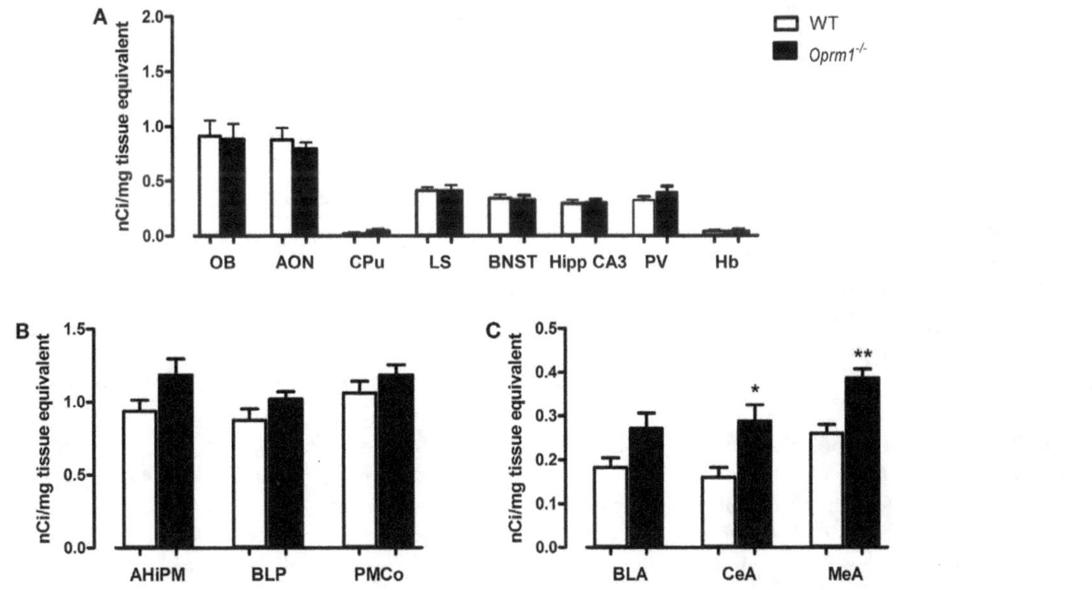


**FIGURE 3 | *Oprm1*$^{-/-}$ mice display increased OXTR expression selectively in the anterior nuclei of the amygdala.** Average regional expression of OXTR defined by [$^{125}$I]-OVTA binding in *Oprm1*$^{-/-}$ mice in comparison with WT mice. **(A)** No differences in OXTR expression were detected in *Oprm1*$^{-/-}$ mice in several brain regions reported to co-express medium-high levels of MOR and OXTR. **(B)** OXTR expression is not influenced by the lack of MOR in the posterior nuclei of the amygdala whereas **(C)** an increase of OXTR is detectable in the anterior nuclei of the amygdala CeA and MeA. Data expressed as mean and SEM of three to four animals. *$p < 0.05$, **$p < 0.01$ compared to WT controls.

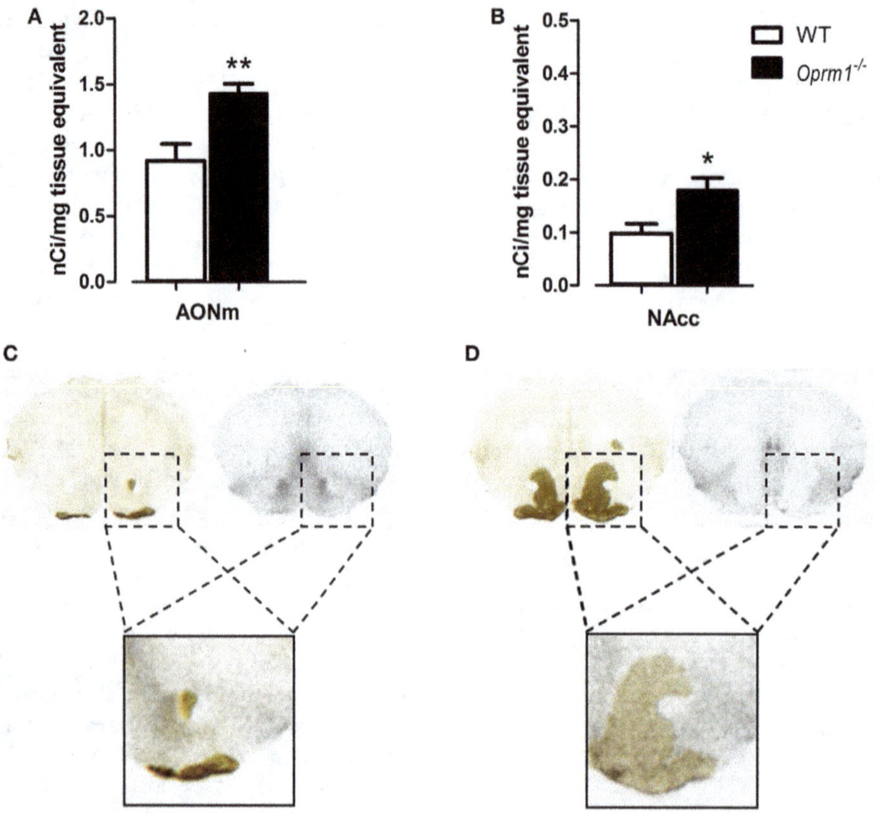


**FIGURE 4 | *Oprm1*$^{-/-}$ mice display increased OXTR expression in the medial AON and the nucleus accumbens.** Average regional expression of OXTR defined by [$^{125}$I]-OVTA binding in *Oprm1*$^{-/-}$ mice in comparison with WT mice. OXTR expression is increased in both **(A)** AONm and **(B)** NAcc of *Oprm1*$^{-/-}$ mice. At the zone of transition between AON and NAcc, distinction between the two structures was determined by AChE staining, which selectively labels the NAcc and the olfactory tubercle. **(C)** The spot of intense [$^{125}$I]-OVTA labeling evident in the autoradiographic picture and the AChE staining, apparently in the same position, do not overlap when the two images are merged (blow-up), indicating that the NAcc doesn't express high levels of OXTR in this area. **(D)** Superimposition of the autoradiogram and the AChE staining of a coronal section of the NAcc where the AONm is not present anymore (blow-up) confirms that this region does not express high levels of OXTR.

the difficulty, in this region, to discriminate between AONm and NAcc in absence of AChE staining, we cannot exclude that the area identified as NAcc in (34) may, instead, correspond to the AONm.

Finally, in the NAcc of *Oprm1*$^{-/-}$ mice, sampled at three different coronal planes, we found an OXTR level twice as high as that observed in WT animals {*t*-test; [$t(5) = 2.767$, $p < 0.05$]} (**Figure 4B**), suggesting that the NAcc is an anatomical field of compensative interaction(s) between the oxytocinergic and the opioidergic systems.

### BEHAVIORAL EFFECTS OF INTRANASAL ADMINISTRATION OF OXYTOCIN IN *Oprm1*$^{-/-}$ MICE

To evaluate the pro-social effects of OXT, we tested sexually naive males during courtship, before the initiation of sexual behavior, during the first minutes of interaction with a female. The behavioral profile of males interacting with females is shown in **Figure 5**. The MANOVA indicated no significant effect of main factors (genotype: $\lambda = 0.90$, $F_{(5/27)} = 0.58$, n.s.; treatment: $\lambda = 0.89$, $F_{(5/27)} = 0.61$, n.s.), but a significant genotype × treatment interaction ($\lambda = 0.62$, $F_{(5/27)} = 3.56$, $p < 0.05$), suggesting that OXT had different effect on mice behavioral profile according to the genotype. Univariate results confirmed significant genotype × treatment effect for locomotion [$F_{(1/31)} = 5.01$, $p < 0.05$], social investigation [$F_{(1/31)} = 4.22$, $p < 0.05$], and USVs [$F_{(1/31)} = 15.29$, $p < 0.001$]. *Post hoc* analysis showed a significant difference at basal conditions between *Oprm1*$^{-/-}$ and WT mice only in ultrasonic vocalizations (*Oprm1*$^{-/-}$ + Veh vs. WT + Veh: $p < 0.01$), and an increase in the number of USVs due to OXT treatment, selectively in the *Oprm1*$^{-/-}$ line (*Oprm1*$^{-/-}$ + Veh vs. *Oprm1*$^{-/-}$ + OXT: $p = 0.01$). By contrast, OXT did not to significantly modify WT males' vocalizations ($p = 0.13$, n.s.) (**Figure 5B**). The deficit shown by *Oprm1*$^{-/-}$ mice in USVs emission in response to social cues does not depend on a general impairment in their capacity to emit high levels of ultrasonic calls or in their sensitivity to olfactory stimuli, in infancy (16) as well as in adulthood (data presented here), but suggests lower motivation to interact with conspecifics.

The low impact of OXT on mutant males' general social behavior (**Figure 5A**) can be related to the role of their mutant (untreated) females that may prefer to avoid their partner. In this respect, the USVs test will result more susceptible to treatment, as

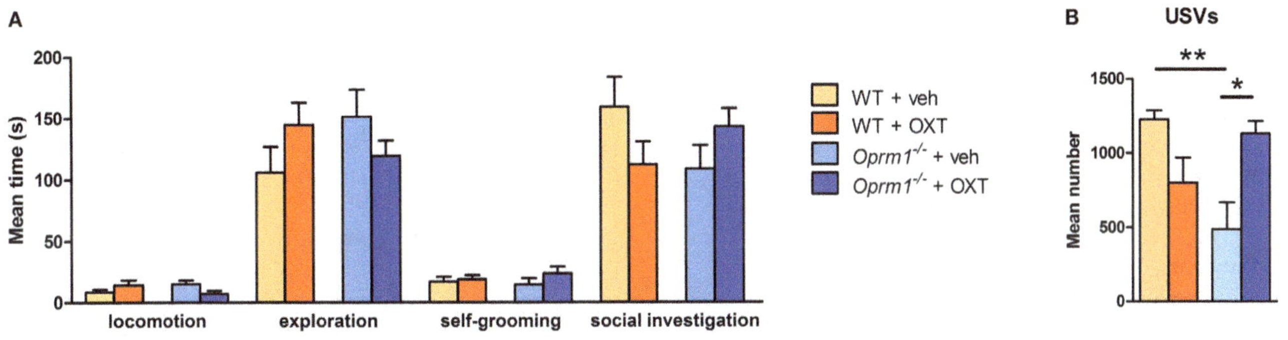


**FIGURE 5 | Acute intranasal administration of OXT rescues the impairments in ultrasound emission in *Oprm1*$^{-/-}$ mice during male–female social interaction**. Effects of acute intranasal OXT administration (600 ng) in *Oprm1*$^{-/-}$ and WT male mice during a 5 min male–female social interaction. **(A)** Genotype and OXT treatment do not affect the amount of time spent in locomotion, exploration, self-grooming, or social investigation during the test. **(B)** *Oprm1*$^{-/-}$ mice emit a reduced number of ultrasound vocalizations during the test in comparison with WT mice, and this deficit is completely rescued by OXT treatment. Data expressed as mean and SEM of eight to nine animals. $*p < 0.05$, $**p < 0.01$ compared to *Oprm1*$^{-/-}$ + veh group.

it only relies on the male behavior, independently on the female receptivity. Adult male mice emit USVs in the presence of female conspecifics and these vocalizations, promoting proximity, facilitate close social interactions, and sexual behavior. The advantage of testing males in this context stands in the consistent amount of ultrasonic calls that characterizes their first approach to the partner, which is independent from female's receptivity and closely associated to the male's motivational state (42–44). As a matter of fact, males emit USVs also when exposed to female's cage bedding or urine (47). When in close proximity, mice can acquire information on the partner's individual characteristics (e.g. sex, rank, sexual experience, and estrous condition) modulating their social behavior, and facilitating or avoiding social interactions. Moreover, the lack of strong deficits during sexual encounters in this mutant line confirms the entirety of their reproductive capabilities. Finally, the absence of significant effects of the intranasal OXT treatment in control male mice is in line with the Huang et al. study, showing only little changes in social investigation toward a female partner in C57BL/6J mice (34).

## DISCUSSION

The aim of this study was to investigate, in *Oprm1*$^{-/-}$ mice, the altered molecular mechanisms underlying the well documented deficits in social behavior presented by this animal model (16–19). In particular, we focused on alterations in the expression of brain OXTRs because they are the target of intranasally administered OXT, a promising new treatment for social deficits in autism (35, 48, 49). Our data show an OXTR up-regulation in specific brain regions of MOR-null mice, such as AONm, CeA, MeA, and NAcc. All these regions are involved in the regulation of social behavior, but, in our study, not all regions involved in social behavior that express OXTR were found to up-regulate the receptor. Furthermore, no correspondence between a high expression level of the OXTR and its up-regulation was observed. In particular: (1) regions that display very high levels of OXTR such as LS and BNST did not show any OXTR up-regulation and (2) of the regions where we observed OXTR up-regulation, three (AON, MeA, and CeA) have a high level of OXTR expression, and one (NAcc) has a medium-low level. Interestingly, a region-selective OXTR up-regulation was also observed in a recent paper in which OXTR expression levels were analyzed in the mouse brain after morphine treatment and withdrawal (50). However, the regions found in the aforementioned pharmacological manipulation study did not overlap with those described in the present study, an observation consistent with multiple patterns of receptor modulation linked to specific genetic, developmental, and pharmacological conditions. AONm, MeA, CeA, and NAcc are, nevertheless, all characterized by a medium-high MOR expression in WT mice (**Table 1**), suggesting a local interplay between the two receptor systems, which may involve neuroanatomical, cellular, or even subcellular interactions.

An open question regards, which is the neurobiological mechanism at the basis of the OXTR up-regulation. It is difficult to answer to this question as the OXT content and capability of OXT release in the hypothalamus of *Oprm1*$^{-/-}$ mice has not been evaluated so far. If reduced, an up-regulation of the OXTR in target sites of the neuropeptide's action may represent a compensatory mechanism to normalize the neuronal responses to reduced levels of secreted OXT. Becker et al. (19) actually found a reduced level of OXT transcript in *Oprm1*$^{-/-}$ mice, but this impairment was restricted to the NAcc, leaving the overall levels of OXT undetermined. A second possibility implies direct molecular interactions between OXTR and MOR. G-protein coupled receptors such as OXTR and MOR, can form homo- (with another molecule of the same receptor) or hetero- (with receptors from other families) dimers and it has been shown that this physical association can modulate receptor binding and function (51). Interestingly, in mice lacking the alpha2A-adrenergic receptor, morphine has a reduced analgesic effect, suggesting that alterations in the noradrenergic system induce alterations in the opioid system (52). Molecular dimerization of MOR and alpha2A-adrenergic receptor has been demonstrated in both cell lines and primary neuronal cultures (53) and it has been shown that, in MOR–alpha2A-adrenergic receptor dimers, the activation of MOR by morphine inhibits the adjacent alpha2A-receptor by blocking its ability to activate the G-proteins even in the presence of noradrenaline (54). If dimeric interactions occur between MOR and OXTR, the lack of MOR may result in specific alterations of OXTR pharmacology in the brain regions in which the two receptors physically interact. Even if only speculative at present, this hypothesis will deserve further investigation.

A second question is: what are the neuroanatomical basis of the specific OXTR up-regulation in NAcc, CeA, MeA, and AONm of MOR-null mice?

As the NAcc is involved in the processing of social motivation and reward, it is not surprising that alterations in OXTR levels in NAcc have been found to be linked to altered social behaviors. First of all, natural variability in OXTR expression in the NAcc has been associated to social organization and mating behavior in voles, being the level of OXTR in the NAcc higher in monogamous voles displaying greater maternal care (55). Many other studies associated OXTR density in the NAcc to the degree of maternal and affiliative behavior and partner preference formation (56–60). Regardless of whether differences in OXTR expression are intrinsic (due to individual or species-related variability) (55, 57, 58), exogenously induced by viral-mediated over expression (35, 59, 60), or physiologically caused by labor and lactation (56), an higher OXTR level in these brain regions correlates with more pronounced social behavior. On the contrary, reduced levels of OXTR binding in the NAcc were observed in voles after paternal deprivation (61). At the neurophysiological level, presynaptic OXTRs have been recently shown to be required for social reward in the NAcc (33). In particular, OXTRs located on axonal terminals of serotoninergic projections coming from the dorsal raphe have been found to elicit Long-Term Depression (LTD) in medium spiny neurons by activation of serotoninergic 5HT1B receptors (33). NAcc neurons express high levels or MOR, but the neuronal populations that mediate all the distinct opiate effects remain elusive; recently, a subpopulation of striatal direct-pathway neurons was shown to support opiate reward-driven behaviors (62), and specific "hotspots" involved in the modulation of hedonic "liking" responses in which opioid receptors might function as hedonic enhancers have been identified (63). Furthermore, activation of MORs within the dorsal striatum appears to be critical to partner preference formation by generating socially motivated behavioral responses (9). OXTR may thus be postulated to act on specific MOR positive NAcc subpopulation(s) to regulate specific aspects or components of social reward, possibly via a presynaptic mechanism similar to that observed for the OXT induced LTP at 5HT1B receptors.

The different nuclei of the amygdala are responsible for the processing of emotional content of both positive and negative experiences. The CeA, as part of the brain's reward circuitry, is important in processing positive emotions and, particularly, in the learning process of stimulus–reward association (64, 65). Moreover, the CeA is strongly implicated in the expression of fear. In mice, a neural circuit within the CeA that gates fear responses activating active strategies of risk assessment or passive expression of fear (freezing) has been described and, in this circuit, the OXTR was found to be a key player (66). Interestingly, as it has been observed that excessively aggressive animals show highest OXTR binding in the CeA (67), it is tempting to speculate that the increased aggressive behavior observed in *Oprm1*$^{-/-}$ mice (19) may be linked to the selective up-regulation of OXTR in the CeA. The MeA is highly activated during social encounters and recognition, thus representing a critical neuroanatomical substrate of social cognition. The recognition of conspecifics is an initial and crucial condition for the establishment of social and sexual behavior. Odor, scent, and pheromones mediate sexual and competitive interactions, and are important in individual and kin recognition and mate selection. In rodents, odor signals are processed by two systems: the main olfactory pathways and the vomeronasal pathway, both directly and indirectly projecting to the MeA, a key region for the processing of chemosensory information (68). OXT-deficient mice are not able to recognize a previously encountered, familiar conspecific, and this social recognition behavior can be restored with a direct microinjection of OXT into the MeA of OXT KO mice, indicating that OXT in the MeA is both necessary and sufficient for social recognition (69, 70). Furthermore, male social interest correlated positively with OXTR in the MeA, while female social interest correlated negatively with OXTR expression in the same region (71). Finally, it has recently been shown that OXT-mediated LTD in the AOB–MeA pathway is directly involved in long-term social recognition memory formation (72). The up-regulation of OXTR in MeA may thus be involved in the pharmacological rescue of intranasal OXT on the social interaction test used in our study.

The up-regulation of OXTR in AONm of *Oprm1*$^{-/-}$ remains of difficult interpretation. The *pars medialis* of the AON can be distinguished from the rest of the AON by cytoarchitectural features and projection patterns (73, 74), suggesting a different role than a station along the main olfactory and the vomeronasal pathways, but the role of OXTR in this region is still undefined.

Finally, what is the pathophysiological meaning of the OXTR up-regulation in *Oprm1*$^{-/-}$ mice? As *Oprm1*$^{-/-}$ mice do have severe defects in social interaction and social memory (19), the up-regulation of OXTR binding sites observed in *Oprm1*$^{-/-}$ mice is apparently unable to normalize social cognition in these animals. Nevertheless, the up-regulation of OXTR may contribute to the rescue effects observed with intranasal OXT in MOR-null animals, as these KO animals completely recovered from communication deficits during the first minutes of social interaction, not differing from wild type animals anymore. Indeed, the present study confirms the efficacy of OXT treatment in reverting social deficits in a mouse model in which the oxytocinergic system underwent a compensatory modulation. These findings are of high relevance in the autism field as they further validate the use of OXT in ASD regardless of the primary etiopathogenetic cause(s) but solely on the basis of the social endophenotype. To fully understand the role of OXTR compensatory roles, it will be very interesting to investigate in detail the time-course of OXTR up-regulation in crucial periods of prenatal and post-natal life, including birth, weaning, and sexual maturity. Similarly, we only investigated male animals, but, due to the sexual dimorphism of OXTR expression in different species and brain areas (75, 76), similar analysis in female animals is warranted, as this may have a profound impact on the design of therapeutic schemes and doses.

In conclusion, the OXT system may act as a downstream effector toward social behaviors, compensating and/or bypassing genetic alterations in upstream circuits that produce social deficits. Such a hypothesis would justify the use of this neuropeptide in a wide variety of human conditions characterized by defects in social cognition and/or reward, such as ASDs, upon demonstration of OXT/OXTR modification(s) in the brain of affected individuals. Moreover, the results presented here further corroborate the hypothesis that alterations in the OXTergic system are involved in the pathophysiology of autism and that administration of OXT to such altered system might restore a balance in the neural circuitries involved in social behavior.

## AUTHOR CONTRIBUTORS

Valentina Gigliucci: performed experiments (autoradiography, Nissl staining, and AChE) and data analysis; wrote the manuscript. Marianna Leonzino: performed data analysis and wrote the manuscript. Marta Busnelli: performed experiments (autoradiography and AChE staining) and data analysis. Alessandra Luchetti: performed experiments (pharmacological treatment and behavioral tests). Viola Stella Palladino: performed experiments (animal genotyping and behavioral tests). Francesca R. D'Amato: conceived and supervised behavior experiments and wrote the manuscript. Bice Chini: conceived and supervised the study and wrote the manuscript.

## ACKNOWLEDGMENTS

Thanks are given to Dr. Diego Oddi for projecting and discussing preliminary data. This study was partly supported by Regione Lazio FILAS for "Sviluppo della Ricerca sul Cervello."

## REFERENCES


1. Association AP. *Diagnostic and Statistical Manual of Mental Disorders*. 5th ed. Arlington, VA: American Psychiatric Publishing (2013).
2. Baron-Cohen S. Social and pragmatic deficits in autism: cognitive or affective? *J Autism Dev Disord* (1988) **18**(3):379–402. doi:10.1007/BF02212194
3. Baron-Cohen S, Leslie AM, Frith U. Does the autistic child have a "theory of mind"? *Cognition* (1985) **21**(1):37–46. doi:10.1016/0010-0277(85)90022-8
4. Kanner L. Autistic disturbances of affective contact. *Nerv Child* (1943) **2**(3):217–50.
5. Chevallier C, Kohls G, Troiani V, Brodkin ES, Schultz RT. The social motivation theory of autism. *Trends Cogn Sci* (2012) **16**(4):231–9. doi:10.1016/j.tics.2012.02.007
6. Panksepp J. A neurochemical theory of autism. *Trends Neurosci* (1979) **2**:174–7. doi:10.1016/0166-2236(79)90071-7
7. Zubieta JK, Ketter TA, Bueller JA, Xu Y, Kilbourn MR, Young EA, et al. Regulation of human affective responses by anterior cingulate and limbic mu-opioid neurotransmission. *Arch Gen Psychiatry* (2003) **60**(11):1145–53. doi:10.1001/archpsyc.60.11.1145
8. Trezza V, Damsteegt R, Achterberg EJ, Vanderschuren LJ. Nucleus accumbens mu-opioid receptors mediate social reward. *J Neurosci* (2011) **31**(17):6362–70. doi:10.1523/JNEUROSCI.5492-10.2011
9. Resendez SL, Dome M, Gormley G, Franco D, Nevarez N, Hamid AA, et al. Mu-opioid receptors within subregions of the striatum mediate pair bond formation through parallel yet distinct reward mechanisms. *J Neurosci* (2013) **33**(21):9140–9. doi:10.1523/JNEUROSCI.4123-12.2013
10. Hsu DT, Sanford BJ, Meyers KK, Love TM, Hazlett KE, Wang H, et al. Response of the mu-opioid system to social rejection and acceptance. *Mol Psychiatry* (2013) **18**(11):1211–7. doi:10.1038/mp.2013.96
11. Troisi A, Frazzetto G, Carola V, Di Lorenzo G, Coviello M, D'Amato FR, et al. Social hedonic capacity is associated with the A118G polymorphism of the mu-opioid receptor gene (OPRM1) in adult healthy volunteers and psychiatric patients. *Soc Neurosci* (2011) **6**(1):88–97. doi:10.1080/17470919.2010.482786
12. Burkett JP, Spiegel LL, Inoue K, Murphy AZ, Young LJ. Activation of mu-opioid receptors in the dorsal striatum is necessary for adult social attachment in monogamous prairie voles. *Neuropsychopharmacology* (2011) **36**(11):2200–10. doi:10.1038/npp.2011.117
13. Miller GM, Bendor J, Tiefenbacher S, Yang H, Novak MA, Madras BK. A mu-opioid receptor single nucleotide polymorphism in rhesus monkey: association with stress response and aggression. *Mol Psychiatry* (2004) **9**(1):99–108. doi:10.1038/sj.mp.4001378
14. Barr CS, Schwandt ML, Lindell SG, Higley JD, Maestripieri D, Goldman D, et al. Variation at the mu-opioid receptor gene (OPRM1) influences attachment behavior in infant primates. *Proc Natl Acad Sci U S A* (2008) **105**(13):5277–81. doi:10.1073/pnas.0710225105
15. Higham JP, Barr CS, Hoffman CL, Mandalaywala TM, Parker KJ, Maestripieri D. Mu-opioid receptor (OPRM1) variation, oxytocin levels and maternal attachment in free-ranging rhesus macaques *Macaca mulatta*. *Behav Neurosci* (2011) **125**(2):131–6. doi:10.1037/a0022695
16. Moles A, Kieffer BL, D'Amato FR. Deficit in attachment behavior in mice lacking the mu-opioid receptor gene. *Science* (2004) **304**(5679):1983–6. doi:10.1126/science.1095943
17. Cinque C, Pondiki S, Oddi D, Di Certo MG, Marinelli S, Troisi A, et al. Modeling socially anhedonic syndromes: genetic and pharmacological manipulation of opioid neurotransmission in mice. *Transl Psychiatry* (2012) **2**:e155. doi:10.1038/tp.2012.83
18. Wohr M, Moles A, Schwarting RK, D'Amato FR. Lack of social exploratory activation in male mu-opioid receptor KO mice in response to playback of female ultrasonic vocalizations. *Soc Neurosci* (2011) **6**(1):76–87. doi:10.1080/17470911003765560
19. Becker JA, Clesse D, Spiegelhalter C, Schwab Y, Le Merrer J, Kieffer BL. Autistic-like syndrome in mu opioid receptor null mice is relieved by facilitated mGluR4 activity. *Neuropsychopharmacology* (2014) **39**(9):2049–60. doi:10.1038/npp.2014.59
20. Lee HJ, Macbeth AH, Pagani JH, Young WS III. Oxytocin: the great facilitator of life. *Prog Neurobiol* (2009) **88**(2):127–51. doi:10.1016/j.pneurobio.2009.04.001
21. Preti A, Melis M, Siddi S, Vellante M, Doneddu G, Fadda R. Oxytocin and autism: a systematic review of randomized controlled trials. *J Child Adolesc Psychopharmacol* (2014) **24**(2):54–68. doi:10.1089/cap.2013.0040
22. Modahl C, Fein D, Waterhouse L, Newton N. Does oxytocin deficiency mediate social deficits in autism? *J Autism Dev Disord* (1992) **22**(3):449–51. doi:10.1007/BF01048246
23. Russell JA, Leng G, Douglas AJ. The magnocellular oxytocin system, the fount of maternity: adaptations in pregnancy. *Front Neuroendocrinol* (2003) **24**(1):27–61. doi:10.1016/S0091-3022(02)00104-8
24. Brown CH, Russell JA, Leng G. Opioid modulation of magnocellular neurosecretory cell activity. *Neurosci Res* (2000) **36**(2):97–120. doi:10.1016/S0168-0102(99)00121-2
25. Haldar J, Sawyer WH. Inhibition of oxytocin release by morphine and its analogs. *Proc Soc Exp Biol Med* (1978) **157**(3):476–80. doi:10.3181/00379727-157-40080
26. Morris MS, Domino EF, Domino SE. Opioid modulation of oxytocin release. *J Clin Pharmacol* (2010) **50**(10):1112–7. doi:10.1177/0091270010361256
27. Nelson EE, Panksepp J. Brain substrates of infant-mother attachment: contributions of opioids, oxytocin, and norepinephrine. *Neurosci Biobehav Rev* (1998) **22**(3):437–52. doi:10.1016/S0149-7634(97)00052-3
28. Neuhaus E, Beauchaine TP, Bernier R. Neurobiological correlates of social functioning in autism. *Clin Psychol Rev* (2010) **30**(6):733–48. doi:10.1016/j.cpr.2010.05.007
29. Kitchen I, Slowe SJ, Matthes HW, Kieffer B. Quantitative autoradiographic mapping of mu-, delta- and kappa-opioid receptors in knockout mice lacking the mu-opioid receptor gene. *Brain Res* (1997) **778**(1):73–88.
30. Slowe SJ, Simonin F, Kieffer B, Kitchen I. Quantitative autoradiography of mu-,delta- and kappa1 opioid receptors in kappa-opioid receptor knockout mice. *Brain Res* (1999) **818**(2):335–45.
31. Erbs E, Faget L, Scherrer G, Matifas A, Filliol D, Vonesch JL, et al. A mu-delta opioid receptor brain atlas reveals neuronal co-occurrence in subcortical networks. *Brain Struct Funct* (2014). doi:10.1007/s00429-014-0717-9

32. Yoshida M, Takayanagi Y, Inoue K, Kimura T, Young LJ, Onaka T, et al. Evidence that oxytocin exerts anxiolytic effects via oxytocin receptor expressed in serotonergic neurons in mice. *J Neurosci* (2009) **29**(7):2259–71. doi:10.1523/JNEUROSCI.5593-08.2009
33. Dolen G, Darvishzadeh A, Huang KW, Malenka RC. Social reward requires coordinated activity of nucleus accumbens oxytocin and serotonin. *Nature* (2013) **501**(7466):179–84. doi:10.1038/nature12518
34. Huang H, Michetti C, Busnelli M, Manago F, Sannino S, Scheggia D, et al. Chronic and acute intranasal oxytocin produce divergent social effects in mice. *Neuropsychopharmacology* (2014) **39**(5):1102–14. doi:10.1038/npp.2013.310
35. Andari E, Duhamel JR, Zalla T, Herbrecht E, Leboyer M, Sirigu A. Promoting social behavior with oxytocin in high-functioning autism spectrum disorders. *Proc Natl Acad Sci U S A* (2010) **107**(9):4389–94. doi:10.1073/pnas.0910249107
36. Neumann ID, Maloumby R, Beiderbeck DI, Lukas M, Landgraf R. Increased brain and plasma oxytocin after nasal and peripheral administration in rats and mice. *Psychoneuroendocrinology* (2013) **38**(10):1985–93. doi:10.1016/j.psyneuen.2013.03.003
37. Ludwig M, Tobin VA, Callahan MF, Papadaki E, Becker A, Engelmann M, et al. Intranasal application of vasopressin fails to elicit changes in brain immediate early gene expression, neural activity and behavioural performance of rats. *J Neuroendocrinol* (2013) **25**(7):655–67. doi:10.1111/jne.12046
38. Suraev AS, Bowen MT, Ali SO, Hicks C, Ramos L, McGregor IS. Adolescent exposure to oxytocin, but not the selective oxytocin receptor agonist TGOT, increases social behavior and plasma oxytocin in adulthood. *Horm Behav* (2014) **65**(5):488–96. doi:10.1016/j.yhbeh.2014.03.002
39. Bales KL, Perkeybile AM, Conley OG, Lee MH, Guoynes CD, Downing GM, et al. Chronic intranasal oxytocin causes long-term impairments in partner preference formation in male prairie voles. *Biol Psychiatry* (2013) **74**(3):180–8. doi:10.1016/j.biopsych.2012.08.025
40. Matthes HW, Maldonado R, Simonin F, Valverde O, Slowe S, Kitchen I, et al. Loss of morphine-induced analgesia, reward effect and withdrawal symptoms in mice lacking the mu-opioid-receptor gene. *Nature* (1996) **383**(6603):819–23. doi:10.1038/383819a0
41. Franklin KB, Paxinos G. *The Mouse Brain in Stereotaxic Coordinates.* 3rd ed. Amsterdam: Elsevier (2007).
42. Nyby J, Wysocki CJ, Whitney G, Dizinno G, Schneider J. Elicitation of male mouse (*Mus musculus*) ultrasonic vocalizations: I. Urinary cues. *J Comp Physiol Psychol* (1979) **93**(5):957–75. doi:10.1037/h0077623
43. Pomerantz SM, Nunez AA, Bean NJ. Female behavior is affected by male ultrasonic vocalizations in house mice. *Physiol Behav* (1983) **31**(1):91–6. doi:10.1016/0031-9384(83)90101-4
44. Hanson JL, Hurley LM. Female presence and estrous state influence mouse ultrasonic courtship vocalizations. *PLoS One* (2012) **7**(7):e40782. doi:10.1371/journal.pone.0040782
45. D'Amato FR, Zanettini C, Lampis V, Coccurello R, Pascucci T, Ventura R, et al. Unstable maternal environment, separation anxiety, and heightened CO2 sensitivity induced by gene-by-environment interplay. *PLoS One* (2011) **6**(4):e18637. doi:10.1371/journal.pone.0018637
46. Holy TE, Guo Z. Ultrasonic songs of male mice. *PLoS Biol* (2005) **3**(12):e386. doi:10.1371/journal.pbio.0030386
47. Costantini F, D'Amato FR. Ultrasonic vocalizations in mice and rats: social contexts and functions. *Acta Zool Sin* (2006) **52**(4):619–33.
48. Bartz J, Simeon D, Hamilton H, Kim S, Crystal S, Braun A, et al. Oxytocin can hinder trust and cooperation in borderline personality disorder. *Soc Cogn Affect Neurosci* (2011) **6**(5):556–63. doi:10.1093/scan/nsq085
49. Zak PJ, Stanton AA, Ahmadi S. Oxytocin increases generosity in humans. *PLoS One* (2007) **2**(11):e1128. doi:10.1371/journal.pone.0001128
50. Zanos P, Georgiou P, Wright SR, Hourani SM, Kitchen I, Winsky-Sommerer R, et al. The oxytocin analogue carbetocin prevents emotional impairment and stress-induced reinstatement of opioid-seeking in morphine-abstinent mice. *Neuropsychopharmacology* (2014) **39**(4):855–65. doi:10.1038/npp.2013.285
51. Ferre S, Casado V, Devi LA, Filizola M, Jockers R, Lohse MJ, et al. G protein-coupled receptor oligomerization revisited: functional and pharmacological perspectives. *Pharmacol Rev* (2014) **66**(2):413–34. doi:10.1124/pr.113.008052
52. Stone LS, MacMillan LB, Kitto KF, Limbird LE, Wilcox GL. The alpha2a adrenergic receptor subtype mediates spinal analgesia evoked by alpha2 agonists and is necessary for spinal adrenergic-opioid synergy. *J Neurosci* (1997) **17**(18):7157–65.
53. Jordan BA, Gomes I, Rios C, Filipovska J, Devi LA. Functional interactions between mu opioid and alpha 2A-adrenergic receptors. *Mol Pharmacol* (2003) **64**(6):1317–24. doi:10.1124/mol.64.6.1317
54. Vilardaga JP, Nikolaev VO, Lorenz K, Ferrandon S, Zhuang Z, Lohse MJ. Conformational cross-talk between alpha2A-adrenergic and mu-opioid receptors controls cell signaling. *Nat Chem Biol* (2008) **4**(2):126–31. doi:10.1038/nchembio.64
55. Insel TR, Shapiro LE. Oxytocin receptor distribution reflects social organization in monogamous and polygamous voles. *Proc Natl Acad Sci U S A* (1992) **89**(13):5981–5. doi:10.1073/pnas.89.13.5981
56. Francis DD, Champagne FC, Meaney MJ. Variations in maternal behaviour are associated with differences in oxytocin receptor levels in the rat. *J Neuroendocrinol* (2000) **12**(12):1145–8. doi:10.1046/j.1365-2826.2000.00599.x
57. Olazabal DE, Young LJ. Oxytocin receptors in the nucleus accumbens facilitate "spontaneous" maternal behavior in adult female prairie voles. *Neuroscience* (2006) **141**(2):559–68. doi:10.1016/j.neuroscience.2006.04.017
58. Olazabal DE, Young LJ. Species and individual differences in juvenile female alloparental care are associated with oxytocin receptor density in the striatum and the lateral septum. *Horm Behav* (2006) **49**(5):681–7. doi:10.1016/j.yhbeh.2005.12.010
59. Ross HE, Freeman SM, Spiegel LL, Ren X, Terwilliger EF, Young LJ. Variation in oxytocin receptor density in the nucleus accumbens has differential effects on affiliative behaviors in monogamous and polygamous voles. *J Neurosci* (2009) **29**(5):1312–8. doi:10.1523/JNEUROSCI.5039-08.2009
60. Keebaugh AC, Young LJ. Increasing oxytocin receptor expression in the nucleus accumbens of pre-pubertal female prairie voles enhances alloparental responsiveness and partner preference formation as adults. *Horm Behav* (2011) **60**(5):498–504. doi:10.1016/j.yhbeh.2011.07.018
61. Cao Y, Wu R, Tai F, Zhang X, Yu P, An X, et al. Neonatal paternal deprivation impairs social recognition and alters levels of oxytocin and estrogen receptor alpha mRNA expression in the MeA and NAcc, and serum oxytocin in mandarin voles. *Horm Behav* (2014) **65**(1):57–65. doi:10.1016/j.yhbeh.2013.11.005
62. Cui Y, Ostlund SB, James AS, Park CS, Ge W, Roberts KW, et al. Targeted expression of mu-opioid receptors in a subset of striatal direct-pathway neurons restores opiate reward. *Nat Neurosci* (2014) **17**(2):254–61. doi:10.1038/nn.3622
63. Castro DC, Berridge KC. Opioid hedonic hotspot in nucleus accumbens shell: mu, delta, and kappa maps for enhancement of sweetness "liking" and "wanting". *J Neurosci* (2014) **34**(12):4239–50. doi:10.1523/JNEUROSCI.4458-13.2014
64. Baxter MG, Murray EA. The amygdala and reward. *Nat Rev Neurosci* (2002) **3**(7):563–73. doi:10.1038/nrn875
65. See RE, Fuchs RA, Ledford CC, McLaughlin J. Drug addiction, relapse, and the amygdala. *Ann N Y Acad Sci* (2003) **985**:294–307. doi:10.1111/j.1749-6632.2003.tb07089.x
66. Gozzi A, Jain A, Giovannelli A, Bertollini C, Crestan V, Schwarz AJ, et al. A neural switch for active and passive fear. *Neuron* (2010) **67**(4):656–66. doi:10.1016/j.neuron.2010.07.008
67. Calcagnoli F, de Boer SF, Beiderbeck DI, Althaus M, Koolhaas JM, Neumann ID. Local oxytocin expression and oxytocin receptor binding in the male rat brain is associated with aggressiveness. *Behav Brain Res* (2014) **261**:315–22. doi:10.1016/j.bbr.2013.12.050
68. Newman SW. The medial extended amygdala in male reproductive behavior. A node in the mammalian social behavior network. *Ann N Y Acad Sci* (1999) **877**:242–57. doi:10.1111/j.1749-6632.1999.tb09271.x
69. Ferguson JN, Aldag JM, Insel TR, Young LJ. Oxytocin in the medial amygdala is essential for social recognition in the mouse. *J Neurosci* (2001) **21**(20):8278–85.
70. Bielsky IF, Young LJ. Oxytocin, vasopressin, and social recognition in mammals. *Peptides* (2004) **25**(9):1565–74. doi:10.1016/j.peptides.2004.05.019
71. Dumais KM, Bredewold R, Mayer TE, Veenema AH. Sex differences in oxytocin receptor binding in forebrain regions: correlations with social interest in brain region- and sex-specific ways. *Horm Behav* (2013) **64**(4):693–701. doi:10.1016/j.yhbeh.2013.08.012
72. Gur R, Tendler A, Wagner S. Long-term social recognition memory is mediated by oxytocin-dependent synaptic plasticity in the medial amygdala. *Biol Psychiatry* (2014) **76**(5):377–86. doi:10.1016/j.biopsych.2014.03.022
73. Haberly LB. Parallel-distributed processing in olfactory cortex: new insights from morphological and physiological analysis of neuronal circuitry. *Chem Senses* (2001) **26**(5):551–76. doi:10.1093/chemse/26.5.551
74. Brunjes PC, Illig KR, Meyer EA. A field guide to the anterior olfactory nucleus (cortex). *Brain Res Brain Res Rev* (2005) **50**(2):305–35. doi:10.1016/j.brainresrev.2005.08.005

75. Smeltzer MD, Curtis JT, Aragona BJ, Wang Z. Dopamine, oxytocin, and vasopressin receptor binding in the medial prefrontal cortex of monogamous and promiscuous voles. *Neurosci Lett* (2006) **394**(2):146–51. doi:10.1016/j.neulet.2005.10.019
76. Uhl-Bronner S, Waltisperger E, Martinez-Lorenzana G, Condes Lara M, Freund-Mercier MJ. Sexually dimorphic expression of oxytocin binding sites in forebrain and spinal cord of the rat. *Neuroscience* (2005) **135**(1):147–54. doi:10.1016/j.neuroscience.2005.05.025

# 5

# Studying autism in rodent models: reconciling endophenotypes with comorbidities

**_Andrew Argyropoulos[1], Krista L. Gilby[1] and Elisa L. Hill-Yardin[2]*_**

[1] *Department of Medicine, The University of Melbourne, Parkville, VIC, Australia*
[2] *Department of Physiology, The University of Melbourne, Parkville, VIC, Australia*

***Edited by:***
*Charles Claudianos, University of Queensland, Australia*

***Reviewed by:***
*Wah Chin Boon, Florey Neuroscience Institutes, Australia*
*Thomas Burne, Queensland Brain Institute, Australia*

****Correspondence:***
*Elisa L. Hill-Yardin, Enteric Neuroscience Laboratory, Department of Physiology, The University of Melbourne, Cnr of Grattan Street and Royal Parade, Parkville, VIC 3010, Australia*
*e-mail: elhill@unimelb.edu.au*

Autism spectrum disorder (ASD) patients commonly exhibit a variety of comorbid traits including seizures, anxiety, aggressive behavior, gastrointestinal problems, motor deficits, abnormal sensory processing, and sleep disturbances for which the cause is unknown. These features impact negatively on daily life and can exaggerate the effects of the core diagnostic traits (social communication deficits and repetitive behaviors). Studying endophenotypes relevant to both core and comorbid features of ASD in rodent models can provide insight into biological mechanisms underlying these disorders. Here we review the characterization of endophenotypes in a selection of environmental, genetic, and behavioral rodent models of ASD. In addition to exhibiting core ASD-like behaviors, each of these animal models display one or more endophenotypes relevant to comorbid features including altered sensory processing, seizure susceptibility, anxiety-like behavior, and disturbed motor functions, suggesting that these traits are indicators of altered biological pathways in ASD. However, the study of behaviors paralleling comorbid traits in animal models of ASD is an emerging field and further research is needed to assess altered gastrointestinal function, aggression, and disorders of sleep onset across models. Future studies should include investigation of these endophenotypes in order to advance our understanding of the etiology of this complex disorder.

**Keywords: autism, epilepsy, sleep, motor deficits, aggression, sensory, gastrointestinal function, anxiety**

Studying endophenotypes in rodent models of Autism spectrum disorder (ASD) can offer insights into the heterogeneity and underlying biological causes of this complex disorder. Patients with ASD demonstrate a high degree of variability in both the severity of core diagnostic symptoms (social communication deficits alongside repetitive behaviors) and in the nature and strength of a range of associated comorbidities. If comorbid traits associated with ASD are integral to the disorder we expect that many of these traits will present in animal models. However, despite the prevalence of comorbidities in patients, studies in animal models to date have largely focused on characterizing core behavioral traits. Here we review findings from salient rodent models of ASD identifying endophenotypes that parallel core ASD deficits in combination with one or more comorbid traits commonly reported in patients.

## ASD: COMORBID TRAITS

Comorbid traits in ASD include seizures, heightened aggression, and anxiety disorders as well as gastrointestinal problems, altered sensory processing, motor deficits, and sleep disorders (**Table 1**). While treatment of these issues can significantly improve quality of life for patients and their families, the biological mechanisms underlying these symptoms and their co-expression are generally unknown in the context of ASD.

Current estimates for the prevalence of epilepsy in ASD patients range between 8 and 25% (Hara, 2007; Jeste, 2011; Sansa et al., 2011; Woolfenden et al., 2012). Recent meta-analysis data show that epilepsy is more common in ASD patients with an intellectual disability (21.5 vs. 8%; Woolfenden et al., 2012). When epilepsy and abnormal EEG data are compared within the general ASD population, 15% of ASD subjects have an epilepsy diagnosis whereas a larger proportion (24.6%) shows interictal epileptiform EEG abnormalities during sleep (Ekinci et al., 2010). Other reports reveal that as many as 25% of ASD patients have comorbid epilepsy, and that 45.5% show non-seizure-related EEG abnormalities (Parmeggiani et al., 2010). Furthermore, one third (34%) of patients with idiopathic ASD have treatment resistant epilepsy (Sansa et al., 2011).

Aggressive behavior and elevated anxiety are frequently reported in children and adolescents with ASD. Caregiver surveys suggest that as many as 68% of ASD patients show episodes of aggression toward them (Kanne and Mazurek, 2011). Pouw et al. (2013) found that aggression behaviors in ASD are most likely due to a relative impairment in the understanding of the emotions of others. It is also estimated that 40% of ASD patients have at least one anxiety disorder (van Steensel et al., 2011). Specific phobias, obsessive compulsive disorder, and social anxiety disorder are most frequently observed.

A significant proportion of patients with ASD also suffer from gastrointestinal problems (42–90%); with constipation, chronic diarrhea, abnormal stool patterns, and stomach cramps frequently reported (Parracho et al., 2005; Valicenti-McDermott et al., 2006; Ibrahim et al., 2009; Buie et al., 2010; Wang et al., 2011a). Alterations in gastrointestinal function in the context

**Table 1 | Clinical comorbidities commonly associated with ASD.**

| Domain | Comorbid symptoms |
|---|---|
| Epilepsy | High prevalence of epilepsy (8–25%) and EEG abnormalities (46%) in ASD patients (Amiet et al., 2008; Parmeggiani et al., 2010; Jeste, 2011)<br>High rate of treatment resistant epilepsy in idiopathic autism (34%) (Dudova et al., 2011; Sansa et al., 2011) |
| Heightened aggression | Approximately 70% of ASD patients exhibit aggression toward caregivers (Kanne and Mazurek, 2011)<br>Reactive aggression correlates with impairments in emotional regulation in children with ASD but not in typically developing children (Pouw et al., 2013) |
| Anxiety | 40% of ASD cases associated with at least one comorbid anxiety disorder (van Steensel et al., 2011) |
| Gastrointestinal disturbances | Up to 90% ASD patients have chronic GI problems, most commonly constipation, also abdominal pain, diarrhea, and bloating (Parracho et al., 2005; Ibrahim et al., 2009; Buie et al., 2010) |
| Sensory | Tactile: heightened sensitivity to vibration and thermal pain in palm and forearm (Blakemore et al., 2006; Cascio et al., 2008)<br>Auditory: atypical change detection of auditory stimuli (Gomot et al., 2006; Kwakye et al., 2011)<br>Visual: superior performance in detail oriented tasks, deficits in motion perception (Dakin and Frith, 2005; Latham et al., 2013; Robertson et al., 2013)<br>Altered olfaction and taste in high-functioning ASD patients (Bennetto et al., 2007; Dudova et al., 2011) |
| Motor impairment | Delays in gross and fine motor domains (Jeste, 2011)<br>Deficits in motor planning, coordination, and gait (Rinehart et al., 2006; Jeste, 2011) |
| Sleep | Sleep disturbances (quality, quantity, latency to sleep) found in 40–80% of children and adolescents with ASD (Allik et al., 2006; Malow et al., 2006; Jeste, 2011)<br>Sleep onset problems and night waking common in 2- to 5-year-olds with ASD (Krakowiak et al., 2008) |

*Comorbid traits observed in patients with ASD are heterogeneous and include enhanced seizure susceptibility, heightened aggression, anxiety, gastrointestinal (GI) disturbances, altered sensory and motor function, and sleep disorders.*

of ASD are thought to be linked to the effects of anxiety and thereby mediated via CNS function; however investigations into mechanisms involving the enteric nervous system have not been reported.

By far the most common changes associated with ASD are those related to sensory processing which are present in over 90% of individuals diagnosed with ASD (Leekam et al., 2007). Patients with Asperger Syndrome show significantly higher sensitivity to high frequency tactile stimuli compared to control subjects (Cascio et al., 2008). Abnormalities in tactile sensitivity, as well as hypersensitivity to hot and cold stimuli have also been reported in adults with ASD (Blakemore et al., 2006). Auditory processing deficits related to the discrimination of temporally separated tones (Kwakye et al., 2011) and impaired odor detection thresholds (Bennetto et al., 2007; Dudova et al., 2011) have been documented in patients with high-functioning autism as well as subtle impairments in identifying tastes (Bennetto et al., 2007). Interestingly, aberrant motion perception can occur alongside superior visual processing performance in detail oriented tasks, highlighting the potential complexity of sensory changes in ASD patients (reviewed in Dakin and Frith, 2005; also see Latham et al., 2013; Robertson et al., 2013).

Motor abnormalities occur in 60–80% of individuals with ASD and include hypotonia, apraxia, and subtle gait anomalies (see Geschwind, 2009 for review). Abnormal fine and gross motor function, as well as delayed motor learning, dyspraxia, and postural abnormalities are also commonly reported in ASD patients (reviewed in Jeste, 2011). Finally, difficulties initiating sleep, frequent night time waking, and insomnia are frequently reported in children with ASD (Allik et al., 2006; Malow et al., 2006; Krakowiak et al., 2008; Jeste, 2011).

The systematic analysis of traits in animal models corresponding to patient comorbidities can potentially provide insight into the underlying biological mechanisms of ASD. Such outcomes may lead to the design of new therapies and benefits to patients.

## ANIMAL MODELS OF ASD

Over the last decade, a substantial number of rodent models of ASD have been generated (reviewed in Silverman et al., 2010a; Peca et al., 2011; Penagarikano et al., 2011; Wang et al., 2011b; Schmeisser et al., 2012; Won et al., 2012) and demonstrate face validity by replicating behavioral traits relevant to ASD. Well-characterized social and communication assessment paradigms and tests for the presence of repetitive behaviors exist for rodent models of ASD (Silverman et al., 2010a). In addition, a battery of tests is available to determine the presence of potential comorbidities including anxiety-like and aggressive behaviors, seizures, disrupted motor activity, sleep dysfunction, and sensory processing deficits (Crawley, 2007) as well as assays for gastrointestinal motility dysfunction (Roberts et al., 2007) in these models. Here we outline findings derived from investigations using these tests (**Table 2**) and highlight areas requiring further research (**Table 3**).

Animal models are discussed in three groups; (i) models with acquired behaviors resulting from environmental insult, (ii) models expressing a human genetic mutation associated with ASD,

**Table 2 | Endophenotypes identified in rodent models relevant to comorbid features of ASD.**

| Domain | Model | Behavior |
|---|---|---|
| Seizure susceptibility | VPA | ↑ Sensitivity to PTZ (Sobrian and Nandedkar, 1986) and electroshock-induced seizures (Kim et al., 2011) |
| | PPA | ↑ Susceptibility to kindling with repeated intracerebroventricular infusions (MacFabe et al., 2007) |
| | Shank3B$^{-/-}$ | Occasional handling-induced seizures (Peca et al., 2011) |
| | CNTNAP2 | Handling-induced seizures common in adults (Penagarikano et al., 2011) |
| | FAST | ↑ Sensitivity to kindling and chemoconvulsant-induced seizures (McIntyre et al., 1999; Xu et al., 2004; Gilby et al., 2005) |
| | EL | Handling-induced seizures (Todorova et al., 1999) |
| | BALB/c | ↑ Audiogenic seizures (Morin et al., 1994; Banko et al., 1997) |
| | C58/J | ↑ Sensitivity to PTZ-induced seizures (Nutt and Lister, 1988) |
| Aggression | Shank2$^{-/-}$ | ↑ Aggression in home cages although no change in resident-intruder test (Schmeisser et al., 2012) |
| | FAST | ↑ (Reinhart et al., 2004) |
| | BALB/c | ↑ (Brodkin, 2007; Velez et al., 2010) |
| Anxiety-like behavior | VPA | ↑ (Mice) (Markram et al., 2008) |
| | Shank3B$^{-/-}$ | ↑ (Peca et al., 2011) |
| | Shank2$^{-/-}$ | ↑ (Schmeisser et al., 2012; Won et al., 2012) |
| | FAST | ↑ Fear-potentiated startle (Anisman et al., 2000) |
| | BALB/c | ↑ (Brodkin, 2007) |
| | BTBR | ↑ Under some conditions (McFarlane et al., 2008; Pobbe et al., 2011) |
| Gastro-intestinal disturbances | BALB/c | Altered intestinal motility compared to C57BL/6 mice in response to serotonin antagonists (Neal et al., 2009) |
| Sensory | VPA | ↓ PPI, ↑ tactile sensitivity (Schneider and Przewlocki, 2005), ↓ olfactory (Schneider and Przewlocki, 2005; Roullet et al., 2010) and pain (Markram et al., 2008) sensitivity |
| | PPA | ↓ Sensorimotor function (increased tendency to slip/fall during beam task; Shultz et al., 2009) |
| | NL3$^{R451C}$ | ↓ Acoustic startle at high decibel levels (Chadman et al., 2008) |
| | Shank3B$^{-/-}$ | ↓ PPI (Peca et al., 2011) |
| | CNTNAP2 | ↑ Pain and olfactory sensitivity (Penagarikano et al., 2011) |
| | FAST | ↓ Acoustic startle (Anisman et al., 2000) |
| | BTBR | ↓ Thermal response (Silverman et al., 2010b) |
| Motor | NL3$^{R451C}$ | ↑ Latency to fall from rotarod (Chadman et al., 2008) |
| | Shank3$^{e4-9}$ | Mild motor impairments (Wang et al., 2011b) |
| | CNTNAP2 | Slight ↑ motor coordination (↑ latency to fall from rotarod Penagarikano et al., 2011) |
| | EL | Delays in visuomotor development (McFadyen-Leussis and Heinrichs, 2005) |
| Sleep | VPA | Abnormal circadian rhythms (Tsujino et al., 2007) |

*Endophenotypes relevant to enhanced seizure susceptibility, altered sensory function, and anxiety-like behavior were observed across environmental, monogenetic, and phenotype first models. However, each model was assessed for only a subset of the endophenotypes listed and further research is required to clarify full endophenotypic profiles. VPA, rodents administered valproate.*

and (iii) naturally occurring rodent strains that demonstrate behavioral endophenotypes relevant to ASD.

## ENVIRONMENTAL MODELS

Autism spectrum disorder-like features exhibited by environmental rodent models are generally elicited in response to an overt insult or developmental challenge, such as exposure to toxins resulting in altered neurological development.

### *Valproate models*

During pregnancy, maternal exposure to the first generation antiepileptic drug valproate has been shown to significantly increase the risk of ASD in children (Rasalam et al., 2005; Meador et al., 2006; Bromley et al., 2008). Valproate is a short-chain fatty acid and is thought to reduce neuronal excitability primarily by increasing concentrations of the inhibitory neurotransmitter GABA and modulating voltage-gated sodium channels (Chapman et al., 1982; Rogawski and Loscher, 2004). In both mice and rats, exposure to valproate during gestation via intraperitoneal injection or orally with food produces deficits in social interaction and repetitive behaviors (Schneider and Przewlocki, 2005; Wagner et al., 2006; Roullet et al., 2010; Kim et al., 2011). These animals also show reduced sensitivity to pain (Markram et al., 2008) and olfactory cues (Schneider and

**Table 3 | An overview of endophenotypes assayed in rodent models of ASD.**

| | Seizure susceptibility | Aggression | Anxiety | Gastrointestinal | Sensory | Motor coordination | Sleep |
|---|---|---|---|---|---|---|---|
| VPA | Increase ↑ | | Increase ↑ | | Mixed/complex | Decrease | Mixed/complex |
| PPA | Increase ↑ | | | | Decrease | No change / Decrease | |
| NL3$^{R451C}$ | | | No change | | Decrease | Increase ↑ | |
| Shank2 | | No change / Increase ↑ | Increase ↑ | | No change | | |
| Shank3 | Increase ↑ | | Increase ↑ | | Decrease | Decrease | |
| CNTNAP2 | Increase ↑ | | No change | | Increase ↑ | Increase ↑ | |
| EL | Increase ↑ | | | | | Decrease | |
| C58/J | Increase ↑ | | | | | | |
| BALB/c | Increase ↑ | Increase ↑ | Increase ↑ | Mixed/complex | | | |
| BTBR | | | No change / Increase ↑ | | Decrease | | |
| FAST | Increase ↑ | Increase ↑ | Increase ↑ | | Decrease | | |

Legend: Increase; Decrease; No change; Not tested; Mixed/complex

*Seizure susceptibility, sensory function, motor coordination, and anxiety-like behaviors are most commonly tested across models. Aggressive behavior, gastrointestinal function, and sleep cycles are generally understudied. Dual colored cells: formal aggression testing in Shank2$^{-/-}$ mice did not yield data suggesting abnormal aggressive behavior, however excessive aggression was observed in home cages; PPA rats had impaired sensorimotor abilities when tested using the beam task but showed no change in swim speed in other assays. VPA, rodents administered valproate.*

Przewlocki, 2005; Roullet et al., 2010), increased tactile sensitivity (Schneider and Przewlocki, 2005), and diminished acoustic pre-pulse inhibition, a test commonly used to index abnormalities in sensorimotor gating (Schneider and Przewlocki, 2005; Markram et al., 2008; Gandal et al., 2010; Roullet et al., 2010). Valproate-exposed adult rats show increased levels of anxiety-like behaviors (Markram et al., 2008) and a reduced threshold for electroshock (Kim et al., 2011) and pentylenetetrazole (PTZ)-induced seizures (Sobrian and Nandedkar, 1986). These rats also show altered circadian rhythms characterized by frequent arousal during the light/sleep phase (Tsujino et al., 2007; **Tables 2** and **3**).

### *Propionic acid model*

The gut microbiota have been suggested to play a role in the etiology of ASD (Mulle et al., 2013). Potential mechanisms contributing to ASD phenotypes are unknown, however excess toxin-producing bacteria have been identified in patients with ASD (Parracho et al., 2005) and increased levels of short-chain fatty acids (such as propionic acid; PPA) produced by enteric bacteria have been studied in rats (MacFabe et al., 2007). In rodent models, administration of the endogenous short-chain fatty acids butyric acid (Thomas et al., 2010), sodium acetate (Shultz et al., 2008, 2009), and PPA directly into the cerebral ventricles produces endophenotypes relevant to ASD (MacFabe et al., 2007, 2011; Shultz et al., 2008, 2009; Thomas et al., 2010). Acute intracerebral ventricular infusion of PPA in rats reduces sociability and learning and also produces sensorimotor impairments (Shultz et al., 2009). This paradigm also results in reduced cognitive flexibility during reversal learning (MacFabe et al., 2011). Furthermore, repeated intraventricular PPA infusion leads to increased susceptibility to kindling-induced seizures and stereotypic behavior (MacFabe et al., 2007, 2011; Shultz et al., 2009; **Tables 2** and **3**).

A small number of ASD patients (5%) show mitochondrial dysfunction along with altered levels of various metabolites suggestive of altered fatty acid processing (Frye et al., 2013). Further investigation to assess the effects of both PPA and valproate on gastrointestinal function (i.e., following oral administration) is needed (see **Table 3**), as the short-chain fatty acid receptor (GPR43) expressed by some mucosal enteroendocrine cells may play a role (Karaki et al., 2006). The effects of orally administered PPA in particular would be of interest and would serve to strengthen construct validity of this model.

## GENETIC MODELS

Many gene mutations associated with ASD code for proteins involved in the formation and maintenance of synapses (Sudhof, 2008; Betancur et al., 2009; Bourgeron, 2009; Chakrabarti et al., 2009; Betancur, 2011; Geschwind, 2011). Here we review findings from monogenic mouse models expressing mutations in four genes modulating synaptic function; the neuroligin-3$^{R451C}$ (NL3$^{R451C}$) mice (Tabuchi et al., 2007; Chadman et al., 2008) two models expressing specific mutations in the Shank3B/ProSAP2 gene [Shank3B knockout mice and Shank3B$^{e4-9}$ partial knockout mice (Peca et al., 2011; Wang et al., 2011b)], as well as two SHANK2 knockout models (Schmeisser et al., 2012; Won et al., 2012) and the contactin associated protein-like 2/Neurexin IV (CNTNAP2/NRXN4; Penagarikano et al., 2011) knockout mouse model (**Table 2**). Electrophysiological studies in these mice report altered glutamatergic and GABAergic synaptic function (Tabuchi et al., 2007; Etherton et al., 2009, 2011; Peca et al., 2011; Wang et al., 2011b; Schmeisser et al., 2012; Won et al., 2012). Each of these models also expresses strong ASD behavioral endophenotypes suggesting a role for these genes in shaping core behaviors relevant to ASD diagnosis. However, it is not well established whether these animal models replicate comorbid traits observed in patients.

#### *Neuroligin-3$^{R451C}$ mice*

Neuroligins are adhesion molecules which interact with a range of post-synaptic scaffolding proteins including Shank3 and CNTNAP2 and bind to members of the presynaptic neurexin family across the synaptic cleft (Sudhof, 2008; Krueger et al., 2012; Verpelli and Sala, 2012). Mutations in the neuroligin family of post-synaptic adhesion molecules were implicated in ASD after a spontaneous point mutation in the gene encoding NL3 was identified in two brothers with ASD; one with comorbid epilepsy (Jamain et al., 2003). Mice expressing the NL3$^{R451C}$ mutation show a subtle reduction in pup distress calls (on post-natal day 8) and reduced acoustic startle (Chadman et al., 2008). Under some conditions and on some genetic backgrounds, NL3$^{R451C}$ mice also show impaired social interaction (Tabuchi et al., 2007; Etherton et al., 2011). Delays in meeting developmental milestones (e.g., slower righting reflexes), which may appear as motor deficits early in development, have also been observed in these mice (Chadman et al., 2008). However, adult NL3$^{R451C}$ mice showed better motor coordination in the accelerating rotarod test compared with wild type littermates (Chadman et al., 2008).

#### *Shank3-related models*

The Shank (SH3 and multiple ankyrin repeat domains) gene family (also known as Proline-rich synapse-associated proteins; ProSAPs) contains three members; Shank1-3 that code for post-synaptic scaffolding proteins involved in the recruitment of several receptors and proteins (including the neuroligins and neurexins) to the excitatory post-synaptic membrane (Irie et al., 1997; Meyer et al., 2004; Baron et al., 2006; Hayashi et al., 2009; Arons et al., 2012). Rare microdeletions within the 22q13 locus (containing Shank3) are associated with intellectual disability, speech delay, and ASD (Nesslinger et al., 1994; Bonaglia et al., 2006; Durand et al., 2007). Mutations in Shank2 are also associated with ASD (Berkel et al., 2010; Kumar, 2010). Two different genetic models in which Shank3 is altered; Shank3B$^{-/-}$ (Peca et al., 2011) and Shank3$^{e4-9}$ (Wang et al., 2011b) in addition to two recently reported Shank2 knockout models (Schmeisser et al., 2012; Won et al., 2012) demonstrate core and comorbid traits relevant to ASD. A third model in which one full length copy of Shank3 is deleted shows core ASD endophenotypes; however the expression of secondary/comorbid features outlined here has not been investigated in these mice (Bozdagi et al., 2010). Shank3B$^{-/-}$ mice lacking the Shank3$\alpha$ and $\beta$ isoforms show increased repetitive behavior (self-injurious grooming) and reduced interaction with a stranger mouse as well as occasional handling-induced seizures (Peca et al., 2011 and reviewed in Herbert, 2011). Shank3$^{e4-9}$ mice (in which exons 4–9 are deleted) show core ASD-like deficits including social impairments, repetitive behaviors, and altered communication (i.e., less complex vocalization patterns), with learning deficits and mild motor abnormalities also evident (Wang et al., 2011b). In addition to a role as a structural protein in the central nervous system, Shank3 is present at enteric nervous system synapses (Huett et al., 2009). The enteric nervous system controls gastrointestinal motility and mucous secretion and therefore gene mutations leading to changes in synaptic function (including many ASD candidate genes) may also affect gastrointestinal function (Gershon and Ratcliffe, 2004). The Shank3 mouse models of ASD are therefore excellent candidates for investigating effects of ASD-associated gene mutations on gastrointestinal motility. Shank2 knockout mice demonstrate abnormal vocal and social behaviors, and increased grooming behaviors. Hyperactivity (e.g., repetitive jumping) and anxiety-like behaviors have also been reported in these mice (Schmeisser et al., 2012; Won et al., 2012). Schmeisser et al. (2012) detected no change in aggressive behaviors in Shank2 knockout mice using a resident-intruder assay. Despite this negative result, a high level of aggression between Shank2 knockout males was observed in home cages (Schmeisser et al., 2012).

#### *CNTNAP2 mice*

Genetic ablation of the contactin associated protein-like 2 (CNTNAP2) gene, a member of the neurexin transmembrane protein superfamily (also known as CASPR2 and Neurexin IV), results in ASD-like deficits in social interaction and stereotypic behaviors in mice (Penagarikano et al., 2011). In addition, CNTNAP2 knockout mice show hyperactivity, impaired nest building, and frequent handling-induced seizures after 6 months of age (Penagarikano et al., 2011). The CNTNAP2 gene has been associated with ASD and a recessive form of epilepsy (Strauss et al., 2006). These mice exhibit sensory endophenotypes including hyper-reactivity to thermal sensory stimuli and superior performance in the buried food test, an assay for olfactory function (Penagarikano et al., 2011). CNTNAP2 knockout mice also showed slightly improved motor coordination on the rotarod compared to wild type littermates. Perhaps surprisingly, the atypical antipsychotic risperidone (prescribed to treat aggression and irritability in some cases of ASD) reversed nest building deficits as well as locomotor hyperactivity in these mice (Penagarikano et al., 2011), demonstrating predictive validity in this model (**Table 2**).

Behavioral analyses in transgenic mouse models of ASD confirm that a range of proteins regulating synaptic function are likely to be integral to this disorder. Most studies involving genetic models have investigated one or two endophenotypes relevant to patient core and comorbid traits (**Tables 2** and **3**). However, to better understand the relationship between these traits a focus on assessing the more subtle secondary endophenotypes is required. Seizure susceptibility, gastrointestinal function, sleep cycles, and aggressive behaviors remain to be investigated in the majority of these genetic models of ASD (**Table 3**). Still, the presence of endophenotypes relevant to comorbid traits of ASD in each of these genetic models suggests that at least some of these traits may be associated with the core behavioral features of the disorder.

### PHENOTYPE FIRST MODELS

Interplay between genomic and non-genomic influences (e.g., maternal effects) is almost certainly involved in the symptom heterogeneity associated with ASD. To further understand their relative degree of contribution, animal models in which clinically relevant endophenotypes occur "naturally" are of great interest. There are currently several rodent models developed via breeding processes alone that exhibit measurable endophenotypes relevant to the diagnostic criteria and comorbid traits associated with ASD. These animal models include the FAST/SLOW rats and the C58/J, BALB/c, BtBR T + tf/J (BTBR), and epileptic-like (EL) mice (**Tables 2** and **3**).

#### *FAST/SLOW rats and EL mice*

The FAST and SLOW rat strains were derived from parent populations of Long Evans Hooded and Wistar rats using selective breeding processes based on relative seizure susceptibility in the amygdala kindling model (Racine et al., 1999). This process ultimately produced a seizure-prone (FAST) and seizure-resistant (SLOW) strain. FAST rats have since proven highly seizure-prone in both the kindling model and in chemoconvulsant (e.g., pilocarpine, kainate) seizure-induction models (McIntyre et al., 1999; Xu et al., 2004; Gilby et al., 2007; Gilby and O'Brien, 2013). EL mice, like FAST rats, were also created via selective breeding based on relative seizure susceptibility and originated from the non-epileptic DDY mouse strain (Meidenbauer et al., 2011). EL mice typically exhibit handling-induced seizures by postnatal day 50–60 (Todorova et al., 1999). Remarkably, the breeding processes used to create heightened seizure sensitivity in both colonies simultaneously produced robust, comorbid ASD-like traits. Both FAST rats and EL mice exhibit significant social impairment (Reinhart et al., 2004, 2006; Gilby et al., 2007; Lim et al., 2007; Turner et al., 2007) and repetitive behaviors (e.g., overgrooming, self-injurious scratching, and/or myoclonic jumping; Gilby, 2008; Meidenbauer et al., 2011) alongside delays in social, physical, and visuomotor development (McFadyen-Leussis and Heinrichs, 2005), learning deficits, impulsivity, and hyperactivity in various testing paradigms (Anisman and McIntyre, 2002; McFadyen-Leussis and Heinrichs, 2005; Azarbar et al., 2010). FAST rats are also more aggressive than their comparison (SLOW) strain (Reinhart et al., 2004, 2006) and show reduced acoustic startle but enhanced fear conditioning (Anisman et al., 2000). Thus, FAST rats and EL mice offer a similar endophenotypic profile relevant to core and comorbid symptoms observed in ASD.

#### *C58/J mice*

C58/J mice naturally exhibit ASD-like traits including poor sociability (Moy et al., 2008; Ryan et al., 2010), relative learning deficits, hyperactivity (Moy et al., 2008), and stereotypic behaviors (i.e., jumping and flipping; Ryan et al., 2010). Interestingly, C58/J mice also demonstrate a reduced threshold for PTZ-induced seizures (Nutt and Lister, 1988). However, in contrast to the ASD-like developmental delays observed in FAST and EL animals, C58/J mice meet developmental milestones earlier than their comparison strain (C57BL/6J; Ryan et al., 2010).

#### *BALB/c and BTBR mice*

The BALB/c and BTBR mouse strains exhibit core ASD traits in the form of impaired social interaction and repetitive behaviors (i.e., overgrooming and/or excessive marble burying; Brodkin, 2007; Shoji and Kato, 2009; Pearson et al., 2011). BTBR mice also demonstrate increased social anxiety-like behavior (Pobbe et al., 2011) although anxiety responses to novel situations are inconsistent (McFarlane et al., 2008). BTBR mice are less reactive to thermal (hotplate) stimuli than the C57Bl/6J standard strain (Silverman et al., 2010b), suggesting subtle sensory changes exist in this model. In addition, several BALB/c substrains displaying distinct behavioral phenotypes offer particular strengths for comorbidity investigation. BALB/cJ mice exhibit altered gastrointestinal function (Neal et al., 2009) and are highly aggressive (Velez et al., 2010) while the epilepsy-prone (EP) BALB/c substrain is susceptible to audiogenic seizures (Morin et al., 1994; Banko et al., 1997). Notably, BTBR and BALB models have a high incidence of corpus callosal agenesis and severely reduced hippocampal commissural volumes (Wahlsten et al., 2003), which may be relevant to reports of reduced corpus callosal volumes in ASD patients (Anderson et al., 2011).

The characterization of ASD-relevant traits in these "natural" models is a relatively new initiative. Still, the documented commonalities thus far are striking; particularly the co-expression of repetitive behaviors and impaired social interaction together with heightened seizure sensitivity (**Table 3**). Finally, while we are aware that a few studies have investigated aggression and sensory processing in these rodent models, further testing using validated assays (Silverman et al., 2010a) should be applied to fully characterize the presence of core and comorbid features in these models.

## SUMMARY

The primary aim of this review was to compare endophenotypic clustering within a selection of animal models of ASD. Here we focus on models expressing at least two core ASD endophenotypes with additional endophenotypes relevant to comorbid traits reported in ASD patients.

### ENDOPHENOTYPING: A NEW APPROACH

We report that models generated via environmental insult, genetic manipulation, and selective breeding processes demonstrate a number of overlapping endophenotypes (**Tables 2** and **3**) relevant to both clinical comorbid (**Table 1**) and core traits of ASD. Detailed investigation into the more subtle endophenotypes associated with these models is a relatively novel approach. Indeed, many clinical traits highlighted here have yet to be investigated in these models or should be re-examined using consistent methodological approaches. Until then any ranking of the clinical relevance of the phenotypic profiles would be premature. Interestingly however, enhanced seizure susceptibility, altered sensory function, anxiety-like behaviors, and changes in motor coordination were the most frequently reported endophenotypes across models (**Table 3**). Although not routinely investigated, several of the models also showed atypical aggressive interactions (**Tables 2** and **3**). Despite evidence for disturbed sleep and abnormal gastrointestinal function in a significant number of ASD patients (see **Table 1**), to our knowledge, circadian rhythms and gastrointestinal function have only been investigated in two models; valproate-exposed rats and BALB/c mice, respectively. As discussed, gastrointestinal motility was insensitive to serotonin antagonists in BALB/c mice in comparison to a control strain (Neal et al., 2009) and valproate-treated rats showed increased arousal during sleep compared to untreated controls (Tsujino et al., 2007; **Tables 2** and **3**).

### OVERLAPPING TRAITS

The presence of both core and comorbid endophenotypes in a range of animal models suggests that at least some of these traits may be interrelated and possibly integral to the etiology of ASD. Some endophenotypes are indeed co-expressed across different model constructs (for example, seizure susceptibility is consistently increased, as are anxiety-like behaviors in examples of environmental, genetic, as well as phenotype first models;

**Table 3**). Both environmental models (i.e., rodents administered the fatty acids valproate and PPA) and phenotype first models show heightened seizure susceptibility and anxiety-like behaviors together with sensory and motor deficits (**Table 3**). In contrast, genetic models show varied changes in sensory and motor domains (**Table 3**) for which the underlying mechanisms are unknown.

## FUTURE DIRECTIONS: POTENTIAL MECHANISMS UNDERLYING ASD ENDOPHENOTYPES

Animal models are an important tool with which to tease apart the biological mechanisms underlying ASD. Given the diverse nature of ASD, it is unlikely that a single cause is responsible for this disorder and more recent research suggests some degree of interaction between the CNS and peripheral systems. Many gene mutations identified in patients with ASD affect synaptic function (Betancur et al., 2009; Bourgeron, 2009; Betancur, 2011). This supports an emerging hypothesis that ASD is primarily a disorder of neuronal communication (Grabrucker et al., 2011; Ebert and Greenberg, 2013) and we suggest that subtle changes in neural function could underlie many of the comorbid traits described here. For example, it is well established that gene mutations coding for ion channels that result in altered synaptic function in the CNS can cause seizures in patients (Helbig et al., 2008; Goldberg and Coulter, 2013). It is also important to acknowledge, however, that many neurotransmitters and receptors that regulate neuronal communication in the CNS are of functional importance in the periphery and may thereby contribute to common comorbid traits in patient subsets. For example, in the case of gastrointestinal issues, many of the synaptic genes associated with ASD including the Shanks, neurexins, and neuroligins are also expressed in the enteric nervous system (Huett et al., 2009; Raab et al., 2010; Zhang et al., 2013), which regulates gastrointestinal motility and secretion. It is, therefore, feasible that synaptic mutations may underlie gastrointestinal symptoms in at least a subset of patients with ASD (Gershon and Ratcliffe, 2004) in addition to altering neuronal communication in the CNS. Future research should explore potential neural mechanisms underlying endophenotypes, in particular, those that are currently understudied (such as gastrointestinal disorders and altered circadian rhythms) in animal models of ASD.

In summary, rigorous endophenotyping in animal models of ASD can assist in identifying the molecular mechanisms underlying these common comorbid traits. Such information may also contribute to the identification of putative patient subsets within this spectrum of disorders and the subsequent tailoring of potential therapies. However, in order to achieve these goals, a more consistent approach in the assessment and comparison of endophenotypes is needed.

## ACKNOWLEDGMENTS

The authors thank Dr. Randal Moldrich, Professor Joel Bornstein, Dr. Emma Burrows, and Professor Terence O'Brien for the critical reading of this manuscript. Elisa L. Hill-Yardin was supported by a Department of Defense (DoD) Office of Congressionally Directed Medical Research Programs (CDMRP) Autism Research Program (ARP) Idea Development Award (AR110134) and an NHMRC Grant (1047674).

## REFERENCES


1. Allik, H., Larsson, J. O., and Smedje, H. (2006). Sleep patterns of school-age children with Asperger syndrome or high-functioning autism. *J. Autism Dev. Disord.* 36, 585–595. doi:10. 1007/s10803-006-0099-9
2. Amiet, C., Gourfinkel-An, I., Bouza- mondo, A., Tordjman, S., Baulac, M., Lechat, P., et al. (2008). Epilepsy in autism is associated with intel- lectual disability and gender: evi- dence from a meta-analysis. *Biol. Psychiatry* 64, 577–582. doi:10.1016/ j.biopsych.2008.04.030
3. Anderson, J. S., Druzgal, T. J., Froehlich, A., Dubray, M. B., Lange, N., Alex- an- der, A. L., et al. (2011). Decreased interhemispheric functional con- nec- tivity in autism. *Cereb. Cortex* 21, 1134–1146. doi:10.1093/cercor/ bhq190
4. Anisman, H., Kelly, O., Hayley, S., Borowski, T., Merali, Z., and McIntyre, D. C. (2000). Acoustic startle and fear-potentiated startle in rats selectively bred for fast and slow kindling rates: relation to monoamine activity. *Eur. J. Neurosci.* 12, 4405–4416. doi: 10.1046/j.0953-816X.2000.01216.x
5. Anisman, H., and McIntyre, D. C. (2002). Conceptual, spatial, and cue learning in the Morris water maze in fast or slow kindling rats: attention deficit comorbidity. *J. Neurosci.* 22, 7809–7817.
6. Arons, M. H., Thynne, C. J., Grabrucker, A. M., Li, D., Schoen, M., Cheyne, J. E., et al. (2012). Autism-associated mutations in ProSAP2/Shank3 impair synaptic transmission and neurexin-neuroligin-mediated transsyn- aptic signaling. *J. Neurosci.* 32, 14966–14978. doi:10.1523/ JNEUROSCI.2215-12.2012
7. Azarbar, A., McIntyre, D. C., and Gilby, K. L. (2010). Caloric restriction alters seizure disposition and behav- ioral profiles in seizure-prone (fast) versus seizure-resistant (slow) rats. *Behav. Neurosci.* 124, 106–114. doi: 10.1037/a0018307
8. Banko, M. L., Allen, K. M., Dolina, S., Neumann, P. E., and Seyfried, T. N. (1997). Genomic imprinting and audiogenic seizures in mice. *Behav. Genet.* 27, 465–475. doi:10.1023/A: 1025626501148
9. Baron, M. K., Boeckers, T. M., Vaida, B., Faham, S., Gingery, M., Sawaya, M. R., et al. (2006). An architectural framework that may lie at the core of the postsynaptic density. *Science* 311, 531–535. doi:10.1126/science. 1118995
10. Bennetto, L., Kuschner, E. S., and Hyman, S. L. (2007). Olfaction and taste processing in autism. *Biol. Psy- chiatry* 62, 1015–1021. doi:10.1016/ j.biopsych.2007.04.019
11. Berkel, S., Marshall, C. R., Weiss, B., Howe, J., Roeth, R., Moog, U., et al. (2010). Muta- tions in the SHANK2 synaptic scaffolding gene in autism spectrum disorder and mental retarda- tion. *Nat. Genet.* 42, 489–491. doi:10.1038/ng.589
12. Betancur, C. (2011). Etiological heterogeneity in autism spec- trum disorders: more than 100 genetic and genomic disorders and still counting. *Brain Res.* 1380, 42–77. doi:10.1016/j.brainres.2010. 11.078
13. Betancur, C., Sakurai, T., and Buxbaum, D. (2009). The emerging role of synaptic cell-adhesion pathways in the pathogenesis of autism spectrum disorders. *Trends Neu- rosci.* 32, 402–412. doi:10.1016/j. tins.2009.04.003
14. Blakemore, S. J., Tavassoli, T., Calo, S., Thomas, R. M., Catmur, C., Frith, U., et al. (2006). Tactile sensitivity in Asperger syndrome. *Brain Cogn.* 61, 5–13. doi:10.1016/j.bandc.2005. 12.013
15. Bonaglia, M. C., Giorda, R., Mani, E., Aceti, G., Anderlid, B. M., Baroncini, A., et al. (2006). Identification of a recurrent breakpoint within the SHANK3 gene in the 22q13.3 deletion syndrome. *J. Med. Genet.* 43, 822–828. doi:10.1136/jmg.2005. 038604
16. Bourgeron, T. (2009). A synaptic trek to autism. *Curr. Opin. Neu- robiol.* 19, 231–234. doi:10.1016/j. conb.2009.06.003
17. Bozdagi, O., Sakurai, T., Papapetrou, D., Wang, X., Dickstein, D. L., Takahashi, N., et al. (2010). Haploin- sufficiency of the autism-associated Shank3 gene leads to deficits in synaptic function, social interaction, and social communication. *Mol. Autism* 1, 15–15. doi:10.1186/2040-2392-1-15
18. Brodkin, E. S. (2007). BALB/c mice: low sociability and other pheno- types that may be relevant to autism. *Behav. Brain Res.* 176, 53–65. doi:10. 1016/j. bbr.2006.06.025
19. Bromley, R. L., Mawer, G., Clayton- Smith, J., and Baker, G. A. (2008). Autism spectrum disorders follow- ing in utero exposure to antiepileptic drugs. *Neurology* 71, 1923–1924. doi:10.1212/01.wnl.0000339399. 64213.1a
20. Buie, T., Fuchs, G. J. III, Furuta, G. T., Kooros, K., Levy, J., Lewis, J. D., et al. (2010). Recommenda- tions for evaluation and treatment of common gastrointestinal prob- lems in children with ASDs. *Pedi- atrics* 125(Suppl. 1), S19–S29. doi: 10.1542/peds.2009-1878D

21. Cascio, C., McGlone, F., Folger, S., Tannan, V., Baranek, G., Pelphrey,A., et al. (2008). Tactile per- ception in adults with autism: a multidimensional psychophysical study. *J. Autism Dev. Disord.* 38, 127–137. doi:10.1007/ s10803-007- 0370-8
22. Chadman, K. K., Gong, S., Scattoni, M. L., Boltuck, S. E., Gandhy, S. U., Heintz, N., et al. (2008). Minimal aberrant behavioral phenotypes of neuroligin-3 R451C knockin mice. *Autism Res.* 1, 147–158. doi:10.1002/ aur.22
23. Chakrabarti, B., Dudbridge, F., Kent, L., Wheelwright, S., Hill-Cawthorne, G., Allison, C., et al. (2009). Genes related to sex steroids, neural growth, and social-emotional behavior are associated with autis- tic traits, empathy, and Asperger syn- drome. *Autism Res.* 2, 157–177. doi: 10.1002/aur.80
24. Chapman, A., Keane, P. E., Meldrum, B. S., Simiand, J., and Vernieres, J. C. (1982). Mechanism of anticonvul- sant action of valproate. *Prog. Neurobiol.* 19, 315–359. doi:10.1016/0301-0082(82)90010-7
25. Crawley, J. N. (2007). Mouse behav- ioral assays relevant to the symp- toms of autism. *Brain Pathol.* 17, 448–459. doi:10.1111/j.1750-3639.2007.00096.x
26. Dakin, S., and Frith, U. (2005). Vagaries of visual perception in autism. *Neuron* 48, 497–507. doi:10.1016/j. neuron.2005.10.018
27. Dudova, I., Vodicka, J., Havlovicova, M., Sedlacek, Z., Urbanek, T., and Hrdlicka, M. (2011). Odor detec- tion threshold, but not odor iden- tification, is impaired in children with autism. *Eur. Child Adolesc. Psy- chiatry* 20, 333–340. doi:10.1007/s00787-011-0177-1
28. Durand, C. M., Betancur, C., Boeck- ers, T. M., Bockmann, J., Chaste, P., Fauchereau, F., et al. (2007). Muta- tions in the gene encoding the synap- tic scaffolding protein SHANK3 are associated with autism spectrum disorders. *Nat. Genet.* 39, 25–27. doi: 10.1038/ng1933
29. Ebert, D. H., and Greenberg, M. E. (2013). Activity-dependent neuronal signalling and autism spec- trum disorder. *Nature* 493, 327–337. doi:10.1038/nature11860
30. Ekinci, O., Arman, A. R., Isik, U., Bez, Y., and Berkem, M. (2010). EEG abnor- malities and epilepsy in autistic spec- trum disorders: clinical and famil- ial correlates. *Epilepsy Behav.* 17, 178–182. doi:10.1016/j.yebeh.2009. 11.014
31. Etherton, M., Foldy, C., Sharma, M., Tabuchi, K., Liu, X., Sham-loo, M., et al. (2011). Autism- linked neuroligin-3 R451C mutation differentially alters hippocampal and cortical synap- tic function. *Proc. Natl. Acad. Sci. U.S.A.* 30, 2115–2129. doi:10.1073/pnas.1111093108
32. Etherton, M. R., Blaiss, C. A., Powell, C. M., and Sudhof, T. C. (2009). Mouse neurexin-1alpha deletion causes correlated electrophysiological and behavioral changes consis- tent with cognitive impairments. *Proc. Natl. Acad. Sci. U.S.A.* 106, 17998–18003. doi:10.1073/pnas. 0910297106
33. Frye, R. E., Melnyk, S., and MacFabe, D. F. (2013). Unique acyl-carnitine profiles are potential biomarkers for acquired mitochondrial disease in autism spectrum disorder. *Transl. Psychiatry* 3, e220. doi:10.1038/tp. 2012.143
34. Gandal, M. J., Edgar, J. C., Ehrlich- man, R. S., Mehta, M., Roberts, T. P., and Siegel, S. J. (2010). Validat- ing gamma oscillations and delayed auditory responses as translational biomarkers of autism. *Biol. Psychi- atry* 68, 1100–1106. doi:10.1016/j. biopsych.2010.09.031
35. Gershon, M. D., and Ratcliffe, E. M. (2004). Developmental biol- ogy of the enteric nervous sys- tem: pathogenesis of Hirschsprung's disease and other congenital dys- motilities. *Semin. Pediatr. Surg.* 13, 224–235. doi:10.1053/j. sempedsurg. 2004.10.019
36. Geschwind, D. H. (2009). Advances in autism. *Annu. Rev. Med.* 60, 367–380. doi:10.1146/annurev.med. 60.053107.121225
37. Geschwind, D. H. (2011). Genetics of autism spectrum disorders. *Trends Cogn. Sci. (Regul. Ed.)* 15, 409–416. doi:10.1016/j.tics.2011.07.003
38. Gilby, K. L. (2008). A new rat model for vulnerability to epilepsy and autism spectrum disorders. *Epilepsia* 49(Suppl. 8), 108–110. doi:10.1111/ j.1528-1167.2008.01851.x
39. Gilby, K. L., Da Silva, A. G., and McIntyre, D. C. (2005). Differential GABA(A) subunit expression fol- lowing status epilepticus in seizure- prone and seizure-resistant rats: a putative mechanism for refractory drug response. *Epilepsia* 46(Suppl. 5), 3–9. doi:10.1111/j.1528-1167. 2005.01001.x
40. Gilby, K. L., and O'Brien, T. J. (2013). Epilepsy, autism, and neurodevelopment: kindling a shared vulnera- bility? *Epilepsy Behav.* 26, 370–374. doi:10.1016/j.yebeh.2012.11.002
41. Gilby, K. L., Thorne, V., Patey, A., and McIntyre, D. C. (2007). Ruling out postnatal origins to attention-deficit/hyperactivity disorder (ADHD)-like behaviors in a seizure-prone rat strain. *Behav. Neurosci.* 121, 370–379. doi:10.1037/0735-7044.121.2.370
42. Goldberg, E. M., and Coulter, D. A. (2013). Mechanisms of epileptogenesis: a convergence on neural circuit dysfunction. *Nat. Rev. Neurosci.* 14, 337–349. doi:10.1038/nrn3482
43. Gomot, M., Bernard, F. A., Davis, M. H., Belmonte, M. K., Ash- win, C., Bullmore, E. T., et al. (2006). Change detection in chil- dren with autism: an auditory event- related fMRI study. *Neuroimage* 29, 475–484. doi:10.1016/j. neuroimage. 2005.07.027
44. Grabrucker, A. M., Schmeisser, M. J., Schoen, M., and Boeckers, T. M. (2011). Postsynaptic ProSAP/Shank scaffolds in the cross-hair of synaptopathies. *Trends Cell Biol.* 21, 594–603. doi:10.1016/j.tcb.2011.07. 003
45. Hara, H. (2007). Autism and epilepsy: a retrospective follow-up study. *Brain Dev.* 29, 486–490. doi:10.1016/j. braindev.2006.12.012
46. Hayashi, M. K., Tang, C., Verpelli, C., Narayanan, R., Stearns, M. H., Xu, R. M., et al. (2009). The postsynaptic density proteins Homer and Shank form a polymeric network structure. *Cell* 137, 159–171. doi:10.1016/j.cell. 2009.01.050
47. Helbig, I., Scheffer, I. E., Mulley, J. C., and Berkovic, S. F. (2008). Navigat- ing the channels and beyond: unrav- elling the genetics of the epilepsies. *Lancet Neurol.* 7, 231–245. doi:10. 1016/S1474-4422(08)70039-5
48. Herbert, M. R. (2011). SHANK3, the synapse, and autism. *N. Engl. J. Med.* 365, 173–175. doi:10.1056/ NEJMcibr1104261
49. Huett, A., Leong, J. M., Podolsky, D. K., and Xavier, R. J. (2009). The cytoskeletal scaffold Shank3 is recruited to pathogen-induced actin rearrangements. *Exp. Cell Res.* 315, 2001–2011. doi:10.1016/j.yexcr. 2009.04.003
50. Ibrahim, S. H., Voigt, R. G., Katu-sic, S. K., Weaver, A. L., and Bar- baresi, W. J. (2009). Incidence of gas- trointestinal symptoms in children with autism: a population-based study. *Pediatrics* 124, 680–686. doi: 10.1542/peds.2008-2933
51. Irie, M., Hata, Y., Takeuchi, M., Ichtchenko, K., Toyoda, A., Hirao, K., et al. (1997). Binding of neu- roligins to PSD-95. *Science* 277, 1511–1515. doi:10.1126/science. 277.5331.1511
52. Jamain, S., Quach, H., Betancur, C., Ras- tam, M., Colineaux, C., Gillberg, I. C., et al. (2003). Mutations of the X-linked genes encoding neuroligins NLGN3 and NLGN4 are associated with autism. *Nat. Genet.* 34, 27–29. doi:10.1038/ng1136
53. Jeste, S. S. (2011). The neurology of autism spectrum disorders. *Curr. Opin. Neurol.* 24, 132–139. doi:10. 1097/WCO.0b013e3283446450
54. Kanne, S. M., and Mazurek, M. O. (2011). Aggression in children and adolescents with ASD: prevalence and risk factors. *J. Autism Dev. Disord.* 41, 926–937. doi:10.1007/s10803-010-1118-4
55. Karaki, S., Mitsui, R., Hayashi, H., Kato, I., Sugiya, H., Iwanaga, T., et al. (2006). Short-chain fatty acid recep- tor, GPR43, is expressed by enteroendocrine cells and mucosal mast cells in rat intestine. *Cell Tissue Res.* 324, 353–360. doi:10.1007/s00441-005-0140-x
56. Kim, K. C., Kim, P., Go, H. S., Choi, C. S., Yang, S. I., Cheong, J. H., et al. (2011). The critical period of val- proate exposure to induce autistic symptoms in Sprague-Dawley rats. *Toxicol. Lett.* 201, 137–142. doi:10. 1016/j. toxlet.2010.12.018
57. Krakowiak, P., Goodlin-Jones, B., Hertz- Picciotto, I., Croen, L. A., and Hansen, R. L. (2008). Sleep problems in children with autism spectrum disorders, developmental delays, and typical development: a population- based study. *J. Sleep Res.* 17, 197–206. doi:10.1111/j.1365-2869. 2008.00650.x
58. Krueger, D. D., Tuffy, L. P., Papadopou- los, T., and Brose, N. (2012). The role of neurexins and neuroligins in the formation, maturation, and func- tion of vertebrate synapses. *Curr. Opin. Neurobiol.* 22, 412–422. doi: 10.1016/j. conb.2012.02.012
59. Kumar, R. A. (2010). SHANK2 redemp- tion: another synaptic protein for mental retardation and autism. *Clin. Genet.* 78, 519–521. doi:10.1111/j. 1399-0004.2010.01530_2.x
60. Kwakye, L. D., Foss-Feig, J. H., Cas- cio, C. J., Stone, W. L., and Wal- lace, M. T. (2011). Altered auditory and multisensory temporal process- ing in autism spectrum disorders. *Front. Integr. Neurosci.* 4:129. doi:10. 3389/ fnint.2010.00129
61. Latham, K., Chung, S. T., Allen, P. M., Tavassoli, T., and Baron-Cohen, S. (2013). Spatial localisation in autism: evidence for differences in early cortical visual processing. *Mol. Autism* 4, 4. doi:10.1186/2040-2392- 4-4
62. Leekam, S. R., Nieto, C., Libby, S. J., Wing, L., and Gould, J. (2007). Describing the sensory abnormal- ities of children and adults with autism. *J. Autism Dev. Disord.* 37, 894–910. doi:10.1007/s10803-006- 0218-7

63. Lim, C. E., Turner, L. H., and Heinrichs, S. C. (2007). Short- term social recognition mem- ory deficit and atypical social and physiological stressor reac- tivity in seizure-susceptible El mice. *Seizure* 16, 59–68. doi:10.1016/j.seizure.2006.10.006
64. MacFabe, D. F., Cain, D. P., Rodriguez- Capote, K., Franklin, A. E., Hoffman, J. E., Boon, F., et al. (2007). Neu- robiological effects of intraventric- ular propionic acid in rats: possi- ble role of short chain fatty acids on the patho- genesis and character- istics of autism spectrum disorders. *Behav. Brain Res.* 176, 149–169. doi: 10.1016/j.bbr.2006.07.025
65. MacFabe, D. F., Cain, N. E., Boon, F., Ossenkopp, K. P., and Cain, D. P. (2011). Effects of the enteric bacterial metabolic product propi- onic acid on object-directed behav- ior, social behavior, cognition, and neuroinflam- mation in adolescent rats: relevance to autism spec- trum disorder. *Behav. Brain Res.* 217, 47–54. doi:10.1016/j.bbr.2010. 10.005
66. Malow, B. A., Marzec, M. L., McGrew, S. G., Wang, L., Henderson, L. M., and Stone, W. L. (2006). Char- acterizing sleep in children with autism spec- trum disorders: a mul- tidimensional approach. *Sleep* 29, 1563–1571.
67. Markram, K., Rinaldi, T., La Mendola, D., Sandi, C., and Markram, H. (2008). Abnormal fear condition- ing and amygdala processing in an animal model of autism. *Neuropsy- chopharmacology* 33, 901–912. doi: 10.1038/sj.npp.1301453
68. McFadyen-Leussis, M. P., and Hein- richs, S. C. (2005). Seizure-prone EL/Suz mice exhibit physical and motor delays and heightened locomotor ac- tivity in response to novelty during development. *Epilepsy Behav.* 6, 312–319. doi:10.1016/j.yebeh.2005.01.010
69. McFarlane, H. G., Kusek, G. K., Yang, M., Phoenix, J. L., Bolivar, V. J., and Crawley, J. N. (2008). Autism-like behavioral phenotypes in BTBR T+tf/J mice. *Genes Brain Behav.* 7, 152–163. doi:10.1111/j.1601-183X. 2007.00330.x
70. McIntyre, D. C., Kelly, M. E., and Dufresne, C. (1999). FAST and SLOW amygdala kindling rat strains: comparison of amygdala, hippocam- pal, piriform and perirhi- nal cortex kindling. *Epilepsy Res.* 35, 197–209. doi:10.1016/S0920-1211(99)00012-1
71. Meador, K. J., Baker, G. A., Finnell, R. H., Kalayjian, L. A., Liporace,J. D., Loring, D. W., et al. (2006). In utero antiepileptic drug exposure: fe- tal death and malformations. *Neu- rology* 67, 407–412. doi:10.1212/01.wnl.0000227919.81208.b2
72. Meidenbauer, J. J., Mantis, J. G., and Seyfried, T. N. (2011). The EL mouse: a natural model of autism and epilepsy. *Epilepsia* 52, 347–357. doi:10.1111/j.1528-1167.2010.02898.x
73. Meyer, G., Varoqueaux, F., Neeb, A., Oschlies, M., and Brose, N. (2004). The complexity of PDZ domain-mediated interactions at glutamatergic synapses: a case study on neuroligin. *Neuropharmacol- ogy* 47, 724–733. doi:10.1016/j. neuropharm.2004.06.023
74. Morin, C. L., Dolina, S., Robertson,R. T., and Ribak, C. E. (1994). An inbred epilepsy-prone substrain of BALB/c mice shows absence of the corpus cal- losum, an abnormal pro- jection to the basal forebrain, and bilateral projec- tions to the thalamus. *Cereb. Cortex* 4, 119–128. doi:10. 1093/cercor/4.2.119
75. Moy, S. S., Nadler, J. J., Poe, M. D., Nonneman, R. J., Young, N. B., Koller, B. H., et al. (2008). Devel- opment of a mouse test for repeti- tive, restricted be- haviors: relevance to autism. *Behav. Brain Res.* 188, 178–194. doi:10.1016/j.bbr.2007.10. 029
76. Mulle, J. G., Sharp, W. G., and Cubells, J. F. (2013). The gut microbiome: a new frontier in autism research. *Curr. Psychiatry Rep.* 15, 337. doi:10. 1007/s11920-012-0337-0
77. Neal, K. B., Parry, L. J., and Born- stein, J. C. (2009). Strain-specific genet- ics, anatomy and function of enteric neural serotonergic pathways in inbred mice. *J. Physiol. (Lond.)* 587, 567–586. doi:10.1113/jphysiol. 2008.160416
78. Nesslinger, N. J., Gorski, J. L., Kur- czynski, T. W., Shapira, S. K., Siegel-Bar- telt, J., Dumanski, J. P., et al. (1994). Clinical, cytogenetic, and molecular characterization of seven patients with deletions of chromosome 22q13.3. *Am. J. Hum. Genet.* 54, 464–472.
79. Nutt, D. J., and Lister, R. G. (1988). Strain differences in response to a benzo- diazepine receptor inverse agonist (FG 7142) in mice. *Psychopharmacology (Berl.)* 94, 335–336. doi:10.1007/BF00174705
80. Parmeggiani, A., Barcia, G., Posar, A., Raimondi, E., Santucci, M., and Scaduto, M. C. (2010). Epilepsy and EEG paroxysmal abnormali- ties in autism spectrum disorders. *Brain Dev.* 32, 783–789. doi:10.1016/ j.brain- dev.2010.07.003
81. Parracho, H. M., Bingham, M. O., Gib- son, G. R., and McCartney, A. L. (2005). Differences between the gut microflora of children with autis- tic spectrum disorders and that of healthy children. *J. Med. Micro- biol.* 54, 987–991. doi:10.1099/jmm. 0.46101-0
82. Pearson, B. L., Pobbe, R. L., Defen- sor, E. B., Oasay, L., Bolivar, V. J., Blanchard, D. C., et al. (2011). Motor and cognitive stereotypies in the BTBR T+tf/J mouse model of autism. *Genes Brain Behav.* 10, 228–235. doi:10.1111/j.1601-183X. 2010.00659.x
83. Peca, J., Feliciano, C., Ting, J. T., Wang, W., Wells, M. F., Venkatra- man, T. N., et al. (2011). Shank3 mutant mice display autistic-like behaviours and striatal dysfunction. *Nature* 472, 437–442. doi:10.1038/ nature09965
84. Penagarikano, O., Abrahams, B. S., Her- man, E. I., Winden, K. D., Gda- lyahu, A., Dong, H., et al. (2011). Absence of CNTNAP2 leads to epilepsy, neuronal migration abnormalities, and core autism-related deficits. *Cell* 147, 235–246. doi:10.1016/j.cell. 2011.08.040
85. Pobbe, R. L., Defensor, E. B., Pearson, B. L., Bolivar,V. J., Blanchard, D. C., and Blanchard, R. J. (2011). General and social anxiety in the BTBR T+ tf/J mouse strain. *Behav. Brain Res.* 216, 446–451. doi:10.1016/j.bbr.2010.08. 039
86. Pouw, L. B., Rieffe, C., Oosterveld, P., Huskens, B., and Stockmann, L. (2013). Reactive/proactive aggres- sion and affective/cognitive empa- thy in children with ASD. *Res. Dev. Disabil.* 34, 1256–1266. doi:10.1016/j.ridd.2012.12.022
87. Raab, M., Boeckers, T. M., and Neuhu- ber, W. L. (2010). Proline-rich syn- apse-associated protein-1 and 2 (ProSAP1/Shank2 and ProSAP2/Shank3)-scaffolding pro- teins are also present in postsynaptic special- izations of the peripheral nervous system. *Neuroscience* 171, 421–433. doi:10.1016/j. neuroscience.2010.08.041
88. Racine, R. J., Steingart, M., and McIn- tyre, D. C. (1999). Development of kindling-prone and kindling- resistant rats: selective breeding and elec- trophysiological studies. *Epilepsy Res.* 35, 183–195. doi:10. 1016/S0920-1211(99)00013-3
89. Rasalam, A. D., Hailey, H., Williams, J. H., Moore, S. J., Turnpenny, P. D., Lloyd, D. J., et al. (2005). Charac- teristics of fetal anticonvulsant syn- drome associated autistic disorder. *Dev. Med. Child Neurol.* 47, 551–555. doi:10.1017/S0012162205001076
90. *Reinhart*, C. J., McIntyre, D. C., Metz, A., and Pellis, S. M. (2006). Play fight- ing between kindling- prone (FAST) and kindling-resistant (SLOW) rats. *J. Comp. Psychol.* 120, 19–30. doi:10.1037/0735-7036.120. 1.19
91. Reinhart, C. J., Pellis, S. M., and McIntyre, D. C. (2004). Develop- ment of play fighting in kindling- prone (FAST) and kindling-resistant (SLOW) rats: how does the retention of phenotypic juvenility affect the complexity of play? *Dev. Psychobiol.* 45, 83–92. doi:10.1002/dev.20016
92. Rinehart, N. J., Tonge, B. J., Iansek, R., McGinley, J., Brereton, A. V., Enti- cott, P. G., et al. (2006). Gait function in newly diagnosed children with autism: cerebellar and basal ganglia related motor disorder. *Dev. Med. Child Neurol.* 48, 819–824. doi:10. 1111/j.1469-8749.2006.tb01229.x
93. Roberts, R. R., Murphy, J. F., Young, M., and Bornstein, J. C. (2007). Devel- opment of colonic motil- ity in the neonatal mouse-studies using spatio- temporal maps. *Am. J. Physiol. Gastrointest. Liver Physiol.* 292, G930–G938. doi:10.1152/ajpgi. 00444.2006
94. Robertson, C., Kravitz, D., Freyberg, J., Baron-Cohen, S., and Baker, C. (2013). Tunnel vision: sharper gra- dient of spatial attention in autism. *J. Neurosci.* 33, 6676–6681. doi:10. 1523/JNEUROSCI.5120-12.2013
95. Rogawski, M. A., and Loscher, W. (2004). The neurobiol- ogy of antiepilep- tic drugs. *Nat. Rev. Neurosci.* 5, 553–564. doi:10.1038/nrn1430
96. Roullet, F. I., Wollaston, L., Decatan- zaro, D., and Foster, J. A. (2010). Be- havioral and molecular changes in the mouse in response to prenatal expo- sure to the anti- epileptic drug valproic acid. *Neuro- science* 170, 514–522. doi:10.1016/j. neuroscience.2010.06.069
97. Ryan, B. C., Young, N. B., Crawley, J. N., Bodfish, J. W., and Moy, S. S. (2010). Social deficits, stereo- typy and early emergence of repet- itive be- havior in the C58/J inbred mouse strain. *Behav. Brain Res.* 208, 178–188. doi:10.1016/j.bbr.2009.11. 031
98. Sansa, G., Carlson, C., Doyle, W., Weiner, H. L., Bluvstein, J., Barr, W., et al. (2011). Medically refrac- tory epilepsy in autism. *Epilepsia* 52, 1071–1075. doi:10.1111/j.1528-1167.2011.03069.x
99. Schmeisser, M. J., Ey, E., Wegener, S., Bockmann, J., Stempel, A. V., Kuebler, A., et al. (2012). Autistic- like behaviours and hyperactivity in mice lacking ProSAP1/Shank2. *Nature* 486, 256–260. doi:10.1038/ nature11015
100. Schneider, T., and Przewlocki, R. (2005). Behavioral alterations in rats pre- na- tally exposed to valproic acid: animal model of autism. *Neuropsycho- phar- macology* 30, 80–89. doi:10.1038/sj. npp.1300518
101. Shoji, H., and Kato, K. (2009). Mater- nal care affects the development of maternal behavior in inbred mice. *Dev. Psychobiol.* 51, 345–357. doi:10. 1002/dev.20375

102. Shultz, S. R., MacFabe, D. F., Martin, S., Jackson, J., Taylor, R., Boon, F., et al. (2009). Intracerebroventricular injections of the enteric bacterial metabolic product propionic acid impair cognition and sensorimo- tor ability in the Long-Evans rat: further development of a rodent model of autism. *Behav. Brain Res.* 200, 33–41. doi:10.1016/j.bbr.2008. 12.023

103. Shultz, S. R., MacFabe, D. F., Ossenkopp, K. P., Scratch, S., Whelan, J., Taylor, R., et al. (2008). Intracerebroven- tricular injection of propionic acid, an enteric bacterial metabolic end- product, impairs social behavior in the rat: implications for an ani- mal model of autism. *Neurophar- macology* 54, 901–911. doi:10.1016/ j.neuropharm.2008.01.013

104. Silverman, J. L., Yang, M., Lord, C., and Crawley, J. N. (2010a). Behavioural phenotyping assays for mouse mod- els of autism. *Nat. Rev. Neurosci.* 11, 490–502. doi:10.1038/nrn2851

105. Silverman, J. L., Yang, M., Turner, S. M., Katz, A. M., Bell, D. B., Koenig, J. I., et al. (2010b). Low stress reactivity and neuroendocrine factors in the BTBR T+tf/J mouse model of autism. *Neu- roscience* 171, 1197–1208. doi:10. 1016/j.neuroscience.2010.09.059

106. Sobrian, S. K., and Nandedkar, A. K. (1986). Prenatal antiepileptic drug exposure alters seizure susceptibility in rats. *Pharmacol. Biochem. Behav.* 24, 1383–1391. doi:10.1016/0091-3057(86)90199-1

107. Strauss, K. A., Puffenberger, E. G., Huentelman, M. J., Gottlieb, S., Dobrin, S. E., Parod, J. M., et al. (2006). Recessive symptomatic focal epilepsy and mutant contactin- associated protein-like 2. *N. Engl. J. Med.* 354, 1370–1377. doi:10.1056/ NEJMoa052773

108. Sudhof, T. C. (2008). Neuroligins and neurexins link synaptic function to cognitive disease. *Nature* 455, 903–911. doi:10.1038/nature07456

109. Tabuchi, K., Blundell, J., Etherton, M. R., Hammer, R. E., Liu, X., Powell, C. M., et al. (2007). A neuroligin-3 mutation implicated in autism increases inhibitory synaptic trans- mission in mice. *Science* 318, 71–76. doi:10.1126/ science.1146221

110. Thomas, R. H., Foley, K. A., Mepham, J. R., Tichenoff, L. J., Possmayer, F., and MacFabe, D. F. (2010). Altered brain phospholipid and acyl- carnitine profiles in propionic acid infused rodents: further develop- ment of a potential model of autism spectrum disorders. *J. Neurochem.* 113, 515–529. doi:10.1111/j.1471- 4159.2010.06614.x

111. Todorova, M. T., Burwell, T. J., and Seyfried, T. N. (1999). Environ- mental risk factors for multifacto- rial epilepsy in EL mice. *Epilepsia* 40, 1697–1707. doi:10.1111/j.1528- 1157.1999.tb01586.x

112. Tsujino, N., Nakatani, Y., Seki, Y., Nakasato, A., Nakamura, M., Sug- awara, M., et al. (2007). Abnormal- ity of circadian rhythm accompa- nied by an increase in frontal cor- tex serotonin in animal model of autism. *Neurosci. Res.* 57, 289–295. doi:10.1016/j.neures.2006.10.018

113. Turner, L. H., Lim, C. E., and Hein- richs, S. C. (2007). Antisocial and seizure susceptibility phenotypes in an animal model of epilepsy are normalized by impairment of brain corticotropin-releasing factor. *Epilepsy Behav.* 10, 8–15. doi:10. 1016/j.yebeh.2006.08.013

114. Valicenti-McDermott, M., McVicar, K., Rapin, I., Wershil, B. K., Cohen, H., and Shinnar, S. (2006). Fre- quency of gastrointestinal symp- toms in children with autistic spec- trum disorders and association with family history of autoimmune dis- ease. *J. Dev. Behav. Pediatr.* 27, S128–S136. doi:10.1097/00004703- 200604002-00011

115. van Steensel, F. J., Bogels, S. M., and Perrin, S. (2011). Anxiety disor- ders in children and adolescents with autistic spectrum disorders: a meta-analysis. *Clin. Child Fam. Psy- chol. Rev.* 14, 302–317. doi:10.1007/s10567-011-0097-0

116. Velez, L., Sokoloff, G., Miczek, K. A., Palmer, A. A., and Dulawa, S. C. (2010). Differences in aggres- sive behavior and DNA copy num- ber variants between BALB/cJ and BALB/cByJ substrains. *Behav. Genet.* 40, 201–210. doi:10.1007/s10519- 009-9325-5

117. Verpelli, C., and Sala, C. (2012). Mole- cular and synaptic defects in intel- lectual disability syndromes. *Curr. Opin. Neurobiol.* 22, 530–536. doi: 10.1016/j.conb.2011.09.007

118. Wagner, G. C., Reuhl, K. R., Cheh, M., McRae, P., and Halladay, A. K. (2006). A new neurobehavioral model of autism in mice: pre- and post-natal exposure to sodium val- proate. *J. Autism Dev. Disord.* 36, 779–793. doi:10.1007/s10803-006- 0117-y

119. Wahlsten, D., Metten, P., and Crabbe, J. C. (2003). Survey of 21 inbred mouse strains in two laboratories reveals that BTBR T/+ tf/tf has severely reduced hippocampal com- missure and absent corpus callosum. *Brain Res.* 971, 47–54.

120. Wang, L. W., Tancredi, D. J., and Thomas, D. W. (2011a). The preva- lence of gastrointestinal problems in children across the United States with autism spectrum disorders from families with multiple affected members. *J. Dev. Behav. Pedi- atr.* 32, 351–360. doi:10.1097/DBP. 0b013e31821bd06a

121. Wang, X., McCoy, P. A., Rodriguiz, R. M., Pan, Y., Je, H. S., Roberts, A. C., et al. (2011b). Synaptic dysfunction and abnormal behaviors in mice lack- ing major isoforms of Shank3. *Hum. Mol. Genet.* 20, 3093–3108. doi:10. 1093/ hmg/ddr212

122. Won, H., Lee, H. R., Gee, H. Y., Mah, W., Kim, J. I., Lee, J., et al. (2012). Autistic-like social behaviour in Shank2-mutant mice improved by restoring NMDA receptor function. *Nature* 486, 261–265. doi:10.1038/ nature11208

123. Woolfenden, S., Sarkozy, V., Ridley, G., Coory, M., and Williams, K. (2012). A systematic review of two out- comes in autism spectrum disorder – epilepsy and mortality. *Dev. Med. Child Neurol.* 54, 306–312. doi:10. 1111/j.1469-8749.2012.04223.x

124. Xu, B., McIntyre, D. C., Fahnestock, M., and Racine, R. J. (2004). Strain dif- ferences affect the induction of sta- tus epilepticus and seizure-induced morphological changes. *Eur. J. Neu- rosci.* 20, 403–418. doi:10.1111/j. 1460-9568.2004.03489.x

125. Zhang, Q., Wang, J., Li, A., Liu, H., Zhang, W., Cui, X., et al. (2013). Expression of neurexin and neuroli- gin in the enteric nervous system and their down-regulated expres- sion levels in Hirschsprung disease. *Mol. Biol. Rep.* 40, 2969–2975. doi: 10.1007/s11033-012-2368-3

# 6

# A "bottom-up" approach to aetiological research in autism spectrum disorders

**_Lisa M. Unwin[1,2]*, Murray T. Maybery[1], John A. Wray[3] and Andrew J. O. Whitehouse[1,2]_**

[1] *School of Psychology, The University of Western Australia, Perth, WA, Australia*
[2] *Telethon Institute for Child Health Research, Centre for Child Health Research, The University of Western Australia, Perth, WA, Australia*
[3] *Child and Adolescent Health Service, State Child Development Centre, Princess Margaret Hospital for Children, Perth, WA, Australia*

***Edited by:***
*Rudi Crncec, South Western Sydney Local Health District, Australia*

***Reviewed by:***
*Roger Blackmore, South Western Sydney Local Health District, Australia*
*Rebecca A. Harrington, Johns Hopkins University, USA*

****Correspondence:***
*Lisa M. Unwin, School of Psychology, The University of Western Australia, M304, 35 Stirling Highway, Crawley, WA 6009, Australia*
*e-mail: 20375262@student.uwa.edu.au*

Autism spectrum disorders (ASD) are currently diagnosed in the presence of impairments in social interaction and communication, and a restricted range of activities and interests. However, there is considerable variability in the behaviors of different individuals with an ASD diagnosis. The heterogeneity spans the entire range of IQ and language abilities, as well as other behavioral, communicative, and social functions. While any psychiatric condition is likely to incorporate a degree of heterogeneity, the variability in the nature and severity of behaviors observed in ASD is thought to exceed that of other disorders. The current paper aims to provide a model for future research into ASD subgroups. In doing so, we examined whether two proposed risk factors – low birth weight (LBW), and *in utero* exposure to selective serotonin reuptake inhibitors (SSRIs) – are associated with greater behavioral homogeneity. Using data from the Western Australian Autism Biological Registry, this study found that LBW and maternal SSRI use during pregnancy were associated with greater sleep disturbances and a greater number of gastrointestinal complaints in children with ASD, respectively. The findings from this "proof of principle" paper provide support for this "bottom-up" approach as a feasible method for creating homogenous groups.

**Keywords: autism spectrum disorders, heterogeneity, autism phenotype**

## INTRODUCTION

Autism spectrum disorders (ASD) are currently diagnosed in the presence of impairments in social interaction and communication, and a restricted range of activities and interests. However, there is considerable variability in the behaviors of different individuals with an ASD diagnosis. Traditionally, researchers have conceptualized ASD as a unitary disorder with a large spectrum, and have sought to discover a single aetiological factor that leads to disorder. However, the behavioral heterogeneity has been mirrored at the genetic level, for instance, many susceptibility loci have been identified, yet each has been found to account for a small amount of variance only (1–2%) (Weiss et al., 2008). A proposition that has gathered momentum over the last decade involves moving away from the traditional conceptualization of ASD as a unitary disorder toward conceptualizing a syndrome of multiple and separate disorders; in essence, re-examining "autism" as "the autisms" (Geschwind and Levitt, 2007; Whitehouse and Stanley, 2013).

Research in this area has traditionally adopted a "top-down approach" by constraining behavioral phenotypes in the hope that this will facilitate the identification of biological subtypes. For example, Buxbaum et al. (2001) reported linkage evidence for a susceptibility gene for Autistic Disorder on chromosome 2. In an analysis of 95 affected-relative pair families with Autistic Disorder they found a maximum multipoint heterogeneity LOD score (HLOD) of 1.96 and a maximum multipoint NPL score of 2.39 on chromosome 2q (at 186cM, for D2s364). When families were grouped according to delayed onset (at age >36 months) of phrase speech, linkage to chromosome 2 increased (HLOD = 2.99, NPL = 3.32). Shao et al. (2002) found further evidence for a susceptibility gene on chromosome 2. In an analysis of 82 sibling pairs with Autistic Disorder they found a HLOD of 0.53 at D2S116. When the analysis was restricted to a subset of 45 families with phrase speech delay (>36 months), linkage to chromosome 2q increased (HLOD = 2.12). Whilst this approach has received the most attention in aetiological research, generally speaking, it has underperformed, with only weak evidence that stratification based on IQ, age at first word, or verbal ability yield a more genetically homogenous population (Geschwind and Levitt, 2007).

A "bottom-up" approach to identify biological subtypes of ASD has not received the same level of research attention. This methodology focuses on known aetiological risk factors, and whether individuals exposed to these risk factors have a more homogenous phenotype. In this paper, we report on this bottom-up approach, focusing on aspects of the phenotype that are not part of the core defining features of the disorder. We know that comorbid medical conditions are highly prevalent in ASD (Bauman, 2010). Sleep problems are thought to affect 40–80% of children on the spectrum (Richdale, 1999) and estimates of gastrointestinal disorders in ASD range from 9 to 70% (Buie et al., 2010). The high prevalence of these comorbid conditions in children with ASD may suggest the presence of important genetic and/or biological markers, which if identified, can refine our ability to be more precise in categorizing clinical and genetic subtypes within the autism spectrum (Bauman, 2010). In this paper, we have adopted a bottom-up approach by stratifying groups based on two previously identified risk factors, namely, maternal use of selective serotonin reuptake inhibitors (SSRIs) during pregnancy and low birth weight (LBW). The second part of our strategy involved examining the homogeneity within the groups based on medical complaints such as sleep problems and gastrointestinal complaints in addition to core features of ASD such as social behavior, language characteristics, and severity.

Selective serotonin reuptake inhibitors use during pregnancy has gained considerable attention over the last 2 years and is thought to be implicated in an increased risk of ASD diagnosis (Croen et al., 2011). Prevalence studies in the US estimate that up to 8% of mothers may be treated with SSRIs during pregnancy for conditions such as anxiety disorders or major depression (Alwan et al., 2011). SSRIs act primarily by blocking the serotonin transporter, thereby raising extracellular serotonin (5-HT) levels (Oberlander et al., 2009). These SSRIs readily cross the placental and blood-brain barriers to the fetus, with the potential to alter central 5-HT signaling (Oberlander et al., 2009). The neuroactive properties of SSRIs are thought to be a potential risk to fetal neurodevelopment, since 5-HT plays such a critical role in regulating diverse processes such as cell division, differentiation, migration, myelination, synaptogenesis, and dendritic pruning (Gaspar et al., 2003). A number of researchers have hypothesized that the increase in ASD diagnoses in recent years may be associated with a commensurate increase in maternal use of antidepressant medication during pregnancy (Croen et al., 2011). A recent population-based case-control study by Croen et al. (2011) reviewed record-based data describing the postnatal development of children exposed to SSRIs *in utero*. This study examined data for children born through a medical care program during the period of 1995–1999. Infants in the sample who were later diagnosed with ASD were considered cases. Children without an ASD diagnosis were randomly sampled from the remaining cohort at a ratio of five control children per one case child. Using this matched sample, Croen et al. (2011) investigated SSRI use throughout pregnancy and found that 70 women who took antidepressant medication the year before the birth of their child had twice the risk of having a child with ASD ($n = 20$ offspring with ASD, 28.57%) compared with 1735 women who did not take any antidepressant medication ($n = 278$ offspring with ASD, 16.02%).

Using a similar population-based nested case-control design, Rai et al. (2013) investigated the extent to which parental depression and maternal antidepressant use during pregnancy were associated with ASDs in offspring. For parental depression, record-based data was available for 4429 cases of ASD and 43277 age- and sex-matched controls, and for maternal antidepressant use, data existed for 1679 ASD cases and 16845 non-ASD controls. They found that a history of maternal but not paternal depression was associated with higher risk of autism in offspring. These associations were largely limited to children of mothers who reported using antidepressants at the first antenatal interview. Antidepressant use during pregnancy was reported by 1.3% of mothers of children with ASD and by 0.6% of control mothers, equating to an almost twofold increase in risk of ASD with use of antidepressants (Rai et al., 2013). Other studies that have examined the effect of maternal SSRI use during pregnancy have observed several atypical behavioral outcomes among offspring, including delay in meeting gross motor milestones (Pedersen et al., 2010), a wide range of feeding difficulties (Oberlander et al., 2006) and sleep disturbances (Zeskind and Stephens, 2004).

Low birth weight (<2500 g) has also been considered an environmental risk factor implicated in a range of psychiatric disorders including ASD, anxiety disorder, and depression (Indredavik et al., 2004; Gardener et al., 2011; Jaspers et al., 2012). Lampi et al. (2012) examined data from the case-control Finnish Prenatal Study of Autism and ASDs and found that children with very LBW (<1500 g) had a greater than threefold increased odds of autism compared with children with normal birth weight (NBW) (2500–3999 g). Interestingly, LBW did not significantly increase the odds of Asperger syndrome (Lampi et al., 2012). In addition to these associated psychiatric disorders, when compared to children with NBW, children with LBW have been found to show pervasive motor impairments, increased socio-emotional issues, increased risk of sleep-disordered breathing, and reductions in language ability (Paavonen et al., 2007; de Kieviet et al., 2009; Spittle et al., 2009; Barre et al., 2011; Scott et al., 2012). Despite evidence supporting the role of these environmental risk factors in the development of ASD, no single factor has been identified that poses a determinant risk for this disorder.

This paper will adopt a "bottom-up" approach to parsing ASD heterogeneity by investigating the behavioral phenotype associated with two possible environmental risk factors. The first study compared the behavioral and developmental phenotype of children with ASD whose mothers used SSRIs during pregnancy with the phenotype for a tightly matched group of children with ASD whose mothers did not use SSRIs during pregnancy. It was hypothesized that those children with ASD whose mothers used SSRIs during pregnancy would display early feeding and sleep disturbances compared to the control group of children with ASD. We also examined whether these children showed a distinguishable behavioral phenotype. Study 2 compared the phenotype of children with ASD born with LBW with a matched group of children with ASD born with NBW. It was hypothesized that those LBW children with ASD would display greater sleep disturbances (e.g., sleep-disordered breathing), language difficulties, and socio-emotional problems compared to the NBW group. This "proof of principle" study seeks to examine two potential risk factors within the context of a "bottom-up" research design. If the hypotheses are supported this paper may provide a blueprint for using the "bottom-up" approach as a feasible method for creating homogenous groups compared with the more costly "top-down" approach which requires large sample sizes.

## STUDY 1

### MATERIALS AND METHODS

#### *Participants*

Participants were part of the Western Australian Autism Biological Registry (WAABR), which is an ongoing study of children with a clinical diagnosis of an ASD and their families taking place at the Telethon Institute for Child Health Research in Perth, Western Australia (see Taylor et al., in press). Diagnosing ASD in Western Australia mandates assessment by a clinical team comprising a Pediatrician, Psychologist, and Speech-Language Pathologist under

DSM-IV guidelines (American Psychiatric Association, 1994). A diagnosis is only made when there is consensus amongst the team. The current study included nine participants from the WAABR whose mothers reported SSRI use during pregnancy (cases). Each of these participants was individually matched on gender and chronological age at assessment (within 15 months) with three further children with ASD ($n = 27$) whose mothers did not take an SSRI during pregnancy.

#### *Measures and procedure*

Prior to attending a face-to-face assessment, families were mailed and asked to complete a comprehensive case-history questionnaire relating to the mother's pregnancy and the ASD child's development. Mothers were asked to provide details of any history of psychological disorder such as major depression or anxiety. They were also asked to provide the name of any prescription or non-prescription medications, the dosage, and the amount they used during pregnancy. A series of questionnaires were also included in this package, including the Social Responsiveness Scale (SRS; Constantino and Gruber, 2002), Children's Sleep Habits Questionnaire (CSHQ; Owens et al., 2000), Children's Communication Checklist-2 (CCC-2; Bishop, 2003), and a gastrointestinal complaints questionnaire (Ibrahim et al., 2009).

The SRS is a 65-item questionnaire used to examine a range of social behaviors characteristic of ASD in children over the last 6 months. A total score can be calculated for the SRS as well as five subscale scores, namely, social communication, autism mannerisms, social motivation, social awareness, and social cognition. Parents respond using a four-point scale ranging from "not true" (1) to "almost always true" (4). A higher total score on this measure is indicative of greater social difficulties. The CSHQ is a 34-item parent-report instrument that was used to examine sleep behavior over a "typical week." Parents were asked to rate how often their child showed behaviors such as "struggle at bedtime" and "show fear at sleeping alone" using a one to three point scale corresponding to "rarely," "sometimes," or "usually," respectively. A total score and eight subscale scores (bedtime resistance, sleep onset delay, sleep duration, sleep anxiety, night wakings, parasomnias, sleep-disordered breathing, and daytime sleepiness) can be calculated for responses on the CSHQ. Higher total scores on the CSHQ indicate that the child has a greater number of sleep problems.

The CCC-2 is a parent-report questionnaire designed to assess the communication skills of children aged 4–16 years. The purposes of the CCC-2 are the identification of pragmatic language impairment, screening of receptive and expressive language skills, and assistance in screening for ASD. The CCC-2 consists of 70 items that are divided into 10 scales, each with 7 items. The first four scales focus on specific aspects of language and communications skills (content and form). The next four scales assess the pragmatic aspects of communication. The last two scales measure behaviors that are usually impaired in children with ASDs. The parent rates the frequency of the communication behavior described in each item from 0 (less than once a week or never) to 3 (several times a day or always). Interpretation is based on a General Communication Composite (GCC), with lower scores indicative of greater language and communication difficulties.

Parents also completed a brief questionnaire related to their child's history of gastrointestinal problems. This questionnaire was developed specifically for the WAABR case-history questionnaire based on the list of complaints in Ibrahim et al. (2009). After reviewing the literature related to gastrointestinal symptoms they identified five categories that have been reported to be common in patients with autism, namely, constipation, diarrhea, gastroesophageal reflux or vomiting, abdominal discomfort/irritability, or feeding issues (Ibrahim et al., 2009). If the parent reported their child had experienced any of the five gastrointestinal complaints for a period of at least a month, resulting in consultation with their doctor, they received a score of one for the indicated complaint(s). Any other reports received a score of zero. Using this scoring method these complaints were analyzed in two ways: (1) individually to see if the frequency of each complaint differed between the two groups and (2) as a summary measure of gastrointestinal complaints (score of one or more) versus no gastrointestinal complaints (score of zero).

Families were then invited to the Telethon Institute for Child Health Research for a face-to-face behavioral assessment. Clinical diagnoses of ASD were confirmed using the Autism Diagnostic Observation Schedule-Generic (ADOS-G; Lord et al., 2000). The present study used the child's age and ADOS module (reflective of their quantity of speech) to calibrate severity scores (0–10) for each participant according to the severity scale of Gotham et al. (2009). This enabled comparisons between the participants, irrespective of the module they completed.

#### *Statistical analyses*

Between-group differences in the quantitative scores of the SRS, CCC-2, CSHQ, and ADOS severity scale were investigated with independent-samples $t$-tests. Responses to the gastrointestinal complaints questionnaire were analyzed according to whether parents reported zero complaints or one or more complaints for their children using chi-square analyses with Fisher's exact test of significance.

### RESULTS

The SSRI case ($n = 9$) and control ($n = 27$) groups did not significantly differ on gestational age [$F(1, 34) = 1.05$, $p > 0.05$] or maternal age at conception [$F(1, 34) = 3.45$, $p > 0.05$]. **Table 1** provides details of the maternal, pregnancy and offspring characteristics of the case group.

Independent-samples $t$-tests revealed that there were no significant differences between the two groups on any of the SRS, CCC-2, CSHQ, or ADOS severity scores (**Table 2**). However, analysis of responses to the gastrointestinal complaints questionnaire found that mothers who used SSRIs during pregnancy were more likely to have a child with ASD who experienced one or more gut problems ($n = 8$, 88.9%), compared to the control group ($n = 13$, 48.1%), $\chi^2(1)$, $p = 0.05$. To further investigate this association, chi-square analyses with Fisher's exact test were performed on the five individual complaints (**Table 3**). The individual complaints did not significantly differentiate between the groups. However, the percentage of constipation complaints was noticeably larger (though, not significantly) for cases compared to controls.

**Table 1 | Study 1: maternal and offspring characteristics of the SSRI case group.**

| | Maternal | | | Offspring | | | | | | |
|---|---|---|---|---|---|---|---|---|---|---|
| | **SSRI taken during pregnancy** | **Period of pregnancy SSRI taken** | **Psychiatric diagnosis** | **Gestational age at birth (weeks)** | **Age at assessment** | **ADOS module administered** | **ADOS severity score** | **CSHQ score** | **SRS score** | **Number of gut problems** |
| Case 1 | Lexapro | Daily | Major depression | 41 | 5, 6 | 2 | 1 | 42 | 146 | 2 |
| Case 2 | Lexapro | Daily | Major depression | 40 | 4, 6 | 2 | 6 | 62 | 157 | 1 |
| Case 3 | Lovan | 3 months | Major depression | 36 | 5, 2 | 2 | 8 | 54 | 158 | 4 |
| Case 4 | Effexor | Daily | Major depression | 38 | 10, 2 | 3 | 3 | 46 | 172 | 2 |
| Case 5 | Not specified | – | Major depression | 38 | 4, 3 | 2 | 7 | 59 | 166 | 0 |
| Case 6 | Escitalopram | Daily | – | 38 | 2, 9 | 1 | 4 | 77 | 207 | 1 |
| Case 7 | Fluoxetine | Daily | Anxiety disorder | 40 | 8, 5 | 3 | 3 | 63 | 145 | 1 |
| Case 8 | Aropax | 1 month | Anxiety disorder | 39 | 3, 1 | 1 | 6 | 54 | 120 | 2 |
| Case 9 | Zoloft | Daily | Depression | 38 | 3, 5 | 1 | 6 | 41 | 90 | 1 |

**Table 2 | Study 1: descriptive statistics and independent-samples *t*-tests for CSHQ, SRS, and ADOS severity scores.**

| | SSRI cases | | Controls | | Statistic | *p* |
|---|---|---|---|---|---|---|
| | ***M*** | **SD** | ***M*** | **SD** | | |
| CSHQ | 55.56 | 11.36 | 51.58 | 11.96 | $t(31) =$ 0.86 | 0.40 |
| Bedtime resistance | 9.56 | 2.79 | 9.83 | 3.25 | | |
| Sleep onset delay | 1.89 | 0.60 | 1.83 | 0.87 | | |
| Sleep duration | 5.11 | 2.42 | 4.96 | 2.39 | | |
| Sleep anxiety | 4.89 | 1.45 | 4.79 | 1.82 | | |
| Night wakings | 6.00 | 1.50 | 5.04 | 2.03 | | |
| Parasomnias | 11.33 | 2.78 | 9.58 | 3.36 | | |
| Sleep dis-breathing | 4.11 | 1.83 | 4.08 | 1.56 | | |
| Daytime sleepiness | 12.67 | 3.16 | 11.46 | 2.95 | | |
| SRS | 151.22 | 32.84 | 145.11 | 25.86 | $t(34) =$ 0.57 | 0.57 |
| Social awareness | 16.56 | 1.81 | 16.44 | 2.94 | | |
| Social cognition | 28.78 | 8.23 | 26.56 | 6.24 | | |
| Social communication | 50.33 | 12.58 | 47.74 | 8.88 | | |
| Social motivation | 25.56 | 5.36 | 24.93 | 5.95 | | |
| Autistic mannerisms | 30.00 | 7.78 | 29.44 | 7.54 | | |
| ADOS severity | 4.89 | 2.26 | 5.93 | 1.96 | $t(34) =$ 1.32 | 0.19 |
| CCC-2 | | | | | | |
| GCC | 30.75 | 6.99 | 36.15 | 16.53 | $t(15) =$ 0.63 | 0.54 |

**Table 3 | Study 1: chi-square analyses using Fisher's exact test for both groups of children for the five gastrointestinal complaints.**

| Gut complaint | SSRI cases *N* (%) | Control *N* (%) | *p* |
|---|---|---|---|
| Constipation | 4 (44.4) | 4 (14.8) | 0.09 |
| Diarrhea | 2 (22.2) | 3 (11.1) | 0.58 |
| Gastro reflux | 2 (22.2) | 3 (11.1) | 0.58 |
| Abdominal | 1 (11.1) | 2 (7.4) | 1.00 |
| Feeding | 5 (55.6) | 8 (29.6) | 0.24 |
| One or more complaints | 8 (88.9) | 13 (48.1) | 0.05 |

## DISCUSSION

This is the first study to examine the relationship between SSRI exposure and ASD phenotype. There were no differences between the cases and individually matched control participants in scores on the SRS, CCC-2, CSHQ, or ADOS-G severity. However, children with ASD whose mothers took SSRIs during pregnancy were significantly more likely to experience gastrointestinal complaints during childhood. Further examination of the relationship between gastrointestinal complaints and *in utero* SSRI exposure revealed that no individual complaint could significantly differentiate the two groups. While this does not support Oberlander et al. (2009) who found evidence for feeding disturbances in typically developing infants exposed to SSRIs *in utero*, it is possible that the small sample size contributed to the null findings for the less-frequent individual complaints.

The current study was limited by the absence of a control group of children whose mothers had affective disorders but who did not take SSRIs during pregnancy, and therefore we are unable to parse out whether the differences in the frequency of gut problems is related to mood disturbances or SSRI use. Rai et al. (2013) reported an association between maternal depression and an increased risk of offspring ASD. Although they found that this association was largely confined to antidepressant use in a subsample of mothers, future studies could build on the findings presented here and in Rai et al. (2013) by comparing the phenotype for children with ASD whose mothers report untreated depression during pregnancy with a matched ASD control group of children. The hypothesized association between ASD and gastrointestinal pathology is the subject of increasing amounts of research. Despite the numerous parental reports of gastrointestinal complaints among their children with ASD, studies have failed to find a significant difference in the prevalence of these complaints between children with ASD and control groups of children (e.g., Ibrahim et al., 2009). The current findings suggest that SSRI exposure *in utero* may be one potential candidate accounting for variance in the gut phenotype in children diagnosed with ASD.

## STUDY 2

### MATERIALS AND METHODS

#### *Participants*

The study involved using data for 16 participants from WAABR whose birth weight was $\leq 2500$ g (LBW). Each of these participants was individually matched on gender and chronological age at assessment (within 18 months) with two further control children with ASD ($n = 32$) whose birth weight was within the normal range (NBW; 2500–3999 g).

#### *Measures and procedure*

Within the case-history questionnaire, mothers were asked to report their child's birth weight. For the purposes of Study 2, data collected for each child using the SRS, CSHQ, ADOS severity, CCC-2, and gastrointestinal complaints questionnaire were analyzed.

#### *Statistical analyses*

Between-group differences in the quantitative scores of the SRS, the CSHQ, CCC-2, and ADOS severity scale were investigated with independent-samples *t*-tests. Responses to the gastrointestinal complaints questionnaire were analyzed using chi-square analyses with Fisher's exact test of significance.

### RESULTS

The LBW ($n = 16$) and the NBW ($n = 32$) groups did not significantly differ on maternal age at conception [$F(1, 45) = 0.07$, $p > 0.05$]. Mean gestational age was significantly lower for the LBW group [$F(1, 43) = 28.53$, $p < 0.05$, $M = 34.25$ weeks, SD = 4.55 weeks] relative to the NBW group ($M = 39.07$ weeks, SD = 1.33 weeks, $p < 0.05$). **Table 4** provides details of the offspring characteristics of the case group. Independent-samples *t*-tests (see **Table 5**) revealed that LBW children with ASD had significantly higher scores relative to the NBW group on the CSHQ for Total Sleep Disturbance and two of the subscales, namely, Sleep-Disordered Breathing and Daytime Sleepiness. There were no significant differences between the two groups on the SRS, CCC-2, or ADOS severity scores (**Table 5**).

Similarly, children with LBW ($n = 16$, 81%) did not experience significantly greater gastrointestinal issues compared to the NBW group ($n = 32$, 53%), $\chi^2(1)$, $p = 0.07$. To further investigate this association, chi-square analyses with Fisher's exact test were performed on the five individual complaints (**Table 6**). The individual complaints did not significantly differentiate between the groups.

### DISCUSSION

The second study examined the phenotype of children with ASD born with LBW relative to a group of children with ASD born with NBW. This study did not find any significant differences between the groups on the gastrointestinal complaints questionnaire, SRS, ADOS-G severity, or CCC-2. This is inconsistent with findings of greater socio-emotional issues and reduced language ability in LBW children compared to NBW children in the absence of an ASD diagnosis (Barre et al., 2011; Scott et al., 2012). The present study did find that children in the LBW group obtained higher mean scores on the CSHQ for total sleep disturbance, Daytime Sleepiness, and Sleep-Disordered Breathing relative to the NBW group. This supports the finding of sleep-disordered breathing in children with LBW without an ASD diagnosis (e.g., Paavonen et al., 2007). Interestingly, compared to norms from typically developing children ($M = 3.24$) and children with ASD ($M = 3.92$) (Hoffman et al., 2006), LBW children with ASD obtained larger mean scores for the Sleep-disordered Breathing subscale ($M = 4.31$).

Currently, there are no norms to describe performance of typically developing LBW children on the CSHQ. It would be interesting to compare sleep disturbance between LBW typically developing children and LBW children with ASD. Thus it may be useful to conduct a more comprehensive study of LBW and NBW children with and without ASD to look more closely at the significance of the present findings. Unsurprisingly, the LBW children

**Table 4 | Study 2: offspring characteristics of the LBW case group.**

| | Birth weight | Gestational age at birth | Age at assessment | ADOS module | ADOS severity score | CSHQ score | SRS score | GCC | Number of gut problems |
|---|---|---|---|---|---|---|---|---|---|
| Case 1 | 600 | 24 | 11; 1 | 3 | 4 | 45 | 152 | 42 | 1 |
| Case 2 | 895 | 27 | 7; 4 | 2 | 6 | 57 | 166 | 32 | 3 |
| Case 3 | 985 | 29 | 5; 6 | 1 | 3 | 39 | 133 | 38 | 1 |
| Case 4 | 1565 | 30 | 4; 7 | 1 | 6 | 42 | 172 | – | 0 |
| Case 5 | 1640 | 37 | 5; 2 | 1 | 6 | 65 | 169 | 40 | 2 |
| Case 6 | 1665 | 37 | 5; 2 | 2 | 4 | 56 | 143 | 49 | 1 |
| Case 7 | 1725 | 35 | 14; 4 | 3 | 4 | 63 | 171 | 28 | 3 |
| Case 8 | 1765 | 34 | 2; 8 | 1 | 7 | 47 | 107 | – | 1 |
| Case 9 | 2097 | 40 | 13; 1 | 1 | 6 | 54 | 183 | – | 2 |
| Case 10 | 2285 | 36 | 5; 2 | 2 | 8 | 54 | 158 | – | 4 |
| Case 11 | 2300 | 37 | 5; 11 | 1 | 7 | 51 | 163 | – | 0 |
| Case 12 | 2426 | 37 | 9; 7 | 1 | 8 | 69 | 200 | - | 1 |
| Case 13 | 2450 | 32 | 4; 7 | 2 | 6 | 52 | 159 | 56 | 1 |
| Case 14 | 2500 | 38 | 4; 3 | 2 | 7 | 59 | 166 | 39 | 0 |
| Case 15 | 2125 | 37 | 11; 3 | 3 | 6 | 66 | 191 | 7 | 1 |
| Case 16 | 2480 | 38 | 4; 6 | 2 | 5 | 66 | 156 | – | 2 |

**Table 5 | Study 2: descriptive statistics and independent-samples *t*-tests for CSHQ, SRS, CCC-2, and ADOS severity score.**

| | LBW | | NBW | | Statistics | *p* |
|---|---|---|---|---|---|---|
| | *M* | SD | *M* | SD | | |
| CSHQ | 55.31 | 9.08 | 47.84 | 8.84 | $t(45) = 2.72$ | 0.01 |
| Bedtime resistance | 9.81 | 2.76 | 8.13 | 2.38 | | |
| Sleep onset delay | 1.88 | 0.72 | 1.52 | 0.68 | | |
| Sleep duration | 5.69 | 2.39 | 4.55 | 1.93 | | |
| Sleep anxiety | 4.63 | 1.63 | 4.74 | 1.86 | | |
| Night wakings | 5.19 | 1.87 | 4.19 | 1.66 | | |
| Parasomnias | 10.44 | 2.71 | 9.97 | 2.56 | | |
| Sleep dis-breathing | 4.31 | 1.49 | 3.29 | 0.82 | $t(45) = 3.04$ | 0.00 |
| Daytime sleepiness | 13.38 | 3.36 | 11.19 | 2.56 | $t(45) = 2.48$ | 0.02 |
| SRS | | | | | $t(45) = 0.75$ | 0.46 |
| Social awareness | 17.31 | 2.73 | 17.97 | 2.33 | | |
| Social cognition | 30.25 | 3.64 | 28.77 | 5.81 | | |
| Social communication | 54.00 | 8.25 | 51.13 | 8.58 | | |
| Social motivation | 27.69 | 4.70 | 26.68 | 4.88 | | |
| Autistic mannerisms | 32.56 | 7.16 | 31.68 | 7.36 | | |
| ADOS severity | 5.81 | 1.47 | 6.56 | 1.98 | $t(46) = 1.34$ | 0.19 |
| CCC-2 | | | | | | |
| GCC | 36.78 | 13.92 | 28.88 | 13.67 | $t(31) = 1.47$ | 0.15 |

**Table 6 | Study 2: chi-square analyses using Fisher's exact test for both groups of children for the five gastrointestinal complaints.**

| Gut complaint | LBW *N* (%) | NBW *N* (%) | *p* |
|---|---|---|---|
| Constipation | 7 (43.8) | 9 (28.1) | 0.22 |
| Diarrhea | 2 (12.5) | 3 (9.4) | 0.55 |
| Gastro reflux | 5 (31.3) | 8 (25) | 0.45 |
| Abdominal | 0 (0) | 4 (12.5) | 0.19 |
| Feeding | 9 (56.3) | 13 (40.6) | 0.24 |
| One or more complaints | 8 (88.9) | 13 (48.1) | 0.05 |

had a significantly lower gestational age at birth than the NBW children, which raises the possibility that gestational age may be driving the findings and not birth weight. However, it is important to note that the study by Lampi et al. (2012), which informed our hypotheses, found that LBW was a better predictor of ASD diagnosis than was prematurity.

## GENERAL DISCUSSION

This present study used a "bottom-up" approach to seek understanding of the heterogeneity of ASD by investigating the behavioral phenotype associated with two suspected environmental risk factors, namely, *in utero* SSRI exposure and LBW. It was hypothesized that children with ASD who were exposed to one of these environmental risk factors would present with a more homogenous phenotype relative to individually matched control groups of children with ASD. There was some preliminary support for this hypothesis. While the children in the LBW and SSRI-exposed groups were no different to their respective control groups in quantitative and qualitative measures of the core symptomatology of autism, there was evidence that the two groups were distinct in the level of their non-core symptomatology such as sleep and gastrointestinal complaints, respectively.

The numbers of children with ASD in the "aetiological risk" subgroups are small, and therefore we urge caution in drawing conclusions from these data. Rather, we seek to highlight a different method for understanding the heterogeneity in the ASD phenotype. We believe that the preliminary findings of increased levels of non-core symptoms of ASD among certain "aetiological risk" subgroups, provides evidence that this "bottom-up" methodology may assist ASD research. Studies including larger samples of children with ASD will build on the research presented here, and provide the opportunity to validate our preliminary findings.

Whilst the present study did not find any differences in core ASD symptoms between LBW and SSRI-exposed children with their respective control groups, we know that each child who is given an ASD diagnosis presents with the triad of core symptoms irrespective of their severity. It is unlikely that a single environmental factor could be attributed to "causing" one of these core impairments. Rather we may expect that the interplay between the environment and a child's genetic profile contributes to the variable expression of autistic-related traits (Ratajczak, 2011). Therefore, it seems reasonable that environmental factors may be related to the expression of non-core ASD symptoms among these children rather than to any variance in core symptomatology.

Recently, Whitehouse and Stanley (2013) reaffirmed an emerging view in the literature with regard to reconceptualizing autism in moving away from a unitary disorder with one cause, and toward an "umbrella" for a collection of behavioral disorders resulting from a range of causal pathways. In their paper they describe how research in cerebral palsy may be analogous to research on autism. Initially cerebral palsy was thought to be a unitary disorder caused by anoxia secondary to trauma occurring during labor and delivery. However, the heterogeneity in symptoms and severity amongst children with cerebral palsy led researchers to hypothesize that there may be many causal pathways. Many other causes were identified for cerebral palsy following this reconceptualization, such as complications of preterm birth, infections, and inflammation *in utero* (McIntyre et al., 2012). For diagnosis, cerebral palsy is now considered an umbrella term covering a wide range of syndromes that arise secondary to a number of brain lesions/anomalies occurring early in development (Badawi et al., 2008).

A key question facing the field is whether the long-held view that autism is a unitary disorder with a single causal pathway is correct, or whether autism may best be conceptualized as an umbrella term for a collection of behavioral disorders resulting from a range of causal pathways, analogous to cerebral palsy. Current evidence suggests that the latter may be a more accurate representation. Heterogeneity in the distal causes of autism is now well-established. It is estimated that between 10 and 15% of individuals with autism have a known genetic aetiology, but the loci and nature of these lesions vary, from known syndromes to observable cytogenetic lesions and rare *de novo* mutations (e.g., copy number variations) (Abrahams and Geschwind, 2008). Among those with idiopathic autism, no single genetic risk variant has been found to occur in more than 1% of individuals (Abrahams and Geschwind, 2008). Similarly, environmental risk factors identified through epidemiological studies and examined in this study – *in utero* exposure to SSRIs (Croen et al., 2011) and LBW (Lampi et al., 2012) – differ considerably in the hypothesized biological paths to disorder, and as yet, no known environmental exposure is deterministic of autism.

Given that diagnosis is currently based on behavior, the question of whether autism is one or multiple disorders is ultimately a query over the proximal causes of these behaviors, and one perhaps best addressed in neuroscience. Neuroscientific studies may help determine whether (a) distal risk factors "fan in" on a common neurobiological substrate that has the capability of underpinning the considerable behavioral heterogeneity in autism (one disorder), or (b) the exact combination of distal risk factors determines the brain regions and functions that are affected, which in turn prescribe the behavioral profile of each individual (multiple disorders). A key research aim will be to investigate the correspondence (if any) between known distal (genetic and environmental) and proximal (neurobiological) risk factors for autistic behaviors, using increasingly sophisticated environmental monitoring, genetic sequencing, and neuroimaging techniques.

Using preliminary data in this study we have demonstrated how a "bottom-up" approach can be applied to current aetiological research. Grouping individuals using this method may facilitate the identification of subtypes of people with ASD. Elucidating the underlying nature of the disorder(s) is a crucial step toward achieving perhaps the "holy grail" of autism research: tailoring intervention to the biological and cognitive makeup of each individual (Whitehouse and Stanley, 2013).

## REFERENCES


1. Abrahams, B. S., and Geschwind, D. H. (2008). Advances in autism genetics: on the threshold of a new neurobi- ology. *Nat. Rev. Genet.* 9, 341–355. doi:10.1038/nrg2346
2. Alwan, S., Reefhuis, J., Rasmussen, S. A., Friedman, J. M., and National Birth Defects Prevention Study. (2011). Patterns of antidepressant medica- tion use among pregnant women in a United States population. *J. Clin. Pharmacol.* 51, 264–270. doi: 10.1177/0091270010373928
3. American Psychiatric Association. (1994). *Diagnostic and Statistical Manual for Mental Disorders*, 4th Edn. Washington DC: American Psychiatric Press.
4. Badawi, N., Watson, L., Petterson, B., Blair, E., Slee, J., Haan, E., et al. (2008). What constitutes cerebral palsy? *Dev. Med. Child Neurol.* 40, 520–527.
5. Barre, N., Morgan, A., Doyle, L. W., and Anderson, P. J. (2011). Lan- guage abilities in children who were very preterm and/or very low birth weight: a meta-analysis. *J. Pediatr.* 158, 766–774. doi:10.1016/j.jpeds. 2010.10.032
6. Bauman, M. L. (2010). Medical comor- bidities in autism: challenges to diag- nosis and treatment. *Neurotherapeu- tics* 7, 320–327. doi:10.1016/j. nurt. 2010.06.001
7. Bishop, D. V. M. (2003). *The Chil- dren's Communication Checklist-2*. London: Psychological Corporation.
8. Buie, T., Campbell, D. B., Fuchs, G. J., Furuta, G. T., Levy, J., Vande- water, J., et al. (2010). Evaluation, diagnosis, and treatment of gas- trointestinal disorders in individu-als with ASDs: a consensus report. *Pediatrics* 125, S1–S18. doi:10.1542/ peds.2009-1878C
9. Buxbaum, J. D., Silverman, J. M., Smith, C. J., Kilifarski, M., Reichert, J., Hollander, E., et al. (2001). Evi- dence for a susceptibility gene for autism on chromosome 2 and for genetic heterogeneity. *Am. J. Hum. Genet.* 68, 1514–1520. doi:10.1086/320588
10. Constantino, J., and Gruber, C. (2002). *The Social Responsiveness Scale*. Los Angeles: Western Psychological Ser- vices.
11. Croen, L. A., Grether, J. K., Yoshida, C. K., Odouli, R., and Hen- drick, V. (2011). Antidepressant use during pregnancy and childhood autism spectrum disorders. *Arch. Gen. Psychiatry* 73, doi:10.1001/ archgenpsychiatry.2011.73
12. de Kieviet, J. F., Piek, J. P., Aarnoudse- Moens, C. S., and Oosterlaan, J. (2009). Motor development in very preterm and very low-birth-weight children from birth to adolescence. *JAMA* 302, 2235–2242. doi:10.1001/ jama.2009.1708
13. Gardener, H., Spiehelman, D., and Buka, S. L. (2011). Perinatal and neonatal risk factors for autism: a comprehensive meta-analysis. *Pedi- atrics* 128, 344–355. doi:10.1542/ peds.2010-1036
14. Gaspar, P., Cases, O., and Maroteaux, L. (2003). The developmental role of serotonin: news from mouse mole- cular genetics. *Nat. Rev. Neurosci.* 4, 1002–1012. doi:10.1038/nrn1256
15. Geschwind, D. H., and Levitt, P. (2007). Autism spectrum disorders: developmental disconnection syn- dromes. *Curr. Opin. Neurobiol.* 17, 103–111. doi:10.1016/j.conb.2007. 01.009
16. Gotham, K., Pickles, A., and Lord, C. (2009). Standardizing ADOS scores for a measure of severity in autism spectrum disorders. *J. Autism Dev. Disord.* 39, 693–705. doi:10.1007/s10803-008-0674-3
17. Hoffman, C. D., Sweeney, D. P., Gilliam,J. E., and Lopez-Wagner, M. (2006). Sleep problems in children with autism and in typically developing children. *Focus Autism Other Dev. Disabl.* 21, 146–152. doi:10.1177/ 10883576060210030301
18. Ibrahim, S. H., Voigt, R. G., Katu-sic, S. K., Weaver, A. L., and Bar- baresi, W. J. (2009). Incidence of gastrointestinal symptoms in chil- dren with autism: a population- based study. *Pediatrics* 124, 680–686. doi:10.1542/peds.2008-2933
19. Indredavik, M. S., Vik, T., Heyerdahl, S., Kulseng, S., Fayers, P., and Brubakk, A. M. (2004). Psychiatric symptoms and disorders in adolescents with low birth weight. *Arch. Dis. Child. Fetal Neonatal Ed.* 89, F445–F450. doi:10.1136/adc.2003.038943
20. Jaspers, M., de Winter, A. F., Veenstra, R., Ormel, J., Verhulst, F. C., and Reijneveld, S. A. (2012). Preventive child health care findings on early childhood predict peer-group social status in early adolescence. *J. Ado- lesc. Health* 51, 637. doi:10.1016/j. jadohealth.2012.03.017
21. Lampi, K. M., Lehtonen, L., Tran, P. L., Suominen, A., Lehti, V., Banerjee, P. N., et al. (2012). Risk of autism spec- trum disorders in low birth weight and small for gestational age infants. *J. Pediatr.* 161, 830. doi:10.1016/j. jpeds.2012.04.058
22. Lord, C., Risi, S., Lambrecht, L., Cook, E. H. Jr., Leventhal, B. L., and DiLavore, P. C. (2000). The autism diagnostic observation schedule – generic: a standard measure of social and com- munication deficits associated with the spectrum of autism. *J. Autism Dev. Disord.* 30, 205–223. doi:10. 1023/A:1005592401947
23. McIntyre, S., Taitz, D., Keogh, J., Gold- smith, S., Badawi, N., and Blair, E. (2012). A systematic review of risk factors for cerebral palsy in children born at term in developed countries. *Dev. Med. Child Neurol.* doi:10.1111/ dmcn.12017
24. Oberlander, T. F., Gingrich, J. A., and Ansorge, M. S. (2009). Sustained neurobehavioral effects of expo- sure to SSRI antidepressants dur- ing development: molecular to clin- ical evidence. *Clin. Pharmacol. Ther.* 86, 672–677. doi:10.1038/clpt.2009. 201
25. Oberlander, T. F., Warburton, W., Misri, S., Aghajanian, J., and Hertzman, C. (2006). Neonatal outcomes after prenatal exposure to selective sero- tonin reuptake inhibitor antidepres- sants and maternal depression using population-based linked health data. *Arch. Gen. Psychiatry* 63, 898. doi:10. 1001/archpsyc.63.8.898
26. Owens, J. A., Spirito, A., and McGuinn, M. (2000). The Children's Sleep Habits Questionnaire (CSHQ): psy- chometric properties of a survey instrument for school-aged chil- dren. *Sleep* 23, 1043–1051.
27. Paavonen, E. J., Strang-Karlsson, S., Räikkönen, K., Heinonen, K., Pesonen, A. K., Hovi, P., et al. (2007). Very low birth weight increases risk for sleep-disordered breathing in young adulthood: the Helsinki Study of Very Low Birth Weight Adults. *Pedi- atrics* 120, 778–784. doi:10.1542/ peds.2007-0540

28. Pedersen, L. H., Henriksen, T. B., and Olsen, J. (2010). Fetal expo- sure to antidepressants and nor- mal milestone development at 6 and 19 months of age. *Pedi- atrics* 125, 600–608. doi:10.1542/peds.2008-3655
29. Rai, D., Lee, B. K., Dalman, C., Gold- ing, G., Lewis, G., and Magnusson, C. (2013). Parental depression, mater- nal antidepressant use during pregnancy, and risk of autism spectrum disorders: population based case- control study. *Br. Med. J.* 349, f2059. doi:10.1136/bmj.f2059
30. Ratajczak, H. V. (2011). Theoretical aspects of autism: causes – a review. *J. Immunotoxicol.* 8, 68–79. doi:10. 3109/1547691X.2010.545086
31. Richdale, A. L. (1999). Sleep problems in autism: prevalence, cause, and inter- vention. *Dev. Med. Child Neurol.* 41, 60–66.
32. Scott, M. N., Taylor, H. G., Fris- tad, M. A., Klein, N., Espy, K. A., Minich, N., et al. (2012). Behavior disorders in extremely preterm/extremely low birth weight children in kindergarten. *J. Dev. Behav. Pediatr.* 33, 202. doi:10.1097/DBP.0b013e3182475287
33. Shao, Y., Raiford, K. L., Wolpert, C. M., Cope, H. A., Ravan, S. A., Ashley-Koch, A. A., et al. (2002). Phenotypic homogeneity provides increased support for linkage on chromosome 2 in autistic disorder. *Am. J. Hum. Genet.* 70, 1058–1061. doi:10.1086/339765
34. Spittle, A. J., Boyd, R. N., Inder, T. E., and Doyle, L. W. (2009). Predicting motor development in very preterm infants at 12 months' corrected age: the role of qualitative mag- netic resonance imaging and gen- eral movements assessments. *Pedi- atrics* 123, 512–517. doi:10.1542/peds.2008-0590
35. Taylor, L., Maybery, M. T., and Whitehouse, A. J. O. (in press). Do the nature of communication impairments in autism spectrum disorders relate to the broader autism phenotype in parents? *J. Autism Dev. Disord.*
36. Weiss, L. A., Shen, Y., Korn, J. M., Ark- ing, D. E., Miller, D. T., Fossdal, R., et al. (2008). Association between microdeletion and microduplica- tion at 16p11. 2 and autism. *N. Engl. J. Med.* 358, 667–675. doi:10.1056/ NEJMoa075974
37. Whitehouse, A. J. O., and Stanley, F. J. (2013). Is autism one or multiple disorders? *Med. J. Aust.* 28, 302–303. doi:10.5694/mja12.11667
38. Zeskind, P. S., and Stephens, L. E. (2004). Maternal selective serotonin reuptake inhibitor use during preg- nancy and newborn neurobehav- ior. *Pediatrics* 113, 368–375. doi:10. 1542/peds.113.2.368

# 7

# On the application of quantitative EEG for characterizing autistic brain: a systematic review

**_Lucia Billeci[1]*, Federico Sicca[2], Koushik Maharatna[3], Fabio Apicella[2], Antonio Narzisi[2,4], Giulia Campatelli[2], Sara Calderoni[2], Giovanni Pioggia[1] and Filippo Muratori[2,4]_**

[1] *Institute of Clinical Physiology, National Council of Research (CNR), Pisa, Italy*
[2] *IRCCS Stella Maris Foundation, Pisa, Italy*
[3] *Electronics and Computer Science, Faculty of Physical and Applied Sciences, University of Southampton, Southampton, United Kingdom*
[4] *Department of Developmental Medicine, University of Pisa, Pisa, Italy*

***Edited by:***
*Andrew Whitehouse, Telethon Institute for Child Health Research, Australia; The University of Western Australia, Australia*

***Reviewed by:***
*Shozo Tobimatsu, Kyushu University, Japan*
*David Steven Cantor, Psychological Sciences Institute, USA*

****Correspondence:***
*Lucia Billeci, Institute of Clinical Physiology, National Council of Research (CNR), Via Moruzzi 1, Pisa 56124, Italy*
*e-mail: lucia.billeci@ifc.cnr.it*

Autism-Spectrum Disorders (ASD) are thought to be associated with abnormalities in neural connectivity at both the global and local levels. Quantitative electroencephalography (QEEG) is a non-invasive technique that allows a highly precise measurement of brain function and connectivity. This review encompasses the key findings of QEEG application in subjects with ASD, in order to assess the relevance of this approach in characterizing brain function and clustering phenotypes. QEEG studies evaluating both the spontaneous brain activity and brain signals under controlled experimental stimuli were examined. Despite conflicting results, literature analysis suggests that QEEG features are sensitive to modification in neuronal regulation dysfunction which characterize autistic brain. QEEG may therefore help in detecting regions of altered brain function and connectivity abnormalities, in linking behavior with brain activity, and subgrouping affected individuals within the wide heterogeneity of ASD. The use of advanced techniques for the increase of the specificity and of spatial localization could allow finding distinctive patterns of QEEG abnormalities in ASD subjects, paving the way for the development of tailored intervention strategies.

**Keywords: autism-spectrum disorder, quantitative electroencephalography, coherence, asymmetry, non-linear techniques**

## INTRODUCTION

Autism-Spectrum Disorders (ASD) are neurodevelopmental conditions characterized by deficits in social communication and interactions and by the presence of repetitive patterns of behavior, interests, and activities (American Psychiatric Association, 2013). These features appear in early childhood, tend to persist life-long, and often lead to poor outcome in adulthood. Recent epidemiological studies estimate the prevalence of ASD to be 1 in 88 children in the USA (Centers for Disease Control and Prevention, 2012). Despite an extensive research, there is still much debate about the morphological, functional, and neuropsychological characteristics of the "autistic" brain (Schipul et al., 2011; Calderoni et al., 2012; Muratori et al., 2012; Narzisi et al., 2012), and thus the neural basis of altered behaviors in ASD remains largely unclear. Several neuroimaging and neurophysiological techniques have been used in order to understand the correlation between brain functionality and autistic behavior. Among them, Quantitative Electroencephalography (QEEG) is currently receiving great interest and it is increasingly used in studies on neurodevelopmental disorders, especially the ASD. It has been found relevant for evaluating heterogeneity of behavioral disorders, treatment responses, and outcomes amongst other issues (Sheikhani et al., 2009). The ease and simplicity of the EEG procedure and its millisecond resolution of brain activity coupled with standardized analysis protocols provides an opportunity for elaborate analysis of brain functions and dysfunctions. Emerging EEG analysis techniques that involve interesting applications of signal analysis protocols have given us new and exciting measures of brain function.

According to the American Academy of Neurology, QEEG is defined as "... The mathematical processing of digitally recorded EEG in order to highlight specific waveform components, transform the EEG into a format or domain that elucidates relevant information, or associate numerical results ..." (Nuwer, 1997). Therefore, QEEG applies computerized mathematical algorithms to transform raw EEG data into a number of frequency bands of interest. Five wide frequency bands are usually studied, typically defined as delta (1.5–3.5 Hz), theta (3.5–7.5 Hz), alpha (7.5–12.5 Hz), beta (12.5–30 Hz), and gamma (30–70 Hz) (Steriade et al., 1990). In addition, although not included in the standard classification of EEG bands, a further alpha-like rhythm, called mu rhythm, has been extensively studied in the research on ASD (Oberman et al., 2005, 2008; Barnier et al., 2007), since mu suppression during the observation of biological actions is thought to reflect mirror neuron system (MNS) functioning and, in its turn, MNS dysfunction has been proposed to explain the core social deficits observed in ASD (Williams et al., 2001). EEG recordings may be performed at rest, in both closed and opened eye conditions, or while subjects perform specific tasks. Normative or control data are usually needed, in order to give meaning to the functional information obtained.

In this article we carried out a systematic survey of existing research to present an integrated view on how QEEG may help in characterizing autistic brain and present the future direction in the same domain. The paper is organized as follows: after briefly describing the fundamentals of QEEG in Section "QEEG Methods," we reviewed the recent works on application of QEEG in characterizing the autistic brain in Section "QEEG in Autism." Three particular directions have been surveyed in detail – QEEG during rest, during specific tasks, and how QEEG may be applied for classifying autistic subgroups. The paper is concluded and future research directions are discussed in Section "Discussion and Conclusion."

## QEEG METHODS

For QEEG analysis raw EEG data are collected non-invasively via a set of electrodes typically following an international 10/10 or 10/20 electrode placement configuration on the scalp. The collected data is then transformed into frequency domain using computerized algorithms (i.e., Fourier Transform, Welch Method) and scalp map of different frequency bands is obtained (Dumermuth and Molinari, 1987).

Absolute and relative spectral power (SP) consists in transforming the EEG traces from time domain into frequency domain providing information about the harmonic content of the signal. The spatial analysis provides information about the distribution of electrical activity in the brain and the interconnectivity among cortical regions measured through coherence and symmetry analyses.

EEG power spectrums are regulated by anatomically complex homeostatic systems in the various frequency bands. Brainstem, thalamic, and cortical processes involving large neuronal populations mediate this regulation, using all the major neurotransmitters. The spectrum is quite stable in healthy individuals because it is regulated by homeostatic regulation of neurotransmitters and can be abnormal in some psychiatric disorders due to the dysfunction of this regulation (Hughes and John, 1999).

Coherence measures the degree of coupling between signals generated by specific neuronal assemblies, which are located in proximity of the recorded electrodes. Coherently oscillating neuronal assemblies exhibit electrical activity with common spectral properties. When a coherent oscillation occurs these neural groups can effectively communicate, because their communication windows for input and for output are open at the same times (Fries, 2005). The coherence pattern is flexible, changing according during specific cognitive or motor task and allowing the maintenance of our cognitive flexibility (Fries, 2005).

Brain asymmetry is due to hemispheric specialization, so that the global neural activity is not the same in the two hemispheres. However it has been shown that hemispheric differences in competence are not fixed and structure-dependent but are subject by dynamic processes. According to this view asymmetry can vary inter- and intra-individually according to arousal or other factors (Hugdahl, 1996).

Taken together, frequency and spatial information, and their modification over consecutive EEG epochs, provides a quantitative view of the dynamic evolution of connectivity between different brain areas, getting therefore cues on the functional organization of underlying neuronal networks in static and dynamic settings.

Before applying a quantitative analysis, a pre-processing step needs to be performed. First of all the signal is segmented in epochs of the same length and visually inspected, in order to reject those epochs with evident artifacts. Any remaining artifact is then removed by using high-pass, low-pass, and notch filters.

In most cases, frequencies below 0.5 Hz, due to movement artifacts, and higher than 60 Hz, afflicted by muscle artifacts, are filtered out, although this latter operation impairs the possibility to analyze gamma band. Notch filter allows removing artifacts caused by electrical power lines (50 or 60 Hz according to the country).

After preprocessing, spectral analysis can be applied to the signal. The Power Spectral Density (PSD) can be calculated by transforming the time domain signal to the frequency domain, using different techniques such as the Fast Fourier Transform (FFT) or the Welch method (Welch, 1967). From PSD the absolute power of the signal can be computed. However, since the absolute power measures may vary significantly in humans, it is more useful to calculate the power ratios among bands, which show less variability among subjects and are less affected by artifacts. Power ratios are expressed as a percentage, and are obtained by dividing the absolute power of a specific band by the total absolute power of the spectrum. Power ratio can be calculated also between only two bands (e.g., $\alpha/\theta$) or between band sets (e.g., $\alpha + \beta/\theta + \delta$).

Classical spectral analysis techniques, like the FFT, are very useful when analyzing stationary signals. Nevertheless, when dealing with non-stationary signals, as is the case of EEG, they show the big disadvantage of not preserving information on the temporal evolution/localization of the frequency components. This occurs because changes in frequency content, at a given time instant, cause changes to all the Fourier coefficients and therefore it is not possible to localize at which times these frequencies occur. In QEEG analysis, temporal information is important to detect and monitor changes in brain activity at different time-scales following a specific event. For this reason in some studies other techniques as the Short-Time Fourier Transform (STFT) have been used (Sheikhani et al., 2007). STFT can be interpreted as the Fourier transform of the signal observed through a sliding time window of finite duration. The STFT allows constructing the signal spectrogram, which is an image representation of the magnitude of Fourier coefficients within that time window and therefore describes the frequency contents of the signal in the neighborhood (bounded by the time window) of the selected time instant (Walter, 1963).

Spectral analysis is often associated with spatial analysis that allows characterizing relationships between activities of different brain areas. The spatial information may be mainly derived from QEEG data through symmetry and coherence analysis. The symmetry between the two hemispheres can be computed using the Brain Symmetry Index (BSI) (John et al., 1977; Van Putten et al., 2004). The BSI captures a particular asymmetry in SP between hemispheres, and is normalized between 0 (perfect symmetry) and 1 (maximal asymmetry). Asymmetry is defined by the difference on the EEG absolute power between homologous contralateral electrodes and it is calculated as:

$$BSI = (LH - RH) / (LH + RH)$$

where LH is the absolute power at one electrode in the left hemisphere and RH at its homologous electrode in the right hemisphere. On the other hand, the coherence function is a measure of the degree of association or coupling of frequency spectra between two EEG signals simultaneously recorded from different scalp locations per frequency band. Mathematically coherence is defined as the squared cross-correlation between two waveforms within a specific frequency band that has been normalized for amplitude (Otnes and Enochson, 1972). It is assumed to be an index of functional coupling between different brain areas. In neuroscience the coherence measure is generally distinct from synchrony, which refers to signals oscillating at the same frequency with identical phases (Singer, 1999).

Finally, another interesting QEEG index, recently introduced by Pop-Jordanova and Pop-Jordanov (2005), is the "brain rate." This is calculated as the EEG spectrum weighted frequency with the following formula:

$$f_b \sum {}_i P_i = \sum {}_i f_i V_i / V \text{ with } V = \sum {}_i V_i$$

where the index corresponds to the frequency band ($i = 1$ for delta, $i = 2$, for theta, etc.), $f_i$ is the mean frequency of the corresponding band and $V_i$ is the mean amplitude of the electric potential associated to each band. The brain rate can thus be defined as an integral state attribute correlated to brain electric, mental, and metabolic activity (Pop-Jordanova and Pop-Jordanov, 2005).

The techniques described above are all linear methods and are the most commonly applied in the analysis of QEEG data. Given the non-linear nature of EEG, however, non-linear methods could be more suitable for the analysis of this signal. Although less conventional, a set of non-linear techniques have been sometimes used in QEEG analysis, allowing to obtain new information not detectable through linear methods, such as non-linear interactions and the complexity and stability of underlying brain sites. Some of these techniques, like higher-order statistical analysis, complexity analysis, and the phase synchronization analysis, have been applied to the study of QEEG signals in ASD.

Finally, the analysis of microstates represents another promising technique although not yet used in ASD research.

Among the higher-order statistical analysis techniques, the bispectral analysis is an advanced technique that quantifies quadratic non-linearities amongst the components of the EEG signal. In particular it measures the phase relationships between different frequency components and on that basis quantifies the degree of dependence amongst these components. Bispectrum is computed by the Fourier transform of the third order cumulant (a statistical measure of correlation). As the bi-spectrum depends not only on phase coupling but also on the power, it can be normalized in order to make it sensitive only to changes in phase coupling. This normalized bispectrum is then termed as bicoherence (for a detailed description of the mathematical bases of the bispectral analysis, see Sigl and Chamoun, 1994).

Another interesting property of EEG signal is complexity, which reflects random fluctuations over multiple time scales in the dynamics of neural networks, thus providing insights about neural connectivity. The most interesting methods employed for computing complexity of EEG signals are entropy and fractality.

Entropy is a physical measure related to the amount of disorder in a system, and it describes the irregularity or unpredictability characteristics of a signal.

Since regularity is not necessarily correlated with complexity, the quantification of complexity of EEG signals can be computed using the multiscale entropy (MSE), which measures the entropy across multiple time scales (Costa et al., 2002). This method is based on the principle that biological systems are modulated by multiple mechanisms, which interact over multiple temporal scales generating complex data. Another quantity that identifies the degree of complexity of a system is the fractal dimension. This is a non-integer number describing the self-similarity of a system: the whole can be fitted by parts of it by shifting and stretching (Mandelbrot, 1977).

The phase synchrony analysis may be useful when needed to analyze the phase relationships between EEG signals at different electrodes, independently of their amplitude (Lachaux et al., 1999). The basic idea of this technique is to generate an analytic signal from which a phase, and a phase difference between two signals, can be defined. On the basis of this phase difference a phase synchronization index can be computed, which will be zero if the signals under investigation are not synchronized and will be one for a constant phase difference.

Finally, the technique of functional microstates allows studying brief transactions occurring in the brain in the time range of milliseconds. Microstates are defined as time periods, of 80–120 ms, during which the potential distribution over the scalp shows stable topographical configuration after which a rapid transition to another stable configuration (another microstate) occurs (Lehmann et al., 1987). Microstates could be considered as the basic blocks of human information processing (Lehmann, 1990), reflecting the interactions between environmental information and the subject's previous knowledge and internal state. Microstates can only repeat several times within a period so that a cluster approach can be adopted to identify different classes of electrical states composing the EEG signal. Several statistical measures can then be extracted and related to the different experimental conditions and microstate class, such as mean microstate duration, mean number of microstates per second, or the percentage time covered by each state (Koenig et al., 2002) (for a detailed mathematical description of the non-linear analysis techniques described above, see Tong and Thakor, 2009).

Quantitative electroencephalography data are usually obtained using commercial or free software that are able to extract the most common features of EEG signals. The use of advanced techniques such as Independent Component Analysis (ICA), and neuroimaging techniques such as Low Resolution Electromagnetic Tomography (LORETA) (Pascual-Marqui et al., 1994) are used to map the actual sources of the cortical rhythms. These advanced techniques may, therefore, represent a promising approach to understand the dynamics and functions of the brain in a number of neurological diseases, including ASD.

## QEEG IN AUTISM

Quantitative electroencephalography has been adopted in several studies for the assessment of ASD with the aim of finding out quantitative indices characterizing brain functions. An understanding of how this evolving technique can aid future research in ASD is very important.

Several studies highlight QEEG capacity to classify subjects with ASD from controls, or different subgroups of ASD. Moreover, QEEG has been also applied as a tool for therapeutic intervention through a neurofeedback approach, although its use in ASD is still poorly reported in literature. A description of neurofeedback methods and of its application in ASD, however, is beyond the aim of this article, and readers may refer to dedicated original researches and reviews (Pineda et al., 2008; Kouijzer et al., 2009, 2010; Coben et al., 2010).

In the following subsections, we will review the main applications of QEEG in three different scenarios: (1) closed or open-eyes rest condition; (2) subjects performing specific tasks; (3) subtyping of ASD through QEEG information. All the studies reviewed here are summarized in **Table 1**. This research provides evidence for the utility of QEEG in extracting objective measures that can characterize brain activity in different conditions.

### QEEG DURING REST

Quantitative electroencephalography during rest conditions represents one of the most used applications of this technique in the field of autism research. Neural oscillations reflect the synchronous firing of large populations of neurons mediated by excitatory/inhibitory interactions and can be registered on the scalp. QEEG at rest may therefore inform, *in vivo*, on the balance between excitatory and inhibitory activities, which in turn could affect the cognitive and social functioning in ASD (Rubenstein and Merzenich, 2003; Bourgeron, 2009). The observation of spontaneous brain activity also allows characterizing different patterns in functional connectivity that might specify functionally relevant brain networks.

Finally, by studying power fluctuations of different bands it is possible to notice deviations from normal patterns that reflect the organization of the underlying system.

One of the first studies on QEEG in autism (Cantor et al., 1986) tried to examine if QEEG analysis could be used to differentiate low-functioning children with ASD from subjects with mental retardation without ASD, age-matched subjects with typical development and toddlers with typical development. Data were acquired during open-eyes rest condition and spectral as well as spatial analysis on the acquired data were performed.

Differences in PSD, coherence, and symmetry were found. In particular, children with ASD showed a significantly greater percentage delta and less alpha activity, higher degree of coherence between and within hemispheres, especially in delta and alpha band, and less amplitude asymmetry in every band. Interestingly, while ASD subjects significantly differentiate from age-matched controls and mentally retarded subjects, the pattern of activation was similar to the one obtained in typical toddlers, suggesting a maturational lag in cerebral functioning of subjects with ASD.

Chan et al. (2007) also studied PSD in children with ASD and in neurotypical controls by recording EEG in an open-eyes condition. In this study both low and high-functioning ASD children were included in the sample set. In consistence with the previous study, the ASD group showed significantly higher absolute delta and lower relative alpha. The authors attempted to localize the abnormalities in EEG signal, and found similar results at each channel suggesting that QEEG characteristics were not regionally specific, but were observed across all the cortex of children with ASD. This conclusion is also consistent with neuroimaging data indicating widespread brain abnormalities in ASD that include increased total intracranial volume (Courchesne et al., 2007), abnormal gray matter (Waiter et al., 2004; McAlonan et al., 2005), altered white matter (Barnea-Goraly et al., 2004; Billeci et al., 2012), and disrupted anatomical functioning (Belmonte and Yurgelun-Todd, 2003; Hubl et al., 2003).

Abnormalities in symmetry in ASD children were also found in the study of Stroganova et al. (2007). They acquired EEGs in open-eyes condition, in a large group of high-functioning children with ASD and in age-matched controls. PSD was calculated for delta, theta, and alpha frequency bands and BSI was computed. Atypical EEG asymmetry in children with ASD was found. In particular: (1) a broad-band leftward EEG asymmetry at the temporal and some adjacent regions that was absent in controls and (2) a symmetrically distributed mu rhythm in ASD across central sites of the left and right hemisphere, whereas in controls it was lateralized to the left. The first result could reflect structural asymmetries in the brain, although research on this issue is still inconclusive. For example, a decrease of deep white matter predominantly in the right hemisphere of ASD individuals has been highlighted in two recent studies (Boddaert et al., 2004; Waiter et al., 2005). However, further research is needed to adequately correlate structural and neurophysiologic data in ASD. Concerning the second result, the asymmetric distribution of mu is known to be linked to motor function and could mean that there is a greater down regulation of sensorimotor areas of the left hemisphere, involved in the control of the dominant right hand. On the contrary, the symmetrical distribution may be linked to a decreased control of motor function of the right hand.

Coben et al. (2008) demonstrated how the closed-eyes condition might cause changes in PSD and in coherence. In this study EEG was acquired on high-functioning children with ASD and controls and absolute and relative PSD for each band were computed. Moreover, intra-hemispheric and inter-hemispheric coherences were calculated. Opposite results in delta and beta band spectra with respect to the open-eyes condition were detected: in fact, a reduction in absolute and relative delta and an increase in absolute beta and relative theta distinguished ASD subjects from controls.

Also the coherence analysis revealed opposite results with respect to the open-eyes condition. In this study ASD subjects showed reduced intra-hemispheric as well as inter-hemispheric coherence in particular in the delta and theta band. Moreover they displayed lower inter-hemispheric coherences in the delta and theta bands in frontal regions, lower coherences in the delta, theta, and alpha bands in temporal regions and lower coherences in delta, theta, and beta bands in the central/parietal/occipital regions. The large amount of significant differences in coherence values in several brain regions, suggests altered connectivity in ASD (Belmonte et al., 2004).

Murias et al. (2007) have studied the eye-closed condition by using a high-density EEG system (124 electrodes) in adults with ASD. Indeed, a high-density approach, by employing more number of electrodes, allows increasing spatial resolution of the EEG potentials and improving signal source localization. A spectral analysis as well as a coherence analysis was performed. In

**Table 1 | Summary of QEEG studies in autism.**

| Study | Design | Participants | Measures | Results in ASD |
|---|---|---|---|---|
| **QEEG DURING REST** | | | | |
| Cantor et al. (1986) | 10/20 System, open eyes | *n* = 11 ASD (age: 4–12 years, IQ = 37.45 ± 11.4)<br>*n* = 88 TD (age: 5–15 years, IQ = 113.35 ± 9.5)<br>*n* = 18 Intellectually disabled (age: 5–15 years, IQ = 71.1 ± 12.6)<br>*n* = 13 TD toddlers (age: 16 months to 5 years, IQ = 121.0 ± 25.4) | PSD, coherence, symmetry | Higher percent delta and less alpha; higher coherence between and within, hemispheres; less asymmetry |
| Chan et al. (2007) | 10/20 System, open eyes | *n* = 66 ASD (age: 5–18 years, TONI = 83.36 ± 21.61)<br>*n* = 90 TD (age: 6–12 years, TONI = 111.42 ± 16.16) | PSD | Higher absolute delta and lower relative alpha; same results for all channel |
| Stroganova et al. (2007) | 32 or 24 Electrode system, open eyes | *n* = 40 ASD (age: 3–8 years, IQ = 111 ± 8.29)<br>*n* = 40 TD (age: 3–8 years) | PSD, asymmetry | Higher prefrontal delta; leftward asymmetry at the temporal regions; symmetric mu rhythm in ASD across central sites |
| Coben et al. (2008) | 10/20 System, closed eyes | *n* = 40 ASD (age: 6–11 years, IQ = 93 ± 16.8)<br>*n* = 40 TD (age: 6–11 years, IQ = 98 ± 15.4) | PSD, coherence | Less absolute (left frontal and posterior region) and relative delta (left frontal and vertex regions) and higher absolute beta (midline regions) and relative theta (right posterior regions); less delta and theta intrahemispheric coherence; less inter-hemispheric coherences in delta and theta in frontal regions in delta, theta, and alpha in temporal regions and in delta, theta, and beta bands central/parietal/occipital regions |
| Murias et al. (2007) | 128 Channels, closed eyes | *n* = 18 ASD (age: 18–38 years, IQ = 107.33 ± 13.96)<br>*n* = 18 TD (age: 18–38 years, IQ = 106.11 ± 13.56) | PSD, coherence | Higher relative theta in primarily frontal and prefrontal regions, less relative alpha in primarily frontal/prefrontal and occipital/parietal regions and higher relative beta in occipital/parietal regions; higher coherence in theta and less coherence in alpha |
| Pop-Jordanova et al. (2010) | 10/20 System, open eyes and closed eyes | *n* = 9 ASD (age: 3–6 years) database of TD | PSD, brain rate | Higher delta/theta; higher beta in open eyes than in closed eyes; reduction of brain rate in all regions |
| Mathewson et al. (2012) | 128 Channels, open eyes and closed eyes | *n* = 15 ASD (age: 19–52 years, IQ = 100.9 ± 18.6)<br>*n* = 18 TD (age: 18–38 years, IQ = 107.1 ± 11.9) | PSD, coherence, correlation with AQ | Higher alpha in eye opens; less alpha suppression in 01; no difference in coherence; negative correlation between alpha and preferential attention to detail in posterior and frontal regions both in eye open and eye closed; negative correlation between attention to details and coherence in eye opened in the right centro-parietal region and in eye closed in the parieto-occipital regions; negative correlation between alpha coherence in eye-open and social functioning in the right fronto-central region; positive correlation between theta coherence in the left centro-parietal region in eye-closed and social functioning |
| Sheikhani et al. (2007) | 10/20 System, closed eyes | *n* = 10 ASD (age: 9.3 ± 1.8 years)<br>*n* = 7 TD (age: 9.2 ± 0.7 years) | PSD (STFT and STFT-BW) and bispectrum | No differences in STFT or bispectrum; significant differences in STFT-BW over Fp1, F3, F7, T3, T5, and O1 |

*(Continued)*

**Table 1 | Continued**

| Study | Design | Participants | Measures | Results in ASD |
|---|---|---|---|---|
| **QEEG DURING REST** | | | | |
| Ahmadlou et al. (2010) | 10/20 System, closed eyes | $n=9$ ASD (age: 6–13 years) $n=6$ TD (age: 7–13 years) | Fractal dimension (HFD and KFD) | Significant difference in HFD in gamma, beta, and alpha and in KFD in gamma, beta, and delta |
| Thatcher et al. (2009) | 10/20 System, open eyes | $n=54$ ASD (age: 2.6–10.74 years) $n=241$ TD (age: 2.2–11 years) | Phase synchronization analysis | Shorter phase shift durations in ASD in the alpha-1 frequency band (8–10 Hz); longer phase lock durations in ASD in the alpha-2 frequency band (10–12 Hz) and; differences in short and long inter-electrode pairs |
| Bosl et al. (2011) | 64 Channels, open eyes | $n=46$ HRA (age: 6–24 months) $n=33$ TD (age: 6–24 months) | Multiscale Entropy (MSE) analysis | Reduced MSE in HRA subjects especially in 9–24 months range; discrimination between HRA and controls at 9 months with 80% of accuracy |
| Duffy and Als (2012) | 32 Channels, open eyes | $n=463$ ASD (age: 1–18 years) $n=571$ TD (age: 1–18 years) | Coherence | High classification success between ASD and TD groups. decrease in short-distance coherence and increase in long-distance coherence in ASD group within a wide spectral range |
| **QEEG DURING SPECIFIC TASKS** | | | | |
| Oberman et al. (2005) | 10/20 System, tasks: (1) moving their own hand, (2) watching a video of a moving hand, (3) watching a video of two bouncing balls (non-biological motion), and (4) watching visual white noise | $n=10$ ASD (age: 9–14 years, IQ > 80) $n=10$ TD (age: 9–14 years) | PSD mu | Decreased mu only during the self-initiated hand movement |
| Orekhova et al. (2007) | 10/20 System, sustained visual attention | $n=40$ ASD (age: 3–8 years) $n=40$ TD (age: 3–8 years) | PSD in high frequency bands | Higher power especially in gamma1 in midline, central, and parietal regions |
| Sheikhani et al. (2009) | 10/20 System, tasks: (1) eye-closed condition, (2) eye-opened condition, (3–5) looking at three samples of Kanizsa shapes, (6) looking at mother's picture upright and (7) inverted, (8) looking at stranger's picture upright, and (9) inverted in frequency bands | $n=15$ ASD (age: 6–11 years, IQ > 85) $n=11$ TD (age: 6–11 years, IQ > 85) | PSD, spectrogram | Lower spectrogram criteria at Fp1, Fp2, and T6 in gamma and higher spectral power at FP1 and FP2 in open-eyes condition; difference in alpha at T3, F7, and C3 in looking at the inverted mother's picture; difference in alpha and beta at F7, F4, F8, C4, Pz. In looking at a stranger's picture inverted |
| Sheikhani et al. (2012) | 128 Channels (reduced to 10/20), sustained visual attention | $n=17$ ASD (age: 6–11 years, IQ > 85) $n=11$ (age: 6–11 years, IQ > 85) | Spectrogram criteria | Lower spectrogram criteria in alpha, beta, and gamma especially in temporal and frontal regions in left hemisphere |
| Chan et al. (2011a) | Object recognition (OR) task | $n=21$ ASD (age: 5–14 years, TONI = 101.86 ± 16.09) $n=21$ TD (age: 5–14 years, TONI = 106 ± 14.59) | Coherence in theta | Elevated fronto-posterior coherences in left hemisphere; higher coherence in the left than in the right hemisphere; negative correlations between memory performance and the inter-hemispheric coherence |

*(Continued)*

**Table 1 | Continued**

| Study | Design | Participants | Measures | Results in ASD |
|---|---|---|---|---|
| **QEEG DURING SPECIFIC TASKS** | | | | |
| Chan et al. (2011b) | 10/20 System, Go/No-Go task | $n = 20$ ASD (age: 7–14 years) $n = 20$ TD (age: 7–14 years) | PSD in theta source localization with LORETA | In the "Go" condition theta decreased in the anterior cingulate cortex (ACC), in the "No-Go" condition in the ACC and in the precuneus |
| Lushchekina et al. (2012) | 10/20 System, tasks: (1) eye-closed condition, (2) counting during eye closed | $n = 27$ ASD (age: 5–7 years) $n = 19$ TD (age: 5–7 years) | PSD, coherence | Higher gamma in baseline condition; right-sided predominance of spectral power in alpha both at rest and during counting |
| Catarino et al. (2011) | 10/20 System, detection tasks: (1) faces, (2) chairs | $n = 15$ ASD (age: 23.79–42.34 years, IQ $= 119 \pm 13$) $n = 15$ TD (age: 21.50–37.77 years, mean IQ $= 119 \pm 14$) | MSE, PSD | Reduced MSE in ASD especially in parietal regions; higher MSE in response to faces in both groups; no differences in PSD |
| **QEEG FOR THE IDENTIFICATION OF AUTISTIC SUBGROUPS** | | | | |
| Dawson et al. (1995) | 10/20 System, open eyes | $n = 28$ ASD (age: 5–19 years, IQ $= 119 \pm 13$) $n = 28$ Chronological-age-matched TD (age: 5–19 years) $n = 24$ Language-age-matched TD (age: 2–7 years) | PSD | Reduced delta and theta in the passive group in all brain regions and reduced alpha in the frontal regions |
| Sutton et al. (2005) | 10/20 System, open eyes and closed eyes | $n = 23$ ASD (age: 9–14 years, IQ: $110.13 \pm 21.21$) $n = 20$ TD (age: 9–14 years IQ: $116.80 \pm 11.69$) | PSD | Higher alpha in anterior, central, and posterior cortical regions; more left-sided mid-frontal and central regions; subgroups with greater left-sided mid-frontal activity had greater social anxiety, greater general anxiety, greater social stress, and less satisfaction with interpersonal relations |

*ASD, autism-spectrum disorder; TD, typical developing; HRA, "high risk" of autism.*

this experiment, ASD group showed an elevated relative theta and reduced relative alpha power primarily in the frontal and prefrontal regions. In addition, a reduced relative alpha and increased relative beta power was observed in the occipital/parietal regions, with bilateral central regions approaching significance. Significant differences in coherence analysis between the two groups were also observed in theta and alpha bands. The results of this study are in agreement with the theory of local overconnectivity and global under-connectivity in ASD (Courchesne and Pierce, 2005). In fact EEG oscillations in the theta range reflect locally dominant neocortical processes, whereas alpha oscillations represent more globally dominant phenomena that are more dependent on cortico-cortical and callosal fibers (Nunez, 2006).

In a more recent study (Pop-Jordanova et al., 2010) both the open-eyes and the closed-eyes conditions were investigated. In this study EEG data obtained on ASD children were compared to data belonging to neurotypical subjects contained in a database. The authors found an increase delta/theta power in ASD in both conditions. Moreover they noticed that in the open-eyes condition there was an increase in beta power with respect to the closed-eyes condition in both groups. These results were only partially in agreement with the previous studies. The authors also have introduced here a new index, namely the spectrum weighted frequency (brain rate), as an indicator of general mental arousal in these subjects. They found a reduction of brain rate in all regions in autistic children compared to the controls, indicating a lower general mental arousal in ASD.

Also in the most recent study by Mathewson et al. (2012) where QEEG technique was applied in the study of high-functioning adults with ASD, both the open-eyes and the closed-eyes condition were analyzed. The novelty of this study is that the features extracted by QEEG analysis related to power and frequency, were correlated to behavioral performances measured with the Autism-Spectrum Quotient (AQ; Baron-Cohen et al., 2001). In particular in this study the scores obtained with this instrument were clustered in two groups: preferential attention to detail and deficits in social interaction. EEG data were continuously recorded by means of a 128-channel system during a resting baseline condition in which eyes-open and eyes-closed conditions alternated. The absolute PSD was calculated for each band separately at each single electrode, however, in order to reduce the computational complexity, power was averaged within four quadrants: left frontal, right frontal, left posterior, and right posterior. The main focus of the study was alpha band because it is thought to indirectly reflect the level of cortical excitability in the regions where it is found. It means that higher resting alpha power might denote cortical deactivation or inactivity (Rihs et al., 2007; Sauseng et al., 2009). Power analysis showed that in the eye-open condition the alpha power was higher in ASD group than in the controls in all regions, while in eye-closed condition no difference was found.

Regarding the other bands, beta, gamma, and theta powers were increased in ASD group. An analysis of the amount of alpha suppression in occipital regions was also performed. The results indicated that at O1 a significantly greater alpha suppression was present in control subjects than in ASD group. This difference in suppression is related to the fact that alpha suppression is associated with optimal neurological functioning that is impaired in ASD. In contradiction with the previous studies, no differences in coherence between the two groups were found.

While correlating the SP with the AQ score it was found that in ASD participants, alpha power was inversely correlated with preferential attention to detail in posterior and frontal regions both in eye-open and eye-closed condition, while no correlation was found in controls. From the coherence analysis, a positive correlation between alpha coherence in eye-closed condition and attention to details was found in the right centro-parietal region in controls, while in ASD group, attention to details was inversely correlated with coherence in eye-opened condition in the right centro-parietal region and in eye-closed condition in the parieto-occipital regions. Moreover in both groups alpha coherence in eye open was inversely correlated to social functioning in the right fronto-central region. For the other bands, increased theta coherence in the left centro-parietal region in eye-closed condition appeared to be related to poorer social functioning in ASD, while increased gamma coherence in the same region and condition appeared to be beneficial to social functioning in controls. The negative correlation between attention to detail and alpha power and coherence in parietal regions in ASD is consistent with the theory of altered parietal functioning in ASD. An explanation of this result could be that in ASD the mapping of attention focus may be exaggerated at the expense of attention prioritizing. Moreover the negative correlation between alpha coherence and attention to details is consistent with the fact that the brain is more receptive to incoming sensory information when neural activity is desynchronized than when it is engaged in performing a specific task.

In a few articles non-linear analysis techniques have been used to study particular properties of EEG signals. In the study of Sheikhani et al. (2007) the authors computed three types of transforms at each electrode for discriminating between ASD and controls: the STFT, the STFT-BW calculated considering the bandwidth of all the spectra as window, and the bispectrum. Data were acquired using a standard 10/20 system during eye-closed condition. The authors did not find any difference in STFT or bispectrum but they found significant differences in STFT-BW over Fp1, F3, F7, T3, T5, and O1. Since the sample of ASD and controls is very small in this study, it is difficult to draw any conclusions from the results. The bispectral analysis needs to be tested in a larger sample of subjects to see if it gives significant results and relevant information on brain activation not evidenced by the most common power spectral analysis.

In another study by Ahmadlou et al. (2010), the complexity of EEG signals in ASD and controls was investigated by using fractal dimension analysis. Data were acquired during eye-closed condition and a wavelet analysis approach aimed at decomposing the signal into the five standard EEG bands was performed. For each band and electrode the fractal dimension was computed using two methods: Higuchi's Fractal Dimension (HFD) (Higuchi, 1988) and Katz's Fractal Dimension (KFD) (Katz, 1988). Significant differences between ASD and controls in HFD were detected, especially in gamma, beta, and alpha and in KFD in gamma, beta, and delta. Differences were most significant for KFD, meaning that this method is a more effective tool for discriminating between ASD and controls. This study shows how fractal dimension, providing additional information about EEG signals, could be an important instrument for the identification of brain abnormalities in ASD.

Thatcher et al. (2009) applied phase analysis for the investigation of phase-reset mechanism in high-functioning children with ASD. Phase reset (PR) is defined as the succession of phase shifts (e.g., 30–80 ms) and phase locking (e.g., 100–800 ms) of clusters and sub-clusters of neurons. This process is regulated by GABA mediated thalamo-cortical circuits that is believed to be compromised in ASD (Orekhova et al., 2008). EEG data were acquired on ASD subjects and age-matched controls during eyes-open resting condition. Complex demodulation was used to compute phase differences between the signals from each pairs of electrodes. Each PR was composed by a phase shift of a finite duration (SD) and a phase locking of an extended duration (LD). SD is the interval of time from the onset of phase shift to its termination, defined by a peak in the first derivative and a peak in the second derivative or inflection on the declining side of the time series of first derivatives. LD was defined as the interval of time between the end of a significant phase shift and the beginning of a subsequent significant phase shift. Both in ASD and in controls SD, LD, and PR were computed for each pairs of electrodes in each EEG band. The comparison between the two groups showed that SD was significantly shorter in ASD than in the controls in particular in alpha-1 frequency band (8–10 Hz). On the contrary, LD was consistently longer in ASD especially in alpha-2 frequency band (10–12 Hz). The results of this study demonstrate an altered mechanism of neural synchronization in ASD, and suggest that increased phase lock periods, that represent the time in which clusters of neurons are synchronized, could reflect less cognitive flexibility and less availability of neural resources. However, higher statistically significant differences were found at short rather than long interelectrode distances, suggesting that the defect in the mechanism of phase locking is particularly present in local neural.

In a recent study by Bosl et al. (2011) a non-linear analysis based on the calculation of MSE was performed. The analysis was applied to EEG signals acquired on a group of infants at "High Risk" because siblings of children with ASD. Data were obtained during resting state eyes open using a 64 channels EEG system. For a more accurate comparison, the sample set was divided in subgroups according to age: 6, 9, 12, 18, and 24 months. The authors found a decrease of MSE in HRA over all EEG channels across all scales and ages. When considering the trajectories of mean MSE with age, it was shown that while the pattern of complexity was almost the same in the two groups in the age range 6–9 months, there was a strong decrease in EEG complexity in the HRA groups in the age range 9–12 months. Several classification approaches were then applied to distinguish between the groups of controls and HRA subjects according to the EEG complexity features. The machine learning approach represents an accurate classification method, especially in the first year of life of the children. As underlined by Griffin and Westbury (2011), in their commentary to the article of Bosl et al. (2011), these results should be viewed with caution because they identify an alteration of MSE in the whole population of HRA subjects without differentiating between the ones who will really develop autism and the ones who will have a typical development or other neuropsychiatric disorders. However, this study could be a promising starting point to carry out further investigation in order to highlight the differences in EEG complexity at the individual level, possibly helping to predict the risk of developing autistic traits.

Another interesting attempt in differentiating ASD and controls group based on a data-driven approach has been recently performed by Duffy and Als (2012). In this study, EEG data were recording on a large sample of ASD and TD subjects during awake state and coherence values were measured for each EEG frequency band.

In a first step, the dimensionality of the coherence data was reduced by applying a Principal Component Analysis (PCA) based on a Singular Value Decomposition (SVD) approach (SVD-based PCA). In the following step a classification algorithm, in particular the Discriminant Function Analysis (DFA), was applied to the variables selected by PCA. This technique allows producing a new canonical variable, the discriminant function, which is based on a weighted combination of the input variables and allows maximally separating the ASD and TD groups.

Given the wide age range of subjects, the classification analysis was applied also to subset of subjects with a narrower age span. The coherence factors given by DFA analysis allowed to accurately classifying ASD and TD across all three age spans. Moreover, it was observed that 70% of the factors were associated with reduced coherence for ASD subjects, in particular in the left temporal regions and frontal (short–distance connections). The decreased connectivity within these regions could be associated to language and communication problems. The other coherence factors showed an increased coherence in ASD subjects in particular in the long-distance connection. This finding could be explained as a compensatory mechanism of the autistic brain which establish atypical, spatially disparate, cortical networks to replace deficit function normally associated to more localized network. These results were quite stable across all broad spectral ranges.

The results of this study are very encouraging because it seems that the coherence factors could be used as a possible useful neurophysiological ASD-phenotype.

### QEEG DURING SPECIFIC TASKS

The application of QEEG processing technique during cognitive tasks can give the possibility to view the dynamic changes which take place in the brain during these conditions, determining in this way which areas of the brain are engaged. Although in the past some researchers have considered that EEG signals acquired during task conditions are destabilized or otherwise corrupted (Thatcher, 1998), recent researches have challenged this conclusion. For example, McEvoy et al. (2000) have demonstrated greater stability of QEEG signals recorded during cognitive tasks, with respect to the resting condition and therefore paving the way for developing task-specific understandings of brain operation.

Oberman et al. (2005) have analyzed the mu (8–13 Hz) power, an index of neuron synchronization or desynchronization, over the sensorimotor cortex during imitation tasks. At rest, sensorimotor neurons spontaneously fire in synchrony, leading to large amplitude EEG oscillations and to elevated power in mu frequency band. Conversely, during action, these neurons fire asynchronously, and therefore the power in mu band decreases. In this investigation, EEG from high-functioning ASD and controls were recorded during observation of biological and non-biological motion. While controls showed a decreased mu power both in self-initiated hand movement and in observed biological motion conditions, the ASD group obtained the same effect only during the first task, suggesting mirror neuron dysfunction in autism.

In fact, sensorimotor neurons could be considered as belonging to the well-known mirror neurons system (Rizzolatti et al., 2001). Several studies have related the imitation deficit in subjects with autism to an impairment of this neural circuitry (Williams et al., 2001; Nishitani et al., 2004; Iacoboni and Dapretto, 2006). Nevertheless, the findings of some recent studies argue against a mirror system dysfunction in ASD (Dinstein et al., 2010; Fan et al., 2010).

Sheikhani et al. (2012) used the spectrogram method to analyze data acquired on a group of children with ASD and age-matched controls during sustained visual attention. The spectrogram criteria – defined as the average of all the frequency component values of spectrogram >70% of the maximum value for each frequency band – as well as the coherence between pairs of different electrodes were computed. The ASD group exhibited lower values of spectrogram criteria in alpha, beta, and gamma bands, whereas no significant difference was observed in the delta band. According to these results, EEG signal show the most significant differences in the temporal and in the frontal regions of the left brain hemisphere. These results agree with several studies showing an impairment of left hemisphere, in particular in temporal and frontal regions, in ASD (Rojas et al., 2002, 2005; Chandana et al., 2005). The authors also showed an increase in the degree of coherence in the ASD group, and suggested increased functional connectivity of temporal lobes with other regions in the gamma band frequency.

In another investigation of the same authors (Sheikhani et al., 2009), children with ASD and controls underwent EEG acquisition in nine different conditions: [(1) eye-closed condition, (2) eye-opened condition, (3–5) looking at three samples of Kanizsa shapes, (6) looking at mother's picture upright and (7) inverted, (8) looking at stranger's picture upright, and (9) inverted in frequency bands]. Spectrogram and PSDs were calculated for each band at each condition. In the relaxed eye-opened condition, children with ASD obtained significant differences in gamma band with lower values of spectrogram criteria and higher values of SP. Spectrogram criteria were also significantly different in the alpha band when ASD and control children looked at the inverted mother's picture, and in alpha, beta, and gamma bands, when they looked at an inverted stranger's picture. Given that gamma band seems to play a role in the synchronization of cortical nets region, especially in recognition and perception, the authors suggested an abnormal functioning on these issues in ASD. Furthermore, since the alpha band is associated with the coordination of wider areas of the brain, and beta band plays a role in integrating neighboring areas, the abnormal spectrogram criteria found in this study might suggest a defect of coordination and integration in ASD.

In a recent study (Chan et al., 2011a), QEEG techniques were employed in order to examine the association between memory performance and fronto-posterior theta coherence in individuals with ASD. Several studies have found associations of theta-band amplitude with the performance of working memory tasks (Klimesch et al., 1994) and long-term memory encoding and retrieval (Larson et al., 1986). Moreover, basic research in animals and neuroimaging studies in humans have shown that during working memory tasks multiple brain areas are activated, in particular the prefrontal and postrolandic association cortices as well as the cingulate cortex and medial temporal areas (Fuster, 1995; Krause et al., 2000; Postle and D'Esposito, 2000). Given these findings, it has been suggested that connectivity abnormalities in these brain areas could be the neural bases of memory deficits in autism (Rippon et al., 2007). In the study by Chan et al. (2011a), EEG data were recorded during an object recognition task. ASD individuals showed elevated fronto-posterior long-range theta coherences, both intra-hemispheric (in the left hemisphere) and inter hemispheric (from left anterior to right posterior regions). Moreover, an opposite asymmetry pattern was observed: coherences in controls were higher in the right than in the left hemisphere, while in ASD children the pattern was opposite. A significant negative correlation between memory performance and inter-hemispheric long-range coherence was present in ASD subjects, whilst no significant correlations were found in controls. The abnormal pattern in ASD children could be explained with a hyper-functional connectivity in theta band with respect to controls that decrease the efficiency of memory processing.

In another study by the same research group (Chan et al., 2011b) the association between the performance of children with ASD in attention and inhibitory control and brain activity was investigated. The analysis was focused on relative PSD within theta band, which is related to attentional and inhibitory processing during a Go/No-Go task.

The authors found a decrease of theta activity in ASD children with respect to controls in the anterior regions for the "Go" and in anterior and centrotemporal regions for the "No-Go" condition. The application of LORETA software allowed a more accurate source localization ad it showed that in the "Go" condition theta decreased occurred in particular in the anterior cingulate cortex (ACC), while in the "No-Go" condition in the ACC and also in the precuneus. Significant correlations were found between theta power and scores obtained at the several tests performed showing an association between depressed brain activity, in particular in the ACC, and poorer performance in attention and inhibition.

Some authors have outlined the importance of studying the high EEG frequencies in order to characterize brain activity in ASD. The paper from Orekhova et al. (2007) aims at analyzing the differences between controls and ASD in high frequency EEG bands. EEG activity was recorded in young children with autism and age-matched controls during sustained visual attention. The mean PSD was calculated in three high frequency bands: beta (13.2–24 Hz), gamma 1 (24.4–44.0 Hz), and gamma 2 (56.0–70 Hz). An enhancement of spontaneous high frequency EEG oscillations in ASD was found, especially in gamma 1 band. The most involved brain areas were the midline, central, and parietal regions. Moreover, a significant positive correlation between the power spectrum value of gamma 1 and the degree of developmental delay in ASD group was detected. The excess of high frequencies in ASD agrees with the theory of an increase in ratio of excitation/inhibition in autism that leads to the formation of "noisy" and unstable cortical networks (Rubenstein and Merzenich, 2003).

In the most recent study (Lushchekina et al., 2012), the authors have tried to identify the neurophysiological components of cognitive abnormalities in ASD. EEG recordings, made in the standard 10/20 scheme were performed at baseline (rest with closed eyes), and during a cognitive task, consisting of counting, adding, and subtracting. SP and mean coherence were studied in the alpha, beta, and gamma ranges. Both typical and ASD subjects showed a marked frontal-occipital alpha gradient in baseline conditions. ASD individuals were characterized by right-sided predominance of PSD in the alpha range, both at rest and during cognitive tasks. In addition, in ASD the PSD of the gamma rhythm in baseline conditions was higher than that in the controls. During the cognitive task in ASD group the SP and mean coherence of fast rhythms did not change.

Another study (Catarino et al., 2011) analyzed EEG data acquired from adult ASD individuals and controls during a visual task (pictures of neutral faces versus pictures of chairs); a complexity analysis was performed using the MSE measure already described (Bosl et al., 2011). The task consisted in the detection of pictures of neutral faces and of chairs. Both a MSE investigation and a more traditional power spectral analysis were performed for each group and condition. While no differences were found in PSD, the authors demonstrated reduced entropy in ASD with respect to controls, especially at higher time scales, confirming that the decrease of MSE can be associated to impairments in brain function and connectivity.

## QEEG FOR THE IDENTIFICATION OF AUTISTIC SUBGROUPS

Clinical observation as well as research data, suggest that ASD are a set of neurodevelopmental disorders with a considerable heterogeneity in the phenotypic presentation (Witwer and Lecavalier, 2008; Georgiades et al., 2013). Among the several methods used to stratify ASD subjects into more homogeneous subgroups, the QEEG may provide more objective and quantitative features characterizing different groups of affected individuals. However, despite the fact that QEEG approach seems very promising, only few studies have so far been directed to this end.

The first investigation on this topic (Dawson et al., 1995) showed how QEEG is not only useful in differentiating subjects with high-functioning ASD from controls, but also in distinguishing amongst subgroups which differ in degree and nature of social impairments. Twenty-eight children with autism were classified according to Wing and Gould (1979) classification system: "Aloof," "Passive," and "Active-but-odd." In particular, the authors studied the "passive" and the "active-but-odd" groups. EEG was acquired during sustained visual attention, and the PSD were calculated for each band. The passive group showed reduced EEG power in delta and theta bands in all brain regions and reduced alpha power in the frontal regions. Since the alpha activity is related to social engagement, a reduced alpha activity could reflect, in this "passive" group, a lack of active engagement in social information processing.

A subsequent study by Sutton et al. (2005), QEEG analysis was performed in order to correlate resting cortical brain activity with social-emotional abilities behaviors in high functioning children with autism (HFA).

Data were acquired on high-functioning ASD children and controls during eyes-opened and closed conditions. The analysis focused on the alpha band, due to its stronger relation with behavioral measures with respect to other frequency bands. Moreover an asymmetry index was calculated for homologous electrode pairs and was used for subgrouping autistic children. Three subgroups were obtained using computer-generated cut points: (1) the most extreme right mid-frontal asymmetry scores (RFA group), (2) the most extreme left medial frontal asymmetry scores (LFA group), and (3) the intermediate frontal asymmetry (IFA group A reduction of alpha power density in anterior, central, and posterior cortical regions of control individuals compared with HFA subjects was detected. Moreover, the HFA group showed a different asymmetry pattern compared to the control group. Finally, some brain-behavior relationship were found: in particular, the LFA group reported greater symptoms of anxiety and social stress, while the RFA group was characterized by a greater social impairment.

## DISCUSSION AND CONCLUSION

This review focuses on key findings of quantitative EEG application in subjects with ASD. Despite conflicting results, literature analysis suggests that QEEG may help in detecting features of altered brain function, in linking behavior with brain activity and in defining more phenotypically homogeneous subgroups within the affected individuals.

Taken together, reviewed studies show that children with ASD present several differences in power spectra, coherence, and symmetry measures with respect to controls. This is true both when the signals are acquired in resting conditions – with either open or closed eyes – and when specific tasks are performed. However, QEEG features strongly depend on the diverse experimental settings (for example EEG recorded during observation of actions or during execution of actions) that may lead to different results. In addition, most parameters such as power spectra, coherence, and asymmetry, change with age and may vary according to behavioral, cognitive, and comorbid features of ASD subjects. The wide heterogeneity of the samples examined in the literature, particularly with regard to the cognitive level and age of subjects, and the different criteria used to diagnose ASD, makes it difficult to compare these studies and achieve unique general conclusions. In addition, drugs could influence the EEG activity (Muroka et al., 1992; Banoczi, 2005) with a potential impact on brain developmental process, especially in the frontal regions, which are the slowest in maturating. While some studies are more restrictive in defining the exclusion criteria of the sample, avoiding the enrollment of subjects taking medication, others do not define strict exclusion/inclusion criteria, or at least there are not clearly mentioned in the participant description. Thus, the variability in medication use across studies may be responsible for mixed findings in the literature reviewed. A possible role of immune dysregulation, toxicant exposures, and metabolic factors on the development of ASD abnormalities has been suggested (for a recent review, see Rossignol and Frye, 2012). However, the evaluation of these issues are often not specified or considered in the studies examined, potentially accounting for variation across studies and within subjects.

In open-eyes condition, the differences between ASD and TD are more pronounced. Studies performed in an eye-open rest condition present some replicated finding, i.e., the constant increase on delta power in ASD with respect to controls and the decrease in high frequency, especially alpha in childhood and adolescents (Cantor et al., 1986; Chan et al., 2007; Stroganova et al., 2007; Pop-Jordanova et al., 2010), but also some contradictory results. The power of alpha band in ASD, with respect to typical controls, was found to be reduced (Cantor et al., 1986; Chan et al., 2007), unchanged (Stroganova et al., 2007), or even increased (Mathewson et al., 2012) in different studies. A greater level of alpha amplitude reflects the inhibition of non-essential activity and consequently a better performance on the task (Klimesch et al., 2007) that could be explained by the *neural efficiency hypothesis* (Doppelmayr et al., 1998).

Also, the degree of asymmetry was found either broad-band decreased in ASD (Cantor et al., 1986) or leftward increased (Stroganova et al., 2007). This latter study also showed a symmetric mu rhythm, which was paradoxically asymmetric in healthy controls. The analysis of coherence between and within hemispheres in ASD subjects revealed an increased (Cantor et al., 1986) or reduced finding (Mathewson et al., 2012).

Several demographic and clinical differences characterize the samples involved in the above-mentioned studies, which may in part explain the conflicting results. In particular, the age range varies among the studies considered: young children (Cantor et al., 1986; Stroganova et al., 2007) children and adolescents (Chan et al., 2007), and adults (Mathewson et al., 2012) were respectively enrolled. Moreover, the cognitive level of ASD children displays a wide range of abilities: low functioning (Cantor et al., 1986), both high and low functioning (Stroganova et al., 2007), and only high-functioning (Chan et al., 2007; Mathewson et al., 2012) ASD subjects were evaluated.

Since QEEG indices are related to brain maturation and development (Clarke et al., 2001), the age represents a critical factor in the interpretation of results.

In typical development children low frequencies tend to decrease with age from childhood to adulthood while high frequencies increase (Gasser et al., 1988a). As regards coherence it broad-band increases with age (Gasser et al., 1988b). Autistic children seems to have a late maturation as they show more slow-wave and less alpha activity, as well as greater coherence than the age-matched typical controls. As coherence increases with age in TD subjects, in adulthood coherence values became comparable between ASD and TD groups (Murias et al., 2007; Mathewson et al., 2012).

In addition, EEG activity is influenced by level of cognitive abilities: in fact, Thatcher et al. (2005) showed that absolute EEG power is positively correlated with full scale, verbal, and performance IQ, while coherence is negatively correlated with these scores.

The comorbidity between ASD and other psychiatric or neurological disorders is a common feature of ASD clinical manifestation (Simonoff et al., 2008). The presence of an additional non-ASD disorder represents a potential confounding factor in EEG research that frequently hasn't been taken into account in the interpretation of results. Thus, future exploration into the EEG presentations of subjects with comorbid psychopathology versus ASD singly may be of seminal importance for a better knowledge of the ASD biological underpinnings.

In closed-eyes condition, results are even more contradictory both in terms of power and coherence (Murias et al., 2007; Coben et al., 2008; Pop-Jordanova et al., 2010; Mathewson et al., 2012). Except for the study of Pop-Jordanova et al. (2010), which do not define the cognitive level, all these studies enrolled high-functioning individuals. In addition, two studies (Murias et al., 2007; Mathewson et al., 2012) have been performed on adults, whereas one investigation (Coben et al., 2008) on scholar children and another (Pop-Jordanova et al., 2010) on pre-scholar children. This suggests again that the different age range of the subjects participating to the different studies may at least in part influence the results. Moreover, the different findings of Murias et al. (2007) and Mathewson et al. (2012) on adult subjects (with respect to both alpha power and coherence) may in part be due to the different methodological approach. By considering all the 128 electrodes in computing power spectrum and coherence, both a decrease in power and coherence in alpha band (Murias et al., 2007), and no differences (Mathewson et al., 2012) were detected. Therefore, the analysis of neural networks with higher spatial resolution seems to allow a thinner characterization of brain activation and connectivity. Source localization using software like LORETA used in the study by Chan et al. (2011b) can also be useful to increase the spatial resolution of EEG.

In closed-eyes condition the increase in slow-way activity is more related to theta than delta. Moreover there is an increase in beta frequencies from childhood to adulthood, which is not observed in open-eyes condition (Murias et al., 2007; Coben et al., 2008). Increase of beta activity is associated with a strengthening of sensory feedback in static motor control when movement has to be resisted or voluntarily suppressed (Lalo et al., 2007; Zhang et al., 2008). In children with ASD the increased beta activity in closed-eyes condition may reflect the difficulty in motor and sensorial regulation that they present in this situation.

With regards to coherence, it seems that increases with age such as controls: in fact, it is decreased in childhood and adolescence and become equal or increased in adulthood.

Although the exact meaning of changes in SP and coherence in ASD children is not easy to understand, in resting state condition, both dysfunction of general state of arousal or of more specific systems of cognitive processing may explain these findings. However, by correlating brain activity findings with behavioral measures, Mathewson et al. (2012) showed that cognitive function and modulation might influence QEEG also at rest.

Acquiring data while children perform specific tasks allows having a better characterization of the link between behavior and brain activation, although the possibility to drive definitive conclusions is limited due to the small number of studies and of sample size. Differences between ASD subjects and controls during tasks mainly involve high frequencies, alpha, beta, and gamma, which have been found increased (Orekhova et al., 2007; Sheikhani et al., 2009; Lushchekina et al., 2012) in ASD population, regardless of the type of task. Moreover some authors also found an increase in coherence during tasks, in ASD with respect to control, supporting the hypothesis of an enhanced functional connection between cortical networks (over-connectivity) at the basis of the aberrant behaviors observed in autism.

In literature, moreover, QEEG was used for subtyping ASD subjects (Dawson et al., 1995; Sutton et al., 2005), suggesting that some QEEG parameters may correlate with different behavioral phenotype The identification of subgroups of subjects with different QEEG profiles could contribute to increase the homogeneity of ASD samples, with the aim to detect specific developmental time course, treatment responses, and possibly pathophysiological underpinnings.

In addition, due to the fact that brain activation and QEEG measures are strictly dependent on age, it is very important evaluating developmental processes in autism. QEEG, in fact, may show different developmental patterns in infants with high and low risk for ASD, and could be therefore used as a promising endophenotype for early diagnosis in at-risk children (Tierney et al., 2012). Non-linear techniques, such as entropy (Bosl et al., 2011) have also been used at this end. This technique, like also fractal dimension or phase coupling (Sheikhani et al., 2007; Thatcher et al., 2009; Ahmadlou et al., 2010; Bosl et al., 2011), is appealing not only in order to characterize autistic brain, but also to obtain potential biomarkers of the disorder, not otherwise detectable with common linear methods.

Overall, it is important to underline that QEEG activity components may also have some individual characteristics that differentiate each subject. The assessment of these features has a crucial importance for establishing a QEEG "baseline," which may be different for each person.

New advanced analysis methods such as entropy or cluster analysis could be useful to identify autistic subgroups with specific neurophysiological characteristics, providing in this way different brain endophenotypes, which may benefit from different intervention strategies. Thus, this sort of metrics on the brain's function could be used, in the future, to develop personalized treatments (for example by using connectivity-guided neurofeedback), and evaluate the effects of therapies through quantitative measures of brain activity. Also in this case, source localization is extremely important: in fact, variation of brain activity in a specific brain area can be a quick and objective indicator to monitor the effect of the treatment.

## ACKNOWLEDGMENTS

The research leading to this work has received funding from the European Union's Seventh Framework Programme (FP7/2007-20013) under grant agreement no. #288241. The financial support of Telethon-Italy (grant no. GGP11188) is gratefully acknowledged. Sara Calderoni was partially supported by the Italian Ministry of Health and Tuscany Region (grant "GR-2010-2317873").

## REFERENCES

1. Ahmadlou, M., Adeli, H., and Adeli, A. (2010). Fractality and a wavelet-chaos-neural network methodology for EEG-based diagnosis of autistic spectrum disorder. *J. Clin. Neu- rophysiol.* 27, 328–333. doi:10.1097/WNP.0b013e3181f40dc8
2. American Psychiatric Association. (2013). *Diagnostic and Statistical Manual of Mental Disorders*, 5th Edn. Washington, DC: American Psychiatric Association.
3. Banoczi, W. (2005). How some drugs affect the electroencephalogram (EEG). *Am. J. Electroneurodiagnostic Technol.* 45, 118–129.
4. Barnea-Goraly, N., Kwon, H., Menon,V., Eliez, S., Lotspeich, L., and Reiss, A. L. (2004). White matter structure in autism: preliminary evidence from diffusion tensor imaging. *Biol. Psy- chiatry* 55, 323–326. doi:10.1016/j. biopsych.2003.10.022
5. Barnier, R., Dawson, G., Webb, S., and Murias, M. (2007). EEG mu rhythm and imitation impairments in indi- viduals with autism spectrum disor- der. *Brain Cogn.* 64, 228–237. doi:10. 1016/j.bandc.2007.03.004
6. Baron-Cohen, S., Wheelwright, S., Skin- ner, R., Martin, J., and Clubley, E. (2001). The autism-spectrum quo- tient (AQ): evidence from Asperger syndrome/high-functioning autism, males and females, scientists and mathematicians. *J. Autism Dev. Disord.* 31, 5–17. doi:10.1023/A: 1005653411471
7. Belmonte, M. K., Allen, G., Beckel- Mitchener, A., Boulanger, L. M., Carper, R. A., and Webb, S. J. (2004). Autism and abnormal devel- opment of brain connectivity. *J. Neurosci.* 24, 9228–9231. doi:10. 1523/JNEUROSCI.3340-04.2004
8. Belmonte, M. K., and Yurgelun- Todd, D. A. (2003). Functional anatomy of impaired selective atten- tion and compensatory process- ing in autism. *Brain Res. Cogn. Brain Res.* 17, 651–664. doi:10.1016/S0926-6410(03)00189-7
9. Billeci, L., Calderoni, S., Tosetti, M., Catani, M., and Muratori, F. (2012). White matter connectivity in chil- dren with autism spectrum disor- ders: a tract-based spatial statistics study. *BMC Neurol.* 12:148. doi:10. 1186/1471-2377-12-148
10. Boddaert, N., Chabane, N., Ger- vais, H., Good, C. D., Bourgeois, M., Plumet, M.-H., et al. (2004). Superior temporal sulcus anatom- ical abnormalities in childhood autism: a voxel-based morphom- etry MRI study. *Neuroimage* 23, 364–369. doi:10.1016/j.neuroimage. 2004.06.016
11. Bosl, W., Tierney, A., Tager-Flusberg, H., and Nelson, C. (2011). EEG complexity as a biomarker for autism spectrum disorder risk. *BMC Med.* 9:18. doi:10.1186/1741-7015-9-18
12. Bourgeron, T. (2009). A synaptic trek to autism. *Curr. Opin. Neu- robiol.* 19, 231–234. doi:10.1016/j. conb.2009.06.003
13. Calderoni, S., Retico, A., Biagi, L., Tancredi, R., Muratori, F., and Tosetti, M. (2012). Female children with autism spectrum disorder: an insight from mass-univariate and pattern classification analyses. *Neu- roimage* 59, 1013–1022. doi:10.1016/ j.neuroimage.2011.08.070
14. Cantor, D. S., Thatcher, R. W., Hry- byk, M., and Kaye, H. (1986). Com- puterized EEG analyses of autistic children. *J. Autism Dev. Disord.* 16, 169–187. doi:10.1007/BF01531728
15. Catarino, A., Churches, O., Baron- Cohen, S., Andrade, A., and Ring, H. (2011). Atypical EEG complex- ity in autism spectrum conditions: a multiscale entropy analysis. *Clin. Neurophysiol.* 122, 2375–2383. doi: 10.1016/j. clinph.2011.05.004
16. Centers for Disease Control and Preven- tion. (2012). Prevalence of autism spectrum disorders – autism and developmental disabilities monitor- ing network, 14 sites, United States, 2008. *MMWR Surveill. Summ.* 61, 1–19.
17. Chan, A. S., Han, Y. M. Y., Sze, S. L., Che-ung, M., Leung, W. W., Chan, R. C. K., et al. (2011a). Disordered con- nectivity associated with memory deficits in children with autism spec- trum disorders. *Res. Autism Spectr. Disord.* 5, 237–245. doi:10.1016/j. rasd.2010.04.007
18. Chan, A. S., Han, Y. M. Y., Sze, S. L., Cheung, M., Leung, W. W., Leung, C., et al. (2011b). Abnormalities in the anterior cingulate cortex associated with attentional and inhibitory control deficits: a neu- rophysiological study on children with autism spectrum disorders. *Res. Autism Spectr. Disord.* 5, 254–266. doi:10.1016/j.rasd.2010. 04.007
19. Chan, A. S., Sze, S. L., and Che- ung, M.-C. (2007). Quantitative electro-encephalographic profiles for children with autistic spectrum dis- order. *Neuropsychology* 21, 74–81. doi:10.1037/0894-4105.21.1.74
20. Chandana, S. R., Behen, M. E., Juhász, C., Muzik, O., Rothermel, R. D., Mangner, T. J., et al. (2005). Sig- nificance of abnormalities in devel- opmental trajectory and asymme- try of cortical serotonin synthe- sis in autism. *Int. J. Dev. Neurosci.* 23, 171–182. doi:10.1016/j.ijdevneu. 2004.08.002
21. Clarke, A. R., Barry, R. J., McCarthy, R., and Selikowitz, M. (2001). Age and sex effects in the EEG: devel- opment of the normal child. *Neuro- physiol. Clin.* 112, 806–814. doi:10. 1016/S1388-2457(01)00488-6
22. Coben, R., Clarke, A. R., Hudspeth, W., and Barry, R. J. (2008). EEG power and coherence in autistic spectrum disorder. *Clin. Neurophys- iol.* 119, 1002–1009. doi:10.1016/j. clinph.2008.01.013
23. Coben, R., Linden, M., and Myers, T. E. (2010). Neurofeedback for autis- tic spectrum *disorder*: a review of the literature. *Appl. Psychophysiol. Biofeedback* 35, 83–105. doi:10.1007/ s10484-009-9117-y
24. Costa, M., Goldberger, A. L., and Peng, C. K. (2002). Multiscale entropy analysis of complex physiologic time series. *Phys. Rev. Lett.* 89, 068102. doi:10.1103/PhysRevLett.89.068102
25. Courchesne, E., and Pierce, K. (2005). Why the frontal cortex in autism might be talking only to itself: local over-connectivity but long-distance disconnection. *Curr. Opin. Neu- robiol.* 15, 225–230. doi:10.1016/j. conb.2005.03.001
26. Courchesne, E., Pierce, K., Schumann, C. M., Redcay, E., Buckwalter, J. A., Kennedy, D. P., et al. (2007). Mapping early brain development in autism. *Neuron* 56, 399–413. doi:10. 1016/j.neuron.2007.10.016
27. Dawson, G., Klinger, L. G., Panagiotides, H., Lewy, A., and Castelloe, P. (1995). Subgroups of autistic children based on social behavior display distinct patterns of brain activity. *J. Abnorm. Child Psychol.* 23, 569–583. doi:10. 1007/BF01447662
28. Dinstein, I., Thomas, C., Humphreys, K., Minshew, N., Behrmann, M., and Heeger, D. J. (2010). Normal move- ment selectivity in autism. *Neuron* 66, 461–469. doi:10.1016/j.neuron. 2010.03.034
29. Doppelmayr, M., Klimesch, W., Pachinger, T., and Rippe, B. (1998). The functional significance of absolute power with respect to event-related desynchroniza- tion. *Brain Topogr.* 11, 133–140. doi:10.1023/A:1022206622348
30. Duffy, F. H., and Als, H. (2012). A stable pattern of EEG spectral coherence distinguishes children with autism from neurotypical controls – a large case control study. *BMC Med.* 10:64. doi:10.1186/1741-7015-10-64
31. Dumermuth, G., and Molinari, L. (1987). Spectral analysis of the EEG: some fundamentals revisited and some open problems. *Neuropsy- chobiology* 17, 85–99. doi:10.1159/000118345
32. Fan, Y. T., Decety, J., Yang, C. Y., Liu, J. L., and Cheng, Y. (2010). Unbroken mirror neurons in autism spectrum disorders. *J. Child Psychol. Psychia- try* 51, 981–988. doi:10.1111/j.1469- 7610.2010.02269.x
33. Fries, P. (2005). A mechanism for cog- nitive dynamics: neuronal communication through neuronal coher- ence. *Trends Cogn. Sci. (Regul. Ed.)* 9, 474–480. doi:10.1016/j.tics.2005.08. 011
34. Fuster, J. M. (1995). *Memory in the Cerebral Cortex – An Empirical Approach to Neural Networks in the Human and Nonhuman Primate.* Cambridge, MA: MIT Press.
35. Gasser, T., Verleger, R., Bacher, P., and Sroka, L. (1988a). Develop- ment of the EEG of school- age children and adolescents. I. Analysis of band power. *Electroen- cephalogr. Clin. Neurophysiol.* 69, 91–99. doi:10.1016/0013-4694(88) 90204-0
36. Gasser, T., Verleger, R., Bacher, P., and Sroka, L. (1988b). Develop- ment of the EEG of school-age chil- dren and adolescents. II. Topogra- phy. *Electroencephalogr. Clin. Neu- rophysiol.* 69, 100–109. doi:10.1016/0013-4694(88)90205-2
37. Georgiades, S., Szatmari, P., Boyle, M., Hanna, S., Duku, E., Zwaigenbaum, L., et al. (2013). Investigating phe- notypic heterogeneity in children with autism spectrum disorder: a factor mixture modeling approach. *J. Child Psychol. Psychiatry* 54, 206–215. doi:10.1111/j.1469-7610. 2012.02588.x
38. Griffin, R., and Westbury, C. (2011). Infant EEG activity as a biomarker for autism: a promising approach or a false promise? *BMC Med.* 9:61. doi:10.1186/1741-7015-9-61

39. Higuchi, T. (1988). Approach to an irregular time series on the basis of the fractal theory. *Physica D* 31, 277–283. doi:10.1016/0167-2789(88)90081-4
40. Hubl, D., Bölte, S., Feineis-Matthews, S., Lanfermann, H., Federspiel, A., Strik, W., et al. (2003). Func- tional imbalance of visual path- ways indicates alternative face pro- cessing strategies in autism. *Neurol- ogy* 61, 1232–1237. doi:10.1212/01. WNL.0000091862.22033.1A
41. Hugdahl, K. (1996). Brain laterality – beyond the basics. *Eur. Psychol.* 3, 206–220. doi:10.1027/1016-9040.1. 3.206
42. Hughes, J. R., and John, E. R. (1999). Conventional and quantitative electroencephalography in psychiatry. *J. Neuropsychiatry Clin. Neurosci.* 11, 190–208.
43. Iacoboni, M., and Dapretto, M. (2006). The mirror neuron system and the consequences of its dysfunction. *Nat. Rev. Neurosci.* 7, 942–951. doi: 10.1038/nrn2024
44. John, E. R., Karmel, B. Z., Corning, W. C., Easton, P., Brown, D., Ahn, H., et al. (1977). Neurometrics. *Sci- ence* 196, 1393–1410. doi:10.1126/ science.867036
45. Katz, M. J. (1988). Fractals and the analysis of waveforms. *Comput. Biol. Med.* 18, 145–156. doi:10.1016/0010-4825(88)90041-8
46. Klimesch, W., Sauseng, P., and Hanslmayr, S. (2007). EEG alpha oscillations: the inhibition-timing hypothesis. *Brain Res. Rev.* 53, 63–88. doi:10.1016/j. brainresrev. 2006.06.003
47. Klimesch, W., Schimke, H., and Schwaiger, J. (1994). Episodic and semantic memory: an analysis in the EEG theta and alpha band. *Electroencephalogr. Clin. Neurophysiol.* 91, 428–441. doi:10.1016/0013-4694(94)90164-3
48. Koenig, T., Prichep, L., Lehmann, D., Sosa, P. V., Braeker, E., Kleinlogel, H., et al. (2002). Millisecond by mil- lisecond, year by year: normative EEG microstates and developmen- tal stages. *Neuroimage* 16, 41–48. doi:10.1006/ nimg.2002.1070
49. Kouijzer, M. E. J., de Moor, J. M. H., Gerrits, B. J. L., Con- gedo, M., and van Schie, H. T. (2010). Neurofeedback improves executive functioning in children with autism spectrum disorders. *Res. Autism Spectr. Disord.* 3, 145–162. doi:10.1016/j.rasd.2008. 05.001
50. Kouijzer, M. E. J., van Schie, H. T., de Moor, J. M. H., Gerrits, B. J. L., and Buitelaar, J. K. (2009). Neurofeedback treatment in autism. Preliminary findings in behavioral, cognitive, and neurophysiological functioning. *Res. Autism Spectr. Dis- ord.* 4, 386–399. doi:10.1016/j.rasd. 2009.10.007
51. Krause, C. M., Sillanmäki, L., Koivisto, M., Saarela, C., Häggqvist, A., Laine, M., et al. (2000). The effects of memory load on event-related EEG desynchronization and syn- chronization. *Clin. Neurophysiol.* 111, 2071–2078. doi:10.1016/S1388- 2457(00)00429-6
52. Lachaux, J. P., Rodriguez, E., Martinerie, J., and Varela, F. J. (1999). Measuring phase synchrony in brain signals. *Hum. Brain Mapp.* 8, 194–208. doi: 10.1002/(SICI)1097-0193(1999)8: 4<194::AID-HBM4>3.0.CO;2-C
53. Lalo, E., Gilbertson, T., Doyle, L., Di Lazzaro, V., Cioni, B., and Brown, P. (2007). Phasic increases in cor- tical beta activity are associated with alterations in sensory process- ing in the human. *Exp. Brain Res.* 177, 137–145. doi:10.1007/s00221- 006-0828-5
54. Larson, J., Wong, D., and Lynch, G. (1986). Patterned stimulation at the theta frequency is opti- mal for the induction of hip- pocampal long-term potentiation. *Brain Res.* 368, 347–350. doi:10. 1016/0006-8993(86)90579-2
55. Lehmann, D. (1990). "Brain electric microstates and cognition: the atoms of thought," in *Machinery of the Mind*, ed. E. R. John (Boston: Birkhauser), 209–224.
56. Lehmann, D., Ozaki, H., and Pal, I. (1987). EEG alpha map series: brain micro-states by space-oriented adaptive seg- mentation. *Electroencephalogr. Clin. Neurophysiol.* 67, 271–288. doi:10.1016/0013-4694(87)90025-3
57. Lushchekina, E. A., Podreznaya, E. D., Lushchekina, V. S., and Strelets, V. B. (2012). A Comparison EEG study in normal and autistic chil- dren. *Neurosci. Behav. Physiol.* 42, 236–243. doi:10.1007/s11055-012- 9558-2
58. Mandelbrot, B. B. (1977). *The Fractal Geometry of Nature*. New York: Freeman and Company.
59. Mathewson, K. J., Jetha, M. K., Drmic, I. E., Bryson, S. E., Goldberg, J. O., and Schmidt, L. A. (2012). Regional EEG alpha power, coher- ence, and behavioral symptomatol- ogy in autism spectrum disorder. *Clin. Neurophysiol.* 123, 1798–1809. doi:10.1016/j.clinph.2012.02.061
60. McAlonan, G. M., Cheung, V., Che- ung, C., Suckling, J., Lam, G. Y., Tai, K. S., et al. (2005). Mapping the brain in autism. A voxel-based MRI study of volumetric differences and intercorrelations in autism. *Brain* 128, 268–276. doi:10.1093/brain/awh332
61. McEvoy, L. K., Smith, M. E., and Gevins, A. (2000). Test-retest reliability of cognitive EEG. *Clin. Neurophysiol.* 111, 457–463. doi:10.1016/S1388- 2457(99)00258-8
62. Muratori, F., Calderoni, S., Apicella, F., Filippi, T., Santocchi, E., Calugi, S., et al. (2012). Tracing back to the onset of abnormal head circumference growth in children with autism spec- trum disorder. *Res. Autism Spectr. Disord.* 6, 442–449. doi:10.1016/j. rasd.2011.07.004
63. Murias, M., Webb, S. J., Greenson, J., and Dawson, G. (2007). Resting state cortical connectivity reflected in EEG coherence in individuals with autism. *Biol. Psychiatry* 62, 270–273. doi:10.1016/j.biopsych.2006.11.012
64. Muroka, M., Tada, K., Nogami, Y., Ishikawa, K., and Nagoya, T. (1992). Residual effects of repeated adminis- tration of triazolam and nitrazepam in healthy volunteers. *Neuropsy- chobiology* 25, 134–139. doi:10.1159/000118823
65. Narzisi, A., Muratori, F., Calderoni, S., Fabbro, F., and Urgesi, C. (2012). Neuropsychological profile in high functioning autism spectrum disorders. *J. Autism Dev. Disord.* 43, 1895–1909. doi:10.1007/s10803-012-1736-0
66. Nishitani, N., Avikainen, S., and Hari, R. (2004). Abnormal imitation- related cortical activation sequences in Asperger's syndrome. *Ann. Neu- rol.* 55, 558–562. doi:10.1002/ana. 20031
67. Nunez, P. L. (2006). *Neocortical Dynam- ics and Human EEG Rhythms*. New York: Oxford University Press.
68. Nuwer, M. (1997). Assessment of digi- tal EEG, quantitative EEG, and EEG brain mapping: report of the Amer- ican Academy of Neurology and the American Clinical Neurophysiology Society. *Neurology* 49, 277–292. doi: 10.1212/WNL.49.1.277
69. Oberman, L. M., Hubbard, E. M., McCleery, J. P., Altschuler, E. L., Ramachandran, V. S., and Pineda, J. A. (2005). EEG evidence for mir- ror neuron dysfunction in autism spectrum disorders. *Brain Res. Cogn. Brain Res.* 24, 190–198. doi:10.1016/ j.cogbrainres.2005.01.014
70. Oberman, L. M., Ramachandran, V. S., and Pineda, J. A. (2008). Modulation of mu suppression in children with autism spec- trum disorders in response to familiar or unfamiliar stimuli: the mirror neuron hypothesis. *Neuropsychologia* 46, 1558–1565. doi:10.1016/j.neuropsychologia. 2008.01.010
71. Orekhova, E. V., Stroganova, T. A., Nygren, G., Tsetlin, M. M., Posik- era, I. N., Gillberg, C., et al. (2007). Excess of high frequency electroen- cephalogram oscillations in boys with autism. *Biol. Psychiatry* 62, 1022–1029. doi:10.1016/j.biopsych. 2006.12.029
72. Orekhova, E. V., Stroganova, T. A., Prokofyev, A. O., Nygren, G., Gill- berg, C., and Elam, M. (2008). Sen- sory gating in young children with autism: relation to age, IQ, and EEG gamma oscillations. *Neurosci. Lett.* 434, 218–223. doi:10.1016/j.neulet. 2008.01.066
73. Otnes, R. K., and Enochson, L. (1972). *Digital Time Series Analysis*. New York: Wiley & Sons.
74. Pascual-Marqui, R. D., Michel, C. M., and Lehmann, D. (1994). Low resolution electromagnetic tomography: a new method for localizing electri- cal activity in the brain. *Int. J. Psy- chophysiol.* 18, 49–65. doi:10.1016/0167-8760(84)90014-X
75. Pineda, J. A., Brang, D., Hecht, E., Edwards, L., Carey, S., Bacon, M., et al. (2008). Positive behavioral and electrophysiological changes follow- ing neurofeedback training in chil- dren with autism. *Res. Autism Spectr. Disord.* 2, 557–581. doi:10.1016/j. rasd.2007.12.003
76. Pop-Jordanova, N., and Pop-Jordanov, J. (2005). Spectrum-weighted EEG frequency ("brain-rate") as a quan- titative indicator of mental arousal. *Prilozi* 26, 35–42.
77. Pop-Jordanova, N., Zorcec, T., Demerdzieva, A., and Gucev, Z. (2010). QEEG characteristics and spectrum weighted fre- quency for children diagnosed as autistic spectrum disorder. *Nonlinear Biomed. Phys.* 4, 4. doi:10.1186/1753-4631-4-4
78. Postle, B. R., and D'Esposito, M. (2000). Evaluating models of the topographical organization of working memory function in frontal cortex with event- related fMRI. *Psychobiology* 28, 132–145.
79. Rihs, T. A., Michel, C. M., and Thut, G. (2007). Mechanisms of selective inhibition in visual spatial atten- tion are indexed by alpha-band EEG synchronization. *Eur. J. Neu- rosci.* 25, 603–610. doi:10.1111/j. 1460-9568.2007.05278.x
80. Rippon, G., Brock, J., Brown, C., and Boucher, J. (2007). Dis- ordered connectivity in the autistic brain: challenges for the "new psychophysiology." *Int. J. Psychophysiol.* 63, 164–172. doi:10.1016/j.ijpsycho.2006.03.012
81. Rizzolatti, G., Fogassi, L., and Gallese, V. (2001). Neurophysiological mecha- nisms underlying the understanding and imitation of action. *Nat. Rev. Neurosci.* 2, 661–670. doi:10.1038/35090060
82. Rojas, D. C., Bawn, S. D., Benkers, T. L., Reite, M. L., and Rogers, S. J. (2002). Smaller left hemi- sphere planum temporale in adults with autistic disorder. *Neurosci. Lett.* 328, 237–240. doi:10.1016/S0304-3940(02)00521-9

83. Rojas, D. C., Camou, S. L., Reite, M. L., and Rogers, S. J. (2005). Planum temporale volume in children and adolescents with autism. *J. Autism Dev. Disord.* 35, 479–486. doi:10. 1007/s10803-005-5038-7
84. Rossignol, D. A., and Frye, R. E. (2012). A review of research trends in physiological abnormalities in autism spectrum disorders: immune dys- regulation, inflammation, oxidative stress, mitochondrial dysfunction and environmental toxicant expo- sures. *Mol. Psychiatry* 17, 389–401. doi:10.1038/mp.2011.165
85. Rubenstein, J. L. R., and Merzenich, M. M. (2003). Model of autism: increased ratio of excita- tion/*inhibition* in key neural systems. *Genes Brain Behav.* 2, 255–267. doi:10.1034/j.1601-183X. 2003.00037.x
86. Sauseng, P., Klimesch, W., Gerloff, C., and Hummel, F. C. (2009). Spontaneous locally restricted EEG alpha activity determines cortical excitability in the motor cortex. *Neuropsychologia* 47, 284–288. doi:10.1016/j.neuropsychologia. 2008.07.021
87. Schipul, S. E., Keller, T. A., and Just, M. A. (2011). Inter-regional brain com- munication and its disturbance in autism. *Front. Syst. Neurosci.* 5:10. doi:10.3389/fnsys.2011.00010
88. Sheikhani, A., Behnam, H., Moham- madi, M. R., Noroozian, M., and Mohammadi, M. (2012). Detection of abnormalities for diagnosing of children with autism disorders using of quantitative electroencephalog- raphy analysis. *J. Med. Syst.* 36, 957–963. doi:10.1007/s10916-010-9560-6
89. Sheikhani, A., Behnam, H., Moham- madi, M. R., Noroozian, M. (2007). "Analysis of EEG background activ- ity in Autsim disease patients with bispectrum and STFT measure," in *Proceedings of the 11th WSEAS International Conference on COMMUNI- CATIONS*, Agios Nikolaos.
90. Sheikhani, A., Behnam, H., Norooz- ian, M., Mohammadi, M. R., and Mohammadi, M. (2009). Abnor- malities of quantitative electroen- cephalography in children with Asperger disorder in various con- ditions. *Res. Autism Spectr. Disord.* 3, 538–546. doi:10.1016/j.rasd.2008. 11.002
91. Sigl, J. C., and Chamoun, N. G. (1994). An introduction to bispectral analysis for the electroencephalogram. *J. Clin. Monit.* 10, 392–404. doi:10. 1007/BF01618421
92. Simonoff, E., Pickles, A., Charman, T., Chandler, S., Loucas, T., and Baird, G. (2008). Psychiatric disorders in children with autism spectrum dis- orders: prevalence, comorbidity, and associated factors in a population- derived sample. *J. Am. Acad. Child Adolesc. Psychiatry* 47, 921–929. doi: 10.1097/CHI.0b013e318179964f
93. Singer, W. (1999). Neuronal synchrony: a versatile code for the definition of relations? *Neuron* 24, 49–65. doi:10. 1016/S0896-6273(00)80821-1
94. Steriade, M., Gloor, P., Llinás, R. R., Lopes de Silva, F. H., and Mesulam, M. M. (1990). Report of IFCN Com- mittee on Basic Mechanisms. Basic mechanisms of cerebral rhythmic activities. *Electroencephalogr. Clin. Neurophysiol.* 76, 481–508. doi:10. 1016/0013-4694(90)90001-Z
95. Stroganova, T. A., Nygren, G., Tsetlin, M. M., Posikera, I. N., Gillberg, C., Elam, M., et al. (2007). Abnormal EEG lateralization in boys with autism. *Clin. Neurophysiol.* 118, 1842–1854. doi:10.1016/j.clinph.2007.05.005
96. Sutton, S. K., Burnette, C. P., Mundy, P. C., Meyer, J., Vaughan, A., Sanders, C., et al. (2005). Resting cortical brain activity and social behavior in higher functioning children with autism. *J. Child Psychol. Psychia- try* 46, 211–222. doi:10.1111/j.1469- 7610.2004.00341.x
97. Thatcher, R. W. (1998). Normative EEG databases and EEG biofeedback. *J. Neurother.* 2, 8–39. doi:10.1300/ J184v02n04_02
98. Thatcher, R. W., North, D. M., Neubran- der, J., Biver, C. J., Cutler, S., and Defina, P. (2009). Autism and EEG phase reset: deficient GABA mediated inhibition in thalamo- cortical circuits. *Dev. Neuropsy- chol.* 34, 780–800. doi:10.1080/87565640903265178
99. Thatcher, R. W., Northa, D., and Bivera,(2005). EEG and intelligence: Relations between EEG coherence, EEG phase delay and power. *Clin. Neurophysiol.* 116, 2129–2141. doi: 10.1016/j.clinph.2005.04.026
100. Tierney, A. L., Gabard-Durnam, L., Vogel-Farley, V., Tager-Flusberg, H., and Nelson, C. A. (2012). Devel- opmental trajectories of resting EEG power: an endophenotype of autism spectrum disorder. *PLoS ONE* 7:e39127. doi:10.1371/journal. pone.0039127
101. Tong, S., and Thakor, N. V. (2009). *Quantitative EEG Analysis Methods and Clinical Applications (Engineer- ing in Medicine & Biology)*. Boston: Artech House, Inc.
102. Van Putten, M. J. A. M., Peters, J. M., Mulder, S. M., De Haas, J. A. M., Bruijninckx, C. M. A., and Tavy, L. J. (2004). A brain symmetry index (BSI) for online EEG mon- itoring in carotid endarterectomy. *Clin. Neurophysiol.* 115, 1189–1194. doi:10.1016/j.clinph.2003.12.002
103. Waiter, G. D., Williams, J. H. G., Mur- ray, A. D., Gilchrist, A., Perrett, D. I., and Whiten, A. (2004). A voxel- based investigation of brain struc- ture in male adolescents with autistic spectrum disorder. *Neuroimage* 22, 619–625. doi:10.1016/j.neuroimage. 2004.02.029
104. Waiter, G. D., Williams, J. H. G., Murray, A. D., Gilchrist, A., Perrett, D. I., and Whiten, A. (2005). Structural white matter deficits in high-functioning individuals with autistic spectrum disorder: a voxel-based investiga- tion. *Neuroimage* 24, 455–461. doi: 10.1016/j.neuroimage.2004.08.049
105. Walter, D. O. (1963). Spectral analysis for electroencephalograms: mathematical determination of neu- rophysiological relationships from records of limited duration. *Exp. Neurol.* 8, 155–181. doi:10.1016/0014-4886(63)90042-6
106. Welch, P. D. (1967). The use of fast Fourier transform for the estimation of power spectra: a method based on time averaging over short, modified periodograms. *IEEE Trans. Acoust.* AU-15, 70–73. doi:10.1109/TAU.1967.1161901
107. Williams, J. H., Whiten, A., Sud- dendorf, T., and Perrett, D. I. (2001). Imitation, mirror neurons and autism. *Neurosci. Biobehav. Rev.* 25, 287–295. doi:10.1016/S0149-7634(01)00014-8
108. Wing, L., and Gould, J. (1979). Severe impairments of social interaction and associated abnormalities in chil- dren: epidemiology and classification. *J. Autism Dev. Disord.* 9, 11–29. doi:10.1007/BF01531288
109. Witwer, A. N., and Lecavalier, L. (2008). Examining the validity of autism spectrum disorder subtypes. *J. Autism Dev. Disord.* 38, 1611–1624. doi:10.1007/s10803-008-0541-2
110. Zhang, Y., Chen, Y., Bressler, S. L., and Ding, M. (2008). Response prepara- tion and inhibition: the role of the cortical sensorimotor beta rhythm. *Neuroscience* 156, 238–246. doi:10. 1016/j.neuroscience.2008.06.061

# 8

# Heterogeneity within autism spectrum disorders: what have we learned from neuroimaging studies?

**_Rhoshel K. Lenroot_** [1,2]* **_and Pui Ka Yeung_** [1,2]

[1] *School of Psychiatry, University of New South Wales, Sydney, NSW, Australia*
[2] *Neuroscience Research Australia, Sydney, NSW, Australia*

**_Edited by:_**
*Andrew Whitehouse, University of Western Australia, Australia*

**_Reviewed by:_**
*Peter G. Enticott, Monash University, Australia*
*Christine Wu Nordahl, University of California at Davis, USA*

**_*Correspondence:_**
*Rhoshel K. Lenroot, Neuroscience Research Australia, Hospital Road, Randwick, Sydney, NSW 2031, Australia*
*e-mail: r.lenroot@unsw.edu.au*

Autism spectrum disorders (ASD) display significant heterogeneity. Although most neuroimaging studies in ASD have been designed to identify commonalities among affected individuals, rather than differences, some studies have explored variation within ASD. There have been two general types of approaches used for this in the neuroimaging literature to date: comparison of subgroups within ASD, and analyses using dimensional measures to link clinical variation to brain differences. This review focuses on structural and functional magnetic resonance imaging studies that have used these approaches to begin to explore heterogeneity between individuals with ASD. Although this type of data is yet sparse, recognition is growing of the limitations of behaviorally defined categorical diagnoses for understanding neurobiology. Study designs that are more informative regarding the sources of heterogeneity in ASD have the potential to improve our understanding of the neurobiological processes underlying ASD.

**Keywords: autism, psychiatry and developmental disabilities, intellectual disability, functional magnetic resonance imaging, structural magnetic resonance imaging**

## INTRODUCTION

The Autism Spectrum Disorders (ASD) are a group of lifelong neurodevelopmental syndromes which manifest in early childhood, defined by the presence of difficulties with social interactions and communication together with restricted, repetitive patterns of interests or behaviors (American Psychiatric Association, 2013). The variety of clinical presentations considered to fall within autism has gradually increased over the past 60 years. Leo Kanner first used the diagnosis in 1943 to describe a relatively homogenous group of individuals with deficits in all three domains but intact intellectual capacity (Kanner, 1968). Work by Lorna Wing and others then went on to place Kanner's subgroup within a broader spectrum that shared some level of deficit in these core domains but was otherwise highly heterogeneous, including allowing a wider spread of cognitive function (Wing, 1981).

In the previous version of the Diagnostic and Statistical Manual IV (American Psychiatric Association, 2000), this heterogeneity was captured primarily through the different categorical diagnoses within the Pervasive Developmental Disorders (PDD). The PDD category included Autism, Asperger's Syndrome, and Pervasive Developmental Disorder not otherwise specified (PDD-NOS), as well as two regressive neurodevelopmental disorders of early childhood frequently associated with autistic symptoms, Rett's syndrome and Childhood Disintegrative Disorder. As research progressed, the clinical and neurobiological validity of the categorical distinctions between Autism, Asperger's Syndrome, and PDD-NOS appeared increasingly doubtful, until they were dropped altogether in the recently released DSM-5 (American Psychiatric Association, 2013). Instead, a broader ASD diagnosis with dimensional specifiers of severity has been adopted, and a new diagnosis of Social Communication Disorder added for those individuals with problems in social communication but without the symptoms in the domain of restrictive and repetitive behaviors (RRIB) required for an ASD diagnosis.

An explicit goal of the recent reformulation of the diagnostic criteria for ASD was to refocus attention on the aspects of heterogeneity within ASD that were likely to be more meaningful than the previous categorical divisions, both clinically and in relation to underlying pathophysiology. This shift in conceptualization of ASD has occurred within a larger context of increasing dissatisfaction with existing diagnostic categories for a variety of psychiatric syndromes, particularly when seeking to link clinical symptoms to specific neurobiological processes (Insel et al., 2010; Lord and Jones, 2012; Uher and Rutter, 2012).

Heterogeneity of clinical presentation among individuals who meet criteria for a specific diagnosis is a particular impediment. One contributor to this heterogeneity is the checklist approach currently used to assign categorical diagnoses. While allowing a good level of reliability between diagnosticians, it has the unfortunate effect of allowing different individuals to meet the threshold for a particular syndrome without necessarily sharing many specific clinical features. A second contributor to heterogeneity of clinical presentations within a particular syndrome such as ASD is the extensive comorbidity between psychiatric diagnoses (Matson and Williams, 2013). It has been estimated that between 14 and 78% of children with ASD also meet criteria for Attention Deficit and Hyperactivity Disorder (ADHD) (Gadow et al., 2005; Gargaro et al., 2011), up to 42% for anxiety disorders (Simonoff et al., 2008; Matson and Williams, 2013), and between 25 and 70% have some level of intellectual disability (ID) (Fombonne, 2009). There are a wide variety of other symptoms not considered as "core" but which are nevertheless prominent in sizeable fractions of individuals with ASD, such as poor attention, seizure disorders, poor sleep, and gastro-intestinal dysfunction (Silver and Rapin, 2012). How these symptoms relate to the pathophysiology of ASD is not clear, but their frequency is suggestive that they may represent at least in part pleiotropic expressions of common processes (Brock, 2011; Rommelse et al., 2011).

In addition to the clinical heterogeneity within ASD, it is associated with a wide variety of different risk factors, implying the potential for many different pathways to generate symptoms (Geschwind, 2009; Herbert, 2010). ASD has been associated with over 100 different genes affecting different aspects of neural development and function (Betancur, 2011), as well as a wide variety of environmental factors (Herbert, 2010). Attempting to understand the links of specific risk factors to autism is further complicated by the different ways risk factors can relate to clinical phenomena, described as *equifinality* and *multifinality* (Cicchetti and Rogosch, 1996). Equifinality refers to the observation that a single clinical syndrome may be associated with many different risk factors. Multifinality describes the converse situation, where a single risk factor can be associated with different clinical outcomes. Examples pertinent to ASD include Fragile X, where up to 45% of affected individuals have been estimated meet criteria for ASD (but 55% do not) (Gallagher and Hallahan, 2012), and 22q11.2d syndrome, which appears to increase risk for ASD in some individuals (Antshel et al., 2007), and schizophrenia in others (Murphy et al., 1999). Research on genetic risk factors for ASD in general has been notable for the lack of specificity to ASD (Betancur, 2011). Risk-genes instead appear to confer vulnerability for a variety of neurodevelopmental disorders (Sahoo et al., 2011; Rapoport et al., 2012), suggesting that understanding the role of genetic risk factors for ASD will require identifying the factors that direct an individual with a risk-gene down the path to one neurodevelopmental disorder versus another as much as identifying the genes themselves (Moreno-De-Luca et al., 2013).

Investigators have taken different approaches to the clinical and neurobiological heterogeneity of ASD. Geschwind and Levitt (2007) drew attention to the variety of associated genetic syndromes, endorsing the view that the field should be considering a multiplicity of "autisms" rather than a single condition. They went on to hypothesize that what these "autisms" shared was a common abnormality in brain connectivity that occurred early in development and most strongly affected the links between frontal and temporal/parietal cortices. A large body of work has accrued using multiple neuroimaging techniques across a variety of presentations and ages that has shown impaired functional and structural connectivity between brain regions (Amaral et al., 2008; Horder and Murphy, 2012; Just et al., 2012; Travers et al., 2012).

However, limitations to this formulation have also been recognized (Vissers et al., 2012). While the evidence of abnormalities in connectivity are convincing, it does not in itself explain either how the observed abnormalities in connectivity explain the heterogeneity of specific presentations, or how they differentiate autism from a variety of other disorders characterized by poor connectivity between similar brain regions, such as ADHD and schizophrenia. Pelphrey et al. (2011) proposed an alternative approach, in which heterogeneity was constrained by narrowing attention to the deficits in social communication felt to be the heart of ASD, and focusing on early failures of the neural systems relevant to these. While acknowledging that disruptions in these systems could arise from many different sources, congruent with the observations of multiple risk factors, they argued that what was relevant to ASD was the convergence of these factors on the development of specific aspects of the social brain network, such as the posterior superior temporal sulcus (Pinkham et al., 2008; Kaiser et al., 2010).

Concerns have been raised that this approach focuses too closely on the social communication aspect of ASD, and thus not only does not address the range of clinically relevant symptoms, but also stands to lose information potentially crucial for determining what types of pathophysiology are relevant to a particular individual. Brock (2011) have argued that a better method is to consider the heterogeneity along with the findings: for example, rather than just determining whether the amygdala is hyper- or hypo-activated, one should characterize what differentiates those with hyperactivity from those with hypoactivity.

This leads to the strategy of tackling heterogeneity by identifying more homogeneous subgroups, with the hypothesis that this will decrease noise due to variation and facilitate detection of meaningful group differences or brain-behavior relationships (Volkmar et al., 2009). Comparing putative subgroups against each other can also test whether a particular feature distinguishing the subgroups is related to brain differences, or conversely, if there is something that appears consistently found in individuals meeting diagnostic criteria despite other heterogeneous aspects of the presentation. The subgroups explored the most to date are the different disorders within the PDD category in DSM-IV (American Psychiatric Association, 2000), but other ways of dividing ASD have also been used, including divisions based on clinical features such as regression or level of ID, or subgroups defined by presence of a specific risk factor such as gender or a known genetic disorder.

Heterogeneity can also be addressed by using a dimensional approach to relate variation in neuroimaging measures to some other aspect of the presentation (Constantino, 2011; Lord and Jones, 2012; Uher and Rutter, 2012). Being able to determine whether some aspect of the brain is predictive of a clinical symptom can both support the relevance of the imaging data, and perhaps, depending on how much is known about the function of those brain regions, inform the larger questions as to what neural processes are responsible for the clinical presentation.

We first briefly discuss which findings appear to be the most consistent in neuroimaging studies of ASD. The second section will review studies that have looked at subgroups within ASD, and the third section work that has instead focused on dimensional approach, both of the features considered as core symptoms of ASD and of common co-occurring conditions.

## WHAT IS COMMON WITHIN NEUROIMAGING FINDINGS IN ASD?

Most imaging studies of ASD done to date have been done taking the categorical diagnosis as their framework, asking the basic question of whether there are one or more brain differences corresponding to the clinical syndrome that can be recognized despite the various sources of heterogeneity. As is the case for other psychiatric disorders, clinical MRIs of individuals with autism do not typically show gross lesions or other abnormalities that can be used to distinguish affected individuals. Instead, alterations in brain structure or function are most easily detectable as differences between groups, and, given the variability of the syndrome, preferably using large samples.

Meta-analysis provides one method of combining data to create larger databases in which to search for patterns. A meta-analysis by Stanfield et al. (2008) included 43 structural neuroimaging studies comprised of data from over 800 subjects between 3 and 30 years of age with ASD and similar number of matched controls. Although there was considerable heterogeneity of results across the studies they included, significant findings on meta-analysis included enlarged total brain volume, hemispheres, cerebellum, and caudate in ASD, and decreased volumes in other brain regions including midbrain regions, regions of the cerebellar vermis, and area of the corpus callosum. Gray and white matter (WM) volumes were not reported separately in this meta-analysis.

Another recent meta-analysis of differences in brain morphometry in ASD limited its scope to fully automated voxel-based morphometry (VBM) studies of gray matter volumes (Via et al., 2011). Twenty studies met inclusion criteria, including 496 adolescents or adults with ASD (a combination of Autism and Asperger's Syndrome) and 471 controls. Of the 17 studies that reported IQ, only one included subjects whose mean IQ was less than 70. This meta-analysis found no differences in global gray matter volume between ASD and controls; regional differences consisted of smaller gray matter volume in the ASD group in the amygdala-hippocampus complex and medial parietal regions. A linked meta-analysis by the same group of WM differences measured with VBM identified 13 eligible studies, including 246 patients with ASD, and 237 controls; while global WM volumes were not different, they did find evidence of increased volumes in regions relevant to language and social cognition (Radua et al., 2011).

Meta-analyses of functional magnetic resonance imaging (fMRI) studies have additional challenges due to the even greater variety of possible tasks and conditions to be compared. Philip et al. (2012) examined available fMRI studies in ASD across six different functional domains: visual processing, executive function and language tasks, basic social processing, and more complex challenges of social cognition. They performed their meta-analysis using the activation likelihood estimation (ALE) method, in which data regarding loci of activations are spatially normalized and then the overlap calculated across different experiments (Eickhoff et al., 2009). Ninety papers met inclusion criteria, with an average sample size of ASD participants of 12. Although the wide variety of tasks used made comparison challenging, there were regions of activation that were significantly different between the ASD subjects and controls in each of the functional domains examined. Notable findings included a tendency for decreased activation in ASD across several prefrontal and subcortical brain regions during tasks tapping executive function. Activation patterns in the superior temporal gyri were significantly different between ASD and controls across several domains, although the direction varied: ASD had decreased activation during tasks related to auditory and language processing, but increased during tasks of simple social processing, and mixed findings as demands became more complex. The authors also provided a qualitative review of available studies of functional connectivity that could not be included in an ALE analysis, finding multiple observations of decreased connectivity between areas of the cortex in ASD across a variety of resting or task based paradigms, and conversely some instead of increased connectivity, particularly between subcortical and cortical areas.

Robustness of findings in imaging studies has been limited by the small sample sizes and methodological variability of the studies available. However, technical advances in methods for data acquisition and automated processing are making multi-site large-scale imaging studies increasingly feasible. One such collaboration is the Autism Brain Imaging Data Exchange (ABIDE[1]), a consortium of investigators in which members contribute both published and unpublished resting-state fMRI data from ASD subjects and controls obtained using similar clinical and imaging protocols. The first paper from this consortium reported on measures of brain connectivity in a dataset collected across 17 sites. Neuroimaging data included in this analysis were limited to that collected from males (360 ASD, 403 controls) who had IQ within 2 standard deviations of the overall sample mean of 108 (Di Martino et al., 2013). The results helped to clarify conflicting results from earlier studies, confirming that both hyper- and hypo-connectivity are characteristic of brain activity in ASD. Hypo-connectivity was much more prominent, affecting to varying degrees all cortico-cortical connections tested, with particularly strong effects in unimodal association areas such as the fusiform and superior temporal gyri, paralimbic regions such as the insula and paracingulate cortex, and connections between hemispheres. Hyperconnectivity was more limited, affecting primarily subcortical nuclei and parietal cortex. The study represented a significant advance in reconciling previously inconsistent observations (Muller et al., 2011; Vissers et al., 2012), although the population studied was limited to the subset of individuals with ASD with normal range IQ, and did not have the younger subjects needed to answer questions around early developmental changes.

In summary, despite the clinical and etiological heterogeneity with ASD, the use of quantitative methods to look for common patterns across datasets collected thus far has detected evidence of some relatively consistent differences in both brain structure and function on a group level. However, a significant contributor to differences in findings among studies of ASD is age.

## AGE EFFECTS

As suggested by the meta-analyses above, structural neuroimaging studies of adolescents and adults have had inconsistent findings, with some reporting enlarged volumes (Piven et al., 1995), but the majority normal or even reduced volumes (Garber et al., 1989), consistent with the meta-analyses of VBM data in older individuals by Via et al. (2011) discussed above (Radua et al., 2011). In contrast, studies of head circumference and brain volumes in children with autism have suggested that brain enlargement is a more consistent finding (Wolff, 2013). In the meta-analysis by Stanfield discussed above, age effects are described for the amygdala, such that the differences in amygdala volume correlated with age, becoming larger in younger subjects. While this analysis did not find similar age effects for total brain volume, unlike what had been reported in

[1] http://fcon_1000.projects.nitrc.org/indi/abide/

a previous meta-analysis (Redcay and Courchesne, 2005), there are increased effect sizes for larger total brain volumes in younger children. These and similar observations have led to the hypothesis that the trajectory of brain development in some individuals with ASD may show a two-step deviation: an early acceleration in brain growth, followed by a flattening of the growth trajectory or even relative loss in brain volume sometime during early adolescence (Aylward et al., 2002; Redcay and Courchesne, 2005).

It should be noted that while increased early brain volume is one of the most consistently reported observations, it has not been found by all studies (Raznahan et al., 2013a). A recent paper re-examining past reports of increased head circumference in ASD found evidence to suggest that much of this could actually due to bias from cohort effects within commonly used population databases such as the CDC. Those studies in which control data had been collected from the same community as the ASD group were less likely to find head circumference differences (Raznahan et al., 2013b). MRI comparisons of global gray and WM volumes in young children have also had mixed results. Studies that limited participants to those that met narrow DSM-IV criteria for Autism were less likely to find group differences, while larger brain volumes were more frequently observed when the patient group was extended to the broader autism spectrum. A recent study of brain volumes in toddlers with regressive versus non-regressive autism (Rogers, 2004; Hansen et al., 2008) of the same clinical severity also only found increased brain volumes in males with the regressive subtypes, while males with non-regressive autism were not different than controls. Brain volumes were not increased in females with either regressive or non-regressive autism, although sample size differences may have affected the ability to detect differences in the latter, as there were many more males in the study than females (114 males/22 females) (Nordahl et al., 2011). These findings, together with the observation that many genetic disorders associated with autism often result in microcephaly (Betancur, 2011), suggest that early increased brain growth is present in only a subset of individuals with ASD (Raznahan et al., 2013a).

There is as yet relatively little work attempting to assess developmental shifts in brain functional activity in ASD. In a recent meta-analysis, Dickstein et al. (2013) addressed developmental questions in fMRI results by using ALE methods to directly compare fMRI study results in children less than 18 years old with those obtained in adults. Tasks were split into those testing aspects of social function, such as theory of mind, face processing, and language, versus non-social capacities such as executive function and reward processing. Forty-two studies met inclusion criteria: 18 studies in children (including 262 ASD participants, average age $12.95 \pm 1.74$ years) and 24 in adults (288 participants, average age $30.55 \pm 4.94$ years), with similar numbers of age-matched controls. They reported that loci of both hyperactivation and hypoactivation were more pronounced in the younger subjects: in the group of social tasks, the convergence of hyperactivation was higher in the children in the left postcentral gyrus, and hypoactivation greater in the right parahippocampal gyrus/hippocampus and right superior temporal gyrus. In the non-social tasks, hyperactivation was greater in the ASD children in areas such as the right insula, right middle frontal gyrus, and left cingulate gyrus, while hypoactivation was more pronounced in the right middle frontal gyrus; there were no instances in either condition where convergences of hypo- or hyperactivation were greater in the adult ASD group. While the results need to be followed up in longitudinal analysis, they do suggest that development stage plays an important role in functional differences in ASD as well.

## SUBGROUPS WITHIN ASD

### SUBGROUPS DEFINED BY CLINICAL FEATURES

#### *Autism and Asperger's syndrome*

As discussed above, until the recent revision of DSM-5, ASD were divided into several categorical diagnoses. The question of whether Autism and Asperger's syndrome should be considered different disorders has been contentious, particularly when comparing individuals with Asperger's syndrome to those with Autism and normal cognitive function (Kozlowski et al., 2012; Planche and Lemonnier, 2012). Studies directly comparing the two have tended to report evidence of more severe brain abnormalities in Autism, with Asperger's syndrome being intermediate (Lotspeich et al., 2004; Schumann et al., 2004). The recent meta-analysis of VBM measures of gray matter volume described above (Via et al., 2011) did not find evidence of significant differences in gray matter volume between Autism and Asperger's syndrome, supporting the hypothesis that the conditions had similar neural substrates with differing levels of severity.

#### *Intellectual disability*

It is estimated that approximately of 60–80% of the total ASD population have mild to severe ID (Fombonne, 2003). How best to understand the relationship of ID to the core features of ASD is not clear – whether they should be considered as arising from the same fundamental process in individuals with both, whether ID should instead be treated as a co-occurring disorder, or whether ID may serve as an "unmasking" element that decreases an individual's ability to compensate for other factors that place them at risk for autistic behaviors (Skuse, 2007).

A handful of studies have compared ASD with and without co-occurring ID, often referred to as "low-functioning autism" (LFA), and "high-functioning autism" (HFA). A study of global brain volumes and amygdala and hippocampal volumes in a group of children and a group of adolescents, divided into the four subgroups of LFA and HFA, Asperger's syndrome and matched controls, did not find significant differences in patterns of neural abnormalities between LFA and HFA; both had significantly enlarged amygdala and hippocampal volumes in the younger children but not adolescents, and global brain volumes were the same as controls throughout (Schumann et al., 2004). A cross-sectional analysis of a subset of the same sample reported differences in cortical folding patterns between the four groups (Nordahl et al., 2007). Cortical morphometry and sulcal depths were modeled using a surface-based registration system (Van Essen et al., 2001). The LFA group had an area of deeper sulci than controls in the left frontal operculum and anterior insula; in the HFA group, sulcal depth was deeper in the left parietal operculum, approximately 12 mm distant from the area affected in the LFA group, and correlated with a similarly affected region in the right hemisphere. In the Asperger's syndrome group, this region was not affected, but there was evidence of greater sulcal depth bilaterally in the intraparietal sulcus.

Shape analysis showed an abnormal region in the pars opercularis portion of the left inferior frontal gyrus of the LFA group, which coincided with the sulcal depth abnormality. The sample was also divided into a younger (7.5–12.5 years) and older (12.75–18.5 years) in order to explore developmental effects: similarly to the study of amygdala size in this cohort, findings were more pronounced in the younger group, despite the smaller sample size, and no longer evident in the adolescent group.

Scanning children with intellectual disabilities is challenging, and relatively few studies have focused on LFA. Riva et al. (2011) compared brain volumes in a group of children with ASD aged 3–10 years, average IQ of approximately 52, against controls with normal IQ. They reported similar global brain volumes between the two groups, but a pattern of regional gray matter deficits in the autistic group. Other studies have used control groups matched on level of ID. Predescu et al. (2010) did not find differences between 15 children aged 2–8 with ASD and 10 age-matched children with developmental delay (DD) in global gray and WM volumes measured using VBM. A slightly larger study of 34 children aged 2–7 years with ASD and 13 controls matched for age and developmental level also did not find any significant differences in brain volumes, although there appeared to be a positive relationship between developmental stage in the developmentally delayed group that was absent in the ASD children (Zeegers et al., 2009). A study in older children with significant DD (27 ASD, 17 controls; both groups had chronologic age of approximately 14 years and developmental age of approximately 4.5 years) reported that the area of the corpus callosum was significantly smaller in the ASD group, although head circumference and cerebellar volumes were not different (Manes et al., 1999). A different approach was taken by Hrdlicka et al. (2005), who used cluster analysis to determine which traits grouped together across several domains, including brain volumes, autistic symptoms, IQ, facial dysmorphism, and comorbidities such as epilepsy. They found that level of ID differentiated between clusters, while ASD symptoms did not; more severe ID was associated with smaller volumes of the amygdala, hippocampus, and corpus callosum genu/splenium, along with higher frequency of epilepsy, facial dysmorphic features, and abnormal early psychomotor development. A significant limitation to the studies available thus far is their relatively small size. Compounding this is that the pathology underlying ID and DD is itself not well understood, and so control groups defined on basis of cognitive function are likely to introduce additional variation related to the causes of the cognitive impairment.

## SUBGROUPS DEFINED BY RISK FACTORS

### *Environmental risk factors*

Another strategy for parsing heterogeneity is subdividing based on the presence of a specific risk factor, either comparing individuals that have a specific risk factor who also have ASD features against those who do not, or comparing individuals with ASD and a specific risk factor against idiopathic ASD (iASD) and controls in order to see if the same patterns of differences is present regardless of the presence of the risk factor. Analyses of this type thus far have been carried out in primarily in regards to genetic risks. Although ASD has also been associated with a variety of environmental risk factors (Herbert, 2010), much less is yet known about how these might relate to brain differences. The strongest environmental risk identified thus far is severe early neglect, which has been associated with development of autistic behavioral features (Rutter et al., 2007), although studies of children raised in these conditions have also shown a capacity for significant improvements on exposure to a socially enriched environment that ASD generally does not. Some small neuroimaging studies have been done in these populations, which have documented decreased brain volumes and abnormal WM architecture, but the relationship of brain findings to autistic symptoms in these subjects is not known (Bos et al., 2011).

Prenatal exposure to maternal autoantibodies has been suggested as another environmental risk factor potentially playing a role in some individuals with ASD. The blood-brain barrier is permeable to maternal IgG during prenatal development, and maternal autoantibodies have been observed to react with fetal brain tissue, with reactivity to several specific antigens in the 37 and 73 kDa range of molecular weight linked to significantly increased risk for ASD in offspring (Braunschweig et al., 2013). Prenatal exposure of rhesus macaques to these autoantibodies from mothers of ASD children resulted in abnormal social function and a more rapid increase in brain volume in the males (although not females) during the first two years of life compared to controls (Bauman et al., 2013). These intriguing findings were followed up by a study of maternal autoantibodies and brain volume in male children with ASD and matched controls (Nordahl et al., 2013). In this study, 7.5% of the mothers of ASD children and none of the mothers of controls had the autoantibodies in the 37/73 kDa range; and the children of this subset had significantly larger brain volumes than the children with ASD who did not have exposure to these autoantibodies. Together, these findings support the hypothesis that there may be a subgroup of individuals with ASD in which pathophysiology is linked to a particular immune-mediated process during prenatal development. There have not been imaging studies yet related to other possible environmental factors such as prenatal maternal influenza.

### *Genetic risk factors*

As extensively reviewed elsewhere, ASD is highly heritable (Ronald and Hoekstra, 2011), and has been linked to a large number of genetic risk factors (Betancur, 2011). The Y chromosome could be considered one of the strongest of these, conferring up to a 4:1 greater risk in males compared to females (Fombonne, 2009). Otherwise, the genes identified to date with the strongest impact on risk for ASD are those associated with known genetic neurodevelopmental disorders which include an increased likelihood of ASD (Fombonne, 2009). Examples include Fragile X syndrome (FXS) (Gallagher and Hallahan, 2012) and 22q11.2d, also known as velocardio-facial syndrome (VCFS) (Antshel et al., 2007). However, even in these disorders, ASD symptoms are only present in a subset of affected individuals, and each of these syndromes increases risk for a number of psychiatric disorders. Neuroimaging has begun to be used to try to determine whether having the ASD phenotype or not in individuals with the same genetic abnormality is reflected in variation in brain structure, and also whether brain differences associated with the ASD phenotype in a specific genetic condition are similar to those in "idiopathic" ASD. Such studies within specific genetic disorders have the additional benefit of allowing comparison of individuals with ASD and ID within a relatively homogeneous cohort. There is an element of controversy regarding the relationship of ASD symptoms to genetic disorders such as FRX, with some arguing that despite appropriate scores on standardized assessments, a closer analysis of clinical features of individuals with genetic syndromes reveals that similarities are superficial, and symptom profiles are not the same as in individuals with iAUT (Moss and Howlin, 2009). An alternative is that the pattern appears atypical precisely because they represent a subgroup associated with a single major genetic risk factor, and so do not display the same characteristics described as averaged observations from a much more heterogeneous group.

### Gender

Autism spectrum disorders is significantly more common in males than females (1 in 54 in boys and 1 in 252 in girls, up to 5 times more frequent in boys; Center for Disease Control and Prevention, 2012), although there has been longstanding debate whether the risk factors disproportionately affects males, or if instead other protective factors tend to make symptoms less noticeable in girls. It has also been uncertain whether the proportion of males and females may change based on the level of ID. Several early studies reported an interaction of gender with ID, such that the ratio of males to females is nearly equal in individuals with ID, and becomes more prominent in the groups with higher IQ (Wing, 1981; Lord et al., 1982; Volkmar et al., 1993). However, some more recent studies have not found a relationship of gender ratio and IQ (Carter et al., 2007; Hartley and Sikora, 2009; Mandy et al., 2012). The preponderance of males in recruitment samples has resulted in many imaging studies excluding females altogether, in order to reduce potential variance related to gender. Those that have included both males and females have generally had insufficient numbers of females to examine effects of gender on outcomes, and there have only been a few MRI studies that have addressed differences in gender directly.

Most studies thus far that have reported on gender effects have not found significant differences in which brain areas are affected, although the magnitude of effects in areas has tended to be larger in females (Bloss and Courchesne, 2007; Schumann et al., 2009, 2010; Calderoni et al., 2012). One study however found reduced cerebral GM and WM volumes and reduced temporal GM volumes in females versus males with ASD; in addition, cerebral, frontal, parietal, and occipital WM volumes were only correlated with age in girls but not in boys (Bloss and Courchesne, 2007). This was consistent with the gender effects observed in a meta-analysis of brain structural differences in ASD, which found that differences in the cerebellum were more likely to be observed when there were fewer males included in the study, suggesting that females may be contributing greater differences (Stanfield et al., 2008).

A notable recent study, the largest to date designed explicitly to examine gender differences, found that brain regions affected in ASD males had little overlap with those affected in ASD females (Lai et al., 2013a). In this study, VBM was used to compare gray and WM global and regional volumes in high-functioning adult males and females with ASD (age range 18–49; 30 males with ASD; 30 females with ASD; 30 male controls and 30 female controls). There were not significant interactions of gender and diagnosis for gray matter volumes. However, for WM, several regions had divergent findings for males and females. In the temporo-parieto-occipital region, females with ASD had larger WM volumes than female controls, while there was no difference in males; while WM in the internal capsule in the area around the basal ganglia was larger in the ASD males than male controls, but smaller in ASD females than female controls. In addition to the difference in direction of findings, there was little spatial overlap between affected regions in males and in females. These findings suggest a difference in neuroanatomical substrates of ASD for males and females, despite similar clinical characteristics. Although in general females who have been identified with ASD have tended to be characterized as clinically more severely affected than males (Dworzynski et al., 2012), suggested by some as due to ascertainment biases, this study as well as the others described above did not find gender differences in their samples in either ID or symptom severity (Bloss and Courchesne, 2007).

There has been one fMRI study to date that targeted gender differences, comprised of a verbal fluency task and a mental rotation task (Beacher et al., 2012). These tasks were chosen based on previous evidence of gender specific performance in health populations: females tend to perform better than males on measures of verbal fluency (Herlitz et al., 1997), and males better than females on tests of mental rotation (Crucian and Berenbaum, 1998; Astur et al., 2004; Parsons et al., 2004; Kozaki and Yasukouchi, 2009). The authors found evidence of interaction of group and gender. On the verbal fluency task, AS males, but not females, had greater activation in the left medial superior frontal gyrus than controls. On the mental rotation task, AS males had greater activation in the left precuneus, bilateral occipital gyri, and left inferior temporal gyrus than controls; the opposite was true for females, with control females having greater activation in the same regions. The authors speculated that differences could have been due to gender differences in cognitive styles.

### Genetic syndrome

Fragile X Syndrome is an X-linked disorder, the most common inherited form of ID, caused by a trinucleotide repeat in the Fragile X mental retardation 1 (FMR1) gene (Gallagher and Hallahan, 2012). It is estimated that 25–47% of individuals with FXS have ASD (Gallagher and Hallahan, 2012), resulting in 2–6% of all ASD cases (Reddy, 2005; Hagerman et al., 2010). Kaufmann et al. (2003) were the first to directly compare children with FXS and ASD, finding hypoplasia of the posterosuperior vermis in both groups compared to controls. A study of 10 adults with FXS, 10 iASD, and 10 TD using VBM also reported decreased volume of the cerebellar vermis in FXS and iASD compared to TD; the FXS group had increased volumes of caudate and dorsolateral prefrontal cortex (PFC), and decreased volumes of left postcentral, middle temporal, and right fusiform gyrus (FG) compared to both ASD and TD (Wilson et al., 2009). Meguid et al. (2010) reported on a comparison of cortical thickness in 10 children with iAUT and 7 children with FXS + AUT; they found that that for the most part there were no significant differences in measures of cortical thickness, gyrification, or sulcal depth between the two groups, except that the iAUT had thinner cortex in the left medial frontal and anterior cingulate cortices, which correlated with an index of social maturity.

A series of reports using different imaging analysis methods have come from work by Hazlett and colleagues regarding a longitudinal study of boys with FXS recruited between 2–4 years of age, including a group who had FXS with autism (FXS + AUT), FXS without autism (FXS-AUT), iASD, and controls (TD, a mix of typically developing and developmentally delayed children). In the baseline study using predefined regions of interest they found that the FXS group, both with and without autism, had enlarged caudate and decreased amygdala volumes, compared to both TD and iAUT. The most significant finding in the iAUT group was enlarged amygdala volume compared to either FXS or TD (Hazlett et al., 2009). At the next time point, when subjects were 5–6 years of age, additional differences were observed. Global volumes were similar between the FXS and iAUT groups, in both cases larger than the TD group, but frontal lobe gray and WM volumes were smaller in the FXS than in iAUT, and temporal WM and cerebellar volumes were larger (Hazlett et al., 2012). A longitudinal analysis of the same cohort using VBM found a complex pattern of differences between the groups. Interestingly, several regions important for social function such as medial PFC, orbitofrontal cortex, superior temporal sulcus, and temporoparietal region appeared to differ in opposite directions, being smaller in the FXS (including FXS + AUT) and larger in the iAUT. There was no significant difference in the overall severity of the autistic symptoms, which the authors interpreted as an example of different patterns of brain structural differences underlying similar symptoms (Hoeft et al., 2011).

Rett's syndrome (RS) is an X-linked genetic disorder commonly associated with autistic features that was previously included within the same PDD category as ASD. Most affected individuals have a mutation in the Methyl-CpG-binding Protein 2 (MECP2), a transcription regulator important in activity-dependent synaptic maturation (Amir et al., 1999). As evidence grows supporting the role of synaptic development as a potential convergent pathway for pathophysiology in ASD, there has been strong interest in the MECP2 mutation as a prototypic model (Neul, 2012). Imaging studies of RS have described decreases in both gray and WM volume affecting frontal, temporal, and parietal regions (Naidu et al., 2001). Decreased volumes are consistent with the characteristic microcephaly, and appear to be more pronounced in individuals with more severe clinical phenotypes (Carter et al., 2008a). Interestingly, a study of the milder preserved speech variant subtype of RS found that while 76% of a cohort of 17 intermediate and high-functioning participants met criteria for ASD, only 3 had microcephaly, 11 had normal head circumference, and 2 were even macrocephalic (Zappella et al., 2001). There have not been studies to date explicitly examining imaging findings in RS in relationship to the autistic phenotype.

Velo-cardio-facial syndrome is caused by a deletion in the 22q11.2 region, and associated with increased risk of ASD (Antshel et al., 2007), as well as schizophrenia and other psychiatric conditions, and DDs (Shprintzen, 2008). One study to date has compared brain structures in VCFS with ASD to those without ASD. This study found that those with an ASD diagnosis had larger right amygdala volume (Antshel et al., 2007), consistent with other reports of increased amygdala size in ASD.

Down's syndrome is the most common genetic cause of ID, and has been reported as being comorbid with ASD in a subset of between 1–11% (Lowenthal et al., 2007). Brain volumes in DS subjects are usually reported as smaller than controls. Findings have been mixed when comparing DS with or without autistic features. Studies that further subdivide DS by presence of autistic features have not found differences total brain volume or total cerebellar volume between those with (DS + AUT, ID + AUT) or without (DS-AUT, ID-AUT) autistic features (Kaufmann et al., 2003; Spencer et al., 2006; Carter et al., 2008b). Some evidence of differences however has been identified in cortical areas related to social functions such as the thalamus and left superior temporal sulcus (Spencer et al., 2006), and associations with motor or RRB in brainstem and cerebellar WM (Kaufmann et al., 2003; Carter et al., 2008b).

#### *Other genetic risk factors*

A large number of other genes not associated with specific genetic disorders have also been linked to increased risk for ASD. Most studies of the effects of these genes on brain structure in relation to ASD thus far have focused on demonstration of the effects of risk-genes on relevant aspects of brain structure or function within healthy subjects (e.g., contactin-associated protein-like 2 (CNTNAP2) (Scott-Van Zeeland et al., 2010a; Tan et al., 2010; Dennis et al., 2011; Whalley et al., 2011); homeobox A1 (HOXA1) (Canu et al., 2009; Raznahan et al., 2012); MET receptor tyrosine kinase (MET) (Hedrick et al., 2012), oxytocin receptor (OXT) (Inoue et al., 2010), and brain-derived neurotrophic factor (BDNF) (Raznahan et al., 2009). However, a few have sought to determine if risk alleles contribute to heterogeneity within ASD and may be useful for intra-diagnostic stratification; i.e., whether ASD subjects with a specific risk-gene allele have differences in brain structure or function from ASD subjects who do not have that particular allele.

Monoamine-oxidase A (MAOA) is an enzyme found in the brain that is a key regulator of serotonin, dopamine, and norepinephrine, all neurotransmitters that have been linked with ASD. VNTR, a polymorphism in the promoter region for the MAOA gene, has been demonstrated to affect the level of activity of this enzyme. A large body of work has linked the low activity (LA) allele to a variety of adverse effects on cognition and behavior, including decreased IQ and worse symptomatology within ASD (Cohen et al., 2003). A study of the relationship of MAOA and ASD compared brain volumes between individuals with the high (HA) versus LA alleles of VNTR, both within a sample of young males with ASD (18–35 months of age, 17 HA, 12 LA) and controls (7–18 years of age, 28 HA, 11 LA). While there was no effect of the allele type in the control subjects, within the ASD sample the LA allele was associated with larger volumes of both gray and WM (Davis et al., 2008).

MET is another candidate genetic risk factor with relatively robust support for a role in ASD. MET is a gene encoding a protein within the ERK/PI3 signaling pathway, and is closely regulated during the development of excitatory neurons during synapse formation in regions of the brain important for social cognition (Levitt and Campbell, 2009). Variations in MET have been linked to increased risk for ASD (Campbell et al., 2010), and in animal models have been associated with developmental abnormalities consistent with ASD phenotypes (Judson et al., 2009). Alleles of rs158830, located within the promoter region of MET, have been of particular interest because of their effects on transcription and protein expression of MET. The presence of the "C" allele of rs158830 has been associated with more severe deficits in social function and communication (Campbell et al., 2010). Rudie et al. (2012) measured the impact of the rs158830 risk allele on structural and functional brain development in a population of 162 children and adolescents with ($n = 75$) and without ($n = 87$) ASD. Participants contributed to one or more of three separate neuroimaging experiments: an fMRI paradigm involving passive viewing emotional faces; a resting fMRI scan; and a diffusion tensor imaging scan. Group differences between ASD and controls were present for both functional imaging paradigms. Independent of diagnosis, the MET risk allele was also associated with abnormalities in brain activation in both paradigms, and with decreased fractional inositropy in several WM tracts in related regions. Notably, the effects of the risk allele were more pronounced in the ASD group than in the controls. Across all three testing conditions, the intermediate heterozygote (GC) within the ASD group were more similar to the high risk homozygote (CC); while within the control group the heterozygote condition was more similar to the low risk (GG) homozygote. The differences between the ASD participants with and without the risk allele supported the value of stratifying samples both by diagnosis and by specific genetic risk factors.

## DIMENSIONAL APPROACHES TO HETEROGENEITY

Although most imaging studies in ASD have concentrated on group comparisons, there have been some which have sought instead to determine whether the variation observed in clinical characteristics could be linked to differences in brain structure and function. Some of these have concerned the different domains considered as part of the core criteria of ASD, while others have started to explore the impact of common co-existing features such as ID, anxiety symptoms, and problems with attention and impulsivity. As the vast majority of the imaging literature is based on DSM-IV criteria, this review will accordingly consider the domains of language, social communication, and repetitive/restricted interests and behaviors separately, rather than following the revised criteria in which language and social interaction are combined (American Psychiatric Association, 2013).

### SOCIAL COGNITION

Impairment in social interactions is the defining feature of ASD. There has been significant progress in delineating the neural systems playing key roles in the enormously complex cognitive processes underlying routine social activity, highlighting brain structures such as the medial frontal and superior temporal cortex, insula, cingulate, and limbic regions (Blakemore, 2008). Neuroimaging studies comparing ASD with controls have demonstrated that these regions among those most consistently showing abnormalities, confirming their likely involvement in the clinical phenomena (Di Martino et al., 2009; Sugranyes et al., 2011).

However, as in other aspects of ASD, the severity of impairment of social function can vary widely. Fewer studies have attempted to determine if MRI measures of these neural systems predicts the clinical symptoms. The amygdala has been one of the regions that has received the most attention, due to its well-established role in relevant aspects of social cognition such as response to facial expressions and threat detection (Adolphs et al., 2005; Adolphs, 2010; Pessoa, 2010), and evidence of abnormal structure and function of the amygdala in ASD (Abell et al., 1999; Baron-Cohen et al., 2000; Howard et al., 2000; Sparks et al., 2002; Schumann et al., 2004, 2009; Hazlett et al., 2009; Mosconi et al., 2009; Groen et al., 2010; Stigler et al., 2011; Nordahl et al., 2012). Studies relating amygdala volume to the degree of social impairment have had mixed results. Two studies found social impairment correlated with decreases in amygdala volume (Nacewicz et al., 2006; Mosconi et al., 2009), one with larger amygdala volume (Schumann et al., 2009), and two others no relationship at all (Dziobek et al., 2006; Juranek et al., 2006). The two studies that found positive correlation assessed social ability by experimental procedures, such as eye-tracking, rating joint attention from camera recordings, or facial emotion recognition tasks (Nacewicz et al., 2006; Mosconi et al., 2009). The other three studies which found no correlation or negative correlation (Dziobek et al., 2006; Juranek et al., 2006; Schumann et al., 2009) instead assessed social ability through clinical interviews such as the Autism Diagnostic Observation Schedule (ADOS) (Lord et al., 2000) or Autism Diagnostic Interview-Revised (ADI-R) (Lord et al., 1994), demonstrating the complexity of characterizing social ability and of relating clinical behaviors to results of cognitive tests. Other areas in which there has been some degree of correlation observed to measures of social function have included the medial PFC (Rojas et al., 2006; Schulte-Ruther et al., 2011), inferior frontal gyrus (Rojas et al., 2006), superior temporal sulcus (Pelphrey et al., 2005), FG (Greimel et al., 2010), temporal-parietal junction (TPJ) (Lombardo et al., 2011), and the anterior cingulate cortex (ACC) (Scott-Van Zeeland et al., 2010b).

### LANGUAGE IMPAIRMENT

Delayed or atypical language development is a core feature of ASD (American Psychiatric Association, 2000). Language ability can vary enormously, from the 25% who never develop functional language to mild abnormalities in prosody (Mody et al., 2013). Neuroimaging studies of language function in autism have focused on language-associated brain regions such lateral inferior frontal cortex, including Broca's area, and temporoparietal cortex, which contains Wernicke's area (Shapleske et al., 1999; Dronkers et al., 2007). Language-associated areas are anatomically and functionally asymmetric, with predominance normally found in the hemisphere opposite the dominant hand. Although results are mixed, observations from multiple studies have suggested that asymmetry is often reduced or reversed in ASD (e.g., Herbert et al., 2002, 2005; Rojas et al., 2002, 2005; Just et al., 2004; McAlonan et al., 2005; Knaus et al., 2009; Anderson et al., 2010; Catarino et al., 2011).

Bigler et al. (2007) reported on gray matter volumes of the superior temporal gyrus in a group of 30 children with ASD compared to 39 controls matched on age and IQ; 13 of the controls had reading deficits. They found that superior temporal gyrus volume correlated with a standardized measure of language ability in the control group, but not the children with ASD. An early fMRI study reported that adults with ASD did not exhibit normal lateralization of brain response to vocal stimuli (Gervais et al., 2004). A more recent fMRI study of brain activity of sleeping toddlers (40 ASD and 40 matched controls, aged 12–48 months) during the reading of a bedtime story found that the ASD group did not show normal left-lateralized responses; there was instead a right-lateralized temporal cortex response which was most pronounced in the children toward the older end of the age range studied, suggesting an increasingly deviant developmental trajectory of laterality. Interestingly, within the ASD group, greater right hemisphere activity correlated with less severe symptoms (Redcay and Courchesne, 2008; Eyler et al., 2012).

These findings are consistent with those from a study comparing ASD and specific language impairment (SLI), a disorder in which delayed language development is present despite preservation of other cognitive abilities, and for which there is evidence of shared genetic risks with ASD (Fisher et al., 2003). This study compared children aged 6–12 years with SLI and typical controls to individuals with ASD with and without language impairment (De Fosse et al., 2004). They found overall larger brain volumes in the children with ASD. However, while reversed asymmetry of language-associated regions was present in the two groups that had language impairment, it was not present in the ASD group with normal language ability, suggesting that the asymmetry was more related to the presence or absence of language impairment than the ASD diagnosis.

### RESTRICTED AND REPETITIVE INTERESTS AND BEHAVIORS

The third core domain of ASD as defined in DSM-IV is the presence of restricted interests and RRIB, including both "higher order" RRIB, such as unusual preoccupations or patterns of interests and compulsive adherence to rituals or routines, and "lower order" RRIB, referring to stereotyped and repetitive motor mannerisms and preoccupation with parts of objects (Lord et al., 1994). Much of the work on RRIB has focused on the relationships between the frontal cortex and basal ganglia, taking as a model conditions with similar features such as obsessive-compulsive disorder (Scarone et al., 1992; Rosenberg et al., 1997) and Tourette syndrome (Peterson et al., 2003; Langen et al., 2012). Volumes of frontal regions have been correlated with RRB severity in ASD (Hardan et al., 2003; Rojas et al., 2006; Ecker et al., 2012), and in fMRI studies of tasks requiring cognitive inhibition, RRB severity has been shown to correlate with abnormal activation in areas including dorsolateral PFC, anterior cingulate, and the intraparietal cortex (Shafritz et al., 2008; Agam et al., 2010). Studies relating RRB symptoms to basal ganglia volumes have had mixed results. In a comparatively large sample of individuals with autism ($n = 99$; TD: $n = 89$), Langen et al. (2009) found that caudate volume was negatively correlated with insistence on sameness within higher order RRB. However, in Hardan et al. (2003), only scores on lower order RRB complex mannerisms were negatively correlated with caudate volume. Two other studies that included subjects across the autism spectrum and did not exclude ID found instead a positive correlation between caudate volume and severity of RRB (Hollander et al., 2005; Rojas et al., 2006).

### SENSORY ABNORMALITIES

Abnormal sensory function, either hyper- or hyposensitivity, is extremely common in ASD. Described as an associated feature in DSM-IV-TR (American Psychiatric Association, 2000), in DSM-5 it was changed to be one of the diagnostic criteria in the restricted/RRIB category (American Psychiatric Association, 2013). Although key brain regions for sensory function such as the primary somatosensory cortex and insula are among those most consistently showing abnormalities in ASD, to date few neuroimaging studies have examined imaging correlates of abnormal sensory function in ASD directly. Cascio et al. (2012) used fMRI to compare responses to pleasant, neutral and unpleasant tactile stimuli between a sample of 13 adults with ASD and 14 matched controls. They found that the subjective descriptions of the sensations were on average similar between the groups, although there was more variability in the ASD responses, highlighting the heterogeneity within the group. Despite the similarity of the subjective reports, there were significant differences in brain activation: the ASD group had significantly less BOLD response to the pleasant and neutral stimuli, but some areas of increased activation during the unpleasant stimuli, including primary somatosensory cortex and insula. Increased activation in the insula correlated with social impairment scores, supporting the theory put forth by some that abnormal sensory function during early development may contribute to abnormal social development (Hilton et al., 2010). The thalamus has also been examined due to its central role in sensory processing. While thalamic volumes have not been found to relate to sensory function, a magnetic resonance spectroscopy study observed indications of a relationship between thalamic brain metabolites (*N*-acetyl aspartate and glutamate + glutamine) and sensory function (Hardan et al., 2008a,b). Another study reported that GM volume in the brainstem and oral sensitivity measures were associated in high-functioning ASD (Jou et al., 2009).

### ANXIETY SYMPTOMS

Anxiety symptoms are also very common in ASD, estimated to affect over 40% (de Bruin et al., 2007; Eussen et al., 2012; Strang et al., 2012). A handful of studies have looked at how varying levels of anxiety affects neuroimaging findings in ASD, most of which have targeted structures in the limbic system. Higher levels of social anxiety (Corbett et al., 2009), and generalized anxiety/depression scores in children (Juranek et al., 2006) have each been correlated with decreased amygdala volume. fMRI studies have been more mixed. Kleinhans et al. (2010) found higher social anxiety scores correlated with reduced activation in the FG and greater activation in the amygdala in adults in response to angry and fearful faces. In contrast, another study in adolescents showed that brain activations were not associated with depression or anxiety scores (Weng et al., 2011).

### POOR ATTENTION AND IMPULSIVITY

Symptoms such as inattention, hyperactivity, and impulsivity (American Psychiatric Association, 2000) are present in a majority of individuals with ASD (Schatz et al., 2002; Goldstein and Schwebach, 2004). The frequency of these types of symptoms in ASD was previously acknowledged through exclusion of a separate diagnosis of ADHD in the presence of PDD. Recognition that this exclusion unfortunately diminished the likelihood of recognition of co-occurring ADHD and associated symptoms resulted in its removal in DSM-5. Although work to date on ADHD and ASD has been largely been done separately, making explicit comparison between the two conditions and difficult, data thus far has demonstrated that there is significant overlap in both affected brain regions and genetic risk factors in the two disorders (Gargaro et al., 2011). This has led to hypotheses that that the underlying biology for both may fall along a continuum, with increasingly prominent social impairments as one moves from ADHD to ASD, and suggestions that more research studies should include both groups to allow direct comparisons (Brieber et al., 2007; Rommelse et al., 2011).

## SUMMARY OF FINDINGS

Most studies in autism have not had understanding heterogeneity as a goal, but instead have effectively treated it as noise in the search for brain differences that correspond to the categorical diagnosis. These efforts have had some success. Findings have implicated many regions with prominent roles in social cognition, such as the superior temporal sulcus, amygdala, and insula (Di Martino et al., 2009). Volumetric and functional differences appear to be more pronounced in younger individuals, with a tendency toward larger volumes earlier in life (Courchesne et al., 2011; Wolff, 2013). With maturation these differences decrease in magnitude, particularly for brain structure, such that by adolescence summative measures such as total brain volume are not significantly different than controls. Other measures of brain structure continue to show differences into adulthood, and newer multivariate techniques have been able to identify subtle and widespread cortical differences consistent with the ongoing differences in function and behavior (Ecker et al., 2010). Abnormalities in structural and functional measures of connectivity are a consistent finding.

Efforts to address the heterogeneity of autism in neuroimaging studies have chiefly taken two forms: the first, to subdivide ASD into more homogeneous subgroups, using a variety of criteria; the second, to take a dimensional approach to examining the relationship between neuroimaging data and clinical features. Far fewer studies have been done using these approaches, and sample sizes are often quite modest; negative findings in particular may reflect lack of statistical power, or that studies using more sensitive measures have not yet been performed.

Clinically defined categories have included subgroups such as Aspergers's versus narrowly defined Autism, ASD with and without significant language impairment, and low-functioning versus high-functioning autism. None of these comparisons have provided a strong case for a neurobiologically robust and distinct subtype, which is not to say variation along these clinical dimensions is not of ongoing interest. The relationship of ID to the pathophysiology of ASD has continued to be a challenging issue, complicated by the fact that brain imaging studies of individuals with significant ID are very difficult to carry out, and so samples including these subjects are often underpowered. This has created a situation where despite the predominance of ID in ASD, most imaging studies, particularly those with the sample sizes necessary for multivariate analyses, are carried out in ASD individuals with normal or near-normal IQ.

There have been a few specific risk factors identified with strong enough associations to ASD to look at affected individuals as specific subgroups. One of these is male gender, whose much higher rates compared to females imply the presence of risk factors unique to males. The few structural imaging studies explicitly designed for gender comparison have generally not found significant differences in the pattern of abnormalities, except for the likelihood of females to show more pronounced brain differences than males. Of other specific genetic risk factors, by far the most work has been done in FXS. Here, the pattern of imaging findings appeared to be driven by the FXS genotype, regardless of whether the individuals met criteria for ASD or not. Some of the brain differences associated with the presence of autistic features in the FXS and non-FXS groups affected similar regions but in opposite directions.

The other most frequently used approach in neuroimaging to heterogeneity with ASD has been through relating dimensional variation in clinical or cognitive measures to brain measures. Although these analyses have been generally intended less to describe heterogeneity than to strengthen the case for the likely relevance of the observed brain differences to the clinical symptoms, they can be informative about whether the variation observed clinically and in imaging measures are likely to be reflective of each other. Although reported findings have been mixed, many have been consistent with what would be expected for brain regions known to be associated with specific functions, as described above.

## CONCLUSION

So, what has neuroimaging told us about heterogeneity in ASD? The main finding may be that neuroimaging provides no refuge from the multiplicity of presentations and candidate risk factors found in the clinic and the genetics laboratory. Studies to date have made progress in identifying patterns of brain abnormalities present in groups of people with ASD, but inconsistency between study results is still more the norm than the exception, and biomarkers robust enough to be meaningful on an individual level have yet to be identified. Adoption of multivariate methods and pattern identification methods based on techniques such as machine learning may improve results, as more reflective of the widespread and subtle morphologic differences that have become apparent with larger scale studies (Ecker et al., 2012), and are consistent with current hypotheses of ASD as being rooted in abnormalities of synaptic development (State and Sestan, 2012). The difficulty with this approach, however, as has been discussed extensively elsewhere (Hyman, 2010), is that it continues to center around a concept of autism, or even the broader range of ASD, as a discrete entity. Such a designation can be highly useful from the practical level of providing a diagnostic label and indications for intervention. However, as a constraint for inquiries into biology, it may more distort than illuminate. Autistic disorders exist not only as a spectrum within the realm of pathology, but also the severe end of a set of continuous traits which extend into the general population, and do not have clear boundaries with other disorders such as ADHD (Lai et al., 2013b). Abundant evidence from epidemiologic, genetic and twin studies supports the common nature of the risk factors affecting autistic traits within individuals meeting criteria for the disorder and in the general population (Robinson et al., 2011; Ronald and Hoekstra, 2011; Lundstrom et al., 2012). ASD might be better considered a name assigned to designate individuals whose expression of a particular set of continuously varying traits has reached a certain threshold of severity (Uher and Rutter, 2012).

These issues have been much discussed of late, prompted by the most recent revision of DSM (Kendler, 2012; Lord and Jones, 2012). Although DSM-5 left the previous categorical system largely intact, acknowledging its clinical utility and the lack of sufficient evidence to support more substantive revision, for research purposes there has been increasing support for decreasing the emphasis on categorical diagnoses (Uher and Rutter, 2012). Proposed alternatives include transdiagnostic dimensional approaches such as the Research Domain Criteria (RDoCs) currently under development at the National Institutes of Mental Health (NIMH) in the U.S.[2] (Insel et al., 2010), which focus on simpler constructs (for example, response to social stimuli, or working memory) that may be more amenable to linking across multiple levels of neural, cognitive, and behavioral function regardless of which clinical syndrome a particular feature is occurring within.

Neuroimaging has revolutionized our understanding of neurodevelopmental disorders by affording observations of brain structure and function *in vivo*, including the tracing of developmental trajectories in children and adolescents from the very first months of life. It should be kept in mind that despite the rapid technical advances in the field, MRI techniques remain limited to a level of spatial and temporal resolution too coarse to visualize the synaptic or neuronal-level abnormalities that may be core features of disorders such as ASD. If this is the level from which heterogeneity arises, neuroimaging may ultimately not be the best tool for parsing these differences. However, in combination with more finely grained methods such as post-mortem tissue analysis and animal models, neuroimaging studies have the potential to provide a critical intermediate step between risk factors such as specific genes and the cognitive or behavioral features of interest. Such approaches, by focusing on the links between genetic, biological, and behavioral domains, allow us the opportunity to deconstruct our conceptions of ASD back to where they can be grounded in biology. Eventually, heterogeneity may no longer be considered as noise in neuroimaging studies of ASD, and instead take its place as a guide to pathophysiology (Brock, 2011; Georgiades et al., 2013).

[2]www.nimh.nih.gov/research-priorities/rdoc

## ACKNOWLEDGMENTS

Rhoshel K. Lenroot and Pui Ka Yeung both contributed to the review of literature and writing of manuscript.

## REFERENCES

1. Abell, F., Krams, M., Ashburner, J., Pass- ingham, R., Friston, K., Frackowiak, R., et al. (1999). The neuroanatomy of autism: a voxel-based whole brain analysis of structural scans. *Neurore- port* 10, 1647–1651. doi:10.1097/00001756-199906030-00005
2. Adolphs, R. (2010). What does the amygdala contribute to social cog- nition? *Ann. N. Y. Acad. Sci.* 1191, 42–61. doi:10.1111/j.1749-6632.2010.05445.x
3. Adolphs, R., Gosselin, F., Buchanan, T. W., Tranel, D., Schyns, P., and Damasio, A. R. (2005). A mecha- nism for impaired fear recognition after amygdala damage. *Nature* 433, 68–72. doi:10.1038/nature03086
4. Agam, Y., Joseph, R. M., Barton, J. J. S., and Manoach, D. S. (2010). Reduced cognitive control of response inhibi- tion by the anterior cingulate cortex in autism spectrum disorders. *Neu- roimage* 52, 336–347. doi:10.1016/j. neuroimage.2010.04.010
5. Amaral, D. G., Schumann, C. M., and Nordahl, C. W. (2008). Neu- roanatomy of autism. *Trends Neu- rosci.* 31, 137–145. doi:10.1016/j. tins.2007.12.005
6. American Psychiatric Association. (2000). *Diagnostic and Statisti- cal Manual of Mental Disorders: DSM-IV. Revised 4th ed.* Wash- ington, DC: American Psychiatric Association.
7. American Psychiatric Association. (2013). *Diagnostic and Statistical Manual of Mental Disorders: DSM-5*, 5th Edn. Arlington, VA: American Psychiatric Association.
8. Amir, R. E., Van den Veyver, I. B., Wan, M., Tran, C. Q., Francke, U., and Zoghbi, H. Y. (1999). Rett syn- drome is caused by mutations in X-linked MECP2, encoding methyl- CpG-binding protein 2. *Nat. Genet.* 23, 185–188. doi:10.1038/13810
9. Anderson, J. S., Lange, N., Froehlich, A., DuBray, M. B., Druzgal, T. J., Froimowitz, M. P., et al. (2010). Decreased left posterior insular activity during auditory language in Autism. *Am. J. Neuroradiol.* 31, 131–139. doi:10.3174/ajnr.A1789
10. Antshel, K., Aneja, A., Strunge, L., Pee- bles, J., Fremont, W., Stallone, K., et al. (2007). Autistic spectrum disor- ders in velo-cardio facial syndrome (22q11.2 Deletion). *J. Autism Dev. Disord.* 37, 1776–1786. doi:10.1007/s10803-006-0308-6
11. Astur, R. S., Tropp, J., Sava, S., Consta-ble, R. T., and Markus, E. J. (2004). Sex differences and correlations in a virtual Morris water task, a virtual radial arm maze, and mental rota- tion. *Behav. Brain Res.* 151, 103–115. doi:10.1016/j.bbr.2003.08.024
12. Aylward, E. H., Minshew, N. J., Field, K., Sparks, B. F., and Singh, N. (2002). Effects of age on brain volume and head circumference in autism. *Neurology* 59, 175–183. doi:10.1212/ WNL.59.2.175
13. Baron-Cohen, S., Ring, H. A., Bullmore, E. T., Wheelwright, S., Ashwin, C., and Williams, S. C. R. (2000). The amygdala theory of autism. *Neurosci. Biobehav. Rev.* 24, 355–364. doi:10. 1016/S0149-7634(00)00011-7
14. Bauman, M. D., Iosif, A. M., Ashwood, P., Braunschweig, D., Lee, A., Schumann, C. M., et al. (2013). Maternal antibodies from mothers of children with autism alter brain growth and social behavior development in the rhesus monkey. *Transl. Psychiatry* 3, e278. doi:10.1038/tp.2013.47
15. Beacher, F., Radulescu, E., Minati, L., Baron-Cohen, S., Lombardo, M. V., Lai, M. C., et al. (2012).
16. Sex differences and autism: brain function during verbal fluency and mental rotation. *PLoS ONE* 7:e38355. doi:10.1371/journal.pone. 0038355
17. Betancur, C. (2011). Etiological hetero- geneity in autism spectrum disorders: more than 100 genetic and genomic disorders and still count- ing. *Brain Res.* 1380, 42–77. doi:10. 1016/j.brainres.2010.11.078
18. Bigler, E. D., Mortensen, S., Nee- ley, E. S., Ozonoff, S., Krasny, L., Johnson, M., et al. (2007). Superior temporal gyrus, language function, and autism. *Dev. Neu- ropsychol.* 31, 217–238. doi:10.1080/87565640701190841
19. Blakemore, S. J. (2008). The social brain in adolescence. *Nat. Rev. Neurosci.* 9, 267–277. doi:10.1038/nrn2353
20. Bloss, C. S., and Courchesne, E. (2007). MRI neuroanatomy in young girls with autism: a preliminary study. *J. Am. Acad. Child Adolesc. Psychi- atry* 46, 515–523. doi:10.1097/chi. 0b013e318030e28b
21. Bos, K., Zeanah, C. H., Fox, N. A., Drury, S. S., McLaughlin, K. A., and Nelson, C. A. (2011). Psy- chiatric outcomes in young chil- dren with a history of institution- alization. *Harv. Rev. Psychiatry* 19, 15–24. doi:10.3109/10673229.2011. 549773
22. Braunschweig, D., Krakowiak, P., Dun- canson, P., Boyce, R., Hansen, R. L., Ashwood, P., et al. (2013). Autism-specific maternal autoanti- bodies recognize critical proteins in developing brain. *Transl. Psychiatry* 3, e277. doi:10.1038/tp.2013.50
23. Brieber, S., Neufang, S., Bruning, N., Kamp-Becker, I., Remschmidt, H., Herpertz-Dahlmann, B., et al. (2007). Structural brain abnormali- ties in adolescents with autism spec- trum disorder and patients with attention deficit/hyperactivity dis- order. *J. Child Psychol. Psychiatry* 48, 1251–1258. doi:10.1111/j.1469-7610.2007.01799.x
24. Brock, J. (2011). Commentary: comple- mentary approaches to the devel- opmental cognitive neuroscience of autism – reflections on Pelphrey etal. (2011). *J. Child Psychol. Psychia- try* 52, 645–646. doi:10.1111/j.1469-7610.2011.02414.x
25. Calderoni, S., Retico, A., Biagi, L., Tancredi, R., Muratori, F., and Tosetti, M. (2012). Female children with autism spectrum disorder: an insight from mass-univariate and pattern classification analyses. *Neu- roimage* 59, 1013–1022. doi:10.1016/ j.neuroimage.2011.08.070

26. Campbell, D. B., Warren, D., Sutcliffe, J. S., Lee, E. B., and Levitt, P. (2010). Association of MET with social and communication phenotypes in indi- viduals with autism spectrum dis- order. *Am. J. Med. Genet. B Neu- ropsychiatr. Genet.* 153B, 438–446. doi:10.1002/ajmg.b.30998
27. Canu, E., Boccardi, M., Ghidoni, R., Benussi, L., Duchesne, S., Testa, C., et al. (2009). HOXA1 A218G polymorphism is associ- ated with smaller cerebellar volume in healthy humans. *J. Neuroimag- ing* 19, 353–358. doi:10.1111/j.1552- 6569.2008.00326.x
28. Carter, A. S., Black, D. O., Tewani, S., Connolly, C. E., Kadlec, M. B., and Tager-Flusberg, H. (2007). Sex differences in toddlers with autism spectrum disorders. *J. Autism Dev. Disord.* 37, 86–97. doi:10.1007/s10803-006-0331-7
29. Carter, J. C., Lanham, D. C., Pham, D., Bibat, G., Naidu, S., and Kaufmann, W. E. (2008a). Selective cerebral vol- ume reduction in Rett syndrome: a multiple-approach MR imaging study. *AJNR Am. J. Neuroradiol.* 29, 436–441. doi:10.3174/ajnr.A0857
30. Carter, J. C., Capone, G. T., and Kaufmann, W. E. (2008b). Neu- roanatomic correlates of autism and stereotypy in children with Down syndrome. *Neuroreport* 19, 653–656. doi:10.1097/WNR. 0b013e3282faa8d8
31. Cascio, C. J., Moana, E. J., Guest, S., Nebel, M. B., Weisner, J., Baranek, T., et al. (2012). Perceptual and neural response to affective tactile texture stimulation in adults with autism spectrum disorders. *Autism Res.* 5, 231–244. doi:10.1002/aur. 1224
32. Catarino, A., Luke, L., Waldman, S., Andrade, A., Fletcher, P. C., and Ring, (2011). An fMRI investigation of detection of semantic incongruities in autistic spectrum conditions. *Eur. J. Neurosci.* 33, 558–567. doi:10. 1111/j.1460-9568.2010.07503.x
33. Center for Disease Control and Preven- tion. (2012). Prevalence of autism spectrum disorders – Autism and developmental disabilities monitor- ing network, 14 Sites, United States, 2006. *MMWR Surveill. Summ.* 61, 1–29.
34. Cicchetti, D., and Rogosch, F. A. (1996). Equifinality and multifinal- ity in developmental psychopathol- ogy. *Dev. Psychopathol.* 8, 597–600. doi:10.1017/S0954579400007318
35. Cohen, I. L., Liu, X., Schutz, C., White, B. N., Jenkins, E. C., Brown, W. T., et al. (2003). Association of autism severity with a monoamine oxidase A functional polymorphism. *Clin. Genet.* 64, 190–197. doi:10.1034/j. 1399-0004.2003.00115.x
36. Constantino, J. N. (2011). The quan- titative nature of autistic social impairment. *Pediatr. Res.* 69(5 Pt 2), 55R–62R. doi:10.1203/PDR. 0b013e318212ec6e
37. Corbett, B. A., Carmean, V., Ravizza, S., Wendelken, C., Henry, M. L., Carter, C., et al. (2009). A functional and structural study of emotion and face processing in children with autism. *Psychiatr. Res.* 173, 196–205. doi:10. 1016/j.pscychresns.2008.08.005
38. Courchesne, E., Campbell, K., and Solso, S. (2011). Brain growth across the life span in autism: age-specific changes in anatomical pathology. *Brain Res.* 1380, 138–145. doi:10. 1016/j.brainres.2010.09.101
39. Crucian, G. P., and Berenbaum, S. A. (1998). Sex differences in right hemisphere tasks. *Brain Cogn.* 36, 377–389. doi:10.1006/brcg.1998.0999
40. Davis, L. K., Hazlett, H. C., Librant, A. L., Nopoulos, P., Sheffield, V. C., Piven, J., et al. (2008). Corti- cal enlargement in autism is associ- ated with a functional VNTR in the monoamine oxidase A gene. *Am. J. Med. Genet. B Neuropsychiatr. Genet.* 147B, 1145–1151. doi:10.1002/ajmg. b.30738
41. De Bruin, E., Ferdinand, R., Meester, S., de Nijs, P., and Verheij, F. (2007). High rates of psychiatric co- morbidity in PDD-NOS. *J. Autism Dev. Disord.* 37, 877–886. doi:10. 1007/s10803-006-0215-x
42. De Fosse, L., Hodge, S. M., Makris, N., Kennedy, D. N., Caviness, V. S., McGrath, L., et al. (2004). Language- association cortex asymmetry in autism and specific language impair- ment. *Ann. Neurol.* 56, 757–766. doi: 10.1002/ ana.20275
43. Dennis, E. L., Jahanshad, N., Rudie, J. D., Brown, J. A., Johnson, K., McMahon, K. L., et al. (2011). Altered structural brain connectivity in healthy carri- ers of the autism risk gene, CNT- NAP2. *Brain Connect.* 1, 447–459. doi:10.1089/brain.2011.0064
44. Di Martino, A., Ross, K., Uddin, L. Q., Sklar, A. B., Castellanos, F. X., and Milham, M. P. (2009). Func- tional brain correlates of social and nonsocial processes in autism spec- trum disorders: an activation likeli- hood estimation meta-analysis. *Biol. Psychiatry* 65, 63–74. doi:10.1016/j. biopsych.2008.09.022
45. Di Martino, A., Yan, C. G., Li, Q., Denio, E., Castellanos, F. X., Alaerts, K., et al. (2013). The autism brain imaging data exchange: towards a large-scale evaluation of the intrin- sic brain architecture in autism. *Mol. Psychiatry.* doi:10.1038/mp.2013.78. [Epub ahead of print].
46. Dickstein, D. P., Pescosolido, M. F., Reidy, B. L., Galvan, T., Kim, K. L., Sey mour, K. E., et al. (2013). Developmental meta-analysis of the functional neural correlates of autism spectrum disorders. *J. Am. Acad. Child Adolesc. Psychiatry* 52, 279e–289e. doi:10.1016/j.jaac.2012. 12.012
47. *Dronkers*, N. F., Plaisant, O., Iba-Zizen, M. T., and Cabanis, E. A. (2007). Paul Broca's historic cases: high res- olution MR imaging of the brains of Leborgne and Lelong. *Brain* 130, 1432–1441. doi:10.1093/brain/ awm042
48. Dworzynski, K., Ronald, A., Bolton, P., and Happe, F. (2012). How different are girls and boys above and below the diagnostic threshold for autism spectrum disorders? *J. Am. Acad. Child Adolesc. Psychiatry* 51, 788–797. doi:10.1016/j.jaac.2012.05. 018
49. Dziobek, I., Fleck, S., Rogers, K., Wolf, T., and Convit, A. (2006). The 'amygdala theory of autism' revis- ited: Linking structure to behavior. *Neuropsychologia* 44, 1891–1899. doi:10.1016/j.neuropsychologia. 2006.02.005
50. Ecker, C., Marquand, A., Mourao- Miranda, J., Johnston, P., Daly, E. M., Brammer, M. J., et al. (2010). Describing the brain in autism in five dimensions – Magnetic resonance imaging-assisted diagnosis of autism spectrum disorder using a multipa- rameter classification approach. *J. Neurosci.* 30, 10612–10623. doi:10. 1523/JNEUROSCI.5413-09.2010
51. Ecker, C., Suckling, J., Deoni, S. C., Lombardo, M. V., Bullmore, E., Baron-Cohen, S., et al. (2012). Brain anatomy and its relationship to behavior in adults with autism spec- trum disorder: a multicenter mag- netic resonance imaging study. *Arch. Gen. Psychiatry* 69, 195–209. doi:10. 1001/archgenpsychiatry.2011.1251
52. Eickhoff, S. B., Laird, A. R., Grefkes, C., Wang, L. E., Zilles, K., and Fox, T. (2009). Activation likelihood estimation meta-analysis of neu- roimaging data: a random-effects approach based on empirical esti- mates of spatial uncertainty. *Hum. Brain Mapp.* 30, 2907–2926. doi:10. 1002/hbm.20718
53. Eussen, M. L., Van Gool, A. R., Verheij, F., De Nijs, P. F., Verhulst, F. C., and Greaves-Lord, K. (2012). The asso- ciation of quality of social relations, symptom severity and intelligence with anxiety in children with autism spectrum disorders. *Autism*. doi:10. 1177/1362361312453882
54. Eyler, L. T., Pierce, K., and Courchesne, E. (2012). A failure of left temporal cortex to specialize for language is an early emerging and fundamental property of autism. *Brain* 135(Pt 3), 949–960. doi:10.1093/brain/awr364
55. Fisher, S. E., Lai, C. S., and Monaco, A. P. (2003). Deciphering the genetic basis of speech and language dis- orders. *Annu. Rev. Neurosci.* 26, 57–80. doi:10.1146/annurev.neuro. 26.041002.131144
56. Fombonne, E. (2003). Epidemiologi- cal surveys of autism and other pervasive developmental disorders: an update. *J. Autism Dev. Dis- ord.* 33, 365–382. doi:10.1023/A: 1024470920898
57. Fombonne, E. (2009). Epidemiology of pervasive developmental disorders. *Pediatr. Res.* 65, 591–598. doi:10. 1203/PDR.0b013e31819e7203
58. Gadow, K. D., Devincent, C. J., Pomeroy, J., and Azizian, A. (2005). Compar- ison of DSM-IV symptoms in ele- mentary school-age children with PDD versus clinic and community samples. *Autism* 9, 392–415. doi:10. 1177/1362361305056079
59. Gallagher, A., and Hallahan, B. (2012). Fragile X-associated disorders: a clinical overview. *J. Neurol.* 259, 401–413. doi:10.1007/s00415-011- 6161-3
60. Garber, H. J., Ritvo, E. R., Chiu, L. C., Griswold, V. J., Kashanian, A., Free- man, B. J., et al. (1989). A mag- netic resonance imaging study of autism: normal fourth ventricle size and absence of pathology. *Am. J. Psy- chiatry* 146, 532–534.
61. Gargaro, B. A., Rinehart, N. J., Brad- shaw, J. L., Tonge, B. J., and Sheppard, D. M. (2011). Autism and ADHD: how far have we come in the comor- bidity debate? *Neurosci. Biobehav. Rev.* 35, 1081–1088. doi:10.1016/j. neubiorev.2010.11.002
62. Georgiades, S., Szatmari, P., and Boyle, M. (2013). Importance of studying heterogeneity in autism. *Neuropsy- chiatry* 3, 123–125. doi:10.2217/npy. 13.8
63. Gervais, H., Belin, P., Boddaert, N., Leboyer, M., Coez, A., Sfaello, I., et al. (2004). Abnormal cortical voice processing in autism. *Nat. Neurosci.* 7, 801–802. doi:10.1038/nn1291
64. Geschwind, D. H. (2009). Advances in autism. *Annu. Rev. Med.* 60, 367–380. doi:10.1146/annurev.med. 60.053107.121225
65. Geschwind, D. H., and Levitt, P. (2007). Autism spectrum disorders: devel- opmental disconnection syndromes. *Curr. Opin. Neurobiol.* 17, 103–111. doi:10.1016/j.conb.2007.01.009
66. Goldstein, S., and Schwebach, A. (2004). The comorbidity of per- vasive developmental disorder and attention deficit hyperactivity dis- order: results of a retrospective chart review. *J. Autism Dev. Disord.* 34, 329–339. doi:10.1023/B:JADD. 0000029554.46570.68
67. Greimel, E., Schulte-Ruther, M., Kircher, T., Kamp-Becker, I., Remschmidt, H., Fink, G. R., et al. (2010). Neural mechanisms of empathy in ado- lescents with autism spectrum dis- order and their fathers. *Neuroim- age* 49, 1055–1065. doi:10.1016/j. neuroimage.2009.07.057

68. Groen, W., Teluij, M., Buitelaar, J., and Tendolkar, I. (2010). Amygdala and Hippocampus enlargement during adolescence in Autism. *J. Am. Acad. Child Adolesc. Psychiatry* 49, 552–560. doi:10.1016/j.jaac. 2009.12.023
69. Hagerman, R. H., Hoem, G., and Hagerman, P. (2010). Fragile X and autism: intertwined at the molecular level leading to targeted treatments. *Mol. Autism* 1, doi:10.1186/2040- 2392-1-12
70. Hansen, R. L., Ozonoff, S., Krakowiak, P., Angkustsiri, K., Jones, C., Deprey, J., et al. (2008). Regression in autism: prevalence and associ- ated factors in the CHARGE study. *Ambul. Pediatr.* 8, 25–31. doi:10. 1016/j. ambp.2007.08.006
71. Hardan, A. Y., Kilpatrick, M., Keshavan, S., and Minshew, N. J. (2003). Motor performance and anatomic magnetic resonance imaging (MRI) of the basal ganglia in autism. *J. Child Neurol.* 18, 317–324. doi:10. 1177/08830738030180050801
72. Hardan, A. Y., Minshew, N. J., Melhem, M., Srihari, S., Jo, B., Bansal, R., et al. (2008a). An MRI and pro- ton spectroscopy study of the thala- mus in children with autism. *Psychi- atr. Res.* 163, 97–105. doi:10.1016/j. pscychres-ns.2007.12.002
73. Hardan, A. Y., Girgis, R. R., Adams, J., Gilbert, A. R., Melhem, N. M., Keshavan, M. S., et al. (2008b). Brief report: abnormal association between the thalamus and brain size in Asperger's disorder. *J. Autism Dev. Disord.* 38, 390–394. doi:10.1007/s10803-007-0385-1
74. Hartley, S. L., and Sikora, D. M. (2009). Sex differences in autism spectrum disorder: an examination of developmental functioning, autis- tic symptoms, and coexisting behav- ior problems in toddlers. *J. Autism Dev. Disord.* 39, 1715–1722. doi:10. 1007/s10803-009-0810-8
75. Hazlett, H. C., Poe, M. D., Lightbody, A. A., Gerig, G., MacFall, J. R., Ross, A. K., et al. (2009). Teasing apart the heterogeneity of autism: same behavior, different brains in toddlers with fragile X syndrome and autism. *J. Neurodev. Disord.* 1, 81–90. doi:10. 1007/s11689-009-9009-8
76. Hazlett, H. C., Poe, M. D., Lightbody, A. A., Styner, M., MacFall, J. R., Reiss, A. L., et al. (2012). Trajectories of early brain volume development in frag- ile X syndrome and autism. *J. Am. Acad. Child Adolesc. Psychiatry* 51, 921–933. doi:10.1016/j.jaac.2012.07. 003
77. Hedrick, A., Lee, Y., Wallace, G. L., Greenstein, D., Clasen, L., Giedd, J. N., et al. (2012). Autism risk gene MET variation and cortical thick- ness in typically developing chil- dren and adolescents. *Autism Res.* 5, 434–439. doi:10.1002/aur.1256
78. Herbert, M. R. (2010). Contributions of the environment and environmentally vulnerable physiology to autism spectrum disorders. *Curr. Opin. Neurol.* 23, 103–110. doi:10. 1097/WCO.0b013e328336a01f
79. Herbert, M. R., Harris, G. J., Adrien, K. T., Ziegler, D. A., Makris, N., Kennedy, D. N., et al. (2002). Abnor- mal asymmetry in language associ- ation cortex in autism. *Ann. Neurol.* 52, 588–596. doi:10.1002/ana.10349
80. Herbert, M. R., Ziegler, D. A., Deutsch, C. K., O'Brien, L. M., Kennedy, D. N., Filipek, P. A., et al. (2005). Brain asymmetries in autism and developmental language disorder: a nested whole-brain analysis. *Brain* 128, 213–226. doi:10.1093/brain/awh330
81. Herlitz, A., Nilsson, L.-G., and Bäckman, L. (1997). Gender differences in episodic memory. *Mem. Cognit.* 25, 801–811. doi:10.3758/BF03211324
82. Hilton, C. L., Harper, J. D., Kueker, R. H., Lang, A. R., Abbacchi, A. M., Todorov, A., et al. (2010). Sen- sory responsiveness as a predictor of social severity in children with high functioning autism spectrum disorders. *J. Autism Dev. Disord.* 40, 937–945. doi:10.1007/s10803-010- 0944-8
83. Hoeft, F., Walter, E., Lightbody, A. A., Hazlett, H. C., Chang, C., Piven, J., et al. (2011). Neuroanatom- ical differences in toddler boys with fragile x syndrome and idio- pathic autism. *Arch. Gen. Psy- chiatry* 68, 295–305. doi:10.1001/ archgenpsychiatry.2010.153
84. Hollander, E., Anagnostou, E., Chaplin, W., Esposito, K., Haznedar, M. M., Licalzi, E., et al. (2005). Striatal volume on magnetic resonance imaging and repetitive behaviors in autism. *Biol. Psychiatry* 58, 226–232. doi:10.1016/j. biopsych. 2005.03.040
85. Horder, J., and Murphy, D. G. M. (2012). Recent advances in neuroimaging in autism. *Neuropsychiatry* 2, 221–229. doi:10.2217/npy.12.25
86. Howard, M. A., Cowell, P. E., Boucher, J., Broks, P., Mayes, A., Farrant, A., et al. (2000). Convergent neuroanatomi- cal and behavioural evidence of an amygdala hypothesis of autism. *Neu- roreport* 11, 2931–2935.
87. Hrdlicka, M., Dudova, I., Beranova, I., Lisy, J., Belsan, T., Neuwirth, J., et al. (2005). Subtypes of autism by cluster analysis based on structural MRI data. *Eur. Child Adolesc. Psy- chiatry* 14, 138–144. doi:10.1007/s00787-005-0453-z
88. Hyman, S. E. (2010). The diagno- sis of mental disorders: the prob- lem of reification. *Annu. Rev. Clin. Psychol.* 6, 155–179. doi:10.1146/ annurev. clinpsy.3.022806.091532
89. Inoue, H., Yamasue, H., Tochigi, M., Abe, O., Liu, X., Kawa- mura, Y., et al. (2010). Associa- tion between the oxytocin recep- tor gene and amygdalar volume in healthy adults. *Biol. Psychiatry* 68, 1066–1072. doi:10.1016/j.biopsych. 2010.07.019
90. Insel, T., Cuthbert, B., Garvey, M., Heinssen, R., Pine, D. S., Quinn, K., et al. (2010). Research domain cri- teria (RDoC): toward a new classi- fication framework for research on mental disorders. *Am. J. Psychiatry* 167, 748–751. doi:10.1176/appi.ajp. 2010.09091379
91. Jou, R. J., Minshew, N. J., Melhem, N. M., Keshavan, M. S., and Hardan, A. Y. (2009). Brainstem volumetric alterations in children with autism. *Psychol. Med.* 39, 1347–1354. doi:10. 1017/S0033291708004376
92. Judson, M. C., Bergman, M. Y., Camp- bell, D. B., Eagleson, K. L., and Levitt, P. (2009). Dynamic gene and protein expression patterns of the autism- associated met receptor tyrosine kinase in the developing mouse fore- brain. *J. Comp. Neurol.* 513, 511–531. doi:10.1002/cne.21969
93. Juranek, J., Filipek, P. A., Berenji, G. R., Modahl, C., Osann, K., and Spence, M. A. (2006). Association between amygdala volume and anxiety level: magnetic resonance imaging (MRI) study in autistic children. *J. Child Neurol.* 21, 1051–1058. doi:10.1177/ 7010.2006.00237
94. Just, M. A., Cherkassky, V. L., Keller, T. A., and Minshew, N. J. (2004). Cortical activation and synchro- nization during sentence com- prehension in high-functioning autism: evidence of undercon- nectivity. *Brain* 127, 1811–1821. doi:10.1093/brain/awh199
95. Just, M. A., Keller, T. A., Malave, V. L., Kana, R. K., and Varma, S. (2012). Autism as a neural systems disor- der: a theory of frontal-posterior underconnectivity. *Neurosci. Biobe- hav. Rev.* 36, 1292–1313. doi:10. 1016/j.neubiorev.2012.02.007
96. Kaiser, M. D., Hudac, C. M., Shultz, S., Lee, S. M., Cheung, C., Berken, A. M., et al. (2010). Neural signa- tures of autism. *Proc. Natl. Acad. Sci. U.S.A.* 107, 21223–21228. doi:10. 1073/pnas.1010412107
97. Kanner, L. (1968). Autistic disturbances of affective contact. *Acta Paedopsychiatr.* 35, 100–136.
98. Kaufmann, W. E., Cooper, K. L., Mostofsky, S. H., Capone, G. T., Kates, W. R., Newschaffer, C. J., et al. (2003). Specificity of cere- bellar vermian abnormalities in autism: a quantitative magnetic res- onance imaging study. *J. Child Neurol.* 18, 463–470. doi:10.1177/08830738030180070501
99. Kendler, K. S. (2012). Levels of explana- tion in psychiatric and substance use disorders: implications for the devel- opment of an etiologically based nosology. *Mol. Psychiatry* 17, 11–21. doi:10.1038/mp.2011.70
100. Kleinhans, N. M., Richards, T., Weaver, K., Johnson, L. C., Greenson, J., Dawson, G., et al. (2010). Associa- tion between amygdala response to emotional faces and social anxiety in autism spectrum disorders. *Neuropsychologia* 48, 3665–3670. doi:10.1016/j.neuropsychologia. 2010.07.022
101. Knaus, T. A., Silver, A. M., Dominick, K. C., Schuring, M. D., Shaffer, N., Lindgren, K. A., et al. (2009). Age- related changes in the anatomy of language regions in autism spec- trum disorder. *Brain Imaging Behav.* 3, 51–63. doi:10.1007/s11682-008- 9048-x
102. Kozaki, T., and Yasukouchi, A. (2009). Sex differences on com- ponents of mental rotation at different menstrual phases. *Int. J. Neurosci.* 119, 59–67. doi:10.1080/00207450802480101
103. Kozlowski, A. M., Matson, J. L., and Sipes, M. (2012). Differences in chal- lenging behaviors between children with high functioning autism and Asperger's disorder. *J. Dev. Phys. Disabil.* 24, 359–371. doi:10.1007/s10882-012-9275-3
104. Lai, M. C., Lombardo, M. V., Suckling, J., Ruigrok, A. N., Chakrabarti, B., Ecker, C., et al. (2013a). Biologi- cal sex affects the neurobiology of autism. *Brain* 136(Pt 9), 2799–2815. doi:10.1093/brain/awt216
105. Lai, M. C., Lombardo, M. V., Chakrabarti, B., and Baron- Cohen, S. (2013b). Subgrouping the autism "spectrum": reflections on DSM-5. *PLoS Biol.* 11:e1001544. doi:10.1371/journal.pbio.1001544
106. Langen, M., Leemans, A., Johnson, P., Ecker, C., Daly, E., Murphy, C., et al. (2012). Fronto-striatal circuitry and inhibitory control in autism: findings from diffusion tensor imaging tractography. *Cortex* 48, 183–193. doi:10.1016/j.cortex.2011.05.018
107. Langen, M., Schnack, H. G., Nederveen, H., Bos, D., Lahuis, B. E., de Jonge, M. V., et al. (2009). Changes in the developmental trajectories of striatum in autism. *Biol. Psychiatry* 66, 327–333. doi:10.1016/j. biopsych. 2009.03.017
108. Levitt, P., and Campbell, D. B. (2009). The genetic and neurobiologic compass points toward common sig- naling dysfunctions in autism spec- trum disorders. *J. Clin. Invest.* 119, 747–754. doi:10.1172/JCI37934
109. Lombardo, M. V., Chakrabarti, B., Bull- more, E. T., Baron-Cohen, S., and Consortium, M. A. (2011). Spe- cialization of right temporo-parietal junction for mentalizing and its rela- tion to social impair-

ments in autism. *Neuroimage* 56, 1832–1838. doi:10. 1016/j.neuroimage.2011.02.067

110. Lord, C., and Jones, R. M. (2012). Annual research review: re-thinking the classification of autism spectrum disorders. *J. Child Psychol. Psychia- try* 53, 490–509. doi:10.1111/j.1469- 7610.2012.02547.x

111. Lord, C., Risi, S., Lambrecht, L., Cook, E. H., Leventhal, B. L., DiLavore, P. C., et al. (2000). The autism diagnos- tic observation schedule-generic: a standard measure of social and com- munication deficits associated with the spectrum of autism. *J. Autism Dev. Disord.* 30, 205–223. doi:10. 1023/A:1005592401947

112. Lord, C., Rutter, M., and Le Cou- teur, A. (1994). Autism diagnostic interview-revised: a revised version of a diagnostic interview for care- givers of individuals with possible pervasive developmental disorders. *J. Autism Dev. Disord.* 24, 659–685. doi:10.1007/BF02172145

113. Lord, C., Schopler, E., and Revicki, D. (1982). Sex differences in autism. *J. Autism Dev. Disord.* 12, 317–330. doi:10.1007/BF01538320

114. Lotspeich, L., Kwon, H., Schumann, C. M., Fryer, S. L., Goodlin-Jones, B. L., Buonocore, M. H., et al. (2004). Investigation of neuroanatomical differences between autism and Asperger syndrome. *Arch. Gen. Psy- chiatry* 61, 291–298. doi:10.1001/ archpsyc.61.3.291

115. Lowenthal, R., Paula, C. S., Schwartz- man, J. S., Brunoni, D., and Mercadante, M. T. (2007). Prevalence of pervasive developmental disorder in Down's syndrome. *J. Autism Dev. Disord.* 37, 1394–1395. doi:10.1007/ s10803-007-0374-4

116. Lundstrom, S., Chang, Z., Rastam, M., Gillberg, C., Larsson, H., Anckarsater, H., et al. (2012). Autism spectrum disorders and autistic like traits: similar etiology in the extreme end and the normal variation. *Arch. Gen. Psychiatry* 69, 46–52. doi:10. 1001/archgenpsychiatry.2011.144

117. Mandy, W., Chilvers, R., Chowdhury, U., Salter, G., Seigal, A., and Skuse, D. (2012). Sex differences in autism spectrum disorder: evidence from a large sample of children and adolescents. *J. Autism Dev. Disord.* 42, 1304–1313. doi:10.1007/s10803- 011-1356-0

118. Manes, F., Piven, J., Vrancic, D., Nan- clares, V., Plebst, C., and Starkstein, S. E. (1999). An MRI study of the corpus callosum and cerebellum in mentally retarded autistic individu- als. *J. Neuropsychiatry Clin. Neurosci.* 11, 470–474.

119. Matson, J. L., and Williams, L. W. (2013). Differential diagnosis and comorbidity: distinguishing autism from other mental health issues. *Neuropsychiatry* 3, 233–243. doi:10. 2217/npy.13.1

120. McAlonan, G. M., Cheung, V., Cheung, C., Suckling, J., Lam, G. Y., Tai, K. S., et al. (2005). Mapping the brain in autism. A voxel-based MRI study of volumetric differences and inter- correlations in autism. *Brain* 128, 268–276. doi:10.1093/brain/awh332

121. Meguid, N., Fahim, C., Yoon, U., Nashaat, N. H., Ibrahim, A. S., Mancini-Marie, A., et al. (2010). Brain morphology in autism and fragile X syndrome correlates with social IQ: first report from the Canadian-Swiss-Egyptian neurodevelopmental study. *J. Child Neurol.* 25, 599–608. doi:10.1177/0883073809341670

122. Mody, M., Manoach, D. S., Guen-ther, F. H., Kenet, T., Bruno, K. A., McDougle, C. J., et al. (2013). Speech and language in autism spec- trum disorder: a view through the lens of behavior and brain imaging. *Neuropsychiatry* 3, 223–232. doi:10. 2217/npy.13.19

123. Moreno-De-Luca, A., Myers, S. M., Challman, T. D., Moreno-De-Luca, D., Evans, D. W., and Ledbetter, D. H. (2013). Developmental brain dysfunction: revival and expan- sion of old concepts based on new genetic evidence. *Lancet Neu- rol.* 12, 406–414. doi:10.1016/S1474-4422(13)70011-5

124. Mosconi, M. W., Cody-Hazlett, H., Poe, M. D., Gerig, G., Gimpel-Smith, R., and Piven, J. (2009). Longitudi- nal study of amygdala volume and joint attention in 2- to 4-year-old children with autism. *Arch. Gen. Psy- chiatry* 66, 509–516. doi:10.1001/ archgenpsychiatry.2009.19

125. Moss, J., and Howlin, P. (2009). Autism spectrum disorders in genetic syndromes: implications for diagno- sis, intervention and understand- ing the wider autism spectrum dis- order population. *J. Intellect. Dis- abil. Res.* 53, 852–873. doi:10.1111/ j.1365-2788.2009.01197.x

126. Muller, R. A., Shih, P., Keehn, B., Deyoe, J. R., Leyden, K. M., and Shukla, D. K. (2011). Underconnected, but how? A survey of functional connectivity MRI studies in autism spectrum dis- orders. *Cereb. Cortex* 21, 2233–2243. doi:10.1093/cercor/bhq296

127. Murphy, K. C., Jones, L. A., and Owen, M. J. (1999). High rates of schizophrenia in adults with velo-cardio- facial syndrome. *Arch. Gen. Psy- chiatry* 56, 940–945. doi:10.1001/ archpsyc.56.10.940

128. Nacewicz, B. M., Dalton, K. M., John- stone, T., Long, M. T., McAuliff, E. M., Oakes, T. R., et al. (2006). Amyg- dala volume and nonverbal social impairment in adolescent and adult males with autism. *Arch. Gen. Psy- chiatry* 63, 1417–1428. doi:10.1001/ archpsyc.63.12.1417

129. Naidu, S., Kaufmann, W. E., Abrams, M. T., Pearlson, G. D., Lan- ham, D. C., Fredericksen, K. A., et al. (2001). Neuroimaging stud- ies in Rett syndrome. *Brain Dev.* 23(Suppl. 1), S62–S71. doi:10.1016/ S0387-7604(01)00381-3

130. Neul, J. L. (2012). The relationship of Rett syndrome and MECP2 disorders to autism. *Dialogues Clin. Neu- rosci.* 14, 253–262.

131. Nordahl, C. W., Braunschweig, D., Iosif, A. M., Lee, A., Rogers, S., Ashwood, P., et al. (2013). Maternal autoan- tibodies are associated with abnormal brain enlargement in a sub- group of children with autism spec- trum disorder. *Brain Behav. Immun.* 30, 61–65. doi:10.1016/j.bbi.2013. 01.084

132. Nordahl, C. W., Dierker, D., Mostafavi, I., Schumann, C. M., Rivera, S. M., Amaral, D. G., et al. (2007). Cortical folding abnormalities in autism revealed by surface- based morphometry. *J. Neurosci.* 27, 11725–11735. doi:10.1523/JNEUROSCI.0777-07.2007

133. Nordahl, C. W., Lange, N., Li, D. D., Barnett, L. A., Lee, A., Buonocore, M. H., et al. (2011). Brain enlarge- ment is associated with regression in preschool-age boys with autism spectrum disorders. *Proc. Natl. Acad. Sci. U.S.A.* 108, 20195–20200. doi:10. 1073/pnas.1107560108

134. Nordahl, C. W., Scholz, R., Yang, X. W., Buonocore, M. H., Simon, T., Rogers, S., et al. (2012). Increased rate of amygdala growth in children aged 2 to 4 years with autism spectrum disorders a longitudinal study. *Arch. Gen. Psychiatry* 69, 53–61. doi:10. 1001/archgenpsychiatry.2011.145

135. Parsons, T. D., Larson, P., Kratz, K., Thiebaux, M., Bluestein, B., Buckwalter, J. G., et al. (2004). Sex differences in mental rota- tion and spatial rotation in a vir- tual environment. *Neuropsycholo- gia* 42, 555–562. doi:10.1016/j. neuropsychologia.2003.08.014

136. Pelphrey, K. A., Morris, J. P., and McCarthy, G. (2005). Neural basis of eye gaze processing deficits in autism. *Brain* 128, 1038–1048. doi: 10.1093/ brain/awh404

137. Pelphrey, K. A., Shultz, S., Hudac, C. M., and Vander Wyk, B. C. (2011). Research review: constraining het- erogeneity: the social brain and its development in autism spectrum disorder. *J. Child Psychol. Psychia- try* 52, 631–644. doi:10.1111/j.1469- 7610.2010.02349.x

138. Pessoa, L. (2010). Emotion and cogni- tion and the amygdala: from"what is it?" to"what's to be done?" *Neuropsy- chologia* 48, 3416–3429. doi:10.1016/ j.neuropsychologia.2010.06.038

139. Peterson, B. S., Thomas, P., Kane, M. J., Scahill, L., Zhang, H., Bronen, R., et al. (2003). Basal ganglia volumes in patients with Gilles de la Tourette Syndrome. *Arch. Gen. Psychiatry* 60, 415–424. doi:10.1001/archpsyc.60.4. 415

140. Philip, R. C. M., Dauvermann, M. R., Whalley, H. C., Baynham, K., Lawrie, S. M., and Stanfield, A. C. (2012). A systematic review and meta-analysis of the fMRI investigation of autism spectrum disorders. *Neurosci. Biobe- hav. Rev.* 36, 901–942. doi:10.1016/j. neubiorev.2011.10.008

141. Pinkham, A. E., Hopfinger, J. B., Pelphrey, K. A., Piven, J., and Penn, D. L. (2008). Neural bases for impaired social cognition in schiz- ophrenia and autism spectrum dis- orders. *Schizophr. Res.* 99, 164–175. doi:10.1016/j. schres.2007.10.024

142. Piven, J., Arndt, S., Bailey, J., Havercamp, S., Andreasen, N. C., and Palmer, P. (1995). An MRI study of brain size in autism. *Am. J. Psychiatry* 152, 1145–1149.

143. Planche, P., and Lemonnier, E. (2012). Children with high- functioning autism and Asperger's syndrome: can we differenti- ate their cognitive profiles? *Res. Autism Spectr. Disord.* 6, 939–948. doi:10.1016/j.rasd.2011.12.009

144. Predescu, E., Sipos, P., Sipos, R., Iftene, F., and Balazsi, R. (2010). Brain vol- umes in autism and developmental delay – a MRI study. *J. Cogn. Behav. Psychother.* 10, 25–38.

145. Radua, J., Via, E., Catani, M., and Mataix-Cols, D. (2011). Voxel- based meta-analysis of regional white-matter volume differ- ences in autism spectrum dis- order versus healthy controls. *Psychol. Med.* 41, 1539–1550. doi:10.1017/S0033291710002187

146. Rapoport, J. L., Giedd, J. N., and Gog- tay, N. (2012). Neurodevelopmental model of schizophrenia: update 2012. *Mol. Psychiatry* 17, 1228–1238. doi:10.1038/mp.2012.23

147. Raznahan, A., Lee, Y., Vaituzis, C., Tran, L., Mackie, S., Tiemeier, H., et al. (2012). Allelic variation within the putative autism spectrum disorder risk gene homeobox A1 and cerebel- lar maturation in typically develop- ing children and adolescents. *Autism Res.* 5, 93–100. doi:10.1002/aur.238

148. Raznahan, A., Lenroot, R., Thurm, A., Gozzi, M., Hanley, A., Spence, S. J., et al. (2013a). Mapping corti- cal anatomy in preschool aged chil- dren with autism using surface- based morphometry. *Neuroimage* 2, 111–119. doi:10.1016/j.nicl.2012.10. 005

149. Raznahan, A., Wallace, G. L., Antezana, L., Greenstein, D., Lenroot, R., Thurm, A., et al. (2013b). Compared to what? Early brain overgrowth in autism and the perils of population norms. *Biol. Psychiatry* 74, 563–575. doi:10.1016/j.biopsych.2013.03.022

150. Raznahan, A., Toro, R., Proitsi, P., Pow- ell, J., Paus, T., Bolton, F. P., et al. (2009). A functional polymorphism of the brain derived neurotrophic factor gene and cortical anatomy in autism spectrum disorder. *J. Neu- rodev. Disord.* 1, 215–223. doi:10. 1007/s11689-009-9012-0

151. Redcay, E., and Courchesne, E. (2005). When is the brain enlarged in autism? A meta-analysis of all brain size reports. *Biol. Psychiatry* 58, 1–9. doi:10.1016/j.biopsych.2005.03.026

152. Redcay, E., and Courchesne, E. (2008). Deviant functional magnetic resonance imaging patterns of brain activity to speech in 2-3-year-old children with autism spectrum disorder. *Biol. Psychiatry* 64, 589–598. doi:10.1016/j. biopsych. 2008.05.020

153. Reddy, K. S. (2005). Cytogenetic abnor- malities and fragile-X syndrome in autism spectrum disorder. *BMC Med. Genet.* 6:3. doi:10.1186/1471- 2350-6-3

154. Riva, D., Bulgheroni, S., Aquino, D., Di Salle, F., Savoiardo, M., and Erbetta, A. (2011). Basal forebrain involve- ment in low-functioning autistic children: a voxel-based morphom- etry study. *Am. J. Neuroradiol.* 32, 1430–1435. doi:10.3174/ajnr.A2527

155. Robinson, E. B., Koenen, K. C., McCormick, M. C., Munir, K., Hal- lett, V., Happe, F., et al. (2011). Evi- dence that autistic traits show the same etiology in the general popula- tion and at the quantitative extremes (5%, 2.5%, and 1%). *Arch. Gen. Psy- chiatry* 68, 1113–1121. doi:10.1001/archgenpsychiatry.2011.119

156. Rogers, S. J. (2004). Developmental regression in autism spectrum disorders. *Ment. Retard. Dev. Disabil. Res. Rev.* 10, 139–143. doi:10.1002/mrdd. 20027

157. Rojas, D. C., Bawn, S. D., Benkers, T. L., Reite, M. L., and Rogers, S. J. (2002). Smaller left hemi- sphere planum temporale in adults with autistic disorder. *Neurosci. Lett.* 328, 237–240. doi:10.1016/S0304- 3940(02)00521-9

158. Rojas, D. C., Camou, S. L., Reite, M. L., and Rogers, S. J. (2005). Planum temporale volume in children and adolescents with autism. *J. Autism Dev. Disord.* 35, 479–486. doi:10. 1007/s10803-005-5038-7

159. Rojas, D. C., Peterson, E., Winter- rowd, E., Reite, M. L., Rogers, S. J., and Tregellas, J. R. (2006). Regional gray matter volumetric changes in autism associated with social and repetitive behavior symptoms. *BMC Psychiatry* 6:56. doi:10.1186/1471- 244X-6-56

160. Rommelse, N. N. J., Geurts, H. M., Franke, B., Buitelaar, J. K., and Hartman, C. A. (2011). A review on cognitive and brain endophe- notypes that may be common in autism spectrum disorder and attention-deficit/hyperactivity dis- order and facilitate the search for pleiotropic genes. *Neurosci. Biobehav. Rev.* 35, 1363–1396. doi:10. 1016/j.neubiorev.2011.02.015

161. Ronald, A., and Hoekstra, R. A. (2011). Autism spectrum disorders and autistic traits: a decade of new twin studies. *Am. J. Med. Genet. B Neu- ropsychiatr. Genet.* 156B, 255–274. doi:10.1002/ajmg.b.31159

162. Rosenberg, D. R., Keshavan, M. S., O'Hearn, K. M., Dick, E. L., Bag-well, W. W., Seymour, A. B., et al. (1997). Frontostriatal measure- ment in treatment-naive children with obsessive-compulsive dis- order. *Arch. Gen. Psychiatry* 54, 824–830. doi:10.1001/archpsyc. 1997.01830210068007

163. Rudie, J. D., Hernandez, L. M., Brown, J. A., Beck-Pancer, D., Colich, N. L., Gorrindo, P., et al. (2012). Autism- associated promoter variant in MET impacts functional and struc- tural brain networks. *Neuron* 75, 904–915. doi:10.1016/j.neuron. 2012.07.010

164. Rutter, M., Kreppner, J., Croft, C., Murin, M., Colvert, E., Beckett, C., et al. (2007). Early adolescent out- comes of institutionally deprived and non-deprived adoptees. III. Quasi-autism. *J. Child Psychol. Psy- chiatry* 48, 1200–1207. doi:10.1111/ j.1469-7610.2006.01688.x

165. Sahoo, T., Theisen, A., Rosenfeld, J. A., Lamb, A. N., Ravnan, J. B., Schultz, R. A., et al. (2011). Copy num- ber variants of schizophrenia sus- ceptibility loci are associated with a spectrum of speech and develop- mental delays and behavior prob- lems. *Genet. Med.* 13, 868–880. doi: 10.1097/ GIM.0b013e3182217a06

166. Scarone, S., Colombo, C., Livian, S., Abbruzzese, M., Ronchi, P., Locatelli, M., et al. (1992). Increased right caudate nucleus size in obsessive- compulsive disorder: detection with magnetic resonance imaging. *Psy- chiatr. Res.* 45, 115–121. doi:10.1016/ 0925-4927(92)90005-O

167. Schatz, A., Weimer, A., and Trauner, D. (2002). Brief report: Attention differences in Asperger syndrome. *J. Autism Dev. Disord.* 32, 333–336. doi:10.1023/A:1016339104165

168. Schulte-Ruther, M., Greimel, E., Markowitsch, H. J., Kamp-Becker, I., Remschmidt, H., Fink, G. R., et al. (2011). Dysfunctions in brain networks supporting empathy: an fMRI study in adults with autism spectrum disorders. *Soc. Neurosci.* 6, 1–21. doi:10.1080/17470911003708032

169. Schumann, C. M., Barnes, C. C., Lord, C., and Courchesne, E. (2009). Amygdala enlargement in toddlers with autism related to severity of social and communication impair- ments. *Biol. Psychiatry* 66, 942–949. doi:10.1016/j.biopsych.2009.07.007

170. Schumann, C. M., Bloss, C. S., Barnes, C. C., Wideman, G. M., Carper, R. A., Akshoomoff, N., et al. (2010). Lon- gitudinal magnetic resonance imag- ing study of cortical development through early childhood in autism. *J. Neurosci.* 30, 4419–4427. doi:10. 1523/JNEUROSCI.5714-09.2010

171. Schumann, C. M., Hamstra, J., Goodlin- Jones, B. L., Lotspeich, L. J., Kwon, H., Buonocore, M. H., et al. (2004). The amygdala is enlarged in children but not adolescents with autism; The hippocampus is enlarged at all ages. *J. Neurosci.* 24, 6392–6401. doi:10. 1523/JNEUROSCI.1297-04.2004

172. Scott-Van Zeeland, A. A., Abrahams, B. S., Alvarez-Retuerto, A. I., Sonnen- blick, L. I., Rudie, J. D., Ghahre- mani, D., et al. (2010a). Altered functional connectivity in frontal lobe circuits is associated with variation in the autism risk gene CNTNAP2. *Sci Transl Med* 2, 56ra80. doi:10. 1126/ scitranslmed.3001344

173. Scott-Van Zeeland, A. A., Dapretto, M., Ghahremani, D. G., Poldrack, R. A., and Bookheimer, S. Y. (2010b). Reward processing in autism. *Autism Res.* 3, 53–67. doi:10.1002/aur.122

174. Shafritz, K. M., Dichter, G. S., Baranek, G. T., and Belger, A. (2008). The neural circuitry mediating shifts in behavioral response and cogni- tive set in autism. *Biol. Psychiatry* 63, 974–980. doi:10.1016/j.biopsych. 2007.06.028

175. Shapleske, J., Rossell, S. L., Woodruff, P. W. R., and David, A. S. (1999). The planum temporale: a system- atic, quantitative review of its structural, functional and clinical signifi- cance. *Brain Res. Rev.* 29, 26–49. doi: 10.1016/S0165-0173(98)00047-2

176. Shprintzen, R. J. (2008). Velo-cardio- facial syndrome: 30 Years of study. *Dev. Disabil. Res. Rev.* 14, 3–10. doi: 10.1002/ddrr.2

177. Silver, W. G., and Rapin, I. (2012). Neu- robiological basis of autism. *Pediatr. Clin. North Am.* 59, 45–61. doi:10. 1016/j.pcl.2011.10.010

178. Simonoff, E., Pickles, A., Charman, T., Chandler, S., Loucas, T., and Baird, G. (2008). Psychiatric disorders in children with autism spectrum disorders: prevalence, comorbidity, and associated factors in a population-derived sample. *J. Am. Acad. Child Adolesc. Psychiatry* 47, 921–929. doi: 10.1097/CHI.0b013e318179964f

179. Skuse, D. H. (2007). Rethinking the nature of genetic vulnerability to autistic spectrum disorders. *Trends Genet.* 23, 387–395. doi:10.1016/j. tig.2007.06.003

180. Sparks, B. F., Friedman, S. D., Shaw, D. W., Aylward, E. H., Echelard, D., Artru, A. A., et al. (2002). Brain structural abnormalities in young children with autism spectrum dis- order. *Neurology* 59, 184–192. doi: 10.1212/ WNL.59.2.184

181. Spencer, M. D., Moorhead, T. M. J., Lymer, G. K. S., Job, D. E., Muir, W. J., Hoare, P., et al. (2006). Structural correlates of intellectual impairment and autistic features in adolescents. *Neuroimage* 33, 1136–1144. doi:10. 1016/j. neuroimage.2006.08.011

182. Stanfield, A. C., McIntosh, A. M., Spencer, M. D., Philip, R., Gaur, S., and Lawrie, S. M. (2008). Towards a neuroanatomy of autism: a systematic review and meta- analysis of structural magnetic res- onance imaging studies. *Eur. Psy- chiatry* 23, 289–299. doi:10.1016/j. eurpsy.2007.05.006

183. State, M. W., and Sestan, N. (2012). Neuroscience. The emerging biology of autism spectrum disorders. *Sci- ence* 337, 1301–1303. doi:10.1126/science.1224989

184. Stigler, K. A., McDonald, B. C., Anand, A., Saykin, A. J., and McDougle, C. J. (2011). Structural and func- tional magnetic resonance imaging of autism spectrum disorders. *Brain Res.* 1380, 146–161. doi:10.1016/j. brainres.2010.11.076

185. Strang, J. F., Kenworthy, L., Daniolos, P., Case, L., Wills, M. C., Martin, A., et al. (2012). Depression and anxiety symptoms in children and adolescents with autism spectrum disorders without intellectual dis- ability. *Res. Autism Spectr. Disord.* 6, 406–412. doi:10.1016/j. rasd.2011. 06.015

186. Sugranyes, G., Kyriakopoulos, M., Cor- rigall, R., Taylor, E., and Frangou, S. (2011). Autism spectrum disorders and schizophrenia: Meta-analysis of the neural correlates of social cog- nition. *PLoS ONE* 6:e25322. doi:10. 1371/journal.pone.0025322

187. Tan, G. C., Doke, T. F., Ashburner, J., Wood, N. W., and Frackowiak, R. S. (2010). Normal variation in fronto-occipital circuitry and cerebellar structure with an autism- associated polymorphism of CNT- NAP2. *Neuroimage* 53, 1030–1042. doi:10.1016/j.neuroimage.2010.02. 018

188. Travers, B. G., Adluru, N., Ennis, C., Tromp do, P. M., Destiche, D., Doran, S., et al. (2012). Diffusion tensor imaging in autism spectrum disorder: a review. *Autism Res.* 5, 289–313. doi:10.1002/aur.1243

189. Uher, R., and Rutter, M. (2012). Basing psychiatric classifica- tion on scientific foundation: problems and prospects. *Int. Rev. Psychiatry* 24, 591–605. doi:10.3109/09540261.2012.721346

190. Van Essen, D. C., Drury, H. A., Dickson, J., Harwell, J., Hanlon, D., and Anderson, C. H. (2001). An integrated software suite for surface-based analyses of cerebral cortex. *J. Am. Med. Inform. Assoc.* 8, 443–459. doi:10.1136/jamia.2001. 0080443

191. Via, E., Radua, J., Cardoner, N., Happe, F., and Mataix-Cols, D. (2011). Meta-analysis of gray matter abnor- malities in autism spectrum disor- der: should Asperger disorder be subsumed under a broader umbrella of autistic spectrum disorder? *Arch. Gen. Psychiatry* 68, 409–418. doi:10.1001/archgenpsychiatry. 2011.27

192. Vissers, M. E., Cohen, M. X., and Geurts, H. M. (2012). Brain connec- tivity and high functioning autism: a promising path of research that needs refined models, method- ological convergence, and stronger behavioral links. *Neurosci. Biobe- hav. Rev.* 36, 604–625. doi:10.1016/j.neubiorev.2011.09.003

193. Volkmar, F. R., State, M., and Klin, A. (2009). Autism and autism spectrum disorders: diagnostic issues for the coming decade. *J. Child Psychol. Psychiatry* 50, 108–115. doi:10.1111/j.1469-7610.2008. 02010.x

194. Volkmar, F. R., Szatmari, P., and Spar- row, S. S. (1993). Sex differences in pervasive developmental disorders. *J. Autism Dev. Disord.* 23, 579–591. doi:10.1007/BF01046103

195. Weng, S. J., Carrasco, M., Swartz, J. R., Wiggins, J. L., Kurapati, N., Liberzon, I., et al. (2011). Neural activation to emotional faces in adolescents with autism spectrum disorders. *J. Child Psychol. Psychiatry* 52, 296–305. doi:10.1111/j.1469-7610.2010. 02317.x

196. Whalley, H. C., O'Connell, G., Suss- mann, J. E., Peel, A., Stanfield, A. C., Hayiou-Thomas, M. E., et al. (2011). Genetic variation in CNT- NAP2 alters brain function during linguistic processing in healthy indi- viduals. *Am. J. Med. Genet. B Neu- ropsychiatr. Genet.* 156B, 941–948. doi:10.1002/ajmg.b.31241

197. Wilson, L. B., Tregellas, J. R., Hager- man, R. J., Rogers, S. J., and Rojas, D. C. (2009). A voxel-based morphom- etry comparison of regional gray matter between fragile X syndrome and autism. *Psychiatr Res.* 174, 138–145. doi:10.1016/j.pscychresns. 2009.04.013

198. Wing, L. (1981). Language, social, and cognitive impairments in autism and severe mental retardation. *J. Autism Dev. Disord.* 11, 31–44. doi:10.1007/BF01531339

199. Wolff, J. J. (2013). On the emergence of autism: neuroimaging findings from birth to preschool. *Neuropsychiatry* 3, 209–222. doi:10.2217/npy.13.11

200. Zappella, M., Meloni, I., Longo, I., Hayek, G., and Renieri, A. (2001). Preserved speech variants of the Rett syndrome: molecular and clinical analysis. *Am. J. Med. Genet.* 104, 14–22. doi:10.1002/ajmg.10005

201. Zeegers, M., Pol, H. H., Durston, S., Nederveen, H., Schnack, H., van Daalen, E., et al. (2009). No dif- ferences in MR-based volumetry between 2-and 7-year-old children with autism spectrum disorder and developmental delay. *Brain Dev.* 31, 725–730. doi:10.1016/j.braindev. 2008.11.002

# 9

# Converging pathways in autism spectrum disorders: interplay between synaptic dysfunction and immune responses

***Irina Voineagu*[1]* *and Valsamma Eapen*[2]**

[1] *School of Biotechnology and Biomolecular Sciences, University of New South Wales, Sydney, NSW, Australia*

[2] *Department of Infant, Child and Adolescent Psychiatry, Academic Unit of Child Psychiatry, University of New South Wales, South West Sydney, Sydney, NSW, Australia*

***Edited by:***
*Charles Claudianos, University of Queensland, Australia*

***Reviewed by:***
*Anthony J. Hannan, University of Melbourne, Australia*
*Elisa L. Hill-Yardin, University of Melbourne, Australia*

***Correspondence:***
*Irina Voineagu, School of Biotechnology and Biomolecular Sciences, University of New South Wales, Biological Science Building, Room 217B, Kensington, Sydney, NSW 2052, Australia*
*e-mail: i.voineagu@unsw.edu.au*

Autism spectrum disorders (ASD) are highly heritable, yet genetically heterogeneous neurodevelopmental conditions. Recent genome-wide association and gene expression studies have provided evidence supporting the notion that the large number of genetic variants associated with ASD converge toward a core set of dysregulated biological processes. Here we review recent data demonstrating the involvement of synaptic dysfunction and abnormal immune responses in ASD, and discuss the functional interplay between the two phenomena.

**Keywords: autism spectrum disorders, immune response, synapses, genomics, gene expression**

## INTRODUCTION

Autism spectrum disorders (ASD) are a spectrum of neurodevelopmental conditions characterized by language deficits, social impairments, and repetitive behaviors (Abrahams and Geschwind, 2008). Typically the disorder is diagnosed around 2–3 years of age and manifests with a regression in acquired language and behavioral skills. However, there are wide variations in the clinical presentation and disease progression. In addition to variable severity of the core symptomatology, ASD patients also present with a variable mix of co-morbid conditions: epilepsy, gastro-intestinal problems, intellectual disability, anxiety, and depression (Kim and Lord, 2013). Mirroring its clinical heterogeneity, ASD is also genetically very heterogeneous (State and Levitt, 2011). Based on the results of genome-wide association (GWAS) studies, candidate gene re-sequencing, and exome-sequencing studies, it is currently estimated that hundreds of genetic variants, including common and rare genetic variants, contribute to the disease (Murdoch and State, 2013). What are the molecular pathways that mediate the phenotypic expression of this myriad of genetic variants into a recognizable triad of symptoms? Here we review recent studies demonstrating a convergence of ASD genetic changes toward two main biological processes: synaptic function and immune responses, and discuss their functional interplay, with a focus on immune modulation of neuronal synapses (**Figure 1**).

## FROM MANY GENES TO COMMON BIOLOGICAL PROCESSES

Results from genome-wide studies are beginning to confirm the long-held hypothesis that the wide variety of genetic variants associated with ASD ultimately converge on a core set of molecular pathways (Murdoch and State, 2013). It is worth noting that pathway enrichment analyses are inherently limited by our current knowledge of signaling pathways and molecular interactions, and thus the identification of distinct pathways by different studies might partially reflect yet uncharacterized complexity of molecular pathways.

Four recent studies undertook exome-sequencing in several hundreds of parent-child trios in order to identify *de novo* single nucleotide variants (SNVs) and copy number variants (CNVs) associated with the disease (Iossifov et al., 2012; Neale et al., 2012; O'Roak et al., 2012; Sanders et al., 2012). The study by O'Roak et al. found that the most disruptive *de novo* mutations converged onto a highly interconnected beta-catenin/chromatin remodeling protein network, which is involved in neuronal differentiation and synaptic formation (Ille and Sommer, 2005). Iossifov et al. found an enrichment of *de novo* variants in genes encoding proteins associated with the fragile X syndrome protein, FMRP, suggesting an involvement in synaptic plasticity. The study by Neale et al. demonstrated that genes carrying functional *de novo* variants were functionally related to each other and to synaptic genes previously implicated in ASD. Using a network-based analysis of genetic association data, Talkowski et al. (2012) showed that rare *de novo* CNVs occurring in ASD cases affect primarily genes related to synapse development, axon targeting, and neuron motility. Collectively, these studies highlighted the fact that genes containing pathogenic DNA sequence variants in ASD patients affected primarily genes involved in various aspects of synaptic function.

While genetic association studies identify genetic loci potentially implicated in the disease, they do not assess the functional consequences of the associated variants. On the other hand, transcriptome analyses comparing disease and control groups assess

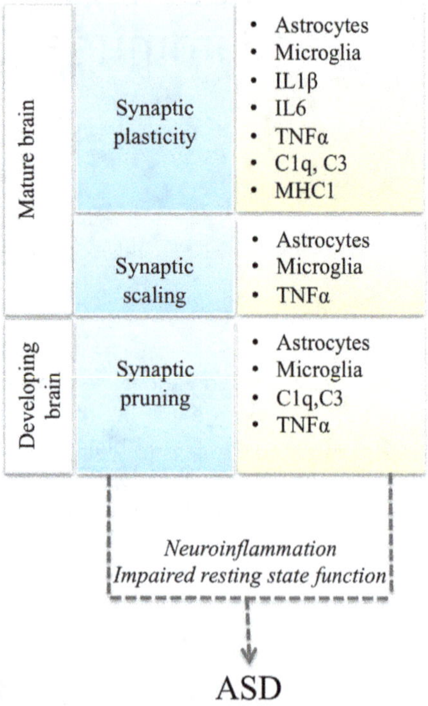


**FIGURE 1 | Interactions between synaptic function and immune molecules and cells, and possible mechanisms leading to ASD.** Multiple aspects of synaptic function (blue boxes) are regulated by astrocytes, microglia, and immune molecules (yellow boxes). Either immune activation during neuroinflammation or impaired resting state activity of immune cells in the brain could impair synaptic function and lead to ASD.

gene function (by quantifying mRNA output), but are liable to environmental variations in gene expression, and functional changes unrelated to the disease. Thus ideally, functional genomic studies should simultaneously assess DNA sequence variation and gene expression, in a disease-relevant tissue. However, the scarce availability of post-mortem brain tissue from ASD cases limits the sample size of such studies below appropriate statistical power. Attempting to address this problem, we performed a genome-wide assessment of gene expression in multiple brain regions (frontal cortex, temporal cortex, and cerebellum) from 19 autism cases and 17 unaffected controls, and integrated these results with previous ASD GWAS data (Wang et al., 2009). Using a network-based approach for the analysis of gene expression data we identified two modules of co-expressed genes dysregulated in a large subset of ASD cases (Voineagu et al., 2011). One of these modules was downregulated in ASD brain and was enriched for neuronal genes involved in synaptic function. A second module was upregulated in ASD brain and contained primarily genes functioning in immune and inflammatory responses. To integrate the gene expression results with previously published GWAS data, we performed a pathway enrichment analysis of ASD GWAS data using the two co-expression modules as pre-defined "pathways." We found that the neuronal genes downregulated in ASD, but not the immune/inflammatory genes, showed an enrichment for genetic association, as measured by a large ASD GWAS study (Wang et al., 2009). These results supported the heritability of synaptic gene dysfunction in ASD and suggested that the upregulation of immune and inflammatory genes is likely environmentally mediated or secondary to the synaptic dysfunction.

Although gene expression analyses of ASD brain are just beginning to emerge, several studies have evaluated gene expression in readily available peripheral tissues (blood and lymphoblast cell lines) from ASD patients (Hu et al., 2006, 2009; Gregg et al., 2008; Enstrom et al., 2009). A common result of these studies was the demonstration of increased expression of immune and inflammatory genes in ASD. Moreover, a comparison of gene expression studies of peripheral tissues in idiopathic autism and related neurodevelopmental disorders showed a convergence of gene expression abnormalities on genes involved in immune responses (Lintas et al., 2012). Interestingly, an analysis of genetic variants nominally associated with ASD found that these variants were enriched in brain expression quantitative trait loci (brain eQTLs), but not lymphoblast eQTLs (Davis et al., 2012). Thus gene expression studies collectively support the concept that (a) immune and inflammatory genes are upregulated in ASD, a phenomenon observed both in the brain and in peripheral tissues, and (b) neuronal synaptic genes are downregulated in ASD brains.

The involvement of synaptic dysfunction and immune responses in ASD had been demonstrated by multiple approaches (Betancur et al., 2009; Pizzarelli and Cherubini, 2011; Wright and Washbourne, 2011; Grabrucker, 2012; Onore et al., 2012; Zoghbi and Bear, 2012; Ebert and Greenberg, 2013), but it was not until large-scale genomic studies that these biological processes could be regarded as points of convergence of the heterogeneous genetic variants underlying ASD.

## INTERPLAY BETWEEN BRAIN IMMUNE PROCESSES AND SYNAPTIC FUNCTION

Microglia, the main resident immune cells in the brain, have been long believed to be active only in response to immune insults, and to exist in a "resting state" in the normal brain. However, this view has dramatically changed over the last decade, and it is becoming increasingly clear that immune cells and molecules play an active role in the normal brain function. Microglia are believed to populate the CNS in the non-vascularized embryonic period and to originate from progenitors from the yolk sac. It has also been proposed that a second wave of microglia, originating from blood monocytes, may populate the CNS during the early postnatal period, a period particularly important for neurodevelopment (Davis and Carson, 2013). Microglia actively survey the brain parenchyma, constantly extending their processes to survey their microenvironment every few hours (Nimmerjahn et al., 2005). Importantly, microglia are required for synaptic pruning during postnatal neurodevelopment (Paolicelli et al., 2011). A recent study (Schafer et al., 2012) demonstrated that microglial synaptic pruning is developmentally regulated and depends on neuronal activity. This process was shown to be mediated by the complement receptor (CR3) pathway, and inhibiting CR3 signaling led to sustained deficits in synaptic connectivity.

Thus immune cells could affect neuronal synaptic function either as a result of their activation during immune responses, or due to a failure of their non-immune roles in the brain (**Figure 1**).

Recent evidence supports the potential involvement of both of these mechanisms in ASD pathogenesis.

Active neuroinflammation has been consistently demonstrated in ASD brains. Prominent activation of microglia (Vargas et al., 2005; Morgan et al., 2010), as well as increased levels of inflammatory cytokines and chemokines [interferon-gamma, IL-1β, IL-6, tumor necrosis factor (TNF)-α] have been documented in post-mortem brain tissue and cerebrospinal fluid from ASD patients (Onore et al., 2012). Recently, activated microglia have also been observed by positron emission tomography in ASD subjects in several brain regions (Suzuki et al., 2013). While it is not clear what is the cause of microglial activation in ASD brain, the cytokines produced by activated microglia have been demonstrated to affect neuronal synaptic function (Onore et al., 2012). TNF-α regulates neuronal cell proliferation and synaptic pruning (Cacci et al., 2005), and modulates synaptic scaling (i.e., the adjustment of synaptic strength for all synapses on a neuronal cell in response to prolonged changes in electrical activity) (Stellwagen and Malenka, 2006). IL-1β regulates long-term potentiation and alters synaptic plasticity (Schneider et al., 1998), while IL-6 has been implicated in behavioral changes associated with maternal immune activation (Patterson, 2009). Mounting evidence suggests that maternal immune activation, particularly during the first and second trimester of pregnancy, may be an important environmental factor in ASD (Onore et al., 2012). Rodent models of maternal immune activation exhibit ASD-like behavioral changes (Patterson, 2009), and the behavioral effects observed in offspring after maternal immune activation appear to be mediated by microglia and IL-6 (Hsiao and Patterson, 2011). In some mouse models increased levels of IL-6 have been sufficient to induce behavioral changes (Onore et al., 2012). Unlike peripheral macrophages, microglia are long-lived, and thus it has been hypothesized that they could maintain an "immunological memory" of an early immune insult, leading to long-term neuronal deficits (Davis and Carson, 2013).

One of the first studies to demonstrate a direct causal relationship between microglial function and a behavioral phenotype, was a mouse model of obsessive-compulsive disorder (Chen et al., 2010). *HOXB8* encodes a homeobox transcription factor expressed in the brain exclusively in bone-marrow-derived microglia. *HOXB8*-null mice exhibit excessive pathological grooming behavior similar to the obsessive-compulsive symptoms of trichotillomania. Chen et al. demonstrated that normal bone marrow transplant could rescue the excessive grooming and hair removal phenotype in the *HOXB8* mutant mouse, and that selective disruption of *HOXB8* in the hematopoietic lineage recapitulates pathological grooming. More recently, a role for non-immune functions of microglia has also been demonstrated in Rett syndrome, a pervasive developmental disorder, belonging to the wider group of ASD. Rett syndrome is caused by loss of function of the methyl-CpG binding protein 2 (*MECP2*) and is characterized by an initial period of normal development of about 5 months followed by deceleration of language development, psychomotor retardation, seizures and loss of social engagement skills (Chahrour and Zoghbi, 2007). It was initially believed that Rett syndrome is primarily due to loss of *MECP2* function in neurons. However several recent studies clearly demonstrated that *MECP2* loss in glial cells impairs neuronal function and contributes to the Rett syndrome symptomatology. *MECP2* deficiency in astrocytes leads to impaired BDNF regulation, cytokine production, and neuronal dendritic arborization (Maezawa et al., 2009). Moreover, *MECP2*-deficient astrocytes are unable to support normal dendritic ramification of wild-type neurons (Ballas et al., 2009). Remarkably, astrocyte-specific expression of *MECP2* in a *MECP2*-null mouse restored the normal neuronal dendritic morphology, improved locomotion, anxiety, and respiratory abnormalities (Lioy et al., 2011). A recent study by Derecki et al. (2012) demonstrated that not only astrocytes but also microglia contribute to the Rett syndrome phenotype. Using irradiation-mediated immune ablation in *MECP2*-null mice, followed by wild-type bone marrow transplantation, this study demonstrated that the wild-type microglia could arrest disease development. In addition, targeted expression of *MECP2* in myeloid cells ameliorated the phenotype in *MECP2*-null mice. These results implicated microglia as important players in the pathophysiology of Rett syndrome, and suggested a potential therapeutic benefit of bone marrow transplantation in Rett syndrome.

## CONCLUSION AND FUTURE DIRECTIONS

Understanding the core biological processes underlying the clinical and genetic heterogeneity of ASD is as yet in incipient stages. Further advances in elucidating the molecular underpinnings of ASD are expected to result from (a) larger cohort sizes of GWAS and exome-sequencing studies, (b) increased availability of archived post-mortem brain tissue for transcriptome studies, and (c) integrative analyses of genomic, transcriptomic, and epigenomic data.

At the same time, understanding the role of immune cells in regulating synaptic function is also a newly developing field. As discussed above, accumulating evidence supports the notion that immune cells play important roles in normal brain function, outside of neuroinflammation. Of particular relevance to ASD is the role of microglia in synaptic pruning during postnatal brain development, a period that coincides with the onset of ASD symptoms. While it has been demonstrated that increased numbers of activated microglia are present in brain parenchyma of ASD patients (Vargas et al., 2005; Morgan et al., 2010; Suzuki et al., 2013), these studies have not captured the early postnatal development window. Future studies, facilitated by early ASD diagnosis, could shed further light on microglial activation occurs during postnatal brain development and on potential changes in the magnitude of this phenomenon across development and adult life in ASD. Notably, abnormal synaptic density, which could result from a deficit of synaptic pruning, is a feature of several ASD animal models [e.g., increased synaptic density in *Fmr1* KO mice, and decreased synaptic density in Rett syndrome mouse models (Delorme et al., 2013)], but it remains to be demonstrated whether it is also a feature of idiopathic ASD in human brain.

Since microglia and astrocytes have been shown to play a role in synaptic formation and maturation, and mutations in neuronal cell adhesion molecules have been associated with ASD, it is also tempting to speculate that ASD neurons might be particularly vulnerable to immune cell dysfunction in the brain.

Given the large amount of data supporting the role of immune responses in ASD and other neuropsychiatric disorders, advances in deciphering the functional interplay between immune cells and neuronal synaptic function will likely provide vital insights into the mechanisms and potential therapy of neurodevelopmental disorders.

## ACKNOWLEDGMENTS

This work was supported by a Ramaciotti Establishment Grant and a NARSAD Young Investigator Award (IV).

## REFERENCES

1. Abrahams, B. S., and Geschwind, D. H. (2008). Advances in autism genetics: on the threshold of a new neurobi- ology. *Nat. Rev. Genet.* 9, 341–355. doi:10.1038/nrg2346
2. Ballas, N., Lioy, D. T., Grunseich, C., and Mandel, G. (2009). Non-cell autonomous influence of MeCP2- deficient glia on neuronal den- dritic morphology. *Nat. Neurosci.* 12, 311–317. doi:10.1038/nn.2275
3. Betancur, C., Sakurai, T., and Buxbaum, J. D. (2009). The emerging role of synaptic cell-adhesion pathways in the pathogenesis of autism spectrum disorders. *Trends Neurosci.* 32, 402- 412. doi:10.1016/j.tins.2009.04.003
4. Cacci, E., Claasen, J. H., and Kokaia, Z. (2005). Microglia-derived tumor necrosis factor-alpha exaggerates death of newborn hippocampal progenitor cells in vitro. *J. Neurosci. Res.* 80, 789–797. doi:10.1002/jnr. 20531
5. Chahrour, M., and Zoghbi, H. Y. (2007). The story of Rett syndrome: from clinic to neurobiology. *Neuron* 56, 422–437. doi:10.1016/j.neuron. 2007.10.001
6. Chen, S. K., Tvrdik, P., Peden, E., Cho, S., Wu, S., Spangrude, G., et al. (2010). Hematopoietic origin of pathologi- cal grooming in Hoxb8 mutant mice. *Cell* 141, 775–785. doi:10.1016/j.cell. 2010.03.055
7. Davis, D. S., and Carson, M. J. (2013). "An introduction to CNS-resident microglia: definitions, assays, and functional roles in health and dis- ease," in *Neural-Immune Interactions in Brain Function and Alcohol Related Disorders*, eds C. Cui, L. Grandi- son, and A. Noronha (New York: Springer), 3–29. doi:10.1007/978-1- 4614-4729-0_1
8. Davis, L. K., Gamazon, E. R., Kistner- Griffin, E., Badner, J. A., Liu, C., Cook, E. H., et al. (2012). Loci nom- inally associated with autism from genome-wide analysis show enrich- ment of brain expression quantita- tive trait loci but not lymphoblastoid cell line expression quantitative trait loci. *Mol. Autism* 3, 3. doi:10.1186/2040-2392-3-3
9. Delorme, R., Ey, E., Toro, R., Leboyer, M., Gillberg, C., and Bourgeron, T. (2013). Progress toward treatments for synaptic defects in autism. *Nat. Med.* 19, 685–694. doi:10.1038/nm. 3193
10. Derecki, N. C., Cronk, J. C., Lu, Z., Xu, E., Abbott, S. B., Guyenet, P. G., et al. (2012). Wild-type microglia arrest pathology in a mouse model of Rett syndrome. *Nature* 484, 105–109. doi:10.1038/nature10907
11. Ebert, D. H., and Greenberg, M. E. (*2013*). Activity-dependent neu- ronal signalling and autism spec- trum disorder. *Nature* 493, 327–337. doi:10.1038/nature11860
12. Enstrom, A. M., Lit, L., Onore, C. E., Gregg, J. P., Hansen, R. L., Pessah, I. N., et al. (2009). Altered gene expression and function of periph- eral blood natural killer cells in children with autism. *Brain Behav. Immun.* 23, 124–133. doi:10.1016/j. bbi.2008.08.001
13. Grabrucker, A. M. (2012). Environmen- tal factors in autism. *Front. Psychiatry* 3:118. doi:10.3389/fpsyt.2012. 00118
14. Gregg, J. P., Lit, L., Baron, C. A., Hertz- Picciotto, I., Walker, W., Davis, R. A., et al. (2008). Gene expression changes in children with autism. *Genomics* 91, 22–29. doi:10.1016/j. ygeno.2007.09.003
15. Hsiao, E. Y., and Patterson, P. H. (2011). Activation of the maternal immune system induces endocrine changes in the placenta via IL-6. *Brain Behav. Immun.* 25, 604–615. doi:10.1016/j. bbi.2010.12.017
16. Hu, V. W., Frank, B. C., Heine, S., Lee, N. H., and Quackenbush, J. (2006). Gene expression profiling of lym- phoblastoid cell lines from monozy- gotic twins discordant in severity of autism reveals differential regula- tion of neurologically relevant genes. *BMC Genomics* 7:118. doi:10.1186/ 1471-2164-7-118
17. Hu, V. W., Nguyen, A., Kim, K. S., Stein- berg, M. E., Sarachana, T., Scully, M. A., et al. (2009). Gene expres- sion profiling of lymphoblasts from autistic and nonaffected sib pairs: altered pathways in neuronal devel- opment and steroid biosynthesis. *PLoS ONE* 4:e5775. doi:10.1371/ journal.pone.0005775
18. Ille, F., and Sommer, L. (2005). Wnt sig- naling: multiple functions in neural development. *Cell. Mol. Life Sci.* 62, 1100–1108. doi:10.1007/s00018-005-4552-2
19. Iossifov, I., Ronemus, M., Levy, D., Wang, Z., Hakker, I., Rosen- baum, J., et al. (2012). De novo gene disruptions in children on the autistic spec- trum. *Neuron* 74, 285–299. doi:10.1016/j.neuron.2012.04.009
20. Kim, S. H., and Lord, C. (2013). "The behavioral manifestations of autism spectrum disorders," in *The Neuro- science of Autism Spectrum Disorders*, ed. J. D. Buxbaum (New York: Else- vier), 25–37.
21. Lintas, C., Sacco, R., and Persico, A. M. (2012). Genome-wide expression studies in autism spectrum disor- der, Rett syndrome, and Down syndrome. *Neurobiol. Dis.* 45, 57–68. doi:10.1016/j.nbd.2010.11.010
22. Lioy, D. T., Garg, S. K., Monaghan, C. E., Raber, J., Foust, K. D., Kaspar, B. K., et al. (2011). A role for glia in the progression of Rett's syndrome. *Nature* 475, 497–500. doi:10.1038/ nature10214
23. Maezawa, I., Swanberg, S., Harvey, D., LaSalle, J. M., and Jin, L. W. (2009). Rett syndrome astrocytes are abnormal and spread MeCP2 deficiency through gap junc- tions. *J. Neurosci.* 29, 5051–5061. doi:10.1523/JNEUROSCI.0324-09. 2009
24. Morgan, J. T., Chana, G., Pardo, C. A., Achim, C., Semendeferi, K., Buckwalter, J., et al. (2010). Microglial activation and increased microglial density observed in the dorsolateral prefrontal cortex in autism. *Biol. Psy- chiatry* 68, 368–376. doi:10.1016/j. biopsych.2010.05.024
25. Murdoch, J. D., and State, M. W. (2013). Recent developments in the genet- ics of autism spectrum disorders. *Curr. Opin. Genet. Dev.* 23, 310–315. doi:10.1016/j.gde.2013.02.003
26. Neale, B. M., Kou, Y., Liu, L., Ma'ayan, A., Samocha, K. E., Sabo, A., et al. (2012). Patterns and rates of exonic de novo mutations in autism spectrum disorders. *Nature* 485, 242–245. doi:10.1038/nature11011
27. Nimmerjahn, A., Kirchhoff, F., and Helmchen, F. (2005). Resting microglial cells are highly dynamic surveillants of brain parenchyma in vivo. *Science* 308, 1314–1318. doi:10.1126/science.1110647
28. Onore, C., Careaga, M., and Ashwood, P. (2012). The role of immune dysfunction in the pathophysiology of autism. *Brain Behav. Immun.* 26, 383–392. doi:10.1016/j.bbi.2011.08. 007
29. O'Roak, B. J., Vives, L., Girirajan, S., Karakoc, E., Krumm, N., Coe, B. P., et al. (2012). Sporadic autism exomes reveal a highly intercon- nected protein network of de novo mutations. *Nature* 485, 246–250. doi:10.1038/nature10989
30. Paolicelli, R. C., Bolasco, G., Pagani, F., Maggi, L., Scianni, M., Pan- zanelli, P., et al. (2011). Synaptic pruning by microglia is necessary for normal brain development. *Sci- ence* 333, 1456–1458. doi:10.1126/science.1202529
31. Patterson, P. H. (2009). Immune involvement in schizophrenia and autism: etiology, pathology and ani- mal models. *Behav. Brain Res.* 204, 313–321. doi:10.1016/j.bbr.2008.12.016
32. Pizzarelli, R., and Cherubini, E. (2011). Alterations of GABAergic signal- ing in autism spectrum disorders. *Neural Plast.* 2011, 297153. doi:10. 1155/2011/297153
33. Sanders, S. J., Murtha, M. T., Gupta, A. R., Murdoch, J. D., Raubeson, M. J., Willsey, A. J., et al. (2012). De novo mutations revealed by whole-exome sequencing are strongly associated with autism. *Nature* 485, 237–241. doi:10.1038/ nature10945
34. Schafer, D. P., Lehrman, E. K., Kautzman, A. G., Koyama, R., Mardinly, A. R., Yamasaki, R., et al. (2012). Microglia sculpt postnatal neural circuits in an activ- ity and complement-dependent manner. *Neuron* 74, 691–705. doi:10.1016/j.neuron.2012.03.026
35. Schneider, H., Pitossi, F., Balschun, D., Wagner, A., del Rey, A., and Besedovsky, H. O. (1998). A neuromod- ulatory role of interleukin-1beta in the hippocampus. *Proc. Natl. Acad. Sci. U.S.A.* 95, 7778–7783. doi:10. 1073/ pnas.95.13.7778
36. State, M. W., and Levitt, P. (2011). The conundrums of understand- ing genetic risks for autism spec- trum disorders. *Nat. Neurosci.* 14, 1499–1506. doi:10.1038/nn.2924
37. Stellwagen, D., and Malenka, R. C. (2006). Synaptic scal- ing mediated by glial TNF- alpha. *Nature* 440, 1054–1059. doi:10.1038/nature04671
38. Suzuki, K., Sugihara, G., Ouchi, Y., Nakamura, K., Futatsubashi, M., Takebayashi, K., et al. (2013). Microglial activation in young adults with autism spectrum disorder. *JAMA Psychiatry* 70, 49–58. doi:10. 1001/jamapsychiatry.2013.272
39. Talkowski, M. E., Maussion, G., Crap- per, L., Rosenfeld, J. A., Blumenthal, I., Hanscom, C., et al. (2012). Dis- ruption of a large intergenic non- coding RNA in subjects with neu- rodevelopmental disabilities. *Am. J. Hum. Genet.* 91, 1128–1134. doi:10. 1016/j.ajhg.2012.10.016

40. Vargas, D. L., Nascimbene, C., Krishnan, C., Zimmerman, A. W., and Pardo, C. A. (2005). Neuroglial activa- tion and neuroinflammation in the brain of patients with autism. *Ann. Neurol.* 57, 67–81. doi:10.1002/ana. 20315
41. Voineagu, I., Wang, X., Johnston, P., Lowe, J. K., Tian, Y., Horvath, S., et al. (2011). Transcriptomic analysis of autistic brain reveals convergent molecular pathology. *Nature* 474, 380–384. doi:10.1038/nature10110
42. Wang, K., Zhang, H., Ma, D., Bucan, M., Glessner, J. T., Abrahams, B. S., et al. (2009). Common genetic vari- ants on 5p14.1 associate with autism spec trum disorders. *Nature* 459, 528–533. doi:10.1038/nature07999
43. Wright, G. J., and Washbourne, P. (2011). Neurexins, neuroligins and LRRTMs: synaptic adhesion get- ting fishy. *J. Neurochem.* 117, 765–778. doi:10.1111/j.1471-4159. 2010.07141.x
44. Zoghbi, H. Y., and Bear, M. F. (2012). Synaptic dysfunction in neurodevelopmental disorders associated with autism and intellectual disabilities. *Cold Spring Harb. Perspect. Biol.* 4, ii:a009886. doi:10.1101/cshperspect. a009886

# 10

# Peer-mediated theatrical engagement for improving reciprocal social interaction in autism spectrum disorder

**Blythe A. Corbett[1,2]*, Lydia R. Qualls[1,2], Blythe Valencia[3], Stéphanie-M. Fecteau[1,2] and Deanna M. Swain[4]**

[1] *Department of Psychiatry, Vanderbilt University, Nashville, TN, USA*
[2] *Vanderbilt Kennedy Center, Nashville, TN, USA*
[3] *Vanderbilt Child Studies, Nashville, TN, USA*
[4] *Virginia Polytechnic Institute and State University, Blacksburg, VA, USA*

***Edited by:***
*Roberto Canitano, University Hospital of Siena, Italy*

***Reviewed by:***
*Liqi Zhu, Chinese Academy of Sciences, China*
*Xiaoming Wang, Duke University, USA*

***Correspondence:**
*Blythe A. Corbett, Vanderbilt University, PMB 40, 230 Appleton Place, Nashville, TN 37203, USA*
*e-mail: blythe.corbett@vanderbilt.edu*

The hallmark characteristic of autism spectrum disorder (ASD) is poor reciprocal social communication. Interventions designed to improve this core deficit are critically needed. Social skills interventions such as direct training, peer mediation, and video modeling have contributed to improvements in various social skills in children with ASD. This paper reviews existing social competence interventions available for children with ASD while highlighting hypothesized critical components for advancing, maintaining, and generalizing skills, which include (1) peer mediation, (2) active learning, and (3) implementation in supportive, natural contexts. As a framework for these approaches, this conceptual paper describes SENSE Theatre, a novel intervention that combines trained peers that facilitate the performance-based theatrical treatment delivered in a supportive, community-based environment. A review of previous research shows early feasibility, setting the stage for more rigorous studies to aid in developing a standardized intervention package.

**Keywords: autism, peer mediation, social skills, active learning, theatre, context**

## INTRODUCTION

Children with autism spectrum disorder (ASD) have difficulty with social interaction, communication, and responding in a flexible way to everyday life (1). A recent report suggested that 1 in 68 individuals are now affected by this complex neurodevelopmental disorder (2). Affected individuals display a wide range of ability in language, sociability, and intellectual functioning. However, the defining characteristic across all levels of functioning is impairment in reciprocal social interaction, which can manifest as limitations in many areas of functioning including social-emotional reciprocity, to-and-fro conversation, play behavior, use of nonverbal communication, and in the development of age-appropriate relationships (1). There is significant diversity in symptom presentation, which can range from spontaneous social approaches with poor understanding of social rules to avoidant behavior with little evidence of social interest (3–5). Similarly, there is significant diversity in repetitive and stereotyped patterns of behavior (6) and a range of hyper- and hypo-sensitivity to sensory experiences (7).

Interacting with others relies on the coordinated effort of many complex and integrated skills to include the ability to recognize, identify, integrate, plan, and respond appropriately to dynamic socioemotional information. This information is conveyed, in part, through the interpretation and expression of verbal (e.g., speech prosody) and non-verbal (e.g., facial expressions and gestures) forms of communication (8), which can be difficult for those affected by ASD to interpret. Additionally, many individuals with ASD have difficulty perceiving, understanding, and remembering emotions (9, 10) and human faces (11–17). In addition to understanding how others feel, children with ASD have limitations in empathizing and predicting how others will think and act (18). Understanding other people's thoughts and feelings is a part of the concept of "theory of mind," which is defined as the ability to attribute mental states, such as beliefs, to other people and then use these ideas to understand and predict other peoples' behavior (18–20). Since sociability is a fundamental and encompassing skill, interventions designed to improve the complexity and diversity of social functioning are critically needed.

During social interaction with peers, many children with ASD experience heightened physiological stress as measured by cortisol, a primary stress hormone in human beings (21–24). Moreover, many children and adolescents with ASD show significant anxiety in social contexts especially as they get older and gain insight into their challenges engaging with others (25, 26). Despite showing improvements in social communication through experience and development, many children with ASD display higher levels of stress as measured by increased cortisol during benign social interactions with same age peers (22, 23, 27). It has been shown that behavioral patterns of approach and avoidance, as well as age factors can contribute to distinct patterns of stress in youth with ASD (22). Thus, stress responsivity may be an important moderator of social interaction for children with ASD and should be considered in programs developed to improve social skills (28, 29).

Currently, there are no known pharmaceutical treatments that have been shown to improve the core symptoms of ASD; thus, behavioral-based interventions designed to improve social skills are essential. There are many different types of social skills interventions available including direct skills training, applied behavior analysis, social skills groups, video modeling, and peer training (30–35). Many training programs produce positive outcomes in children with ASD; however, only a few meet strict criteria for empirical support (e.g., inclusion of control groups and randomization) (33) in order to distinguish observed effects attributed to the intervention from natural improvements over time (36–38).

## BACKGROUND

The current paper briefly introduces some existing social skills interventions available for children with ASD that are relevant to the concepts outlined below. Comprehensive reviews of social skills program and treatment options for children with ASD are more thoroughly reviewed elsewhere [e.g., Ref. (38–41)]. Teaching appropriate social skills to children with ASD by direct didactic training in either a group or one-on-one format has received empirical support (33, 42, 43). Qualified psychologists and paraprofessionals often teach these training sessions in clinic settings, which have demonstrated immediate, in-context gains for targeted skills. While participating children with ASD may learn specific social skills such as initiating interaction using priming (35), improving conversation skills through direct instruction with caregivers (44), or enhancing perspective taking from teaching theory of mind and social skills (45), acquired skills often do not generalize across people, contexts, or everyday environments (38, 46). Thus, the strong context-dependent learning in children with ASD is the most common barrier to behavioral change in children and adolescents with ASD (47). Thus, the inclusion of typically developing peers in the training and active practice of social skills can significantly contribute to the acquisition, maintenance, and generalization of sociability. Moreover, as described below, the context in which treatment is delivered also can impact social skill development.

Rather than reviewing or critiquing a broad range of social skills programs, the strengths of the approaches that are relevant to our theatre-based social engagement treatment are highlighted. In the context of the paper, three key components are discussed that we hypothesize to be necessary for advancing, maintaining, and generalizing social interaction abilities in children and youth with ASD, which include (1) peer mediation, (2) active learning, and (3) implementation in supportive, natural contexts. Moreover, these central ideas involve the inclusion of the recipient or target of the treatment in the intervention model to achieve changes in self-efficacy. Additionally, the conceptual paper presents SENSE Theatre, a novel intervention that combines trained peers that facilitate the performance-based theatrical approach delivered in a supportive, community-based environment.

## PEER MEDIATION

Peers can have a profound impact on the psychological, social, and physiological functioning of other children, including children with ASD (22–24, 27). Peer-mediated interventions utilize typically developing peers as agents of change, facilitating the development of social behavior and engagement in children with ASD (48–50). Peer mediation programs vary in the degree to which peers are trained in the delivery of social skills. One widely used peer-mediated program for children with ASD in school settings involves a one-on-one assistant who helps the child throughout the school day and is given the task of helping the child integrate socially with others (51). Although well intended, if the peers are untrained, the approach may produce unwelcome effects as it may label the child with social deficits as "different," possibly leading to stigmatization and greater social isolation. Peers' negative expectations of the target children must be managed in order to prevent this effect, and peer training is an effective way to achieve more positive expectations (52). For example, studies utilizing students who participated in trained mediation groups show greater generalization of skills for children with ASD (53). Peers should not simply be a social partner but also an active model of appropriate social behavior (54). In some programs, peers are extensively trained in how to elicit certain target behaviors through modeling, reinforcement, scripts, and other program-specific methods (55, 56). Thus, peers may serve as the optimal agent of change because they are not only the interventionists but they are also the intended recipients of improved socialization.

Since the primary objective for any social skills program is for children to be able to interact more competently with peers in natural settings (52), the inclusion of trained peers in treatment is both logical and beneficial. Moreover, it may be economical; utilizing peers as a resource for learning has the potential for reducing the demands on teachers and parents (57). Utilizing peers increases the number of training models for practice (49), which supplements instruction provided by parents and professionals. Zhang and Wheeler (58) performed a meta-analysis of peer-mediated interventions for children aged 8 years and younger and found them highly effective for increasing social interactive behavior. Additionally, Lang et al. (57) performed an analysis of several studies that utilized recess time to improve social skills and found that use of peer mediation increased social interaction for children with ASD. Further, peers participating as mediators can increase peer acceptance and engagement with others, and this in turn can be a powerful agent of change for children with ASD (51).

Peer-mediated interventions not only benefit the child with ASD but they also provide positive results for the typically developing children delivering the intervention. While it can be argued that school-based peer mediation takes away valuable learning opportunities for those administering the intervention, Hunt and Goetz (59) report that these peers demonstrate positive social-emotional growth and participation does not interfere with academic performance. As an added benefit, participating peers often develop positive and accepting attitudes when they observe the capability of their peers with a disability (60).

Kasari and colleagues (51) performed one of the first randomized controlled studies that compared the effectiveness of one-on-one direct social skills training to a peer-mediated model for high-functioning children with ASD. Peers received extensive instruction (40 min per week for 6 weeks) and training in how to recognize and lend social support to those who may have social difficulties. Results showed that children who received the peer-mediated intervention had increased involvement in classroom social networks as rated by teachers and untrained peers in the classroom, as well as less isolation on the playground. These treatment gains persisted to a 3-month follow-up. Despite these improvements, reciprocal friendships remained low for children with ASD and they still exhibited isolated play on the playground, although to a lesser extent.

While the previous study shows that peer mediation may be an independently superior treatment than simply direct skills training, using the treatments in combination should also be considered when creating an efficacious social skills intervention. Banda et al. (61) conducted a study that combined direct instruction and peer training for increasing social skills in two elementary students with ASD. They had teachers in a classroom setting model to participants and peers how to initiate questions and answer with appropriate responses, while praising students for properly asking and responding to questions. Results showed an increase in participant initiating and responding. A similar study had an interventionist teach a participant and two peers various phrases and skills to promote cooperative play at recess and provide cues during appropriate times of play. All three participants had higher rates of communicative acts during the intervention sessions than at baseline (62). Schmidt and Stichter (63) had adolescent peer mediators interact with three target students with ASD who had just completed a direct skills training program delivered in a school setting and found that the addition of the peer mediators lead to improved skill generalization for all three students with ASD. As these studies illustrate, adult supervision using direct skills training in concert with peer intervention may be a strategic combination for improving the social engagement of children with ASD.

## SOCIAL LEARNING IS ACTIVE *"PRACTICE IS THE KEY TO SOCIAL SUCCESS"*

Whether by direct skills didactic training or peer-mediated interventions, social learning theory posits that much of human behavior is learned by watching and imitating others (64). In fact, four processes are deemed necessary to promote the acquisition of social behavior, namely, attention, retention, production, and motivation. In other words, despite the misleading title, observational learning is not a passive task of merely watching others; it is an active and engaging process. Thus, programs that include techniques to activate learning and engage the participant through the actual performance and practice of social skills can advance learning (65–68). As discussed below, acting is fundamentally active and thereby may provide the opportunity to enhance observational learning and the practice of social skills.

Reciprocal social interaction requires active engagement and practice. While it is helpful to teach social rules and strategies, there are a variety of possible encounters and, therefore, the proficiency, spontaneity, and improvement in socialization is gained through interacting with a variety of partners. In infancy and early childhood, many fundamental social skills are acquired by imitating others; yet, children with autism have difficulty with imitation (69), which includes knowing who to model, what behaviors to imitate, and in what context to apply the behaviors learned (70). Since imitation is one of the ways in which children learn social rules, early deficits in this ability could impair a child's social development (71).

As a key component in social learning (64), imitation is not a passive process, rather, it is a volitional, effortful, and active process (72). Studies show that children with autism are impaired in imitating various actions and emotions compared to peers with other developmental delays or typical development (69). In this study, Rogers and colleagues postulate that imitation deficits in children with autism may lead to a lack of active imitation practice due in part to a diminished interest in socially motivating rewards (69). This suggests that in order to engage children with autism to practice imitating others, they must be motivated to observe and imitate the actions of others. One approach shown to capture the motivation of children with ASD is video modeling (31, 73, 74).

Video modeling is an effective way to work with children on the autism spectrum to capture and transfer the targeted skills into their repertoire. In video modeling, an individual watches specific skills presented on a video, then imitates through active practice of the performed skills often in the form of a role-play that may be initially guided by a trained paraprofessional or parent. Video modeling has consistently gained empirical support across a number of studies for improving various aspects of social functioning and teaching adaptive behaviors, such as reciprocal play and promoting social language verbalizations in children with autism (30, 31, 75–81). The use of video can facilitate observational learning and generalization of behavior because it is an inherently motivating medium (28, 31, 73, 74). Since video modeling involves not only watching the performance of others but also includes role-play with another person, it is complimentary to several acting approaches used in theatre outlined below.

## NATURAL AND SUPPORTIVE CONTEXTS

It is well established that the context in which an individual learns can significantly impact the retention and transfer of skills in typically developing children (82, 83) and ASD (37, 57). Motivation is a key component in active learning, and is influenced by external factors, including the learning context (84). An environment that is perceived as naturally stimulating and supportive leads to greater motivation and participation compared to restrictive and controlled settings (85). This is shown in children with ASD as well as other developmental disabilities demonstrated by Gresham and colleagues (86), who state that social skills interventions with poor generalization outcomes usually take place in more restrictive settings that are unlike the child's usual environment. In contrast, the positive impact of social skills training with or without peers can be enhanced when conducted in natural settings, thereby leading to greater generalization and maintenance (46, 87, 88). Providing a least restrictive environment allows children of all achievement and developmental needs to receive an adequate and effective education (89). Peer-assisted learning strategies implemented within an inclusive classroom environment can provide reciprocal learning when delivered in a supportive and structured manner (90). In the process, children can benefit from different instructional procedures that are conducive to individual learning needs while allowing the teacher the opportunity to supervise a variety of instructional methods simultaneously (90).

The context in which typically developing peers and children with developmental needs are brought together is especially critical. For example, an increase in communication and interaction was demonstrated in children with ASD utilizing peer mediation at recess where it is possible to *encourage* appropriate social interactions with peers, although the authors acknowledge that such an approach lacks structure and close adult supervision (62). Kasari and Smith (91) propose that contexts outside of school that mimic the school environment could be an effective compromise between the naturalistic environment of a cafeteria or playground and the structure of a clinic setting. Ideally, a combined supportive structure may be the best. For example, Sansosti (92) proposes a multitier framework to teach social skills for children with ASD that includes core (e.g., positive behavior support), targeted (social skills groups), and intensive (individualized videos) intervention strategies.

In treatment, the contextual framework plays an integral role in the development and transfer of skills (37, 57, 82). In order for treatment to be successful, interventionists have the responsibility of cultivating applicable learning environments that will lead to successful dissemination within the community (93). Effective learning conditions ought to be natural, motivating, and supportive (46, 84, 85, 87, 88). Moreover, the study of an intervention needs to be applied within the same context and under the same conditions for which it was developed (93). In short, context is not an extraneous variable, it is a critical factor. The SENSE Theatre intervention discussed below fosters these principal conditions while providing a supportive context in which there is clear structure and one-to-one peer supervision, with many adults in close contact with the participants.

## SENSE THEATRE, A NOVEL, PEER-MEDIATED, PERFORMANCE-BASED PROGRAM DELIVERED IN A COMMUNITY-BASED INTERVENTION

While there is an inherent drive in science, and intervention research in particular, to reveal the key contributing components or mechanisms that lead to change, the treatment of such complex skills will naturally require several components. Nevertheless, we argue that a few important components are critical for the acquisition, maintenance, and generalization of sociability in ASD. As previously described, peer mediation, active practice, and training conducted in a supportive, natural context can significantly impact the acquisition of important reciprocal social interaction skills. Here, we highlight the importance of these techniques that are integral to a novel program called SENSE Theatre that includes these important elements as well as a unique form of treatment delivery, the use of theatre, and acting techniques.

Acting is an interactive process that involves many aspects of socializing, namely, observing, perceiving, interpreting, and expressing thoughts and ideas. For example, an actor must pay attention to the other actors, listen and react to their cues, and express the thoughts and feelings of their characters. It also encompasses other important elements known to be problematic in individuals with ASD, theory of mind and empathy (18, 19). An actor must learn to take on the perspective of another character, which includes their beliefs and feelings. The process can lead to enhanced awareness and increased understanding of the experiences of other people. Thus, in the process, children with ASD may gain greater insight and ability to attribute mental states and feelings onto oneself and others. In fact the inclusion of various theatrical approaches into earlier intervention programs for individuals with typical development and ASD have shown improvement in relevant areas of social functioning, such as empathy and perspective taking (28, 94–98). In the SENSE Theatre program, a variety of acting techniques are employed to include role-play, scripts, and improvisation that provide an opportunity for the participant with ASD to explore and practice social interaction skills in a safe and supportive environment (28, 29). Participants engage in peer-mediated theatre games, such as mirroring, which involve imitating a partner's actions, thoughts, or feelings. Acting provides the opportunity for the children with ASD to interact with peers and indirectly practice social skills. For example, role-play exercises require verbal and non-verbal turn taking, which can facilitate reciprocal communication and interaction skills. Improvisation is also an active and dynamic process in which scenarios are presented to perform without preparation, which engages the child's imagination and allows more flexible thought and behavior.

### PEERS AS AN EXPERT MODEL

The SENSE Theatre intervention utilizes highly interactive peers to facilitate social interaction in children with ASD. While there are different types of models that can be employed in treatment studies, the utilization of an expert model can provide direct instruction from persons that characterize optimal functioning. For example, integrated playgroup models have been used in which *expert players* help instruct the *novice players* on particular skills (99, 100). In the current theatre intervention, each participant with ASD is paired with a typically developing child with acting skills who, in addition to being a co-actor in a play, serves as the participant's peer model. In the SENSE approach, youth actors are conceptualized as "experts" of reciprocal social interaction skills that include verbal and non-verbal communication, socioemotional perception, and expression, as well as behavioral and affective control. It has been shown that learning from an expert with instructional cues can enhance learning (101). Learning by watching and interacting with the expert models in a to-and-fro social exchange develops the skills in an efficient and precise manner.

In fact, the peers are selected, in part, based on their exceptional skills in key areas of social functioning, which are often found in actors (e.g., empathy, social communication) (102). While testing of peers for inclusion is not required, prior to training, we recently identified some of the underlying characteristics of many of the peers. Based on self-report measures, the majority of peers score highly on empathy (103) and self-efficacy (104). It is likely that these key attributes are fundamental to peer mediation such that strong empathy skills allow the peers to be concerned about the welfare of the child with ASD and that high confidence allows them to serve as an expert model. Although this is currently conjecture, efforts are underway to examine these hypotheses.

Prior to the start of the intervention, peer actors receive comprehensive training in key topics including characteristics of ASD, a variety of established behavioral intervention techniques, and the SENSE Theatre manualized approach. When peer training is included in an intervention, it is important to examine the integrity of the training by testing the acquisition of knowledge [e.g., Ref. (63)]. In the SENSE Theatre program, this is conducted immediately before and after peer training.

Moreover, to ensure that training is implemented appropriately especially when working with peers or students, delivery fidelity is recommended (105, 106). To assess fidelity of implementation of the behavioral techniques and core objectives of the program, raters behaviorally code the peers during semi-structured activities at three time points in the course of the program. For SENSE Theatre, to achieve fidelity, the peer must obtain a minimum performance of skill implantation (e.g., 80%) on each of the techniques and objectives observed. Research personnel supervise the application of the technique using objective and reliable coding throughout the program. If individual peers have difficulty implementing the techniques or maintaining a high level of skill, then booster sessions and individualized feedback are employed.

#### PERFORMANCE

Through *in vivo* and video modeling with expert peer models, children with ASD are given the opportunity to practice and perform the skills necessary for acquisition. One of the goals of repeated performance of newly learned skills is to reach the status of automaticity (107) in which domain-specific skills became a natural part of the child's repertoire. Moreover, as part of the SENSE Theatre program, the children perform in a multi-context manner, specifically, in the theatre with their peers and practice at home via video modeling (29), and also perform their skills and roles for the public. Thus, the program is performance-based, enhancing the ability of children to exercise their new and developing social skills for each other, as well as for the public in the form of a play.

#### CONTEXT

The foundational work of Vygotsky has shown that the context in which learning occurs is critical (83). As part of his theory of the zone of proximal development, a child benefits from training that bridges their actual developmental level with his or her potential developmental level. In SENSE Theatre, one of the core principals is to create an environment that provides the opportunity to advance the child's learning while supporting the child's current ability. As noted above, motivation is an important part of active learning, which is influenced by the learning context (84). Social interaction with peers can be challenging and stressful for children with ASD; however, they can be motivated by the inclusion of peers, modeling of positive social engagement, and playful group activities. SENSE Theatre, with the inclusion of supportive theatre games and peers, is naturally stimulating thereby contributing to enhanced motivation and participation (85).

The SENSE Theatre program has been conducted in natural, community-based environments that are supportive and less restrictive, which likely contributes to greater maintenance and generalization of learned skills (46, 87–90). Training is implemented in a hierarchical manner via supervised large group, small groups, and one-on-one peer-mediated teaching allowing individualized support, as needed (92). Additionally, snack breaks are provided fostering less formal engagement and *in vivo* modeling. Thus, the delivery of treatment in a context outside of the child's school; yet, in the community or school theatre merges the feel of a natural setting with the oversight of a clinical setting (91). Video modeling approaches allow participants to view and practice daily with videotaped peers from home via a password protected website to extend the learning practice (29). Finally, the program includes multiple trained peers that engage directly or indirectly with the participants; as such, the variability and diversity of modeled behavior is more representative of natural social interactions (108).

Thus, acting and the theatrical techniques used in the SENSE Theatre program help to teach social skills through the use of expert peers models who provide multiple opportunities for socialization in real and imagined supportive contexts. Children with ASD require clear and repetitive exemplars, which are delivered in the role-plays and exercises. Simultaneously, the use of improvisation and theatre games stimulates imagination and fosters more flexible thinking and behavior. Moreover, the positive reinforcement received from the peers can enhance social motivation to engage with others. Since ASD has been conceptualized as a disorder of social motivation (3, 4), treatments that show the benefits of socialization set the stage for targeting a core deficit. Acting is interactive, a dynamic process that can fundamentally enhance the attention to, practice of, and motivation to engage in reciprocal social interaction.

### RESEARCH FINDINGS

The SENSE Theatre intervention has been offered to dozens of children with ASD and formally examined in two published studies that included a pre-test, post-test design in which measures were assessed immediately before and following the intervention (28, 29). Briefly, the first study was conducted in a community theatre model including approximately 40 intervention hours delivered over a 2 1/2-month duration. Practices were held approximately one to two nights per week including several days of rehearsal the week before the public performance. Participants included eight children with ASD (seven boys and one girl) ranging in age from 7 to 18 years that were paired with typically developing peers. Dependent measures included neuropsychological, biological (cortisol and oxytocin), and behavioral scales to assess social perception, hormone levels, and adaptive behaviors. Primary dependent neuropsychological measures included subtests from the NEPSY (109) to measure memory for faces, affect recognition, and theory of mind, all hypothesized to show skill improvement following the intervention. Cortisol, a measure of stress responsivity, was hypothesized to show initial rise followed by gradual decline as the participants acclimated to the social intervention. The participants with ASD showed moderate improvement in face identification and theory of mind skills following the intervention. Additionally, they demonstrated a reduction in cortisol levels over time (28). The findings suggested changes in social perception and adaptation to the social environment.

Recently, we reported findings on the implementation of a summer camp model that included a comparable dose of 10 sessions. However, it was conducted over a shorter duration and more concentrated dose intensity. Specifically, the treatment was delivered over 2 weeks for 3 1/2 h per day in a summer camp model. Sixteen youth with ASD between 8 and 17 years completed the treatment and 12 participated in the research. A multilevel approach was again employed in which examination of neuropsychological, biological, and behavioral variables was measured. Significant differences in social perception on the NEPSY (109) (memory for faces), social function on the Social Responsiveness Scale (SRS), (110) (awareness, cognition), and adaptive skills on the Adaptive Behavior Assessment System (ABAS (111)) (home living, self-care) were observed. Stress reduction as measured by salivary cortisol was also observed (29).

Since this initial model was implemented, subsequent camp interventions have been delivered using a pre-test, post-test design. In a combined cohort of participants ($N = 20$) from the 2012 and 2013 SENSE Theatre summer camps, several findings were replicated using paired samples $t$-tests. Specifically, social perception in the form of memory for faces immediate [$t(18) = -2.612$, $p = 0.018$] and memory for faces delayed [$t(18) = -4.194$, $p = 0.001$] showed significant change upon post testing. In regard to generalized social functioning based on parental report using the SRS (110), improvement was reported on total social responsiveness [$t(19) = 2.665$, $p = 0.015$], and social cognition [$t(19) = 3.523$, $p = 0.002$] in particular. These results further support the findings that the SENSE Theatre intervention produces improvement in core areas of functioning for many children with ASD, namely, gains in social cognition, memory, and behavior. Moreover, in the most recent data, increases in adaptive skills were reported for functional academics [$t(18) = -2.617$, $p = 0.017$] and self-direction [$t(18) = -2.179$, $p = 0.043$] suggesting that the treatment has positive impact beyond the targeted social communication skills.

Improvements in social functioning have likewise been reported in other peer-mediated social skills interventions previously mentioned (51, 57, 58). In addition, the randomized social skills program given by Solomon and colleagues (33), which targeted emotional awareness, theory of mind, and problem solving, led to improvement in social perception. Also, another program that used theatre techniques to improve social skills (96) similarly found increases in social perception, social assertiveness, and reduction in social problems.

The observed gains in children with ASD in social perception, social functioning, and adaptive skills, which are important building blocks of reciprocal social interaction, provide support for the utilization of theatre-based approaches. While randomized experimental studies are warranted, these preliminary studies collectively provide strong support for the SENSE Theatre model (28, 29).

## DISCUSSION

The hallmark characteristic of ASD is poor reciprocal social communication and a variety of interventions have been employed to improve functioning in these critical skills. Promising approaches, such as peer mediation have contributed to improvements in various specific social skills in children with ASD. The inclusion of typically developing peers in social interaction programs can improve social development and engagement in children with ASD (48–50). Peers can be trained to elicit target behaviors using behavioral approaches such as modeling, reinforcement, and scripting that can enhance generalization (53, 55, 56). In addition to working *in vivo*, video modeling has been shown to be a promising approach to teach a variety of skills to children with ASD (30, 31, 75, 76, 80, 112, 113).

The aforementioned efficacious behavioral approaches have been combined with performance-based theatrical techniques in SENSE Theatre to address barriers to behavioral change and explicitly advance the learning and application of social functioning in youth with ASD. While theatrical techniques such as role playing, improvisation, and character development are rarely used in the treatment of ASD, they have been shown to target core deficits in reciprocal social communication (28, 29, 96, 114). Acting is explicitly active, requiring the performance of thoughts, ideas, and actions thereby providing the child with ASD the opportunity to practice social skills in a supportive albeit dynamic setting. As in acting, interacting with others relies on the ability to recognize, identify, integrate, plan, and respond appropriately to dynamic socioemotional information; therefore, utilizing theatre techniques provides the opportunity to learn and practice these social skills. The trained typically developing peer actors are the primary agents of change and in the process serve as both teacher and recipient of reciprocal social exchange. The program is also enhanced by treatment delivery in a community setting, demonstrating that promising interventions can be delivered in natural contexts while maintaining the rigor of a clinic setting.

The SENSE Theatre model suggests that the inclusion of these approaches in combination with the core theatre methods enhances the training, social experience, and motivation of the participants to engage with peers (28, 29). Combining treatments that have been independently effective has been shown to demonstrate even greater gains when delivered in combination (115). While previous efforts lend preliminary support for SENSE Theatre for improving social interaction skills in ASD, we are conducting a randomized, waitlist control group study with a large sample of participants enrolled in a 10-week model of the SENSE Theatre treatment. Additionally, a manual is in final development, which will allow the treatment to be delivered systematically by other interventionists in various settings to increase reliability and determine efficacy. Some may insist on trying to discover the turnkey ingredient that contributes to the promising results for this or any other treatment. For a complex set of behaviors, such as reciprocal social skills, it is highly unlikely that a single basic factor will be identified to target or explain the benefits when remediated. Indeed, the aforementioned theatrical treatment framework provides evidence that synthesizing peer mediation, active learning, and a supportive, natural context can promote the advancement, maintenance, and generalization of skills for youth with ASD.

## CONCLUDING REMARKS

Interventions aimed at improving core impairment in reciprocal social communication in children with ASD are critically needed. Evidence is presented highlighting important components for advancing, maintaining, and generalizing social competence, which include peer mediation, active learning, and the implementation of interventions in supportive, natural contexts. Moreover, acting specifically targets the core ASD impairment in reciprocal social communication and rigid, inflexible thought and behavior by having the child actively engage in activities such as role-playing and improvisation to develop these skills. SENSE Theatre, a promising treatment for youth with ASD, serves as a model for utilizing these elements by combining trained peers that facilitate the performance-based theatrical treatment delivered in a supportive, community-based environment.

## AUTHOR CONTRIBUTIONS

Blythe A. Corbett conceptualized the paper, developed the SENSE Theatre program, wrote the initial draft of the paper, and revised the final manuscript. Lydia R. Qualls researched peer mediation and active practice, assisted with writing the first full draft, and revised and copyedited the final version of the manuscript.

Blythe Valencia researched the importance of context and natural environments in learning, as well as the section on peers as expert models, and helped draft those sections of the manuscript. Stéphanie-M. Fecteau contributed background information regarding autism spectrum disorders and peer mediation, and helped with the revision of the manuscript. Deanna M. Swain contributed to early ideas regarding peer mediation and video modeling strategies for ASD and contributed to the original draft of the paper. All authors have read the final work and agree to be accountable for its accuracy and integrity.

## ACKNOWLEDGMENTS

This work was supported in part by the National Institute of Mental Health (NIMH; R34 MH 097793, Blythe A. Corbett). The content is solely the responsibility of the authors and does not necessarily represent the official views of the NIMH or the National Institute of Health. The NIHM had no further role in study design; in the collection, analysis, and interpretation of the data; in the writing of the report; and in the decision to submit the paper for publication. We would like to acknowledge all the peers that have served as extraordinary models for our children with ASD through their participation in the SENSE Theatre intervention research program.

## REFERENCES

1. APA. *Diagnostic and Statistical Manual of Mental Disorders, Fifth Edition (DSM-5)*. Washington, DC: American Psychiatric Association (2013).
2. CDC. *Autism and Developmental Disabilities Monitoring (ADDM) Network*. (2014). Available from: http://www.cdc.gov/ncbddd/autism/research.html
3. Chevallier C, Kohls G, Troiani V, Brodkin ES, Schultz RT. The social motivation theory of autism. *Trends Cogn Sci* (2012) **16**(4):231–9. doi:10.1016/j.tics.2012.02.007
4. Dawson G, Carver L, Meltzoff AN, Panagiotides H, McPartland J, Webb SJ. Neural correlates of face and object recognition in young children with autism spectrum disorder, developmental delay, and typical development. *Child Dev* (2002) **73**(3):700–17. doi:10.1111/1467-8624.00411
5. Wing L, Gould J. Severe impairments of social interaction and associated abnormalities in children: epidemiology and classification. *J Autism Dev Disor* (1979) **9**(1):11–29. doi:10.1007/BF01531288
6. Esbensen AJ, Seltzer MM, Lam KS, Bodfish JW. Age-related differences in restricted repetitive behaviors in autism spectrum disorders. *J Autism Dev Disord* (2009) **39**(1):57–66. doi:10.1007/s10803-008-0599-x
7. Dunn W. The sensations of everyday life: empirical, theoretical, and pragmatic considerations. *Am J Occup Ther* (2001) **55**(6):608–20. doi:10.5014/ajot.55.6.608
8. Etcoff NL. The neuropsychology of emotional expression. *Adv Clin Neuropsychol* (1986) **3**:127–79. doi:10.1007/978-1-4613-2211-5_5
9. Celani G, Battacchi MW, Arcidiacono L. The understanding of the emotional meaning of facial expressions in people with autism. *J Autism Dev Disord* (1999) **29**(1):57–66. doi:10.1023/A:1025970600181
10. Macdonald H, Rutter M, Howlin P, Rios P, Le Conteur A, Evered C, et al. Recognition and expression of emotional cues by autistic and normal adults. *J Child Psychol Psychiatry* (1989) **30**(6):865–77. doi:10.1111/j.1469-7610.1989.tb00288.x
11. Adolphs R, Sears L, Piven J. Abnormal processing of social information from faces in autism. *J Cogn Neurosci* (2001) **13**(2):232–40. doi:10.1162/089892901564289
12. Ashwin C, Wheelwright S, Baron-Cohen S. Finding a face in the crowd: testing the anger superiority effect in Asperger syndrome. *Brain Cogn* (2006) **61**(1):78–95. doi:10.1016/j.bandc.2005.12.008
13. Baron-Cohen S, Ring HA, Wheelwright S, Bullmore ET, Brammer MJ, Simmons A, et al. Social intelligence in the normal and autistic brain: an fMRI study. *Eur J Neurosci* (1999) **11**(6):1891–8. doi:10.1046/j.1460-9568.1999.00621.x
14. Critchley HD, Daly EM, Bullmore ET, Williams SC, Van Amelsvoort T, Robertson DM, et al. The functional neuroanatomy of social behaviour: changes in cerebral blood flow when people with autistic disorder process facial expressions. *Brain* (2000) **123**(Pt 11):2203–12. doi:10.1093/brain/123.11.2203
15. Dalton KM, Nacewicz BM, Johnstone T, Schaefer HS, Gernsbacher MA, Goldsmith HH, et al. Gaze fixation and the neural circuitry of face processing in autism. *Nat Neurosci* (2005) **8**(4):519–26. doi:10.1038/nn1421
16. Davies S, Bishop D, Manstead AS, Tantam D. Face perception in children with autism and Asperger's syndrome. *J Child Psychol Psychiatry* (1994) **35**(6):1033–57. doi:10.1111/j.1469-7610.1994.tb01808.x
17. Schultz RT, Gauthier I, Klin A, Fulbright RK, Anderson AW, Volkmar F, et al. Abnormal ventral temporal cortical activity during face discrimination among individuals with autism and Asperger syndrome. *Arch Gen Psychiatry* (2000) **57**(4):331–40. doi:10.1001/archpsyc.57.4.331
18. Baron-Cohen S, Leslie AM, Frith U. Does the autistic child have a "theory of mind"? *Cognition* (1985) **21**(1):37–46. doi:10.1016/0010-0277(85)90022-8
19. Frith U, Frith CD. Development and neurophysiology of mentalizing. *Philos Trans R Soc Lond B Biol Sci* (2003) **358**(1431):459–73. doi:10.1098/rstb.2002.1218
20. Happe F, Frith U. *Theory of Mind in Autism*. New York: Plenum Press (1995).
21. Corbett BA, Schupp CW, Levine S, Mendoza S. Comparing cortisol, stress and sensory sensitivity in children with autism. *Autism Res* (2009) **2**:32–9. doi:10.1002/aur.64
22. Corbett BA, Schupp CW, Simon D, Ryan N, Mendoza S. Elevated cortisol during play is associated with age and social engagement in children with autism. *Mol Autism* (2010) **1**(1):13. doi:10.1186/2040-2392-1-13
23. Corbett BA, Swain DM, Newsom C, Wang L, Song Y, Edgerton D. Biobehavioral profiles of arousal and social motivation in autism spectrum disorders. *J Child Psychol Psychiatry* (2013) **55**(8):924–34. doi:10.1111/jcpp.12184
24. Lopata C, Volker MA, Putnam SK, Thomeer ML, Nida RE. Effect of social familiarity on salivary cortisol and self-reports of social anxiety and stress in children with high functioning autism spectrum disorders. *J Autism Dev Disord* (2008) **38**(10):1866–77. doi:10.1007/s10803-008-0575-5
25. Gillott A, Furniss F, Walter A. Anxiety in high-functioning children with autism. *Autism* (2001) **5**(3):277–86. doi:10.1177/1362361301005003005
26. Kuusikko S, Pollock-Wurman R, Jussila K, Carter AS, Mattila ML, Ebeling H, et al. Social anxiety in high-functioning children and adolescents with autism and Asperger syndrome. *J Autism Dev Disord* (2008) **38**(9):1697–709. doi:10.1007/s10803-008-0555-9
27. Schupp CW, Simon D, Corbett BA. Cortisol responsivity differences in children with autism spectrum disorders during free and cooperative play. *J Autism Dev Disord* (2013) **43**(10):2405–17. doi:10.1007/s10803-013-1790-2
28. Corbett BA, Gunther JR, Comins D, Price J, Ryan N, Simon D, et al. Brief report: theatre as therapy for children with autism spectrum disorder. *J Autism Dev Disord* (2011) **41**(4):505–11. doi:10.1007/s10803-010-1064-1
29. Corbett BA, Swain DM, Coke C, Simon D, Newsom C, Houchins-Juarez N, et al. Improvement in social deficits in autism spectrum disorders using a theatre-based, peer-mediated intervention. *Autism Res* (2014) **7**:4–16. doi:10.1002/aur.1341
30. Charlop-Christy MH, Le L, Freeman KA. A comparison of video modeling with in vivo modeling for teaching children with autism. *J Autism Dev Disord* (2000) **30**(6):537–52. doi:10.1023/A:1005635326276
31. Corbett BA. Video modeling: a window into the world of autism. *Behav Analyst Today* (2003) **4**(3):367–77.
32. Kamps D, Royer J, Dugan E, Kravits T, Gonzalez-Lopez A, Garcia J, et al. Peer training to facilitate social interaction for elementary students with autism and their peers. *Except Child* (2002) **68**(2):173–87.
33. Solomon M, Goodlin-Jones BL, Anders TF. A social adjustment enhancement intervention for high functioning autism, Asperger's syndrome, and pervasive developmental disorder NOS. *J Autism Dev Disord* (2004) **34**(6):649–68. doi:10.1007/s10803-004-5286-y
34. Strain PS, Schwartz I. ABA and the development of meaningful social relations for young children with autism. *Focus Autism Relat Disord* (2001) **16**:120–8. doi:10.1177/108835760101600208
35. Zanolli K, Daggett J, Adams T. Teaching preschool age autistic children to make spontaneous initiations to peers using priming. *J Autism Dev Disord* (1996) **26**(4):407–22. doi:10.1007/BF02172826

36. Reichow B, Volkmar FR, Cicchetti DV. Development of the evaluative method for evaluating and determining evidence-based practices in autism. *J Autism Dev Disord* (2008) **38**(7):1311–9. doi:10.1007/s10803-007-0517-7
37. Chan JM, Lang R, Rispoli M, O'Reilly MF, Sigafoos J, Cole H. Use of peer-mediated interventions in the treatment of autism spectrum disorders: a systematic review. *Res Autism Spectr Disord* (2009) **3**:876–89. doi:10.1016/j.rasd.2009.04.003
38. White SW, Keonig K, Scahill L. Social skills development in children with autism spectrum disorders: a review of the intervention research. *J Autism Dev Disord* (2007) **37**(10):1858–68. doi:10.1007/s10803-006-0320-x
39. Camargo SP, Rispoli M, Ganz J, Hong ER, Davis H, Mason R. A review of the quality of behaviorally-based intervention research to improve social interaction skills of children with ASD in inclusive settings. *J Autism Dev Disord* (2014) **44**(9):2096–116. doi:10.1007/s10803-014-2060-7
40. Kasari C, Patterson S. Interventions addressing social impairment in autism. *Curr Psychiatry Rep* (2012) **14**(6):713–25. doi:10.1007/s11920-012-0317-4
41. Reichow B, Steiner AM, Volkmar F. Cochrane review: social skills groups for people aged 6 to 21 with autism spectrum disorders (ASD). *Evid Based Child Health* (2013) **8**(2):266–315. doi:10.1002/ebch.1903
42. Bellini S, Peters JK. Social skills training for youth with autism spectrum disorders. *Child Adolesc Psychiatr Clin N Am* (2008) **17**(4):857–73. doi:10.1016/j.chc.2008.06.008
43. Mesibov GB. Social skills training with verbal autistic adolescents and adults: a program model. *J Autism Dev Disord* (1984) **14**(4):395–404. doi:10.1007/BF02409830
44. Chin HY, Bernard-Opitz V. Teaching conversational skills to children with autism: effect on the development of a theory of mind. *J Autism Dev Disord* (2000) **30**(6):569–83. doi:10.1023/A:1005639427185
45. Feng H, Lo Y, Tsai S, Cartledge G. The effects of theory-of-mind and social skills training on the social competence of a sixth-grade student with autism. *J Posit Behav Intervent* (2008) **10**(4):228–42. doi:10.1177/1098300708319906
46. Bellini S, Akullian J, Hopf A. Increasing social engagement in young children with autism spectrum disorders use video self-modeling. *School Psych Rev* (2007) **16**:80–90.
47. Qian N, Lipkin RM. A learning-style theory for understanding autistic behaviors. *Front Hum Neurosci* (2011) **5**:77. doi:10.3389/fnhum.2011.00077
48. Barry TD, Klinger LG, Lee JM, Palardy N, Gilmore T, Bodin SD. Examining the effectiveness of an outpatient clinic-based social skills group for high-functioning children with autism. *J Autism Dev Disord* (2003) **33**(6):685–701. doi:10.1023/B:JADD.0000006004.86556.e0
49. Egel AL, Richman GS, Koegel RL. Normal peer models and autistic children's learning. *J Appl Behav Anal* (1981) **14**(1):3–12. doi:10.1901/jaba.1981.14-3
50. Odom SL, Strain PS. Peer-mediated approaches to promoting children's social interaction: a review. *Am J Orthopsychiatry* (1984) **54**(4):544–57. doi:10.1111/j.1939-0025.1984.tb01525.x
51. Kasari C, Rotheram-Fuller E, Locke J, Gulsrud A. Making the connection: randomized controlled trial of social skills at school for children with autism spectrum disorders. *J Child Psychol Psychiatry* (2012) **53**(4):431–9. doi:10.1111/j.1469-7610.2011.02493.x
52. DiSalvo C, Oswald D. Peer-mediated interventions to increase the social interaction of children with autism: consideration of peer expectancies. *Focus Autism Dev Disabil* (2002) **17**(4):198–207. doi:10.1177/10883576020170040201
53. Kamps D, Leonard B, Vernon S, Dugan E, Delquadri J, Gershon B, et al. Teaching social skills to students with autism to increase peer interactions in an integrated first-grade classroom. *J Appl Behav Anal* (1992) **25**:281–8. doi:10.1901/jaba.1992.25-281
54. Prendeville JA, Prelock PA, Unwin G. Peer play interventions to support the social competence of children with autism spectrum disorders. *Semin Speech Lang* (2006) **27**(1):32–46. doi:10.1055/s-2006-932437
55. McConnell SR. Interventions to facilitate social interaction for young children with autism: review of available research and recommendations for educational intervention and future research. *J Autism Dev Disord* (2002) **32**(5):351–72. doi:10.1023/A:1020537805154
56. Banda DR, Copple KS, Koul RK, Sancibrian SL, Bogschutz RJ. Video modelling interventions to teach spontaneous requesting using AAC devices to individuals with autism: a preliminary investigation. *Disabil Rehabil* (2010) **32**(16):1364–72. doi:10.3109/09638280903551525
57. Lang R, Kuriakose S, Lyons G, Mulloy A, Boutot A, Britt C, et al. Use of school recess time in the education and treatment of children with autism spectrum disorders: a systematic review. *Res Autism Spectr Disord* (2011) **5**(4):1296–305. doi:10.1016/j.rasd.2011.02.012
58. Zhang J, Wheeler JJ. A meta-analysis of peer-mediated interventions for young children with autism spectrum disorders. *Educ Train Autism Dev Disabil* (2011) **46**(1):62–77.
59. Hunt P, Goetz L. Research on inclusive educational programs, practices, and outcomes for students with severe disabilities. *J Spec Educ* (1997) **31**(1):3–29. doi:10.1177/002246699703100102
60. Ferraioli SJ, Harris SL. Effective educational inclusion of students on the autism spectrum. *J Contemp Psychother* (2011) **41**(1):19–28. doi:10.1007/s10879-010-9156-y
61. Banda DR, Hart SL, Liu-Gitz L. Impact of training peers and children with autism on social skills during center time activities in inclusive classrooms. *Res Autism Spectr Disord* (2010) **4**(4):619–25. doi:10.1016/j.rasd.2009.12.005
62. Mason R, Kamps D, Turcotte A, Cox S, Feldmiller S, Miller T. Peer mediation to increase communication and interaction at recess for students with autism spectrum disorders. *Res Autism Spectr Disord* (2014) **8**:334–44. doi:10.1016/j.rasd.2013.12.014
63. Schmidt C, Stichter JP. The use of peer-mediated interventions to promote the generalization of social competence for adolescents with high-functioning autism and Asperger's syndrome. *Exceptionality* (2012) **20**(2):94–113. doi:10.1080/09362835.2012.669303
64. Bandura A. *Social Foundations of Thought and Action: A Social Cognitive Theory*. Englewood Cliffs, NJ: Prentice-Hall (1986).
65. Davies RR, Rogers ES. Social skills training with persons who are mentally retarded. *Ment Retard* (1985) **23**(4):186–96.
66. Falloon IR, Lindley P, McDonald R, Marks IM. Social skills training of outpatient groups. A controlled study of rehearsal and homework. *Br J Psychiatry* (1977) **131**:599–609. doi:10.1192/bjp.131.6.599
67. Laugeson EA, Park MN. Using a CBT approach to teach social skills to adolescents with autism spectrum disorder and other social challenges: the PEERS® method. *J Rat Emot Cogn Behav Ther* (2014) **32**(1):84–97. doi:10.1007/s10942-014-0181-8
68. Senatore V, Matson JL, Kazdin AE. A comparison of behavioral methods to train social skills to mentally retarded adults. *Behav Ther* (1982) **13**(3):313–24. doi:10.1016/S0005-7894(82)80040-3
69. Rogers SJ, Hepburn SL, Stackhouse T, Wehner E. Imitation performance in toddlers with autism and those with other developmental disorders. *J Child Psychol Psychiatry* (2003) **44**(5):763–81. doi:10.1111/1469-7610.00162
70. Vivanti G, Rogers SJ. Autism and the mirror neuron system: insights from learning and teaching. *Philos Trans R Soc Lond B Biol Sci* (2014) **369**(1644):20130184. doi:10.1098/rstb.2013.0184
71. McIntosh DN, Reichmann-Decker A, Winkielman P, Wilbarger JL. When the social mirror breaks: deficits in automatic, but not voluntary, mimicry of emotional facial expressions in autism. *Dev Sci* (2006) **9**(3):295–302. doi:10.1111/j.1467-7687.2006.00492.x
72. Butterworth G. Neonatal imitation: existence, mechanisms and motives. In: Butterworth JNG, editor. *Imitation in Infancy*. Cambridge, England: Cambridge University Press (1999). p. 63–88.
73. Corbett BA, Abdullah M. Video modeling: why does it work for children with autism? *J Early Inten Behav Intervent* (2005) **2**(1):2–8.
74. Jones J, Lerman DC, Lechago S. Assessing stimulus control and promoting generalization via video modeling when teaching social responses to children with autism. *J Appl Behav Anal* (2014) **47**(1):37–50. doi:10.1002/jaba.81
75. Charlop MH, Milstein JP. Teaching autistic children conversational speech using video modeling. *J Appl Behav Anal* (1989) **22**(3):275–85. doi:10.1901/jaba.1989.22-275
76. LeBlanc LA, Coates AM, Daneshvar S, Charlop-Christy MH, Morris C, Lancaster BM. Using video modeling and reinforcement to teach perspective-taking skills to children with autism. *J Appl Behav Anal* (2003) **36**(2):253–7. doi:10.1901/jaba.2003.36-253
77. Haring TG, Kennedy CH, Adams MJ, Pitts-Conway V. Teaching generalization of purchasing skills across community settings to autistic youth using videotape modeling. *J Appl Behav Anal* (1987) **20**(1):89–96. doi:10.1901/jaba.1987.20-89

78. MacDonald R, Sacramone S, Mansfield R, Wiltz K, Ahearn WH. Using video modeling to teach reciprocal pretend play to children with autism. *J Appl Behav Anal* (2009) **42**(1):43–55. doi:10.1901/jaba.2009.42-43
79. Maione L, Mirenda P. Effects of video modeling and video feedback on peer-directed social language skills of a child with autism. *J Posit Behav Intervent* (2006) **8**:106–18. doi:10.1177/10983007060080020201
80. Nikopoulos CK, Keenan M. Using video modeling to teach complex social sequences to children with autism. *J Autism Dev Disord* (2007) **37**(4):678–93. doi:10.1007/s10803-006-0195-x
81. Odluyurt S. A comparison of the effects of direct modeling and video modeling provided by peers to students with autism who are attending in rural play teaching in an inclusive setting. *Kuram Uygul Egit Bil* (2013) **13**(1):536–40.
82. Stokes TF, Baer DM. An implicit technology of generalization. *J Appl Behav Anal* (1977) **10**(2):349–67. doi:10.1901/jaba.1977.10-349
83. Vygotsky LS. *Mind in Society: The Development of Higher Mental Processes.* Cambridge, MA: Harvard University Press (1978).
84. Pintrich PR, De Groot EV. Motivational and self-regulated learning components of classroom academic performance. *J Educ Psychol* (1990) **82**:33–40. doi:10.1037/0022-0663.82.1.33
85. Ryan AM, Patrick H. The classroom social environment and changes in adolescents' motivation and engagement during middle school. *Am Educ Res J* (2001) **38**(2):437–60. doi:10.3102/00028312038002437
86. Gresham FM, Sugai G, Horner RH. Interpreting outcomes of social skills training for students with high-incidence disabilities. *Except Child* (2001) **67**(3):331–44.
87. Harper CB, Symon JB, Frea WD. Recess is time-in: using peers to improve social skills of children with autism. *J Autism Dev Disord* (2008) **38**(5):815–26. doi:10.1007/s10803-007-0449-2
88. Owen-DeSchryver JS, Carr EG, Cale SI, Blakeley-Smith A. Prompting social interactions between students with autism spectrum disorders and their peers in inclusive school settings. *Focus Autism Dev Disabil* (2008) **23**(1):15–28. doi:10.1177/1088357608314370
89. Fuchs LS, Fuchs D. Treatment validity: a unifying concept for ceconceptualizing the identification of learning disabilities. *Learn Disabil Res Pract* (1998) **13**:204–19.
90. Fuchs D, Fuchs LS. Peer-assisted learning strategies: promoting word recognition, fluency, and reading comprehension in young children. *J Spec Educ* (2005) **39**(1):34–44. doi:10.1177/00224669050390010401
91. Kasari C, Smith T. Interventions in schools for children with autism spectrum disorder: methods and recommendations. *Autism* (2013) **17**(3):254–67. doi:10.1177/1362361312470496
92. Sansosti FJ. Teaching social skills to children with autism spectrum disorders using tiers of support: a guide for school-based professionals. *Psychol Sch* (2010) **47**(3):257–81. doi:10.1002/pits.20469
93. Dingfelder HE, Mandell DS. Bridging the research-to-practice gap in autism intervention: an application of diffusion of innovation theory. *J Autism Dev Disord* (2011) **41**(5):597–609. doi:10.1007/s10803-010-1081-0
94. Goldstein H, Cisar CL. Promoting interaction during sociodramatic play: teaching scripts to typical preschoolers and classmates with disabilities. *J Appl Behav Anal* (1992) **25**(2):265–80. doi:10.1901/jaba.1992.25-265
95. Goldstein TR. Correlations among social-cognitive skills in adolescents involved in acting or arts classes. *Mind Brain Edu* (2011) **5**:97–103. doi:10.1111/j.1751-228X.2011.01115.x
96. Lerner MD, Mikami AY, Levine K. Socio-dramatic affective-relational intervention for adolescents with Asperger syndrome & high functioning autism: pilot study. *Autism* (2011) **15**(1):21–42. doi:10.1177/1362361309353613
97. Webb BJ, Miller SP, Pierce TB, Strawser S, Jones PS. Effects of social skill instruction for high-functioning adolescents with autism spectrum disorders. *Focus Autism Dev Disabil* (2004) **19**(1):53–62. doi:10.1177/10883576040190010701
98. Williams TI. A social skills group for autistic children. *J Autism Dev Disord* (1989) **19**(1):143–55. doi:10.1007/BF02212726
99. Wolfberg PJ. *Peer Play and the Autism Spectrum: The Art of Guiding Children's Socialization and Imagination.* Shawnee Mission, KS: Autism Asperger Publishing Co (2003).
100. Yang TR, Wolfberg PJ, Wu SC, Hwu PY. Supporting children on the autism spectrum in peer play at home and school: piloting the integrated play groups model in Taiwan. *Autism* (2003) **7**(4):437–53. doi:10.1177/1362361303007004009
101. Zetou E, Tzetzis G, Vernadakis N, Kioumourtzoglou E. Modeling in learning two volleyball skills. *Percept Mot Skills* (2002) **94**(3 Pt 2):1131–42. doi:10.2466/pms.2002.94.3c.1131
102. Goldstein TR, Winner E. Enhancing empathy and theory of mind. *J Cogn Dev* (2012) **13**(1):19–37. doi:10.1080/15248372.2011.573514
103. Jolliffe D, Farrington DP. Development and validation of the basic empathy scale. *J Adolesc* (2006) **29**(4):589–611. doi:10.1016/j.adolescence.2005.08.010
104. Brown L, Alexander J. *Self-Esteem Index.* Austin, TX: Pro-Ed Inc (1991).
105. Ory MG, Jordan PJ, Bazzarre T. The behavior change consortium: setting the stage for a new century of health behavior-change research. *Health Educ Res* (2002) **17**(5):500–11. doi:10.1093/her/17.5.500
106. Stichter JP, Laffey J, Galyen K, Herzog M. iSocial: delivering the social competence intervention for adolescents (SCI-A) in a 3D virtual learning environment for youth with high functioning autism. *J Autism Dev Disord* (2014) **44**(2):417–30. doi:10.1007/s10803-013-1881-0
107. Logan GD. Toward an instance theory of automatization. *Psychol Rev* (1988) **95**(4):492–527. doi:10.1037/0033-295X.95.4.492
108. Laushey KM, Heflin LJ. Enhancing social skills of kindergarten children with autism through the training of multiple peers as tutors. *J Autism Dev Disord* (2000) **30**(3):183–93. doi:10.1023/A:1005558101038
109. Korkman M, Kirk U, Kemp S. *NEPSY 2nd Edition.* San Antonio, TX: Harcourt Assessment (2007).
110. Constantino JN, Gruber CP. *Social Responsiveness Scale.* Los Angeles: Western Psychological Services (2005).
111. Harrison PL. *Adaptive Behavior Assessment System.* San Antonio, TX: Psychological Corporation (2000).
112. Nikopoulos CK, Keenan M. Effects of video modeling on social initiations by children with autism. *J Appl Behav Anal* (2004) **37**(1):93–6. doi:10.1901/jaba.2004.37-93
113. Sherer M, Pierce KL, Paredes S, Kisacky KL, Ingersoll B, Schreibman L. Enhancing conversation skills in children with autism via video technology. Which is better, "self" or "other" as a model? *Behav Modif* (2001) **25**(1):140–58. doi:10.1177/0145445501251008
114. Guli LA. The effects of creative drama based intervention for children with deficits in social perception [dissertation]. (2004). p. 1–174.
115. March J, Silva S, Vitiello B, Team T. The treatment for adolescents with depression study (TADS): methods and message at 12 weeks. *J Am Acad Child Adolesc Psychiatry* (2006) **45**(12):1393–403. doi:10.1097/01.chi.0000237709.35637.c0

# 11

# Mapping pathological phenotypes in reelin mutant mice

**Caterina Michetti[1,2†], Emilia Romano[3,4†], Luisa Altabella[5], Angela Caruso[1,6], Paolo Castelluccio[1], Gaurav Bedse[2], Silvana Gaetani[2], Rossella Canese[5]*, Giovanni Laviola[3§] and Maria Luisa Scattoni[1*§]**

[1] Neurotoxicology and Neuroendocrinology Section, Department of Cell Biology and Neuroscience, Istituto Superiore di Sanità, Rome, Italy
[2] Department of Physiology and Pharmacology "V. Erspamer," Sapienza University of Rome, Rome, Italy
[3] Behavioural Neuroscience Section, Department of Cell Biology and Neuroscience, Istituto Superiore di Sanità, Rome, Italy
[4] Bambino Gesù Children's Hospital, Istituto Di Ricovero e Cura a Carattere Scientifico, Rome, Italy
[5] Molecular and Cellular Imaging Section, Department of Cell Biology and Neuroscience, Istituto Superiore di Sanità, Rome, Italy
[6] Department of Psychology, School of Behavioural Neuroscience, Sapienza University of Rome, Rome, Italy

***Edited by:***
*Yuri Bozzi, University of Trento, Italy*

***Reviewed by:***
*Elizabeth M. Powell, University of Maryland, USA*
*Emanuel DiCicco-Bloom, University of Medicine and Dentistry of New Jersey, USA*

****Correspondence:***
*Rossella Canese, Molecular and Cellular Imaging Section, Department of Cell Biology and Neuroscience, Istituto Superiore di Sanità, Viale Regina Elena 299, I-00161 Rome, Italy*
*e-mail: rossella.canese@iss.it;*
*Maria Luisa Scattoni, Neurotoxicology and Neuroendocrinology Section, Department of Cell Biology and Neuroscience, Istituto Superiore di Sanità, Viale Regina Elena, 299, I-00161 Rome, Italy*
*e-mail: marialuisa.scattoni@iss.it*

*† These authors contributed equally to this work.*
*§ These authors also contributed equally to this work.*

Autism Spectrum Disorders (ASD) are neurodevelopmental disorders with multifactorial origin characterized by social communication deficits and the presence of repetitive behaviors/interests. Several studies showed an association between the *reelin* gene mutation and increased risk of ASD and a reduced reelin expression in some brain regions of ASD subjects, suggesting a role for *reelin* deficiency in ASD etiology. Reelin is a large extracellular matrix glycoprotein playing important roles during development of the central nervous system. To deeply investigate the role of *reelin* dysfunction as vulnerability factor in ASD, we assessed the behavioral, neurochemical, and brain morphological features of reeler male mice. We recently reported a genotype-dependent deviation in the ultrasonic vocal repertoire and a general delay in motor development of reeler pups. We now report that adult male heterozygous (Het) reeler mice did not show social behavior and communication deficits during male–female social interactions. Wildtype and Het mice showed a typical light/dark locomotor activity profile, with a peak during the central interval of the dark phase. However, when faced with a mild stressful stimulus (a saline injection) only Het mice showed an over response to stress. In addition to the behavioral studies, we conducted high performance liquid chromatography and magnetic resonance imaging and spectroscopy to investigate whether *reelin* mutation influences brain monoamine and metabolites levels in regions involved in ASD. Low levels of dopamine in cortex and high levels of glutamate and taurine in hippocampus were detected in Het mice, in line with clinical data collected on ASD children. Altogether, our data detected subtle but relevant neurochemical abnormalities in reeler mice supporting this mutant line, particularly male subjects, as a valid experimental model to estimate the contribution played by *reelin* deficiency in the global ASD neurobehavioral phenotype.

**Keywords: autism spectrum disorders, reeler mice, ultrasonic vocalizations, social interaction, stress response, dopamine, glutamate, circadian cycle**

## INTRODUCTION

Autism Spectrum Disorders (ASD) are neurodevelopmental disorders with multifactorial origin characterized by persistent deficits in social communication and interaction and restricted and repetitive patterns of behavior, interests, or activities (1). Several studies showed that abnormal reelin expression in the brain is involved in a number of neuropsychiatric disorders including lissencephaly, schizophrenia, and autism (2–8).

Clinical studies have shown reduced levels of reelin protein in blood serum and in post-mortem brain of ASD patients (9–12). Genetic variants in RELN have been investigated as risk factors of ASD in numerous epidemiologic studies but with inconclusive results (13–19). However, recent data collected on much larger samples and with more advanced genetic approaches indicated a relationship between *reelin* gene mutation and increase risk of autism, suggesting that *reelin* deficiency may be a vulnerability factor in the etiology of this neurodevelopmental disorder (20–27).

Animal models in which reelin expression is reduced or absent, provide important information about the role of *reelin* deficiency in the onset of neurodevelopmental disorders such as ASD. Homozygous reeler mice show decreased brain volume, increased ventricles volume, (28–30), a non-foliated cerebellum (30), reduced number of Purkinje cells (31), deficits in lamination of the hippocampus (Hip), and disorganization of the amygdala (30). Some of these abnormalities are comparable with the ones found in post-mortem studies on autistic brain such as: increased ventricle volume, altered cortical lamination, heterotopias, dysplastic changes, and reduced number of Purkinje cells (32–39). These morphological changes in homozygous reeler mice are also associated with serious physical impairments and for this reason these mice are not considered as a reliable animal model for basic behavioral research but their use has been so far limited to the study of neuronal migration and of etiology of human lissencephaly (4, 5).

Heterozygous reeler mice, which exhibit the 50% reduction in reelin expression, do not display a reeler phenotype but express a number of abnormal traits including loss of Purkinje cells of the cerebellum (40, 41) and decrease in the number of dendritic spines in cortical and hippocampal neurons (42). Reduced levels of reelin are also associated with an increased anxiety profile (43, 44), cognitive deficits in the operant conditioning (44, 45), executive functions (46), fear conditioning learning (47, 48), olfactory conditioning learning (49), latent inhibition (50), and attentional set-shifting (51).

Surprisingly, only limited studies have investigated the contribution of *reelin* deficiency to the establishment of the social/communicative deficits, first ASD core symptom as indicated in the DSM 5 (1). Adult social responses in heterozygous (Het) reeler mice have been tested so far in two studies assessing either direct male–male and female–female social interactions (52) or performance in a modified version of the three-chamber sociability test (51). In both studies, only social behavioral performances have been assessed but a detailed evaluation of the ultrasonic vocalizations (USVs) emitted during the interaction was missing. To this aim, we deeply investigated the social and vocal repertoire of wildtype (Wt) and Het reeler mice during courtship (53), to evaluate the presence of qualitative alterations in social interaction and communication in this mutant line. In addition, we evaluated the baseline circadian locomotor activity in the home-cage as well as the response to a mild stressful stimulus represented by a saline injection (54–57) to check for abnormalities in the spontaneous locomotor activity that could affect the behavioral performances. To investigate whether *reelin* mutation influences brain metabolism, brain morphology, and levels of monoamines and their metabolites into selected brain regions involved in ASD and social behavior, we performed *in vivo* quantitative magnetic resonance imaging (MRI), spectroscopy, and high performance liquid chromatography (HPLC) analyses.

## MATERIALS AND METHODS

### ANIMALS AND HOUSING

Breeding pairs were originally purchased from The Jackson Laboratory (Bar Harbor, ME, USA) and bred in our laboratory at ISS. About 2 weeks after pairing for breeding (15 Het × Het crosses), the females were individually housed and subsequently inspected daily for pregnancy and delivery. After weaning on postnatal day (pnd) 25, mice were housed by sex in mixed genotype groups (B6C3Fe Wt and Het) of two to three per cage. All mice were housed in a colony room with temperature maintained at 21 ± 1°C and humidity at 60 ± 10% with food (Enriched standard diet purchased from Mucedola, Settimo Milanese, Italy) and water available *ad libitum*. The colony room was maintained on a 12:12 light/dark cycle with lights on at 18.30 h. Mice genotype was determined at pnd 21 by polymerase chain reaction (PCR) analysis on tale samples and the animals were marked by an ear punching for identification. Consistent with the higher prevalence of autism in human males, only male mice were tested. Homozygous reeler mice were not tested due to their serious physical impairments after weaning. The same cohort of adult male mice was tested for male–female reciprocal social interaction with concomitant USVs (3 months of age), locomotor activity in the home-cage (6 months), and HPLC (7 months). A separate cohort of mice was subjected to *in vivo* quantitative MRI and spectroscopy at 4 months of age. All procedures were conducted in strict compliance with the European Communities guidelines (EC Council Directive 86/609), Italian legislation on animal experimentation (Decreto L.Vo 116/92).

### ADULT MALE–FEMALE SOCIAL INTERACTIONS

Three-month-old male mice ($N = 9$ Wt, $N = 21$ Het) were evaluated in the male–female social interaction test as in Ref. (53). Each male subject was isolated 1 h before testing and the vaginal estrous condition of each stimulus female was assessed as in Ref. (58). Only females in estrous were selected for the test. The unfamiliar stimulus C57BL/6J female mouse was placed into the home-cage of the isolated male mouse and behaviors and USVs were recorded for a 3-min test session. Stimulus mice (C57BL/6J females) were purchased from Jackson Laboratories (Bar Harbor, ME, USA) and maintained in our colony room in social groups of three per home-cage. Each female was used only twice and were matched to the subject mice by age and body weight.

Social interaction test was conducted between 09.00 and 13.00 h, during the dark phase, under red light. In addition to the isolated mouse, the cage contained litter (1.5-cm deep) and the lid was removed during the test. For video recordings, the video-camera (Panasonic monochrome charge-coupled device camera) was mounted facing the side of the cage and the subsequent scoring of social investigation parameters was conducted with Noldus Observer 10XT software (Noldus Information Technology, Leesburg, VA, USA).

Social interactions were scored from the videotapes for the frequencies and durations of the following behavioral responses performed by the subject mouse: *anogenital sniffing* (direct contact with the anogenital area), *body sniffing* (sniffing or snout contact with the flank area), *head sniffing* (sniffing or snout contact with the head/neck/mouth area), *locomotor activity*, *rearing* up against the wall of the home-cage, *digging* in the bedding, and *grooming* (self-cleaning, licking any part of its own body). No observations of *mounting*, *fighting*, *tail rattling*, and *wrestling* behaviors were observed. Scoring was conducted by two investigators uninformed of the genotype. Inter-rater reliability was 98%.

For audio recordings, the ultrasonic microphone (Avisoft UltraSoundGate condenser microphone capsule CM16, Avisoft Bioacoustics, Berlin, Germany) was mounted 20 cm above the cage and the USVs recorded using Avisoft RECORDER software version 3.2. Settings included sampling rate at 250 kHz; format 16 bit. The ultrasonic microphone was sensitive to frequencies between 10 and 180 kHz. For acoustical analysis, recordings were transferred to Avisoft SASLabPro (version 4.40) and a fast Fourier transformation (FFT) was conducted as previously described (59). Start times for the video and audio files were synchronized. Parameters analyzed included number and mean duration of calls, qualitative and quantitative analyses of sound frequencies measured in terms of frequency, and amplitude at the maximum of the spectrum. Waveform patterns of calls [a total of 17195 (Wt) and 8454 (Het) calls] were examined in depth in the sonograms collected from every mouse tested. Each call was identified as one of eight distinct categories, based on internal pitch changes, lengths, and shapes, as in our previously published studies (53, 59, 60).

Inter-rater reliability in scoring the call categories was 98%. Scoring was conducted by two investigators blind to the mouse genotype. Call category data were subjected to two different analyses: (1) Genotype-dependent effects on the probability of producing calls (proportion of calls in each category for each subject) from each of the eight categories of USV, as described below under statistical analysis; (2) a descriptive analysis that included genotype-dependent effects on the percentage of calls emitted by each subject in each of the eight categories of USV.

### LOCOMOTOR ACTIVITY IN THE HOME-CAGE

At 6 months of age, male mice ($N = 9$ Wt, $N = 10$ Het) were individually housed in standard cages (33 cm × 13 cm × 14 cm) and assigned to a continuous monitoring of spontaneous locomotor activity. The assessment of daily spontaneous activity in the home-cage was carried out by means of an automatic device using small passive infrared sensors positioned on the top of each cage (Activiscope system, see the website: www.newbehavior.com) (61–63). The system operated continuously for 13 days and after 2 days of acclimation the experimental procedure began. The sensors (20 Hz) detected any movement of mice. Data were recorded by an IBM computer with dedicated software. No movements were detected by the sensors when mice were sleeping, inactive, or performed moderate self-grooming. Scores were obtained during 30-min intervals and expressed as counts per minute (cpm). The 24-h profile of activity was obtained by averaging 7 days of continuous registration. The position of Wt and Het mouse cages in the rack was equally distributed in rows and columns. Animals were provided with tap water and food pellets *ad libitum*. After the first 7 days of spontaneous activity, all animals were subjected to an injection of saline (a mild stressful stimulus), at 11 h (dark phase), and locomotor activity monitored up to 3 days later. The analysis of the locomotor profile over a period of 7 h (11–18) after saline injection was performed to evaluate the immediate stress response.

### MONOAMINES AND THEIR METABOLITES: HPLC DETERMINATION

Subsequently to behavioral studies, male mice ($N = 9$ Wt, $N = 10$ Het) were sacrificed, their brains removed and rapidly dissected on ice to obtain the olfactory bulb, frontal cortex, striatum, Hip, and cerebellum for HPLC analysis. All samples were immediately flash frozen on dry ice, and then stored at −80°C until further processing. HPLC was performed according to Ref. (64). In particular, each brain region was weighed, ultrasonicated in 0.1 M perchloric acid, centrifuged for 20 min at 15,000 g (4°C) and the supernatant was used for monoamine neurotransmitters and their metabolites detection. The endogenous levels of 5-HT and 5-HT metabolite (5-hydroxyindolacetic acid; 5-HIAA), dopamine (DA) and final DA metabolite (homovanillic acid; HVA), and norepinephrine (NA) and NA metabolite (4-hydroxy-3-methoxyphenyl-glycol, MOPEG) were assayed by HPLC using a SphereClone 150 mm × 2 mm column (3-μm packing). Detection was accomplished with a Unijet cell (BAS) with a 6-mm-diameter glassy carbon electrode at +650 mV versus an Ag/AgCl reference electrode, connected to an electrochemical amperometric detector (INTRO, Antec Leyden, The Netherlands). For each analysis, a set of standards containing various concentrations of each compound (monoamines and their metabolites) was prepared in the perchloric acid solution, and calibration curves were calculated by a linear regression. The retention time of calibration standards was used to identify peaks, and areas under each peak were used to quantify monoamine levels. Results were normalized to the weight of wet tissue.

### MAGNETIC RESONANCE IMAGING AND SPECTROSCOPY

At 4 months of age, a separate cohort of male mice ($N = 7$ Wt, $N = 7$ Het), was subjected to *in vivo* MRI and magnetic resonance spectroscopy (MRS). During the MR analyses, animals were anesthetized with 2.5–2.0% isoflurane in oxygen 1 l/min (Isoflo, Abbott SpA, Latina, Italy). An integrated heating system allowed maintaining the animal body temperature at 37.0 ± 0.1°C. All MRI and MRS experiments were conducted on a 4.7 T Varian/Agilent Inova animal system (Agilent Inc., Palo Alto, CA, USA), equipped with actively shielded gradient system (max 200 mT/m, 12 cm bore size). A 6-cm diameter volume coil was used for transmission in combination with an electronically decoupled receive-only surface coil (Rapid Biomedical, Rimpar, Germany). Spin-echo sagittal anatomical images (TR/TE = 3000/60 ms, 13 consecutive slices of 0.8 mm thickness, FOV = 20 mm × 20 mm, matrix of 128 × 128, 2 averages) were acquired for accurate positioning the voxel for the MRS study. Single voxel localized $^1$H MR spectra (PRESS, TR/TE = 4000/23 ms, ns = 256 or 512) were collected from relevant brain areas: Hip (11.7 μl), striatum (STR, 10.4 μl), thalamus (Th, 12.96 μl), and cerebellum (Cb, 7.45 μl), as shown in **Figure 1A** and defined in the mouse brain atlas (65). Quantitative MRS protocol, including water T2 measurements, was applied (66) and T2 measurements were performed on water signal in order to identify any change in the mutant mice. Unsuppressed water signal was used for metabolite quantification (assuming 79.9% for gray matter water content). Spectra were analyzed using LCModel (67). Only those metabolites that were estimated to have Cramer–Rao lower bounds (CRLB) <20%, which corresponded to an estimated concentration error <0.2 μmol/g, were included into the quantitative analysis. In some cases, metabolites that have resonance overlapped or very close are also given as their sum. An example of spectra and its LCModel analysis is shown in **Figure 1B**.

Multislice fast spin-echo axial images (TR/TEeff = 3200/60 ms, ns = 4, slice thickness 0.6 mm, 24 slices, matrix 256 × 256, FOV = 25 mm × 25 mm, which correspond to voxel resolution of 98 × 98 × 600 $\mu m^3$) were also acquired for volumetric analyses.

Motor cortex thickness was measured at +1.32 from bregma as shown in **Figure 1C**. Volumetric analyses of the whole brain have been performed from olfactory bulb to cerebellum excluded. Ventricles and cerebellum volumes were also measured. Brains were manually segmented for forebrain, ventricles, and cerebellum using Varian/Agilent Imaging Browser, which perform a 3D-volume calculation by summing the pixels areas on the center of each slices and interpolating the cross sectional areas between the center of the other slices (Agilent Inc., Palo Alto, USA) on MR images. Manual segmentation of the ventricles was facilitated by

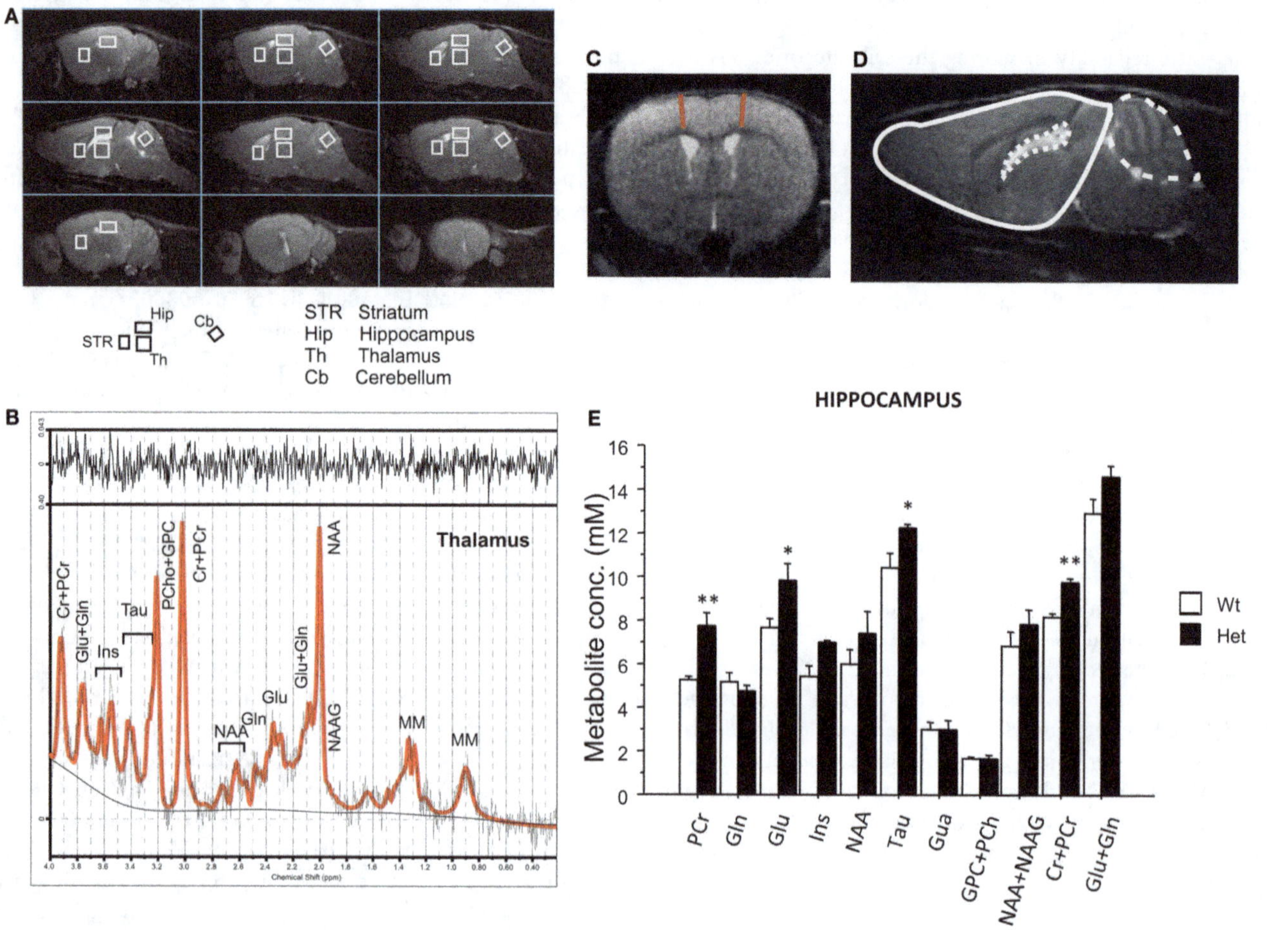


**FIGURE 1 | Magnetic resonance imaging and spectroscopy performed in 4-month-old reeler mutant mice.** **(A)** MRI panel – example of *in vivo* sagittal T2-weighted spin-echo images (TR/TE = 3000/70 ms, slice thickness 0.8 mm, NS = 2, FOV = 20 mm × 20 mm, matrix 128 × 128). Voxels localized on STR, Hip, Th, and Cb are indicated by the white rectangles. **(B)** MRS panel – examples of *in vivo* 1H spectra (as a black trace), acquired from the thalamus (PRESS, TR/TE = 4000/23 ms, NS = 256). The result of LCModel fit is shown as a red trace superimposed on the spectrum. Metabolite assignments: Ins, inositol; Cr, creatine; PCr, phospho-creatine; Glu, glutamate; Gln, glutamine; Tau, taurine; PCho, phospho-choline; GPC, glicero-phospho-choline; NAA, *N*-acetyl-aspartate; NAAG, *N*-acetyl-aspartyl-glutamate; MM, macromolecules. **(C)** Examples of axial fast T2-weighted MR images from reeler heterozygous (Het) mice, respectively (TR/TEeff = 3200/60 ms, ns = 4, slice thickness 0.6 mm, 24 slices, matrix 256 × 256, FOV = 25 mm × 25 mm, which correspond to voxel resolution of 98 × 98 × 600 μm³). The red lines show the motor cortex thickness measure. **(D)** Example of brain segmentation for volumetric analyses of brain (plain line), cerebellum (dashed line), and ventricles (dotted line). **(E)** The histogram shows metabolite concentrations in hippocampus (Hip) for the two groups. Data are expressed as mean + SEM, $*P < 0.05$, $**P < 0.005$ between wildtype and heterozygous reeler mice. $N = 7$ Wt and $N = 7$ Het.

the high contrast that cerebrospinal fluid has in the MR images. **Figure 1D** shows an example of segmentation (slice central to the brain in sagittal images).

## STATISTICAL ANALYSIS

A mixed-model ANOVA with repeated measures was used to analyze: (1) sniffing of different body areas (anogenital, body, or head), (2) spontaneous locomotor activity in the home-cage, (3) number of USVs for each minute of interaction, and (4) probability of vocalizations in eight call categories with genotype as between-subject factor. Probability of vocalizations within each genotype was calculated as number of calls in each category for each subject/total number of calls analyzed in each subject and standardized by angular transformation.

Data relative to MRI and MRS were analyzed by a one way ANOVA with genotype as the independent factor and MRI/MRS parameters (values of water T2, metabolite levels in each brain region and volume of each brain region) as dependent factor. Differences between genotypes in each brain region with respect to serotoninergic, dopaminergic, and noradrenergic systems (5-HT, 5-HIAA, and 5-HT turnover for serotoninergic system; DA, HVA, DOPAC, and DA turnover for dopaminergic system; and NA, MOPEG, and NA turnover for noradrenergic system) were determined by a multivariate analysis of variance (MANOVA), due to the potentially high correlation between these dependent variables within each system. Pillai's statistic was used. Univariate ANOVAs were conducted for each variable (Statview II, Abacus Concepts, CA, USA).

For all comparisons, data are expressed as mean ± SEM and significance was set at $P < 0.05$. *Post hoc* comparisons were performed using Tukey's test only when a significant $F$-value was determined.

## RESULTS

### MALE–FEMALE SOCIAL INTERACTION TEST

To assess the presence or absence of a social communication deficit in Het reeler mice, we evaluated the behaviors and the USVs emitted by a male mouse during the interaction with an estrus C57BL/6J female. Analysis of the social sniffing response on different body areas (head, body, and anogenital) did not reveal significant effects of genotype [frequency, $F(2,56) = 0.15$, $P = 0.858$, (data not shown); duration, $F(2,56) = 1.74$; $P = 0.183$, **Figure 2A**]. No genotype effect was detected on explorative behaviors such as *rearing* [frequency, $F(1,28) = 0.27$, $P = 0.610$ and duration, $F(1,28) = 0.30$, $P = 0.589$] and *digging* [frequency, $F(1,28) = 0.75$, $P = 0.392$ and duration, $F(1,28) = 1{,}15$, $P = 0.292$] (data not shown).

Analysis of the USVs emitted by male mice during the social interaction test did not detect significant differences between Het reeler and Wt mice: number of USVs [number of calls × genotype, $F(2,56) = 0.89$, $P = 0.41$, **Figure 2B**], mean duration [$F(2,54) = 0.79$, $P = 0.457$ (data not shown)], peak frequency [$F(2,54) = 0.43$, $P = 0.650$ (data not shown)], and peak amplitude [$F(2,54) = 0.14$, $P = 0.863$ (data not shown)]. As a whole, the pattern of sonographic structures did not differ between Het reeler and Wt mice indicating a comparable vocal repertoire in both genotypes (see pie graphs in **Figure 2C**).

### LOCOMOTOR ACTIVITY IN THE HOME-CAGE

Sleep problems and irregular sleep–wake cycles have been identified in several ASD children (68–71). Alterations in circadian rhythm lead to anxiety-like, impulsive, and depressive behaviors both in humans and mice (72–74). In the present study, we evaluated baseline circadian locomotor activity in the home-cage as well as response to a mild stressful stimulus represented by a saline injection to check for abnormalities in the spontaneous locomotor activity that could affect the behavioral performances.

Analysis of spontaneous locomotor activity measured in the home-cage for 7 days revealed, as expected, an increased activity in mice of both genotypes during the dark phase of the light/dark cycle [phase effect, $F(1,17) = 239.05$, $P < 0.001$] (see **Figure 3**). No genotype differences were found [light phase: genotype, $F(1,17) = 2.99$, $P = 0.102$; dark phase: genotype, $F(1,17) = 1.34$, $P = 0.263$].

The analysis of the locomotor profile over a period of 7 h after saline injection (11–18, dark phase) was performed to evaluate the immediate stress response. Het reeler mice increased significantly their locomotor activity as compared to Wt mice [genotype, $F(1,17) = 5.63$, $P = 0.029$] thus revealing a genotype-dependent increased sensitivity to mild stress challenge (see graph on the top right of **Figure 3**). After this 7-h-period, locomotor activity goes back to the normal activity profile [genotype effect, $F(1,17) = 0.226$, $P = 0{,}64$; genotype × hours, $F(1,23) = 0.38$, $P = 0.99$; data not shown].

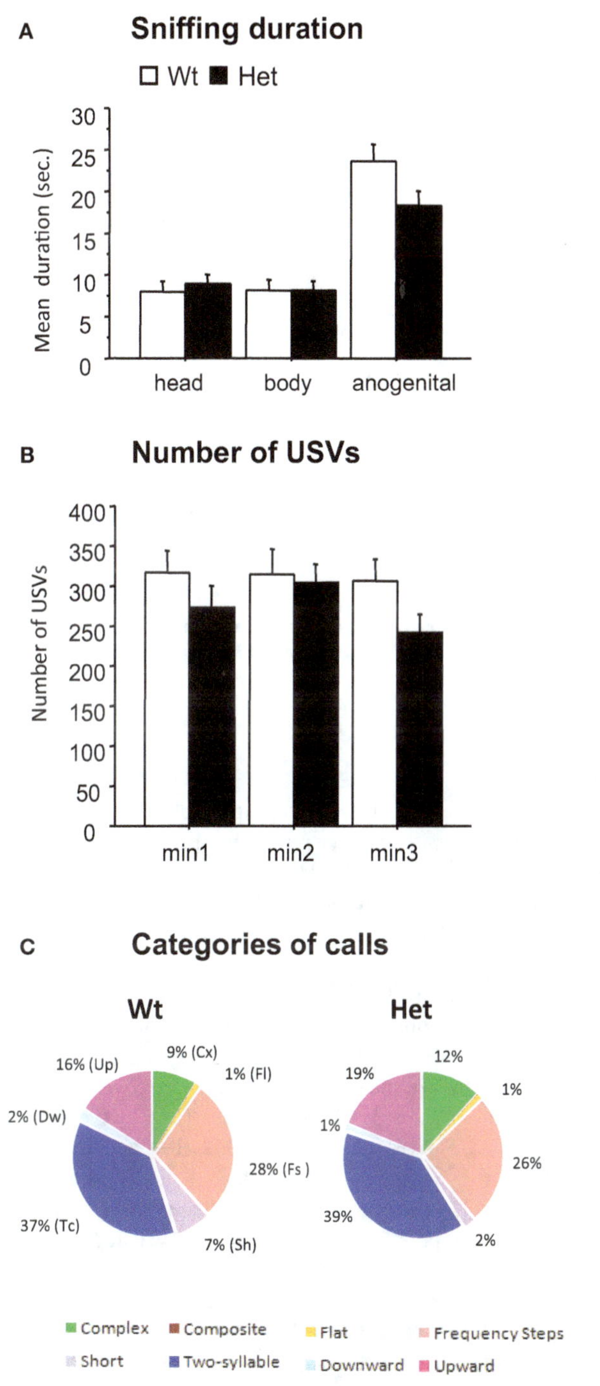


**FIGURE 2 | Male–female social interaction test (3-min-session) performed in 3-month-old reeler mutant mice.** Parameters measured during a direct interaction between a male with a sexually receptive C57BL/6J female. **(A)** Sniffing duration. **(B)** Number of ultrasonic vocalizations. Data are expressed as mean + SEM. **(C)** Pie graphs show the percentages of the different call categories emitted by Wt and Het reeler mice. Percentages were calculated in each genotype as number of calls in each category for each subject/total number of calls analyzed for each subject. Number of calls analyzed: 17195 in Wt and 8454 in Het. $N = 9$ Wt and $N = 21$ Het.

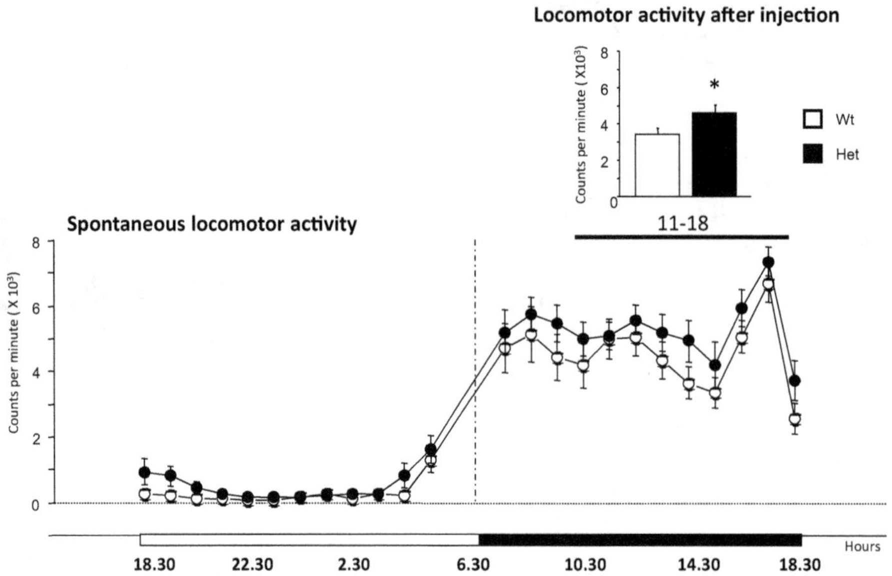


**FIGURE 3 | Locomotor activity expressed spontaneously in the home-cage by 6-month-old wildtype and heterozygous reeler male mice.** The main graph indicates spontaneous locomotor activity monitored for 1 week. The graph on the top right shows the spontaneous locomotor activity monitored for 7 h after a mild stressful stimuli represented by a saline injection at 11 h (dark phase). Data are expressed as mean ± SEM, $*P < 0.05$, between wildtype and heterozygous reeler mice. $N = 9$ Wt and $N = 10$ Het.

### MONOAMINES AND THEIR METABOLITES: HPLC DETERMINATION

High performance liquid chromatography determination has been applied to investigate whether *reelin* mutation influences the different monoamine systems. MANOVA revealed a significant genotype effect on several components of the dopaminergic system in hypothalamus [Pillai's Trace: $F(4,13) = 9.73$, $P < 0.001$] and in Hip [Pillai's Trace: $F(4,13) = 4.97$, $P = 0.005$]. ANOVA showed a strong reduction of DA levels [genotype effect, $F(1,16) = 5.29$, $P = 0.035$] and a consequent increase in the DA turnover [genotype effect, $F(1,16) = 7.43$, $P = 0.015$] in the cortex of Het reeler as compared to Wt mice (see **Table 1**). Moreover, Het reeler mice showed an increase of DOPAC and HVA levels [genotype effect: DOPAC, $F(1,16) = 18.88$, $P < 0.001$; HVA, $F(1,16) = 11.47$, $P = 0.003$] in hypothalamus. ANOVA evidenced also a decrease of HVA levels [$F(1,16) = 6.43$, $P = 0.022$] and an increase of DA turnover [genotype effect, $F(1,16) = 6.14$, $P = 0.025$] in Hip of Het mice.

Heterozygous mice showed an higher DA levels [genotype effect, $F(1,16) = 4.38$, $P = 0.052$] and a lower DA turnover in olfactory bulb [genotype effect, $F(1,16) = 6.87$, $P = 0.018$] than Wt mice. No genotype related differences were found on noradrenergic and serotoninergic systems in each brain areas analyzed.

### MAGNETIC RESONANCE IMAGING

To acquire deeper information into the functional state of brain areas involved in ASD, we assessed a $^1$H magnetic resonance in adult reeler male mice. Enlarged ventricles and reduced cerebellum are typical features of reeler mice (75). Volumetric analyses confirmed a cerebellum reduction [genotype effect, $F(1,10) = 15.50$, $P = 0.002$] and an enlargement of ventricles volume [genotype effect, $F(1,11) = 8.01$, $P = 0.016$] in Het reeler when compared to Wt mice. No genotype differences were detected in volume [genotype effect, $F(1,11) = 0.86$, $P = 0.374$] and medial motor cortex (MC) thickness [genotype effect, $F(1,11) = 3.62$, $P = 0.083$] (see **Table 2**).

### MAGNETIC RESONANCE SPECTROSCOPY

To investigate the possible alterations in brain metabolism of adult reeler male mice, we performed MRS. The high quality spectra allowed reliable quantification (%SD <20%) not only for the commonly observed *N*-acetyl-aspartate (NAA), total creatine (Cr + PCr) and total choline resonances (NAA + NAAG), but also for glutamine (Gln), glutamate (Glu), taurine (Tau), and inositol (Ins) in all the investigated brain regions.

Water T2 analyses confirmed that no changes between the genotypes occurred in the T2s in Hip [$F(1,10) = 2.52$, $P = 0.143$], Striatum [$F(1,10) = 0.02$, $P = 0.883$], Thalamus [$F(1,10) = 1.15E-5$, $P = 0.977$], and Cerebellum [$F(1,10) = 0.32$, $P = 0.584$] (data not shown).

Metabolic changes were detected in Hip while no differences have been found for any metabolite in thalamus, striatum, and cerebellum. Het reeler mice showed increased levels of Glu [genotype effect, $F(1,11) = 4.61$, $P = 0.044$], Tau [genotype effect, $F(1,11) = 4.82$, $P = 0.050$], PCr [genotype effect, $F(1,7) = 18.08$, $P = 0.003$], and total amount of PCr + Cr [genotype effect, $F(1,11) = 24.68$, $P < 0.001$] in Hip as compared to Wt mice (see **Figure 1E**).

## DISCUSSION

Reelin is a glycoprotein playing a crucial role during development: it regulates neuronal migration and brain lamination (6, 8, 29, 30, 76, 77) and its reduced or complete lack of signaling impairs

**Table 1 | Levels of monoamines and their metabolites detected *ex vivo* in cortex, bulbs, hypothalamus, striatum, hippocampus, and cerebellum (mean ± SEM: picogram per milligram of wet tissue)**.

| Brain region | Genotype | Neurotransmitter, metabolite concentration picogram per milligram wet brain weight) | | | | | | |
|---|---|---|---|---|---|---|---|---|
| | | Noradrenergic system | | Dopaminergic system | | | Serotoninergic system | |
| | | NA | MOPEG | DA | DOPAC | HVA | 5-HT | 5-HIAA |
| Cortex | Wt | 469.60 ± 22.99 | 102.74 ± 7.53 | 874.14 ± 268.95 | 134.50 ± 19.85 | 252.97 ± 35.58 | 523.10 ± 29.72 | 341.42 ± 17.59 |
| | Het | 440.84 ± 28.76 | 102.47 ± 6.20 | 296.37 ± 69.32* | 108.65 ± 18.65 | 184.52 ± 40.76 | 470.09 ± 31.15 | 285.37 ± 14.32 |
| Bulbs | Wt | 291.82 ± 24.28 | 46.35 ± 5.94 | 312.11 ± 33.66 | 100.26 ± 8.63 | 152.87 ± 15.49 | 247.65 ± 25.63 | 191.88 ± 16.88 |
| | Het | 346.10 ± 14.98 | 66.26 ± 6.28 | 396.15 ± 23.84* | 102.06 ± 6.83 | 154.78 ± 8.95 | 131.53 ± 20.97 | 192.13 ± 9.76 |
| Hypothalamus | Wt | 1789.74 ± 80.36 | 205.08 ± 23.06 | 394.87 ± 16.83 | 116.63 ± 6.12 | 362.10 ± 13.19 | 518.33 ± 22.43 | 934.82 ± 42.78 |
| | Het | 1742.52 ± 81.41 | 183.74 ± 7.50 | 540.86 ± 163.65 | 144.44 ± 5.48** | 444.55 ± 13.27** | 487.36 ± 29.79 | 864.22 ± 19.73 |
| Striatum | Wt | 129.71 ± 32.78 | 339.05 ± 49.89 | 12521.13 ± 1661.54 | 2718.95 ± 326.72 | 4310.08 ± 383.59 | 453.07 ± 30.88 | 654.30 ± 23.09 |
| | Het | 128.12 ± 19.16 | 261.70 ± 25.90 | 12275.97 ± 1376.40 | 2847.63 ± 196.75 | 4583.34 ± 398.19 | 109.34 ± 26.48 | 679.84 ± 24.65 |
| Hippocampus | Wt | 508.02 ± 33.64 | 115.37 ± 6.77 | 82.16 ± 7.61 | 18.21 ± 1.33 | 69.47 ± 8.48 | 505.52 ± 61.78 | 540.99 ± 37.90 |
| | Het | 423.67 ± 39.12 | 108.17 ± 8.75 | 84.80 ± 13.48 | 25.16 ± 4.81 | 42.01 ± 6.93* | 580.54 ± 33.18 | 503.31 ± 53.05 |
| Cerebellum | Wt | 402.46 ± 28.48 | 48.85 ± 3.12 | 5.09 ± 1.06 | 12.52 ± 2.38 | 80.66 ± 5.09 | 115.60 ± 17.51 | 129.05 ± 6.03 |
| | Het | 433.56 ± 17.08 | 46.17 ± 3.42 | 6.75 ± 2.68 | 18.77 ± 7.55 | 79.52 ± 3.59 | 118.94 ± 21.13 | 126.85 ± 6.04 |

| Brain region | Genotype | Neurotransmitter turnover | | |
|---|---|---|---|---|
| | | NA | DA | 5-HT |
| Cortex | Wt | 0.22 ± 0.01 | 0.24 ± 0.05 | 0.66 ± 0.03 |
| | Het | 0.24 ± 0.01 | 0.45 ± 0.05* | 0.62 ± 0.03 |
| Bulbs | Wt | 0.16 ± 0.02 | 0.33 ± 0.02 | 0.80 ± 0.05 |
| | Het | 0.19 ± 0.01 | 0.26 ± 0.02* | 0.86 ± 0.05 |
| Hypothalamus | Wt | 0.11 ± 0.01 | 0.30 ± 0.02 | 1.81 ± 0.09 |
| | Het | 0.11 ± 0.01 | 0.35 ± 0.04 | 1.83 ± 0.11 |
| Striatum | Wt | 4.09 ± 1.01 | 0.23 ± 0.03 | 1.47 ± 0.06 |
| | Het | 2.86 ± 0.7E | 0.26 ± 0.03 | 1.71 ± 0.10 |
| Hippocampus | Wt | 0.23 ± 0.01 | 0.23 ± 0.02 | 0.95 ± 0.11 |
| | Het | 0.26 ± 0.02 | 0.29 ± 0.02* | 0.87 ± 0.07 |
| Cerebellum | Wt | 0.12 ± 0.01 | 2.83 ± 0.51 | 1.25 ± 0.13 |
| | Het | 0.11 ± 0.01 | 6.76 ± 2.45 | 1.36 ± 0.23 |

**P* < 0.05, ***P* < 0.005 between wildtype and heterozygous reeler mice.*

**Table 2 | Analysis for forebrain, cerebellum, and ventricles volume.**

| | Forebrain volume (μ1) | Ventricles volume (μ1) | Cerebellum volume (μ1) | Medial cortex thickness (mm) |
|---|---|---|---|---|
| Wt | 366.17 ± 2.6 | 3.29 ± 0.5 | 59.18 ± 1.2 | 1.16 ± 0.1 |
| Het | 369.85 ± 3.0 | 5.25 ± 0.4* | 53.03 ± 1.1* | 1.22 ± 0.1 |

*Data are expressed as mean ± SEM. *P < 0.05, between wildtype and heterozygous reeler mice.*

neuronal connectivity and synaptic plasticity (43, 78). Moreover, recent data suggest that a defect in reelin signaling pathway confers greater susceptibility to autism (20–25, 27).

For these reasons, we consider Het reeler mice, haploinsufficient for *reelin* and sharing some neurochemical and behavioral features with autistic patients, a suitable animal model for studying the effects of *reelin* deficiency in determining social communication deficits and in changing brain monoamine and brain metabolites levels. Unfortunately, no comparison can be drawn with homozygous mutant mice, since adult knockout reeler mice did not survive longer than weaning (79–82).

## NO DEFICITS IN SOCIAL AND VOCAL REPERTOIRES DURING COURTSHIP

To our knowledge, this is the first time that a detailed analysis of the adult male vocal repertoire has been performed in this mutant line. Only behavioral data on same-sex interactions or approaching/recognizing a conspecific have been collected (44, 51, 52).

Recently, we characterized vocal and motor repertoires on homozygous and Het reeler pups (60) evidencing a general delay in vocal and motor development during the first 2 weeks of postnatal life, in line with the alterations in the same two systems observed in children with ASD. In addition, a preferential use of a specific call category (two-components) at pnd 2 and 6 was detected in both mutants (Het and homozygous), whereas an increased number of vocalizations characterized only Het pup's emission.

Contrary to what we found in pups, adult Het male mice did not show deficits on USVs emitted during courtship of a female in estrous. Social behaviors, generally associated to this vocal emission, were not affected either. These results are in contrast with the reduction in anogenital sniffing and/or the number of USVs found in other ASD animal models such as BTBR, En2, NMDA-Nr1, NLG3, NLg4, Dlg4, and FmR1 mice (53, 83–87), but in line with data collected on Shank3 mice, carrying a mutation strongly implicated in autism and Phelan-McDermid 22q13 deletion syndrome, where male knockout mice did not present alterations in social communication and interaction (88).

These data thus confirm that adult Het reeler mice present deficits on cognitive performances but not on social domains (44–47, 49–52). It is worth of notice that intellectual disabilities are present in about 50% of autistic individuals. Due to the cerebellar alteration leading to death shortly after weaning, no data could be collected on mice with the complete deletion in the reelin gene, thus we cannot exclude an impairment of the social domain only related to the complete deletion of *reelin*.

## OVER RESPONSE TO A MILD STRESS STIMULI

Previous studies indicated that Het reeler mice have several abnormalities in their brain architecture (40–42), but, at a first sight, their phenotype is absolutely "normal" (7, 44, 89). Some behavioral deficits become evident only after a "second hit" (7, 63, 90, 91) supporting the "double-hit" theory postulating a gene–environment interaction in the pathogenesis of several neurodevelopmental disorders such ASD (89). Depending on the features of environmental factors and the time-window of insult interacting with reelin expression, an individual could thus develop one neurodevelopmental disorder rather than another one (i.e., schizophrenia versus ASD).

Our previous evidence shows that either an environmental pollutant or, for example, an activated stress reactivity caused by repeated separation from the dams, elicits different responses as a function of the mouse genotype (91). In line with these data, in the present study, no significant genotype differences were found in basal activity levels of mice monitored in their home-cages for 1 week. By contrast, after a saline injection (a mild stressful stimulus), the Het male displayed a higher locomotor activity profile as compared to Wt male mice. Already in a previous study, our group showed a hyperactive profile in Het adolescent reeler mice following handling plus saline injections (63). Altogether, these data indicate that Het reeler mice show a different response to environmental stimuli, confirming the suitability of such mutant line for the study of gene–environment interactions (7, 92).

Moreover, a deficit in behavioral inhibition has been reported as a core alteration of Het reeler mice, associated with dysfunctions of mesolimbic DA transmission (93) and reduced GABAergic transmission in central nervous system (40, 94–96).

## IMPAIRMENT IN THE DOPAMINERGIC PATHWAY

To correlate observed behavioral abnormalities to the neural systems reportedly affected by *reelin* mutation, we conducted HPLC analyses in different brain areas involved in autism, detecting impairments in the dopaminergic system. Specifically, Het reeler mice had decreased DA levels in cortex and increased levels in the olfactory bulb, whereas DA turnover was altered in cortex, bulb, and Hip.

A disruption of DA maturation in *reelin* haploinsufficient mice had been already suggested: a reduced locomotor activation by D-amphetamine in reeler mice was associated with an exaggerated drug-induced stereotyped behavioral syndrome (90). Moreover, Ballmaier et al. (93) reported alterations in the mesolimbic DA pathway of Het reeler mice. In particular, they found that Het mice exhibit a reduction in DA transporter immunoreactivity and D2 receptor mRNA in the limbic striatum and the ventral tegmental area (93). In agreement with our study, they did not find any significant alteration in the dopaminergic markers examined in the nigrostriatal pathway of Het reeler mice.

Alterations in DA levels and its turnover have been found in brain areas primarily associated to reward. Individuals with ASD show reduced responsiveness to reward stimuli, a feature that appears to be especially prominent with social reinforces such as facial expressions, spoken language, and gestures (97, 98). No effects have been found in the striatum where DA contributes to motor performances.

In addition, the neurotransmitter DA plays a pivotal modulatory role on executive functions and learning (99, 100), thus a dysfunctional DA system could underlying the cognitive deficits detected in Het mice.

## GLUTAMATE AND TAURINE INCREASED LEVELS IN HIPPOCAMPUS

To gain deeper insights into the functional state of brain areas involved in ASD, we carried out a $^{1}$H MRI guided spectroscopy examination in adult reeler mice. MRS is a powerful, non-invasive tool for monitoring neurological diseases (101) and it is also used in clinical studies on autistic individuals (102). Abnormalities in neurotransmitter pathways have been associated to ASD, with evidence for a possible implication of glutamatergic, GABAergic, and serotonergic imbalances (102).

In the Hip, as compared to Wt in Het mice, MRS showed increased levels of glutamate, taurine, phospho-creatine, and of the total amount of phospho-creatine plus creatine. Glutamate is the main brain excitatory neurotransmitter involved in cognitive functions, although in excessive quantities can cause neuronal damages typical of neurodegenerative diseases (for example, Alzheimer's and Huntington's diseases) (103–105). The higher levels of glutamate in the Hip of Het reeler mice are in agreement with previous findings reporting an increase of glutamate in Hip (106) and cortex (107) of ASD patients; altogether these evidences support the hypothesis of an imbalance between excitatory and inhibitory (GABA) systems as one of the possible causes of autism (107).

Recently, clinical trials with glutamate antagonists have been initiated, since they have been proved to be effective in rescuing social deficits and repetitive behaviors in selected animal models of autism (108). Also the presence of high levels of taurine in the Hip could be correlated to high levels of glutamate. In fact, taurine appears to have a protective action against glutamate excitotoxicity (109) and it is widely considered a general index of neuronal functionality.

The largest meta analysis performed on ASD patients showed evidence that ASD is characterized by age-dependent fluctuations in metabolite levels across the whole brain. In particular, significant reduction in the level of a cerebral metabolites, NAA, a specific neuronal marker, in whole gray matter of ASD children as well as significant increase in the total pool of creatine (phospho-creatine plus creatine) in adult subjects were observed (110). The observed differences in creatine as a function of age and brain region, suggest caution in the use of Cr-based ratio measures of metabolites. For this reason, we adopt a quantitative approach for brain metabolites level determination, which has been validated on phantom (111) as well as on other animal models of psychiatric and neurodevelopmental diseases (51, 112–114).

## CONCLUSION

In the literature, Het reeler mice are widely considered a reliable animal model of either autism or schizophrenia. Genetic and molecular evidences showed that reelin messenger-RNA and its protein are downregulated in cortical, hippocampal, and cerebellar neurons of patients suffering of schizophrenia and autism (3, 8, 10, 20, 115, 116). In particular, these mutant mice are characterized by decreased contextual fear conditioning (48), prepulse inhibition (43, 117), impaired executive functions (45), and associative learning (48), all typical traits of schizophrenia. In addition, Het reeler mice yielded autistic-like deficits in social behavior and communication in the first two postnatal weeks of age (60) and perseverative (51) and hyperactive behaviors (44) at adulthood. Discordant evidences exist on this model, possibly associated with differences in the genetic background, age of mice, training and testing protocols, and rearing conditions (52, 89).

Overall, our results, together with data previously collected by our (Laviola and collaborators) and other groups suggest that Het reeler mice have common behavioral traits to both these neurodevelopmental disorders. Moreover, these studies indicate the suitability of this mutant line to investigate the role of *reelin* as vulnerability factor on the etiology of both disorders. In addition, Het reeler mutant mice may represent a useful animal model to develop novel treatment strategies for these devastating human disorders. For example, our HPLC and MRS results favor further studies to evaluate the effects of DA agonist or glutamate antagonist treatments on behavioral and neurochemical responses.

## ACKNOWLEDGMENTS

Supported by the Italian Ministry of Health Grant (GR3), Young Researcher 2008, "Non-invasive tools for early detection of Autism Spectrum Disorders." We thank Flavia Chiarotti for the statistical advice.

## REFERENCES

1. American Psychiatric Association, Washington D. *Diagnostic and Statistical Manual of Mental Disorders DSM-5*. Washington, DC: American Psychiatric Publishing (2013).
2. Impagnatiello F, Guidotti AR, Pesold C, Dwivedi Y, Caruncho H, Pisu MG, et al. A decrease of reelin expression as a putative vulnerability factor in schizophrenia. *Proc Natl Acad Sci U S A* (1998) **95**:15718–23. doi:10.1073/pnas.95.26.15718
3. Guidotti A, Auta J, Davis JM, Di-Giorgi-Gerevini V, Dwivedi Y, Grayson DR, et al. Decrease in reelin and glutamic acid decarboxylase67 (GAD67) expression in schizophrenia and bipolar disorder: a postmortem brain study. *Arch Gen Psychiatry* (2000) **57**:1061–9. doi:10.1001/archpsyc.57.11.1061
4. Hong SE, Shugart YY, Huang DT, Shahwan SA, Grant PE, Hourihane JO, et al. Autosomal recessive lissencephaly with cerebellar hypoplasia is associated with human RELN mutations. *Nat Genet* (2000) **26**:93–6. doi:10.1038/79246
5. Fatemi SH. Reelin mutations in mouse and man: from reeler mouse to schizophrenia, mood disorders, autism and lissencephaly. *Mol Psychiatry* (2001) **6**:129–33. doi:10.1038/sj.mp.4000129
6. Keller F, Persico AM. The neurobiological context of autism. *Mol Neurobiol* (2003) **28**:1–22. doi:10.1385/MN:28:1:1
7. Laviola G, Ognibene E, Romano E, Adriani W, Keller F. Gene-environment interaction during early development in the heterozygous reeler mouse: clues for modelling of major neurobehavioral syndromes. *Neurosci Biobehav Rev* (2009) **33**:560–72. doi:10.1016/j.neubiorev.2008.09.006
8. Folsom TD, Fatemi SH. The involvement of Reelin in neurodevelopmental disorders. *Neuropharmacology* (2013) **68**:122–35. doi:10.1016/j.neuropharm.2012.08.015
9. Keller F, Persico AM, Zelante L, Gasperial P, D'agruma N, Maiorano N, et al. Reelin gene alleles and haplotypes are associated with autistic disorder. *Society for Neuroscience*. New Orleans (2000) **26**:77 (31.11).
10. Fatemi SH, Stary JM, Halt AR, Realmuto GR. Dysregulation of Reelin and Bcl-2 proteins in autistic cerebellum. *J Autism Dev Disord* (2001) **31**:529–35. doi:10.1023/A:1013234708757
11. Fatemi SH, Stary JM, Egan EA. Reduced blood levels of reelin as a vulnerability factor in pathophysiology of autistic disorder. *Cell Mol Neurobiol* (2002) **22**:139–52. doi:10.1023/A:1019857620251
12. Fatemi SH, Snow AV, Stary JM, Araghi-Niknam M, Reutiman TJ, Lee S, et al. Reelin signaling is impaired in autism. *Biol Psychiatry* (2005) **57**:777–87. doi:10.1016/j.biopsych.2004.12.018

13. Krebs MO, Betancur C, Leroy S, Bourdel MC, Gillberg C, Leboyer M. Absence of association between a polymorphic GGC repeat in the 5' untranslated region of the reelin gene and autism. *Mol Psychiatry* (2002) **7**:801–4. doi:10.1038/sj.mp.4001071
14. Zhang H, Liu X, Zhang C, Mundo E, Macciardi F, Grayson DR, et al. Reelin gene alleles and susceptibility to autism spectrum disorders. *Mol Psychiatry* (2002) **7**:1012–7. doi:10.1038/sj.mp.4001124
15. Bonora E, Beyer KS, Lamb JA, Parr JR, Klauck SM, Benner A, et al. Analysis of reelin as a candidate gene for autism. *Mol Psychiatry* (2003) **8**:885–92. doi:10.1038/sj.mp.4001310
16. Serajee FJ, Zhong H, Mahbubul Huq AH. Association of Reelin gene polymorphisms with autism. *Genomics* (2006) **87**:75–83. doi:10.1016/j.ygeno.2005.09.008
17. Dutta S, Guhathakurta S, Sinha S, Chatterjee A, Ahmed S, Ghosh S, et al. Reelin gene polymorphisms in the Indian population: a possible paternal 5'UTR-CGG-repeat-allele effect on autism. *Am J Med Genet B Neuropsychiatr Genet* (2007) **144B**:106–12. doi:10.1002/ajmg.b.30419
18. Dutta S, Sinha S, Ghosh S, Chatterjee A, Ahmed S, Usha R. Genetic analysis of reelin gene (RELN) SNPs: no association with autism spectrum disorder in the Indian population. *Neurosci Lett* (2008) **441**:56–60. doi:10.1016/j.neulet.2008.06.022
19. He Y, Xun G, Xia K, Hu Z, Lv L, Deng Z, et al. No significant association between RELN polymorphism and autism in case-control and family-based association study in Chinese Han population. *Psychiatry Res* (2011) **187**:462–4. doi:10.1016/j.psychres.2010.04.051
20. Persico AM, D'agruma L, Maiorano N, Totaro A, Militerni R, Bravaccio C, et al. Reelin gene alleles and haplotypes as a factor predisposing to autistic disorder. *Mol Psychiatry* (2001) **6**:150–9. doi:10.1038/sj.mp.4000850
21. Skaar DA, Shao Y, Haines JL, Stenger JE, Jaworski J, Martin ER, et al. Analysis of the RELN gene as a genetic risk factor for autism. *Mol Psychiatry* (2005) **10**:563–71. doi:10.1038/sj.mp.4001614
22. Ashley-Koch AE, Jaworski J, Ma De Q, Mei H, Ritchie MD, Skaar DA, et al. Investigation of potential gene-gene interactions between APOE and RELN contributing to autism risk. *Psychiatr Genet* (2007) **17**:221–6. doi:10.1097/YPG.0b013e32809c2f75
23. Li H, Li Y, Shao J, Li R, Qin Y, Xie C, et al. The association analysis of RELN and GRM8 genes with autistic spectrum disorder in Chinese Han population. *Am J Med Genet B Neuropsychiatr Genet* (2008) **147B**:194–200. doi:10.1002/ajmg.b.30584
24. Holt R, Barnby G, Maestrini E, Bacchelli E, Brocklebank D, Sousa I, et al. Linkage and candidate gene studies of autism spectrum disorders in European populations. *Eur J Hum Genet* (2010) **18**:1013–9. doi:10.1038/ejhg.2010.69
25. Fu X, Mei Z, Sun L. Association between the g.296596G > A genetic variant of RELN gene and susceptibility to autism in a Chinese Han population. *Genet Mol Biol* (2013) **36**:486–9. doi:10.1590/S1415-47572013005000037
26. Sharma JR, Arieff Z, Gameeldien H, Davids M, Kaur M, Van Der Merwe L. Association analysis of two single-nucleotide polymorphisms of the RELN gene with autism in the South African population. *Genet Test Mol Biomarkers* (2013) **17**:93–8. doi:10.1089/gtmb.2012.0212
27. Wang Z, Hong Y, Zou L, Zhong R, Zhu B, Shen N, et al. Reelin gene variants and risk of autism spectrum disorders: an integrated meta-analysis. *Am J Med Genet B Neuropsychiatr Genet* (2014) **165B**:192–200. doi:10.1002/ajmg.b.32222
28. Hamburgh M. Analysis of the postnatal developmental effects of "reeler," a neurological mutation in mice. A study in developmental genetics. *Dev Biol* (1963) **8**:165–85. doi:10.1016/0012-1606(63)90040-X
29. Tissir F, Goffinet AM. Reelin and brain development. *Nat Rev Neurosci* (2003) **4**:496–505. doi:10.1038/nrn1113
30. Boyle MP, Bernard A, Thompson CL, Ng L, Boe A, Mortrud M, et al. Cell-type-specific consequences of Reelin deficiency in the mouse neocortex, hippocampus, and amygdala. *J Comp Neurol* (2011) **519**:2061–89. doi:10.1002/cne.22655
31. Mariani J, Crepel F, Mikoshiba K, Changeux JP, Sotelo C. Anatomical, physiological and biochemical studies of the cerebellum from Reeler mutant mouse. *Philos Trans R Soc Lond B Biol Sci* (1977) **281**:1–28. doi:10.1098/rstb.1977.0121
32. Bailey AJ. The biology of autism. *Psychol Med* (1993) **23**:7–11. doi:10.1017/S0033291700038794
33. Casanova MF, Buxhoeveden DP, Switala AE, Roy E. Minicolumnar pathology in autism. *Neurology* (2002) **58**:428–32. doi:10.1212/WNL.58.3.428
34. Courchesne E, Carper R, Akshoomoff N. Evidence of brain overgrowth in the first year of life in autism. *JAMA* (2003) **290**:337–44. doi:10.1001/jama.290.3.337
35. Palmen SJ, Van Engeland H, Hof PR, Schmitz C. Neuropathological findings in autism. *Brain* (2004) **127**:2572–83. doi:10.1093/brain/awh287
36. Bauman ML, Kemper TL. Neuroanatomic observations of the brain in autism: a review and future directions. *Int J Dev Neurosci* (2005) **23**:183–7. doi:10.1016/j.ijdevneu.2004.09.006
37. Wegiel J, Kuchna I, Nowicki K, Imaki H, Wegiel J, Marchi E, et al. The neuropathology of autism: defects of neurogenesis and neuronal migration, and dysplastic changes. *Acta Neuropathol* (2010) **119**:755–70. doi:10.1007/s00401-010-0655-4
38. Schumann CM, Nordahl CW. Bridging the gap between MRI and postmortem research in autism. *Brain Res* (2011) **1380**:175–86. doi:10.1016/j.brainres.2010.09.061
39. Fatemi SH, Aldinger KA, Ashwood P, Bauman ML, Blaha CD, Blatt GJ, et al. Consensus paper: pathological role of the cerebellum in autism. *Cerebellum* (2012) **11**:777–807. doi:10.1007/s12311-012-0355-9
40. Biamonte F, Assenza G, Marino R, D'amelio M, Panteri R, Caruso D, et al. Interactions between neuroactive steroids and reelin haploinsufficiency in Purkinje cell survival. *Neurobiol Dis* (2009) **36**:103–15. doi:10.1016/j.nbd.2009.07.001
41. Maloku E, Covelo IR, Hanbauer I, Guidotti A, Kadriu B, Hu Q, et al. Lower number of cerebellar Purkinje neurons in psychosis is associated with reduced reelin expression. *Proc Natl Acad Sci U S A* (2010) **107**:4407–11. doi:10.1073/pnas.0914483107
42. Pappas GD, Kriho V, Pesold C. Reelin in the extracellular matrix and dendritic spines of the cortex and hippocampus: a comparison between wild type and heterozygous reeler mice by immunoelectron microscopy. *J Neurocytol* (2001) **30**:413–25. doi:10.1023/A:1015017710332
43. Tueting P, Costa E, Dwivedi Y, Guidotti A, Impagnatiello F, Manev R, et al. The phenotypic characteristics of heterozygous reeler mouse. *Neuroreport* (1999) **10**:1329–34. doi:10.1097/00001756-199904260-00032
44. Ognibene E, Adriani W, Granstrem O, Pieretti S, Laviola G. Impulsivity-anxiety-related behavior and profiles of morphine-induced analgesia in heterozygous reeler mice. *Brain Res* (2007) **1131**:173–80. doi:10.1016/j.brainres.2006.11.007
45. Krueger DD, Howell JL, Hebert BF, Olausson P, Taylor JR, Nairn AC. Assessment of cognitive function in the heterozygous reeler mouse. *Psychopharmacology (Berl)* (2006) **189**:95–104. doi:10.1007/s00213-006-0530-0
46. Brigman JL, Padukiewicz KE, Sutherland ML, Rothblat LA. Executive functions in the heterozygous reeler mouse model of schizophrenia. *Behav Neurosci* (2006) **120**:984–8. doi:10.1037/0735-7044.120.4.984
47. Marrone MC, Marinelli S, Biamonte F, Keller F, Sgobio CA, Ammassari-Teule M, et al. Altered cortico-striatal synaptic plasticity and related behavioural impairments in reeler mice. *Eur J Neurosci* (2006) **24**:2061–70. doi:10.1111/j.1460-9568.2006.05083.x
48. Qiu S, Korwek KM, Pratt-Davis AR, Peters M, Bergman MY, Weeber EJ. Cognitive disruption and altered hippocampus synaptic function in Reelin haploinsufficient mice. *Neurobiol Learn Mem* (2006) **85**:228–42. doi:10.1016/j.nlm.2005.11.001
49. Larson J, Hoffman JS, Guidotti A, Costa E. Olfactory discrimination learning deficit in heterozygous reeler mice. *Brain Res* (2003) **971**:40–6. doi:10.1016/S0006-8993(03)02353-9
50. Ammassari-Teule M, Sgobio C, Biamonte F, Marrone C, Mercuri NB, Keller F. Reelin haploinsufficiency reduces the density of PV+ neurons in circumscribed regions of the striatum and selectively alters striatal-based behaviors. *Psychopharmacology (Berl)* (2009) **204**:511–21. doi:10.1007/s00213-009-1483-x
51. Macri S, Biamonte F, Romano E, Marino R, Keller F, Laviola G. Perseverative responding and neuroanatomical alterations in adult heterozygous reeler mice are mitigated by neonatal estrogen administration. *Psychoneuroendocrinology* (2010) **35**:1374–87. doi:10.1016/j.psyneuen.2010.03.012
52. Podhorna J, Didriksen M. The heterozygous reeler mouse: behavioural phenotype. *Behav Brain Res* (2004) **153**:43–54. doi:10.1016/j.bbr.2003.10.033
53. Scattoni ML, Ricceri L, Crawley JN. Unusual repertoire of vocalizations in adult BTBR T+tf/J mice during three types of social encounters. *Genes Brain Behav* (2011) **10**:44–56. doi:10.1111/j.1601-183X.2010.00623.x

54. Liu X, Hubbard JA, Fabes RA, Adam JB. Sleep disturbances and correlates of children with autism spectrum disorders. *Child Psychiatry Hum Dev* (2006) **37**:179–91. doi:10.1007/s10578-006-0028-3
55. Malow BA, Marzec ML, Mcgrew SG, Wang L, Henderson LM, Stone WL. Characterizing sleep in children with autism spectrum disorders: a multidimensional approach. *Sleep* (2006) **29**:1563–71.
56. Goldman SE, Surdyka K, Cuevas R, Adkins K, Wang L, Malow BA. Defining the sleep phenotype in children with autism. *Dev Neuropsychol* (2009) **34**:560–73. doi:10.1080/87565640903133509
57. May T, Cornish K, Conduit R, Rajaratnam SM, Rinehart NJ. Sleep in high-functioning children with autism: longitudinal developmental change and associations with behavior problems. *Behav Sleep Med* (2013). doi:10.1080/15402002.2013.829064
58. Rugh R. *The Mouse: Its Reproduction and Development*. New York: Oxford University Press (1990).
59. Scattoni ML, Gandhy SU, Ricceri L, Crawley JN. Unusual repertoire of vocalizations in the BTBR T+tf/J mouse model of autism. *PLoS One* (2008) **3**:e3067. doi:10.1371/journal.pone.0003067
60. Romano E, Michetti C, Caruso A, Laviola G, Scattoni ML. Characterization of neonatal vocal and motor repertoire of reelin mutant mice. *PLoS One* (2013) **8**:e64407. doi:10.1371/journal.pone.0064407
61. Dell'Omo G, Vannoni E, Vyssotski AL, Di Bari MA, Nonno R, Agrimi U, et al. Early behavioural changes in mice infected with BSE and scrapie: automated home cage monitoring reveals prion strain differences. *Eur J Neurosci* (2002) **16**:735–42. doi:10.1046/j.1460-9568.2002.02128.x
62. Adriani W, Caprioli A, Granstrem O, Carli M, Laviola G. The spontaneously hypertensive-rat as an animal model of ADHD: evidence for impulsive and non-impulsive subpopulations. *Neurosci Biobehav Rev* (2003) **27**:639–51. doi:10.1016/j.neubiorev.2003.08.007
63. Romano E, Fuso A, Laviola G. Nicotine restores Wt-like levels of reelin and GAD67 gene expression in brain of heterozygous reeler mice. *Neurotox Res* (2013) **24**:205–15. doi:10.1007/s12640-013-9378-3
64. Cassano T, Gaetani S, Morgese MG, Macheda T, Laconca L, Dipasquale P, et al. Monoaminergic changes in locus coeruleus and dorsal raphe nucleus following noradrenaline depletion. *Neurochem Res* (2009) **34**:1417–26. doi:10.1007/s11064-009-9928-5
65. Paxinos G, Franklin K. *The Mouse Brain in Stereotaxic Coordinates*. San Diego: Elsevier Academic Press (2001).
66. Canese R, Pisanu ME, Mezzanzanica D, Ricci A, Paris L, Bagnoli M, et al. Characterisation of in vivo ovarian cancer models by quantitative 1H magnetic resonance spectroscopy and diffusion-weighted imaging. *NMR Biomed* (2012) **25**:632–42. doi:10.1002/nbm.1779
67. Provencher SW. Estimation of metabolite concentrations from localized in vivo proton NMR spectra. *Magn Reson Med* (1993) **30**:672–9. doi:10.1002/mrm.1910300604
68. Johnson KP, Giannotti F, Cortesi F. Sleep patterns in autism spectrum disorders. *Child Adolesc Psychiatr Clin N Am* (2009) **18**:917–28. doi:10.1016/j.chc.2009.04.001
69. Glickman G. Circadian rhythms and sleep in children with autism. *Neurosci Biobehav Rev* (2010) **34**:755–68. doi:10.1016/j.neubiorev.2009.11.017
70. Rzepecka H, Mckenzie K, Mcclure I, Murphy S. Sleep, anxiety and challenging behaviour in children with intellectual disability and/or autism spectrum disorder. *Res Dev Disabil* (2011) **32**:2758–66. doi:10.1016/j.ridd.2011.05.034
71. Kotagal S, Broomall E. Sleep in children with autism spectrum disorder. *Pediatr Neurol* (2012) **47**:242–51. doi:10.1016/j.pediatrneurol.2012.05.007
72. Fonken LK, Finy MS, Walton JC, Weil ZM, Workman JL, Ross J, et al. Influence of light at night on murine anxiety- and depressive-like responses. *Behav Brain Res* (2009) **205**:349–54. doi:10.1016/j.bbr.2009.07.001
73. Menet JS, Rosbash M. When brain clocks lose track of time: cause or consequence of neuropsychiatric disorders. *Curr Opin Neurobiol* (2011) **21**:849–57. doi:10.1016/j.conb.2011.06.008
74. Griesauer I, Diao W, Ronovsky M, Elbau I, Sartori S, Singewald N, et al. Circadian abnormalities in a mouse model of high trait anxiety and depression. *Ann Med* (2014) **46**:148–54. doi:10.3109/07853890.2013.866440
75. Badea A, Nicholls PJ, Johnson GA, Wetsel WC. Neuroanatomical phenotypes in the reeler mouse. *Neuroimage* (2007) **34**:1363–74. doi:10.1016/j.neuroimage.2006.09.053
76. Niu S, Renfro A, Quattrocchi CC, Sheldon M, D'Arcangelo G. Reelin promotes hippocampal dendrite development through the VLDLR/ApoER2-Dab1 pathway. *Neuron* (2004) **41**:71–84. doi:10.1016/S0896-6273(03)00819-5
77. Stranahan AM, Erion JR, Wosiski-Kuhn M. Reelin signaling in development, maintenance, and plasticity of neural networks. *Ageing Res Rev* (2013) **12**:815–22. doi:10.1016/j.arr.2013.01.005
78. Costa E, Davis J, Grayson DR, Guidotti A, Pappas GD, Pesold C. Dendritic spine hypoplasticity and downregulation of reelin and GABAergic tone in schizophrenia vulnerability. *Neurobiol Dis* (2001) **8**:723–42. doi:10.1006/nbdi.2001.0436
79. Falconer DS. Two new mutants, 'trembler' and 'reeler', with neurological actions in the house mouse (*Mus musculus* L.). *J Genet* (1951) **50**:192–201. doi:10.1007/BF02996215
80. Caviness VS Jr, Sidman RL. Time of origin or corresponding cell classes in the cerebral cortex of normal and reeler mutant mice: an autoradiographic analysis. *J Comp Neurol* (1973) **148**:141–51. doi:10.1002/cne.901480202
81. Goffinet AM. An early development defect in the cerebral cortex of the reeler mouse. A morphological study leading to a hypothesis concerning the action of the mutant gene. *Anat Embryol (Berl)* (1979) **157**:205–16. doi:10.1007/BF00305160
82. D'Arcangelo G, Curran T. Reeler: new tales on an old mutant mouse. *Bioessays* (1998) **20**:235–44. doi:10.1002/(SICI)1521-1878(199803)20:3<235::AID-BIES7>3.0.CO;2-Q
83. Jamain S, Radyushkin K, Hammerschmidt K, Granon S, Boretius S, Varoqueaux F, et al. Reduced social interaction and ultrasonic communication in a mouse model of monogenic heritable autism. *Proc Natl Acad Sci U S A* (2008) **105**:1710–5. doi:10.1073/pnas.0711555105
84. Radyushkin K, Hammerschmidt K, Boretius S, Varoqueaux F, El-Kordi A, Ronnenberg A, et al. Neuroligin-3-deficient mice: model of a monogenic heritable form of autism with an olfactory deficit. *Genes Brain Behav* (2009) **8**:416–25. doi:10.1111/j.1601-183X.2009.00487.x
85. Brielmaier J, Matteson PG, Silverman JL, Senerth JM, Kelly S, Genestine M, et al. Autism-relevant social abnormalities and cognitive deficits in engrailed-2 knockout mice. *PLoS One* (2012) **7**:e40914. doi:10.1371/journal.pone.0040914
86. Gandal MJ, Anderson RL, Billingslea EN, Carlson GC, Roberts TP, Siegel SJ. Mice with reduced NMDA receptor expression: more consistent with autism than schizophrenia? *Genes Brain Behav* (2012) **11**:740–50. doi:10.1111/j.1601-183X.2012.00816.x
87. Rotschafer SE, Trujillo MS, Dansie LE, Ethell IM, Razak KA. Minocycline treatment reverses ultrasonic vocalization production deficit in a mouse model of Fragile X Syndrome. *Brain Res* (2012) **1439**:7–14. doi:10.1016/j.brainres.2011.12.041
88. Yang M, Bozdagi O, Scattoni ML, Wohr M, Roullet FI, Katz AM, et al. Reduced excitatory neurotransmission and mild autism-relevant phenotypes in adolescent Shank3 null mutant mice. *J Neurosci* (2012) **32**:6525–41. doi:10.1523/JNEUROSCI.6107-11.2012
89. Salinger WL, Ladrow P, Wheeler C. Behavioral phenotype of the reeler mutant mouse: effects of RELN gene dosage and social isolation. *Behav Neurosci* (2003) **117**:1257–75. doi:10.1037/0735-7044.117.6.1257
90. Laviola G, Adriani W, Gaudino C, Marino R, Keller F. Paradoxical effects of prenatal acetylcholinesterase blockade on neuro-behavioral development and drug-induced stereotypies in reeler mutant mice. *Psychopharmacology (Berl)* (2006) **187**:331–44. doi:10.1007/s00213-006-0426-z
91. Ognibene E, Adriani W, Macri S, Laviola G. Neurobehavioural disorders in the infant reeler mouse model: interaction of genetic vulnerability and consequences of maternal separation. *Behav Brain Res* (2007) **177**:142–9. doi:10.1016/j.bbr.2006.10.027
92. Ognibene E, Adriani W, Caprioli A, Ghirardi O, Ali SF, Aloe L, et al. The effect of early maternal separation on brain derived neurotrophic factor and monoamine levels in adult heterozygous reeler mice. *Prog Neuropsychopharmacol Biol Psychiatry* (2008) **32**:1269–76. doi:10.1016/j.pnpbp.2008.03.023
93. Ballmaier M, Zoli M, Leo G, Agnati LF, Spano P. Preferential alterations in the mesolimbic dopamine pathway of heterozygous reeler mice: an emerging animal-based model of schizophrenia. *Eur J Neurosci* (2002) **15**:1197–205. doi:10.1046/j.1460-9568.2002.01952.x
94. Owens DF, Kriegstein AR. Is there more to GABA than synaptic inhibition? *Nat Rev Neurosci* (2002) **3**:715–27. doi:10.1038/nrn919

95. Watanabe M, Maemura K, Kanbara K, Tamayama T, Hayasaki H. GABA and GABA receptors in the central nervous system and other organs. *Int Rev Cytol* (2002) **213**:1–47. doi:10.1016/S0074-7696(02)13011-7
96. Wang L, Bruce G, Spary E, Deuchars J, Deuchars SA. GABA(B) mediated regulation of sympathetic preganglionic neurons: pre- and postsynaptic sites of action. *Front Neurol* (2010) **1**:142. doi:10.3389/fneur.2010.00142
97. Dawson G, Webb SJ, Mcpartland J. Understanding the nature of face processing impairment in autism: insights from behavioral and electrophysiological studies. *Dev Neuropsychol* (2005) **27**:403–24. doi:10.1207/s15326942dn2703_6
98. Schultz RT. Developmental deficits in social perception in autism: the role of the amygdala and fusiform face area. *Int J Dev Neurosci* (2005) **23**:125–41. doi:10.1016/j.ijdevneu.2004.12.012
99. Pezze MA, Feldon J. Mesolimbic dopaminergic pathways in fear conditioning. *Prog Neurobiol* (2004) **74**:301–20. doi:10.1016/j.pneurobio.2004.09.004
100. Rinaldi A, Mandillo S, Oliverio A, Mele A. D1 and D2 receptor antagonist injections in the prefrontal cortex selectively impair spatial learning in mice. *Neuropsychopharmacology* (2007) **32**:309–19. doi:10.1038/sj.npp.1301176
101. Tran T, Ross B, Lin A. Magnetic resonance spectroscopy in neurological diagnosis. *Neurol Clin* (2009) **27**:21–60,xiii. doi:10.1016/j.ncl.2008.09.007
102. Chugani DC. Neuroimaging and neurochemistry of autism. *Pediatr Clin North Am* (2012) **59**:63–73,x. doi:10.1016/j.pcl.2011.10.002
103. Olney JW, de Gubareff T. Glutamate neurotoxicity and Huntington's chorea. *Nature* (1978) **271**:557–9. doi:10.1038/271557a0
104. Tsai VW, Scott HL, Lewis RJ, Dodd PR. The role of group I metabotropic glutamate receptors in neuronal excitotoxicity in Alzheimer's disease. *Neurotox Res* (2005) **7**:125–41. doi:10.1007/BF03033782
105. Estrada-Sanchez AM, Montiel T, Segovia J, Massieu L. Glutamate toxicity in the striatum of the R6/2 Huntington's disease transgenic mice is age-dependent and correlates with decreased levels of glutamate transporters. *Neurobiol Dis* (2009) **34**:78–86. doi:10.1016/j.nbd.2008.12.017
106. Page LA, Daly E, Schmitz N, Simmons A, Toal F, Deeley Q, et al. In vivo 1H-magnetic resonance spectroscopy study of amygdala-hippocampal and parietal regions in autism. *Am J Psychiatry* (2006) **163**:2189–92. doi:10.1176/appi.ajp.163.12.2189
107. Bejjani A, O'neill J, Kim JA, Frew AJ, Yee VW, Ly R, et al. Elevated glutamatergic compounds in pregenual anterior cingulate in pediatric autism spectrum disorder demonstrated by 1H MRS and 1H MRSI. *PLoS One* (2012) **7**:e38786. doi:10.1371/journal.pone.0038786
108. Silverman JL, Smith DG, Rizzo SJ, Karras MN, Turner SM, Tolu SS, et al. Negative allosteric modulation of the mGluR5 receptor reduces repetitive behaviors and rescues social deficits in mouse models of autism. *Sci Transl Med* (2012) **4**:131ra151. doi:10.1126/scitranslmed.3003501
109. Wu JY, Wu H, Jin Y, Wei J, Sha D, Prentice H, et al. Mechanism of neuroprotective function of taurine. *Adv Exp Med Biol* (2009) **643**:169–79. doi:10.1007/978-0-387-75681-3_17
110. Ipser JC, Syal S, Bentley J, Adnams CM, Steyn B, Stein DJ. 1H-MRS in autism spectrum disorders: a systematic meta-analysis. *Metab Brain Dis* (2012) **27**:275–87. doi:10.1007/s11011-012-9293-y
111. Canese R, Pisanu ME, Mezzanzanica D, Ricci A, Paris L, Bagnoli M, et al. Characterisation of in vivo ovarian cancer models by quantitative 1H magnetic resonance spectroscopy and diffusion-weighted imaging. *NMR Biomed* (2011) **25**:632–42. doi:10.1002/nbm.1779
112. Adriani W, Canese R, Podo F, Laviola G. 1H MRS-detectable metabolic brain changes and reduced impulsive behavior in adult rats exposed to methylphenidate during adolescence. *Neurotoxicol Teratol* (2007) **29**:116–25. doi:10.1016/j.ntt.2006.11.010
113. Marco EM, Adriani W, Canese R, Podo F, Viveros MP, Laviola G. Enhancement of endocannabinoid signalling during adolescence: modulation of impulsivity and long-term consequences on metabolic brain parameters in early maternally deprived rats. *Pharmacol Biochem Behav* (2007) **86**:334–45. doi:10.1016/j.pbb.2006.10.006
114. De Filippis B, Fabbri A, Simone D, Canese R, Ricceri L, Malchiodi-Albedi F, et al. Modulation of RhoGTPases improves the behavioral phenotype and reverses astrocytic deficits in a mouse model of Rett syndrome. *Neuropsychopharmacology* (2011) **37**:1152–63. doi:10.1038/npp.2011.301
115. Fatemi SH, Stary JM, Earle JA, Araghi-Niknam M, Eagan E. GABAergic dysfunction in schizophrenia and mood disorders as reflected by decreased levels of glutamic acid decarboxylase 65 and 67 kDa and Reelin proteins in cerebellum. *Schizophr Res* (2005) **72**:109–22. doi:10.1016/j.schres.2004.02.017
116. Eastwood SL, Harrison PJ. Cellular basis of reduced cortical reelin expression in schizophrenia. *Am J Psychiatry* (2006) **163**:540–2. doi:10.1176/appi.ajp.163.3.540
117. Tremolizzo L, Carboni G, Ruzicka WB, Mitchell CP, Sugaya I, Tueting P, et al. An epigenetic mouse model for molecular and behavioral neuropathologies related to schizophrenia vulnerability. *Proc Natl Acad Sci U S A* (2002) **99**:17095–100. doi:10.1073/pnas.262658999

# 12

# Intellectual development in autism spectrum disorders: new insights from longitudinal studies

***Giacomo Vivanti*** [1,2] ****, Josephine Barbaro*** [1]***, Kristelle Hudry*** [1]***, Cheryl Dissanayake*** [1] ***and Margot Prior*** [1,3]

[1] *Olga Tennison Autism Research Centre, School of Psychological Science, La Trobe University, Melbourne, VIC, Australia*
[2] *Victorian Autism Specific Early Learning and Care Centre, La Trobe University, Melbourne, VIC, Australia*
[3] *Melbourne School of Psychological Sciences, University of Melbourne, Melbourne, VIC, Australia*

**Edited by:**
*Andrew Whitehouse, University of Western Australia, Australia*

**Reviewed by:**
*Wendy Heller, University of Illinois, USA*
*Sue Woolfenden, Sydney Children's Hospital, Australia*
*Amelia Walter, Academic Unit of Child Psychiatry South West Sydney, Australia*

***Correspondence:**
*Giacomo Vivanti, Olga Tennison Autism Research Centre, School of Psychological Science, La Trobe University, Bundoora Campus, Bundoora, VIC 3086, Australia*
*e-mail: g.vivanti@latrobe.edu.au*

The presence/absence of Intellectual Disability (ID) is considered to be the most critical factor affecting outcomes in individuals with Autism Spectrum Disorders (ASD). However, the question of the specific nature of ID in ASD has received little attention, with the current view being that ID is a comorbid condition (i.e., one that is unrelated in etiology and causality from the ASD itself). Recent advances in developmental neuroscience, highlighting the importance of early exposure to social experiences for cognitive development, support an alternative view; that ID in ASD might emerge as a consequence of severe social-communication deficits on the experience-dependent mechanisms underlying neurocognitive development. We tested this prediction in two independent samples of young children with ASD ($Ns = 23$ and 60), finding that children with greater ASD severity at an initial assessment were more likely to present with poorer cognitive outcomes at a later assessment, irrespective of initial cognitive level. The results of this proof of principle study suggest that ASD symptom severity contributes to the extent to which the environmental input required to support "typical" brain development can be processed by the individual, so that the risk of developing ID increases as the number and severity of ASD social-communicative impairments increase.

**Keywords: autism, intellectual disability, cognitive development, comorbidity, developmental cognitive neuroscience**

## INTRODUCTION

Intellectual Disability (ID) is characterized by significant limitations in intellectual functioning and in adaptive behavior as expressed in conceptual, social, and practical adaptive skills, with age of onset before age 18 years (Schalock et al., 2010). Approximately two thirds of individuals with Autism Spectrum Disorders (ASD) have co-occurring ID (Dykens and Lense, 2011), and the presence/absence of ID is considered to be the most critical factor affecting outcomes in this population (Howlin et al., 2004; Henninger and Taylor, 2013). However, the question of the nature of the association between ID and ASD has received little attention. One common view in the current conceptualization of ASD is that ID is a *comorbid* condition that occurs over and above ASD symptomatology in some individuals with ASD (Nordin and Gillberg, 1998; Cashin et al., 2009; Matson and Worley, 2013). The term "comorbidity" is used in medicine to denote clinical entities "unrelated in etiology or causality to the principal diagnosis" (e.g., cancer diagnosed after a stroke), and therefore conceptually distinct from complications or sequelae of the principal diagnosis (Greenfield, 1989; Iezzoni, 1994, p. 52; see also Lilienfeld et al., 1994). Other authors suggest that ID and ASD are related in terms of their etiology (i.e., that which causes ID also causes ASD) but they are not themselves causally related (e.g., Waterhouse, 2013). The perspective according to which ID is a distinct additional entity to ASD is reflected in many aspects of ASD research. For example, many studies report that participants with "comorbid ID" were excluded, to allow for the study of "pure autism"; that is, autism not confounded by ID.

The main argument supporting the idea of ID as a comorbid feature of ASD is the notion that a person can have either one without also having the other. While we do not disagree that such dissociation is possible, we argue that the presence of such a situation is not sufficient to demonstrate the independence of the two conditions. We will provide a number of counter arguments supporting an alternative view that severe ASD symptoms increase the risk of an individual also developing ID. We propose a theoretical model indicating the specific mechanisms through which the risk of having ID is related to the severity of ASD symptoms, and we provide novel data from two independent studies to support this model.

### THEORETICAL ARGUMENTS FOR THE ASSOCIATION OF ID AND ASD

The notion of ID and ASD as independent clinical entities reflects a modular conceptualization of cognition, according to which one processing domain/module (in the case of ASD, the processing of social information) can be selectively disrupted without negative repercussions on the rest of cognitive system (that is, other domains will not be affected). According to this framework, "pure autism" is the exemplification of a "modular impairment" involving selective difficulties with social processing, while in the situation of "autism confounded by ID," additional (non-social) processing domains happen to be disrupted as well, albeit for a different reason (i.e., the occurrence of a distinct clinical entity which is causally unrelated to ASD). However, an alternative to this account on the relationship between ID and ASD can be advanced within a developmental neuroscience framework (see Thomas and Karmiloff-Smith, 2002). Recent research emphasizes the experience-dependent nature of early brain development (e.g., Grossmann and Johnson, 2007; Kuhl, 2007; Makinodan et al., 2012), pointing to the crucial role of early exposure to social experience opportunities for cognitive development. For example, education and active engagement in a socially rich environment is associated with both structural and functional brain changes, whilst rearing in minimally stimulating environments (e.g., some orphanages) has a negative impact on brain functioning (Blakemore and Frith, 2005; Cicchetti and Cohen, 2006; Nelson, 2007).

Given the relevance of social input for normal brain development (Kuhl, 2007), it has been hypothesized that a decrease in the attentional and processing weight assigned to social information, in children with ASD, might preclude the usual social experiences that are necessary for "normal" cognitive development during early sensitive periods (Dawson, 2008; Klin et al., 2009; see also Hobson, 2004). This process would affect a number of different domains. For example, as noted by Whitehouse et al. (2007) language impairments in this population might be a secondary consequence of ASD symptoms. If infants with ASD do not have access to the appropriate input that supports the efficient organization and specialization of the brain in neurotypical development, this might ultimately result in the child also having an ID. A corollary of this model is that the more severe the ASD symptoms, the more the child would be "at risk" for developing an ID. Therefore, according to this view, ID is not a comorbid condition (i.e., an unrelated clinical entity), but a developmental *consequence* of the virtual "social deprivation" caused by the ASD symptoms. In this model, we do not imply that the presence of ASD necessarily results in ID in all children, regardless of symptom severity. Rather, we argue that ASD symptoms put the child "at risk" for ID, and that this risk will increase as the severity of ASD symptoms increase. One objection to this perspective is that the severity of ASD and ID are unrelated, so that ID can be equally present in children with mild or severe ASD symptoms. We turn to recent literature suggesting that this is not the case.

#### EMPIRICAL ARGUMENTS FOR THE ASSOCIATION OF ID AND ASD

If the notion that ID is a comorbid feature of ASD is correct, then measures of ASD severity and of cognitive abilities should be independent in the ASD population, so that a child could have mild ASD with severe ID, or severe ASD with mild ID. Empirical data, however, appear more consistent with our reasoning, showing that ID is more likely to be present in children with more severe ASD symptoms than in those with milder presentations. A review by Dykens and Lense (2011) using diagnostic categories from DSM-IV-TR (American Psychiatric Association, 2000) indicates that IQ levels vary substantially across diagnoses under the umbrella of the Pervasive Developmental Disorders (i.e., ASD), with more severe forms associated with lower cognitive scores. Furthermore, a recent longitudinal study by Gotham et al. (2012), involving a sample of 345 participants, documented that individuals with more severe autism symptoms had lower IQ, leading the authors to conclude that autism characteristics and cognitive functioning are not entirely independent features.

Another argument supporting our position derives from recent research on intervention in this population by Dawson et al. (2010). This study, focusing on the efficacy of the Early Start Denver Model – an intervention program specifically targeting ASD symptoms in very young children – found that children undergoing this program experience significant gains on measures of cognitive development and adaptive behavior. If ASD symptoms and ID (defined by low cognitive ability and adaptive functioning) are independent features, how is it that intervention targeting ASD symptoms results in gains in cognitive and adaptive functioning?

#### CURRENT AIMS AND HYPOTHESES

Based on the aforementioned arguments, we conducted a proof of principle study testing the hypothesis that severity of ASD in early childhood is associated with poorer development of cognitive abilities. We did this by collating secondary data across two independent samples of young children with ASD, each followed longitudinally. We predicted that (1) children with more severe ASD symptom presentation would be more likely to also demonstrate lower overall levels of cognitive ability, and (2) that these children would make slower gains in cognitive skills across time.

## MATERIALS AND METHODS

#### PARTICIPANTS

Data for this study were available from two pre-existing, independent samples of young children with ASD; one comprising preschoolers with ASD diagnoses given by expert autism assessment teams in the community, and the other comprising toddlers with ASD prospectively identified and diagnosed from a low-risk, community-based sample following developmental surveillance. Ethics approval for each of these was provided via the La Trobe University Human Ethics Committee; HEC 10-084 and HEC06-94, respectively. We present data from each study as collected across two visits (hereafter, Time 1 and Time 2). Initial characterization data for each sample at Time 1 is presented in **Table 1**.

**Table 1 | Sample characteristics at time 1; mean (SD) range.**

| | Preschoolers with ASD (community diagnosis) | Toddlers with ASD (developmental surveillance) |
|---|---|---|
| Chronological age (months) | 40 (11) 22–60 | 25 (2) 23–33 |
| ADOS-G[a] total algorithm | 14.9 (4.6) 6–21 | 14.0 (4.1) 6–20 |
| MSEL[b] Age-equivalence (months) | | |
| Overall mental age | 21.4 (12) 8–54.5 | 16.7 (3.4) 8–26 |
| Subscales | | |
| Visual reception | 22.6 (8.9) 10–54 | 18.9 (3.2) 10–29 |
| Fine motor | 26.3 (10.7) 13–68 | 21.6 (3.7) 9–30 |
| Receptive language | 17.4 (10.7) 1–47 | 12.2 (5.1) 1–25 |
| Expressive language | 19.8 (11.5) 3–43 | 14.2 (4.1) 3–26 |

[a]*Autism diagnostic observation schedule – generic (Lord et al., 1999).*
[b]*Mullen scales of early learning (Mullen, 1995).*

***Sample 1: preschoolers with community-based ASD diagnosis***

Data for 23 children with ASD (1 female), aged 22–60 months at Time 1, were available from their enrollment and ongoing participation at a community early intervention center (see Vivanti et al., 2013). Children were accepted into the center on the basis of having an existing (or provisional) ASD diagnosis given by a community professional. This was confirmed at Time 1 via administration of the Autism Diagnostic Observation Schedule – Generic (ADOS-G; Lord et al., 1999) by an independent clinician with demonstrated research-reliability in the use of this measure. All participants were free from other medical conditions, and any visual, hearing, or motor impairment. Cognitive abilities for each child were assessed at entry to the early intervention center (Time 1) and again 1 year later (Time 2).

***Sample 2: toddlers with ASD identified via developmental surveillance***

Data for 60 toddlers with ASD (15 female), aged 23–33 months at Time 1, were drawn from a larger pool of participants identified within the Social Attention and Communication Study (SACS; Barbaro and Dissanayake, 2010; Barbaro et al., 2011). This longitudinal, community-based developmental surveillance study investigated the utility of a set of early markers in infants and toddlers for the prospectively identification of ASD at 12-, 18-, and 24 months of age. A sample of 110 children were identified at "at risk" for ASD on the SACS, and assessed at 24 months using the ADOS-G (Lord et al., 1999) and ADI-R (Lord et al., 1994), administered by a researcher with demonstrated reliability in using these measures. Of these, 89 toddlers were identified as having ASD at 24 months of age (Time 1), with 60 returning for a follow-up assessment 2 years later (Time 2; mean age 50 months, SD = 4.8). The current sample therefore comprises those 60 toddlers for whom an ASD diagnosis was initially given and for whom longitudinal cognitive ability data were available at follow-up.

### MEASURES

Common measures of autism symptoms and cognitive ability were used to characterize children across the two samples. As already noted, the ADOS-G (Lord et al., 1999) was administered at Time 1 for all children (early intervention entry for the preschoolers, and initial diagnostic assessment visit for the toddlers). This standardized tool is considered the gold-standard observational measure for use in quantifying symptoms relevant to a diagnosis of ASD; that is, impairments in the areas of communication, reciprocal social interaction, and restricted/repetitive behaviors. While serving to inform diagnostic decisions around ASD, ADOS-G total algorithm scores (comprising communication and social interaction items only) can also be considered to index relative symptom severity, in so far as a range of scores is available beyond that considered to signal the "cut-off" for an ASD. Total algorithm scores for Module 1 (minimally verbal young children) plausibly range from 0 to 26, with a cut-off score of 7 used to identify an ASD (and with higher scores indexing greater symptom expression). As shown in **Table 1**, Time 1 ADOS scores varied substantially across the available range within each of our samples, showing clear individual differences on this measure.

Cognitive ability was assessed for all children at both Time 1 and Time 2 (following 1 year of early intervention for the preschoolers, and at a 2-year follow-up, post diagnosis, for the toddlers). This was achieved using the Mullen Scales of Early Learning (MSEL; Mullen, 1995), a standardized measure of ability across four domains important for cognitive functioning in early development; Visual Reception, Fine Motor, Receptive Language, and Expressive Language. The MSEL yields standardized $T$-Scores for each domain. However, as these can be of limited use for samples where children have ASD, as floor-level performance is often observed, we instead report Age-Equivalence (AE) scores here. These scores demonstrate good variability and can be meaningfully interpreted (i.e., a typically developing child should be expected to have an AE score in line with their own chronological age, and to make gains of 12 months' AE over a 1-year period). As shown in **Table 1**, Time 1 MSEL scores varied substantially, showing clear individual differences on this measure within each sample.

### DESIGN AND ANALYTIC PROCEDURE

Associations between autism symptom presentation and cognitive ability were evaluated, separately within each sample, using Pearson Product Moment Correlation Coefficients. First, we examined concurrent associations among our indices of autism symptoms and cognitive ability at Time 1. Second, we computed a measure of gains in cognitive ability between Time 1 and 2 assessments (subtracting the former from the latter, for each child) and then examined the association of ASD symptoms at Time 1 with this measure of cognitive AE gains.

## RESULTS AND DISCUSSION

### SAMPLE 1: PRESCHOOLERS WITH COMMUNITY-BASED ASD DIAGNOSIS

For the sample of 23 preschoolers with ASD, a significant association, of large effect size, was evident between ASD symptoms and cognitive AE scores assessed concurrently at Time 1 (i.e., early intervention intake); $r = -0.49$, $p = 0.010$, $d = 0.9$. Longitudinally, a significant association, of larger effect size, was evident for this sample between Time 1 ASD symptoms and gains in cognitive AE made between Time 1 and Time 2 assessments; $r = -0.65$, $p = 0.001$, $d = 1.2$. Average cognitive AE scores increased from 21.4 months (SD = 12) to 30.4 months (SD = 18) over the 1-year period, representing an average growth of 9 months within this time. The results from the correlational analyses indicated that those preschoolers with more severe ASD symptoms also presented with lower concurrent cognitive ability. Moreover, they also had fewer gains in cognitive ability over the following year. **Figures 1** and **2** present individual data-points for these associations.

### SAMPLE 2: TODDLERS WITH ASD IDENTIFIED VIA DEVELOPMENTAL SURVEILLANCE

Among the sample of 60 toddlers prospectively identified via developmental surveillance and meeting criteria for ASD at 2 years of age, a significant association, of medium effect size, was evident among concurrent ASD symptoms and cognitive AE assessed at Time 1 (i.e., initial diagnostic assessment); $r = -0.52$, $p < 0.001$, $d = 0.7$. A significant association, also of medium effect size, was

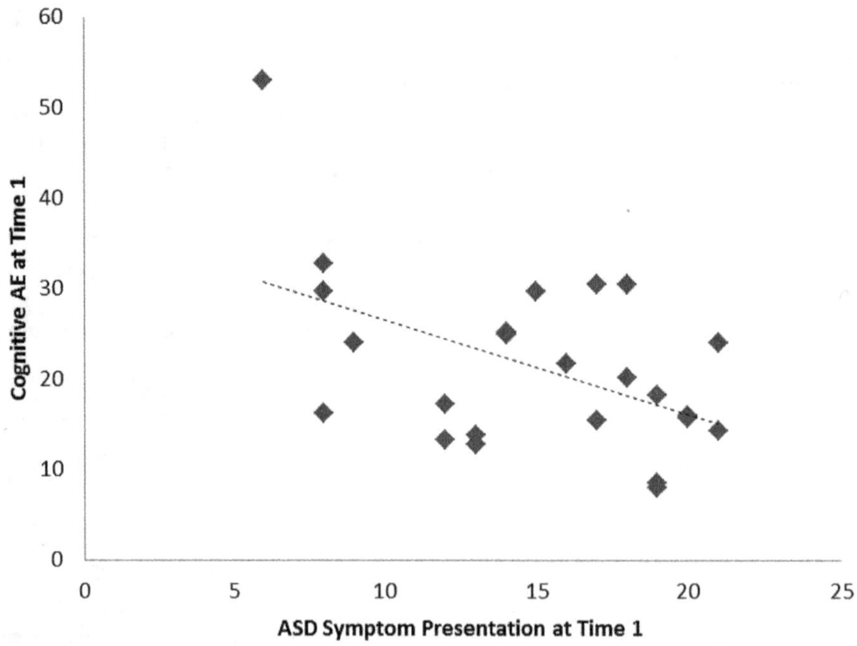


**FIGURE 1 | Scatterplots for 23 preschoolers with community ASD diagnoses presenting associations among Time 1 ASD symptoms and concurrent cognitive age-equivalence scores.**

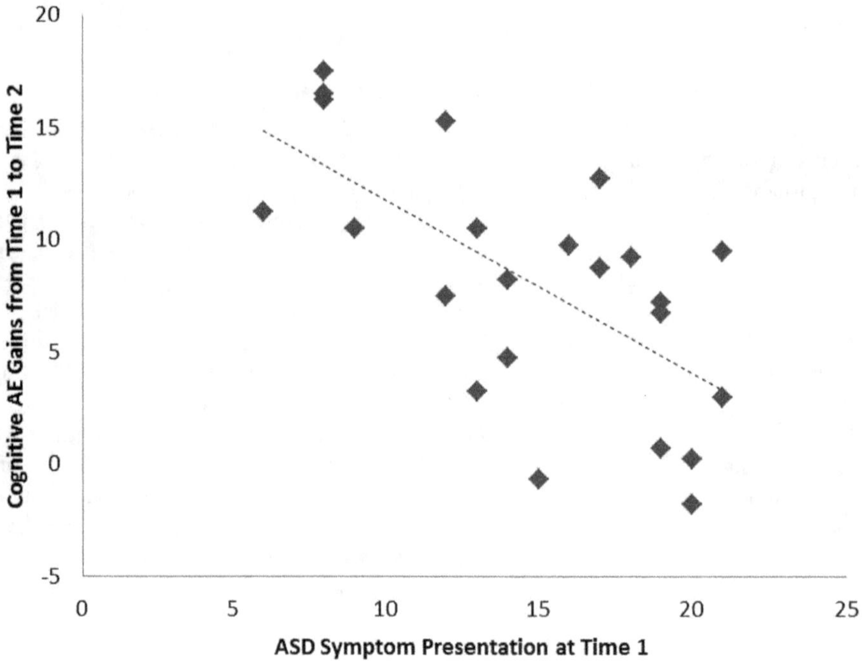


**FIGURE 2 | Scatterplots for 23 preschoolers with community ASD diagnoses presenting associations among Time 1 ASD symptoms and gains in cognitive age-equivalence over a 1-year follow-up period.**

also evident for this sample between ASD symptom presentation at Time 1 and gains in cognitive AE made between Time 1 and Time 2 assessments; $r = -0.32$, $p = 0.007$, $d = 0.7$. On average, cognitive AE scores increased from 16.7 months (SD = 3.4) to 37.5 months (SD = 11.5) over the 2-year period, representing an average growth of 20.8 months during this time (or around 10.4 months per year).

As with our findings for the preschoolers with ASD, and in keeping with our hypothesis, toddlers with more severe ASD symptoms showed lower cognitive ability at concurrent assessment and also made more limited cognitive gains across the following 2 years. These associations are shown in **Figures 3** and **4**, and a summary of our data across both samples is presented in **Table 2**.

### CROSS-SAMPLE SIMILARITIES AND DIFFERENCES

Across these two independent samples of young children with ASD, similar magnitude of associations between Time 1 ASD symptom scores and concurrent cognitive AE are noted. However, effect sizes for the correlations between Time 1 ASD symptoms and longitudinal gains in cognitive AE were of quite different magnitude, albeit presenting a negative association for both groups. A somewhat stronger effect was observed here for our sample of preschoolers, followed across a 1-year period, with a more modest one apparent for our toddlers who were observed across a 2-year period. This variation in effect sizes may be due to sample differences. First, while our toddler sample included a greater number of individuals ($N = 60$) than our preschool sample ($N = 23$), the former comprised a relatively homogenous group, while the latter presented greater heterogeneity in terms of chronological age at each assessment and Time 1 cognitive AE scores (see standard deviation metrics in **Table 1**). Differences in the range of scores present within the groups may account, at least in part, for the differing magnitudes of effect size we observed. Variability in Time 1 ASD symptom presentation was relatively well balanced across the samples. However, by Time 2, cognitive AE scores were more varied in each of the groups. As such, this is unlikely to provide a full explanation for our finding.

The most likely potential contributing factor for the difference in effect size lies in the different intervals spanning Time 1 and Time 2 assessments for each group. In the case of the preschoolers, intake assessment to the community center was followed with an outcome evaluation 1 year later. For toddlers, by contrast, ASD diagnosis was made at a visit when children were ~2 years of age (having been referred to the study across infancy and toddlerhood via developmental surveillance in the SACS) and the follow-up visit was scheduled ~2 years later. This longer-interval, over which gains were evaluated, may explain the more modest effect size observed here between early ASD symptom presentation and change in cognitive AE ability.

### GENERAL DISCUSSION

Autism Spectrum Disorder is defined in terms of limitations in social-communication and behavioral flexibility, and ID is defined in terms of limitations in intellectual functioning and in adaptive behavior as expressed in conceptual, social, and practical skills. Whilst the validity of ASD as a specific construct independent from ID and other factors (e.g., language) is well established, the majority of individuals with ASD also have co-occurring ID, posing the problem of the nature of this association. One possibility, which is widely accepted in the ASD field, is that ID represents a comorbid condition in ASD (i.e., one that is unrelated in etiology and causality from ASD). In this paper, we outlined a number of theoretical and empirical arguments indicating that this notion is questionable. Whilst there is clear evidence that mild ASD symptoms are compatible with normative or superior IQ, the evidence is less clear with regards to severe ASD symptoms, with recent data (including the novel data presented here) suggesting that the more "autism

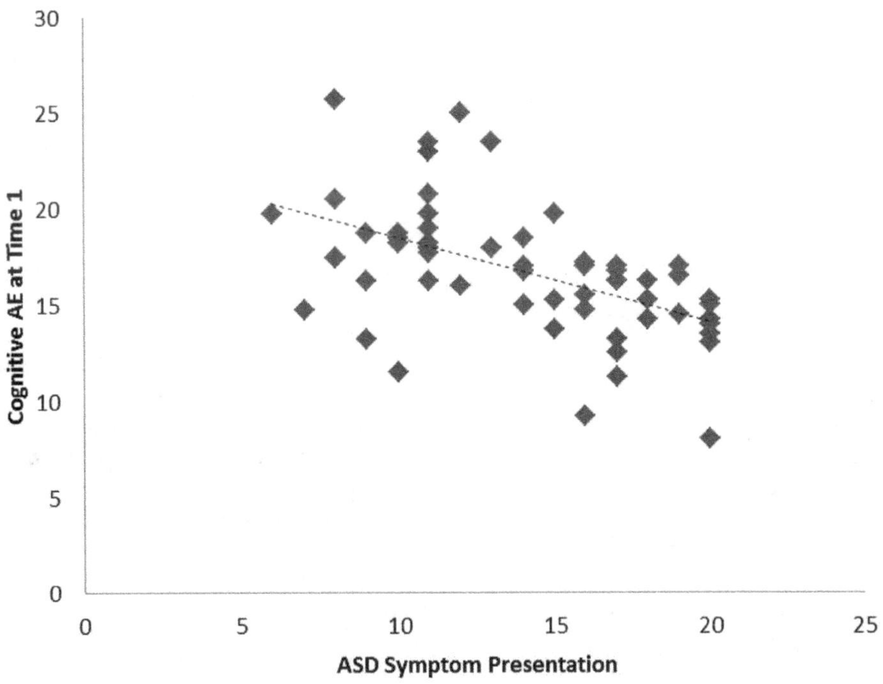


**FIGURE 3 | Scatterplots for 60 toddlers with ASD identified via developmental surveillance presenting associations among Time 1 ASD symptoms and concurrent cognitive age-equivalence scores.**

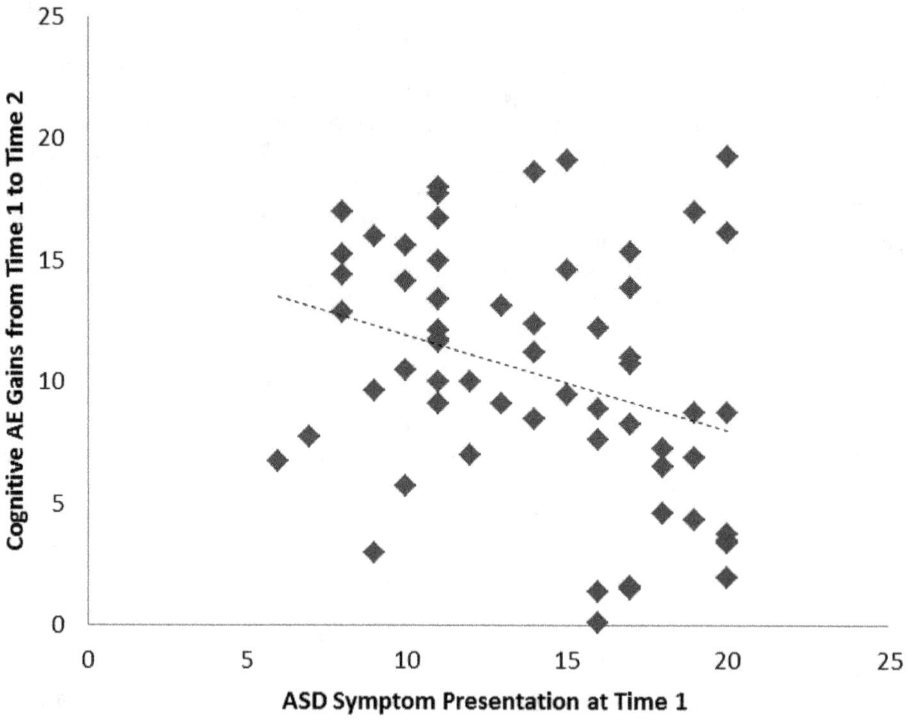


**FIGURE 4 | Scatterplots for 60 toddlers with ASD identified via developmental surveillance presenting associations among Time 1 ASD symptoms and gains in cognitive age-equivalence over a 2-year follow-up period.**

**Table 2 | Summary of the strengths of association across the two samples.**

| | Preschoolers with ASD (community diagnosis) | Toddlers with ASD (developmental surveillance) |
|---|---|---|
| Concurrent associations | | |
| Time 1 ADOS[a] and MSEL[b] | $r = -0.49$, $p = 0.010$, $d = 0.9$ | $r = -0.52$, $p < 0.001$, $d = 0.7$ |
| Longitudinal associations | | |
| Time 1 ADOS[a] and Time 2 MSEL[b] | $r = -0.65$, $p = 0.001$, $d = 1.2$ | $r = -0.32$, $p = 0.007$, $d = 0.7$ |
| Interval between Time 1 and 2 | 1 year | 2 years |

[a] *Autism diagnostic observation schedule – generic (Lord et al., 1999).*
[b] *Mullen scales of early learning (Mullen, 1995).*

specific" symptoms a child has, the more at risk he or she is of poor cognitive outcome. Moreover, early behavioral intervention targeting ASD symptoms results in positive changes in IQ, again indicating some inter-dependence, rather than independence, of these two dimensions.

We argue that the presence of severe ASD symptoms is a risk factor for low IQ, in the same way that severe hypertension or severe obesity increases the risk of cardiovascular events (Flynn et al., 2011). Advances in developmental neuroscience, emphasizing the experience-dependent nature of early brain development (e.g., Grossmann and Johnson, 2007; Kuhl, 2007), allow us to explain this association of ID and ASD from a neurodevelopmental perspective. Based on this framework, we suggest that ASD symptom severity moderates the extent to which the environmental input required to support "typical" brain development can be processed by the individual, so that the risk of poor cognitive developmental outcomes increases as the number and severity of ASD social-communication impairments increase. That is, emerging social-communication deficits early in development might deprive the developing brain from receiving important environmental inputs, with downstream effects on global cognitive development. The result is lower IQ in those individuals with the most severe ASD symptoms.

According to this perspective, we argue that the practice of excluding children with ID in ASD research to study "pure autism unconfounded by ID" is ill considered, just as studying the risk of cardiovascular events in individuals who are slightly overweight, or who have mild presentation of hypertension, would not be informative on the most relevant aspects affecting the outcomes of individuals with those conditions. Rather, research should target those factors that place affected individuals at an increased risk of negative outcomes, by investigating the mechanisms underlying symptoms and their sequelae, and identifying prevention/remediation strategies to foster positive developmental outcomes.

## LIMITATIONS AND FUTURE DIRECTIONS

There were several limitations of the current study. First, we do not have data on participants' adaptive behavior level, which form part of the criteria required for the diagnosis of ID. Second, whilst all of the children involved in this study would likely have been enrolled in community early intervention programs, we have not collected details on the specific programs the children were involved in, nor on the amounts of intervention being received. As such, this potentially critical factor mediating the impact of ASD severity on cognition could not be taken into account in the current study. Future research will involve collecting data on adaptive behavior and participation in intervention in order to build on the results from the current study.

Whilst the aim of this proof of principle study was to test the notion that the severity of ASD symptoms has a negative influence on cognitive development, it is important to mention various other risk factors that are known to affect cognitive development in other groups of children. These include demographic factors, preterm birth, maternal age and education, and birth weight, among others (Zeanah, 2009). In order to disentangle the relative importance of ASD symptom severity from that of other potentially significant factors on cognitive development, more empirical research is needed that utilizes prospective research designs and includes larger sample sizes.

## CONCLUSION

Intellectual Disability is known to result from a number of different risk factors. Here, we have argued that the presence of severe (but not mild) symptoms of ASD is one such risk factor, so that ID is unlikely to be a comorbid condition to ASD but, rather, one that is intimately linked to certain ASD presentations. Consistent with Ockham's razor (Popper, 1992), the presence of ID in the majority of the ASD population, in particular in those individuals who are more severely affected with ASD, can be more parsimoniously explained by positing a relationship between these two frequently co-occurring clinical entities than by claiming their independence. A developmental neuroscience framework provides a good explanatory model on the nature of such a relationship, indicating that it is plausible that children with very severe disabilities affecting social understanding and social learning are more vulnerable to poor cognitive outcomes (Coch et al., 2007). As the poor outcomes associated with the presence of ID in ASD result in large human and societal costs, it is important that future research systematically investigate the risk and protective factors associated with the development of ID in ASD. Indeed, excluding individuals with ID from research in ASD only renders more difficult the ultimate goal of fostering positive outcomes for individuals with ASD.

## ACKNOWLEDGMENTS

We would like to acknowledge the children and parents involved in each of these studies. We also thank the nursing staff who undertook developmental surveillance and referred toddlers for assessment in the SACS and we thank the staff at the Margot Prior Wing who worked with our preschool sample. Thanks also to Donata Pagetti Vivanti for the inspiring discussions on this theme.

## REFERENCES

1. American Psychiatric Association. (2000). *Diagnostic and Statistical Manual of Mental Disorders, (4th Edn, Text Revised).* Washington, DC: American Psychiatric Association.
2. Barbaro, J., and Dissanayake, C. (2010). Prospective identification of autism spectrum disorders in infancy and toddlerhood using developmen- tal surveillance: the social atten- tion and communication study. *J. Dev. Behav. Pediatr.* 31, 376–385. doi:10.1097/DBP.0b013e3181df7f3c
3. Barbaro, J., Ridgway, L., and Dis- sanayake, C. (2011). Developmental surveillance of infants and toddlers by maternal and child health nurses in an Australian community-based setting: promoting the early identi- fication of autism spectrum disor- ders. *J. Pediatr. Nurs.* 26, 334–347. doi:10.1016/j.pedn.2010.04.007
4. Blakemore, S. J., and Frith, U. (2005). *The Learning Brain.* Malden, MA: Blackwell.
5. Cashin, A., Sci, D. A., and Barker, P. (2009). The triad of impair- ment in autism revisited. *J. Child Adolesc. Psychiatr. Nurs.* 22, 189–193. doi:10.1111/j.1744- 6171.2009.00198.x
6. Cicchetti, D., and Cohen, D. J. (eds). (2006). *Developmental Psychopathology: Developmental Neuroscience*, 2nd Edn, Vol. 2. New York: Wiley.
7. Coch, D., Dawson, G., and Fischer, K. (eds). (2007). *Human Behavior and the Developing Brain.* New York: Guilford Press.
8. Dawson, G. (2008). Early behavioral intervention, brain plastic- ity, and the prevention of autism spectrum disorder. *Dev. Psychopathol.* 20, 775–803. doi:10.1017/S0954579408000370
9. Dawson, G., Rogers, S., Munson, J., Smith, M., Winter, J., Greenson, J., et al. (2010). Randomized, controlled trial of an intervention for toddlers with autism: the Early Start Den- ver Model. *Pediatrics* 125, e17–e23. doi:10.1542/peds.2009-0958
10. Dykens, E. M., and Lense, M. (2011). "Intellectual disabilities and autism spectrum disorder: a cautionary note," in *Autism Spectrum Disor- ders*, eds D. Amaral, G. Dawson, and D. Geschwind (New York: Oxford University Press), 261–269.
11. Flynn, J. T., Ingelfinger, J., and Port- man, R. (2011). *Pediatric Hypertension*, 2nd Edn. New York: Humana Press.
12. Gotham, K., Pickles, A., and Lord, C. (2012). Trajectories of autism sever- ity in children using standardized ADOS scores. *Pediatrics* 130, e1278–e1284. doi:10.1542/peds.2011-3668
13. Greenfield, S. (1989). The state of out- comes research: are we on target? *N. Engl. J. Med.* 320, 1142. doi:10. 1056/NEJM198904273201710
14. Grossmann, T., and Johnson, M. H. (2007). The development of the social brain in human infancy. *Eur. J. Neurosci.* 25, 909–919. doi:10.1111/j.1460-9568.2007.05379.x
15. Henninger, N. A., and Taylor, J. L. (2013). Outcomes in adults with autism spectrum disorders: a histor- ical perspective. *Autism* 17, 103–116. doi:10.1177/1362361312441266
16. Hobson, R. P. (2004). *The Cradle of Thought: Exploring the Origins of Thinking.* Oxford, NY: Oxford Uni- versity Press.
17. Howlin, P., Goode, S., Hutton, J., and Rutter, M. (2004). Adult outcome for children with autism. *J. Child Psychol. Psychiatry* 45, 212–229. doi:10.1111/j.1469- 7610.2004.00215.x
18. Iezzoni, L. I. (1994). *Risk Adjustment for Measuring Health Care Outcomes.* Ann Arbor, MI: Health Administra- tion Press.
19. Klin, A., Lin, D. J., Gorrindo, P., Ramsay, G., and Jones, W. (2009). Two-year- olds with autism orient to non-social contingencies rather than biolo- gi- cal motion. *Nature* 459, 257–261. doi:10.1038/nature07868
20. Kuhl, P. K. (2007). Is speech learn- ing 'gated' by the social brain? *Dev. Sci.* 10, 110–120. doi:10.1111/j.1467- 7687.2007.00572.x
21. Lord, C., Rutter, M., DiLavore, P., and Risi, S. (1999). *Autism Diagnostic Observation Schedule.* Los Angeles, CA: Western Psychological Services. Lord, C., Rutter, M., and LeCou- teur, A. (1994). Autism Diagnostic Interview-Revised – a revised ver- sion of a diagnostic interview for caregivers of individuals with pos- sible pervasive developmental dis- orders. *J. Autism Dev. Disord.* 24, 659–685. doi:10.1007/BF02172145
22. Lilienfeld, S. O., Waldman, I. D., and Israel, A. C. (1994). A critical examination of the use of the term "comorbidity" in psychopathol- ogy research. *Clin. Psychol. Sci. Pract.* 1, 71–83. doi:10.1111/j.1468- 2850.1994.tb00007.x
23. Makinodan, M., Rosen, K. M., Ito, S., and Corfas, G. (2012). A critical period for social experience- dependent oligodendrocyte maturation and myelina- tion. *Science* 337, 1357–1360. doi:10.1126/science.1220845
24. Matson, J., and Worley, M. (2013). "The diagnostic process," in *Encyclopae- dia of Autism Spectrum Disorders*, ed. F. Vokmar (New York: Springer), 940–944.

25. Mullen, E. M. (1995). *Mullen Scales of Early Learning*. Circle Pines, MN: American Guidance Service.
26. Nelson, C. A. (2007). A neuro- biological perspective on early human deprivation. *Child Dev. Per- spect.* 1, 13–18. doi:10.1111/j.1750- 8606.2007.00004.x
27. Nordin, V., and Gillberg, C. (1998). The long-term course of autistic disorders: update on follow-up studies. *Acta Psychiatr. Scand.* 97, 99–108. doi:10.1111/j.1600-0447.1998.tb09970.x
28. Popper, K. (1992). "*7. Simplicity.*" *The Logic of Scientific Discovery*, 2nd Edn. London: Routledge.
29. Schalock, R. L., Borthwick-Duffy, S. A., *Bradley*, V. J., Buntinx, W. H. E., Coulter, D. L., Craig, E. M., et al. (2010). *Intellectual dis- ability: Definition, Classification, and Systems of Supports.* Wash- ington: American Association on Intellectual and Developmental Disabilities.
30. Thomas, M., and Karmiloff-Smith, A. (2002). Are developmental disor- ders like cases of brain dam- age? Implications from connection- ist modelling. *Behav. Brain Sci.* 25, 727–787. doi:10.1017/S0140525X02 000134
31. Vivanti, G., Dissanayake, C., Zierhut, C., Roger, S. J, and the Victorian ASELCC Team (2013). Brief report: predictors of outcomes in the early start denver model delivered in a group setting. *J. Autism Dev. Disord.* 43, 1717–1724. doi:10.1007/s10803-012-1705-7
32. Waterhouse, L. (2013). *Rethinking Autism: Variation and Complexity*. London: Academic Press.
33. Whitehouse, A. J. O., Barry, J. G., and Bishop, D. V. M. (2007). The broader language pheno- type of autism: a comparison with specific language *impair-* ment. *J. Child Psychol. Psychiatry* 42, 822–830. doi:10.1111/j.1469-7610.2007.01765.x
34. Zeanah, C. H. (eds). (2009). *Hand- book of Infant Mental Health.* 472–485. New York: Guilford Press.

# 13

# New experimental treatments for core social domain in autism spectrum disorders

**Roberto Canitano***

*Division of Child Neuropsychiatry, University Hospital of Siena, Siena, Italy*

***Edited by:***
*Yuri Bozzi, University of Trento, Italy*

***Reviewed by:***
*Maria Luisa Scattoni, Istituto Superiore di Sanità, Italy*
*Latha Soorya, Rush University Medical Center, USA*

***Correspondence:***
*Roberto Canitano, Division of Child Neuropsychiatry, University Hospital of Siena, Viale Bracci 14, Siena 53100, Italy*
*e-mail: r.canitano@ao-siena.toscana.it*

Current therapeutics in autism spectrum disorders (ASD) only treat the associated symptoms, without addressing core social dysfunctions. A paradigm shift in research of the pathogenesis of ASD, its synaptic abnormalities and altered signaling in multiple dynamic systems, have led to new experimental treatments for treating the core social abnormalities of ASD. NMDA antagonists, especially memantine, have been introduced in clinical trials addressing glutamatergic transmission in children and adolescents with ASD. GABAergic signaling has been targeted in trials using the $GABA_B$ receptor agonist arbaclofen for ASD patients with promising results. Oxytocin has been recognized as implicated in social development and affiliative behaviors. Preliminary findings from clinical trials using oxytocin in children with ASD show encouraging improvements in social cognition, but larger studies are needed. In two of the single gene disorders associated with ASD, Insulin Growth Factor (IGF-1) is a new treatment that has been tested in Rett syndrome and Phelan-McDermid syndrome (Chromosome 22 deletion syndrome). IGF-1 has been demonstrated to reverse the reduction in the number of excitatory synapses and the density of neurons that characterize these conditions in animal studies and it is being introduced as an experimental treatment. As a novel approach to verify treatment efficacy, neural processing modifications were recently evaluated by fMRI after a pivotal response training intervention. Another study of neural changes in response to treatment examined variations in EEG signaling in patients after an Early Start Denver Model (ESDM) intervention.

**Keywords: autism spectrum disorders, experimental treatments, preclinical models, clinical trials, childhood and adolescence**

## INTRODUCTION

Autism spectrum disorders (ASD) are early-onset neurodevelopmental disorders characterized by major difficulties in social interaction, communication, and repetitive or restricted interests and behaviors. Autism is defined as a spectrum disorder due to the heterogeneity of clinical presentation, the degree of social impairment, intellectual ability, associated symptoms, and possible etiology. ASD are included in the diagnostic category of neurodevelopmental disorders in the Diagnostic and Statistical Manual of Mental Disorders V (1). The diagnosis of ASD is based on two major symptoms: social-communication deficits, restricted and repetitive interests, and behaviors. By definition, these symptoms must occur during the early childhood of individuals with ASD.

The currently accepted prevalence of ASD, based on consistent reports from multiple sources in different populations, is about 1% worldwide. ASDs are therefore among the most common pervasive developmental disorders and there is great concern regarding its growing incidence (2–4).

To date, the only FDA-approved treatments for ASD are the atypical antipsychotics risperidone and aripiprazole, which are mainly directed at treating the associated symptoms and not the core social dysfunctions that characterize this heterogeneous group of disorders. Treatments with these two medications have been demonstrated to reduce and attenuate irritability (e.g., tantrums, aggression, hyperactivity, and self-injurious behaviors) in children and adolescents with ASD (5–8). Improvements in social interaction and reciprocity have been observed as well, but this is probably a secondary effect of an overall reduction in maladaptive behaviors and not a primary therapeutic effect of these medications.

Targeted treatments for ASD are developed through the understanding of molecular and cellular abnormalities that guide specific interventions, hypothesizing that the wide variety of genetic variants in ASD converge in a core set of molecular pathways that mediate phenotypic expression in some identifiable core symptoms (9). Most research for new therapeutics currently uses preclinical models, such as "knockout" mice displaying specific molecular abnormalities. Genetic studies of ASD and related neurodevelopmental disorders have provided classes of potentially useful compounds. Proof-of-principle assays with agents that reversed phenotypes in mouse models have paved the way for clinical trials (10).

## EXCITATORY/INHIBITORY IMBALANCE IN ASD AND NEW TREATMENTS

An imbalance of excitatory (glutamate) to inhibitory (GABA) neurotransmission (E/I imbalance) is thought to be implicated in the pathogenesis of ASD (11–13). Excessive excitatory glutamatergic neurotransmission with a loss of inhibitory GABA transmission, as well as abnormalities in synaptic plasticity due to dysfunctions in the NMDA, AMPA, and/or GABA receptor systems, have been detected in mouse models and support this conceptualization of ASD pathogenesis (10). Pharmacological evidence emerged from mouse models with deletions in synaptic genes Fmrl, Mecp2, and Shank2, and the BTBR inbred strain, which have demonstrated favorable outcomes from treatments with glutamatergic agents, including memantine (14). After these preclinical investigations, clinical trials were carried out to test the potential role of glutamatergic and GABAergic agents in reversing core social dysfunction in ASD.

## GLUTAMATERGIC TARGETING IN ASD

Altered glutamatergic excitatory transmission involves different receptors, including down-regulation of AMPA receptors, abnormalities of NMDA receptor-mediated plasticity, and altered metabotropic glutamate receptor subtype 5(mGluR5) signal transduction. The mGluR5 antagonists have been tested in preclinical models of autism with variable effects on social and stereotypic behaviors (15). MPEP, an antagonist of the mGluR5 receptor, reduced repetitive self-grooming in BTBR mice. BTBR is an autism mouse model with behavioral abnormalities in social interaction and communication, as well as repetitive movements and behaviors. Risperidone also reduced repetitive self-grooming in BTBR, but only at doses that induced sedation (16). GRN-259, a selective negative allosteric modulator of the mGluR5 receptor, was tested in BTBR mice. GRN-529 reduced repetitive behaviors in three cohorts of BTBR mice and it attenuated social withdrawal with an associated increase in communication, providing overall improvement in behavioral conditions (17). Treatment with the two AMPAKINE compounds CX1837 and CX1739, agents active on AMPA receptors that enhance excitatory glutamatergic action, succeeded in recovering social impairment but it did not attenuate the high levels of repetitive self-grooming in BTBR (18). In 4-week-old Balb/c mice, the NMDA receptor agonist D-cycloserine was found to improve both sociability and repetitive behaviors, emphasizing the potential role of NMDA agents in modulating the core social dysfunctions of ASD (19). Studies of Shank3 heterozygous mice detected a reduction in basal neurotransmission, reflecting reduced AMPA receptor-mediated transmission, which was targeted with insulin growth factor (IGF-1) treatment (20, 21).

Clinical trials followed the preclinical phase of investigation with glutamatergic agents. Memantine, an NMDA receptor antagonist, was tested in children and adolescents with ASD. Overall, the memantine trials conducted so far have yielded inconsistent findings due to methodological flaws, thus they did not allow for firm conclusions. No recommendations on the use of memantine or of other glutamatergic agents in ASD treatment are warranted as yet (22).

## GABAergic TARGETING IN ASD

GABAergic signaling has been demonstrated to be implicated in E/I imbalance in ASD (23). Engrailed2 (En2) knockout mice have been proposed as a model for ASD. In this mutant, the cerebellum and hippocampus have been shown to have abnormal synaptic transmission, altered developmental processes and defective GABA transmission convergent with ASD pathways. A link between altered function of En2, deficits of GABAergic forebrain neurons, and the pathogenesis of ASD has been postulated (24, 25). In addition, social and cognitive abnormalities have been detected in En2 knockout mice, further highlighting its role in ASD. Deficits in reciprocal social interactions growing over time were found in En2 null mutants (26). Interestingly, mice lacking Mecp2 from GABA-releasing neurons demonstrated Rett syndrome and autistic features, including repetitive behaviors. In these mice, MeCP2-deficient GABAergic neurons showed a presynaptic reduction in glutamic acid decarboxylase 1 (Gad1) and glutamic acid decarboxylase 2 (Gad2) levels, and GABA immunoreactivity (27).

In clinical trials, GABA signaling has been probed with specific compounds. Arbaclofen, a $GABA_B$ receptor agonist that acts upstream of mGluR5 receptor signaling and is thought to augment inhibitory neurotransmission, was investigated. Initially, a preclinical study (28) followed by a clinical trial with arbaclofen was carried out in Fragile X syndrome, the most common cause of intellectual disability and ASD (29), and favorable findings were reported regarding social domains (30). A recent open-label trial with STX209, a form of Arbaclofen, was conducted in ASD patients (31). Safety, tolerability, and efficacy were tested in ASD individuals in an 8-week open-label trial enrolling 32 children and adolescents with a score of $\geq 17$ on the aberrant behavior checklist (ABC)-irritability subscale. STX209 was generally well tolerated. Improvements were reported on several outcome measures, including the ABC-Irritability (the primary endpoint) and the Lethargy/Social Withdrawal subscales, and the Social Responsiveness Scale. Randomized controlled trials are needed to confirm these preliminary positive findings.

## mTOR TARGETING IN ASD

The mammalian target of rapamycin (mTOR) pathway is central to synaptic protein synthesis and it integrates inputs from different sources, including NMDA and metabotropic glutamate receptors. In addition, it is directly involved in the maintenance of the physiological synaptic E/I ratio. Abnormalities in mTOR signaling have been found in ASD (32). Activation of mTORC1 promotes the formation of the eIF4F initiation complex. Mutations in genes upstream of mTOR, as detected in tuberous sclerosis complex (TSC1/2), neurofibromatosis 1(NF1), phosphatase and tensin homolog (PTEN), or the Fragile X syndrome gene (FMR1) cause hyperactivity of the mTORC1–eIF4E pathway and lead to syndromic forms of ASDs (33, 34). Accordingly, mTOR inhibitors are first line candidates for the treatment of ASD in TSC (35). Everolimus, an mTOR inhibitor, is currently being studied in a double-blind controlled trial in children and adolescents (6–21 years old) with TSC, ASD and seizures (NCT01289912).[1] The primary aim of this trial is improvement in cognition, while ASD symptoms attenuation and seizure frequencies are secondary objectives. Rapamycin, an mTORC1 inhibitor and immune-suppressor, was investigated in a recent preclinical study as an agent to ameliorate social behaviors and attenuate stereotypies in BTBR mice. Rapamycin was found to improve many components of sociability in the BTBR mouse,

[1] http://clinicaltrials.gov

pointing to mTOR overactivation as a therapeutic target in ASD. However, no effects of rapamycin on stereotypic behaviors were detected (36).

An important regulatory action was recently described in the other component of this pathway, the downstream effectors of mTOR. Signaling molecules in the downstream of the mTOR pathway have been demonstrated to play crucial roles in ASD pathogenesis, further highlighting its role (37, 38). Furthermore, 4E-BP2 inhibits protein translation by competing with eIF4G for eIF4E binding. The deletion of the gene encoding 4E-BP2 (EIF4ebp2) leads to autistic-like behaviors in mice. It was demonstrated that the removal of 4E-BP2, or overexpression of eIF4E, enhances protein translation; increased translation of neuroligins (NLGNs) is the next step that in turn causes an increased synaptic E/I ratio, which may eventually lead to ASD phenotypes. Pharmacological inhibition of eIF4E reversed social behavior deficits in EIF4ebp2 knockout mice and restored the E/I balance (37). These findings thus established a strong link between eIF4E-dependent translational control of NLGNs, E/I balance, and the development of ASD-like behaviors. Pharmacological targeting of downstream effectors of mTOR may represent promising experimental therapeutics in ASDs.

## SINGLE GENE DISORDERS WITH ASD AND EXPERIMENTAL TREATMENTS

Single gene disorders associated with high rates of comorbid ASD, such as Rett syndrome and Phelan-McDermid syndrome (PMS) have provided significant models of targeted interventions with novel experimental treatments.

### IGF-1 IN PHELAN-McDERMID SYNDROME (CHROMOSOME 22q13 DELETION SYNDROME)

The loss of a functional copy of the SHANK3 gene leads to 22q13 deletion syndrome, a complex clinical condition known as PMS. Haploinsufficiency of SHANK3 accounts for about 0.5% of cases of ASD and/or developmental delay (39). There is mounting evidence for a wider role of SHANK3 and glutamate signaling abnormalities in ASD and related conditions. IGF-1 regulates synapse formation, neurotransmitter release, and neuronal excitability via posttranslational modification of NMDA and AMPA receptors (40).

Therapeutic approaches with IGF-1 aimed at reversing deficits in SHANK3-haploinsufficiency have been carried out in mice. IGF-1 has been demonstrated to reverse the reduction in excitatory synapse numbers and density of neurons. Administration of daily intraperitoneal injections of human IGF-1 over a 2-week period was found to reverse deficits in hippocampal AMPA signaling, long-term potentiation (LTP), and motor performance in Shank3-deficient mice (41). These findings led to a current trial of IGF-1 as a treatment in PMS, which is still underway and expected to provide important clues on its role in the treatment of this ASD subtype (see text footnote 1 NCT0152590).

In a recent study, induced pluripotent stem cells (iPSCs) from individuals with PMS and autism were used to produce functional neurons. It was demonstrated that PMS neurons have reduced SHANK3 expression and major defects in excitatory, but not inhibitory, synaptic transmission. IGF-1 treatment promoted the formation of mature excitatory synapses that lack SHANK3 but contain PSD95 and NMDA receptors with fast deactivation kinetics. These findings provided evidence for a disruption in the ratio of E/I in PMS neurons, and they point to a molecular pathway that can be recruited to restore it (42).

### IGF-1 IN RETT SYNDROME

Studies in mouse and human neuronal models of Rett syndrome also demonstrated benefits with IGF-1 administration. In 90% of cases, Rett syndrome is caused by abnormalities on the MECP2 gene, by either deletions or mutations. IGF-1, highly expressed during brain development and very important for spine maturation, has been tested to overcome MECP2 deficit. Synaptic abnormalities have been observed in Rett syndrome related to genetic defects on the MECP2 gene (43). Treatment with IGF-1 in a mouse model of Rett syndrome has been shown to increase synaptic growth and to rescue phenotype defects (44). A phase II randomized placebo-controlled trial is underway to evaluate the safety and efficacy of IGF-1 in treating ASD symptoms and respiratory/autonomic dysfunction in patients with Rett syndrome (see text footnote 1 NCT01777542).

## INTRANASAL OXYTOCIN IN ASD

There has been growing interest in oxytocin as it is recognized to be implicated in social development and affiliative behaviors. Intranasal oxytocin has been shown to increase social initiative and motivation (45), as well as social cognition (46), and to reduce repetitive and restricted behaviors in ASD. Previous studies with oxytocin in ASD were conducted by single-dose administration to adults, therefore, the long-term effect of nasal oxytocin and its effect on children must still be clarified (47).

There have been only a few trials with intranasal oxytocin in children with ASD, and most were pilot studies on small numbers of patients. In one of the first double-blind studies, oxytocin nasal spray was found to improve emotion recognition in 16 male youth aged 12–19 with ASD (48). In a recent pilot study, 15 children and adolescents with ASD with verbal IQs of $\geq 70$ participated in a trial on the safety and tolerability of intranasal oxytocin. Repeated measures of regression analysis controlled for week, dose, age, and sex were employed. The highest dose evaluated, 0.4 IU/kg, was found to be well tolerated. Over 3 months of treatment, social cognition, repetitive behaviors, and anxiety were improved with the maintenance of effect for 3 months after discontinuation of treatment (49). In an open-label study, oxytocin was administered intranasaly over a long term of 7 months to eight male youths with ASD (10–14 years of age; IQ: 20–101). Six of the eight participants had improvement in the communication and social interaction domains at ADOS-G evaluation and at *T*-scores of the CBCL; however, no statistically significant improvement was found in the ABC (50). In a double-blind study with a controlled design, a group of 38 male youths (7–16 years old) with ASD were administered 24 or 12 IU, depending on weight, of intranasal placebo or oxytocin once daily over four consecutive days. The oxytocin or placebo was administered in a dynamic social condition, i.e., during parent–child interaction training sessions. In this study, intranasal oxytocin did not significantly improve social interaction skills, however it must be mentioned that it was an untested behavioral intervention, limiting the interpretation of results (51). Collectively, these studies demonstrated mixed results as to the outcome of core social impairment, with a tendency toward an improvement in social domains. Large-scale, double-blind placebo-controlled studies are needed to confirm the role of intranasal oxytocin in core social ASD dysfunction.

A randomized, double-blind cross over fMRI trial with intranasal oxytocin was conducted in a group of 17 ASD children and adolescents (age 8–16.5 years) to evaluate neural circuit modifications hypothesized after oxytocin administration (52). The Reading the Mind in the Eyes Test (RMET), a social cognition test (53) was used to investigate the brain areas under examination, and a remarkable variation was observed 45 min after oxytocin administration. Structures and circuits within the so-called social brain, such as the dorsal and ventral striatum, premotor cortex, posterior cingulate, and posterior–superior temporal sulcus, demonstrated enhanced activity after oxytocin administration. Moreover, changes in salivary oxytocin concentrations from baseline to 30 min post administration were positively associated with increased activity in the right amygdala and orbito-frontal cortex during social vs. non-social judgments. Furthermore, it was highlighted that oxytocin enhanced the salience of social stimuli, thus positively interfering with social cognition. These changes in the relevant brain areas of interest were observed following a single oxytocin administration and further research to test the persistence of these changes over time in long-term treatments is needed.

## NEW APPROACHES TO VERIFY TREATMENT EFFICACY

Neural circuit modification following treatment for ASD is a novel field of research that could shed light on the mechanisms involved in neural changes and in the search for the biomarkers of treatment response (54). Functional MRI is the main instrument for a dynamic investigation of the neural substrate. A case study in two children with ASD was carried out with functional MRI performed before and after an intensive intervention of 4 months of pivotal response training (PRT). PRT is an empirically validated behavioral treatment that has widespread positive effects on communication, behavior, and social skills in young children with ASD. Neural processing modifications during a biological motion task, a form of social information, were evaluated by fMRI. Outcome measures included the evaluation of dysfunctional areas identified in children with ASD, compared to typically developing children (right amygdala, bilateral fusiform gyri, left ventrolateral prefrontal, and right posterior superotemporal sulcus). After treatment, ASD children showed increased activation in the above listed areas, indicating that neural modifications had occurred and they overlapped with the brain area activations of their typically developing peers (55).

Another study, investigating neural changes in response to treatment, examined variations in EEG signaling after an intervention with the Early Start Denver Model (ESDM) in a group of 48 children with ASD, aged 18–30 months. Children with ASD were randomized into two groups; one received an ESDM intervention for 2 years and the other received only their previous treatment in the community. A typically developing group of children served as controls. Event related potentials (ERP) and EEG activity (spectral power) were detected during the presentation of faces versus objects. The ESDM group demonstrated a better outcome in ASD symptoms, IQ, language, and adaptive behavior than the others. Increased cortical activation, i.e., a reduction in alfa power and increased theta band, was detected in this group of children as well as in typically developing children when viewing faces, in contrast to the community intervention group that showed the opposite pattern with greater cortical activation when viewing objects. The limitation of this research was that it lacked a baseline evaluation (56).

## CONCLUSION AND FUTURE DIRECTIONS

Currently available medications mostly act upon selective symptoms of ASD, possibly offering a chance to further explore the specific mechanisms and circuits involved in etiological factors. Synaptic or circuit mechanisms associated with circumscribed aspects of ASD, e.g., social and communication domains, need to be thoroughly evaluated at the molecular and synaptic levels and possibly separated from the other symptoms/domains. Core mechanisms that cover distinct fractions of ASD would parallel the concept of core symptoms in ASD, based on the hypothesis that a group of protein factors converges on common pathways to be targeted (13). The next generation of animal models carrying human mutations will be of the utmost importance in uncovering the neural and molecular bases of ASD and to pave the way for clinical trials of treatments for core social domains. A homogeneous group of ASD individuals with phenotype and synaptic defects should be enrolled in pharmacological trials to test the efficacy and the safety of specific compounds. These trials would measure outcomes in the core social domain of ASD and also identify specific biomarkers for a wider perspective of treatment outcomes. Investigations of dynamic brain changes in ASD patients, using fMRI after treatments, would be extremely valuable in order to shed light on the neural underpinnings of core social impairment in these individuals.

## REFERENCES

1. Grzadzinski R, Huerta M, Lord C. DSM-5 and autism spectrum disorders (ASDs): an opportunity for identifying ASD subtypes. *Mol Autism* (2013) **4**:12. doi:10.1186/2040-2392-4-12
2. Centers for Disease Control. Prevalence of autism spectrum disorders – autism and developmental disabilities monitoring network, 14 sites, United States, 2008. *MMWR Surveill Summ* (2012) **61**(3):1–19.
3. Pedersen A, Pettygrove S, Meaney FJ, Mancilla K, Gotschall K, Kessler DB, et al. Prevalence of autism spectrum disorders in Hispanic and non-Hispanic white children. *Pediatrics* (2012) **129**(3):e629–35. doi:10.1542/peds.2011-1145
4. Zaroff CM, Uhm SY. Prevalence of autism spectrum disorders and influence of country of measurement and ethnicity. *Soc Psychiatry Psychiatr Epidemiol* (2012) **47**(3):395–8. doi:10.1007/s00127-011-0350-3
5. McCracken JT, McGough J, Shah B, Cronin P, Hong D, Aman MG, et al. Research units on pediatric psychopharmacology autism network (2002). Risperidone in children with autism and serious behavioral problems. *N Engl J Med* (2002) **347**:314–21. doi:10.1056/NEJMoa013171
6. Aman MG, Arnold LE, McDougle CJ, Vitiello B, Scahill L, Davies M, et al. Acute and long-term safety and tolerability of risperidone in children with autism. *J Child Adolesc Psychopharmacol* (2005) **15**:869–84. doi:10.1089/cap.2005.15.869
7. Ching H, Pringsheim T. Aripiprazole for autism spectrum disorders (ASD). *Cochrane Database Syst Rev* (2012) **16**(5):CD009043. doi:10.1002/14651858.CD009043.pub2

8. Farmer CA, Aman MG. Aripiprazole for the treatment of irritability associated with autism. *Expert Opin Pharmacother* (2011) **2011**(12):635–40. doi:10.1517/14656566.2011.557661
9. Murdoch JD, State MW. Recent developments in the genetics of autism spectrum disorders. *Curr Opin Genet Dev* (2013) **23**:310–5. doi:10.1016/j.gde.2013.02.003
10. Silverman JL, Crawley JN. The promising trajectory of autism therapeutics discovery. *Drug Discov Today* (2013). doi:10.1016/j.drudis.2013.12.007
11. Rubenstein JL, Merzenich MM. Model of autism: increased ratio of excitation/inhibition in key neural systems. *Genes Brain Behav* (2003) **2**:255–67. doi:10.1034/j.1601-183X.2003.00037.x
12. Yizhar O, Fenno LE, Prigge M, Schneider F, Davidson TJ, O'Shea DJ, et al. Neocortical excitation/inhibition balance in information processing and social dysfunction. *Nature* (2011) **477**(7363):171–8. doi:10.1038/nature10360
13. Won H, Mah W, Kim E. Autism spectrum disorder causes, mechanisms, and treatments: focus on neuronal synapses. *Front Mol Neurosci* (2013) **6**:19. doi:10.3389/fnmol.2013.00019
14. Wei H, Dobkin C, Sheikh AM, Malik M, Brown WT, Li X. The therapeutic effect of memantine through the stimulation of synapse formation and dendritic spine maturation in autism and Fragile X syndrome. *PLoS One* (2012) **7**:e36981. doi:10.1371/journal.pone.0036981
15. Burket JA, Herndon AL, Winebarger EE, Jacome LF, Deutsch SI. Complex effects of mGluR5 antagonism on sociability and stereotypic behaviors in mice: possible implications for the pharmacotherapy of autism spectrum disorders. *Brain Res Bull* (2011) **86**:152–8. doi:10.1016/j.brainresbull.2011.08.001
16. Silverman JL, Tolu SS, Barkan CL, Crawley JN. Repetitive self-grooming behavior in the BTBR mouse model of autism is blocked by the mGluR5 antagonist MPEP. *Neuropsychopharmacology* (2010) **35**(4):976–89. doi:10.1038/npp.2009.201
17. Silverman JL, Smith DG, Rizzo SJ, Karras MN, Turner SM, Tolu SS, et al. Negative allosteric modulation of the mGluR5 receptor reduces repetitive behaviors and rescues social deficits in mouse models of autism. *Sci Transl Med* (2012) **4**(131):131ra51. doi:10.1126/scitranslmed.3003501
18. Silverman JL, Oliver CF, Karras MN, Gastrell PT, Crawley JN. AMPAKINE enhancement of social interaction in the BTBR mouse model of autism. *Neuropharmacology* (2013) **64**:268–82. doi:10.1016/j.neuropharm.2012.07.013
19. Deutsch SI, Pepe GJ, Burket JA, Winebarger EE, Herndon AL, Benson AD. D-cycloserine improves sociability and spontaneous stereotypic behaviors in 4-week old mice. *Brain Res* (2012) **1439**:96–107. doi:10.1016/j.brainres.2011.12.040
20. Bozdagi O, Sakurai T, Papapetrou D, Wang X, Dickstein DL, Takahashi N, et al. Haploinsufficiency of the autism-associated Shank3 gene leads to deficits in synaptic function, social interaction, and social communication. *Mol Autism* (2010) **17**:1–15. doi:10.1186/2040-2392-1-15
21. Yang M, Bozdagi O, Scattoni ML, Wöhr M, Roullet FI, Katz AM, et al. Reduced excitatory neurotransmission and mild autism-relevant phenotypes in adolescent Shank3 null mutant mice. *J Neurosci* (2012) **32**(19):6525–41. doi:10.1523/JNEUROSCI.6107-11.2012
22. Canitano R, Scandurra V. Glutamatergic agents in ASD: current trends. *Res Autism Spectr Disord* (2014) **8**:255–65. doi:10.1016/j.rasd.2013.12.009
23. Coghlan S, Horder J, Inkster B, Mendez MA, Murphy DG, Nutt DJ. GABA system dysfunction in autism and related disorders: from synapse to symptoms. *Neurosci Biobehav Rev* (2013) **36**(9):2044–55. doi:10.1016/j.neubiorev.2012.07.005
24. Sgadò P, Genovesi S, Kalinovsky A, Zunino G, Macchi F, Allegra M, et al. Loss of GABAergic neurons in the hippocampus and cerebral cortex of Engrailed-2 null mutant mice: implications for autism spectrum disorders. *Exp Neurol* (2013) **247**:496–505. doi:10.1016/j.expneurol.2013.01.021
25. Sgadò P, Provenzano G, Dassi E, Adami V, Zunino G, Genovesi S, et al. Transcriptome profiling in engrailed-2 mutant mice reveals common molecular pathways associated with autism spectrum disorders. *Mol Autism* (2013) **4**(1):51. doi:10.1186/2040-2392-4-51
26. Brielmaier J, Matteson PG, Silverman JL, Senerth JM, Kelly S, Genestine M, et al. Autism-relevant social abnormalities and cognitive deficits in engrailed-2 knockout mice. *PLoS One* (2012) **7**(7):e40914. doi:10.1371/journal.pone.0040914
27. Chao HT, Chen H, Samaco RC, Xue M, Chahrour M, Yoo J, et al. Dysfunction in GABA signaling mediates autism-like stereotypies and Rett syndrome phenotypes. *Nature* (2010) **468**(7321):263–9. doi:10.1038/nature09582
28. Henderson C, Wijetunge L, Kinoshita MN, Shumway M, Hammond RS, Postma FR, et al. Reversal of disease-related pathologies in the fragile X mouse model by selective activation of GABAB receptors with arbaclofen. *Sci Transl Med* (2012) **4**(152):ra128. doi:10.1126/scitranslmed.3004218
29. Wang T, Bray SM, Warren ST. New perspectives on the biology of fragile X syndrome. *Curr Opin Genet Dev* (2012) **22**:256–63. doi:10.1016/j.gde.2012.02.002
30. Berry-Kravis EM, Hessl D, Rathmell B, Zarevics P, Cherubini M, Walton-Bowen K, et al. Effects of STX209 (arbaclofen) on neurobehavioral function in children and adults with fragile X syndrome: a randomized, controlled, phase 2 trial. *Sci Transl Med* (2012) **4**(152):ra127. doi:10.1126/scitranslmed.3004214
31. Erickson CA, Veenstra-Vanderweele JM, Melmed RD, McCracken JT, Ginsberg LD, Sikich L, et al. STX209 (arbaclofen) for autism spectrum disorders: an 8-week open-label study. *J Autism Dev Disord* (2013) **44**:958–64. doi:10.1007/s10803-013-1963-z
32. Wang H, Doering LC. Reversing autism by targeting downstream mTOR signaling. *Front Cell Neurosci* (2013) **7**:28. doi:10.3389/fncel.2013.00028
33. Bateup HS, Takasaki KT, Saulnier JL, Denefrio CL, Sabatini BL. Loss of Tsc1 *in vivo* impairs hippocampal mGluR-LTD and increases excitatory synaptic function. *J Neurosci* (2011) **31**:8862–9. doi:10.1523/JNEUROSCI.1617-11.2011
34. Luikart BW, Schnell E, Washburn EK, Bensen AL, Tovar KR, Westbrook GL. PTEN knockdown *in vivo* increases excitatory drive onto dentate granule cells. *J Neurosci* (2011) **31**:4345–54. doi:10.1523/JNEUROSCI.0061-11.2011
35. Sahin M. Targeted treatment trials for tuberous sclerosis and autism: no longer a dream. *Curr Opin Neurobiol* (2012) **22**:1–7. doi:10.1016/j.conb.2012.04.008
36. Burket JA, Benson AD, Tang AH, Deutsch SI. Rapamycin improves sociability in the BTBR T(+)Itpr3(tf)/J mouse model of autism spectrum disorders. *Brain Res Bull* (2014) **100**:70–5. doi:10.1016/j.brainresbull.2013.11.005
37. Gkogkas CG, Khoutorsky A, Ran I, Rampakakis E, Nevarko T, Weatherill DB, et al. Autism-related deficits via dysregulated eIF4E-dependent translational control. *Nature* (2013) **493**:371–7. doi:10.1038/nature11628
38. Santini E, Huynh TN, MacAskill AF, Carter AG, Pierre P, Ruggero D, et al. Exaggerated translation causes synaptic and behavioural aberrations associated with autism. *Nature* (2013) **493**:411–5. doi:10.1038/nature11782
39. Boccuto L, Lauri M, Sarasua SM, Skinner CD, Buccella D, Dwivedi A, et al. Prevalence of SHANK3 variants in patients with different subtypes of autism spectrum disorders. *Eur J Hum Genet* (2013) **21**:310–6. doi:10.1038/ejhg.2012.175
40. Torres-Aleman I. Toward a comprehensive neurobiology of IGF-I. *Dev Neurobiol* (2010) **70**:384–96. doi:10.1002/dneu.20778
41. Bozdagi O, Tavassoli T, Buxbaum JD. Insulin-like growth factor-1 rescues synaptic and motor deficits in a mouse model of autism and developmental delay. *Mol Autism* (2013) **27**(4):9. doi:10.1186/2040-2392-4-9
42. Shcheglovitov A, Shcheglovitova O, Yazawa M, Portmann T, Shu R, Sebastiano V, et al. SHANK3 and IGF1 restore synaptic deficits in neurons from 22q13 deletion syndrome patients. *Nature* (2013) **503**:267–71. doi:10.1038/nature12618
43. Banerjee A, Castro J, Sur M. Rett syndrome: genes, synapses, circuits, and therapeutics. *Front Psychiatry* (2012) **3**:34. doi:10.3389/fpsyt.2012.00034
44. Tropea D, Giacometti E, Wilson NR, Beard C, McCurry C, Fu DD, et al. Partial reversal of Rett syndrome-like symptoms in MeCP2 mutant mice. *Proc Natl Acad Sci U S A* (2009) **106**:2029–34. doi:10.1073/pnas.0812394106
45. Andari E, Duhamel JR, Zalla T, Herbrecht E, Leboyer M, Sirigu A. Promoting social behavior with oxytocin in high-functioning autism spectrum disorders. *Proc Natl Acad Sci U S A* (2010) **107**:4389–94. doi:10.1073/pnas.0910249107
46. Bartz JA, Hollander E. Oxytocin and experimental therapeutics in autism spectrum disorders. *Prog Brain Res* (2008) **170**:451–62. doi:10.1016/S0079-6123(08)00435-4
47. Baribeau DA, Anagnostou E. Social communication is an emerging target for pharmacotherapy in autism spectrum disorder – a review of the literature on potential agents. *J Can Acad Child Adolesc Psychiatry* (2014) **23**:20–30.
48. Guastalla AJ, Einfeld SL, Gray KM, Rinehart NJ, Tonge BJ, Lambert TJ, et al. Intranasal oxytocin improves emotion recognition for youth with autism spectrum disorders. *Biol Psychiatry* (2010) **67**:692–4. doi:10.1016/j.biopsych.2009.09.020
49. Anagnostou E, Soorya L, Brian J, Dupuis A, Mankad D, Smile S, et al. Intranasal oxytocin in the treatment of autism spectrum disorders: a review of literature and early safety and efficacy data in youth. *Brain Res* (2014). doi:10.1016/j.brainres.2014.01.049
50. Tachibana M, Kagitani-Shimono K, Mohri I, Yamamoto T, Sanefuji W, Nakamura A, et al. Long-term administration of intranasal oxytocin is a safe and promising therapy for early adolescent boys with autism spectrum disorders. *J Child Adolesc Psychopharmacol* (2013) **23**:123–7. doi:10.1089/cap.2012.0048

51. Dadds MR, Macdonald E, Cauchi A, Williams K, Levy F, Brennan J. Nasal oxytocin for social deficits in childhood autism: a randomized controlled trial. *J Autism Dev Disord* (2014) **44**:521–31. doi:10.1007/s10803-013-1899-3
52. Gordon I, Vander Wyk BC, Bennett RH, Cordeaux C, Lucas MV, Eilbott JA, et al. Oxytocin enhances brain function in children with autism. *Proc Natl Acad Sci U S A* (2013) **110**:20953–8. doi:10.1073/pnas.1312857110
53. Baron-Cohen S, Wheelwright S, Hill J, Raste Y, Plumb I. The "reading the mind in the eyes" test, revised version: a study with normal adults, and adults with Asperger syndrome or high-functioning autism. *J Child Psychol Psychiatry* (2001) **42**:241–51. doi:10.1111/1469-7610.00715
54. Ventola PE, Oosting D, Anderson LC, Pelphrey KA. Brain mechanisms of plasticity in response to treatment for core deficits in autism. *Prog Brain Res* (2013) **207**:255–72. doi:10.1016/B978-0-444-63327-9.00007-2
55. Voos AC, Pelphrey KA, Tirrell J, Bolling DZ, Vander Wyk B, Kaiser MD, et al. Neural mechanisms of improvements in social motivation after pivotal response treatment: two case studies. *J Autism Dev Disord* (2013) **43**:1–10. doi:10.1007/s10803-012-1683-9
56. Dawson G, Jones EJ, Merkle K, Venema K, Lowy R, Faja S, et al. Early behavioral intervention is associated with normalized brain activity in young children with autism. *J Am Acad Child Adolesc Psychiatry* (2012) **51**:1150–9. doi:10.1016/j.jaac.2012.08.018

# 14

# Autism as a disorder of biological and behavioral rhythms: toward new therapeutic perspectives

**Sylvie Tordjman[1,2]*, Katherine S. Davlantis[3], Nicolas Georgieff[4], Marie-Maude Geoffray[4], Mario Speranza[5], George M. Anderson[6], Jean Xavier[7], Michel Botbol[1,8], Cécile Oriol[2], Eric Bellissant[9,10], Julie Vernay-Leconte[11], Claire Fougerou[9,10], Anne Hespel[9,10], Aude Tavenard[9,10], David Cohen[7], Solenn Kermarrec[1,2], Nathalie Coulon[1], Olivier Bonnot[1] and Geraldine Dawson[3]**

[1] *Laboratoire Psychologie de la Perception, Université Paris Descartes, CNRS, UMR 8158, Paris, France*
[2] *Pôle Hospitalo-Universitaire de Psychiatrie de l'Enfant et de l'Adolescent (PHUPEA), Centre Hospitalier Guillaume Régnier, Université de Rennes 1, Rennes, France*
[3] *Department of Psychiatry and Behavioral Sciences, Duke University School of Medicine, Durham, NC, USA*
[4] *Department of Child and Adolescent Psychiatry, Centre Hospitalier Le Vinatier, Lyon, France*
[5] *Department of Child and Adolescent Psychiatry, Centre Hospitalier de Versailles, Université de Versailles Saint-Quentin-en-Yvelines, Le Chensay, France*
[6] *Child Study Center, Yale University School of Medicine, New Haven, CT, USA*
[7] *Department of Child and Adolescent Psychiatry, Assistance Publique – Hôpitaux de Paris, Groupe Hospitalier Pitié-Salpêtrière, CNRS FRE 2987, University Pierre and Marie Curie, Paris, France*
[8] *Service Hospitalo-Universitaire de Psychiatrie de l'Enfant et de l'Adolescent, CHU de Brest, Université de Bretagne Occidentale, Brest, France*
[9] *Clinical Investigation Center, INSERM CIC 0203, University Hospital, Rennes 1 University, Rennes, France*
[10] *Department of Clinical Pharmacology, University Hospital, Rennes 1 University, Rennes, France*
[11] *Pôle Hospitalo-Universitaire de Psychiatrie Adulte (PHUPA), Centre Hospitalier Guillaume Régnier, Université de Rennes 1, Rennes, France*

***Edited by:***
*Roberto Canitano, University Hospital of Siena, Italy*

***Reviewed by:***
*Rajshekhar Bipeta, Gandhi Medical College and Hospital, India*
*Felipe Ortuño, Clínica Universidad de Navarra, Spain*
*Roberto Canitano, University Hospital of Siena, Italy*

****Correspondence:***
*Sylvie Tordjman, Hospitalo-Universitaire de Psychiatrie de l'Enfant et de l'Adolescent, 154 rue de Châtillon, Rennes 35200, France*
*e-mail: s.tordjman@yahoo.fr*

There is a growing interest in the role of biological and behavioral rhythms in typical and atypical development. Recent studies in cognitive and developmental psychology have highlighted the importance of rhythmicity and synchrony of motor, emotional, and interpersonal rhythms in early development of social communication. The synchronization of rhythms allows tuning and adaptation to the external environment. The role of melatonin in the ontogenetic establishment of circadian rhythms and the synchronization of the circadian clocks network suggests that this hormone might be also involved in the synchrony of motor, emotional, and interpersonal rhythms. Autism provides a challenging model of physiological and behavioral rhythm disturbances and their possible effects on the development of social communication impairments and repetitive behaviors and interests. This article situates autism as a disorder of biological and behavioral rhythms and reviews the recent literature on the role of rhythmicity and synchrony of rhythms in child development. Finally, the hypothesis is developed that an integrated approach focusing on biological, motor, emotional, and interpersonal rhythms may open interesting therapeutic perspectives for children with autism. More specifically, promising avenues are discussed for potential therapeutic benefits in autism spectrum disorder of melatonin combined with developmental behavioral interventions that emphasize synchrony, such as the Early Start Denver Model.

**Keywords: autism spectrum disorder, biological rhythms, motor, emotional and relational rhythms, synchronization of rhythms, melatonin, Early Start Denver Model, therapeutics**

## INTRODUCTION

Endogenous physiological variations involved in biological rhythms reflect adaptation to the environment. Thus, the sleep–wake rhythm associated with biological circadian rhythms can be viewed as an adaptation to the day–night cycle. Circadian rhythms allow temporal organization of biological functions in relation to environmental changes (1). The periodicity of activities applies to all biological, physiological, and psychological functions; recently, the science of biological rhythms, chronobiology, has emerged with its own theory, science, and education (2).

Furthermore, recent studies in the field of cognitive and developmental psychology have highlighted the importance of rhythmicity and synchrony of motor, emotional, and relational rhythms in early development of social communication. Given the major role of the sleep hormone melatonin in the ontogenetic establishment of diurnal rhythms, the synchronization of peripheral oscillators (also termed clocks) and the regulation of human circadian rhythms (1), melatonin might be involved in the synchrony of motor, emotional, and relational rhythms.

Indeed, relationships might exist, based on the hypothesis of ergodicity (3), between cellular communication networks involving a cellular synchrony (synchronization of cellular oscillations by melatonin) and early social communication development involving a synchrony of motor, emotional, and interpersonal rhythms. Autism spectrum disorder (ASD) – a developmental disorder characterized by social communication impairments associated with repetitive interests and behaviors – provides an interesting and challenging model of abnormal melatonin production in early developmental disorders and its possible relationship with autistic behavioral impairments.

This article proposes a central role of rhythmicity and synchrony of rhythms in typical child development and offers a new integrative approach, which considers autism as a disorder of biological and behavioral rhythms. In this perspective, promising avenues will be discussed in this article for potential therapeutic benefits in ASD of melatonin and developmental behavioral interventions that emphasize rhythms and synchronization, such as the Early Start Denver Model (ESDM).

## PHYSIOLOGICAL AND BEHAVIORAL RHYTHM DISTURBANCES IN AUTISM

### AUTISM AS A DISORDER OF BIOLOGICAL RHYTHMS

Alterations in circadian sleep–wake rhythm have frequently been reported in autism (4, 5). More specifically, reduced total sleep and longer sleep latency as well as nocturnal and early morning awakenings are often observed in individuals with ASD (6–12). Furthermore, prior studies on melatonin in autism have all reported abnormalities in melatonin secretion (see **Table 1**). In addition, abnormalities in cortisol circadian rhythm have also been reported in autism [for a review, see Tordjman et al. (13)]. In particular, significantly higher frequency of absence of circadian variation in melatonin and cortisol levels was observed in individuals with autism compared to typically developing controls. Golombek et al. (14) described the effects of circadian desynchronization that can enhance susceptibility to certain disorders (metabolic, immune, cognitive, and somatic disorders including cancer). It is noteworthy that congenitally blind children with consequently abnormal melatonin secretion and synchronization [the production of pineal-derived melatonin depends on the light acting through the retinohypothalamic tract (15)] very frequently display autism [up to 42% (16)], whereas hearing impaired children, including hearing loss, show autism less frequently [up to 10% (17)]. More specifically, abnormally low daytime and nighttime melatonin secretion was associated with an absence of melatonin circadian variation in some individuals with autism (18, 19), which in turn, given the role of synchronizer of melatonin, also has consequences on the circadian rhythms network, including the cortisol circadian rhythm (13, 20).

This blunted circadian rhythmicity with no or little variability might be related to the difficulties in adapting to changes typically observed in individuals with autism. Thus, children with autism who are confronted with physiological continuity due to absent circadian rhythms may have difficulties adapting to changes in either their external or their internal environment (26). Indeed, as previously underlined, the circadian clocks network, synchronized by melatonin and involving an internal system of continuity/discontinuity, allows adaptation to environmental changes.

Similarly, blunted circadian rhythmicity may explain the difficulty observed in many children with autism in adapting to

**Table 1 | Studies of melatonin levels in individuals with autism.**

| Study | Sample | Study group | Measured variable | Results |
|---|---|---|---|---|
| Ritvo et al. (21) | Urine | Young adults with autism ($N = 10$) | Melatonin concentration | Increased daytime values compared to typically developing controls<br>Similar nighttime values compared to typically developing controls |
| Nir et al. (22) | Serum | Young men with autism ($N = 10$) | Melatonin concentration | Increased daytime values compared to typically developing controls<br>Decreased nighttime values compared to typically developing controls |
| Kulman et al. (19) | Serum | Children with autism ($N = 14$) | Melatonin concentration (24-h circadian rhythm) | Decreased nighttime values compared to typically developing controls<br>No circadian variation in 10/14 (71.4%) children with autism<br>Inverted rhythm in 4/14 (28.6%) children with autism |
| Tordjman et al. (23) | Urine | Children and adolescents with autism ($N = 49$) | 6-Sulphatoxymelatonin excretion rate (12-h collection) | Decreased nighttime values compared to typically developing controls |
| Melke et al. (24) | Plasma | Adolescents and young adults with autism ($N = 43$) | Melatonin concentration | Decreased daytime values compared to typically developing controls |
| Mulder et al. (25) | Urine | Children and adolescents with autism ($N = 20$) | 6-Sulphatoxymelatonin excretion rate (24-h collection) | Trend to lower 24-h melatonin excretion rate in hyperserotonemic compared to normoserotonemic individuals with autism |
| Tordjman et al. (18) | Urine | Post-pubertal adolescents and young adults with autism ($N = 43$) | 6-Sulphatoxymelatonin excretion rate (split 24-h collection) | Decreased daytime values compared to typically developing controls<br>Decreased nighttime values compared to typically developing controls<br>No circadian variation in 10/43 (23.2%) individuals with autism |

changes in rhythms of their external and internal environment. Thus, rapid rhythms of sensory stimuli in their external environment (e.g., repeated visual stimuli provided by a stroboscopic light) can provoke epileptic seizure in some individuals with autism [approximately one-third of children with autism have epilepsy (27)]. Interestingly, EEG changes tended to be correlated with an abnormal rhythm of melatonin in young adults with autism (22). Furthermore, some parents have reported that their daughters with autism experience epileptic seizures toward the 14th day of their menstrual cycle, which is when luteinizing hormone (LH) levels peak (Tordjman, personal communication), suggesting quite tentatively that individuals with autism may have difficulties adapting to periodic hormonal changes in their internal environment. We can state the following hypothesis: a change in rhythm associated with excessive environmental stimuli might strongly increase arousal and lead to physiological stress which, for some individuals with autism, can disturb the rhythmic activity of a particular brain area, leading it to fall out of sync with the rest of the brain and causing its population of neurons to fire (depolarization and occurrence of an epileptic seizure). This underlines the importance of stable physiological rhythms.

Finally, significant relationships have been found between lower nocturnal melatonin excretion and increased severity of autistic social communication impairments, especially for verbal communication and social imitative play (18, 23). These findings are in agreement with studies suggesting an association between reduced melatonin production and language impairment (22, 28). Along the same line, the systemic administration in the animal model of Zebra Finch of a melatonin-1B receptor antagonist at the beginning of the night shortens the song and motif length and affects the song syllable lengths produced the next day (29). Reduced melatonin activity might create timing problems in biological clocks with physiological and psychological effects that might be, according to Boucher's model of autism (30) and Wimpory's theory (31), involved in autistic impairments, notably in autistic social communication impairments. It is noteworthy that deficiency in oxytocin [oxytocin is considered a bonding hormone (32, 33)] has also been reported in autism (34, 35) and bonding is involved in the development of very early social interaction in infants. Interestingly, the release of oxytocin by the posterior pituitary gland follows a robust circadian rhythm in mammals. Further studies are needed to better understand the underlying mechanisms of oxytocin anomalies in autism and to explore, in particular, possible oxytocin rhythm disturbances in ASD. The importance of the synchrony of rhythms in the development of social interaction and communication is detailed in the next section.

## IMPORTANCE OF SYNCHRONY OF RHYTHMS FOR SOCIAL COMMUNICATION IN TYPICAL DEVELOPMENT AND AUTISM SPECTRUM DISORDER

Several studies, based on animal models and human perinatal development, suggest that stable patterns of repeated stimuli in the form of maternal physiological rhythms, involving cross-modal perception such as regular cardiac rhythm, which provides the fetus with auditory and vibratory stimuli, allow the fetus to integrate sensory information facilitating prenatal perceptual learning and develop a coherent representation of his or her internal and external environment (36–38). Fluctuations in the physiological rhythms (variants), such as variations in the maternal cardiac rhythm and also variations in hormone levels involved in the circadian rhythms that are already present during the fetus life (the fetus' circadian rhythms are the mother's ones), occurring in a background of regular repetition of identical sequences (invariants), may help the fetus to develop the ability to adapt to change in an environment characterized by high regularity. As previously emphasized (38), very early mother–infant relations provide a secure environment based on the repetition of invariants, while at the same time promoting adaptation to change through the presence of variants. It is through the regular repetition of identical sequences of discontinuity, such as circadian rhythms, that a continuum is constructed associated with the development of adaptation to changes.

The development of the very earliest form of communication relies on the sharing of emotions between mother and infant, when, for example, the infant is suckling in his or her mother's arms, through emotional synchrony that enhances the integration of sensory inputs (39, 40). Concerning memory processes, emotions enable to "fix" events, just as a photographic fixing agent sets images (38). Cortisol (a stress and arousal neurohormone) crosses the placental barrier. The cortisol circadian rhythm, as well as the melatonin circadian rhythm in the fetus and infant after birth, are those of maternal cortisol and melatonin. Indeed, the infant's circadian cortisol and melatonin rhythms are only established between 2 and 3 months of age in typical development, at the same time that infants begin to have more regular sleep–wake cycles associated with nighttime sleep lasting 6–8 h (41, 42). Interestingly, this period coincides in typical development with the emergence of social smiling by the second month of life (43), the advent of mirror self-recognition at around 3 months of age (44), and increased brain activation to speech occurring between 3 and 4 months of age (45).

At birth, the human immaturity of the cerebral cortex allows initial learning to influence the neural architecture through perceptual-action mapping (46, 47). The infant's social skills, especially including imitation, shared attention, and empathic understanding, also contribute to the development of learning (46, 48). Social synchrony can be defined as the dynamic and reciprocal adaptation of the temporal structure of behaviors between interactive partners (49). In typically developing children, the quality of social interaction depends on an active dialog between the parent and the infant (50, 51). Numerous studies have been emphasizing the importance of parent–infant synchrony and the construction of shared timing in social communication development (52).

Also, biological markers were associated with relational synchrony. First, oxytocin administration to parent enhances infant physiological and behavioral readiness for social engagement and parallels an oxytocin increase in infants (32). Second, neural correlates were found using hyper-scanning recordings of EEG brain activity and measures of neural synchronization between distant brain regions of interacting individuals through a free imitation task (53). Dumas and colleagues' study (53) was the first to record dual EEG activity in dyads of subjects during spontaneous non-verbal interaction. Eleven same-sex pairs were scanned. They found that interpersonal rhythmic oscillations were correlated with the emergence of synchronization in the brain's alpha–mu band between the right centro-parietal regions (an area involved in social interaction) of both participants. Developmental psychologists now study interaction not only as the addition of two behaviors but also as a global phenomenon in which synchrony is considered as social *per se*. To describe the dialog between two partners engaged in behavioral and affective exchange, developmental psychologists more and more take into consideration rhythm and temporal course of both behavior and affect, regarded as key expressions of adaptation during interaction (49, 52).

Only a few studies have addressed the importance of infant–caregiver synchrony/reciprocity in the development of social communication involving infants who subsequently are diagnosed with autism. It appears appropriate in the field of autism to consider the combined domain of social communication, as the most recent version of the ADOS scale does, as well as the recently released DSM-5 American classification. Methods to investigate this issue include studies using early home videos (54), parental interviews focusing on early abnormalities (55), and prospective assessment of children at risk of ASD (e.g., siblings) (56, 57). Studies have revealed a pervasive developmental course in infants who were later diagnosed with ASD. Thus, the first signs were abnormalities in eye contact, imitation, disengagement, joint attention, orienting to name, and body language. These behaviors are parts of the affective tuning disturbances; the term affective tuning, defined by Stern (58) as the "execution of behaviors expressing the emotional ownership of a shared affective state," refers to infant–caregiver emotional communication based on rhythmic similarity from the second semester of life onward. Also, these behaviors are important precursors of later-developing symptoms. However, whether these first signs impair early infant–parent interactions and whether they reflect already autistic behavioral impairments in the infant remain to be explored. In two related studies based on home movies of children later diagnosed with autism, Saint-Georges et al. (54) and Cohen et al. (59) showed that motor and emotional asynchrony was present between infants and parents before 12 months of age, and parents perceived weaker initiatives from their children. In addition, parents experienced weaker interactive responsiveness from their children and increasingly tried to compensate this perceived deficit by soliciting behaviors through touching the infant. This was particularly observed after 12 months of age for the fathers of infants who were later diagnosed with autism.

Many authors have studied imitation in children with autism (imitation of other people's faces, gestures, or vocal signals) in order to better understand the development of autistic social communication impairments. This specific type of imitation is referred to as "spatial" imitation to highlight the capacity to produce an instantaneous copy of the form of the signal. However, another way to communicate with others is to perform a "temporal" imitation of their behavior (60). This is what humans do through rhythmic finger or foot taping, dancing, singing, and drumming in synchrony with others (61). Xavier et al. (62) highlighted the importance of rhythmicity and synchrony in the development of children's imitative exchanges with peers. From birth, a child has a predisposition to engage, intersubjectively, with the rhytmic actions and awareness of other persons, and to move in synchrony with them (44, 63). Synchronic imitation is an important preverbal way to communicate among peers (64, 65). This reciprocal experience concerns two children able and motivated to coordinate their behavior with the non-ritualized behavior of the other, in both form and timing and to alternate turns between model and imitator (66). The impression of fluidity in the coordination of movements between partners is underlined by mutual attention, engagement, continuous adaptation, and turn taking (67). This rhythmic process made of ludic spontaneous imitation reveals moments of discontinuity occurring in a background of continuity. Neural bases of this coupling activity are constituted by the neuron mirrors system (68), with the same evidence showing that the neuronal structures involved when a mental state is experienced, are also recruited during the observation of others. Guionnet et al. (69) designed a free imitation paradigm in an fMRI study to examine some neural correlates of social interaction. Their results agree with those previously evidenced (70, 71) concerning the core circuit of imitation, but they found different activations between the situation of imitating and that of being imitated.

A special quality of temporal imitation is the ability to use different motor movements in order to communicate. Thus, simple finger tapping can be synchronized with another's head nodding or trunk movements, whether entrained by one of the movements or in response to external synchronizing stimuli such as music. Although animals and humans can perceive rhythms and produce rhythmic motor patterns, only humans can adapt their rhythmic movements to external rhythms (72) [with the exception of the cockatoo (73)]. The ability to be rhythmically synchronized with the environment appears important for infant development in the emotional, cognitive, social, and sensorimotor realms (44, 74). It has been demonstrated that the human fetus and newborn already have the capacity to perceive and produce rhythms (75). The ability to produce temporally adapted motor patterns comes later and depends on the specific motor system involved and the relationship between the beat presented and the spontaneously occurring motor tempo of the infant (76, 77). It should be fruitful to longitudinally examine children with autism in terms of ability to adapt their own rhythm to external rhythms. Interestingly, clinical observations suggest that some children with autism are able to respond to an external rhythmic vocalization by a similar rhythmic motor pattern such as hand flapping (Tordjman, personal communication). However, previous studies reported disorganized rhythms, stereotypies, and poor synchrony in most of these children (78), which might be related to the low melatonin levels reported to be associated in autism with the severity of verbal communication and social imitative play impairments (18, 23). Melatonin, as a regulator of physiological rhythms and oscillations, might enhance the capacity of children with ASD to synchronize their movements with movements of others (this synchronization of movements is needed for imitative play) and with external rhythmic auditory stimuli (such as music and/or human voice enhancing their verbal skills). Interestingly, in a study of social smiling in infants (79), there was no difference in frequency of smiling between 2- and 5-month-old infants with and without ASD during infant–caregiver face-to-face interactions. However, whereas typically developing infants showed a significant increase in smiling rate when caregivers were smiling, smiling in infants later diagnosed with ASD was not synchronized with smiling in caregivers and was not contingent upon caregiver behavior (caregiver facial expressions and vocalizations). Furthermore, it is noteworthy that, as previously indicated in this section, the infant's melatonin circadian rhythm is established between 2 and 3 months of age, and a study (80) reported that eye contact was normal in 2-month-old infants later diagnosed with autism but declined between 2 and 6 months of age, suggesting an additional argument in favor of a possible relationship between the well-replicated nocturnal melatonin deficit in autism (see **Table 1**) and the development of autistic social communication impairments.

### REPETITIVE BEHAVIORS AND INTERESTS

Repetitive behaviors and interests are defined, according to DSM-5 criteria (81), as a repetition of identical sequences of behaviors for motor stereotypies (motor stereotypies involve repetitive maladaptive movements) or thoughts for restrictive patterns of interests (restrictive and repetitive interests involve fixated interests, adherence to routines, or ritualized and rigid thinking patterns). Thus, repetitive behaviors and interests can be viewed as behavioral responses to the need to create discontinuity that is repeated at regular intervals, which could have been fundamentally lacking in the physiological development of children with autism due to the melatonin deficit reported in autism. Our finding (18) observed in a sample of 43 adolescents and young adults with autism (nocturnal excretion of 6-SM was significantly negatively correlated with repetitive use of objects), taken together with improvement of stereotyped behaviors following administration of melatonin in 24 children and adolescents with ASD (82), supports this hypothesis.

The autistic deficit in melatonin secretion might lead to physiological rhythm disturbances in autism impairing biological circadian rhythms and even, in certain cases, to an "endless" physiological continuity provoked by the absence of variation in melatonin levels. From this perspective, stereotyped behaviors and interests can be seen as offering to children with autism rhythmic forms providing rhythmicity and discontinuity through the creation of repeated identical patterns. Albert Goldbeter (83), director of the Chronobiology Unit at the Brussels Sciences University, underlines that life is rhythm. It is noteworthy that the word pineal comes from pine cone that is a Mesopotamian symbol representing the source of life and the power of regeneration. In Asia, the pineal gland is considered as the 7th chakra and represents the location of the soul and the highest level of consciousness.

Donald Winnicott (84) emphasized that "the main problem for a typically developing child is to be able to create a continuum out of discontinuity." According to him, the first optimal container ("holding environment") for the newborn is the progressive internalization of the rhythmic structures of feeding (rhythmic ebb and flow corresponding to the kinesthetic experience of suckling), providing a sense of continuing existence. We can nevertheless hypothesize, as we did in the previous section and in a prior article (26), that this internalization process starts far earlier, in the womb, through maternal physiological rhythms; conversely, based on clinical observations in autism, children with autism create discontinuity out of continuity. We can also state the hypothesis that children with autism, confronted with an "endless" physiological continuity (or at least with an absence of physiological discontinuities repeated at regular intervals), would develop anxiety and stress due to the lack of secure stable rhythms, and would therefore try to create by themselves rhythmicity in order to control them through stereotyped behaviors. However, the relationships between stereotyped behaviors and stress responses or anxiety need to be clarified given discrepant results reported in some studies (85, 86).

Finally, it should be noted that several studies have also recently opened new behavioral, neurobiological, and pharmacological perspectives on autistic repetitive behaviors, especially on self-injurious behaviors [for a review, see Adler et al. (87), Minshawi et al. (88), and Stigler (89)]. Thus, research on potential therapeutic effects for repetitive behaviors and interests should investigate benefits of melatonin in ASD (see next section) but should not be limited to the administration of melatonin.

## THERAPEUTIC BENEFITS OF MELATONIN IN AUTISM SPECTRUM DISORDER

Published melatonin treatment studies in autism are presented in **Table 2**. Many have been most concerned with effects of melatonin on sleep. Reviews, commentaries, and meta analyses of melatonin treatment studies are presented in **Table 3**. These two tables come from a prior article of our team (26).

As previously discussed (26), the treatment studies have a number of limitations. In some studies individuals covering a wide age range were included with pre-pubertal, pubertal, and post-pubertal individuals being studied (102, 103, 105). Reported differences in pineal melatonin secretion according to age and pubertal stage, coupled with the clearly developmental nature of autism, suggests that therapeutic effects of melatonin might vary considerably with age and pubertal status (23). Studies have also been limited by small sample sizes (90–93, 95, 96, 98, 102, 104). In larger studies, heterogeneous groups are often examined and have included blind individuals and individuals with various neurological disabilities with concomitant intellectual disability. In such studies, often results seen for the autism subgroup are not separately presented (97, 100, 103–107). The specificity and interpretation of the results with respect to autism are often unclear. Additional research is needed to determine whether and which findings might be specific to autism or whether melatonin's effect might be similar across groups. It can be hypothesized that melatonin's effects are due to actions on certain behavioral dimensions and that they can be observed across disorders. However, it should be pointed out that in our studies (18, 23), lower melatonin excretion was significantly associated with social communication impairments rather than with sleep problems. Future studies of melatonin in ASD should simultaneously examine melatonin levels, sleep problems, autistic behavioral impairments, and level of functioning so that a more complete picture can emerge.

It is worth noting that just a few of the therapeutic trials of melatonin have assessed effects on autistic behavioral impairments. These include reports of improved communication (105), reduced social withdrawal (82, 99), decreased stereotyped behaviors and rigidity (82, 102), and reduced anxiety (99, 103). Furthermore, at time the improvements noted were not sufficiently detailed. For example, Wright et al. (105) reported significant

**Table 2 | Studies on potential therapeutic benefits of melatonin in autism.**

| Study | Journal | Population | Design | Duration of treatment | Melatonin (formulation, dose) | Time of intake | Main outcome measures | Effects on sleep | Other outcomes | Comments |
|---|---|---|---|---|---|---|---|---|---|---|
| **SINGLE CASE REPORTS** | | | | | | | | | | |
| Horrigan and Barnhill (90) | *J Am Acad Child Adolesc Psychiatry* | 17-year-old boy with Asperger's Syndrome (AS) | – | Not given | 3 mg | 20–30 min before bedtime (BB) | Sleep | Sleep improvement. No side effects | Daytime behavior improvement | – |
| Hayashi (91) | *Psychiatry Clin Neurosci* | 14-year-old boy with autistic disorder, severe intellectual disability and phase delay with polyphasic sleep | – | 4 months | Immediate release (IR) 6 mg | 11:00 p.m. | Sleep | Melatonin increased sleep duration. No side effects | None | – |
| Jan et al. (92) | *Dev Med Child Neurol* | 12-year-old boy with AS and complex sleep disturbance (phase delay and parasomnias) | – | 6 months | Controlled release (CR) 5 mg | 30 min BB | Sleep | Normalization of the sleep–wake rhythm and disappearance of parasomnias. No side effects | None | – |
| **RETROSPECTIVE STUDIES** | | | | | | | | | | |
| Gupta and Hutchins (93) | *Arch Dis Child* | 9 cases of children with autistic disorder (AD) aged from 2 to 11 years. Chronic sleep problems | Not given | 1 week to 1 year | IR 2.5–5 mg | 45 min BB | Parental evaluation of sleep | 56% showed improvement in total sleep duration | None | No standardized collection of sleep variables |
| Andersen et al. (94) | *J Child Neurol* | 107 children and adolescents aged from 2 to 18 years with ASD (DSM-IV): 71% AD, 5% AS, 19% PDDNOS (pervasive developmental disorder not otherwise specified) | Not given | Mean duration: 1.8 years | IR in 91% of the cases. Dose escalation protocol from 1 to 6 mg based upon age | 30–60 min BB | Parental evaluation of sleep | Parents reported full (25%) or partial (60%) improvement. Beneficial effects of melatonin seem to stop after 3–12 months despite the use of higher doses. Side effects observed in 3 children: sleepiness, fogginess, increased enuresis | None | No standardized collection of sleep variables. The loss of response to melatonin treatment is discussed in the text |
| Galli-Carminatti et al. (95) | *Swiss Med Wkly* | 6 adult patients with AD (CIM-10) and intellectual disability, aged from 19 to 52 years | Not given | 6 months | IR. Dose escalation protocol from 3 to 9 mg if clinically required | 45 min BB | Sleep (CGI-S and CGI-I) | Improvement in sleep onset latency, night and early morning awakenings. No side effects | None | No standardized collection of sleep variables. Two to four associated psychotropic drugs per patient |
| **OPEN-LABEL TRIALS** | | | | | | | | | | |
| Jan et al. (96) | *Dev Med Child Neurol* | 15 children with multiple neurological disabilities and severe sleep disorders | Not given | Not given | 2–10 mg | Bedtime | Not given | Partial improvement in sleep disorders. No side effects | Behavior and social improvement | Heterogeneous sleep disorders and neurological disabilities |
| Ishizaki et al. (97) | *No To Hattatsu* | 50 children and young adults with autism ($n = 27$) or mental retardation ($n = 20$) or severe motor/intellectual disability ($n = 3$) aged from 3 to 28 years with sleep disorders | Not given | Not given | Not given | Not given | Sleep disorders and emotional/behavior disturbances | 34 patients experienced improvement in response to melatonin. Side effects reported in 17 patients | Improvements in excitability when sleep also improved. No change in contrariness, stereotyped behavior and in school/workshop refusal | Various types of insomnia and diagnoses |

*(Continued)*

**Table 2 | Continued**

| Study | Journal | Population | Design | Duration of treatment | Melatonin (formulation, dose) | Time of intake | Main outcome measures | Effects on sleep | Other outcomes | Comments |
|---|---|---|---|---|---|---|---|---|---|---|
| Paavonen et al. (98) | *J Child Adolesc Psychopharmacol* | 15 children with AS (DSM-IV) aged from 6 to 17 years with severe sleep problems for at least 3 months | Not given | 14 days | IR 3 mg | 30 min BB | Sleep (72 h-period actigraphy, sleep diaries), daytime behavior (Karolina Sleepiness Scale; KSS), Child Behavior Checklist (CBCL) | Melatonin treatment was associated with significant decrease in sleep onset latency and nocturnal activity. Discontinuation of melatonin led to a significant decrease in sleep duration and more nocturnal activity. Side effects in 20% of the cases: tiredness, headaches, severe sleepiness, dizziness, diarrhea | Significant improvement of daytime behavior (CBCL) | No principal outcome specified. KSS is not validated in children nor in ASD |
| Giannotti et al. (99) | *J Autism Dev Disord* | 29 children with AD (DSM-IV) aged from 2 to 9 years with current sleep problems | Controlled-release melatonin | 6 months | Dose escalation protocol from 3 mg (1 mg of IR + 2 mg of CR) to 6 mg when clinically required, based upon age (max 4 mg under 4 years old and max 6 mg over 6 years old) | 08:00 p.m. | Sleep (diaries and Children's Sleep Habits Questionnaire CSHQ), daytime behavior, Childhood Autism Rating Scale (CARS) | Melatonin treatment was associated with improvement in sleep onset latency, night awakenings, and sleep duration, which vanished after melatonin discontinuation. No side effects | Parents reported less irritability, less anxiety, and better mood. Significant improvement of depression, anxiety, and withdrawal symptoms during melatonin treatment in children with AS. No effect was reported on the CARS | No principal outcome specified. Missing data: analyses on 25 patients |
| De Leersnyder et al. (100) | *Pediatr Neurol* | 88 children with heterogeneous neurodevelopmental disorders (Smith-Magenis syndrome, mental retardation, encephalopathy, Angelman syndrome, Rett syndrome, Bourneville syndrome, blindness, and autism) aged from 5 to 20 years. Seven patients with autism, mean age 12 years old | 6 years of open-label follow up | 3 months | CR 2–4 mg (<40 kg) or 6 mg (>40 kg) based upon weight | 60 min BB | Parental evaluation of sleep and mood (self-constructed questionnaire) | According to parental reports, both sleep latency and sleep duration improved within 3 months such as night awakenings, sleep quality, and daytime napping. Eleven children experienced adverse events (daytime nap, difficulties in swallowing tablets) that the parents attributed to melatonin treatment | 12% of the parents reported improvements of mood in their children | Heterogeneous neurodevelopmental disorders. Results cannot apply to a population with autism spectrum disorders. No standardized collection of sleep and mood parameters. Mean dose for patients with autism: 5.7 mg |
| Malow et al. (82) | *J Autism Dev Disord* | 24 children with ASD (DSM-IV, ADOS): AD, AS, and PDDNOS aged from 3 to 9 years. Sleep onset delay of 30 min or longer confirmed on actigraphy. Exclusion of neurodevelopmental disabilities such as fragile X, Down, and Rett syndromes | Before treatment families received structured sleep education and children underwent a treatment acclimatation phase in order to be sure the melatonin will be taken | 14 weeks | CR. Dose escalation protocol from 2 to 9 mg when clinically required | 30 min BB | Sleep (actigraphy, Children's Sleep Habits Questionnaire; CSHQ, diaries), daytime behavior (Child Behavior Checklist; CBCL, Repetitive Behavior Scale-Revised), parental stress (Parenting Stress Index Short Form), side effects (Hague Side Effects Scale) | Significant improvement in sleep latency within the first week of treatment but not for other sleep parameters such as night awakenings and sleep quality | Significant improvement in children's behavior (withdrawal, affective problems, attention-deficit hyperactivity, stereotyped, and compulsive behaviors). Significant improvement in parental stress | No placebo |

*(Continued)*

**Table 2 | Continued**

| Study | Journal | Population | Design | Duration of treatment | Melatonin (formulation, dose) | Time of intake | Main outcome measures | Effects on sleep | Other outcomes | Comments |
|---|---|---|---|---|---|---|---|---|---|---|
| **PLACEBO-CONTROLLED TRIAL** | | | | | | | | | | |
| McArthur and Budden (101) | *Dev Med Child Neurol* | 9 children and adolescents with Rett syndrome aged from 4 to 17 years. Mean age: 10 years old | Randomized double-blind crossover trial | 2 periods of 4 weeks with a wash out period of 1 week | 2.5–7.5 mg based on weight | 60 min BB | Sleep (actigraphy, diaries) | Significant improvement in total sleep time. No side effects | None | – |
| Garstang and Wallis (102) | *Child Care Health Dev* | 11 children and adolescents with ASD aged from 5 to 15 years with chronic sleep disorders resistant to behavioral treatment | Randomized double-blind crossover trial | 2 periods of 4 weeks with a wash out period of 1 week | IR 5 mg | 60 min BB | Sleep (diary) | Melatonin and placebo were associated with significantly decreased sleep latency and nocturnal awakenings, increased total sleep time. No side effects | Several parents and class teachers commented that their children were easier to manage and less rigid in their behavior while taking melatonin | ASD criteria were not consensual. Only 7 children completed the trial. Investigators found that some of the placebo capsules were empty. Missing data |
| Wasdell et al. (103) | *J Pineal Res* | 51 children and adolescents with neurodevelopmental disabilities (16 patients with ASD) aged from 2 to 18 years. Sleep delay phase syndrome and impaired sleep maintenance with resistant to sleep hygiene intervention | Randomized double-blind crossover trial. Three weeks trial followed by a 3-month open-label study. Behavioral sleep treatment before inclusion | 2 periods of 10 days with a wash out period of 3–5 days | Dose escalation protocol based on unspecified conditions: from 5 mg (1 mg FR + 4 mg CR) to 15 mg | 20–30 min BB | Sleep (actigraphy, diaries, CGI-S, CGI-I), familial stress (family stress scale) | Significant improvement in total sleep duration and sleep latency as well as reduced stress levels in parents in the melatonin arm | Half of the patients with ASD had their dose increased during the open-label phase with no additional improvement in sleep latency or sleep duration, but caregivers reported less anxiety | Unspecified ASD criteria. Fifty patients completed the trial and 47 completed the open-label phase. Selection bias due to previous melatonin treatment (25% of the cases). At the end of the trial, 29 patients received a dose of 10 or 15 mg. Higher doses were necessary in patients with bilateral cerebral lesions |
| Wirojanan et al. (104) | *J Clin Sleep Med* | 12 children and adolescents with unspecified sleep problems, aged from 2 to 15 years: 5 patients with AD (ADOS and ADI-R), 3 patients with fragile X syndrome with AD, 3 patients with AD and fragile X syndrome, and 1 patient with fragile X premutation | Randomized double-blind crossover trial | 2 periods of 2 weeks. No wash out period | IR 3 mg | 30 min BB | Sleep (actigraphy, diary) | Significant, but mild improvement in total sleep time (+21 min) and decrease in sleep latency (−28 min) | None | Missing data: only 12 patients completed the trial (order bias). No subgroup analysis in AD patients. No side effects |
| Wright et al. (105) | *J Autism Dev Disord* | 22 children and adolescents aged from 3 to 16 years with ASD (ICD-10, ADOS, ADI-R): AD (70%), AS (10%), and AA (20%). No fragile X or Rett syndrome. Current sleeplessness (confirmed on a 1-month-diary) and resistant to behavioral treatment | Randomized double-blind crossover trial | 2 periods of 3 months separated by 1 month of washout | IR. Dose escalation protocol from 2 to 10 mg when clinically required | 30–40 min BB | Sleep (sleep difficulties questionnaire, diary), daytime behavior (Developmental Behavior Checklist), side effect questionnaire | Significant improvement in sleep latency (−47 min) and total sleep duration (+52 min) in the melatonin arm. No improvement in night awakenings. The side effect profile was not significantly different between the 2 groups | Improvement in children's behavior in the melatonin arm that was significant for communication ($p = 0.045$) | Missing data. Analysis on 16 patients. No actigraphy. Mean melatonin dose: 7 mg |

*(Continued)*

**Table 2 | Continued**

| Study | Journal | Population | Design | Duration of treatment | Melatonin (formulation, dose) | Time of intake | Main outcome measures | Effects on sleep | Other outcomes | Comments |
|---|---|---|---|---|---|---|---|---|---|---|
| Cortesi et al. (106) | *J Sleep Res* | 160 children with ASD (DSM-IV, ADI-R, ADOS) aged from 4 to 10 years with sleep onset insomnia and impaired sleep maintenance | Randomized placebo-controlled. Randomization in 4 groups: (1) melatonin alone (2) melatonin+ cognitive behavioral therapy (CBT) (3) CBT alone (4) placebo | 12 weeks | CR 3 mg | 09:00 p.m. | Sleep (actigraphy, Children's Sleep Habits Questionnaire, diaries) | 144 patients completed the trial and 134 were analyzed. Combination group showed greater significant improvements on sleep followed by the melatonin alone and the CBT alone compared to placebo group. No side effects | None | – |
| Gringas et al. (107) | *BMJ* | 146 children aged from 3 to 15 years with neurodevelopmental disorders (60 patients with ASD) and severe sleep disorders that did not respond to standardized sleep advice | Double-blind randomized multicentre placebo-controlled phase III trial | 12 weeks | Immediate release melatonin (dose escalation protocol from 0.5 to 12 mg) or matching placebo | 45 min before bedtime | Total sleep time after 12 weeks (sleep diaries and actigraphy); sleep onset latency; child behavior (Aberrant Behavior Checklist); family functioning; adverse events | Melatonin increased total sleep time by 22.4 min (diaries) and 13.3 (actigraphy); reduced sleep onset latency by 37.5 min (diaries) and 45.3 (actigraphy). Children in the melatonin group woke up earlier than the children in the placebo group. Melatonin was most effective in children with longest sleep latency. Adverse events were similar between the 2 groups | Child behavior and family functioning outcomes showed some (but not significant) improvement and favored use of melatonin | The results are not specified by category of developmental disorder |

communication improvement without reporting separate verbal or non-verbal scores. In other instances, investigators did not use validated instruments; thus, Garstang and Wallis (102) reported improvements in rigidity based solely on parents' and teachers' comments, while Wasdell et al. (103) reported reductions in anxiety based on caregivers' comments. All of the published clinical trials of melatonin in autism/ASD have used sleep measures as their main outcome variable and none have studied the dose–response relationship for melatonin. To reiterate, there is a real need for further studies on the therapeutic effects of melatonin that are conducted on large, relatively homogeneous samples and that employ validated behavioral assessments.

## SYNCHRONIZATION OF MOTOR, EMOTIONAL, AND RELATIONAL RHYTHMS: THERAPEUTIC BENEFITS OF THE EARLY START DENVER MODEL IN AUTISM SPECTRUM DISORDER

Although there is a growing interest in the role of motor, emotional, and interpersonal rhythms in autism, there have been only a few attempts to focus on behavioral synchronization of social communication during therapeutic and educational intervention in autism. The ESDM, developed by Sally Rogers and Geraldine Dawson (119, 120), is a comprehensive behavioral and developmental early intervention approach designed for delivery to 12- to 60-month-old children. The model uses the knowledge of how typical infants, toddlers, and pre-schoolers develop, in addition to knowledge of the ways in which autism affects early development, in order to facilitate an appropriate developmental trajectory in young children with autism beginning at the earliest ages. The goals of the ESDM are to reduce the severity of disabling autism symptoms in very young children, and to accelerate children's developmental rates in a multitude of domains, including cognitive, social–emotional, and language domains. In order to do so, there is a strong focus on interpersonal engagement marked by synchrony and reciprocity during teaching, as research demonstrates that these are closely tied to successful developmental outcomes (121–124). Within the ESDM, the therapist and child work together to develop and sustain coordinated, synchronous activity routines into which teaching opportunities are embedded. The ESDM reflects an understanding of the importance of synchrony of motor, emotional, and relational rhythms for the early development of young children with autism.

Thus, the ESDM allows one to initiate interaction with the child by synchronizing the therapist's motor, emotional, and relational rhythms with the child's rhythms (providing invariants/continuity). For example, if the child uses an object with a rhythmic motor pattern, the therapist will reproduce this behavior with exactly the same rhythmic pattern. The evolution of the child is then facilitated by introducing new and different rhythms (providing variants/discontinuity). In addition, the adjustment of the therapist's behaviors, movements, level of arousal, and posture (for example, standing up, lying down, or sitting) to those of the child contributes to foundational invariants necessary during the initial phase. Furthermore, the ESDM requires the program to be implemented in different environments (such as home, school, and caregiver settings), which also contributes to the introduction of variants.

**Table 3 | Review, meta-analysis, and discussion of therapeutic uses of melatonin in autism.**

| REVIEW/META-ANALYSIS | | |
|---|---|---|
| Jan and O'Donnel (108) | *J Pineal Res* | Review based on100 individuals with chronic sleep disorders, aged from 3 months to 21 years. Half of these 100 patients presented visual impairment or blindness. Melatonin dose ranged from 2.5 to 10 mg. Higher doses were needed in patients with impaired sleep maintenance. Partial or total improvement in sleep parameters was found in 82% of the cases. No side effects |
| Jan et al. (109) | *Dev Med Child Neurol* | Systematic review of studies on melatonin in children. Twenty-four studies found, most of them were case reports or uncontrolled studies with small samples. Mean age: 10 years old. Associated diagnosis: blindness and neurodevelopmental disabilities, 1 single case of an adolescent with AS (76). Doses ranged from 0.5 to 20 mg. Improvement in sleep in all the studies |
| Phillips and Appleton (110) | *Dev Med Child Neurol* | Only three studies, reporting a total of 35 children, fulfilled the criteria for inclusion (randomized controlled clinical trials). Two of them reported a significant decrease in time to sleep onset |
| Braam et al. (111) | *Dev Med Child Neurol* | Meta-analysis of placebo-controlled randomized trials of melatonin in individuals with intellectual disabilities and sleep problems. Nine studies were included. Various doses and formulations of melatonin were given. Melatonin decreased sleep latency by a mean of 34 min ($p < 0.001$), significantly decreased mean number of wakes per night ($p = 0.024$), and increased total sleep time by 50 min ($p < 0.001$). Specified reports on adverse effects were given in four studies. Adverse effects were minor and their incidence in both melatonin and placebo phases were the same. Patient groups in studies included in this meta-analysis were very heterogeneous |
| Guénolé et al. (112) | *Sleep Med Rev* | Systematic review of efficacy and safety of exogenous melatonin for treating disordered sleep in individuals with autism spectrum disorders: 4 case reports, 3 retrospective studies, 2 open-label clinical trials, 3 placebo-controlled trials. All studies supported the existence of a beneficial effect of melatonin on sleep in individuals with ASD with minor side effects. Limitations are: small sample, clinical heterogeneity of ASD and sleep disorders, varying methods used to measure sleep, confounding factors such as behavioral interventions and cross over design (no analysis of intention to treat). Melatonin doses ranged from 0.75 to 10 mg/day. The authors propose that future research on the efficacy of melatonin in children with ASD should include daytime functioning as a principal outcome measure. Only 6 patients of 205 presented side effects: daytime sleepiness, fogginess, dizziness, nocturnal enuresis, tiredness, headache, and diarrhea |
| Doyen et al. (113) | *Eur Child Adolesc Psychiatry* | Systematic review on pharmacokinetics data on melatonin and its role in sleep disorders and autism spectrum disorders. Authors reviewed 17 studies on effectiveness and side effects of melatonin in patients with AD, AS, PDDNOS, and Rett syndrome. Effectiveness on sleep disorders was found in all the studies, side effects were reported in 5 studies. Melatonin doses ranged from 0.5 to 10 mg. Melatonin seems to have anxiolytic properties. Most frequent reported side effects: infections, flu, epilepsy, intestinal disorders, and agitation |
| Rossignol and Frye (114) | *Dev Med Child Neurol* | Aim of the study: investigate melatonin-related findings in ASD including AD, AS, Rett syndrome, and PDDNOS. Eighteen studies on melatonin treatment on ASD patients were identified (5 RCT), 12 of them reported improvement in sleep with melatonin in 67% to 100% of the patients. Six studies reported improvement in daytime behavior (less behavioral rigidity, ease of management for parents and teachers, better social interaction, fewer temper tantrums, less irritability, more playfulness, better academic performance, and increased alertness). Melatonin doses ranged from 0.75 to 15 mg, age of patients ranged from 2 to 18 years, treatment duration ranged from 2 weeks to 4 years. Twelve studies explored side effects (headache, tiredness, dizziness, and diarrhea) in which 7 studies reported no side effects. Nine studies found low levels or abnormal circadian rhythm of melatonin in ASD. A correlation between these abnormal levels and autistic behaviors was found in 4 studies. Night time urinary excretion of melatonin metabolite (6-SM) was reported to be inversely correlated with the severity of impairments in verbal communication, play, and daytime sleepiness in patients with ASD. Five studies found genetic abnormalities of melatonin receptor and enzymes involved in melatonin synthesis |
| Reading (115) | *Child Care Health Dev* | Correlation between plasmatic levels of melatonin and autistic behaviors was found. Melatonin groups showed improvements in total sleep duration and sleep onset latency versus placebo groups but not on night awakenings |

*(Continued)*

**Table 3 | Continued**

| | | |
|---|---|---|
| **LETTER TO THE EDITOR** | | |
| Guénolé and Baleyte (116) | *Dev Med Child Neurol* | Response to the Rossignol and Frye review (73); Authors proposed that studies should separately explore sleep disorders in patients with ASD and sleep disorders in patients with Rett syndrome |
| Guénolé and Baleyte (117) | *Pediatr Neurol* | Response to the De Leersnyder et al. study (86) of open-label trial. The definition of «chronic sleep disorder» did not refer to international classifications. Half of the children manifested Smith-Magenis syndrome that involves specific abnormalities of melatonin secretion. Thus, results cannot apply to a population with ASD. The effects of melatonin should be studied separately in each neurodevelopmental disorder and with specific sleep diagnoses |
| **DISCUSSION/COMMENTARY** | | |
| Jan and Freeman (92) | *Dev Med Child Neurol* | Discussion on melatonin use in children with ADHD, ASD, neurodevelopmental disabilities, epilepsy, and blindness. Exogenous melatonin seems to regulate endogenous melatonin secretion. It seems to be more effective in sleep–wake cycle disorders with sleep onset delay disorders. Night and morning awakenings seem to be more difficult to treat, such as sleep problems associated with cerebral lesions. The more the child shows mental or motor comorbidities, the more the melatonin dose is high |
| Lord (118) | *J Autism Dev Disord* | General brief discussion of melatonin and its potential for treating sleep problems in autism |

The ESDM is both a curriculum and a set of teaching practices. A specific developmental curriculum, administered every 3 months in typical practice, defines the skills to be taught at any given time. In addition, a manual of teaching practices outlines the ways in which these skills are to be taught. Embedded within both the curriculum and the set of teaching practices is a focus on rhythms and synchrony. In other words, when therapists are working within the model, a focus on rhythms permeates both what they teach and how they teach it.

The ESDM curriculum outlines skills to be taught in multiple areas, including cognitive, social–emotional, and language domains. The curriculum focuses heavily upon the teaching of skills that promote engagement with other people in a synchronous, rhythmic way. Many young children with autism enter an ESDM program with weaknesses in these skills, such as imitation, joint attention, orienting to name, and eye contact, and these have broad influences upon the manner in which these children can engage with others. It is well recognized that learning occurs within a social context and that social skills, such as imitation and shared attention, provide a foundation for many aspects of learning, including language, cognitive, and social–emotional abilities. Thus, the ESDM focuses heavily on the development of social engagement and interactional synchrony early on in order to further support learning of a wide range of skills.

One area of focus within the ESDM, which is closely tied to the concept of rhythmicity, is imitation. Young children with autism often exhibit deficits in their imitation skills, including those of imitating others' facial expressions and movements, gestures, body actions, and actions on objects. From the beginning of a young child's ESDM program, teaching of imitation is stressed, from basic imitation of actions on objects to more nuanced imitation of sound effects produced in play. Spontaneous and appropriate imitation of others is typically rhythmic and marked by mutual attention, continuous adaptation, and turn taking. The beginning stages of facilitating imitation and social engagement often start with imitating the child, thereby entering into a rhythmic interaction with the child. By imitating the child's movements and establishing a synchronous interaction, eye contact and mutual engagement in the interaction are promoted (125).

Rhythmicity is also involved in the way teaching occurs within the ESDM upon multiple levels, from the basic structure of each interactive routine to the ways in which adults engage with children during interaction. Social communication is about sharing moments of synchrony with others, and the ESDM supports the emergence of interactional synchrony. The therapist facilitates the occurrence of synchronous moments and strings them together into routines into which the therapist can naturally embed teaching opportunities. The primary vehicle through which all teaching is accomplished in this model is the joint activity routine, which is permeated by moments of rhythmic, synchronous interaction, and enriched with positive affect. Adult and child are attuned to one another, both taking the lead, both following the other's lead, taking turns, and creating a positive and motivating activity in conjunction with one another.

The joint activity routine, although flexible and naturalistic, adheres to a four-part structure: (1) opening, (2) theme, (3) elaboration, and (4) closing. This structure provides a set of invariants, against which multiple variants can occur at differing levels. In order to begin engagement within a joint activity routine, the adult works hard to *find the child's smile*. This can often be accomplished by getting into the child's own rhythm (imitating a child's actions is a very powerful tool to facilitate motivated response and interaction) or by finding a rhythm that the child likes. For example, perhaps a child finds a toy drum and begins banging on it with his hand. In the ESDM, the therapist would join the child and would likely take her/his own drum and imitate the child's actions, joining his rhythm. This would be considered the opening phase of the joint activity routine.

Next, the child and adult would develop a theme. This can be considered a continuation of the rhythm introduced during the opening phase – in our example, banging a drum slowly with hands. The adult and child would take turns doing so, each leading and each following. The skillful adult would embed teaching opportunities into these turns – perhaps a focus on eye contact during dyadic engagement, or on imitation of actions on objects, or on giving and taking objects with eye contact. Both partners then play within this rhythm for a while, until one introduces a variant, or elaboration. In the ESDM, elaboration occurs by introducing a change into the joint activity routine, a change in the rhythm which often allows different teaching targets to be practiced. In this example, the child and adult might start to play peek-a-boo behind the drums. A new rhythm would need to be established, and both partners would work together in order to do so. An elaboration of this sort is a rhythmic fluctuation occurring against a background of invariants (e.g., the same interactive partner, the same material, the same setting), which allows the child to learn to adapt to change and teaches the child how to engage with people and materials differently. Finally, this rhythm would likely begin to fade, the teaching value of the activity would start to diminish, and/or the child would begin to lose motivation. The fourth stage of the joint activity routine – the closing – is the last part of the joint activity routine. Adult and child might help one another clean up the materials, and then both partners would begin an entirely new joint activity routine. This could often involve a change in location, activity level, or teaching domain, and an entirely new set of coordinated interactions would be developed.

Within the joint activity routine, synchrony pervades within several different levels and in several different areas. Adult and child are attuned to one another and responsive to one another in terms of sensory input and output, motor actions, and emotions. Coordinated dyadic engagement, well-balanced in terms of leader and follower, pervades a high-quality joint activity routine. It is quite natural to view this ever-present synchrony in terms of a focus on shared nuanced rhythms.

There is also a focus on rhythmicity within some of the broader teaching practices of the ESDM; for example, in the way in which a teaching session is constructed. As mentioned above, teaching is delivered within joint activity routines. For a therapist-delivered session, these routines are strung together within a session to occupy a full 1- or 2-h time period. Within that time period, therapist and child move around to occupy several spaces. In a well-coordinated way, they engage together in a joint activity routine at the table, and then may move onto the floor for the next. They may sit together, then they may stand or walk or run. The child's level of arousal is carefully monitored, and the session is marked by alternations of quiet thoughtfulness and active play, all coordinated artfully by a skilled adult. All of these changes occur against a stable background, as the session is marked by stability and continuity, with the introduction of variants when appropriate. The ESDM, a comprehensive, behavioral, and developmental early intervention designed for infants and toddlers with autism, is rooted within a sense of and appreciation for rhythmicity and synchrony at multiple levels, ranging from the specific skills that are taught to how those skills are taught, woven together and supported by a broader structure focused on maintaining a well-coordinated, synchronous set of dyadic interactions.

## CONCLUSION: TOWARD AN INTEGRATIVE APPROACH COMBINING THE USE OF MELATONIN WITH THE ESDM

Taken all together, ASD could be seen as a disorder of rhythmicity with, more specifically, impairments in the synchrony of rhythms. Alternatively, such asynchrony might play an important role in a possibly large subgroup of individuals that forms part of the heterogeneous ASD category. In this article, we proposed an integrative approach to study desynchronization in biological and psychological rhythms in ASD and develop an etiopathogenic hypothesis as well as therapeutic perspectives for ASD based on this integrative approach. Indeed, this integrated physiological and psychological approach opens important therapeutic perspectives for ASD based on regulation of physiological rhythms (in particular, through the use of chronobiotics such as melatonin, and also through light exposure, use of regularly scheduled bedtime, wake up, meals, or activities) combined with synchronization of motor, emotional, and relational rhythms through developmental behavioral intervention such as the ESDM. Further studies are required to better ascertain the underlying mechanisms of physiological alterations induced by temporal desynchronization and to better understand the role of biological rhythms and rhythmicity in the development of social communication, repetitive behaviors, and interests or adaptation to changes, and therefore in the development of autism involving impairments in these domains.

## REFERENCES


1. Pevet P, Challet E. Melatonin: both master clock output and internal time-giver in the circadian clocks network. *J Physiol Paris* (2011) **105**:170–82. doi:10.1016/j.jphysparis.2011.07.001
2. Botbol M, Cabon P, Kermarrec S, Tordjman S. Biological and psychological rhythms: an integrative approach to rhythm disturbances in autistic disorder. *J Physiol Paris* (2013) **107**(4):298–309. doi:10.1016/j.jphysparis.2013.03.009
3. Molenaar PCM, Campbell CG. The new person-specific paradigm in psychology. *Curr Dir Psychol Sci* (2009) **18**(2):112–7. doi:10.1111/j.1467-8721.2009.01619.x
4. Glickman G. Circadian rhythms and sleep in children with autism. *Neurosci Biobehav Rev* (2010) **34**(5):755–68. doi:10.1016/j.neubiorev.2009.11.017
5. Kotagal S, Broomall E. Sleep in children with autism spectrum disorder. *J Pediatr Neurol* (2012) **47**(4):242–51. doi:10.1016/j.pediatrneurol.2012.05.007
6. Honomichl RD, Goodlin-Jones BL, Burnham M, Gaylor E, Anders T. Sleep patterns of children with pervasive developmental disorders. *J Autism Dev Disord* (2002) **32**:553–61. doi:10.1023/A:1021254914276
7. Hoshino Y, Wanatabe H, Yashima Y, Kaneko M, Kumashiro H. An investigation on the sleep disturbance of autistic children. *Folia Psychiatr Neurol Jpn* (1984) **38**:45–51.
8. Johnson CR. Sleep problems in children with mental retardation and autism. *Child Adolesc Psychiatr Clin N Am* (1996) **5**:673–83.
9. Patzold LM, Richdale AL, Tonge BJ. An investigation into sleep characteristics of children with autism and Asperger's disorder. *J Paediatr Child Health* (1998) **34**:528–33. doi:10.1046/j.1440-1754.1998.00291.x
10. Richdale AL, Prior MR. The sleep-wake rhythm in children with autism. *Eur Child Adolesc Psychiatry* (1995) **4**:175–86. doi:10.1007/BF01980456
11. Richdale AL. Sleep problems in autism: prevalence, cause, and intervention. *Dev Med Child Neurol* (1999) **41**:60–6. doi:10.1017/S0012162299000122
12. Schreck KA, Mullick JA. Parental reports of sleep problems in children with autism. *J Autism Dev Disord* (2000) **30**:127–35. doi:10.1023/A:1005407622050
13. Tordjman S, Anderson GM, Kermarrec S, Olivier Bonnot O, Geoffray MM, Brailly-Tabard S, et al. Altered circadian patterns of salivary cortisol in low-functioning children and adolescents with autism. *Psychoneuroendocrinology* (2014) **50**:227–45. doi:10.1016/j.psyneuen.2014.08.010
14. Golombek DA, Casiraghi LP, Agostino PV, Paladino N, Duhart JM, Plano SA, et al. The times they're a-changing: effects of circadian desynchronization on physiology and disease. *J Physiol Paris* (2013) **107**(4):310–22. doi:10.1016/j.jphysparis.2013.03.007

15. Revell VL, Skene DJ. Light-induced melatonin suppression in humans with polychromatic and monochromatic light. *Chronobiol Int* (2007) **24**:1125–35. doi:10.1080/07420520701800652
16. Brown R, Hobson RP, Lee A, Stevenson J. Are there "autistic-like" features in congenitally blind children? *J Child Psychol Psychiatry* (1997) **38**(6):693–703. doi:10.1111/j.1469-7610.1997.tb01696.x
17. Donaldson AI, Heavner KS, Zwolan TA. Measuring progress in children with autism spectrum disorder who have cochlear implants. *Arch Otolaryngol Head Neck Surg* (2004) **130**:666–71. doi:10.1001/archotol.130.5.666
18. Tordjman S, Anderson GM, Bellissant E, Botbol M, Charbuy H, Camus F, et al. Day and nighttime excretion of 6-sulphatoxymelatonin in adolescents and young adults with autistic disorder. *Psychoneuroendocrinology* (2012) **37**:1990–7. doi:10.1016/j.psyneuen.2012.04.013
19. Kulman G, Lissoni P, Rovelli F, Roselli MG, Brivio F, Sequeri P. Evidence of pineal endocrine hypofunction in autistic children. *Neuro Endocrinol Lett* (2000) **20**:31–4.
20. Tordjman S, Anderson GM, McBride PA, Hertzig M, Snow M, Hall L, et al. Plasma beta-endorphin, adrenocorticotropin hormone and cortisol in autism. *J Child Psychol Psychiatry* (1997) **38**(6):705–16. doi:10.1111/j.1469-7610.1997.tb01697.x
21. Ritvo ER, Ritvo R, Yuliwer A, Brothers A, Freeman BJ, Plotkin S. Elevated daytime melatonin concentration in autism. *Eur Child Adolesc Psychiatry* (1993) **2**:75–8. doi:10.1007/BF02098862
22. Nir I, Meir D, Zilber N, Knobler H, Hadjez J, Lerner Y. Brief report: circadian melatonin, thyroid-stimulating hormone, prolactin, and cortisol levels in serum of young adults with autism. *J Autism Dev Disord* (1995) **25**:641–54. doi:10.1007/BF02178193
23. Tordjman S, Anderson GM, Pichard N, Charbuy H, Touitou Y. Nocturnal excretion of 6-sulphatoxymelatonin in children and adolescents with autistic disorder. *Biol Psychiatry* (2005) **57**:134–8. doi:10.1016/j.biopsych.2004.11.003
24. Melke J, Goubran Botros H, Chaste P, Betancur C, Nygren G, Anckarssater H, et al. Abnormal melatonin synthesis in autism spectrum disorder. *Mol Psychiatry* (2008) **13**(1):90–8. doi:10.1038/sj.mp.4002016
25. Mulder EJ, Anderson GM, Kemperman RFJ, Oosterloo-Duinkerken A, Minderaa RB, Kema IP. Urinary excretion of 5-hydroxyindoleacetic acid, serotonin and 6-sulphatoxymelatonin in normoserotonemic and hyperserotonemic autistic individuals. *Neuropsychobiology* (2010) **61**:27–32. doi:10.1159/000258640
26. Tordjman S, Najjar I, Bellissant E, Anderson GM, Barburoth M, Cohen D, et al. Advances in the research of melatonin in autism spectrum disorders: literature review and new perspectives. *Int J Mol Sci* (2013) **14**(10):20508–42. doi:10.3390/ijms141020508
27. Amiet C, Gourfinkel-An I, Bouzamondo A, Tordjman S, Baulas M, Lechat P, et al. Epilepsy in autism is associated with intellectual disability and gender: evidence from a meta-analysis. *Biol Psychiatry* (2008) **64**(7):577–82. doi:10.1016/j.biopsych.2008.04.030
28. Hu VW, Sarachana T, Kim KS, Nguyen A, Kulkarni S, Steinberg ME, et al. Gene expression profiling differentiates autism case-controls and phenotypic variants of autism spectrum disorders: evidence for circadian rhythm dysfunction in severe autism. *Autism Res* (2009) **2**:78–97. doi:10.1002/aur.73
29. Jansen R, Metzdorf R, Van der Roest M, Fusani L, ter Maat A, Gahr M. Melatonin affects the temporal organization of the song of the zebra finch. *FASEB J* (2005) **19**:848–50. doi:10.1096/fj.04-2874fje
30. Boucher J. Lost in a sea of time: Time parsing and autism. In: Hoerl C, McCormack T, editors. *Time and Memory: Issues in Philosophy and Psychology*. Oxford: Oxford University Press (2001). p. 111–36.
31. Wimpory D, Nicholas B, Nash S. Social timing clock genes and autism: a new hypothesis. *J Intellect Disabil Res* (2002) **46**:352–8. doi:10.1046/j.1365-2788.2002.00423.x
32. Weisman O, Zagoory-Sharon O, Feldman R. Oxytocin administration to parent enhances infant physiological and behavioral readiness for social engagement. *Biol Psychiatry* (2012) **72**:982–9. doi:10.1016/j.biopsych.2012.06.011
33. Insel TR. Oxytocin – a neuropeptide for affiliation: evidence from behavioral, receptor autoradiographic, and comparative studies. *Psychoneuroendocrinology* (1992) **17**(1):3–35. doi:10.1016/0306-4530(92)90073-G
34. Modahl C, Fein D, Waterhouse L, Newton N. Does oxytocin deficiency mediate social deficits in autism? *J Autism Dev Disord* (1992) **2**(3):449–51. doi:10.1007/BF01048246
35. Modahl C, Green LA, Fein D, Morris M, Waterhouse L, Feinstein C, et al. Plasma oxytocin levels in autistic children *Biol. Psychiatry* (1998) **43**(4):270–7.
36. Guedeney A, Guedeney N, Tereno S, Dugravier R, Greacen T, Welniarz B, et al. Infant rhythms versus parental time: promoting parent-infant synchrony. *J Physiol Paris* (2011) **105**(4–6):195–200. doi:10.1016/j.jphysparis.2011.07.005
37. Lickliter R, Bahrick LE, Honeycutt H. Intersensory redundancy facilitates prenatal perceptual learning in bobwhite quail (*Colinus virginianus*) embryos. *Dev Psychol* (2002) **38**:15–23. doi:10.1037/0012-1649.38.1.15
38. Tordjman S. At the crossroads between psychoanalysis and neuroscience: the importance of subjectivity. *J Physiol Paris* (2010) **104**(5):232–42. doi:10.1016/j.jphysparis.2010.08.001
39. Wallon H. *L'enfant Turbulent*. Paris: *PUF* (1984).
40. Haag G, Botbol M, Graignic R, Perez-Diaz F, Bronsard G, Kermarrec S, et al. The autism psychodynamic evaluation of changes (APEC) scale: a reliability and validity study on a newly developed standardized psychodynamic assessment for youth with pervasive developmental disorders. *J Physiol Paris* (2010) **104**(6):323–36. doi:10.1016/j.jphysparis.2010.10.002
41. Price DA, Close GC, Fielding BA. Age of appearance of circadian rhythm in salivary cortisol values in infancy. *Arch Dis Child* (1983) **58**:454–6. doi:10.1136/adc.58.6.454
42. Joseph D, Chong NW, Shanks ME, Rosato E, Taub NA, Petersen SA, et al. Getting rhythm: how do babies do it? *Arch Dis Child Fetal Neonatal Ed* (2014) **100**(1):F50–4. doi:10.1136/archdischild-204-306104
43. Lavelli M, Fogel A. Developmental changes in the relationship between the infant's attention and emotion during early face-to-face communication: the 2-month transition. *Dev Psychol* (2005) **41**(1):265. doi:10.1037/0012-1649.41.1.265
44. Trevarthen C, Aitken KJ. Infant intersubjectivity: research, theory, and clinical applications. *J Child Psychol Psychiatry* (2001) **2**:3–48. doi:10.1111/1469-7610.00701
45. Shultz S, Vouloumanos A, Bennett RH, Pelphrey K. Neural specialization for speech in the first months of life. *Dev Sci* (2014) **17**(5):766–74. doi:10.1111/desc.12151
46. Meltzoff AN, Kuhl PK, Movellan J, Sejnowski TJ. Foundations for a new science of learning. *Science* (2009) **325**:284–8. doi:10.1126/science.1175626
47. Kuhl PK. Early language acquisition: cracking the speech code. *Nat Rev Neurosci* (2004) **5**:831–43. doi:10.1038/nrn1533
48. Goldstein MH, King AP, West MJ. Social interaction shapes babbling: testing parallels between birdsong and speech. *Proc Natl Acad Sci U S A* (2003) **100**:8030–5. doi:10.1073/pnas.1332441100
49. Delaherche E, Chetouani M, Mahdhaoui A, Saint-Georges C, Viaux S, Cohen D. Interpersonal synchrony: a survey of evaluation methods across disciplines. *IEEE Trans Affect Comput* (2012) **3**:349–65. doi:10.1109/T-AFFC.2012.12
50. Crown CL, Feldstein S, Jasnow MD, Beebe B, Jaffe J. The cross-modal coordination of interpersonal timing: six-week-olds infants' gaze with adults' vocal behavior. *J Psycholinguist Res* (2002) **31**(1):1–23. doi:10.1023/A:1014301303616
51. Stormark KM, Braarud HC. Infants' sensitivity to social contingency: a "double video" study of face-to-face communication between 2-and 4-month-olds and their mothers. *Infant Behav Dev* (2004) **27**(2):195–203. doi:10.1016/j.infbeh.2003.09.004
52. Feldman R. Parent-infant synchrony and the construction of shared timing; physiological precursors, developmental outcomes, and risk conditions. *J Child Psychol Psychiatry* (2007) **48**(3–4):329–54. doi:10.1111/j.1469-7610.2006.01701.x
53. Dumas GJ, Nadel R, Soussignan J, Martinerie L, Garnero L. Inter-brain synchronization during social interaction. *PLoS One* (2010) **5**(8):e12166. doi:10.1371/journal.pone.0012166
54. Saint-Georges C, Mahdhaoui A, Chetouani M, Cassel R, Laznik MC, Apicella F, et al. Do parents recognize autistic deviant behavior long before diagnosis? Taking into account interaction using computational methods. *PLoS One* (2011) **6**(7):e22393. doi:10.1371/journal.pone.0022393
55. Guinchat V, Chamak B, Bonniau B, Bodeau N, Perisse D, Cohen D, et al. Very early signs of autism reported by parents include many concerns not specific to autism criteria. *Res Autism Spectr Disord* (2012) **6**:589–601. doi:10.1016/j.rasd.2011.10.005
56. Zwaigenbaum L, Bryson S, Rogers T, Roberts W, Brian J, Szatmari P. Behavioral manifestations of autism in the first year of life. *Int J Dev Neurosci* (2005) **23**(2–3):143–52. doi:10.1016/j.ijdevneu.2004.05.001

57. Elsabbagh M, Johnson MH. Getting answers from babies about autism. *Trends Cogn Sci* (2010) **14**(2):81–7. doi:10.1016/j.tics.2009.12.005
58. Stern D. *Le monde interpersonnel du nourrisson.* Paris: PUF (1989).
59. Cohen D, Cassel RS, Saint-Georges C, Mahdhaoui A, Laznik MC, Apicella F, et al. Do parentese prosody and fathers' involvement in interacting facilitate social interaction in infants who will later develop autism? *PLoS One* (2013) **8**(5):e61402. doi:10.1371/journal.pone.0061402
60. Watanabe K. Behavioral speed contagion: automatic modulation of movement timing by observation of body movements. *Cognition* (2008) **106**:514–24. doi:10.1016/j.cognition.2007.06.001
61. Mauk MD, Buonomano DV. The neural basis of temporal processing. *Annu Rev Neurosci* (2004) **27**:307–40. doi:10.1146/annurev.neuro.27.070203.144247
62. Xavier J, Tilmont E, Bonnot O. Children's synchrony and rhythmicity in imitation of peers: toward a developmental model of empathy. *J Physiol Paris* (2013) **107**(4):291–7. doi:10.1016/j.jphysparis.2013.03.012
63. Trevarthen C. what is like to be a person who knows nothing? Defining the active intersubjective mind of a newborn human being. *Infant Child Dev* (2011) **20**:119–35. doi:10.1002/icd.689
64. Nadel J. *Imiter Pour Grandir. Développement du bébé et de l'enfant avec autisme.* Paris: Dunod (2011).
65. Nadel-Brulfert J, Baudonnière PM. The social function of reciprocal imitation in 2-years-old peers. *Int J Behav Dev* (1982) **5**:95–109. doi:10.1177/016502548200500105
66. Nadel J, Baudonnière PM, Fontaine AM. Les comportements sociaux imitatifs. *Recherches Psychologie Sociale* (1983) **5**:15–29.
67. Ikegami T, Iizuka H. Turn-taking interaction as acooperative and co-creative process. *Infant Behav Dev* (2007) **30**:278–88. doi:10.1016/j.infbeh.2007.02.002
68. Rizzolatti G, Craighero L. The mirror-neuron system. *Annu Rev Neurosci* (2004) **27**:169–92. doi:10.1146/annurev.neuro.27.070203.144230
69. Guionnet S, Nadel J, Bertasi E, Sperduti M, Delaveau P, Fossati P. Reciprocal imitation: toward a neural basis of social interaction. *Cereb Cortex* (2012) **22**:971–8. doi:10.1093/cercor/bhr177
70. Decety J, Chaminade T, Grezes J, Meltzoff AN. A PET exploration of the neural mechanisms involved in reciprocal imitation. *Neuroimage* (2002) **15**:265–72. doi:10.1006/nimg.2001.0938
71. Iacoboni M. Neural mechanisms of imitation. *Curr Opin Neurobiol* (2005) **15**:632–7. doi:10.1016/j.conb.2005.10.010
72. Nettl B. An ethnomusicologist contemplates universals in musical sound and musical culture. In: Wallin NL, Merker B, Brown S, editors. *The Origins of Music.* Cambridge, MA: MIT Press (2000). p. 463–72.
73. Patel AD, Iversen JR, Bregman MR, Schulz I. Experimental evidence for synchronization to a musical beat in a nonhuman animal. *Curr Biol* (2009) **19**:827–30. doi:10.1016/j.cub.2009.03.038
74. Feldman R. Parent-infant synchrony biological foundations and developmental outcomes. *Curr Dir Psychol Sci* (2007) **16**:340–5. doi:10.1111/j.1467-8721.2007.00532.x
75. Winkler I, Háden GP, Ladinig O, Sziller I, Honing H. Newborn infants detect the beat in music. *Proc Natl Acad Sci U S A* (2009) **106**:2468–71. doi:10.1073/pnas.0809035106
76. Provasi J, Bobin-Begue A. Spontaneous motor tempo and rhythmical synchronisation in 2-1/2 and 4-year-old children. *Int J Behav Dev* (2003) **27**:220–31. doi:10.1080/01650250244000290
77. Bobin-Bègue A, Provasi J, Marks A, Pouthas V. Influence of an auditory tempo on the endogenous rhythm of non-nutritive sucking. *Eur Rev Appl Psychol* (2006) **56**:239–45. doi:10.1016/j.erap.2005.09.006
78. Trevarthen C, Stuart Daniel S. Disorganized rhythm and synchrony: early signs of autism and Rett syndrome. *Brain Dev* (2005) **27**:S25–34. doi:10.1016/j.braindev.2005.03.016
79. Sandercock R, Jones W, Klin A, Shultz S. Contingent smiling behavior in 2- to 5-month-old infants with and without ASD during dyadic interactions. *International Meeting for Autism Research (IMFAR).* Atlanta, GA (2015).
80. Jones W, Klin A. Attention to eyes is present but in decline in 2-6-month-old infants later diagnosed with autism. *Nature* (2013) **504**(7480):4427–31. doi:10.1038/nature12715
81. American Psychiatric Association. *Diagnostic and Statistical Manual of Mental Disorders, Fifth Edition (DSM-5).* 5th ed. Washington, DC: American Psychiatric Association (2013).
82. Malow B, Adkins K, McGrew S, Wang L, Goldman S, Fawkes D. Melatonin for sleep in children with autism: a controlled trial examining dose, tolerability and outcomes. *J Autism Dev Disord* (2011) **42**(8):1729–37. doi:10.1007/s10803-011-1418-3
83. Goldbeter A. *La vie Oscillatoire.* Paris: Odile Jacob (2010).
84. Winnicott DW. *Collected Papers: Through Pediatrics to Psychoanalysis.* London: Tavistock Publications (1958).
85. Fureix C, Benhajali H, Henry S, Bruchet A, Prunier A, Ezzaouia M, et al. Plasma cortisol and faecal cortisol metabolites concentrations in stereotypic and non-stereotypic horses: do stereotypic horses cope better with poor environmental conditions? *BMC Vet Res* (2013) **9**:3. doi:10.1186/1746-6148-9-3
86. Gabriels RL, Agnew JA, Pan Z, Holt KD, Reynolds A, Laudensiager ML. Elevated repetitive behaviors are associated with lower diurnal salivary cortisol levels in autism spectrum disorder. *Biol Psychol* (2013) **93**(2):262–8. doi:10.1016/j.biopsycho.2013.02.017
87. Adler BA, Wink LK, Early M, Shaffer R, Minshawi N, McDougle CJ, et al. Drug-refractory aggression, self-injurious behavior, and severe tantrums in autism spectrum disorders: a chart review study. *Autism* (2015) **19**(1):102–6. doi:10.1177/1362361314524641
88. Minshawi NF, Hurwitz S, Morriss D, McDougle CJ. Multidisciplinary assessment and treatment of self-injurious behavior in autism spectrum disorder and intellectual disability: integration of psychological and biological theory and approach. *J Autism Dev Disord* (2014). doi:10.1007/s10803-014-2307-3
89. Stigler KA. Psychopharmacologic management of serious behavioral disturbance in ASD. *Child Adolesc Psychiatr Clin N Am* (2014) **23**(1):73–82. doi:10.1016/j.chc.2013.07.005
90. Horrigan JP, Barnhill LJ. More on melatonin. *J Am Acad Child Adolesc Psychiatry* (1997) **36**(8):1014. doi:10.1097/00004583-199708000-00002
91. Hayashi E. Effect of melatonin on sleep-wake rhythm: the sleep diary of an autistic male. *Psychiatry Clin Neurosci* (2000) **54**:383–4. doi:10.1046/j.1440-1819.2000.00725.x
92. Jan JE, Freeman RD, Wasdell MB, Bomben MM. A child with severe night terrors and sleep-walking responds to melatonin therapy'. *Dev Med Child Neurol* (2004) **46**(11):789. doi:10.1017/S0012162204231358
93. Gupta R, Hutchins J. Melatonin: a pancea for desperate parents? (Hype or truth). *Arch Dis Child* (2005) **90**(9):986–7. doi:10.1136/adc.2005.075218
94. Andersen IM, Kaczmarska J, McGrew SG, Malow BA. Melatonin for insomnia in children with autism spectrum disorders. *J Child Neurol* (2008) **23**(5):482–5. doi:10.1177/0883073807309783
95. Galli-Carminati G, Deriaz N, Bertschy G. Melatonin in treatment of chronic sleep disorders in adults with autism: retrospective study. *Swiss Med Wkly* (2009) **139**(19–20):293–6.
96. Jan JE, Espezel H, Appleton RE. The treatment of sleep disorders with melatonin. *Dev Med Child Neurol* (1994) **36**:97–107. doi:10.1111/j.1469-8749.1994.tb11818.x
97. Ishizaki A, Sugama M, Takeuchi N. Usefulness of melatonin for developmental sleep and emotional/behaviour disorders – studies of melatonin trial on 50 patients with developmental disorders. *No To Hattatsu* (1999) **31**(5):428–37.
98. Paavonen EJ, Nieminen-von Wendt T, Vanhala R, Aronen ET, von Wendt L. Effectiveness of melatonin in the treatment of sleep disturbances in children with Asperger disorder. J *Child Adolesc Psychopharmacol* (2003) **13**(1): 83-95. doi:10.1089/104454603321666225
99. Giannotti F, Cortesi F, Cerquiglini A, Bernabei P. An open-label study of controlled-release melatonin in treatment of sleep disorders in children with autism. *J Autism Dev Disord* (2006) **36**(6):741–52. doi:10.1007/s10803-006-0116-z
100. De Leersnyder H, Zisapel N, Laudon M. Prolonged-release melatonin for children with neurodevelopmental disorders. *Pediatr Neurol* (2011) **45**:23–6. doi:10.1016/j.pediatrneurol.2011.02.001
101. MacArthur AJ, Budden SS. Sleep dysfonction in Rett syndrome: a trial of exogenous melatonin treatment. *Dev Med Child Neurol* (1998) **40**:186–92. doi:10.1111/j.1469-8749.1998.tb15445.x
102. Garstang J, Wallis M. Randomized controlled trial of melatonin for children with autistic spectrum disorders and sleep problems. *Child Care Health Dev* (2006) **32**(5):585–9. doi:10.1111/j.1365-2214.2006.00616.x
103. Wasdell MB, Jan JE, Bomben MM, Freeman RD, Rietveld WJ, Tai J, et al. A randomized, placebo-controlled trial of controlled release melatonin treatment of delayed sleep phase syndrome and impaired sleep maintenance in

children with neurodevelopmental disabilities. *J Pineal Res* (2008) **44**(1):57–64. doi:10.1111/j.1600-079X.2007.00528.x

104. Wirojanan J, Jacquemont S, Diaz R, Bacalman S, Anders TF, Hagerman RJ, et al. The efficacy of melatonin for sleep problems in children with autism, fragile X syndrome, or autism and fragile X syndrome. *J Clin Sleep Med* (2009) **5**(2):145–50.
105. Wright B, Sims D, Smart S, Alwazeer A, Alderson-Day B, Allgar V, et al. Melatonin versus placebo in children with autism spectrum conditions and severe sleep problems not amenable to behaviour. management strategies: a randomised controlled crossover trial. *J Autism Dev Disord* (2011) **41**(2):175–84. doi:10.1007/s10803-010-1036-5
106. Cortesi F, Giannotti F, Sebastiani T, Panunzi S, Valente D. Controlled-release melatonin, singly and combined with cognitive behavioural therapy, for persistent insomnia in children with autism spectrum disorders: a randomized placebo-controlled trial. *J Sleep Res* (2012) **21**(6):700–9. doi:10.1111/j.1365-2869.2012.01021.x
107. Gringas P, Gamble C, Jones AP, Wiggs L, Williamson PR, Sutcliffe A, et al. Melatonin for sleep problems in children with neurodevelopmental disorders: randomised double masked placebo controlled trial. *BMJ* (2012) **345**:1–16. doi:10.1136/bmj.e6664
108. Jan JE, O'Donnel ME. Use of melatonin in the treatment of paediatric sleep disorders. *J Pineal Res* (1996) **21**:193–9. doi:10.1111/j.1600-079X.1996.tb00286.x
109. Jan JE, Connolly MB, Hamilton D, Freeman RD, Laudon M. Melatonin treatment of non-epileptic myoclonus in children. *Dev Med Child Neurol* (1999) **41**(4):255–9. doi:10.1111/j.1469-8749.1999.tb00593.x
110. Phillips L, Appleton RE. Systematic review of melatonin treatment in children with neurodevelopmental disabilities and sleep impairment. *Dev Med Child Neurol* (2004) **46**:771–5. doi:10.1017/S001216220400132X
111. Braam W, Smits MG, Didden R, Korzilius H, Van Geijlswijk M, Curfs LMG. Exogenous melatonin for sleep problems in individuals with intellectual disability: a meta-analysis. *Dev Med Child Neurol* (2009) **51**:340–9. doi:10.1111/j.1469-8749.2008.03244.x
112. Guénolé F, Godbout R, Nicolas A, Franco P, Claustrat B, Baleyte JM. Melatonin for disordered sleep in individuals with autism spectrum disorders: systematic review and discussion. *Sleep Med Rev* (2011) **15**(6):379–87. doi:10.1016/j.smrv.2011.02.001
113. Doyen C, Mighiu D, Kaya K, Colineaux C, Beaumanoir C, Mouraeff Y, et al. Melatonin in children with autistic spectrum disorders: recent and practical-data. *Eur Child Adolesc Psychiatry* (2011) **20**(5):231–9. doi:10.1007/s00787-011-0162-8
114. Rossignol DA, Frye RE. Melatonin in autism spectrum disorders: a systematic review and meta-analysis. *Dev Med Child Neurol* (2011) **53**:783–92. doi:10.1111/j.1469-8749.2011.03980.x
115. Reading R. Melatonin in autism spectrum disorders: a systematic review and meta-analysis. *Child Care Health Dev* (2012) **38**(2):301–2.
116. Guénolé F, Baleyte JM. Meta-analysing the effectiveness of melatonin for sleep-disturbed individuals with autism spectrum conditions: should Rett syndrome be included? *Dev Med Child Neurol* (2011) **53**(11):1063. doi:10.1111/j.1469-8749.2011.04071.x
117. Guénolé F, Baleyte JM. Effects of melatonin should be studied separately in each neurodevelopmental disorder and with specific sleep diagnoses. *Pediatr Neurol* (2012) **46**(1):60. doi:10.1016/j.pediatrneurol.2011.11.001
118. Lord C. What is melatonin? Is it a useful treatment for sleep problems in autism? *J Autism Dev Disord* (1998) **28**(4):345–6. doi:10.1023/A:1026020600723
119. Dawson G, Rogers SJ, Munson J, Smith M, Winter J, Greenson J, et al. Randomized controlled trial of an intervention for toddlers with autism: the early start Denver model. *Pediatrics* (2010) **25**(1):e17–23. doi:10.1542/peds.2009-0958
120. Rogers SJ, Dawson G. *Early Start Denver Model for Children with Autism: Promoting Language, Learning, and Engagement.* New York, NY: Guilford Press (2010).
121. Feldman R, Masalha S. Parent-child and triadic antecedents of children's social competence: cultural specificity, shared process. *Dev Psychol* (2010) **46**(2):455–67. doi:10.1037/a0017415
122. Leerkes EM, Blankson AN, O'Brien M. Differential effects of maternal sensitivity to infant distress and nondistress on social-emotional functioning. *Child Dev* (2009) **80**(3):762–75. doi:10.1111/j.1467-8624.2009.01296.x
123. Paavola L, Kemppinen K, Kumpulainen K, Moilanen I, Ebeling H. Maternal sensitivity, infant co-operation and early linguistic development: some predictive relations. *Eur J Dev Psychol* (2006) **3**(1):13–30. doi:10.1080/17405620500317789
124. Shonkoff JP, Phillips DA, editors. *From Neurons to Neighborhoods: The Science of Early Childhood Development.* Washington, DC: National Academy Press (2000).
125. Lewy A, Dawson G. Social stimulation and joint attention deficits in young autistic children. *J Abnorm Child Psychol* (1992) **20**:555–66. doi:10.1007/BF00911240

# 15

# Social communication and theory of mind in boys with autism and fragile X syndrome

**Molly Losh[1]*, Gary E. Martin[2,3], Jessica Klusek[2,3], Abigail L. Hogan-Brown[1] and John Sideris[2]**

[1] Roxelyn and Richard Pepper Department of Communication Sciences and Disorders, Northwestern University, Evanston, IL, USA
[2] Frank Porter Graham Child Development Institute, University of North Carolina at Chapel Hill, Chapel Hill, NC, USA
[3] Division of Speech and Hearing Sciences, Department of Allied Health Sciences, University of North Carolina at Chapel Hill, Chapel Hill, NC, USA

**Edited by:**
Daniela Plesa Skwerer, Boston University, USA

**Reviewed by:**
Teresa Mitchell, University of Massachusetts Medical School, USA
Audra Sterling, University of Wisconsin-Madison, USA
Lizbeth Finestack, University of Minnesota, USA

***Correspondence:**
Molly Losh, Roxelyn and Richard Pepper Department of Communication Sciences and Disorders, Northwestern University, Frances Searle, Evanston, IL 60208, USA.
e-mail: m-losh@northwestern.edu

Impairments in the social use of language, or pragmatics, constitute a core characteristic of autism. Problems with pragmatic language have also been documented in fragile X syndrome (FXS), a monogenic condition that is the most common known genetic cause of autism. Evidence suggests that social cognitive ability, or theory of mind, may also be impaired in both conditions, and in autism, may importantly relate to pragmatic language ability. Given the substantial overlap observed in autism and FXS, this study aimed to better define those social-communicative phenotypes that overlap in these two conditions by comparing pragmatic language ability and theory of mind in children with idiopathic autism and children with FXS, with and without autism, as well as children with Down syndrome and typically developing controls. We further examined correlations between these cognitive-behavioral phenotypes and molecular genetic variation related to the Fragile X Mental Retardation-1 gene (*FMR1*) in the FXS group. Results indicated that children with idiopathic autism and those with FXS and autism performed comparably on direct-assessment measures of pragmatic language and theory of mind, whereas those with FXS only did not differ from controls. Theory of mind was related to pragmatic language ability in all groups. Pragmatic language and theory of mind also correlated with genetic variation at the *FMR1* locus (Cytosine-Guanine-Guanine repeats and percent methylation). These results point toward substantial overlap in the social and language phenotypes in autism and FXS and suggest a molecular genetic basis to these phenotypic profiles.

**Keywords: autism, fragile X syndrome, pragmatic language, social communication, theory of mind**

Autism and fragile X syndrome (FXS) are genetically based neurodevelopmental disorders that share a number of cognitive and behavioral characteristics, including impairments in social communication, or pragmatic language. Pragmatic language is a complex skill grounded deeply in the capacity to apprehend and contend with social information. Mastering pragmatic language skills (e.g., politeness strategies, adopting different registers, or styles of communication depending upon addressee, conversational, and narrative practices, etc.) hinges on the ability to anticipate others' interests, infer the background knowledge brought by each interlocutor to the communicative interaction, monitor participants' involvement, and appreciate cultural conventions for social and communicative interaction (Grice, 1975; Brown and Levinson, 1987; Sperber and Wilson, 2002; Wilson and Sperber, 2004). Such abilities may be considered aspects of social cognition or "theory of mind," namely, the ability to attribute thoughts, emotions, beliefs, and desires to others, and to appreciate that others may hold thoughts and feelings that are different than one's own. Important evidence for the role of theory of mind in pragmatic language ability has come from studies of autism, where autistic groups' theory of mind difficulties appear strongly associated with the pragmatic language impairments observed in this population (Loveland and Tunali, 1993; Tager-Flusberg and Sullivan, 1995; Surian et al., 1996; Capps et al., 1998, 2000; Tager-Flusberg, 2000; Losh and Capps, 2003). Ultimately, such findings from neurogenetic populations may provide clues to the brain and gene basis of complex human traits such as social communication and theory of mind, by providing links between gene, brain, and behavior. In other words, characterizing pragmatic language impairments in autism and related neurogenetic disorders such as FXS could help to clarify how underlying genetic variation and resultant changes in brain development might give rise to specific phenotypes such as pragmatic language or theory of mind impairment.

Whereas the genetic basis of autism is complex, with the disorder still defined behaviorally (American Psychiatric Association, 1994), FXS is a monogenic X-linked disorder that is the most common inherited cause of intellectual disability (ID) and the most common known genetic cause of autism. Because FXS is more etiologically homogeneous than idiopathic autism, careful study of autism-related phenotypes in the context of this single-gene disorder can provide an important avenue for identifying pathophysiological mechanisms underlying the symptoms of autism, and informing the genetic basis of complex human skills such as pragmatic language and theory of mind.

In this study, we compared pragmatic language ability in children with idiopathic autism and children with FXS, with and without autism, in order to better define those social-communicative phenotypes that overlap in these two conditions. We further examined theory of mind in these groups, both to characterize groups' abilities and to determine whether there exists phenotypic overlap in this important domain, as well as to examine theory of mind as a potential underpinning factor in the pragmatic language impairments in each group. As noted, strong links have been documented between pragmatic language impairment and theory of mind in autism, but to our knowledge, these relationships have not yet been studied in FXS. Finally, we examined molecular genetic correlates of pragmatic language and theory of mind in the FXS group, with the goal of detecting gene-behavior associations that may have implications for the genetic basis of social communication and theory of mind. Below we present a brief review of FXS and rationale for comparison of pragmatic language and theory of mind in autism and FXS.

## INTRODUCTION TO FXS AND ITS OVERLAP WITH AUTISM

Fragile X syndrome is the most frequent known hereditary cause of ID (Dykens et al., 2000; Hagerman and Hagerman, 2002), with the full mutation estimated to occur in approximately 1 in 2,500 to 1 in 5,000 individuals (Hagerman, 2008; Coffee et al., 2009; Fernandez-Carvajal et al., 2009). On the X chromosome, an expansion of Cytosine-Guanine-Guanine (CGG) repeats in the Fragile X Mental Retardation-1 gene (*FMR1*) results in methylation (i.e., shutting down) of the gene and reduced or absent production of the Fragile X Mental Retardation Protein (FMRP). FMRP is thought to be critical for typical brain development (Devys et al., 1993; Jin and Warren, 2003), and its deficiency in FXS is believed to underlie the physical and cognitive-behavioral characteristics of the syndrome. Males with FXS typically experience moderate or severe ID (Bennetto and Pennington, 2002; Abbeduto and Chapman, 2005) and more severe impairments than females overall, because females possess one unaffected X chromosome in addition to one affected chromosome (Hagerman and Hagerman, 2002; Loesch et al., 2003; Reiss and Dant, 2003; Bailey et al., 2008, 2009). Commonly co-occurring conditions include social anxiety (Bregman et al., 1988; Hagerman, 2002; Cordeiro et al., 2011), attentional deficits (Hooper et al., 2000; Wilding et al., 2002), and autism (Hagerman and Hagerman, 2002).

Autistic characteristics observed in individuals with FXS include stereotypic and repetitive behaviors, poor eye contact, and social avoidance (Reiss and Freund, 1992; Hagerman and Hagerman, 2002). FXS is the most common known single-gene disorder linked to autism (Hagerman and Hagerman, 2002). Results of studies using gold standard diagnostic measures indicate that 20–50% of males with FXS may also have autism and as many as three-quarters may meet ASD criteria (Rogers et al., 2001; Kaufmann et al., 2004; Philofsky et al., 2004; Clifford et al., 2007; Hall et al., 2008). In addition, approximately 2–6% of individuals with autism test positive for the fragile X mutation (Hagerman, 2006).

Language development is impaired in males with FXS beyond expectations for cognitive level, with greater deficits in language production compared with comprehension (Roberts et al., 2001, 2008; Abbeduto et al., 2007; Finestack et al., 2009). Early investigations of pragmatic language in FXS reported poor topic maintenance with inappropriate responses, rambling, automatic phrases, and perseveration or repetitive language (Hanson et al., 1986; Madison et al., 1986). However, these studies included small samples and lacked comparison groups. Compared with controls with typical development or Down syndrome (DS), males with FXS have greater difficulty maintaining topics of conversation and produce more off-topic or tangential contributions to the topic (Wolf-Schein et al., 1987; Sudhalter and Belser, 2001) as well as more perseveration (Wolf-Schein et al., 1987; Sudhalter et al., 1990; Roberts et al., 2007a). Young individuals with FXS may also be less likely than MA-matched typically developing (TD) children to report actions during story retelling (Estigarribia et al., 2011) and to request clarification or additional information in the face of unclear messages from a communication partner (Abbeduto et al., 2008). Compared with individuals with idiopathic autism, males with FXS without autism produced more turns per topic and less echolalia but more perseveration in one study (Sudhalter et al., 1990).

Autism status of participants with FXS was handled differently across the studies reviewed above – individuals with FXS and comorbid autism were either excluded (Sudhalter et al., 1990; Abbeduto et al., 2008), included as a separate group (Roberts et al., 2007a; Estigarribia et al., 2011), or autism status was not reported (Hanson et al., 1986; Madison et al., 1986; Wolf-Schein et al., 1987; Sudhalter and Belser, 2001). Several studies have directly examined the role of autism in language in FXS. On global language assessments, males with FXS and comorbid autism show more severe language deficits than males without autism (Bailey et al., 2001; Rogers et al., 2001; Philofsky et al., 2004). Findings are more mixed with respect to specific language domains, however. In several studies, groups of males with FXS did not differ by autism status in either receptive or expressive vocabulary (Price et al., 2007; Roberts et al., 2007a; Kover and Abbeduto, 2010; McDuffie et al., 2012) or syntax (Price et al., 2007, 2008; Kover and Abbeduto, 2010; McDuffie et al., 2012). However, individuals with FXS and comorbid autism performed more poorly than those with only FXS in receptive vocabulary and syntax in one study (Lewis et al., 2006), and autism severity may be negatively related to receptive vocabulary skill when a continuous analytical approach is taken (McDuffie et al., 2012). In two studies, boys with both FXS and autism did not differ from those without autism but did differ from TD controls (whereas boys with only FXS did not) in expressive vocabulary (Roberts et al., 2007b) and overall story retelling ability (Estigarribia et al., 2011), perhaps suggesting that autism in FXS negatively impacts these language areas as well. Boys with FXS and comorbid ASD have been shown to produce more off-topic or tangential language than boys with only FXS (Roberts et al., 2007a). Children and adolescents with both FXS and autism were also rated higher than those without autism in the current use of stereotyped utterances/delayed echolalia and reciprocal conversation on the Communication domain of the Autism Diagnostic Interview-Revised (ADI-R; Lord et al., 1994) in another recent study (McDuffie et al., 2010).

## THEORY OF MIND IN FXS

For the most part, theory of mind performance in FXS appears to be on par with cognitive expectations, and children with FXS score comparably to children with DS or ID of unknown etiology (Mazzocco et al., 1994; Garner et al., 1999; Cornish et al., 2005). Children with FXS also perform similarly on false belief theory of mind tasks to younger, non-verbal mental age-matched TD children (Abbeduto et al., 2001). However, some studies have reported theory of mind deficits in FXS that cannot be explained by cognitive impairment. In a recent comparison of 30 boys with FXS to 15 boys with unspecified ID, Grant et al. (2007) found poorer overall performance on standard false belief tasks among the FXS group (Grant et al., 2007). Similar findings were reported by Garner et al. (1999), who found that a small group of eight boys with FXS performed significantly worse than a matched ID group on a deceptive box false belief task, although these findings may have been sporadic as no group differences were detected on a secondary false belief task (the Sally–Anne task), nor on a second-order false belief task (Garner et al., 1999).

A few studies have examined the impact of autism comorbidity on theory of mind abilities in FXS syndrome, and suggest that autism status may play a role in theory of mind ability in FXS. Lewis et al. (2006) compared non-verbal IQ-matched groups of children with FXS with and without comorbid autism, and found that the children with FXS who met criteria for autism showed worse performance on false belief tasks, despite similar cognitive ability (Lewis et al., 2006). The study by Grant et al. (2007) failed to detect differences in false belief performance among children with FXS with and without autism, although there was a non-significant trend toward poorer performance in the comorbid autism group (Grant et al., 2007).

## RATIONALE FOR THE PRESENT STUDY

In spite of considerable overlap between autism and FXS, and evidence that both disorders are characterized by difficulties in pragmatic language, and likely theory of mind as well (at least in those individuals with comorbid FXS and autism), few direct population comparisons exist to allow precise comparison of these populations and drawing ties between known underlying genetic variation and the social phenotypes of interest. Additionally, whether impairments in pragmatic language and theory of mind may be related in both populations is not known. This study addressed these questions by comparing pragmatic language ability and theory of mind in children with idiopathic autism, children with FXS with and without autism, children with DS (included as a comparison group to control for general cognitive delays), and TD children. Further, correlations with genetic variation at the *FMR1* locus were examined to inform the potential genetic underpinnings of pragmatic language and theory of mind profiles observed.

## MATERIALS AND METHODS

### PARTICIPANTS

Study participants were 28 boys with idiopathic autism (autism only; ASD-O), 40 boys with both FXS and ASD (FXS-ASD), 21 boys with FXS only (FXS-O), 21 boys with DS, and 20 TD boys participating in a large-scale longitudinal study of speech, language, and social-behavioral profiles in children with neurodevelopmental disabilities. Boys with autism, FXS, and DS were recruited from the Research Participant Registry Core of the Carolina Institute for Developmental Disabilities (CIDD) at the University of North Carolina at Chapel Hill (UNC), genetic clinics, and parent support groups in the Southeastern, Eastern, and Midwestern U.S. TD boys were recruited through the CIDD Participant Registry Core, schools, and childcare centers in North Carolina. Study procedures were approved by the institutional review boards at UNC and Northwestern University.

Participants included only boys since females with FXS are less severely impaired than males (Hagerman and Hagerman, 2002; Loesch et al., 2002) and less likely to have autism (Clifford et al., 2007; Bailey et al., 2008). Upon enrollment, parents reported that all boys were combining three or more words. For all children, English was the primary language spoken in their homes. A composite score of Peabody Picture Vocabulary Test-Third Edition (PPVT-III; Dunn and Dunn, 1997) and Expressive Vocabulary Test (EVT; Williams, 1997) raw scores was used to match groups on receptive and expressive lexical skills to help ensure that any differences detected in social communication and theory of mind were not due to differences in structural language ability (see below for description of vocabulary measures and **Table 1** for group means and standard deviations). Pairwise $t$-tests indicated no significant differences between groups (all $p$ between 0.09 and 0.85, with the comparisons between DS vs. FXS-O and TD as well as between FXS-ASD vs. TD with $p > 0.30$). Age equivalent scores from both measures were included as covariates in all statistical models. All boys with FXS had a diagnosis of the full mutation. Boys were excluded for having an average hearing threshold greater than 30 dB HL in the better ear, determined from a hearing screening across 500; 1,000; 2,000; and 4,000 Hz with a MAICO MA 40 audiometer. Boys with DS and TD were screened for autism with the Social Communication Questionnaire (SCQ; Rutter et al., 2003) and also subsequently excluded for scoring as "autism" or "autism spectrum" on the Autism Diagnostic Observation Schedule (ADOS; Lord et al., 2001), described below. **Table 1** provides background characteristics of participants in each group.

### ASSESSMENTS

Boys were tested in a quiet space in a school, home, or in a laboratory setting. The full assessment lasted approximately 4–6 h, with several breaks to prevent fatigue. Assessments were video-recorded with a Sony Digital8 video camera (Model DCR-TVR27) and audio-recorded with a Marantz portable solid-state recorder (PMD670).

#### *Autism classification*

The ADOS (Lord et al., 2001) was used to confirm autism in boys with ASD-O and to classify boys with FXS according to autism status. The ADOS consists of developmentally appropriate activities that are structured to provide a child with opportunities to show diagnostic symptoms of autism, and yields classifications of "autism," "spectrum," and "no autism." Trained examiners coded administrations from video, with scoring based on the revised algorithms (Gotham et al., 2007, 2008). Coders included one research assistant who was reliable with an independent ADOS trainer, and one coder who was reliable with the aforementioned research assistant. Twenty-four boys with ASD-O were identified by the ADOS as having "autism" and three as having "spectrum." One additional boy with ASD-O did not meet criteria for autism or spectrum on the ADOS, scoring 6 (ASD cutoff is 7). However, because his scores on the Autism Diagnostic Interview – Revised (Lord et al., 1994) all exceeded diagnostic cutoffs and medical

**Table 1 | Group characteristics.**

| | ASD-O $N = 28$ | FXS-ASD $N = 40$ | FXS-O $N = 21$ | DS $N = 21$ | TD $N = 20$ |
|---|---|---|---|---|---|
| | Mean (SD) (Range) | Mean (SD) (Range) | Mean (SD) (Range) | Mean (SD) (Range) | Mean (SD) (Range) |
| Chronological age | 9.21 (2.22) (4.16–12.74) | 10.55 (2.42) (6.58–15.07) | 9.61 (3.03) (6.06–14.98) | 10.86 (2.07) (6.81–14.86) | 4.84 (1.34) (3.23–8.78) |
| Non-verbal mental age[1] | 5.88 (1.32) (3.92–10.50) | 5.02 (0.49) (3.50–6.00) | 5.44 (0.95) (4.42–8.25) | 5.33 (0.83) (4.33–8.25) | 5.49 (1.45) (3.58–9.17) |
| Expressive vocabulary age[2] | 5.62 (1.59) (3.42–8.92) | 4.99 (0.99) (2.67–7.25) | 5.42 (1.56) (2.75–9.25) | 5.41 (1.30) (3.58–8.58) | 5.87 (2.14) (2.92–12.33) |
| Receptive vocabulary age[3] | 5.76 (1.81) (3.08–10.00) | 5.67 (1.39) (2.42–8.83) | 6.36 (2.55) (3.42–13.83) | 5.18 (1.44) (2.42–7.50) | 6.12 (2.01) (2.17–11.58) |
| Mean length of utterance (morphemes) | 4.18 (0.94) (2.22–5.49) | 3.49 (0.69) (2.18–4.88) | 3.98 (0.74) (2.27–4.74) | 3.14 (0.75) (1.76–4.76) | 4.87 (0.54) (4.12–6.05) |

[1] *Leiter-R, age equivalent in years.*
[2] *Expressive Vocabulary Test (EVT), age equivalent in years.*
[3] *Peabody Picture Vocabulary Test – 3rd Edition (PPVT-III), age equivalent in years.*

records confirmed a clinical diagnosis by an independent diagnostician, he was not dropped from analyses. Thirty-three boys with FXS were identified by the ADOS as having "autism," seven as having "spectrum," and 21 as having "no autism." Those meeting criteria for either autism or spectrum formed the group of boys with FXS-ASD.

### *Pragmatic language*

The participants' pragmatic language skills were assessed with the Pragmatic Judgment subtest of the Comprehensive Assessment of Spoken Language (CASL; Carrow-Woolfolk, 1999) and the Children's Communication Checklist-Second Edition, U.S. Edition (Bishop, 2006). The Pragmatic Judgment subtest is a direct-assessment tool for examining general pragmatic language understanding and use. The examiner reads aloud a script representing a particular part of daily life, and children are either asked to judge the appropriateness of language used in a particular situation, or they are asked to provide a pragmatically appropriate response. Test-retest reliability coefficients for the Pragmatic Judgment subtest for the age ranges included in this study exceed 0.80, suggesting that this subtest is a reliable index of pragmatic language skill. Age equivalents were computed for the current study except in the case of a raw score of 0, which for analysis was considered missing. Four boys with ASD-O, two boys with DS, and one boy with FXS-ASD received a raw score of 0.

The CCC-2 was developed to measure social language use (although it also assesses structural language domains), and requires parents and/or teachers to rate a variety of communication difficulties or strengths according to how often the behavior in question is observed in everyday settings. For this study, teacher ratings were used. The checklist includes 70 items and yields 10 scaled scores. The scales of primary interest for pragmatic language assessment included the following: Initiation, Scripted Language, Context, Non-verbal Communication, Social Relations, and Interests. We also compared the Speech, Syntax, Semantics, and Coherence scales as variables of secondary interest. Scaled scores range from 1 to 19, with a higher value indicating better communication. The General Communication Composite (GCC) standard score was also calculated (ranging from 40 to 160) and based on the sum of 8 scaled scores (all except Social Relations and Interests).

### *Theory of mind*

Theory of mind was assessed using one of two comparable batteries of tasks. The first version included the following tests: Perspective Taking, Diverse Desires, Diverse Belief, False Belief, Knowledge Access, and Explicit False Belief (Wellman and Liu, 2004; Slaughter et al., 2007). This version involved more complex, primarily verbal, presentation of the tasks. Results from initial assessments indicated that the tasks in the original battery were too difficult for some lower functioning children, and that the heavy verbal load impacted performance above and beyond children's levels of social cognitive competence. Thus, more basic tasks assessing intentionality and understanding of desires were added to the battery (detailed below), and administration of the false belief tasks was also modified such that scenarios were enacted, rather than read as a story involving abstract characters, to decrease verbal and cognitive load (Flavell et al., 1983; Lewis and Mitchell, 1994; Repacholi and Gopnik, 1997; Matthews et al., 2003; Slaughter et al., 2007). It was not necessary to alter the Perspective Taking Task as the protocol was already interaction-based. Two, more basic, tasks were added to tap metarepresentational skills in children who were not capable of performing the original, more advanced battery – Simple Desires and Appearance-Reality – which have been used with children as young as 14 months and 3 years, respectively, and are described in the Appendix. Each participant received either the original or the modified battery of tasks, depending on when they were tested. All assessments were second-scored by a trained research assistant. See Appendix for further task description and scoring procedures.

To produce a single composite theory of mind score for all children (and ensure comparability across the initial and modified batteries), factor analysis scores were derived. First, the two batteries were tested in separate confirmatory factor analytic (CFA) models. Both factor models were estimated under weighted least squares using MPlus (Muthen and Muthen, 2006). The commonality of the Perspective Taking Task across both batteries provided an anchor that enabled us to ensure score equivalence across forms. This task was used to set the metric for the latent variable. The CFA for the older battery was run first. In the model of the newer battery, we fixed the factor loading and threshold parameters for the Perspective Taking Task to be equal to those parameters from the model of the older battery. Thus, estimates of the latent variable, theory of mind, were equivalent across both models. That is, a given respondent would be expected to receive the same score regardless of which form of the test he or she was given. Results indicated very good model fit for the one factor solution in both models (older form: RMSEA = 0.003, CFI = 1.00; newer form: RMSEA = 0.000, CFI = 1.00). Finally, we used the factor models to estimate and export theory of mind scores for each individual. To aid in interpretability, these scores were then standardized to have a mean of 10 and a standard deviation of 1.

#### *Non-verbal cognitive ability*

Non-verbal cognition was assessed with the Brief IQ composite of the Leiter-R (Roid and Miller, 1997), which includes Sequential Order, Figure Ground, Form Completion, and Repeated Patterns subtests. Age equivalents were calculated based on the published norms.

#### *Structural language*

Receptive vocabulary, expressive vocabulary, and expressive syntax were measured with the Peabody Picture Vocabulary Test-Third Edition (PPVT-III; Dunn and Dunn, 1997), EVT (Williams, 1997), and mean length of utterance (MLU; Brown, 1973), respectively. Age equivalents for the PPVT-III and EVT were calculated according to published norms. MLU in morphemes was calculated from 100 child utterances produced during the ADOS. The language samples were transcribed using Systematic Analysis of Language Transcripts (SALT) software conventions (Miller and Chapman, 2008) and using ELAN transcription software (Max Planck Institute for Psycholinguistics, 2002; Sloetjes and Wittenburg, 2008), which allowed transcribers to sync visual information from video recording with separate high-quality audio recordings. All transcribers achieved 80% reliability against two gold standard transcripts for each diagnostic group prior to transcribing samples for the present study. A random subset of the transcripts (10% or more from each group) was independently transcribed by a second research assistant, and morpheme-to-morpheme agreement between the original and reliability transcripts was 77% overall.

#### *Molecular profile characterization in FXS*

Measures of *FMR1*-related variation were derived from blood samples and included the number of CGG expansion repeats, percentage of gene methylation, and percentage of lymphocytes producing FMRP. The number of CGG expansion repeats was determined using PCR analysis to determine repeat size and Southern blot to confirm PCR results for expanded alleles. Phosphorimaging was performed to determine percent methylation. Blood smears were analyzed by immunocytochemistry to determine FMRP expression. The majority of blood samples (85%) were analyzed by Kimball Genetics, Inc., with remaining analyses completed by one of several other laboratories.

### DATA ANALYSIS

#### *Group Comparisons*

Between group differences in pragmatic language (indexed by the Pragmatic Judgment subtest of the CASL and select scales of the CCC-2) were examined using analysis of covariance (ANCOVA) models, with the following covariates: age equivalent scores for receptive and expressive vocabulary measured by the PPVT-III and EVT, respectively; MLU; and general cognitive ability measured by the Leiter-R. Planned *post hoc* contrasts were used to test for specific between group differences. Group differences in theory of mind were also examined with diagnosis as the primary predictor and PPVT-III, EVT, MLU, and Leiter-R included as covariates.

Given the large number of models, omnibus $F$-tests were adjusted using the Benjamini and Hochberg (1995) procedure to control for false discovery.

#### *Genetic correlates of pragmatic language and theory of mind in FXS groups*

Simple correlations were run with the FXS group as a whole (to increase power), between the genetic variables and measures of structural language (PPVT-III, EVT, MLU, and structural language subscales of the CCC), general cognition (Leiter-R), pragmatic language (CASL and pragmatic language subscales of the CCC-2), and theory of mind. Because the number of CGG expansion repeats and percent methylation were highly skewed, these variables were log-transformed prior to analyses.

## RESULTS

### GROUP COMPARISONS OF PRAGMATIC LANGUAGE

Comparisons of group performance on the Pragmatic Judgment subscale of the CASL, controlling for structural language and general cognitive abilities, were statistically significant, $F(4, 108) = 5.49$, $p < 0.001$. *Post hoc* tests (see **Figure 1**) indicated that the ASD-O group scored lower than the FXS-O ($d$[1] $= 0.64$), DS ($d = 0.41$), and TD ($d = 0.69$) groups ($ps < 0.05$). The FXS-ASD group showed a similar pattern, with significantly lower scores than both FXS-O ($p = 0.021$, $d = 0.35$) and TD groups ($p = 0.029$, $d = 0.41$), but did not differ significantly from the DS group ($p = 0.403$). The ASD-O and FXS-ASD groups performed comparably ($p = 0.100$).

Model tests and adjusted means are presented in **Table 2** for the subscales of the CCC-2. The models for the Social Relations and Interests subscales were not significant, and *post hoc* comparisons are therefore not presented for these subscales. Significant group differences were detected for all other subscales.

[1] Cohen's $d$ (Cohen, 1988) is a measure of effect size where 0.2 is considered small, 0.5 is considered medium, and 0.8 is considered large.

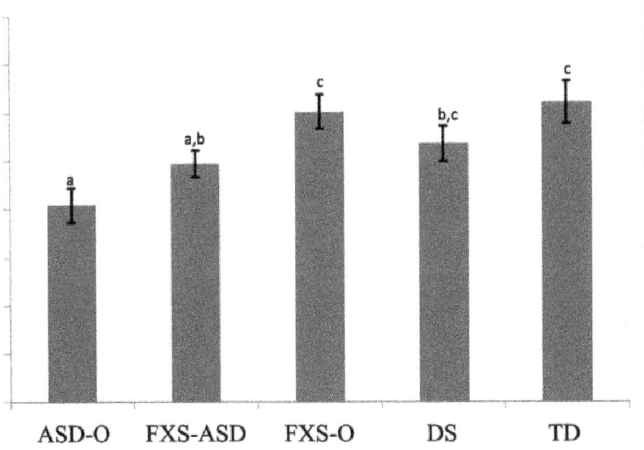


**FIGURE 1 | Model Adjusted Pragmatic Judgment Scores on the CASL.** Notes: groups not sharing superscripts are significantly different from each other ($p < 0.05$). $F$ for Diagnosis (4, 107) = 4.39, $p < 0.001$.

The TD group scored significantly higher on the CCC-2 total score than all other groups (all $d > 1.4$) with no other between group differences. This pattern was repeated for the Syntax, Semantics, Coherence, Scripted Language, and Context subscales (all $d$ for the comparison with TD > 1.3). On the Speech subscale, the DS group also had significantly lower scores than both the ASD-O ($d = 0.34$) and FXS-O ($d = 0.76$) groups, but was not different from children with FXS-ASD. TD children had higher speech scores than all other groups (all $d$ for the comparison with TD > 1.3). The FXS-ASD group scored lower than both the DS ($d = 0.65$) and ASD-O ($d = 0.71$) groups on the Initiation subscale, with TD boys scoring higher than all groups but ASD-O (all $d$ for the significant comparisons with TD > 0.70). The pattern of means was most notably different for the Non-verbal Communication subscale. This was the only outcome, other than Social Relations and Interests, where the DS sample did not score significantly lower than the TD sample. The TD group scored significantly higher in non-verbal communication than the ASD-O, FXS-ASD, and FXS-O groups.

## THEORY OF MIND AND PRAGMATIC LANGUAGE

Comparing scores on the battery of theory of mind tasks, which were standardized to have a mean of 10 and a standard deviation of 1, covarying language and cognitive ability indicated that the TD group performed better than ASD-O, FXS-ASD, and DS groups (all $d > 0.70$). The difference between TD and FXS-O approached significance ($p = 0.082$, $d = 0.56$). There were no other significant group differences (see **Figure 2**).

Significant correlations between theory of mind and performance on the CASL Pragmatic Judgment subscale were found for all groups (see **Table 3**). Theory of mind was additionally related to the "Initiation" subscale of the CCC-2 in the autism group ($r = 0.56$, $p < 0.05$) and in the FXS group, it was related to the CCC-2's "Coherence" subscale ($r = 0.36$, $p < 0.01$).

## MOLECULAR GENETIC CORRELATES OF PRAGMATIC LANGUAGE IN FXS

Correlations were conducted to examine potential associations between molecular genetic variables (CGG repeat number, FMRP,

**Table 2 | Model adjusted scores on pragmatic language and general language subscales of the CCC-2.**

| Group | Scripted language | Initiation | Non-verbal communication | Social relations | Interests | Context | Speech | Syntax | Semantics | Coherence | CCC-2 Standard Score |
|---|---|---|---|---|---|---|---|---|---|---|---|
| | Mean (SE) | Mean (SE) | Mean (SE) | Mean (SE) | Mean (SE) | Mean (SE) | Mean (SE) | Mean (SE) | Mean (SE) | Mean (SE) | Mean (SE) |
| ASD-O | 5.43 (0.78)$^{a}$ | 7.46 (0.76)$^{a,c}$ | 4.76 (0.72)$^{a}$ | 5.46 (0.71) | 6.22 (0.89) | 5.09 (0.65)$^{a}$ | 5.97 (0.89)$^{a}$ | 5.09 (0.75)$^{a}$ | 6.78 (0.65)$^{a}$ | 4.49 (0.77)$^{a}$ | 73.56 (3.95)$^{a}$ |
| FXS-ASD | 5.50 (0.58)$^{a}$ | 4.91 (0.56)$^{b}$ | 4.45 (0.54)$^{a}$ | 6.31 (0.54) | 6.90 (0.66) | 4.80 (0.47)$^{a}$ | 4.28 (0.65)$^{a,b}$ | 4.33 (0.55)$^{a}$ | 5.16 (0.49)$^{a}$ | 3.98 (0.55)$^{a}$ | 67.94 (2.85)$^{a}$ |
| FXS-O | 4.90 (0.68)$^{a}$ | 6.21 (0.63)$^{a,b}$ | 4.55 (0.61)$^{a}$ | 6.76 (0.59) | 8.01 (0.72) | 5.23 (0.54)$^{a}$ | 5.77 (0.74)$^{a}$ | 4.94 (0.64)$^{a}$ | 5.50 (0.55)$^{a}$ | 4.66 (0.62)$^{a}$ | 69.64 (3.29)$^{a}$ |
| DS | 6.70 (0.74)$^{a}$ | 6.87 (0.76)$^{a}$ | 6.10 (0.70)$^{a,b}$ | 6.98 (0.68) | 7.52 (0.85) | 5.71 (0.64)$^{a}$ | 3.06 (0.85)$^{b}$ | 3.80 (0.72)$^{a}$ | 5.73 (0.64)$^{a}$ | 4.60 (0.69)$^{a}$ | 72.65 (3.81)$^{a}$ |
| TD | 9.90 (0.85)$^{b}$ | 9.48 (0.83)$^{c}$ | 7.86 (0.79)$^{b}$ | 7.31 (0.77) | 10.15 (0.97) | 9.56 (0.70)$^{b}$ | 9.63 (0.97)$^{c}$ | 9.13 (0.81)$^{b}$ | 9.07 (0.73)$^{b}$ | 9.28 (0.80)$^{b}$ | 96.63 (4.08)$^{b}$ |
| F for Diagnosis | (3, 63) = 6.36** | (3, 63) = 4.73* | (3, 64) = 4.16** | (3, 62) = 1.16 | (3, 63) = 2.97 | (3, 63) = 8.80** | (3, 64) = 6.45** | (3, 63) = 6.74** | (3, 64) = 4.77** | (3, 60) = 8.15** | (3, 57) = 8.58** |

*Groups not sharing superscripts within a column are significantly different from each other ($p < 0.05$).*

*$*p < 0.05$, $**p < 0.01$.*

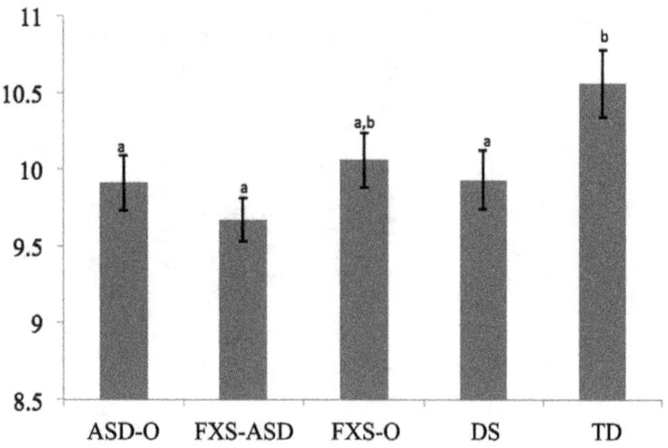


**FIGURE 2 | Model Adjusted Theory of Mind Scores.** Notes: groups not sharing superscripts are significantly different from each other ($p < 0.05$). $F$ for Diagnosis $(4, 106) = 2.87$, $p < 0.05$.

**Table 3 | Correlations between theory of mind and pragmatic language on the CASL.**

| | Theory of mind | | | |
|---|---|---|---|---|
| | **ASD-O** | **FXS (all)** | **DS** | **TD** |
| CASL pragmatic judgment age equivalent (*n*) | 0.56* 21 | 0.36** 57 | 0.51* 21 | 0.54** 19 |

*$p < 0.05$, **$p < 0.01$.

**Table 4 | Genetic correlations with language (structural and pragmatic language), general cognition, and theory of mind in the FXS group.**

| | CGG Repeats | Log-transformed FMRP | Log-transformed percent methylation |
|---|---|---|---|
| PPVT | −0.33* | 0.33 | −0.32 |
| *n* | 36 | 33 | 33 |
| EVT | −0.11 | 0.31 | −0.41* |
| *n* | 36 | 33 | 33 |
| Leiter | −0.36* | 0.34 | −0.30 |
| *n* | 36 | 33 | 33 |
| MLU | −0.35* | 0.10 | −0.34 |
| *n* | 36 | 32 | 32 |
| CASL Pragmatic judgment | −0.40* | 0.33 | −0.36* |
| (*n*) | 36 | 33 | 33 |
| Theory of mind | −0.32 | 0.24 | −0.45* |
| *n* | 35 | 33 | 32 |

*$p < 0.05$.

and percent methylation) and measures of structural language (PPVT-III, EVT, MLU, and relevant subscales of the CCC-2), general cognition (Leiter-R), pragmatic language (Pragmatic Judgment on the CASL, and the pragmatic language subscales of the CCC-2), and theory of mind. Because CGG repeat numbers and methylation values were very skewed, these variables were log-transformed prior to analysis. **Table 4** presents these results, with the exception of the CCC-2, where no significant correlations were detected. No significant associations were observed with FMRP, but higher CGG repeat numbers and increased methylation were associated with lower CASL pragmatic judgment scores. Increased methylation was also significantly related to poorer theory of mind. Measures of structural language and general cognition also showed some relationship with CGG repeat length and methylation.

## DISCUSSION

By comparing the pragmatic language abilities of children with idiopathic autism or FXS (both with and without autism), with children with DS and TD children, this study aimed to determine the extent to which pragmatic language impairment may overlap in autism and FXS, and may potentially be tied to underlying molecular genetic variation related to *FMR1*, the gene that causes FXS. Additionally, we explored theory of mind ability as a potential correlate of pragmatic language across groups. Prior studies have reported a link between impaired theory of mind and pragmatic language use in autism, but to our knowledge this question has not yet been addressed in FXS.

Results indicated that the ASD-O and FXS-ASD groups looked quite similar on direct-assessment of pragmatic language using the CASL, with both groups performing more poorly than the FXS-O, DS, and TD groups. Yet on teacher report findings were more divergent (e.g., Initiation, where the FXS-ASD group scored significantly lower than the ASD-O group). It could be the case that a global measure of pragmatic language ability such as the CASL obscures actual differences between these groups. Alternatively, informant-based methods such as the CCC-2 may introduce measurement error that complicates group comparisons (e.g., different teachers may have different thresholds for ratings, based on their prior experience, the composition of their classrooms, etc.). Further research comparing these groups using direct-assessment measures of specific types of pragmatic language ability will be valuable in addressing this question and determining the extent of overlap in pragmatic language impairment in autism and FXS.

Analyses of theory of mind ability revealed patterns of performance quite similar to those observed in the CASL test of pragmatic language – the ASD-O and FXS-ASD groups performed most poorly, and children with FXS-O did not differ significantly from controls. In this case, however, the DS group performed more like the ASD-O and FXS-ASD groups. We also found that theory of mind ability was associated with pragmatic language on the CASL for all groups, where better theory of mind scores were associated with more pragmatic language competence. Although we cannot draw definitive causal conclusions from the present data, these findings certainly support the hypothesis that the ability to understand and predict one's own and others' thoughts, feelings, intentions, and desires is a critical skill underpinning competent pragmatic language use (Sperber and Wilson, 2002; Wilson and

Sperber, 2004). When theory of mind is impaired, as was the case for the ASD-O and FXS-ASD groups, children may be ill equipped to contend with the demands of social discourse, and less apt to glean information necessary for developing pragmatic language skills. Such a relationship has been demonstrated across a range of pragmatic language skills in autism (Loveland and Tunali, 1993; Tager-Flusberg and Sullivan, 1995; Surian et al., 1996; Capps et al., 1998, 2000; Tager-Flusberg, 2000), and our findings suggest a similarly important role in the pragmatic language problems observed in a subgroup of children with FXS who show pragmatic language impairments as well. That significant associations were detected in all groups, even those who did not show significant pragmatic language impairment, may demonstrate the important role of theory of mind in supporting more fluent pragmatic language use as well. It is of course also possible that theory of mind tasks and pragmatic language are tapping some additional mediating (or moderating) abilities.

Patterns observed in the FXS-O and DS groups may also be informative, particularly with regard to defining syndrome-specific language and social cognitive profiles across these different groups. In particular, whereas social skills are generally considered to represent a relative strength in individuals with DS, the literature on pragmatic language in DS is actually quite mixed, with documented challenges compared with MA-matched TD children including initiation and elaboration of topics (Tannock, 1988; Roberts et al., 2007a), initiation of communicative repairs (Abbeduto et al., 2008), and clarity of messages (Abbeduto et al., 2006). Thus, our finding that boys with DS performed comparably to boys with FXS-ASD is not necessarily surprising. On the otherhand, we may have found significant differences between FXS-ASD and DS groups with a larger sample size or if we examined particular aspects of pragmatic language with direct-assessment measures (and it is important to note that the DS group did not differ significantly from the TD group, whereas the FXS-ASD group did perform significantly more poorly than the TD group). Thus, interpretation of these similarities with the present data is not straightforward.

In the FXS-O group, these data indicated that pragmatic language and theory of mind were relative strengths, and deficits in these areas may be restricted only to those with FXS-ASD, suggesting that pragmatic language deficit (or theory of mind) is not a core characteristic of FXS but rather autism in FXS. This is consistent with findings from Roberts et al. (2007a), who found that boys with FXS-O did not produce more non-contingent language than TD boys, but that the FXS-ASD group produced more non-contingent language than both of these groups. However, it is important to note that the difference between the TD and FXS-O groups approached significance so may have revealed true differences with a larger sample.

Though not a primary focus of the current study, findings do have some important clinical implications. Given that boys with FXS-ASD showed more pragmatic language impairment than boys with FXS-O, performing comparably to boys with idiopathic autism on a direct-assessment measure, the diagnosis of ASD in boys with FXS should be considered during assessment and clinicians may consider interventions that have been studied in the context of ASD when tailoring intervention approaches for boys with FXS-ASD. Our divergent findings depending on assessment method also support the use of multiple assessments, including natural language samples, to fully characterize pragmatic language ability and identify specific targets for intervention which may differ across groups and individuals.

The group similarities in directly assessed pragmatic language ability and theory of mind in ASD-O and FXS-ASD may have important implications for furthering knowledge of the brain and gene basis of these complex skills. In particular, because much is known about the molecular and neurobiological basis of FXS, the considerable overlap observed with ASD-O may help to define specific phenotypes associated with known genetic variation, in this case variation in the *FMR1*. We observed correlations with molecular genetic variables that support this association – pragmatic language on the CASL and theory of mind were both associated with *FMR1*-related variation in the FXS group. Specifically, greater methylation was associated with lower theory of mind performance and more impaired pragmatic language ability. Higher CGG repeat numbers were also related to poorer pragmatic language skills. Genetic variables showed additional associations with general cognition and structural language, which is perhaps not surprising given that general cognitive and language functioning certainly contribute to pragmatic language and theory of mind abilities. By providing a link between genetic and phenotypic variation, these findings may offer a foothold for understanding gene-behavior relationships in atypical and typical development alike.

This study has some limitations. First, we determined autism status primarily with the ADOS, but future studies should utilize information from both the ADOS and ADI-R for all participants to confirm autism status. Second, we did not examine all potential underlying mechanisms of social communication, such as anxiety or various aspects of executive function. Third, we examined social communication and theory of mind at one time point and in boys only. Future studies should assess these skills longitudinally and in both boys and girls.

In sum, this study identified pragmatic language and theory of mind as important abilities that are impaired in autism, and in a subgroup of children with FXS who also meet criteria for autism. This considerable phenotypic overlap between autism and a known monogenic condition suggests that impairments in pragmatic language ability and theory of mind may be tied to a particular genetic variant – the *FMR1*. Further studies are needed to clarify those particular types of pragmatic language difficulties common to both conditions, given that results from the pragmatic language subscales on the informant-based CCC-2 were not as straightforward as those obtained from direct-assessment of pragmatic language ability, or theory of mind for that matter. An additional important area for further study concerns the brain basis of these abilities, and the extent to which impairments may stem from similar neural architectural differences. By integrating detailed phenotypic analysis with neuroimaging studies in autism and FXS, future research may provide important insights into the role of *FMR1* in social-communicative phenotypes.

## ACKNOWLEDGMENTS

We are grateful to the families who participated in this research. We also gratefully acknowledge the support of grants R01HD038819-06A2, R01HD038819-09S1, R01DC010191-01A1, R01HD044935-06A1, and R03DC010880-01A1, and the support of the Research Participant Registry Core of the Carolina Institute for Developmental Disabilities (P30 HD03110).

## REFERENCES

1. Abbeduto, L., Brady, N., and Kover, S. T. (2007). Language develop- ment and fragile X syndrome: profiles, syndrome-specificity, and within-syndrome differences. *Ment. Retard Dev. Disabil. Res. Rev.* 13, 36–46.
2. Abbeduto, L., and Chapman, R. (2005). "Language development in Down syndrome and fragile X syndrome: current research and implications for theory and prac- tice," in *Developmental Theory and Language Disorders*, eds P. Fletcher and J. F. Miller (Amsterdam: John Benjamins Publishing Co.), 53–72.
3. Abbeduto, L., Murphy, M. M., Kover, S. T., Giles, N. D., Karadottir, S., Amman, A., Bruno, L., Kim, J. S., Schroeder, S., Anderson, J. A., and Nollin, K. A. (2008). Signaling noncomprehension of language: a comparison of fragile X syndrome and Down syndrome. *Am. J. Ment. Retard.* 113, 214–230.
4. Abbeduto, L., Murphy, M. M., Rich- mond, E. K., Amman, A., Beth, P., Weissman, M. D., Kin, J., Cawthon, S. W., Karadottir, S., and Dykens, D. (2006). Collaboration in referen- tial communication: comparison of youth with down syndrome or frag- ile X syndrome. *Am. J. Ment. Retard.* 111, 170–183.
5. Abbeduto, L., Pavetto, M., Kesin, E., Weissman, M. D., Karadottir, S., O'Brien, A., and Cawthon, S. (2001). The linguistic and cognitive pro- file of Down syndrome: evidence from a comparison with fragile X syndrome. *Down Syndr. Res. Pract. Down Syndr. Educ. Trust* 7, 9–15.
6. American Psychiatric Association. (1994). *Diagnostic and Statisti- cal Manual of Mental Disorders*. Washington: American Psychiatric Association.
7. Bailey, D. B. Jr., Hatton, D. D., Skin- ner, M., and Mesibov, G. (2001). Autistic behavior, FMR1 protein, and developmental trajectories in young males with fragile X syn- drome. *J. Autism Dev. Disord.* 31, 165–174.
8. Bailey, D. B. Jr., Raspa, M., Olm- sted, M., and Holiday, D. B. (2008). Co-occurring conditions associated with FMR1 gene variations: findings from a national parent survey. *Am. J. Med. Genet. A* 146A, 2060–2069.
9. Bailey, D. B., Raspa, M., Holiday, D., Bishop, E., and Olmsted, M. (2009). Functional skills of individuals with fragile x syndrome: a lifespan cross-sectional analysis. *Am. J. Intellect. Dev. Disabil.* 114, 289–303.
10. Benjamini, Y., and Hochberg, Y. (1995). Controlling the false discovery rate: a practical and powerful approach to multiple testing. *J. R. Stat. Soc. Series B Stat. Methodol.* 57, 289–300.
11. Bennetto, L., and Pennington, B. F. (2002). "Neuropsychology," in *Frag- ile X Syndrome: Diagnosis, Treat- ment, and Research*, 3rd Edn, eds R. J. Hagerman and P. J. Hagerman (Bal- itmore: Johns Hopkins University Press), 206–248.
12. Bishop, D. V. M. (2006). *Children's Com- munication Checklist-2*. San Antonio: Pearson.
13. Bregman, J. D., Leckman, J. F., and Ort, S. I. (1988). Fragile X syn- drome: genetic predisposition of psychopathy. *J. Autism Dev. Disord.* 18, 343–354.
14. Brown, P., and Levinson, S. C. (1987). *Politeness: Some Universals in Language Usage*. Cambridge: Cambridge University Press.
15. Brown, R. (1973). *A First Language; the Early Stages*. Cambridge: Harvard University Press.
16. Capps, L., Kehres, J., and Sigman, M. (1998). Conversational abili- ties among children with autism and developmental delay. *Autism* 2, 325–344.
17. Capps, L., Losh, M., and Thurber, C. (2000). The frog ate a bug and made his mouth sad: narrative competence in children with autism. *J. Abnorm. Child. Psychol.* 28, 193–204.
18. Carrow-Woolfolk, E. (1999). *CASL: Comprehensive Assessment of Spoken Language*. Circle Pines: American Guidance Services.
19. Clifford, S., Dissanayake, C., Bui, Q. M., Huggins, R., Taylor, A. K., and Loesch, D. Z. (2007). Autism spectrum phenotype in males and females with fragile X full muta- tion and premutation. *J. Autism Dev. Disord.* 37, 738–747.
20. Coffee, B., Keith, K., Albizua, I., Mal- one, T., Mowrey, J., Sherman, S. L., and Warren, S. T. (2009). Inci- dence of fragile X syndrome by newborn screening for methylated FMR1 DNA. *Am. J. Hum. Genet.* 85, 503–514.
21. Cohen, J. (1988). *Statistical Power Analysis for the Behavioral Sci- ences*. Hillsdale: L. Erlbaum Associates.
22. Cordeiro, L., Ballinger, E., Hagerman, R., and Hessl, D. (2011). Clini- cal assessment of DSM-IV anx- iety disorders in fragile X syn- drome: prevalence and character- ization. *J. Neurodev. Disord.* 3, 57–67.
23. Cornish, K., Burack, J. A., Rahman, A., Munir, F., Russo, N., and Grant, C. (2005). Theory of mind deficits in children with fragile X syn- drome. *J. Intellect. Disabil. Res.* 49, 372–378.
24. Devys, D., Lutz, Y., Rouyer, N., Bel-locq, J. P., and Mandel, J. L. (1993). The FMR-1 protein is cytoplas- mic, most abundant in neurons and appears normal in carriers of a frag- ile X premutation. *Nat. Genet.* 4, 335–340.
25. Dunn, L. M., and Dunn, D. M. (1997). *Peabody Picture Vocabulary Test*. Circle Pines: American Guidance Ser- vice.
26. Dykens, E., Hodapp, R. M., and Fin- ucane, B. M. (2000). *Genetics and Mental Retardation Syndromes: A New Look at Behavior and Interven- tions*. Baltimore: Paul H. Brookes.
27. Estigarribia, B., Martin, G. E., Roberts, J. E., Spencer, A., Gucwa, A., and Sideris, J. (2011). Narrative skill in boys with *fragile* X syndrome with and without autism spectrum disorder. *Appl. Psycholinguist.* 32, 359–388.
28. Fernandez-Carvajal, I., Walichiewicz, P., Xiaosen, X., Pan, R., Hager-man, P. J., and Tassone, F. (2009). Screening for expanded alleles of the FMR1 gene in blood spots from newborn males in a Span- ish population. *J. Mol. Diagn.* 11, 324–329.
29. Finestack, L. H., Richmond, E. K., and Abbeduto, L. (2009). Language development in individuals with fragile X syndrome. *Top. Lang. Dis- ord.* 29, 133–148.
30. Flavell, J. H., Flavell, E. R., and Green, F. L. (1983). Development of the appearance – reality distinction. *Cogn. Psychol.* 15, 95–120.
31. Garner, C., Callias, M., and Turk, J. (1999). Executive function and the- ory of mind performance of boys with fragile-X syndrome. *J. Intellect. Disabil.* 43, 466–474.
32. Gotham, K., Risi, S., Dawson, G., Tager- Flusberg, H., Joseph, R., Carter, A., Hepburn, S., McMahon, W., Rodier, P., Hyman, S. L., Sigman, M., Rogers, S., Landa, R., Spence, M. A., Osann, K., Flodman, P., Volkmar, F., Hol- lander, E., Buxbaum, J., Pickles, A., and Lord, C. (2008). A replication of the Autism Diagnostic Observa- tion Schedule (ADOS) revised algo- rithms. *J. Am. Acad. Child Adolesc. Psychiatry* 47, 642–651.
33. Gotham, K., Risi, S., Pickles, A., and Lord, C. (2007). The autism diag- nostic observation schedule: revised algorithms for improved diagnostic validity. *J. Autism Dev. Disord.* 37, 613–627.
34. Grant, C. M., Apperly, I., and Oliver, C. (2007). Is theory of mind understanding impaired in males with fragile X syndrome. *J. Abnorm. Child. Psychol.* 35, 17–28.
35. Grice, H. P. (1975). "Logic and con- versation," in *Syntax and Semantics Vol. 3: Speech Acts*, eds P. Cole and J. L. Morgan (New York: Academic Press), 41–58.
36. Hagerman, P. (2008). The fragile X prevalence paradox. *J. Med. Genet.* 45, 498–499.
37. Hagerman, R. (2002). "The physical and behavioral phenotype," in *Frag- ile X Syndrome: Diagnosis, Treat- ment, and Research*, 3rd Edn, eds R. J. Hagerman and P. J. Hagerman (Bal- timore: Johns Hopkins University Press), 3–87.
38. Hagerman, R. (2006). Lessons from fragile X regarding neurobiology, autism, and neurodegeneration. *J. Dev. Behav. Pediatr.* 27, 63–74.
39. Hagerman, R., and Hagerman, P. (eds). (2002). *Fragile X Syndrome: Diagnosis, Treatment, and Research*, 3rd Edn. Baltimore: Johns Hopkins University Press.
40. Hall, S. S., Lightbody, A. A., and Reiss, A. L. (2008). Compulsive, self- injurious, and autistic behavior in children and adolescents with frag- ile X syndrome. *Am. J. Ment. Retard.* 113, 44–53.
41. Hanson, D. M., Jackson, A. W. III, and Hagerman, R. J. (1986). Speech disturbances (cluttering) in mildly impaired males with the Martin-Bell/fragile X syn- drome. *Am. J. Med. Genet.* 23, 195–206.
42. Hooper, S. R., Hatton, D. D., Baranek,
43. G. T., Roberts, J. P., and Bai- ley, D. B. (2000). Nonverbal assessment of IQ, attention, and memory abilities in children with fragile-X syndrome using the Leiter-R. *J. Psychoeduc. Assess.* 18, 255–267.

44. Jin, P., and Warren, S. T. (2003). New insights into fragile X syn- drome: from molecules to neurobe- haviors. *Trends Biochem. Sci.* 28, 152–158.
45. Kaufmann, W. E., Cortell, R., Kau, A. S., Bukelis, I., Tierney, E., Gray, R. M., Cox, C., Capone, G. T., and Stanard, (2004). Autism spectrum disorder in fragile X syndrome: communica- tion, social interaction, and specific behaviors. *Am. J. Med. Genet.* 129, 225–234.
46. Kover, S. T., and Abbeduto, L. (2010). Expressive language in male ado- lescents with fragile X syndrome with and without comorbid autism. *J. Intellect. Disabil. Res.* 54, 246–265.
47. Lewis, C., and Mitchell, P. (eds.). (1994). *Children's Early Understanding of Mind.* East Sussex: Lawrence Erl- baum Associates Publishers.
48. Lewis, P., Abbeduto, L., Murphy, M., Richmond, E., Giles, N., Bruno, L., and Schroeder, S. (2006). Cogni- tive, language and social-cognitive skills of individuals with fragile X syndrome with and without autism. *J. Intellect. Disabil. Res.* 50, 532–545.
49. Loesch, D. Z., Bui, Q. M., Grigsby, J., Butler, E., Epstein, J., Hug- gins, R. M., Taylor, A. K., and Hagerman, R. J. (2003). Effect of the fragile X status categories and the fragile X mental retar- dation protein levels on executive functioning in males and females with fragile X. *Neuropsychology* 17, 646–657.
50. Loesch, D. Z., Huggins, R. M., Bui, M., Epstein, J. L., Taylor, A. K., and Hagerman, R. J. (2002). Effect of the deficits of fragile X men- tal retardation protein on cogni- tive status of fragile X males and females assessed by robust pedigree analysis. *J. Dev. Behav. Pediatr.* 23, 416–423.
51. Lord, C., Rutter, M., DiLavore, P. C., and Risi, S. (2001). *Autism Diagnostic Observation Schedule.* Los Angeles: Western Psychological Services.
52. Lord, C., Rutter, M., and Le Cou- teur, A. (1994). Autism diagnos- tic interview-revised: a revised ver- sion of a diagnostic interview for caregivers of individuals with possible pervasive developmental disorders. *J. Autism Dev. Disord.* 24, 659–685.
53. Losh, M., and Capps, L. (2003). Narra- tive ability in high-functioning chil- dren with autism or Asperger's syn- drome. *J. Autism Dev. Disord.* 33, 239–251.
54. Loveland, K. A., and Tunali, B. (1993). "Narrative language in autism and the theory of mind hypothesis: a wider perspective," in *Understand- ing Other Minds: Perspectives from Autism*, eds S. Baron-Cohen, H. Tager-Flusberg, and D. J. Cohen (Oxford: Oxford University Press), 247–266.
55. Madison, L. S., George, C., and Moeschler, J. B. (1986). Cogni- tive functioning in the fragile- X syndrome: a study of intel- lectual, memory and communica- tion skills. *J. Ment. Defic. Res.* 30, 129–148.
56. Matthews, R., Dissanayake, C., and Pratt, C. (2003). The relationship between the theory of mind and con- servation abilities in children using active/inactive paradigm. *Aust. J. Psychol.* 55, 35–42.
57. Max Planck Institute for Psy- cholinguistics. (2002). *ELAN.* Nijmegen. Available at: http://www.lat-mpi.eu/tools/elan/
58. Mazzoco, M. M., Pennington, B. F., and Hagerman, R. J. (1994). Social cogni- tion skills among females with frag- ile X. *J. Autism Dev. Disord.* 24, 473–485.
59. McDuffie, A., Abbeduto, L., Lewis, P., Kover, S., Kim, J. S., Weber, A., and Brown, W. T. (2010). Autism spectrum disorder in chil- dren and adolescents with fragile X syndrome: within-syndrome dif- ferences and age-related changes. *Am. J. Autism Dev. Disord.* 115, 307–326.
60. McDuffie, A., Kover, S., Abbeduto, L., Lewis, P., and Brown, T. (2012). Profiles of receptive and expressive lan- guage abilities in boys with comor- bid fragile x syndrome and autism. *Am. J. Intellect. Dev. Disabil.* 117, 18–32.
61. Miller, J. F., and Chapman, R. S. (2008). *Systematic Analysis of Lan- guage Transcripts (SALT).* Madison: University of Wisconsin-Madison.
62. Muthen, L. K., and Muthen, B. (2006). *Mplus* User's *Guide (Version 4).* Los Angeles: Muther & Muthen.
63. Philofsky, A., Hepburn, S. L., Hayes, A., Hagerman, R., and Rogers, S. J. (2004). Linguistic and cognitive functioning and autism symptoms in young children with fragile X syn- drome. *Am. J. Ment. Retard.* 109, 208–218.
64. Price, J., Roberts, J., Vandergrift, N., and Martin, G. (2007). Language comprehension in boys with fragile X syndrome and boys with Down syndrome. *J. Intellect. Disabil. Res.* 51, 318–326.
65. Price, J. R., Roberts, J. E., Hennon, E. A., Berni, M. C., Anderson, K. L., and Sideris, J. (2008). Syntactic complex- ity during conversation of boys with fragile X syndrome and Down syn- drome. *J. Speech Lang. Hear. Res.* 51, 3–15.
66. Reiss, A. L., and Dant, C. C. (2003). The behavioral neurogenetics of fragile X syndrome: analyzing gene-brain- behavior relationships in child developmental psychopatholo- gies. *Dev. Psychopathol.* 15, 927–968.
67. Reiss, A. L., and Freund, L. (1992). Behavioral phenotype of fragile X syndrome: DSM-III-R autistic behavior in male children. *Am. J. Med. Genet.* 43, 35–46.
68. Repacholi, B. M., and Gopnik, A. (1997). Early reasoning about desires: evidence from 14- and 18-month-olds. *Dev. Psychol.* 33, 12–21.
69. Roberts, J., Martin, G. E., Moskowitz, L., Harris, A. A., Foreman, J., and Nelson, L. (2007a). Discourse skills of boys with fragile X syndrome in comparison to boys with Down syn- drome. *J. Speech Lang. Hear. Res.* 50, 475–492.
70. Roberts, J., Price, J., Barnes, E., Nel- son, L., Burchinal, M., Hennon, E. A., Moskowitz, L., Edwards, A., Malkin, C., Anderson, K., Misenheimer, J., and Hooper, S. R. (2007b). Recep- tive vocabulary, expressive vocabu- lary, and speech production of boys with fragile X syndrome in com- parison to boys with Down syn- drome. *Am. J. Ment. Retard.* 112, 177–193.
71. Roberts, J. E., Chapman, R. S., Mar- tin, G. E., and Moskowitz, L. (2008). "Language of preschool and school-age children with Down syn- drome and fragile X syndrome," in *Speech and Language Development and Intervention in Down Syndrome and Fragile X Syndrome*, eds J. E. Roberts, R. S. Chapman, and S. War- ren (Baltimore: Paul H. Brookes), 77–115.
72. Roberts, J. E., Mirrett, P., and Burchi- nal, M. (2001). Receptive and expres- sive communication development of young males with fragile X syndrome. *Am. J. Ment. Retard.* 106, 216–230.
73. Rogers, S. J., Wehner, D. E., and Hager- man, R. (2001). The behavioral phenotype in fragile X: symptoms of autism in very young children with fragile X syndrome, idiopathic autism, and other developmental disorders. *J. Dev. Behav. Pediatr.* 22, 409–417.
74. Roid, G. H., and Miller, L. J. (1997). *Leiter International Perfor- mance Scale-Revised.* Wood Dale: Stoelting.
75. Rutter, M., Bailey, A., and Lord, C. (2003). *SCQ: The Social Com- munication Questionnaire.* Los Angeles: Western Psychological Services.
76. Slaughter, V., Peterson, C. C., and Mackintosh, E. (2007). Mind what mother says: narrative input and theory of mind in typi- cal children and those on the autism spectrum. *Child Dev.* 78, 839–858.
77. Sloetjes, H., and Wittenburg, P. (2008). "Annotation by category – ELAN and ISO DCR," in *Proceedings of the 6th International Conference on Language Resources and Evaluation (LREC 2008)*, Nijinegen.
78. Sperber, D., and Wilson, D. (2002). Pragmaticas, modularity, and mind-reading. *Mind Lang.* 17, 2–23.
79. Sudhalter, V., and Belser, C. (2001). Conversational characteristics of children with fragile X syndrome: tangential language. *Am. J. Ment. Retard.* 106, 389–400.
80. Sudhalter, V., Cohen, I. L., Silver- man, W., and Wolf-Schein, E. G. (1990). Conversational analyses of males with fragile X, Down syn- drome, and autism: comparison of the emergence of deviant lan- guage. *Am. J. Ment. Retard.* 94, 431–441.
81. Surian, L., Baron-Cohen, S., and Van der Lely, H. (1996). Are children with autism deaf to Gricean maxims? *Cogn. Neuropsychiatry* 1, 55–71.
82. Tager-Flusberg, H. (2000). "Language and understanding minds: con- nections in autism," in *Under- standing Other Minds: Perspectives from Developmental Cognitive Neu- roscience*, eds S. Baron-Cohen, H. Tager-Flusberg, and D. J. Cohen (Oxford: Oxford University press), 124–149.
83. Tager-Flusberg, H., and Sullivan, K. (1995). Attributing mental states to story characters: a comparison of narratives produced by autis- tic and mentally retarded indi- viduals. *Appl. Psycholinguist.* 16, 241–256.
84. Tannock, R. (1988). Mothers' directive- ness in their interactions with their children with and without Down syndrome. *Am. J. Ment. Retard.* 93, 154–165.
85. Wellman, H., and Liu, D. (2004). Scaling of theory-of-mind tasks. *Child Dev.* 75, 523–541.
86. Wilding, J., Cornish, K., and Munir, F. (2002). Further delineation of the executive deficit in males with fragile-X syndrome. *Neuropsycholo- gia* 40, 1343–1349.
87. Williams, K. T. (1997). *Expressive Vocab- ulary Test.* Circle Pines: American Guidance Service.
88. Wilson, D., and Sperber, D. (2004)."Rel- evance theory," in *The Handbook of Pragmatics*, eds L. R. Horn and G. Ward (Oxford: Blackwell), 607–632.
89. Wolf-Schein, E. G., Sudhalter, V., Cohen, I. L., Fisch, G. S., Hanson, D., Pfadt, A. G., Hagerman, R., Jenkins, E., and Brown, W. T. (1987). Speech-language and the fragile X syndrome: initial findings. *ASHA* 29, 35–38.

## APPENDIX

| Task | Materials/set-up | Script | Control/test questions |
|---|---|---|---|
| Perspective taking[a] | Clear picture frame with blue fish on one side, white fish on the other. Examiner sits across from participant | "We are going to look at a picture of a fish. What color is the fish? Okay let's switch spots. (*Examiner switches seats with participant, without moving orientation of frame*). Now what color is the fish?" | Control: none<br>Test: "What color fish do I see over here? |
| Diverse desires[b] | Picture of a broccoli and cookie; female adult figurine | "Here's Grandma. It's snack-time. Grandma wants a snack to eat. Here are two snacks, broccoli and a cookie. Which do you like best? Well that's a good choice, but Grandma really likes [opposite]. She doesn't like [participant's choice]. What she likes best is [opposite]" | Control: none<br>Test: "Now it's time to eat. Grandma can only choose one snack, just one. Which snack will Grandma choose?" |
| Diverse belief[b] | Girl figurine, displayed midway between a picture of a bush and a garage | "Here's Amy. She wants to find her cat. Her cat might be hiding in the bushes or it might be hiding in the garage. Where do you think the cat is? Well, that's a good idea but Amy thinks her cat is in the [opposite]" | Control: none<br>Test: "Where will Amy look for her cat?" |
| False belief[b] | Goldfish crackers box with plastic toy dog inside; boy figurine | "Here's a Goldfish box, what do you think is inside the Goldfish box? Let's see. It's really a dog inside! Okay, what is in the box?" "Here comes Sam. Sam has never looked inside this Goldfish box" | Control: "Did Sam look inside this box?"<br>Test: "What does Sam think is in the box?" |
| Knowledge access[b] | Box with a ball inside; girl figurine | "Here's a box. What do you think is inside the box? Let's see... It's really a ball inside! So, what is in the box? Here's Amy. She's never looked inside this box" | Control: "Did Amy look inside this box?"<br>Test: "Does Amy know what is in the box? |
| Explicit false belief[b] | Picture of a backpack and closet; boy figurine | "Here's Sam. Sam really wants to find his game. Sam's game may be in his backpack. Or it may be in the closet. Well, really Sam's game is in his backpack. But Sam thinks his game is in the closet" | Control: "Where is Sam's game really?"<br>Test: "Where will Sam look for his game?" |
| Unexpected contents false belief[c,d] | Cardboard M and M's box filled with buttons. Second examiner, who has left the room | "What do you think is in this box? Lets' look inside and see. What's in here?" | Control: "When I first showed you the box, what did you think was inside it before you opened it?"<br>Test: "[Second examiner] has never seen what is in this box. What will she think is in the box?" |
| Unexpected transfer false belief[c,d] | A pen. Second examiner places the pen on the table and announces "I need to go find my bag in the other room- I'll leave my pen right here where it is safe" | "I know, let's play a trick on [second examiner]. Let's hide her pen. Where do you want to hide it?" | Control: "Where is the pen really?"<br>Test: "When [second examiner] comes back, where will she look for her pen?" |
| Simple desires[e] | Bowl of Goldfish crackers and bowl of rice cakes | "It's snack-time! Which do you like better? (*Examiner tastes each food*). Mmm [opposite of child's preferred snack]! Mmm, I tasted the [opposite]! Mmm! Eww [child's choice]! Eww, I tasted [child's choice]. Eww!" | Control: none<br>Test: "Can you give me some?" (*Examiner holds out hand*) |
| Appearance-reality[f] | Sponge that looks like a rock; Candle that is shaped like a crayon; Doll that is covered with a ghost cloth; White card covered by translucent pink cellophane | "When you look at this, what does it look like? | Control: none<br>Test: "What is it really? But what does it look like?" |

*[a]Slaughter et al. (2007); [b]Wellman and Liu (2004); [c]Matthews et al. (2003); [d]Lewis and Mitchell (1994); [e]Repacholi and Gopnik (1997); [f]Flavell et al. (1983).*

# 16

# Are there cultural differences in parental interest in early diagnosis and genetic risk assessment for autism spectrum disorder?

**Claire Amiet[1,2]*, Elizabeth Couchon[3], Kelly Carr[4], Jerôme Carayol[1] and David Cohen[2,5]**

[1] IntegraGen, Evry, France
[2] Department of Child and Adolescent Psychiatry, AP-HP, Groupe Hospitalier Pitié-Salpêtrière, Université Pierre et Marie Curie, Paris, France
[3] IntegraGen Inc., Cambridge, MA, USA
[4] University of Notre Dame, South Bend, IN, USA
[5] CNRS UMR 7222, Institut des Systèmes Intelligents et Robotiques, Université Pierre et Marie Curie, Paris, France

***Edited by:***
*Roberto Canitano, University Hospital of Siena, Italy*

***Reviewed by:***
*Munis Dundar, Erciyes University, Turkey*
*Jean Marc Guilé, Université Picardie Jules Verne, France*

****Correspondence:***
*Claire Amiet, IntegraGen, 5 Rue Henri Desbruères, Genopole Campus 1, Genavenir 8, Evry 91000, France*
*e-mail: claire.amiet@integragen.com*

**Background:** There are many societal and cultural differences between healthcare systems and the use of genetic testing in the US and France. These differences may affect the diagnostic process for autism spectrum disorder (ASD) in each country and influence parental opinions regarding the use of genetic screening tools for ASD.

**Methods:** Using an internet-based tool, a survey of parents with at least one child with ASD was conducted. A total of 162 participants from the US completed an English version of the survey and 469 participants from France completed a French version of the survey. Respondents were mainly females (90%) and biological parents (94.3% in the US and 97.2% in France).

**Results:** The mean age of ASD diagnosis reported was not significantly different between France ($57.5 \pm 38.4$ months) and the US ($56.5 \pm 52.7$ months) ($p = 0.82$) despite significant difference in the average age at which a difference in development was first suspected [29.7 months ($\pm 28.4$) vs. 21.4 months ($\pm 18.1$), respectively, $p = 7 \times 10^{-4}$]. Only 27.8% of US participants indicated that their child diagnosed with ASD had undergone diagnostic genetic testing, whereas 61.7% of the French participants indicated this was the case ($p = 2.7 \times 10^{-12}$). In both countries, the majority of respondents (69.3% and 80% from France and the US, respectively) indicated high interest in the use of a genetic screening test for autism.

**Conclusion:** Parents from France and the US report a persistent delay between the initial suspicion of a difference in development and the diagnosis of ASD. Significantly fewer US participants underwent genetic testing although this result should be regarded as exploratory given the limitations. The significance of these between country differences will be discussed.

**Keywords: autism spectrum disorders, survey, parents' opinion, genetics, France, US**

## BACKGROUND

Autism spectrum disorders (ASDs) are a group of highly heritable developmental disorders characterized by early impairments in communication and social interaction, and restricted interests, and repetitive behaviors (1, 2). Recent reports estimate the median prevalence rate to be 62/10,000 (3) but there is clear evidence that rates have increased over time. In the US, the CDC estimates that the prevalence of ASD is approximately 1 in 88 children (4). In France, the most recent epidemiological survey confirmed this increase and found a prevalence rate among 8 year olds of 33.5/10,000 (5).

In terms of treatment, a combination of developmental and behavioral approaches is now recommended focusing on early, intensive intervention and parental collaboration (6). Recently, several meta-analyses were published suggesting that comprehensive early intensive behavioral interventions programs lead to positive effects regarding intellectual functioning, language skill, and adaptive behavior outcome (7–10). However, there were many differences between meta-analyses and potential confounds and limitations that might have lead to discrepant findings across these studies (11). The only randomized controlled trial of an early intensive behavioral intervention [the early start Denver model (ESDM)] demonstrated significant gains in visual processing and improvements in language abilities, with subsequent gains in intellectual quotient and adaptive behaviors, among children receiving the ESDM (6). Moreover, a secondary outcome measurement from this trial suggested that ESDM is associated with normalized brain activity patterns related to social attention and engagement, and that these normalized brain activity patterns are correlated with improvements in social behavior (12).

Despite an increase in ASD research in recent years, there continues to be much debate on autism leading to extensive media coverage (13). For example, between psychiatric care and educational and behavioral methods (14), between parent's advocacy groups and associations of individuals with autism (15), and between media presentation of research advances and evidence-based data *per se* (16). Among the many issues debated, much focus has been given to early diagnosis and the contribution of genetic factors to the cause of autism. Although the importance of early diagnosis and treatment of autism is well accepted, the methods used to achieve early diagnosis are debated (17). To date, specific clinical screening instruments do not show high sensitivity despite acceptable specificity (18). Delays in diagnosis are not only due to a shortage of accessible specialists, but also due to clinical and developmental limitations regarding infant/toddler assessment tools (19). In many instances, parents' initial concerns regarding their child's development are not specific to autism and may be associated with many other conditions in the differential diagnosis (20). Moreover, some clinicians consider that sharing a possible diagnosis of ASD with parents may alter the way these parents will interact with their child as shown in siblings at-risk of ASD (21). Finally, the cost of general population screening is also a concern in countries that do not have free access to healthcare. The use of family history (one or more older siblings with ASD) (22) or perinatal factors (e.g., prematurity) (23) has been suggested as an alternative method to general population screening in identifying children at-risk for ASD.

In regard to genetic risk for ASD, the majority of research has consistently shown that ASDs have a strong genetic component with heritability rates ranging from 60 to 80% (24, 25) and close to 40% in the largest recent twin study (26). Therefore, there is little doubt of the importance of genetic factors in autism (27–29). However, most authors agree that the number of ASD cases explained by a single genetic abnormality is limited to approximately 15–20%. These include single gene mutations (e.g., Fragile X syndrome) or copy number variants (CNVs) (e.g., at 15q11–q13 locus). Although other causal factors (e.g., pre-, peri-, post-natal factors) have been studied in autism (20, 30), interest in the media and in high-impact scientific journals has been limited (31). Yet, they may account for some part in the recent increase in prevalence rate (32). As a result, the majority of cases of autism are often described as a combination of (1) rare genetic variants with high effect size, (2) common genetic variants with low effect size, and (3) environmental (or non-genetic) risk factors (29, 31, 33). A recent study addressed the challenges of early diagnosis and use of genetic risk factors by reviewing the research related to biomarkers associated with ASD (16). The authors recognized the widespread hope that the discovery of valid biomarkers for autism will enable earlier diagnosis and treatment. However, careful review of the literature shows major scientific challenges and ethical concerns related to the development of biomarkers and their clinical application (16).

In addition, societal and cultural attitudes and practices may also contribute to differing opinions regarding ASD as seen with other neurodevelopmental conditions. For example, there is considerable controversy regarding the use of medications in children (34) or the diagnosis of pediatric bipolar disorder (35) despite similar national recommendations in the US and Europe. Healthcare systems are also very different in Europe and the US, which may influence both expectations and access to care. Finally, regulations related to genetic testing and societal acceptance of genetic contributions to ASD may differ drastically influencing both standard of care and patients' willingness to undergo genetic testing.

To investigate the impact of societal and cultural differences in the approach to health care and autism on the diagnostic experience and parental attitudes regarding genetic risk assessment testing for autism, we conducted two parallel web surveys in the US (36) and France. These countries were chosen due to their cultural and social contrasts regarding both healthcare systems and genetic testing regulations (**Table 1**). The French healthcare system combines universal coverage with a public–private mix of hospital and ambulatory care, whereas the US healthcare system depends on private, for-profit health insurance. Although France has a higher volume of service provisions than the US (37), millions of Americans have inadequate or limited access to care because they have inadequate or no health insurance. Data from the 2011 National Health Interview Survey (NHIS) show that the percentage of person uninsured at the time of interview was 15.1% (46.3 million) for persons of all ages and 7% (5.2 million) for children below 8 years (38). Regarding early developmental risk, both the US and French pediatric associations recommend careful early follow-up and systematic examinations during the first 2 years of life to screen for early-onset condition and disabilities. However, only a few states in the US support specific programs for low-income families, whereas in France, these examinations are supported by two parallel regulations: (1) seven free medical examinations during pregnancy[1] and 20 pediatric free examinations during the first 6 years (Code of Public Health – article L.2132-2); (2) free access "dispensaries" funded by the *Protection Materno-Infantile* program located in all areas that offer medico-social action to promote maternal and child health (Code of Public Health – article R2112-1 to R.2112-8). When a diagnosis of autism is suspected, the child can be referred to local mental health ambulatory services and/or to the Regional Center de Resources for Autism where the diagnosis is confirmed (39). Again, within the French healthcare system, these services are free. In the US, first-line primary care services and specialty clinics for ASD are also available, but access to the services is variable as explained above. In terms of diagnosis classification, the DSM-IV is the standard in the US, whereas in France, clinicians use DSM-IV, ICD-10, or CFTMEA. Correspondence algorithms are available (40).

Similarly, regulations for genetic testing differ in the two countries. Genetic tests for over 2,000 diseases are currently available for use in clinical settings in the US. In addition, a growing number of tests are being developed to look at multiple genes that may increase or decrease a person's risk of common diseases. In 2008, the former Secretary's Advisory Committee on Genetics, Health and Society of the US Department of Health and Human Services released a report identifying gaps in the regulation, oversight, and usefulness of genetic testing. However, few recommendations have been addressed[2]. In France, regulations are more stringent.

[1] http://www.ameli.fr/professionnels-de-sante/sages-femmes/exercer-au-quotidien/formalites/la-maternite.php
[2] http://www.cdc.gov/genomics/gtesting/index.htm

**Table 1 | A brief overview of the use of genetic testing in the US and France.**

| | U.S. | France |
|---|---|---|
| **GENERAL CONTEXT** | | |
| Health care system insurance | No universal coverage<br>Mainly private services, for-profit health insurance | Universal coverage<br>Mix of private and public services |
| Access to genetic testing | Few recommendations<br>Variable insurance coverage | Governed by law<br>Fully covered |
| **SPECIFIC CONTEXT OF ASD** | | |
| **Classification for ASD** | **DSM-IV** | **DSM-IV, ICD-10, CFTMEA** |
| Diagnosis | Occurs mainly in private settings | Occurs mainly through free and prepaid public services for child early development (pediatrician) and mental health including public clinics for autism |
| Treatment setting | Mainly private, and through special education | Mix of public health, private non-profit care and special education |
| Recommended genetic testing | High-resolution karyotype study<br>Fragile X | High-resolution karyotype study<br>Fragile X |
| Genetic diagnostic test | Numerous chromosomal microarray tests<br>Numerous sequencing tests for ASD | No genetic diagnostic test available |
| Genetic screening tests for ASD | One genetic screening test for siblings | No genetic screening test available |

Only DNA analyses for medical, legal, or scientific purposes are authorized by law, and the numerous predictive genetic analyses being developed and available online are raising ethical and legal questions (41).

Regarding ASD, the clinical genetic tests currently available are limited to diagnostic use and serve to identify the underlying genetic etiology of a child already diagnosed with an ASD. They include chromosomal microarray, Fragile X analysis, and tests for known genetic syndromes associated with ASD. In the US and France, it is recommended that a child diagnosed with ASD undergo high-resolution karyotype studies and Fragile X testing (42, 43). Clinical chromosome microarray tests are commonly available in the US through medical prescription, but insurance reimbursement for such testing is variable. In France, chromosomal microarray analyses are also commonly available. Reimbursement is systematic after medical prescription. Recently, based on studies showing the combined effect of common single nucleotide polymorphisms (SNPs) on ASD susceptibility (44), an SNP-based DNA test has become available in the U.S which assesses the risk of ASD in children who have an older sibling diagnosed with ASD (ARISk Test; IntegraGen, Cambridge, MA, USA). This test is also only available through a medical prescription by a qualified, licensed, medical professional.

In summary, the aim of this study was to compare the diagnostic experience with ASD, access to genetic testing and parental attitudes regarding the use of a genetic risk assessment tool to aid in the earlier diagnosis of ASD between France and US families considering the differences in healthcare models, genetic testing regulations and early screening and diagnostic practices for ASD between the two countries. To our knowledge, no similar study comparing France and US population samples has been published previously.

## MATERIALS AND METHODS

### POPULATION

Two self-administered internet-based surveys were administered consecutively using software available from SurveyMonkey[3]. The initial survey was conducted in English only and limited to US residents who were parents or guardians of one or more children with ASD. Requests for participation were e-mailed to potential participants by representatives from local and regional autism advocacy groups [for more details see Ref. (36)]. Responses to the survey were collected from February 13, 2012, until March 23, 2012. The second survey was conducted in French only and was administered to parents or guardians from France or other French-speaking countries with one or more children with ASD. Participants were recruited over a web link posted on the blog "autisme infantile,"[4] the Facebook group "handicap et éducation spécialisée,"[5] and the association "Ecolalie." The survey was conducted from June 27, 2012, until July 9, 2012.

### SURVEY DESIGN

The survey was designed to assess parental opinions regarding the ASD diagnostic process for their child and genetic testing related to ASD. It consisted of four sections: (1) parental perceptions regarding the ASD diagnostic process related to the respondent's most recently diagnosed child. This included questions regarding the timing of initial suspicion of a difference in development, the referral process, and age at diagnosis; (2) parental experiences with genetic testing for their child diagnosed with ASD. This sections also included questions focused on the perceived role of genetics

[3]http://www.surveymonkey.com
[4]http://autismeinfantile.com/
[5]http://www.facebook.com/groups/chapellier/

in ASD; (3) for parents who reported having a younger, undiagnosed child younger than 48 months, parental opinion regarding whether they would want to have their younger child receive a genetic test which assessed the child's risk of ASD, even if it could not confirm a diagnosis; (4) demographic data of the respondent including age, gender, and education level. Participants who did not have a child with ASD were excluded from the survey. Survey questions were yes/no, multiple choice answers or 4-point Likert scale (1 – highly likely; 2 – somewhat likely; 3 – somewhat unlikely; 4 – not likely). All questions were presented in a fixed order. Respondents were allowed to change their responses to any question prior to submitting as "final" the survey, after which no further changes could be made.

The survey was reviewed and pilot tested with select parents of children with ASD and with specialists who provide clinical care and diagnostic services for children with developmental delays and/or ASD. All surveys were completed anonymously and no information was collected that permitted the identification of any individuals completing the survey.

Descriptive statistics included means, medians, ranges, and/or percentages. Responses from French and US participants were compared using the $\chi^2$ test.

## RESULTS

### CHARACTERISTICS OF THE SAMPLES

A total of 162 participants completed the US survey and 554 participants (469 from France, 40 from Canada, and 45 from other countries) completed the French survey. For the purpose of this study, only participants from the US and France were included. Their characteristics are detailed in **Table 2**. In both samples, most of the participants were females (90%). The majority of responders (97.2 and 94.3% in France and the US, respectively) indicated that they were biological parents, the remaining were adoptive parents, stepfathers, grandparents, aunts/uncles, or guardians. French respondents were significantly younger, although more than 40% of respondents in both groups were between the ages of 36 and 45 years. Approximately 76% of the US respondents and only 55% of the French respondents had at least a college degree, meaning that socioeconomic status was on average lower in the French sample.

### AGE OF FIRST CONCERN AND AGE OF DIAGNOSIS

We identified a significant difference in the average age at which a difference in development was first suspected between the two populations with a mean age of 29.7 months (±28.4) reported in the French sample and 21.4 months (±18.1) reported in the US sample ($p = 7 \times 10^{-4}$). However, the mean reported age when ASD was diagnosed was 57.5 months (±38.4) in the French sample compared to 56.5 months (±52.7) in the US sample ($p = 0.82$), reflecting no statistical difference in the age at diagnosis between the US and France.

### ACCESS TO GENETIC TESTING

Most participants declared that they believed genetic factors contributed to the cause of ASD. Eighty-two percent of the US participants and 59% of the French participants indicated that ASD was a combination of genetic and environmental factors. Twelve percent of US participants and 24% of French participants indicated that ASD was almost entirely a result of genetic factors ($p = 0.0005$). However, only 27.8% of US participants indicated that their child diagnosed with ASD had undergone genetic testing, whereas 61.7% of French participants indicated so ($p = 2.7 \times 10^{-12}$) (**Table 3**).

**Table 2 | Sample characteristics.**

| | France, *N* (%) | US, *N* (%) | *p* |
|---|---|---|---|
| **GENDER OF THE RESPONDERS** | | | |
| M | 42 (9.3) | 16 (11.0) | 0.555 |
| F | 410 (90.7) | 130 (89.0) | |
| **AGE OF THE RESPONDERS** | | | |
| <36 | 178 (37.0) | 33 (23.6) | $3 \times 10^{-8}$ |
| 36–45 | 202 (42) | 58 (41.4) | |
| 46–55 | 45 (9.4) | 38 (27.1) | |
| >55 | 56 (6.9) | 11 (7.9) | |
| **EDUCATION LEVEL OF THE RESPONDERS** | | | |
| Less than high school | 88 (20.0) | 0 (0) | 0.004 |
| High school/GED | 110 (25.1) | 35 (23.5) | 0.98 |
| College degree | 159 (36.2) | 59 (39.6) | 0.97 |
| Graduate degree | 82 (18.7) | 55 (36.9) | 0.01 |
| **RESPONDERS INVOLVED IN A PARENTS ASSOCIATION** | | | |
| Yes | 242 (54.5) | 74 (50) | 0.34 |
| No | 202 (45.5) | 74 (50) | |
| **REPORTED DIAGNOSIS** | | | |
| Autistic disorder | 185 (42.6) | 86 (54.9) | 0.15 |
| PDD-NOS | 209 (48.2) | 31 (19.1) | 0.71 |
| Asperger syndrome | 40 (9.2) | 35 (21.6) | 0.04 |
| Unknown | 35 (7.5) | 4 (4.3) | |

**Table 3 | Reported rates of genetic testing perfomed in affected individuals.**

| | France, *N* (%) | US, *N* (%) | *p* |
|---|---|---|---|
| Yes | 284 (61.7) | 42 (27.8) | $3.5 \times 10^{-13}$ |
| Genetic testing recommended but declined | 17 (3.7) | 12 (7.9) | 0.03 |
| No genetic testing recommended | 150 (32.6) | 93 (61.6) | $1.3 \times 10^{-10}$ |
| Don't know | 9 (2.0) | 4 (2.7) | |

### RISK OF AUTISM IN THE SIBLING

Twenty-five participants from the US survey and 101 participants from the French survey reported that their family included a sibling, as of yet not diagnosed with an ASD and under the age of 48 months. Of these, 13 (52%) respondents from the U.S and 48 (47%) respondents from the French survey felt that the younger sibling was somewhat or highly likely to develop ASD. However, 15 respondents (60%) from the US survey and 58 respondents (57%) from the French survey indicated that they had a somewhat or very low level of anxiety regarding the younger sibling's risk of ASD. Seventy respondents from the French survey (69.3%) and 20 respondents from the US sample (80%) with a younger undiagnosed child, <48 months old, indicated that they would want their child tested if a genetic test were available that could identify risk for ASD, even if it could not confirm or rule out the diagnosis.

## DISCUSSION

France and the US differ in many sociocultural aspects such as healthcare systems and the regulation of genetic testing (**Table 1**). These differences may have consequences on early autism diagnosis and parental opinions about genetic testing and access to it. In our study, the mean age of first concern was significantly later in the French sample than in the US sample. However, our results are not strictly consistent with previous French studies (45, 46). In the largest study conducted to date ($N = 424$), the mean age when French parents first reported early signs of ASD in their children was 19 months (±11.7), and 27 months (±17.5) when their children were first evaluated by a medical professional (20). However, in both the US and French samples, the mean reported age of ASD diagnosis was approximately 57 months. These results coincide with reports in the literature suggesting that children may not receive a formal diagnosis until the age of 4 (4, 46, 47). Recently, French parents' advocacy organizations have claimed that a delay in diagnosis is still ongoing in France. However, the current results contradict these claims and are consistent with Chamak et al.'s (46) recent study, showing that the age of diagnosis of autism has decreased over the years in France since the beginning of the 1990s (**Figure 1**).

With a majority of the participants from France (59%) and the US (82%) indicating that ASD was a result of the genetics and non-genetic factors, most of participants' knowledge in both countries is in accordance with the state of the art. Significantly more participants from France (24%) than from the US (12%) indicated that ASD was almost entirely a result of genetic factors. This result may be surprising considering the numerous genetic tests currently available for clinical use in the US. However, this may reflect the influence in French popular opinion regarding the role of genetic factors in the origin of autism (13, 15).

A significantly higher number of children diagnosed with ASD were reported to have undergone clinical genetic testing in the French sample (60%) compared to the US sample (28%). Despite the American Academy of Pediatrics suggestion that primary care physicians should obtain high-resolution chromosome studies and Fragile X testing when the diagnosis of an ASD is made (48) and the American College of Medical Genetics recommendation that a genetic consultation should be offered to all persons and families with ASD (43), only 28% of the US participants indicated that their child diagnosed with ASD had undergone genetic testing. This result may be consistent with Selkirk et al.'s study performed in the US reporting that only 24% of 255 parents whose children were diagnosed with an ASD reported seeing a genetic counselor (49). Similarly, in a recent qualitative study of parents' experience, Chen et al. reported that only 28% of 42 parents with at least one child diagnosed with ASD had reported that their child had undergone genetic testing. Moreover, 63% of the parents whose children had not undergone genetic testing for ASD reported that they had never heard of such testing before the interview (50). Sixty percent of French respondents indicated that their child had undergone genetic testing, as recommended since 2005 by the French *Haute Autorité de Santé* (HAS). This is in accordance with

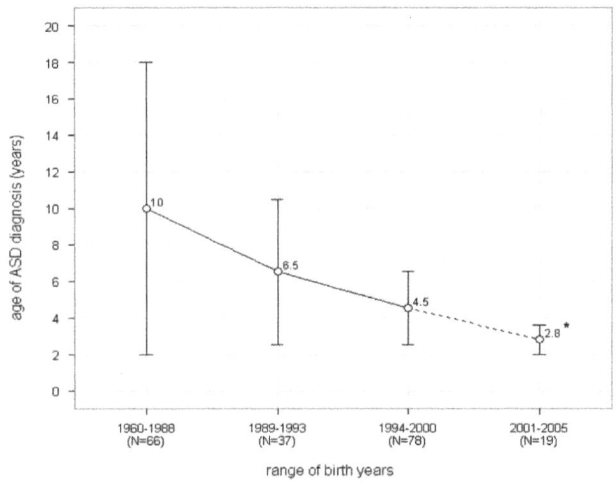


**FIGURE 1 | Changes in age of ASD diagnosis in France during the last 40 years [extracted from Ref. (46); courtesy of Claude Bursztejn].** *The dot line indicates that the 2001–2005 result should be regarded with caution as based on only $N = 19$ cases.

Chamak et al. who reported that 51.5% of the individuals with ASD in a French sample of 200 families had undergone clinical genetic testing (personal communication).

With 60% of the parents from the US reporting that no genetic testing was recommended, the low rate of genetic testing reported for the children from the US (28%) may be mainly attributed to a lack of healthcare provider's referral. This observation is consistent with previous findings showing the importance of physicians referral in accessing genetics services for children with ASD (51); ASD, Down syndrome and/or mental retardation (52); or hearing loss (53). However, little information is available in the literature about healthcare provider's attitudes toward genetic testing. Recently, a literature review of genetic testing in psychiatry found that not all psychiatrists felt competent about their genetic knowledge (9–70%) or ability to offer and interpret genetic test (54). More recently, a large e-mailed survey explored psychiatrists' and neurologists' (mostly with an adult practice) practices and knowledge concerning genetic testing and found that only 33% of respondents felt confident about how to order and where to send genetic tests (55). Almost half of neurologists and over 75% of psychiatrists were not aware of a genetic counselor or geneticist to whom to refer patients (55). One may also be questioning physician knowledge about the inheritance of autism: in 2008, nearly half of a small group of randomly selected psychiatrists were found to rate that genetics has a "weak influence" or "no influence" on the heritability of autism (56). Moreover, because evidence-based interventions for ASD are primarily behavioral, the healthcare provider may not see the need for genetic testing.

The impact of free access to care may also be a key factor in determining the frequency with which clinical genetic testing is used in autism. Considering that (1) higher education, as seen in the US sample, is related to better genetic knowledge and increased access to genetic testing (50); and (2) regulations regarding genetic testing are more stringent in France, a higher rate of genetic testing would have been expected in the US sample rather than the French sample. It is likely that free access to care in France may in part explain the better accordance with genetic testing recommendations in ASD found in this country.

This study should be interpreted in the context of its numerous limitations. First, the comparative survey relied on retrospective self-reporting data collection from parents with numerous biases due to recollection. Second, the parents who responded to the survey may not be representative of the population of families with ASD in France and in the US since most of the parents were contacted via advocacy organizations indicating a higher degree of involvement, and all participants had to have access to a computer. It is probable that the rates reported here are overestimated. Moreover, it is not possible to determine the response rate for an internet survey and it is unknown whether respondents differed in salient ways from non-respondents. For example, families who do not have regular access to a computer or time to respond a survey may not be reflected in the survey. Third, internet-based survey is considered less reliable than direct or e-mail interviews and does not permit clinical diagnosis confirmation of included patients. Also, the collection of ethnicity data was not allowed by the French National Informatics and Liberty Commission (*Commission nationale de l'informatique et des libertés*, CNIL), therefore no comparison could be done with the US data. Fourth, survey participants were not asked to indicate the gender and the age of the affected child. Considering recent changes in the US and French guidelines regarding ASD screening and diagnostic practices, it is unclear whether our results reflect these changes or not, and as a consequence whether older patients could have skewed the results. Indeed, most of what we know about genetics and autism has been learned in the past 20 years. We cannot exclude that the results from the US sample reflect unavailability of genetic testing for older patients. However, the percentage of US families reporting genetic testing in our survey is similar to that found in two recent studies based on a direct interview (50) and an anonymous survey (49). Finally, possible biases due to local variation of accessibility to genetic testing cannot be adjusted in such an internet survey as far as anonymity prevented collection of participant's addresses. This may be an issue for the US sample given that France is no more than a regular US state in terms of surface.

## CONCLUSION

Parents from France and the US report a persistent delay between the initial suspicion of a difference in development and the diagnosis of ASD. Age of diagnosis was about 4.5 years in both countries. Additionally, most parents from both countries with a younger undiagnosed child reported that they would pursue genetic risk assessment testing that could identify risk for ASD in a younger sibling even if it could not confirm or rule out a diagnosis. However, significantly fewer US participants underwent genetic testing. We hypothesize that this is the result of economic issues.

## AUTHOR CONTRIBUTIONS

Claire Amiet participated in the design of the internet survey, the acquisition and the interpretation of data, and to draft the manuscript. Elizabeth Couchon participated in the design of the internet survey, the acquisition and the interpretation of data, and to draft the manuscript. Kelly Carr participated in the design of the internet survey and the acquisition of data. Jerôme Carayol performed the statistical analysis and participated to the interpretation of data. David Cohen participated in the interpretation of data and to draft the manuscript. All authors read and approved the final manuscript.

## REFERENCES


1. WHO. *The ICD-10 Classification of Mental and Behavioral Disorders: Diagnostic Criteria for Research*. Geneva: World Health Organisation (1993).
2. APA. *Diagnostic and Statistical Manual of Mental States Disorders. DSM IV*. Washington, DC: APA (1994).
3. Elsabbagh M, Divan G, Koh YJ, Kim YS, Kauchali S, Marcín C, et al. Global prevalence of autism and other pervasive developmental disorders. *Autism Res* (2012) **5**(3):160–79. doi:10.1002/aur.239
4. Autism and Developmental Disabilities Monitoring Network Surveillance Year 2008 Principal Investigators; Centers for Disease Control and Prevention. Prevalence of autism spectrum disorders – autism and developmental disabilities monitoring network, 14 sites, United States, 2008. *MMWR Surveill Summ* (2012) **61**(3):1–19.
5. Delobel M, Van Bakel M-E, Klapouszczak D, Vignes C, Maffre T, Raynaud J-P, et al. Prévalence de l'autisme et autres troubles envahissants du développement: données des registres français de population. Générations 1995-2002. *Neuropsychiatr Enfance Adolesc* (2013) **61**:23–30. doi:10.1016/j.neurenf.2012.09.007
6. Dawson G, Rogers S, Munson J, Smith M, Winter J, Greenson J, et al. Randomized, controlled trial of an intervention for toddlers with autism: the early start Denver model. *Pediatrics* (2010) **125**(1):e17–23. doi:10.1542/peds.2009-0958
7. Eldevik S, Hastings RP, Hughes JC, Jahr E, Eikeseth S, Cross S. Meta-analysis of early intensive behavioral intervention for children with autism. *J Clin Child Adolesc Psychol* (2009) **38**(3):439–50. doi:10.1080/15374410902851739
8. Reichow B, Wolery M. Comprehensive synthesis of early intensive behavioral interventions for young children with autism based on the UCLA young autism project model. *J Autism Dev Disord* (2009) **39**(1):23–41. doi:10.1007/s10803-008-0596-0
9. Virues-Ortega J. Applied behavior analytic intervention for autism in early childhood: meta-analysis, meta-regression and dose-response meta-analysis of multiple outcomes. *Clin Psychol Rev* (2010) **30**(4):387–99. doi:10.1016/j.cpr.2010.01.008
10. Strauss K, Mancini F; SPC Group, Fava L. Parent inclusion in early intensive behavior interventions for young children with ASD: a synthesis of meta-analyses from 2009 to 2011. *Res Dev Disabil* (2013) **34**(9):2967–85. doi:10.1016/j.ridd.2013.06.007
11. Reichow B. Overview of meta-analyses on early intensive behavioral intervention for young children with autism spectrum disorders. *J Autism Dev Disord* (2012) **42**(4):512–20. doi:10.1007/s10803-011-1218-9
12. Dawson G, Jones EJ, Merkle K, Venema K, Lowy R, Faja S, et al. Early behavioral intervention is associated with normalized brain activity in young children with autism. *J Am Acad Child Adolesc Psychiatry* (2012) **51**(11):1150–9. doi:10.1016/j.jaac.2012.08.018
13. Chamak B. La prise en charge de l'autisme: le traitement médiatique. *Neuropsychiatr Enfance Adolesc* (2013) **61**:231–5. doi:10.1016/j.neurenf.2012.12.004
14. Hochmann J. Le devenir des idées en pédopsychiatrie, à travers l'histoire de l'autisme – the development of child psychiatry through the history of autism as a looking glass. *Neuropsychiatr Enfance Adolesc* (2012) **60**:207–15. doi:10.1016/j.neurenf.2011.11.003
15. Chamak B. Autism and social movements: French parents' associations and international autistic individuals' organisations. *Sociol Health Illn* (2008) **30**(1):76–96. doi:10.1111/j.1467-9566.2007.01053.x
16. Walsh P, Elsabbagh M, Bolton P, Singh I. In search of biomarkers for autism: scientific, social and ethical challenges. *Nat Rev Neurosci* (2011) **12**(10):603–12. doi:10.1038/nrn3113
17. Saint-Georges C, Guinchat V, Chamak B, Apicella F, Muratori F, Cohen D. Signes précoces d'autisme: D'où vient-on? Où va-t-on? *Neuropsychatrie de l'Enfance et de l'Adolescence* (2013) **61**(7–8):400–8. doi:10.1016/j.neurenf.2013.05.005
18. Dereu M, Raymaekers R, Warreyn P, Schietecatte I, Meirsschaut M, Roeyers H. Can child care workers contribute to the early detection of autism spectrum disorders? A comparison between screening instruments with child care workers versus parents as informants. *J Autism Dev Disord* (2012) **42**(5):781–96. doi:10.1007/s10803-011-1307-9

19. Saint-Georges C, Cassel RS, Cohen D, Chetouani M, Laznik M-C, Maestro S, et al. What studies of family home movies can teach us about autistic infants: a literature review. *Res Autism Spectr Disord* (2010) **4**:355–66. doi:10.1016/j.rasd.2009.10.017
20. Guinchat V, Chamak B, Bonniau B, Bodeau N, Perisse D, Cohen D, et al. Very early signs of autism reported by parents include many concerns not specific to autism criteria. *Res Autism Spectr Disord* (2012) **6**(2):589–601. doi:10.1016/j.rasd.2011.10.005
21. Wan MW, Green J, Elsabbagh M, Johnson M, Charman T, Plummer F, et al. Parent–infant interaction in infant siblings at risk of autism. *Res Dev Disabil* (2012) **33**(3):924–32. doi:10.1016/j.ridd.2011.12.011
22. Newschaffer CJ, Croen LA, Fallin MD, Hertz-Picciotto I, Nguyen DV, Lee NL, et al. Infant siblings and the investigation of autism risk factors. *J Neurodev Disord* (2012) **4**(1):7. doi:10.1186/1866-1955-4-7
23. Lipkin PH. Lessons and opportunities from autism screening in high-risk children. *Dev Med Child Neurol* (2012) **54**(6):485. doi:10.1111/j.1469-8749.2012.04285.x
24. Steffenburg S, Gillberg C, Hellgren L, Andersson L, Gillberg IC, Jakobsson G, et al. A twin study of autism in Denmark, Finland, Iceland, Norway and Sweden. *J Child Psychol Psychiatry* (1989) **30**(3):405–16. doi:10.1111/j.1469-7610.1989.tb00254.x
25. Bailey A, Le Couteur A, Gottesman I, Bolton P, Simonoff E, Yuzda E, et al. Autism as a strongly genetic disorder: evidence from a British twin study. *Psychol Med* (1995) **25**(1):63–77. doi:10.1017/S0033291700028099
26. Hallmayer J, Cleveland S, Torres A, Phillips J, Cohen B, Torigoe T, et al. Genetic heritability and shared environmental factors among twin pairs with autism. *Arch Gen Psychiatry* (2011) **68**(11):1095–102. doi:10.1001/archgenpsychiatry.2011.76
27. Cohen D, Pichard N, Tordjman S, Baumann C, Burglen L, Excoffier E, et al. Specific genetic disorders and autism: clinical contribution towards their identification. *J Autism Dev Disord* (2005) **35**(1):103–16. doi:10.1007/s10803-004-1038-2
28. Abrahams BS, Geschwind DH. Advances in autism genetics: on the threshold of a new neurobiology. *Nat Rev Genet* (2008) **9**(5):341–55. doi:10.1038/nrg2346
29. State MW, Levitt P. The conundrums of understanding genetic risks for autism spectrum disorders. *Nat Neurosci* (2011) **14**(12):1499–506. doi:10.1038/nn.2924
30. Gardener H, Spiegelman D, Buka SL. Prenatal risk factors for autism: comprehensive meta-analysis. *Br J Psychiatry* (2009) **195**(1):7–14. doi:10.1192/bjp.bp.108.051672
31. Cohen D. Controverse actuelles dans le champ de l'autisme. *Ann Méd Psychol* (2012) **170**:517–25. doi:10.1016/j.amp.2012.06.019
32. Weintraub K. The prevalence puzzle: autism counts. *Nature* (2011) **479**(7371):22–4. doi:10.1038/479022a
33. Guinchat V, Thorsen P, Laurent C, Cans C, Bodeau N, Cohen D. Pre-, peri- and neonatal risk factors for autism. *Acta Obstet Gynecol Scand* (2012) **91**(3):287–300. doi:10.1111/j.1600-0412.2011.01325.x
34. Cohen D, Bonnot O, Bodeau N, Consoli A, Laurent C. Adverse effects of second-generation antipsychotics in children and adolescents: a Bayesian meta-analysis. *J Clin Psychopharmacol* (2012) **32**(3):309–16. doi:10.1097/JCP.0b013e3182549259
35. Carlson GA. Broadening bipolar disorder – by design or by accident? *World Psychiatry* (2011) **10**(3):195–6.
36. Narcisa V, Discenza M, Vaccari E, Rosen-Sheidley B, Hardan AY, Couchon E. Parental interest in a genetic risk assessment test for autism spectrum disorders. *Clin Pediatr (Phila)* (2012) **52**(2):139–46. doi:10.1177/0009922812466583
37. Rodwin VG. The health care system under French national health insurance: lessons for health reform in the United States. *Am J Public Health* (2003) **93**(1):31–7. doi:10.2105/AJPH.93.1.31
38. Cohen RA, Martinez ME. *Health Insurance Coverage: Early Release of Estimates From the National Health Interview Survey, 2011.* National Center for Health Statistics (2012). Available from: http://www.cdc.gov/nchs/nhis/releases.htm
39. Pernon E, Aussilloux C. Une pratique nouvelle au centre de ressources autisme du Languedoc-Roussillon: l'évaluation sur site. *Neuropsychiatr Enfance Adolesc* (2005) **53**(8):453–6. doi:10.1016/j.neurenf.2005.10.007
40. Misès R, Bursztejn C, Botbol M, Coincon Y, Durand B, Garrabe J, et al. Une nouvelle version de la classification française des troubles mentaux de l'enfant et de l'adolescent: la CFTMEA R 2012, corresponsances et transcodages avec l'ICD 10. *Neuropsychiatr Enfance Adolesc* (2012) **60**(6):414–8. doi:10.1016/j.neurenf.2012.05.578
41. Committee on Bioethics. *Document de consultation sur la Prédictivité, les Tests Génétiques et l'Assurance.* Council of Europe (2012). p. 1–47. Available from: http://www.coe.int/t/dg3/healthbioethic/Source/Final%20F%20consult%20doc.pdf
42. Baghdadli A. *Recommandations pour la pratique professionnelle du diagnostic de l'autisme.* Fédération française de psychiatrie, Haute Autorité de Santé (2005). p. 1–15. Available from: http://www.has-sante.fr/portail/upload/docs/application/pdf/recommandations_autisme.pdf
43. Schaefer GB, Mendelsohn NJ. Clinical genetics evaluation in identifying the etiology of autism spectrum disorders. *Genet Med* (2008) **10**(4):301–5. doi:10.1097/GIM.0b013e31816b5cc9
44. Klei L, Sanders SJ, Murtha MT, Hus V, Lowe JK, Willsey AJ, et al. Common genetic variants, acting additively, are a major source of risk for autism. *Mol Autism* (2012) **3**(1):9. doi:10.1186/2040-2392-3-9
45. Baghdadli A, Picot MC, Pascal C, Pry R, Aussilloux C. Relationship between age of recognition of first disturbances and severity in young children with autism. *Eur Child Adolesc Psychiatry* (2003) **12**(3):122–7. doi:10.1007/s00787-003-0314-6
46. Chamak B, Bonniau B, Oudaya L, Ehrenberg A. The autism diagnostic experiences of French parents. *Autism* (2011) **15**(1):83–97. doi:10.1177/1362361309354756
47. Shattuck PT, Durkin M, Maenner M, Newschaffer C, Mandell DS, Wiggins L, et al. Timing of identification among children with an autism spectrum disorder: findings from a population-based surveillance study. *J Am Acad Child Adolesc Psychiatry* (2009) **48**(5):474–83. doi:10.1097/CHI.0b013e31819b3848
48. Johnson CP, Myers SM. Identification and evaluation of children with autism spectrum disorders. *Pediatrics* (2007) **120**(5):1183–215. doi:10.1542/peds.2007-2361
49. Selkirk CG, McCarthy Veach P, Lian F, Schimmenti L, LeRoy BS. Parents' perceptions of autism spectrum disorder etiology and recurrence risk and effects of their perceptions on family planning: recommendations for genetic counselors. *J Genet Couns* (2009) **18**(5):507–19. doi:10.1007/s10897-009-9233-0
50. Chen LS, Xu L, Huang TY, Dhar SU. Autism genetic testing: a qualitative study of awareness, attitudes, and experiences among parents of children with autism spectrum disorders. *Genet Med* (2013) **15**(4):274–81. doi:10.1038/gim.2012.145
51. Vande Wydeven K, Kwan A, Hardan AY, Bernstein JA. Underutilization of genetics services for autism: the importance of parental awareness and provider recommendation. *J Genet Couns* (2012) **21**(6):803–13. doi:10.1007/s10897-012-9494-x
52. McGrath RJ, Laflamme DJ, Schwartz AP, Stransky M, Moeschler JB. Access to genetic counseling for children with autism, Down syndrome, and intellectual disabilities. *Pediatrics* (2009) **124**(Suppl 4):S443–9. doi:10.1542/peds.2009-1255Q
53. Palmer CG, Lueddeke JT, Zhou J. Factors influencing parental decision about genetics evaluation for their deaf or hard-of-hearing child. *Genet Med* (2009) **11**(4):248–55. doi:10.1097/GIM.0b013e318195aad9
54. Lawrence RE, Appelbaum PS. Genetic testing in psychiatry: a review of attitudes and beliefs. *Psychiatry* (2011) **74**(4):315–31. doi:10.1521/psyc.2011.74.4.315
55. Salm M, Abbate K, Appelbaum P, Ottman R, Chung W, Marder K, et al. Use of genetic tests among neurologists and psychiatrists: knowledge, attitudes, behaviors, and needs for training. *J Genet Couns* (2013) **23**(2):156–63. doi:10.1007/s10897-013-9624-0
56. Hoop JG, Roberts LW, Green Hammond KA, Cox NJ. Psychiatrists' attitudes, knowledge, and experience regarding genetics: a preliminary study. *Genet Med* (2008) **10**:439–49. doi:10.1097/GIM.0b013e318177014b

# 17

# The use of medications approved for Alzheimer's disease in autism spectrum disorder: a systematic review

***Daniel A. Rossignol[1]* and Richard E. Frye[2]***

[1] *Rossignol Medical Center, Irvine, CA, USA*
[2] *Arkansas Children's Hospital Research Institute, University of Arkansas for Medical Sciences, Little Rock, AR, USA*

***Edited by:***
*Roberto Canitano, University Hospital of Siena, Italy*

***Reviewed by:***
*Karen M. Smith, University of Louisiana at Lafayette, USA*
*Xiaoming Wang, Duke University, USA*

****Correspondence:***
*Daniel A. Rossignol, Rossignol Medical Center, 16251 Laguna Canyon Road Suite 175, Irvine, CA 92618, USA*
*e-mail: rossignolmd@gmail.com*

Autism spectrum disorder (ASD) is a neurodevelopmental disorder that affects 1 in 68 children in the United States. Even though it is a common disorder, only two medications (risperidone and aripiprazole) are approved by the U.S. Food and Drug Administration (FDA) to treat symptoms associated with ASD. However, these medications are approved to treat irritability, which is not a core symptom of ASD. A number of novel medications, which have not been approved by the FDA to treat ASD have been used off-label in some studies to treat ASD symptoms, including medications approved for Alzheimer's disease. Interestingly, some of these studies are high-quality, double-blind, placebo-controlled (DBPC) studies. This article systematically reviews studies published through April, 2014, which examined the use of Alzheimer's medications in ASD, including donepezil (seven studies, two were DBPC, five out of seven reported improvements), galantamine (four studies, two were DBPC, all reported improvements), rivastigmine (one study reporting improvements), tacrine (one study reporting improvements), and memantine (nine studies, one was DBPC, eight reported improvements). An evidence-based scale was used to rank each medication. Collectively, these studies reported improvements in expressive language and communication, receptive language, social interaction, irritability, hyperactivity, attention, eye contact, emotional lability, repetitive or self-stimulatory behaviors, motor planning, disruptive behaviors, obsessive–compulsive symptoms, lethargy, overall ASD behaviors, and increased REM sleep. Reported side effects are reviewed and include irritability, gastrointestinal problems, verbal or behavioral regression, headaches, irritability, rash, tremor, sedation, vomiting, and speech problems. Both galantamine and memantine had sufficient evidence ranking for improving both core and associated symptoms of ASD. Given the lack of medications approved to treat ASD, further studies on novel medications, including Alzheimer's disease medications, are needed.

**Keywords: autism, Alzheimer's disease, acetylcholinesterase inhibitors, NMDA antagonist, medications**

## BACKGROUND

Autism spectrum disorder (ASD) is a heterogenous neurodevelopmental disorder that is defined by behavioral observations and characterized by developmental delays in communication and social interaction and by repetitive behaviors and/or restricted interests. The most recent prevalence of ASD in the United States (U.S.) is now 1 in 68 children, including 1 in 42 boys (1). Only two medications have been approved by the U.S. Food and Drug Administration (FDA) for ASD and these medications, risperidone and aripiprazole, are indicated to treat irritability, an associated but not core symptom of ASD (2, 3). Since irritability is not a core feature of ASD, there are currently no U.S. FDA approved medications for treating the core symptoms of ASD.

A number of novel medications have been used to treat the symptoms of ASD (4, 5). Some of these medications are approved for the treatment of Alzheimer's disease. A connection between Alzheimer's disease and autism has been proposed by some investigators (6) and will be reviewed below. Because of the evidence of this connection, several medications approved for Alzheimer's disease have been investigated for use in ASD. To date, five medications have been approved by the U.S. FDA for the treatment of Alzheimer's disease: Tacrine (Cognex®, 1993), Donepezil (Aricept®, 1996), Rivastigmine (Exelon®, 2000), Galantamine (Razadyne®, 2001), and Memantine (Namenda®, 2003). Donepezil, galantamine, rivastigmine, and tacrine are cholinesterase inhibitors, and work by preventing the breakdown of acetylcholine. Galantamine also stimulates nicotinic cholinergic receptors and therefore can increase the release of acetylcholine (7). Memantine is distinct from these other medications and modulates glutamate neurotransmission.

Several lines of evidence have implicated abnormalities in the cholinergic system in ASD (8). First, studies examining post-mortem brain samples from individuals with ASD have reported abnormalities in the cholinergic system (9–11). Early studies compared the cholinergic system in frontal, parietal, hippocampus, and cerebellar tissue from typically developing adults to similarly aged autistic adults with intellectual disability. One of these studies found decreases in muscarinic $M_1$ receptors in the parietal cortex and nicotinic receptors in the frontal and parietal cortexes, with a decrease in $\alpha_4$ and $\beta_2$ nicotinic subtypes confirmed by immunochemistry in the parietal cortex (9). Another study found significant changes in nicotinic receptors but no significant changes in muscarinic receptors or in the presynaptic cholinergic enzyme choline acetyltransferase in the cerebellum. Consistent nicotinic receptor changes included decreases in the $\alpha_4$ receptor subtype in several types of cells including granule and Purkinje cells, as well as increases in the $\alpha_7$ receptor subtype in the granule cell layer (11). In contrast, using quantitative receptor autoradiographic studies, no changes in cholinergic receptor binding were found in the hippocampus (12). Later, a study comparing typically developing and autistic adults showed a decrease in $\alpha_7$ and $\beta_2$ but not $\alpha_4$ nicotinic acetylcholine receptor subunits in the thalamus (10). Secondly, a positron emission tomography study reported a decrease in acetylcholinesterase activity in the bilateral fusiform gyri in ASD adults, as compared to typically developing adults, with this decrease correlated with objective scales of individual participant social disability (13). Thirdly, functional analysis of gene networks altered in individuals with ASD implicate synaptic cholinergic receptor families of genes (14) and epigenetic changes in both ASD and Rett syndrome have been linked to decreased expression of the CHRNA7 gene encoding the nicotinic receptor subtype $\alpha_7$ (15). Lastly, some studies have implicated cholinergic abnormalities in an animal model of ASD. The BTBR ASD mouse model demonstrates lower basal levels of extracellular acetylcholine in the prefrontal cortex (16) and injection of the acetylcholinesterase inhibitor donepezil into the BTBR mouse (systemically or directly) in the dorsomedial striatum, the rodent homolog of the caudate nucleus, ameliorated many core ASD behaviors (17). Thus, there is substantial support for the idea that treatments that modulate the cholinergic system might be helpful in ASD (18).

Several lines of scientific evidence have also pointed to abnormalities in glutamate metabolism in individuals with ASD as identified by imaging, genetic, and post-mortem studies. Proton magnetic resonance spectroscopy has demonstrated abnormalities in glutamate metabolism in individuals with ASD. For example, the glutamate + glutamine peak has been found to be increased in individuals with ASD as compared to controls in the auditory cortex (19), anterior cingulate cortex (20, 21), and basal ganglia (22). Another study found that the glutamate/glutamine ratio in the amygdala–hippocampal region was increased in ASD individuals as compared to controls (23), while one study found an increase in glutamate/creatine in the putamen in individuals with ASD (24). Interestingly, the magnetic resonance spectroscopy glutamate + glutamine peak in the basal ganglia of ASD individuals was correlated with a measure of impairment in social communication (22) and the glutamate/creatine ratio in the putamen was correlated with ASD symptoms (social interaction) (24). However, studies examining glutamate in frontal brain regions have demonstrated inconsistent results. For example, as compared to controls, individuals with ASD demonstrated a decrease in the GABA/glutamate ratio in the frontal cortex in one study (25) while the glutamate + glutamine peak was not different between ASD and control individuals in the prefrontal cortex in another study (22). The glutamate/creatine ratio was decreased in ASD individuals in the frontal lobes, as compared to controls, in another study (26).

Genetic studies have implicated abnormalities in ionotropic glutamate receptors in ASD. Genetic studies have associated ASD with abnormalities in subunits of *N*-methyl-D-aspartate (NMDA) (27–30), α-amino-3-hydroxy-5-methyl-4-isoxazolepropionic acid (AMPA) (31), and kainate (32, 33) receptors and the mitochondrial aspartate/glutamate carrier (34–36). Genetic syndromes that have a high prevalence of ASD features demonstrate abnormalities in glutamate neurotransmission. For example, haploinsufficiency of SHANK3, a gene that encodes postsynaptic scaffolding proteins for glutamate receptors, is characteristic of many patients with Phelan–McDermid syndrome, a genetic disorder with a high prevalence of ASD (37). Interestingly, genetic animal models of ASD have also demonstrated involvement of glutamate receptors. For example, one of the main areas of research is the Fragile X mouse model where abnormalities in metabotropic glutamate receptor subtype 5 (mGluR5) have been linked to behavioral and cognitive abnormalities that overlap symptoms associated with ASD (38).

Lastly, post-mortem studies have also implicated glutamate abnormalities. Cerebellum samples from individuals with ASD have demonstrated an increase in mRNA for AMPA 1, 2, and 3 receptors and glutamate/aspartate transporter 1 and 2, an increase in protein levels of glutamate/aspartate transporter 1 and 2 and AMPA 1 and NMDA 1 receptors, but a decrease in AMPA receptor density (39). In addition, other studies have demonstrated an increase in mGluR5 protein in the vermis (40) and superior frontal cortex (41) of children with ASD. One study reported decreased levels of kidney-type glutaminase in the anterior cingulate cortex of individuals with ASD (42), while another study demonstrated an increase in the mitochondrial aspartate/glutamate carrier in the prefrontal cortex but not in the cerebellum of individuals with ASD (43). Thus, there is substantial evidence for glutamate abnormalities in individuals with ASD, suggesting the treatments that modulate glutamate may be helpful in ASD.

Memantine is an NMDA receptor antagonist and regulates the activity of glutamate, a neurotransmitter involved in memory and learning. Normally glutamate attaches to NMDA receptors allowing calcium to then enter freely into cells. Memantine prevents this by partially blocking NMDA receptors. Memantine has been reported to help obsessive–compulsive disorder (OCD) as well as impulsive behaviors in open-label (44–48), single blind (49), and placebo-controlled studies (50, 51). In animal models, memantine has also been shown to decrease evidence of neuroinflammation (52).

Given this background, this article reviews studies that have been published to date, which have reported on the use of these Alzheimer's medications in ASD individuals. Overall, this review demonstrates that there is significant scientific support for some of these medications in the treatment of core ASD symptoms, suggesting that further clinical trials may be helpful to help define the role for some of these medications for the treatment of individuals with ASD.

## METHODS

### SEARCH STRATEGY

A computer-aided search of PUBMED [website (http://www.ncbi.nlm.nih.gov/entrez)] and Google Scholar databases from

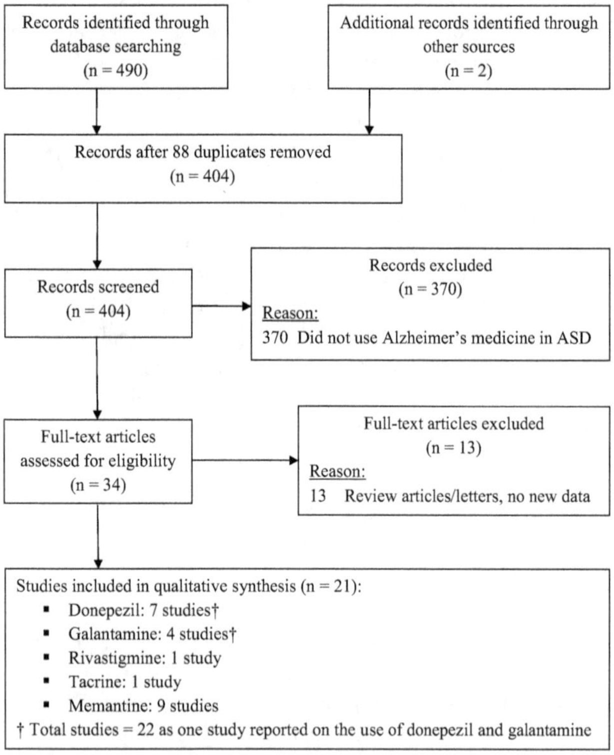


**FIGURE 1 | Study flow chart.**

**Table 1 | Levels of evidence.**

| Level | Description |
|---|---|
| 1a | SR or meta-analysis of RCTs with homogeneity or Cochrane review with favorable findings |
| 1b | Prospective high-quality RCT |
| 2a | SR of cohort (prospective, non-randomized) studies with homogeneity |
| 2b | Individual cohort (prospective, non-randomized) study or low-quality RCT |
| 3a | SR of case–control (retrospective) studies with homogeneity |
| 3b | Individual case–control (retrospective) study |
| 4 | Case-series or reports |
| 5 | Expert opinion without critical appraisal or based on physiology or bench research |

*RCT, randomized controlled trial; SR, systematic review.*

**Table 2 | Grade of recommendation.**

| Grade | Description |
|---|---|
| A | At least one level 1a study or two level 1b studies |
| B | At least one level 1b, 2a, or 3a study, or two level 2b or 3b studies |
| C | At least one level 2b or 3b study, or two level 4 studies |
| D | Level 5 evidence, or troublingly inconsistent or inconclusive studies of any level, or studies reporting no improvements |
| N | No studies identified |

inception through the end of April, 2014 was conducted to identify pertinent articles using the search terms "autism," "autistic," "ASD," "pervasive developmental disorder," "PDD," and "Asperger" in all combinations with the terms: "donepezil," "galantamine," "memantine," "rivastigmine," "tacrine," "Alzheimer," "cholinesterase inhibitor," and "NMDA antagonist." The references cited in identified articles were also searched to locate additional studies (two studies total). **Figure 1** depicts the studies identified during the search process.

### STUDY SELECTION

Studies were included if they: (1) involved individuals with ASD, and (2) administered a medication approved for Alzheimer's disease to at least one individual with ASD. Articles that did not present new or unique data (such as review articles or letters to the editor) and animal studies were excluded. Studies on Rett syndrome and Childhood Disintegrative Disorder were also excluded. One reviewer screened titles and abstracts of all potentially relevant studies. After screening all records, 34 publications were identified and independently reviewed by both reviewers; 21 studies met inclusion criteria (see **Figure 1**). Within each section of this review, strengths and limitations of studies are discussed and recommendations for additional research are offered.

### LEVEL OF EVIDENCE RATINGS

Although we considered conducting a meta-analysis on identified treatments, the lack of standard outcomes and the limitations in study design prevented a meta-analysis of any identified treatment. As an alternative, we provide a grade of recommendation (GOR) for each treatment based on the level of evidence (LOE). Using a well-established scale (53), each study was individually assessed to determine the LOE, ranging from level 1 to 5 (**Table 1**). After assessing all identified studies for each treatment, a GOR ranging from A (solid evidence) to D (limited, inconsistent, or inconclusive evidence) was assigned (**Table 2**). Since a treatment could be a GOR of D for several reasons, we specified if the treatment received this rating because the evidence was a single case report or series (SC), was only based on bench research (BR), demonstrated an overall neutral effect (NE), or was found to be possibly detrimental (DE). If no studies were identified for a treatment, a GOR of N (no studies) was assigned. The overall ratings of Alzheimer disease medications used for ASD are found in **Table 3**. **Table 4** lists the types of symptoms improved with each particular medication, while **Table 5** compiles the side effects by medication.

## RESULTS

### DONEPEZIL

Seven studies reported on the use of donepezil in individuals with ASD, with five studies (71%) reporting improvements. Five studies were open-label or retrospective case-series. The first identified study was an uncontrolled, retrospective, open-label study of eight children (LOE 4) with autistic disorder (mean age 11.0 ± 4.1 years) and reported improvements in irritability and hyperactivity with donepezil (up to 10 mg/day) after at least 2 months of use; side effects included mild irritability (one patient) and gastrointestinal problems (nausea and vomiting in 1 patient) (54). Another uncontrolled, retrospective case-series (LOE 4) of eight children with PDD (ages 10–17 years) used donepezil (2.5–30 mg/day; mean 18 weeks of treatment) for ADHD-type symptoms and reported improvements in ADHD symptoms, communication, and socialization; one patient had to stop the medication due to side effects (tremor, irritability, and distractibility) (55). An uncontrolled, open-label study (LOE 4) of five children with ASD (ages 2.5–6.9 years) with deficits in REM sleep administered donepezil, which increased the percentage of REM sleep as measured by polysomnography after 1 month of treatment (56). In a case report (LOE 4) of a 5-year-old child with ASD, treatment with donepezil (5 mg at bedtime) over 6 weeks led to significant improvements in communication, eye contact, and hyperactivity (57). Finally, one case report (LOE 4) of three adults with autism treated with galantamine reported that the use of donepezil (dose not reported) led to verbal and behavioral regression in one adult (58).

Two studies were double-blind, placebo-controlled (DBPC) studies. The first DBPC study contained 43 children (LOE 1b) with autism (mean age 6.8 years) and administered donepezil or placebo over 6 weeks and reported improvements in expressive and receptive speech and a decrease in overall autistic behaviors in the treatment group; side effects included diarrhea and stomach

**Table 3 | Overall ratings of Alzheimer disease medications used for autism spectrum disorder.**

| Medication | Uncontrolled studies positive (positive/total) | Controlled studies positive (positive/total) | Grade of recommendation |
|---|---|---|---|
| Donepezil | 80% (4/5) | 50% (1/2) | D - NE |
| Galantamine | 100% (2/2) | 100% (2/2) | B |
| Rivastigmine | 100% (1/1) | | D - SC |
| Tacrine | 100% (1/1) | | D - SC |
| Memantine | 88% (7/8) | 100% (1/1) | B |

**Table 4 | Improvements reported in studies of Alzheimer disease medications in ASD.**

| Symptom | Donepezil | Galantamine | Rivastigmine | Tacrine | Memantine |
|---|---|---|---|---|---|
| Expressive language | X | X | X | X | X |
| Receptive language | X | | | | X |
| Social interaction | X | X | | | X |
| Irritability | X | X | | X | X |
| Hyperactivity | X | X | | X | X |
| Attention | X | X | | | X |
| Eye contact | X | X | | X | X |
| Emotional lability | | X | | | |
| Repetitive or self-stimulatory behaviors | | | | | X |
| Motor planning | | | | | X |
| Disruptive behaviors | | | | | X |
| Obsessive–compulsive behaviors | | | | | X |
| Lethargy | | X | | | |
| Overall ASD symptoms | X | | X | | |
| Increased REM sleep | X | | | | |

**Table 5 | Reported side effects of Alzheimer disease medications in ASD.**

| Side effect | Donepezil | Galantamine | Rivastigmine | Tacrine | Memantine |
|---|---|---|---|---|---|
| Irritability | X | | | | X |
| Gastrointestinal problems | X | | | | X |
| Verbal or behavioral regression | X | X | | | |
| Headaches | | X | | | |
| Worsened behaviors | | | | | X |
| Irritability | | | | | X |
| Rash | | | | | X |
| Excessive sedation | | | | | X |
| Vomiting | | | | | X |
| Speech problems | | | | | X |
| Tremor | X | | | | |
| Distractibility | X | | | | |
| Increased seizures | | | | | X |

cramps (59). In the second DBPC study of 34 children (LOE 1b) with ASD (age range 8–17 years), donepezil (dose 5–10 mg/day), or placebo was administered over 10 weeks, with a 10-week open-label trial of the medication for children in the placebo group who did not respond. No significant improvements were found in the donepezil group compared to the placebo group; no serious adverse events were observed (60).

Overall, the evidence for donepezil is inconsistent for improvements in ASD symptoms as one of the two DBPC studies was negative and one of the five case-series reported detrimental effects rather than beneficial effects of donepezil. As two case-series reported improvements in ADHD symptoms and one case-series demonstrated improvements in REM sleep, donepezil may have favorable effects on subsets of children with ASD who have these specific symptoms. Clearly, several studies have demonstrated favorable effects of donepezil, suggesting that further studies focused on specific symptoms may be warranted in the future.

### GALANTAMINE

Four studies reported on the use of galantamine in individuals with ASD, with all four studies reporting improvements. Two of the studies were uncontrolled, open-label, or case-series (LOE 4). In the first case-series (LOE 4) of three adults with autism (21 to 42 years old), galantamine 4–16 mg/day was reported to increase expressive language and communication; however; one individual had a regression when put on donepezil (58). The second study was a 12-week, uncontrolled, open-label study (LOE 4) of galantamine in 13 children with autism (mean age $8.8 \pm 3.5$ years), which reported improvements in parent-rated social withdrawal and irritability on the Aberrant Behavior Checklist (ABC) and improvements in attention and emotional lability on the Conner's Parent Rating Scale – Revised; eight patients were rated as improved on the Clinical Global Impression Scale (CGI); no significant adverse effect were found except for headaches in one child (61).

Two studies were DBPC. The first DBPC study of 20 children (LOE 2b) with autism (mean age $7.4 \pm 3.2$ years) reported a significant improvement with galantamine (dose not noted) compared to placebo on the ABC in irritability, eye contact, hyperactivity, and inappropriate speech; side effects were minimal (62). The second DBPC study of 40 children (LOE 1b) with autism (ages 4–12 years) reported that galantamine (up to 24 mg/day) for 10 weeks led to significant improvements in lethargy/social withdrawal and irritability on the ABC compared to placebo; side effects were similar in both groups (18).

Given that galantamine has been shown to improve both core and associated ASD symptoms in both open-label and DBPC studies (one high-quality and one of lower quality), it is given a GOR of B. Given this preliminary positive evidence, it is clear that large multicenter high-quality controlled trials should be conducted to provide efficacy data to further define the role of galantamine in the treatment of ASD.

### RIVASTIGMINE

An open-label study of 32 children (LOE 4) with autism used rivastigmine (0.4–0.8 mg twice a day) for 12 weeks and reported improvements in expressive speech and overall autism symptoms (63). Given the limited number of studies on rivastigmine for the treatment of ASD, this treatment is given a GOR of D – SC. Because of the positive preliminary results and the fact that it was well tolerated, further larger open-label or blinded studies may be warranted for this treatment in ASD.

### TACRINE

An open-label study of three individuals (LOE 4) with ASD (mean age $17.4 \pm 33.2$ years) administered 20 mg of tacrine daily and reported mild improvements in irritability, hyperactivity, eye contact, and inappropriate speech as rated by combined parent and teacher scales (ABC); no significant side effects were reported (64). Given the limited number of studies on tacrine for the treatment of ASD, this treatment is given a GOR of D – SC. Because of the positive preliminary results and the fact that it was well tolerated, further studies may be warranted for this treatment in ASD to see if a wider number of children with ASD respond to this treatment.

### MEMANTINE

Nine studies reported on the use of memantine in individuals with ASD, with eight studies (89%) reporting improvements. Eight studies were open-label or retrospective case-series. In the first study, Chez et al. (63) administered open-label (LOE 4) memantine (mean dose 8.1 mg/day, range 2.5–10 mg/day) in 30 children (mean age 8.92 years) with ASD and reported that for those treated more than 8 weeks (mean duration 18 weeks, range 8–40 weeks), 16 (53%) demonstrated significant improvements and 10 (33%) showed more mild improvements in attention, eye contact, language (expressive and receptive), repetitive behaviors, and motor planning; no significant side effects were observed (65). One case report (LOE 4) described the effects of memantine on a 23-year-old man with autistic disorder and observed improvements in disruptive behavior with memantine 10 mg/day over an 8-month period (66). An uncontrolled, open-label (LOE 4) study of 151 individuals with ASD (ages 2.58–26.33 years old) used memantine at a dose ranging from 2.5 to 30 mg and reported improvements in language, self-stimulatory behaviors, and social behavior; 22 patients (15%) had worsened behavior as a side effect (67).

An uncontrolled, open-label, and retrospective study (LOE 4) examined the effects of memantine (maximum dose 20 mg/day; duration of use 1.5–56 weeks) in 18 children with ASD (age 6–19 years) and reported improvements in social withdrawal and inattention; 7 patients (39%) had side effects including irritability (4 patients), rash (1 patient), excessive sedation and vomiting (1 patient), and an increase in seizures (1 patient); 4 patients had to discontinue memantine (68). An uncontrolled, open-label (LOE 4) study of four patients with ASD (mean age $17.4 \pm 33.2$ years) administered memantine 20 mg daily for 4 weeks and reported significant improvements on combined parent and teacher ratings on the ABC in irritability, hyperactivity, and inappropriate speech ($p < 0.05$ for all three); no side effects were reported (69). An uncontrolled, open-label study (LOE 4) used memantine (starting at 5 mg, increasing every 2 weeks up to 20 mg/day; mean final dose $18.3 \pm 2.6$ mg/day; mean use $34.7 \pm 36.5$ weeks, range 8–104 weeks) in six individuals with Fragile X and concomitant PDD (mean age $18.3 \pm 3.8$ years, range 13–22 years; four had autistic disorder and two had PDD). Four of the six patients were rated as "much improved" or "very much improved" on the CGI; non-significant improvements were observed on the ABC and SRS; two individuals experienced irritability, which led to drug discontinuation (70). A case report (LOE 4) of a 15-year-old boy with Asperger disorder, OCD, and Tourette disorder described the use of memantine (2.5 mg increasing to 10 mg/day) to treat the OCD symptoms and observed a significant reduction in OCD symptoms, including rituals and intrusive thoughts as well as improvements in social interaction; no significant adverse events were observed (71). One case study (LOE 4) reported stuttering and speech loss in two children with ASD who were taking memantine; in one child the speech improved with stopping the medication, while in the other child it improved while continuing the medication (72).

Only one study was DBPC and was a 10-week study of 40 children (LOE 1b) with ASD (ages 4–2 years). This study administered memantine (up to 15 mg/day if 10–40 kg; 20 mg/day if over 40 kg) compared to placebo and reported significant improvements on the ABC in irritability ($p < 0.001$), stereotypy ($p < 0.01$), and hyperactivity/non-compliance ($p < 0.01$); side effects were similar in both groups (73).

Given that the majority of clinical studies, including a DPBC study, provide positive evidence of improvements in both core and associated ASD symptoms, a GOR of B is provided for memantine for the treatment of ASD. Several studies have outlined adverse effects in certain patients with memantine treatment. Interestingly, memantine has been reported to both improve and worsen irritability. This suggests that there might be specific subgroups of children with ASD that respond optimally to memantine. Clearly larger, well-designed, and blinded studies are needed to further evaluate the efficacy of memantine in children with ASD as well as define the subgroups that might optimally respond to this medication.

## DISCUSSION

This manuscript reviews the evidence for the use of medications which are FDA approved for Alzheimer's disease in individuals with ASD. These medications target two neurotransmitter systems, acetylcholine and glutamate, which are both neurotransmitter systems with abnormalities associated with ASD. Overall five medications, four which target acetylcholine neurotransmission and one that targets glutamate neurotransmission, which are FDA indicated for Alzheimer's disease have been used in individuals with ASD. To provide recommendations on the evidence for the potential usefulness of these medications for the treatment of ASD, we used an objective scale to rate the evidence for the utility of these medications for treating core and associated symptoms of ASD. Overall, we found that one medication that targets acetylcholine neurotransmission, galantamine, and one medication that targets glutamate neurotransmission, memantine, have reasonable evidence for the treatment of core and associated symptoms of ASD, although both require larger controlled studies to provide further efficacy data and define subgroups of individuals with ASD who may best respond to these treatments with limited adverse effects. Two medications, rivastigmine and tacrine, both of which target the acetylcholine neurotransmitter system, have only preliminary uncontrolled studies to support their use, so further studies need to be performed before recommendations can be made. One medication that targets acetylcholine, donepezil, has several studies investigating its use in individuals with ASD but the results of some of the studies, particularly the DBPC studies, are inconsistent, making recommendations difficult at this time, although in certain subgroups (ADHD symptoms or REM sleep problems) it might be of use.

Given the fact that there is no FDA approved medication for the core symptoms of ASD and considering the limited proven effective treatments for ASD, studies are needed to identify novel treatments. Because several of the medications reviewed here show promising evidence for effectiveness for treating core and associated ASD symptoms, such medications should undergo further study in clinical trials to confirm their effectiveness for treating individuals with ASD.

## ACKNOWLEDGMENTS

The review did not receive any financial or grant support from any sources.

## REFERENCES

1. Developmental Disabilities Monitoring Network Surveillance Year 2010 Principal Investigators; Centers for Disease Control and Prevention (CDC). Prevalence of autism spectrum disorder among children aged 8 years – autism and developmental disabilities monitoring network, 11 sites, United States, 2010. *MMWR Surveill Summ* (2014) **63**(Suppl 2):1–21.
2. Scott LJ, Dhillon S. Risperidone: a review of its use in the treatment of irritability associated with autistic disorder in children and adolescents. *Paediatr Drugs* (2007) **9**(5):343–54. doi:10.2165/00148581-200709050-00006
3. Ghanizadeh A, Sahraeizadeh A, Berk M. A head-to-head comparison of aripiprazole and risperidone for safety and treating autistic disorders, a randomized double blind clinical trial. *Child Psychiatry Hum Dev* (2014) **45**(2):185–92. doi:10.1007/s10578-013-0390-x
4. Frye RE, Rossignol D, Casanova MF, Brown GL, Martin V, Edelson S, et al. A review of traditional and novel treatments for seizures in autism spectrum disorder: findings from a systematic review and expert panel. *Front Public Health* (2013) **1**:31. doi:10.3389/fpubh.2013.00031
5. Rossignol DA. Novel and emerging treatments for autism spectrum disorders: a systematic review. *Ann Clin Psychiatry* (2009) **21**(4):213–36.
6. Sokol DK, Maloney B, Long JM, Ray B, Lahiri DK. Autism, Alzheimer disease, and fragile X: APP, FMRP, and mGluR5 are molecular links. *Neurology* (2011) **76**(15):1344–52. doi:10.1212/WNL.0b013e3182166dc7
7. Woodruff-Pak DS, Vogel RW III, Wenk GL. Galantamine: effect on nicotinic receptor binding, acetylcholinesterase inhibition, and learning. *Proc Natl Acad Sci U S A* (2001) **98**(4):2089–94. doi:10.1073/pnas.98.4.2089
8. Deutsch SI, Urbano MR, Neumann SA, Burket JA, Katz E. Cholinergic abnormalities in autism: is there a rationale for selective nicotinic agonist interventions? *Clin Neuropharmacol* (2010) **33**(3):114–20. doi:10.1097/WNF.0b013e3181d6f7ad
9. Perry EK, Lee ML, Martin-Ruiz CM, Court JA, Volsen SG, Merrit J, et al. Cholinergic activity in autism: abnormalities in the cerebral cortex and basal forebrain. *Am J Psychiatry* (2001) **158**(7):1058–66. doi:10.1176/appi.ajp.158.7.1058
10. Ray MA, Graham AJ, Lee M, Perry RH, Court JA, Perry EK. Neuronal nicotinic acetylcholine receptor subunits in autism: an immunohistochemical investigation in the thalamus. *Neurobiol Dis* (2005) **19**(3):366–77. doi:10.1016/j.nbd.2005.01.017
11. Lee M, Martin-Ruiz C, Graham A, Court J, Jaros E, Perry R, et al. Nicotinic receptor abnormalities in the cerebellar cortex in autism. *Brain* (2002) **125**(Pt 7):1483–95. doi:10.1093/brain/awf160
12. Blatt GJ, Fitzgerald CM, Guptill JT, Booker AB, Kemper TL, Bauman ML. Density and distribution of hippocampal neurotransmitter receptors in autism: an autoradiographic study. *J Autism Dev Disord* (2001) **31**(6):537–43. doi:10.1023/A:1013238809666
13. Suzuki K, Sugihara G, Ouchi Y, Nakamura K, Tsujii M, Futatsubashi M, et al. Reduced acetylcholinesterase activity in the fusiform gyrus in adults with autism spectrum disorders. *Arch Gen Psychiatry* (2011) **68**(3):306–13. doi:10.1001/archgenpsychiatry.2011.4

14. Lee TL, Raygada MJ, Rennert OM. Integrative gene network analysis provides novel regulatory relationships, genetic contributions and susceptible targets in autism spectrum disorders. *Gene* (2012) **496**(2):88–96. doi:10.1016/j.gene.2012.01.020
15. Yasui DH, Scoles HA, Horike S, Meguro-Horike M, Dunaway KW, Schroeder DI, et al. 15q11.2-13.3 chromatin analysis reveals epigenetic regulation of CHRNA7 with deficiencies in Rett and autism brain. *Hum Mol Genet* (2011) **20**(22):4311–23. doi:10.1093/hmg/ddr357
16. McTighe SM, Neal SJ, Lin Q, Hughes ZA, Smith DG. The BTBR mouse model of autism spectrum disorders has learning and attentional impairments and alterations in acetylcholine and kynurenic acid in prefrontal cortex. *PLoS One* (2013) **8**(4):e62189. doi:10.1371/journal.pone.0062189
17. Karvat G, Kimchi T. Acetylcholine elevation relieves cognitive rigidity and social deficiency in a mouse model of autism. *Neuropsychopharmacology* (2014) **39**(4):831–40. doi:10.1038/npp.2013.274
18. Ghaleiha A, Ghyasvand M, Mohammadi MR, Farokhnia M, Yadegari N, Tabrizi M, et al. Galantamine efficacy and tolerability as an augmentative therapy in autistic children: a randomized, double-blind, placebo-controlled trial. *J Psychopharmacol* (2014) **28**(7):677–85. doi:10.1177/0269881113508830
19. Brown MS, Singel D, Hepburn S, Rojas DC. Increased glutamate concentration in the auditory cortex of persons with autism and first-degree relatives: a (1)H-MRS study. *Autism Res* (2013) **6**(1):1–10. doi:10.1002/aur.1260
20. Bejjani A, O'Neill J, Kim JA, Frew AJ, Yee VW, Ly R, et al. Elevated glutamatergic compounds in pregenual anterior cingulate in pediatric autism spectrum disorder demonstrated by 1H MRS and 1H MRSI. *PLoS One* (2012) **7**(7):e38786. doi:10.1371/journal.pone.0038786
21. Bernardi S, Anagnostou E, Shen J, Kolevzon A, Buxbaum JD, Hollander E, et al. In vivo 1H-magnetic resonance spectroscopy study of the attentional networks in autism. *Brain Res* (2011) **1380**:198–205. doi:10.1016/j.brainres.2010.12.057
22. Horder J, Lavender T, Mendez MA, O'Gorman R, Daly E, Craig MC, et al. Reduced subcortical glutamate/glutamine in adults with autism spectrum disorders: a [(1)H]MRS study. *Transl Psychiatry* (2013) **3**:e279. doi:10.1038/tp.2013.53
23. Page LA, Daly E, Schmitz N, Simmons A, Toal F, Deeley Q, et al. In vivo 1H-magnetic resonance spectroscopy study of amygdala-hippocampal and parietal regions in autism. *Am J Psychiatry* (2006) **163**(12):2189–92. doi:10.1176/appi.ajp.163.12.2189
24. Doyle-Thomas KA, Card D, Soorya LV, Wang AT, Fan J, Anagnostou E. Metabolic mapping of deep brain structures and associations with symptomatology in autism spectrum disorders. *Res Autism Spectr Disord* (2014) **8**(1):44–51. doi:10.1016/j.rasd.2013.10.003
25. Harada M, Taki MM, Nose A, Kubo H, Mori K, Nishitani H, et al. Non-invasive evaluation of the GABAergic/glutamatergic system in autistic patients observed by MEGA-editing proton MR spectroscopy using a clinical 3 tesla instrument. *J Autism Dev Disord* (2011) **41**(4):447–54. doi:10.1007/s10803-010-1065-0
26. Kubas B, Kulak W, Sobaniec W, Tarasow E, Lebkowska U, Walecki J. Metabolite alterations in autistic children: a 1H MR spectroscopy study. *Adv Med Sci* (2012) **57**(1):152–6. doi:10.2478/v10039-012-0014-x
27. O'Roak BJ, Vives L, Girirajan S, Karakoc E, Krumm N, Coe BP, et al. Sporadic autism exomes reveal a highly interconnected protein network of de novo mutations. *Nature* (2012) **485**(7397):246–50. doi:10.1038/nature10989
28. Yoo HJ, Cho IH, Park M, Yang SY, Kim SA. Family based association of GRIN2A and GRIN2B with Korean autism spectrum disorders. *Neurosci Lett* (2012) **512**(2):89–93. doi:10.1016/j.neulet.2012.01.061
29. Barnby G, Abbott A, Sykes N, Morris A, Weeks DE, Mott R, et al. Candidate-gene screening and association analysis at the autism-susceptibility locus on chromosome 16p: evidence of association at GRIN2A and ABAT. *Am J Hum Genet* (2005) **76**(6):950–66. doi:10.1086/430454
30. Tarabeux J, Kebir O, Gauthier J, Hamdan FF, Xiong L, Piton A, et al. Rare mutations in *N*-methyl-D-aspartate glutamate receptors in autism spectrum disorders and schizophrenia. *Transl Psychiatry* (2011) **1**:e55. doi:10.1038/tp.2011.52
31. Ramanathan S, Woodroffe A, Flodman PL, Mays LZ, Hanouni M, Modahl CB, et al. A case of autism with an interstitial deletion on 4q leading to hemizygosity for genes encoding for glutamine and glycine neurotransmitter receptor sub-units (AMPA 2, GLRA3, GLRB) and neuropeptide receptors NPY1R, NPY5R. *BMC Med Genet* (2004) **5**:10. doi:10.1186/1471-2156-5-10
32. Jamain S, Betancur C, Quach H, Philippe A, Fellous M, Giros B, et al. Linkage and association of the glutamate receptor 6 gene with autism. *Mol Psychiatry* (2002) **7**(3):302–10. doi:10.1038/sj.mp.4000979
33. Shuang M, Liu J, Jia MX, Yang JZ, Wu SP, Gong XH, et al. Family-based association study between autism and glutamate receptor 6 gene in Chinese Han trios. *Am J Med Genet B Neuropsychiatr Genet* (2004) **131B**(1):48–50. doi:10.1002/ajmg.b.30025
34. Hong CJ, Liou YJ, Liao DL, Hou SJ, Yen FC, Tsai SJ. Association study of polymorphisms in the mitochondrial aspartate/glutamate carrier SLC25A12 (aralar) gene with schizophrenia. *Prog Neuropsychopharmacol Biol Psychiatry* (2007) **31**(7):1510–3. doi:10.1016/j.pnpbp.2007.07.010
35. Ramoz N, Reichert JG, Smith CJ, Silverman JM, Bespalova IN, Davis KL, et al. Linkage and association of the mitochondrial aspartate/glutamate carrier SLC25A12 gene with autism. *Am J Psychiatry* (2004) **161**(4):662–9. doi:10.1176/appi.ajp.161.4.662
36. Segurado R, Conroy J, Meally E, Fitzgerald M, Gill M, Gallagher L. Confirmation of association between autism and the mitochondrial aspartate/glutamate carrier SLC25A12 gene on chromosome 2q31. *Am J Psychiatry* (2005) **162**(11):2182–4. doi:10.1176/appi.ajp.162.11.2182
37. Phelan K, McDermid HE. The 22q13.3 Deletion Syndrome (Phelan-McDermid Syndrome). *Mol Syndromol* (2012) **2**(3–5):186–201.
38. D'Antoni S, Spatuzza M, Bonaccorso CM, Musumeci SA, Ciranna L, Nicoletti F, et al. Dysregulation of group-I metabotropic glutamate (mGlu) receptor mediated signalling in disorders associated with Intellectual Disability and Autism. *Neurosci Biobehav Rev* (2014). doi:10.1016/j.neubiorev.2014.02.003
39. Purcell AE, Jeon OH, Zimmerman AW, Blue ME, Pevsner J. Postmortem brain abnormalities of the glutamate neurotransmitter system in autism. *Neurology* (2001) **57**(9):1618–28. doi:10.1212/WNL.57.9.1618
40. Fatemi SH, Folsom TD, Kneeland RE, Liesch SB. Metabotropic glutamate receptor 5 upregulation in children with autism is associated with underexpression of both Fragile X mental retardation protein and GABAA receptor beta 3 in adults with autism. *Anat Rec (Hoboken)* (2011) **294**(10):1635–45. doi:10.1002/ar.21299
41. Fatemi SH, Folsom TD. Dysregulation of fragile x mental retardation protein and metabotropic glutamate receptor 5 in superior frontal cortex of individuals with autism: a postmortem brain study. *Mol Autism* (2011) **2**:6. doi:10.1186/2040-2392-2-6
42. Shimmura C, Suzuki K, Iwata Y, Tsuchiya KJ, Ohno K, Matsuzaki H, et al. Enzymes in the glutamate-glutamine cycle in the anterior cingulate cortex in postmortem brain of subjects with autism. *Mol Autism* (2013) **4**(1):6. doi:10.1186/2040-2392-4-6
43. Lepagnol-Bestel AM, Maussion G, Boda B, Cardona A, Iwayama Y, Delezoide AL, et al. SLC25A12 expression is associated with neurite outgrowth and is upregulated in the prefrontal cortex of autistic subjects. *Mol Psychiatry* (2008) **13**(4):385–97. doi:10.1038/sj.mp.4002120
44. Aboujaoude E, Barry JJ, Gamel N. Memantine augmentation in treatment-resistant obsessive-compulsive disorder: an open-label trial. *J Clin Psychopharmacol* (2009) **29**(1):51–5. doi:10.1097/JCP.0b013e318192e9a4
45. Grant JE, Odlaug BL, Mooney M, O'Brien R, Kim SW. Open-label pilot study of memantine in the treatment of compulsive buying. *Ann Clin Psychiatry* (2012) **24**(2):119–26.
46. Pasquini M, Biondi M. Memantine augmentation for refractory obsessive-compulsive disorder. *Prog Neuropsychopharmacol Biol Psychiatry* (2006) **30**(6):1173–5. doi:10.1016/j.pnpbp.2006.04.013
47. Feusner JD, Kerwin L, Saxena S, Bystritsky A. Differential efficacy of memantine for obsessive-compulsive disorder vs. generalized anxiety disorder: an open-label trial. *Psychopharmacol Bull* (2009) **42**(1):81–93.
48. Grant JE, Chamberlain SR, Odlaug BL, Potenza MN, Kim SW. Memantine shows promise in reducing gambling severity and cognitive inflexibility in pathological gambling: a pilot study. *Psychopharmacology (Berl)* (2010) **212**(4):603–12. doi:10.1007/s00213-010-1994-5
49. Stewart SE, Jenike EA, Hezel DM, Stack DE, Dodman NH, Shuster L, et al. A single-blinded case-control study of memantine in severe obsessive-compulsive disorder. *J Clin Psychopharmacol* (2010) **30**(1):34–9. doi:10.1097/JCP.0b013e3181c856de
50. Ghaleiha A, Entezari N, Modabbernia A, Najand B, Askari N, Tabrizi M, et al. Memantine add-on in moderate to severe obsessive-compulsive disorder: randomized double-blind placebo-controlled study. *J Psychiatr Res* (2013) **47**(2):175–80. doi:10.1016/j.jpsychires.2012.09.015

51. Haghighi M, Jahangard L, Mohammad-Beigi H, Bajoghli H, Hafezian H, Rahimi A, et al. In a double-blind, randomized and placebo-controlled trial, adjuvant memantine improved symptoms in inpatients suffering from refractory obsessive-compulsive disorders (OCD). *Psychopharmacology (Berl)* (2013) **228**(4):633–40. doi:10.1007/s00213-013-3067-z
52. Rosi S, Vazdarjanova A, Ramirez-Amaya V, Worley PF, Barnes CA, Wenk GL. Memantine protects against LPS-induced neuroinflammation, restores behaviorally-induced gene expression and spatial learning in the rat. *Neuroscience* (2006) **142**(4):1303–15. doi:10.1016/j.neuroscience.2006.08.017
53. Howick J, Chalmers I, Glasziou P, Greenhalgh T, Heneghan C, Liberati A, et al. *The Oxford 2011 Levels of Evidence: Oxford Centre for Evidence-Based Medicine.* (2011). Available from: http://www.cebm.net/index.aspx?o=5653
54. Hardan AY, Handen BL. A retrospective open trial of adjunctive donepezil in children and adolescents with autistic disorder. *J Child Adolesc Psychopharmacol* (2002) **12**(3):237–41. doi:10.1089/104454602760386923
55. Doyle RL, Frazier J, Spencer TJ, Geller D, Biederman J, Wilens T. Donepezil in the treatment of ADHD-like symptoms in youths with pervasive developmental disorder: a case series. *J Atten Disord* (2006) **9**(3):543–9. doi:10.1177/1087054705284091
56. Buckley AW, Sassower K, Rodriguez AJ, Jennison K, Wingert K, Buckley J, et al. An open label trial of donepezil for enhancement of rapid eye movement sleep in young children with autism spectrum disorders. *J Child Adolesc Psychopharmacol* (2011) **21**(4):353–7. doi:10.1089/cap.2010.0121
57. Srivastava RK, Agarwal M, Pundhir A. Role of donepezil in autism: its conduciveness in psychopharmacotherapy. *Case Rep Psychiatry* (2011) **2011**:563204. doi:10.1155/2011/563204
58. Hertzman M. Galantamine in the treatment of adult autism: a report of three clinical cases. *Int J Psychiatry Med* (2003) **33**(4):395–8. doi:10.2190/JE5Q-1NFT-FL40-7PMW
59. Chez MG, Buchanan TM, Becker M, Kessler J, Aimonovitch MC, Mrazek SR. Donepezil hydrochloride: a double-blind study in autistic children. *J Pediatr Neurol* (2003) **1**(2):83–8.
60. Handen BL, Johnson CR, McAuliffe-Bellin S, Murray PJ, Hardan AY. Safety and efficacy of donepezil in children and adolescents with autism: neuropsychological measures. *J Child Adolesc Psychopharmacol* (2011) **21**(1):43–50. doi:10.1089/cap.2010.0024
61. Nicolson R, Craven-Thuss B, Smith J. A prospective, open-label trial of galantamine in autistic disorder. *J Child Adolesc Psychopharmacol* (2006) **16**(5):621–9. doi:10.1089/cap.2006.16.621
62. Niederhofer H, Staffen W, Mair A. Galantamine may be effective in treating autistic disorder. *BMJ* (2002) **325**(7377):1422. doi:10.1136/bmj.325.7377.1422/a
63. Chez MG, Aimonovitch M, Buchanan T, Mrazek S, Tremb RJ. Treating autistic spectrum disorders in children: utility of the cholinesterase inhibitor rivastigmine tartrate. *J Child Neurol* (2004) **19**(3):165–9.
64. Niederhofer H. Treating autism pharmacologically: also tacrine might improve symptomatology in some cases. *J Child Neurol* (2007) **22**(8):1054. doi:10.1177/0883073807305857
65. Chez M, Hung PC, Chin K, Memon S, Kirschner S. Memantine experience in children and adolescents with autistic spectrum disorders. *Ann Neurol* (2004) **56**(8 Suppl):109. doi:10.1002/ana.20263
66. Erickson CA, Chambers JE. Memantine for disruptive behavior in autistic disorder. *J Clin Psychiatry* (2006) **67**(6):1000. doi:10.4088/JCP.v67n0619h
67. Chez MG, Burton Q, Dowling T, Chang M, Khanna P, Kramer C. Memantine as adjunctive therapy in children diagnosed with autistic spectrum disorders: an observation of initial clinical response and maintenance tolerability. *J Child Neurol* (2007) **22**(5):574–9. doi:10.1177/0883073807302611
68. Erickson CA, Posey DJ, Stigler KA, Mullett J, Katschke AR, McDougle CJ. A retrospective study of memantine in children and adolescents with pervasive developmental disorders. *Psychopharmacology (Berl)* (2007) **191**(1):141–7. doi:10.1007/s00213-006-0518-9
69. Niederhofer H. Glutamate antagonists seem to be slightly effective in psychopharmacologic treatment of autism. *J Clin Psychopharmacol* (2007) **27**(3):317–8. doi:10.1097/01.jcp.0000270082.30500.69
70. Erickson CA, Mullett JE, McDougle CJ. Open-label memantine in fragile X syndrome. *J Autism Dev Disord* (2009) **39**(12):1629–35. doi:10.1007/s10803-009-0807-3
71. Bernhardt EB, Walsh KH, Posey DJ, McDougle CJ. Memantine for comorbid obsessive-compulsive disorder and Asperger disorder suggests a link in glutamatergic dysregulation. *J Clin Psychopharmacol* (2011) **31**(5):673–5. doi:10.1097/JCP.0b013e31822c92d4
72. Alaghband-Rad J, Nikvarz N, Tehrani-Doost M, Ghaeli P. Memantine-induced speech problems in two patients with autistic disorder. *Daru* (2013) **21**(1):54. doi:10.1186/2008-2231-21-54
73. Ghaleiha A, Asadabadi M, Mohammadi MR, Shahei M, Tabrizi M, Hajiaghaee R, et al. Memantine as adjunctive treatment to risperidone in children with autistic disorder: a randomized, double-blind, placebo-controlled trial. *Int J Neuropsychopharmacol* (2013) **16**(4):783–9. doi:10.1017/S1461145712000880

# 18

# Treatments for biomedical abnormalities associated with autism spectrum disorder

**Richard Eugene Frye[1]* and Daniel A. Rossignol[2]**

[1] Department of Pediatrics, Arkansas Children's Hospital Research Institute, University of Arkansas for Medical Sciences, Little Rock, AR, USA
[2] Rossignol Medical Center, Irvine, CA, USA

**Edited by:**
Roberto Canitano, University Hospital of Siena, Italy

**Reviewed by:**
Andrew Walter Zimmerman, Harvard Medical School, USA
Robert Hendren, University of California San Francisco, USA

***Correspondence:**
Richard Eugene Frye, Arkansas Children's Hospital Research Institute, Slot 512-41B, 13 Children's Way, Little Rock, AR 72202, USA
e-mail: refrye@uams.edu

Recent studies point to the effectiveness of novel treatments that address physiological abnormalities associated with autism spectrum disorder (ASD). This is significant because safe and effective treatments for ASD remain limited. These physiological abnormalities as well as studies addressing treatments of these abnormalities are reviewed in this article. Treatments commonly used to treat mitochondrial disease have been found to improve both core and associated ASD symptoms. Double-blind, placebo-controlled (DBPC) studies have investigated L-carnitine and a multivitamin containing B vitamins, antioxidants, vitamin E, and co-enzyme Q10 while non-blinded studies have investigated ubiquinol. Controlled and uncontrolled studies using folinic acid, a reduced form of folate, have reported marked improvements in core and associated ASD symptoms in some children with ASD and folate related pathway abnormities. Treatments that could address redox metabolism abnormalities include methylcobalamin with and without folinic acid in open-label studies and vitamin C and *N*-acetyl-L-cysteine in DBPC studies. These studies have reported improved core and associated ASD symptoms with these treatments. Lastly, both open-label and DBPC studies have reported improvements in core and associated ASD symptoms with tetrahydrobiopterin. Overall, these treatments were generally well-tolerated without significant adverse effects for most children, although we review the reported adverse effects in detail. This review provides evidence for potentially safe and effective treatments for core and associated symptoms of ASD that target underlying known physiological abnormalities associated with ASD. Further research is needed to define subgroups of children with ASD in which these treatments may be most effective as well as confirm their efficacy in DBPC, large-scale multicenter studies.

**Keywords: autism spectrum disorders, mitochondria, folate receptor alpha, folinic acid, folate metabolism, redox regulation, oxidative stress, tetrahydrobiopterin**

## BACKGROUND

The autism spectrum disorders (ASD) are a group of behaviorally defined neurodevelopmental disorders with lifelong consequences. They are defined by impairments in communication and social interaction along with restrictive and repetitive behaviors (1). The definition of ASD has recently undergone revision. Previously, the Diagnostic Statistical Manual (DSM) Version IV Text Revision divided ASD into several diagnoses including autistic disorder, Asperger syndrome, and pervasive developmental disorder-not otherwise specified. The new revision of the DSM now does not differentiate between these ASD subtypes and considers communication and social impairments together in one symptom class (2). Complicating this change is the fact that over the past several decades, most research has used a framework from the former DSM versions.

Autism spectrum disorder has been recently estimated to affect 1 out of 68 individuals in the United States (3) with four times more males than females being affected (4). Over the past two decades, the prevalence of the ASDs has grown dramatically, although the reasons for this increase are continually debated. Despite decades of research on ASD, identification of the causes of and treatments for ASD remain limited. The standard-of-care treatment for ASD is behavioral therapy that requires full-time engagement of a one-on-one therapist typically requiring many years of treatment, and recent reviews have pointed out that controlled studies on commonly used behavior therapies are generally lacking (5). The only medical treatments approved by the United States of America Food and Drug Administration for ASD are antipsychotic medications. However, these medications only treat a symptom associated with ASD, irritability, but not any core ASD symptom. In children, these medications can be associated with significant adverse effects, including detrimental changes in body weight as well as triglyceride, cholesterol, and blood glucose concentrations within a short time (6) and they also increase the risk of type 2 diabetes (7). In some studies, the percentage of children experiencing these side effects is quite high. For example, one recent study reported that 87% of ASD children had side effects with risperidone, including drowsiness, weight gain, and rhinorrhea (8).

A great majority of ASD research has concentrated on genetic causes of ASD (9) despite the fact that inherited single gene and chromosomal defects are only found in the minority of cases

(10). In fact, several recent studies that have conducted genome wide searches for common genetic defects across large samples of ASD children have only identified rare *de novo* mutations, thereby pointing to acquired mutations and/or mutations secondary to errors in DNA maintenance rather than inherited genetic syndromes (11, 12). As research in the field of ASD continues, it is becoming clear that the etiology of most ASD cases involves complicated interactions between genetic predisposition and environmental exposures or triggers. Indeed, a recent study of dizygotic twins estimated that the environment contributes a greater percentage of the risk of developing autistic disorder as compared to genetic factors (13). Another study of over two million children reported that environmental risk factors accounted for approximately 50% of ASD risk (14). Recent reviews have outlined the many environmental factors that are associated with ASD and have described how polymorphisms in specific genes can combine with the environment to cause neurodevelopmental problems (15).

Recent studies have suggested that ASD is associated with impairments in basic physiological processes such as redox (16) and mitochondrial (9) metabolism as well as abnormalities in regulating essential metabolites such as folate (17), tetrahydrobiopterin (18–20), glutathione (21–23), cholesterol (24), carnitine (25–28), and branch chain amino acids (29). Although many of these studies have based their findings on peripheral markers of abnormal metabolism, many studies have documented some of these same abnormalities in the brain of individuals with ASD, including mitochondrial dysfunction and oxidative stress (30) and one study has demonstrated a link between oxidative stress, inflammation, and mitochondrial dysfunction in the brain of individuals with ASD (23). Interestingly, several of these physiological abnormalities are also observed in genetic syndromes associated with ASD. For example, mitochondrial dysfunction is prevalent in both idiopathic ASD (31) and is associated with Rett syndrome (32–34), PTEN mutations (35), Phelan-McDermid syndrome (36), 15q11-q13 duplication syndrome (37, 38), Angelman syndrome (39), Septo-optic dysplasia (40), and Down syndrome (41, 42).

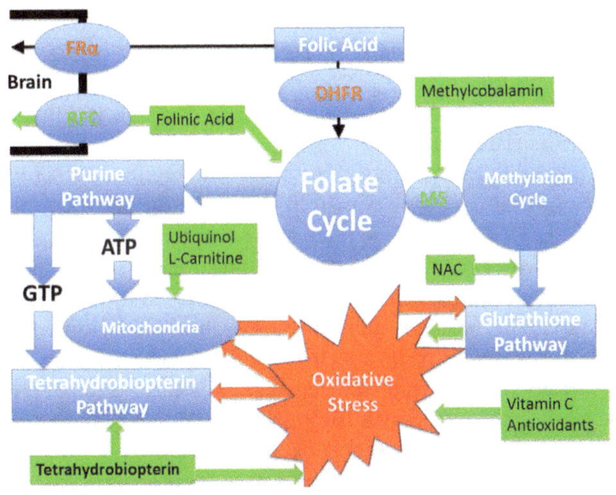


**FIGURE 1 | Pathways affected in autism spectrum disorder that are discussed in this article as well as the treatments discussed with their points of action**. Pathways are outlined in blue while treatments are outlined in green. Oxidative stress is outlined in red and the red arrows demonstrate how it can negatively influence metabolic pathways. Certain pathways such as glutathione and tetrahydrobiopterin pathways have an antioxidant effect and a reciprocal relationship with oxidative stress such that they can improve oxidative stress but at the same time oxidative stress has a direct detrimental effect on them. Mitochondrial dysfunction and oxidative stress have mutually negative effects on each other such that oxidative stress causes mitochondrial dysfunction while mitochondrial dysfunction worsens oxidative stress. Dihydrofolate reductase (DHFR) is colored in red since polymorphisms in this gene, that are commonly seen in individuals with autism, have a detrimental effect on the reduction of folic acid such that the entry of folic acid into the folate cycle is decreased. Folinic acid enters the folate cycle without requiring this enzyme. Similarly the folate receptor alpha can be impaired in individuals with autism by autoantibodies and by mitochondrial dysfunction. In such cases, folinic acid can cross the blood–brain barrier by the reduced folate carrier. Methionine synthase (MS) connects the folate and methylation cycles and requires methylcobalamin as a cofactor.

Identifying the metabolic or physiological abnormalities associated with ASD is important, as treatments for such abnormalities may be possible. Thus, a better understanding of these abnormalities may allow for the development of novel treatments for children with ASD. Below the evidence for metabolic abnormalities related to ASD that may be amenable to treatment are discussed along with the evidence of potential treatments for these disorders. **Figure 1** provides a summary of the pathways and demonstrates which pathways are targeted by the better studied treatments. In addition, a section on the common adverse effects of these treatments follows the discussion of treatments.

## REVIEW OF TREATABLE CONDITIONS AND THEIR POTENTIAL TREATMENTS

### MITOCHONDRIAL DYSFUNCTION

Recent studies suggested that 30–50% of children with ASD possess biomarkers consistent with mitochondrial dysfunction (31, 43) and that the prevalence of abnormal mitochondrial function in immune cells derived from children with ASD is exceedingly high (44, 45). Mitochondrial dysfunction has been demonstrated in the postmortem ASD brain (23, 30, 46–49) and in animal models of ASD (50). Novel types of mitochondrial dysfunction have been described in children with ASD (28, 51, 52) and in cell lines derived from children with ASD (53, 54). Several studies suggest that children with ASD and mitochondrial dysfunction have more severe behavioral and cognitive disabilities compared with children who have ASD but without mitochondrial dysfunction (55–57). Interestingly, a recent review of all of the known published cases of mitochondrial disease and ASD demonstrated that only about 25% had a known genetic mutation that could account for their mitochondrial disease (31).

Treatments that are typically used for patients with mitochondrial disease have been shown to improve functioning in some children with ASD (31). Several studies, including two double-blind, placebo-controlled (DBPC) studies (58, 59) and case reports (25, 37, 60–63) have reported improvements in core and associated ASD behaviors with L-carnitine treatment. Two DBPC studies using a multivitamin containing B vitamins, antioxidants, vitamin E, and co-enzyme Q10 reported various improvements in ASD symptoms compared to placebo (64, 65). Several other antioxidants (66), including vitamin C (67), methylcobalamin (68–70), *N*-acetyl-L-cysteine (71–73), ubiquinol (74), and carnosine (75), have also reported to demonstrate significant improvements in ASD behaviors and may function to improve mitochondrial function.

Thus, many treatments that are believed to improve mitochondrial function have been shown to be helpful for some children with ASD. However, none of these studies have specifically selected children with mitochondrial dysfunction or disease to study, so it is difficult to know if individuals with ASD and mitochondrial dysfunction would benefit the most from these treatments or whether these treatments are effective for a wider group of children with ASD. One study did demonstrate that the multivitamin used for treatment resulted in improvements in biomarkers of energy metabolism (as well as oxidative stress) suggesting that the effect of the multivitamin may have been at least partially related to improvements in mitochondrial function (65). Clearly, this is a fertile area for research but there remain several complications that could impede moving forward in a systematic way. For example, given the inconsistency in the prevalence estimates of mitochondrial disease and dysfunction across studies (ranging from about 5–80%), the notion that mitochondrial abnormalities are even associated with ASD is somewhat controversial. This may be, in part, due to the unclear distinction between mitochondrial disease and dysfunction. However, even the lower bound of the prevalence estimate of 5% is significant, as mitochondrial disease is only believed to affect <0.1% of individuals in the general population and given the current high prevalence of ASD, a disorder that affects even 5% of individuals with ASD would add up to millions of individuals who have the potential to have a treatable metabolic abnormality. Other complicating factors include the fact that there are many treatments for mitochondrial disease and these treatments have not been well-studied (76). Hopefully, the increased interest in treatments for mitochondrial disease will help improve our knowledge of how to best treat mitochondrial disease so that such information can be applied to children who have mitochondrial disease and dysfunction with ASD. Other recent approaches include the *in vitro* assessment of compounds that may improve mitochondrial function in individuals with ASD (53).

## FOLATE METABOLISM

Several lines of evidence point to abnormalities in folate metabolism in ASD. Several genetic polymorphisms in key enzymes in the folate pathway have been associated with ASD. These abnormalities can cause decreased production of 5-methyltetrahydrofolate, impair the production of folate cycle metabolites and decrease folate transport across the blood–brain barrier and into neurons. Indeed, genetic polymorphisms in methylenetetrahydrofolate reductase (22, 77–85), dihydrofolate reductase (86) and the reduced folate carrier (22) have been associated with ASD.

Perhaps the most significant abnormalities in folate metabolism associated with ASD are autoantibodies to the folate receptor alpha (FRα). Folate is transported across the blood–brain barrier by an energy-dependent receptor-mediated system that utilizes the FRα (87). Autoantibodies can bind to the FRα and greatly impair its function. These autoantibodies have been linked to cerebral folate deficiency (CFD). Many cases of CFD carry a diagnosis of ASD (88–94) and other individuals with CFD are diagnosed with Rett syndrome, a disorder closely related to ASD within the pervasive developmental disorder spectrum (95–97). Given that the FRα folate transport system is energy-dependent and consumes ATP, it is not surprising that a wide variety of mitochondrial diseases (91, 94, 97–102) and novel forms of mitochondrial dysfunction related to ASD (52) have been associated with CFD. Recently, Frye et al. (17) reported that 60% and 44% of 93 children with ASD were positive for the blocking and binding FRα autoantibody, respectively. This high rate of FRα autoantibody positivity was confirmed by Ramaekers et al. (103) who compared 75 ASD children to 30 non-autistic controls with developmental delay. The blocking FRα autoantibody was positive in 47% of children with ASD but in only 3% of the control children.

Many children with ASD and CFD have marked improvements in clinical status when treated with folinic acid – a reduced form of folate that can cross the blood–brain barrier using the reduced folate carrier rather than the FRα transport system. Several case reports (89) and case series (90, 91) have described neurological, behavioral, and cognitive improvements in children with documented CFD and ASD. One case series of five children with CFD and low-functioning autism with neurological deficits found complete recovery from ASD symptoms with the use of folinic acid in one child and substantial improvements in communication in two other children (90). In another study of 23 children with low-functioning regressive ASD and CFD, 2 younger children demonstrated full recovery from ASD and neurological symptoms, 3 older children demonstrated improvements in neurological deficits but not in ASD symptoms, and the remainder demonstrated improvements in neurological symptoms and partial improvements in some ASD symptoms with folinic acid; the most prominent improvement was in communication (91). Recently, in a controlled open-label study, Frye et al. (17) demonstrated that ASD children who were positive for at least one of the FRα autoantibodies experienced significant improvements in verbal communication, receptive and expressive language, attention, and stereotypical behavior with high-dose (2 mg/kg/day in two divided doses; maximum 50 mg/day) folinic acid treatment with very few adverse effects reported.

Thus, there are several lines of converging evidence suggesting that abnormalities in folate metabolism are associated with ASD. Evidence for treatment of these disorders is somewhat limited but it is growing. For example, treatment studies have mostly concentrated on the subset of children with ASD who also possess the FRα autoantibodies. These studies have only examined one form of reduced folate, folinic acid, and have only examined treatment response in limited studies. Thus, large DBPC studies would be very helpful for documenting efficacy of this potentially safe and effective treatment. In addition, the role of other abnormalities in the folate pathway beside FRα autoantibodies, such as genetic polymorphisms, in treatment response needs to be investigated. It might also be important to investigate the role of treatment with other forms of folate besides folinic acid, but it might also be wise to concentrate research on one particular form of folate for the time being so as to optimize the generalizability of research studies in order to have a more solid understanding of the role of folate metabolism in ASD. Given the ubiquitous role of folate in many metabolic pathways and the fact that it has a role in preventing ASD during the preconception and prenatal periods (104), this line of research has significant potential for being a novel treatment for many children with ASD.

### REDOX METABOLISM

Several lines of evidence support the notion that some children with ASD have abnormal redox metabolism. Two case-control studies have reported that redox metabolism in children with ASD is abnormal compared to unaffected control children (22, 105). This includes a significant decrease in reduced glutathione (GSH), the major intracellular antioxidant, and mechanism for detoxification, as well as a significant increase in the oxidized disulfide form of glutathione (GSSG). The notion that abnormal glutathione metabolism could lead to oxidative damage is consistent with studies which demonstrate oxidative damage to proteins and DNA in peripheral blood mononuclear cells and postmortem brain from ASD individuals (23, 30, 106), particularly in cortical regions associated with speech, emotion, and social behavior (30, 107).

Treatments for oxidative stress have been shown to be of benefit for children with ASD. In children with ASD, studies have demonstrated that glutathione metabolism can be improved with subcutaneously injected methylcobalamin and oral folinic acid (69, 105), a vitamin and mineral supplement that includes antioxidants, co-enzyme Q10, and B vitamins (65) and tetrahydrobiopterin (20). Interestingly, recent DBPC studies have demonstrated that *N*-acetyl-L-cysteine, a supplement that provides a precursor to glutathione, was effective in improving symptoms and behaviors associated with ASD (72, 73). However, glutathione was not measured in these two studies.

Small (64, 67), medium (72, 73), and large (108) sized DPBC trials and small and medium-sized open-label clinical trials (68, 70) demonstrate that novel treatments for children with ASD, which can address oxidative stress are associated with improvements in core ASD symptoms (68, 70, 72), sleep and gastrointestinal symptoms (64), hyperactivity, tantruming, and parental impression of general functioning (108), sensory-motor symptoms (67), and irritability (72, 73). These novel treatments include *N*-acetyl-L-cysteine (72, 73), methylcobalamin with (69, 70) and without (68) oral folinic acid, vitamin C (67), and a vitamin and mineral supplement that includes antioxidants, co-enzyme Q10, and B vitamins (64, 65).

Several other treatments that have antioxidant properties (66), including carnosine (75), have also been reported to significantly improve ASD behaviors, suggesting that treatment of oxidative stress could be beneficial for children with ASD. Many antioxidants can also help improve mitochondrial function (31), suggesting that clinical improvements with antioxidants may occur through a reduction of oxidative stress and/or an improvement in mitochondrial function.

These studies suggest that treatments that address oxidative stress may improve core and associated symptoms of ASD. Furthermore, these treatments are generally regarded as safe with a low prevalence of adverse effects. Unfortunately many studies that have looked at antioxidants and treatments that potentially support the redox pathway did not use biomarkers to measure redox metabolism status in the participants or the effect of treatment on redox pathways. Including biomarkers in future studies could provide important information regarding which patients may respond to treatments that address redox metabolism and can help identify the most effective treatments. Since there are many treatments used to address oxidative stress and redox metabolism abnormalities in clinical practice and in research studies, the most effective treatments need to be carefully studied in DBPC studies to document their efficacy and effectiveness. Overall, the treatments discussed above have shown some promising results and deserve further study.

### TETRAHYDROBIOPTERIN METABOLISM

Tetrahydrobiopterin ($BH_4$) is a naturally occurring molecule that is an essential cofactor for several critical metabolic pathways, including those responsible for the production of monoamine neurotransmitters, the breakdown of phenylalanine, and the production of nitric oxide (19). $BH_4$ is readily oxidized by reactive species, leading it to be destroyed in the disorders where oxidative stress is prominent such as ASD (18). Abnormalities in several $BH_4$ related metabolic pathways or in the products of these pathways have been noted in some individuals with ASD, and the cerebrospinal fluid concentration of $BH_4$ has been reported to be depressed in some individuals with ASD (19). Clinical trials conducted over the past 25 years have reported encouraging results using sapropterin, a synthetic form of $BH_4$, to treat children with ASD (19). Three controlled (109–111) and several open-label trials have documented improvements in communication, cognitive ability, adaptability, social abilities, and verbal expression with sapropterin treatment in ASD, especially in children younger than 5 years of age and in those who are relatively higher functioning at the beginning of the trial (19).

Frye has shown that the ratio of serum citrulline-to-methionine is related to the $BH_4$ concentration in the cerebrospinal fluid, suggesting that abnormalities in both oxidative stress and nitric oxide metabolism may be related to central $BH_4$ deficiency (18). More recently, Frye et al. demonstrated, in an open-label study, that sapropterin treatment improves redox metabolism and fundamentally alters $BH_4$ metabolism in children with ASD. Interestingly, serum biomarkers of nitric oxide metabolism were found to predict response to sapropterin treatment in children with ASD (20), thereby suggesting that the therapeutic effect of $BH_4$ supplementation may be specific to its effect on nitric oxide metabolism.

The potential positive effects on nitric oxide metabolism by $BH_4$ supplementation could be significant for several reasons. The literature supports an association between ASD and abnormalities in nitric oxide metabolism. Indeed studies have documented alterations in nitric oxide synthase genes in children with ASD (112, 113). In the context of low $BH_4$ concentrations, nitric oxide synthase produces peroxynitrite, an unstable reactive nitrogen species that can result in oxidative cellular damage. Indeed, nitrotyrosine, a biomarker of reactive nitrogen species, has been shown to be increased in multiple tissues in children with ASD, including the brain (22, 23, 107, 114, 115). Thus, $BH_4$ supplementation could help stabilize nitric oxide synthase as well as act as an antioxidant and improve monoamine neurotransmitter production. Further

DBPC studies using biomarkers of metabolic pathways related to $BH_4$ metabolism will be needed to determine which children with ASD will most benefit from formulations of $BH_4$ supplementation like sapropterin.

## POTENTIAL ADVERSE EFFECTS

Although many of the treatments discussed within this manuscript are considered safe and are generally well-tolerated, it is important to understand that these treatments are not without potential adverse effects. In general, these treatments are without serious adverse effects but some children may not tolerate all treatments well. Systematic and controlled studies are best at providing data on adverse effects, so the true adverse effects of the supplements discussed will only be based on the limited treatments that have been studied in such a fashion. It is also important to understand that because of the complicated nature of the effects of these treatments, they should only be used under the care of a medical professional with appropriate expertise and experience.

Controlled studies for treatments that address mitochondrial disorders include L-carnitine and a multivitamin with various mitochondrial supplements. In one small DBPC study, there were no significant adverse events reported in the 16 children treated with L-carnitine (59) while a second small DBPC trial reported no differences between the adverse effects reported by the treatment and placebo groups; notably, more patients in the placebo group withdrew from the study because of adverse effects (58). Thus, there is no data to suggest that L-carnitine has any significant adverse effects. In the large DBPC multivitamin study, about equal numbers of children in the treatment and placebo groups withdrew from the study because of behavior or gastrointestinal issues (65). In another small DBPC study, the investigators noted that two children began to have nausea and emesis when they started receiving the treatment at nighttime on an empty stomach (64). This adverse effect resolved when the timing of the treatment was adjusted. Thus, with proper dosing of this multivitamin, it appears rather safe and well-tolerated.

Controlled studies for folate pathway abnormalities only include folinic acid. In a medium-sized, open-label controlled study, 44 children with ASD and the FRα autoantibody were treated with high-dose folinic acid (2 mg/kg/day in two divided doses; maximum 50 mg/day) and four children discontinued the treatment because of an adverse effect (17). Of the four children who discontinued the treatment, three children, all being concurrently treated with risperidone, demonstrated increased irritability soon after starting the high-dose folinic acid while the other child experienced increased insomnia and gastroesophageal reflux after 6 weeks of treatment. Since there was no placebo in this study, the significance of these adverse effects is difficult to determine. For example, it is not clear whether this was related to concurrent risperidone treatment or was related to a baseline high irritability resulting in the needed for risperidone. All other participants completed the trial without significant adverse effects. Due to the timing of the adverse events in the children on risperidone in this trial, to be safe, the authors suggested caution when using folinic acid in children already on antipsychotic medications.

Clinical studies for treatments that could address redox metabolism include *N*-acetyl-L-cysteine, methylcobalamin, methylcobalamin combined with oral folinic acid and a multivitamin (as previous mentioned). One small open-label study that provided 25–30 μg/kg/day (1500 μg/day maximum) of methylcobalamin to 13 patients found no adverse effects (68) while a medium-sized, open-label trial that provided 75 μg/kg subcutaneously injected methylcobalamin given every 3 days along with twice daily oral low-dose (800 μg/day) folinic acid to 44 children noted some mild adverse effects (69, 70). Four children discontinued the treatment, two because their parents were uncomfortable given injections and two because of hyperactivity and reduced sleep. The most common adverse effect in the participants that remained in the study was hyperactivity, which resolved with a decrease in the folinic acid to 400 μg/day. Lastly, two medium sized, DBPC studies examined *N*-acetyl-L-cysteine, one as a primary treatment and another as an add-on to risperidone. The trial that used *N*-acetyl-L-cysteine as a primary treatment noted no significant differences in adverse events between the treatment and placebo groups, although both groups demonstrated a high rate of gastrointestinal symptoms and one participant in the active treatment phase required termination due to increased agitation (72). In the add-on study, one patient in the active treatment group withdrew due to severe sedation (73). In this latter study, adverse effects were not compared statistically between groups, but most adverse effects were mild and had a low prevalence. Such adverse effects included constipation, increased appetite, fatigue, nervousness, and daytime drowsiness. Lastly, a small DPBC study using vitamin C did not report any adverse effects from the treatment (67). Thus, there are several relatively safe and well-tolerated treatments for addressing abnormal redox metabolism, but there does appear to be a low rate of adverse effects, reinforcing the notion that a medical professional should guide treatment.

Three DBPC studies, one small (110), one medium (111), and one medium-to-large (109) sized, were conducted using sapropterin as a treatment for ASD. None of these studies have reported a higher prevalence of adverse effects in the treatment group as compared to the placebo group and none of these studies attributed any dropouts to the treatment. Thus, sapropterin appears to be a well-tolerated treatment.

## DISCUSSION

One advantage of the treatments outlined above is that the physiological mechanisms that they address are known and biomarkers are available to identify children who may respond to these treatments. Preliminary studies suggest that there are a substantial number of ASD children with these metabolic abnormalities. For example, mitochondrial abnormalities may be seen in 5–80% of children with ASD (31, 43–45, 53, 54) and FRα autoantibodies may be found in 47% (103) to 75% (17) of children with ASD. Clearly, further studies will be required to clarify the percentage of these subgroups.

Further large-scale, multicenter DBPC clinical trials are needed for these promising treatments in order to document the efficacy and define the subgroups that best respond to these treatments. As more treatable disorders are documented and as data accumulates to demonstrate the efficacy of treatments for these disorders, clinical algorithms to approach the work-up for a child with ASD need to be developed by a consensus of experts. Indeed, developing guidelines will be the next step for applying many of these scientific findings. Clearly many children with ASD may be able to benefit from such treatments, which are focused on improving dysfunctional physiology. Given the fact that no approved medical treatment exists which addresses the underlying pathophysiology or core symptoms of ASD, these treatments could make a substantial difference in the lives of children with ASD and their families. With the high prevalence of ASD, treatments that successfully treat even only a fraction of children affected with ASD would translate into substantial benefits for millions of individuals with ASD and their families. In summary, it appears that many of these treatments may provide benefit for a substantial proportion of children with ASD.

## REFERENCES


1. American Psychiatric Association. *Diagnostic and Statistical Manual of Mental Disorders*. Washington, DC: American Psychiatric Association (1994).
2. Volkmar FR, McPartland JC. From Kanner to DSM-5: autism as an evolving diagnostic concept. *Annu Rev Clin Psychol* (2013) **10**:193–212. doi:10.1146/annurev-clinpsy-032813-153710
3. Developmental Disabilities Monitoring Network Surveillance 2010 Year Principal Investigators; Centers for Disease Control and Prevention. Prevalence of autism spectrum disorder among children aged 8 years – autism and developmental disabilities monitoring network, 11 sites, United States, 2010. *MMWR Surveill Summ* (2014) **63**:1–21.
4. Autism and Developmental Disabilities Monitoring Network Surveillance Year 2002 Principal Investigators; Centers for Disease Control and Prevention. Prevalence of autism spectrum disorders – autism and developmental disabilities monitoring network, 14 sites, United States, 2002. *MMWR Surveill Summ* (2007) **56**:12–28.
5. Reichow B, Barton EE, Boyd BA, Hume K. Early intensive behavioral intervention (EIBI) for young children with autism spectrum disorders (ASD). *Cochrane Database Syst Rev* (2012) **10**:CD009260. doi:10.1002/14651858.CD009260.pub2
6. Correll CU, Manu P, Olshanskiy V, Napolitano B, Kane JM, Malhotra AK. Cardiometabolic risk of second-generation antipsychotic medications during first-time use in children and adolescents. *JAMA* (2009) **302**:1765–73. doi:10.1001/jama.2009.1549
7. Bobo WV, Cooper WO, Stein CM, Olfson M, Graham D, Daugherty J, et al. Antipsychotics and the risk of type 2 diabetes mellitus in children and youth. *JAMA Psychiatry* (2013) **70**:1067–75. doi:10.1001/jamapsychiatry.2013.2053
8. Boon-Yasidhi V, Jearnarongrit P, Tulayapichitchock P, Tarugsa J. Adverse effects of risperidone in children with autism spectrum disorders in a naturalistic clinical setting at Siriraj Hospital, Thailand. *Psychiatry J* (2014) **2014**:136158. doi:10.1155/2014/136158
9. Rossignol DA, Frye RE. A review of research trends in physiological abnormalities in autism spectrum disorders: immune dysregulation, inflammation, oxidative stress, mitochondrial dysfunction and environmental toxicant exposures. *Mol Psychiatry* (2012) **17**:389–401. doi:10.1038/mp.2011.165
10. Schaefer GB, Mendelsohn NJ. Genetics evaluation for the etiologic diagnosis of autism spectrum disorders. *Genet Med* (2008) **10**:4–12. doi:10.1097/GIM.0b013e31815efdd7
11. Neale BM, Kou Y, Liu L, Ma'ayan A, Samocha KE, Sabo A, et al. Patterns and rates of exonic de novo mutations in autism spectrum disorders. *Nature* (2012) **485**:242–5. doi:10.1038/nature11011
12. Sanders SJ, Murtha MT, Gupta AR, Murdoch JD, Raubeson MJ, Willsey AJ, et al. De novo mutations revealed by whole-exome sequencing are strongly associated with autism. *Nature* (2012) **485**:237–41. doi:10.1038/nature10945
13. Hallmayer J, Cleveland S, Torres A, Phillips J, Cohen B, Torigoe T, et al. Genetic heritability and shared environmental factors among twin pairs with autism. *Arch Gen Psychiatry* (2011) **68**:1095–102. doi:10.1001/archgenpsychiatry.2011.76
14. Sandin S, Lichtenstein P, Kuja-Halkola R, Larsson H, Hultman CM, Reichenberg A. The familial risk of autism. *JAMA* (2014) **311**:1770–7. doi:10.1001/jama.2014.4144
15. Rossignol DA, Genuis SJ, Frye RE. Environmental toxicants and autism spectrum disorders: a systematic review. *Transl Psychiatry* (2014) **4**:e360. doi:10.1038/tp.2014.4
16. Frye RE, James SJ. Metabolic pathology of autism in relation to redox metabolism. *Biomark Med* (2014) **8**:321–30. doi:10.2217/bmm.13.158
17. Frye RE, Sequeira JM, Quadros EV, James SJ, Rossignol DA. Cerebral folate receptor autoantibodies in autism spectrum disorder. *Mol Psychiatry* (2013) **18**:369–81. doi:10.1038/mp.2011.175
18. Frye RE. Central tetrahydrobiopterin concentration in neurodevelopmental disorders. *Front Neurosci* (2010) **4**:52. doi:10.3389/fnins.2010.00052
19. Frye RE, Huffman LC, Elliott GR. Tetrahydrobiopterin as a novel therapeutic intervention for autism. *Neurotherapeutics* (2010) **7**:241–9. doi:10.1016/j.nurt.2010.05.004
20. Frye RE, Delatorre R, Taylor HB, Slattery J, Melnyk S, Chowdhury N, et al. Metabolic effects of sapropterin treatment in autism spectrum disorder: a preliminary study. *Transl Psychiatry* (2013) **3**:e237. doi:10.1038/tp.2013.14
21. Evangeliou A, Vlachonikolis I, Mihailidou H, Spilioti M, Skarpalezou A, Makaronas N, et al. Application of a ketogenic diet in children with autistic behavior: pilot study. *J Child Neurol* (2003) **18**:113–8. doi:10.1177/08830738030180020501
22. James SJ, Melnyk S, Jernigan S, Cleves MA, Halsted CH, Wong DH, et al. Metabolic endophenotype and related genotypes are associated with oxidative stress in children with autism. *Am J Med Genet B Neuropsychiatr Genet* (2006) **141B**:947–56. doi:10.1002/ajmg.b.30366
23. Rose S, Melnyk S, Pavliv O, Bai S, Nick TG, Frye RE, et al. Evidence of oxidative damage and inflammation associated with low glutathione redox status in the autism brain. *Transl Psychiatry* (2012) **2**:e134. doi:10.1038/tp.2012.61
24. Tierney E, Bukelis I, Thompson RE, Ahmed K, Aneja A, Kratz L, et al. Abnormalities of cholesterol metabolism in autism spectrum disorders. *Am J Med Genet B Neuropsychiatr Genet* (2006) **141B**:666–8. doi:10.1002/ajmg.b.30368
25. Gargus JJ, Lerner MA. Familial autism with primary carnitine deficiency, sudden death, hypotonia and hypochromic anemia. *Am J Human Gen* (1997) **61**:A98.
26. Filipek PA, Juranek J, Nguyen MT, Cummings C, Gargus JJ. Relative carnitine deficiency in autism. *J Autism Dev Disord* (2004) **34**:615–23. doi:10.1007/s10803-004-5283-1
27. Celestino-Soper PB, Violante S, Crawford EL, Luo R, Lionel AC, Delaby E, et al. A common X-linked inborn error of carnitine biosynthesis may be a risk factor for nondysmorphic autism. *Proc Natl Acad Sci U S A* (2012) **109**:7974–81. doi:10.1073/pnas.1120210109
28. Frye RE, Melnyk S, Macfabe DF. Unique acyl-carnitine profiles are potential biomarkers for acquired mitochondrial disease in autism spectrum disorder. *Transl Psychiatry* (2013) **3**:e220. doi:10.1038/tp.2012.143
29. Novarino G, El-Fishawy P, Kayserili H, Meguid NA, Scott EM, Schroth J, et al. Mutations in BCKD-kinase lead to a potentially treatable form of autism with epilepsy. *Science* (2012) **338**:394–7. doi:10.1126/science.1224631
30. Rossignol DA, Frye RE. Evidence linking oxidative stress, mitochondrial dysfunction, and inflammation in the brain of individuals with autism. *Front Physiol* (2014) **5**:150. doi:10.3389/fphys.2014.00150
31. Rossignol DA, Frye RE. Mitochondrial dysfunction in autism spectrum disorders: a systematic review and meta-analysis. *Mol Psychiatry* (2012) **17**:290–314. doi:10.1038/mp.2010.136
32. Condie J, Goldstein J, Wainwright MS. Acquired microcephaly, regression of milestones, mitochondrial dysfunction, and episodic rigidity in a 46,XY male with a de novo MECP2 gene mutation. *J Child Neurol* (2010) **25**:633–6. doi:10.1177/0883073809342004
33. Gibson JH, Slobedman B, Kaipananickal H, Williamson SL, Minchenko D, El-Osta A, et al. Downstream targets of methyl CpG binding protein 2 and their abnormal expression in the frontal cortex of the human Rett syndrome brain. *BMC Neurosci* (2010) **11**:53. doi:10.1186/1471-2202-11-53
34. Grosser E, Hirt U, Janc OA, Menzfeld C, Fischer M, Kempkes B, et al. Oxidative burden and mitochondrial dysfunction in a mouse model of Rett syndrome. *Neurobiol Dis* (2012) **48**:102–14. doi:10.1016/j.nbd.2012.06.007
35. Napoli E, Ross-Inta C, Wong S, Hung C, Fujisawa Y, Sakaguchi D, et al. Mitochondrial dysfunction in Pten haplo-insufficient mice with social deficits and repetitive behavior: interplay between Pten and p53. *PLoS One* (2012) **7**:e42504. doi:10.1371/journal.pone.0042504
36. Frye RE. Mitochondrial disease in 22q13 duplication syndrome. *J Child Neurol* (2012) **27**:942–9. doi:10.1177/0883073811429858

37. Filipek PA, Juranek J, Smith M, Mays LZ, Ramos ER, Bocian M, et al. Mitochondrial dysfunction in autistic patients with 15q inverted duplication. *Ann Neurol* (2003) **53**:801–4. doi:10.1002/ana.10596
38. Frye RE. 15q11.2-13 Duplication, mitochondrial dysfunction, and developmental disorders. *J Child Neurol* (2009) **24**:1316–20. doi:10.1177/0883073809333531
39. Su H, Fan W, Coskun PE, Vesa J, Gold JA, Jiang YH, et al. Mitochondrial dysfunction in CA1 hippocampal neurons of the UBE3A deficient mouse model for Angelman syndrome. *Neurosci Lett* (2011) **487**:129–33. doi:10.1016/j.neulet.2009.06.079
40. Schuelke M, Krude H, Finckh B, Mayatepek E, Janssen A, Schmelz M, et al. Septo-optic dysplasia associated with a new mitochondrial cytochrome b mutation. *Ann Neurol* (2002) **51**:388–92. doi:10.1002/ana.10151
41. Pallardo FV, Lloret A, Lebel M, D'Ischia M, Cogger VC, Le Couteur DG, et al. Mitochondrial dysfunction in some oxidative stress-related genetic diseases: ataxia-Telangiectasia, Down syndrome, Fanconi anaemia and Werner syndrome. *Biogerontology* (2010) **11**:401–19. doi:10.1007/s10522-010-9269-4
42. Pagano G, Castello G. Oxidative stress and mitochondrial dysfunction in Down syndrome. *Adv Exp Med Biol* (2012) **724**:291–9. doi:10.1007/978-1-4614-0653-2_22
43. Frye RE. Biomarker of abnormal energy metabolism in children with autism spectrum disorder. *N A J Med Sci* (2012) **5**:141–7.
44. Giulivi C, Zhang YF, Omanska-Klusek A, Ross-Inta C, Wong S, Hertz-Picciotto I, et al. Mitochondrial dysfunction in autism. *JAMA* (2010) **304**:2389–96. doi:10.1001/jama.2010.1706
45. Napoli E, Wong S, Hertz-Picciotto I, Giulivi C. Deficits in bioenergetics and impaired immune response in granulocytes from children with autism. *Pediatrics* (2014) **133**:e1405–10. doi:10.1542/peds.2013-1545
46. Chauhan A, Gu F, Essa MM, Wegiel J, Kaur K, Brown WT, et al. Brain region-specific deficit in mitochondrial electron transport chain complexes in children with autism. *J Neurochem* (2011) **117**:209–20. doi:10.1111/j.1471-4159.2011.07189.x
47. Anitha A, Nakamura K, Thanseem I, Yamada K, Iwayama Y, Toyota T, et al. Brain region-specific altered expression and association of mitochondria-related genes in autism. *Mol Autism* (2012) **3**:12. doi:10.1186/2040-2392-3-12
48. Anitha A, Nakamura K, Thanseem I, Matsuzaki H, Miyachi T, Tsujii M, et al. Downregulation of the expression of mitochondrial electron transport complex genes in autism brains. *Brain Pathol* (2013) **23**:294–302. doi:10.1111/bpa.12002
49. Tang G, Gutierrez Rios P, Kuo SH, Akman HO, Rosoklija G, Tanji K, et al. Mitochondrial abnormalities in temporal lobe of autistic brain. *Neurobiol Dis* (2013) **54**:349–61. doi:10.1016/j.nbd.2013.01.006
50. Kriaucionis S, Paterson A, Curtis J, Guy J, Macleod N, Bird A. Gene expression analysis exposes mitochondrial abnormalities in a mouse model of Rett syndrome. *Mol Cell Biol* (2006) **26**:5033–42. doi:10.1128/MCB.01665-05
51. Graf WD, Marin-Garcia J, Gao HG, Pizzo S, Naviaux RK, Markusic D, et al. Autism associated with the mitochondrial DNA G8363A transfer RNA(Lys) mutation. *J Child Neurol* (2000) **15**:357–61. doi:10.1177/088307380001500601
52. Frye RE, Naviaux RK. Autistic disorder with complex IV overactivity: a new mitochondrial syndrome. *J Pediatr Neurol* (2011) **9**:427–34. doi:10.3233/JPN-2001-0507
53. Rose S, Frye RE, Slattery J, Wynne R, Tippett M, Melnyk S, et al. Oxidative stress induces mitochondrial dysfunction in a subset of autistic lymphoblastoid cell lines. *Transl Psychiatry* (2014) **4**:e377. doi:10.1038/tp.2014.15
54. Rose S, Frye RE, Slattery J, Wynne R, Tippett M, Pavliv O, et al. Oxidative stress induces mitochondrial dysfunction in a subset of autism lymphoblastoid cell lines in a well-matched case control cohort. *PLoS One* (2014) **9**:e85436. doi:10.1371/journal.pone.0085436
55. Minshew NJ, Goldstein G, Dombrowski SM, Panchalingam K, Pettegrew JW. A preliminary 31P MRS study of autism: evidence for under synthesis and increased degradation of brain membranes. *Biol Psychiatry* (1993) **33**:762–73. doi:10.1016/0006-3223(93)90017-8
56. Mostafa GA, El-Gamal HA, El-Wakkad ASE, El-Shorbagy OE, Hamza MM. Polyunsaturated fatty acids, carnitine and lactate as biological markers of brain energy in autistic children. *Int J Child Neuropsychiatry* (2005) **2**:179–88.
57. Frye RE, Delatorre R, Taylor H, Slattery J, Melnyk S, Chowdhury N, et al. Redox metabolism abnormalities in autistic children associated with mitochondrial disease. *Transl Psychiatry* (2013) **3**:e273. doi:10.1038/tp.2013.51
58. Geier DA, Kern JK, Davis G, King PG, Adams JB, Young JL, et al. A prospective double-blind, randomized clinical trial of levocarnitine to treat autism spectrum disorders. *Med Sci Monit* (2011) **17**:I15–23. doi:10.12659/MSM.881792
59. Fahmy SF, El-Hamamsy MH, Zaki OK, Badary OA. L-carnitine supplementation improves the behavioral symptoms in autistic children. *Res Autism Spectr Disord* (2013) **7**:159–66. doi:10.1016/j.rasd.2012.07.006
60. Poling JS, Frye RE, Shoffner J, Zimmerman AW. Developmental regression and mitochondrial dysfunction in a child with autism. *J Child Neurol* (2006) **21**:170–2. doi:10.1177/08830738060210021401
61. Gargus JJ, Imtiaz F. Mitochondrial energy-deficient endophenotype in autism. *Am J Biochem Biotech* (2008) **4**:198–207. doi:10.3844/ajbbsp.2008.198.207
62. Pastural E, Ritchie S, Lu Y, Jin W, Kavianpour A, Khine Su-Myat K, et al. Novel plasma phospholipid biomarkers of autism: mitochondrial dysfunction as a putative causative mechanism. *Prostaglandins Leukot Essent Fatty Acids* (2009) **81**:253–64. doi:10.1016/j.plefa.2009.06.003
63. Ezugha H, Goldenthal M, Valencia I, Anderson CE, Legido A, Marks H. 5q14.3 Deletion manifesting as mitochondrial disease and autism: case report. *J Child Neurol* (2010) **25**:1232–5. doi:10.1177/0883073809361165
64. Adams JB, Holloway C. Pilot study of a moderate dose multivitamin/mineral supplement for children with autistic spectrum disorder. *J Altern Complement Med* (2004) **10**:1033–9. doi:10.1089/acm.2004.10.1033
65. Adams JB, Audhya T, McDonough-Means S, Rubin RA, Quig D, Geis E, et al. Effect of a vitamin/mineral supplement on children and adults with autism. *BMC Pediatr* (2011) **11**:111. doi:10.1186/1471-2431-11-111
66. Rossignol DA. Novel and emerging treatments for autism spectrum disorders: a systematic review. *Ann Clin Psychiatry* (2009) **21**:213–36.
67. Dolske MC, Spollen J, McKay S, Lancashire E, Tolbert L. A preliminary trial of ascorbic acid as supplemental therapy for autism. *Prog Neuropsychopharmacol Biol Psychiatry* (1993) **17**:765–74. doi:10.1016/0278-5846(93)90058-Z
68. Nakano K, Noda N, Tachikawa E, Urano MAN, Takazawa M, Nakayama T, et al. A preliminary study of methylcobalamin therapy in autism. *J Tokyo Womens Med Univ* (2005) **75**:64–9. doi:10.1016/j.chc.2013.03.002
69. James SJ, Melnyk S, Fuchs G, Reid T, Jernigan S, Pavliv O, et al. Efficacy of methylcobalamin and folinic acid treatment on glutathione redox status in children with autism. *Am J Clin Nutr* (2009) **89**:425–30. doi:10.3945/ajcn.2008.26615
70. Frye RE, Melnyk S, Fuchs G, Reid T, Jernigan S, Pavliv O, et al. Effectiveness of methylcobalamin and folinic acid treatment on adaptive behavior in children with autistic disorder is related to glutathione redox status. *Autism Res Treat* (2013) **2013**:609705. doi:10.1155/2013/609705
71. Ghanizadeh A, Derakhshan N. N-acetylcysteine for treatment of autism, a case report. *J Res Med Sci* (2012) **17**:985–7.
72. Hardan AY, Fung LK, Libove RA, Obukhanych TV, Nair S, Herzenberg LA, et al. A randomized controlled pilot trial of oral N-acetylcysteine in children with autism. *Biol Psychiatry* (2012) **71**:956–61. doi:10.1016/j.biopsych.2012.01.014
73. Ghanizadeh A, Moghimi-Sarani E. A randomized double blind placebo controlled clinical trial of N-acetylcysteine added to risperidone for treating autistic disorders. *BMC Psychiatry* (2013) **13**:196. doi:10.1186/1471-244X-13-196
74. Gvozdjakova A, Kucharska J, Ostatnikova D, Babinska K, Nakladal D, Crane FL. Ubiquinol improves symptoms in children with autism. *Oxid Med Cell Longev* (2014) **2014**:798957. doi:10.1155/2014/798957
75. Chez MG, Buchanan CP, Aimonovitch MC, Becker M, Schaefer K, Black C, et al. Double-blind, placebo-controlled study of L-carnosine supplementation in children with autistic spectrum disorders. *J Child Neurol* (2002) **17**:833–7. doi:10.1177/08830738020170111501
76. Avula S, Parikh S, Demarest S, Kurz J, Gropman A. Treatment of mitochondrial disorders. *Curr Treat Options Neurol* (2014) **16**:292. doi:10.1007/s11940-014-0292-7
77. Boris M, Goldblatt A, Galanko J, James SJ. Association of MTHFR gene variants with autism. *J Am Phys Surg* (2004) **9**:106–8.
78. Goin-Kochel RP, Porter AE, Peters SU, Shinawi M, Sahoo T, Beaudet AL. The MTHFR 677C–>T polymorphism and behaviors in children with autism: exploratory genotype-phenotype correlations. *Autism Res* (2009) **2**:98–108. doi:10.1002/aur.70
79. Mohammad NS, Jain JM, Chintakindi KP, Singh RP, Naik U, Akella RR. Aberrations in folate metabolic pathway and altered susceptibility to autism. *Psychiatr Genet* (2009) **19**:171–6. doi:10.1097/YPG.0b013e32832cebd2

80. Pasca SP, Dronca E, Kaucsar T, Craciun EC, Endreffy E, Ferencz BK, et al. One carbon metabolism disturbances and the C677T MTHFR gene polymorphism in children with autism spectrum disorders. *J Cell Mol Med* (2009) **13**:4229–38. doi:10.1111/j.1582-4934.2008.00463.x
81. Liu X, Solehdin F, Cohen IL, Gonzalez MG, Jenkins EC, Lewis ME, et al. Population- and family-based studies associate the MTHFR gene with idiopathic autism in simplex families. *J Autism Dev Disord* (2011) **41**:938–44. doi:10.1007/s10803-010-1120-x
82. Frustaci A, Neri M, Cesario A, Adams JB, Domenici E, Dalla Bernardina B, et al. Oxidative stress-related biomarkers in autism: systematic review and meta-analyses. *Free Radic Biol Med* (2012) **52**:2128–41. doi:10.1016/j.freeradbiomed.2012.03.011
83. Guo T, Chen H, Liu B, Ji W, Yang C. Methylenetetrahydrofolate reductase polymorphisms C677T and risk of autism in the Chinese Han population. *Genet Test Mol Biomarkers* (2012) **16**:968–73. doi:10.1089/gtmb.2012.0091
84. Schmidt RJ, Tancredi DJ, Ozonoff S, Hansen RL, Hartiala J, Allayee H, et al. Maternal periconceptional folic acid intake and risk of autism spectrum disorders and developmental delay in the CHARGE (childhood autism risks from genetics and environment) case-control study. *Am J Clin Nutr* (2012) **96**:80–9. doi:10.3945/ajcn.110.004416
85. Pu D, Shen Y, Wu J. Association between MTHFR gene polymorphisms and the risk of autism spectrum disorders: a meta-analysis. *Autism Res* (2013) **6**:384–92. doi:10.1002/aur.1300
86. Adams M, Lucock M, Stuart J, Fardell S, Baker K, Ng X. Preliminary evidence for involvement of the folate gene polymorphism 19bp deletion-DHFR in occurrence of autism. *Neurosci Lett* (2007) **422**:24–9. doi:10.1016/j.neulet.2007.05.025
87. Wollack JB, Makori B, Ahlawat S, Koneru R, Picinich SC, Smith A, et al. Characterization of folate uptake by choroid plexus epithelial cells in a rat primary culture model. *J Neurochem* (2008) **104**:1494–503. doi:10.1111/j.1471-4159.2007.05095.x
88. Ramaekers VT, Blau N. Cerebral folate deficiency. *Dev Med Child Neurol* (2004) **46**:843–51. doi:10.1111/j.1469-8749.2004.tb00451.x
89. Moretti P, Sahoo T, Hyland K, Bottiglieri T, Peters S, Del Gaudio D, et al. Cerebral folate deficiency with developmental delay, autism, and response to folinic acid. *Neurology* (2005) **64**:1088–90. doi:10.1212/01.WNL.0000154641.08211.B7
90. Ramaekers VT, Rothenberg SP, Sequeira JM, Opladen T, Blau N, Quadros EV, et al. Autoantibodies to folate receptors in the cerebral folate deficiency syndrome. *N Engl J Med* (2005) **352**:1985–91. doi:10.1056/NEJMoa043160
91. Ramaekers VT, Blau N, Sequeira JM, Nassogne MC, Quadros EV. Folate receptor autoimmunity and cerebral folate deficiency in low-functioning autism with neurological deficits. *Neuropediatrics* (2007) **38**:276–81. doi:10.1055/s-2008-1065354
92. Moretti P, Peters SU, Del Gaudio D, Sahoo T, Hyland K, Bottiglieri T, et al. Brief report: autistic symptoms, developmental regression, mental retardation, epilepsy, and dyskinesias in CNS folate deficiency. *J Autism Dev Disord* (2008) **38**:1170–7. doi:10.1007/s10803-007-0492-z
93. Ramaekers VT, Sequeira JM, Blau N, Quadros EV. A milk-free diet downregulates folate receptor autoimmunity in cerebral folate deficiency syndrome. *Dev Med Child Neurol* (2008) **50**:346–52. doi:10.1111/j.1469-8749.2008.02053.x
94. Shoffner J, Hyams L, Langley GN, Cossette S, Mylacraine L, Dale J, et al. Fever plus mitochondrial disease could be risk factors for autistic regression. *J Child Neurol* (2010) **25**:429–34. doi:10.1177/0883073809342128
95. Ramaekers VT, Hansen SI, Holm J, Opladen T, Senderek J, Hausler M, et al. Reduced folate transport to the CNS in female Rett patients. *Neurology* (2003) **61**:506–15. doi:10.1212/01.WNL.0000078939.64774.1B
96. Ramaekers VT, Sequeira JM, Artuch R, Blau N, Temudo T, Ormazabal A, et al. Folate receptor autoantibodies and spinal fluid 5-methyltetrahydrofolate deficiency in Rett syndrome. *Neuropediatrics* (2007) **38**:179–83. doi:10.1055/s-2007-991148
97. Perez-Duenas B, Ormazabal A, Toma C, Torrico B, Cormand B, Serrano M, et al. Cerebral folate deficiency syndromes in childhood: clinical, analytical, and etiologic aspects. *Arch Neurol* (2011) **68**:615–21. doi:10.1001/archneurol.2011.80
98. Allen RJ, Dimauro S, Coulter DL, Papadimitriou A, Rothenberg SP. Kearns-Sayre syndrome with reduced plasma and cerebrospinal fluid folate. *Ann Neurol* (1983) **13**:679–82. doi:10.1002/ana.410130620
99. Pineda M, Ormazabal A, Lopez-Gallardo E, Nascimento A, Solano A, Herrero MD, et al. Cerebral folate deficiency and leukoencephalopathy caused by a mitochondrial DNA deletion. *Ann Neurol* (2006) **59**:394–8. doi:10.1002/ana.20746
100. Garcia-Cazorla A, Quadros EV, Nascimento A, Garcia-Silva MT, Briones P, Montoya J, et al. Mitochondrial diseases associated with cerebral folate deficiency. *Neurology* (2008) **70**:1360–2. doi:10.1212/01.wnl.0000309223.98616.e4
101. Hasselmann O, Blau N, Ramaekers VT, Quadros EV, Sequeira JM, Weissert M. Cerebral folate deficiency and CNS inflammatory markers in Alpers disease. *Mol Genet Metab* (2010) **99**:58–61. doi:10.1016/j.ymgme.2009.08.005
102. Frye RE, Rossignol DA. Mitochondrial dysfunction can connect the diverse medical symptoms associated with autism spectrum disorders. *Pediatr Res* (2011) **69**:41R–7R. doi:10.1203/PDR.0b013e318212f16b
103. Ramaekers VT, Quadros EV, Sequeira JM. Role of folate receptor autoantibodies in infantile autism. *Mol Psychiatry* (2013) **18**:270–1. doi:10.1038/mp.2012.22
104. Suren P, Roth C, Bresnahan M, Haugen M, Hornig M, Hirtz D, et al. Association between maternal use of folic acid supplements and risk of autism spectrum disorders in children. *JAMA* (2013) **309**:570–7. doi:10.1001/jama.2012.155925
105. James SJ, Cutler P, Melnyk S, Jernigan S, Janak L, Gaylor DW, et al. Metabolic biomarkers of increased oxidative stress and impaired methylation capacity in children with autism. *Am J Clin Nutr* (2004) **80**:1611–7.
106. Rose S, Melnyk S, Trusty TA, Pavliv O, Seidel L, Li J, et al. Intracellular and extracellular redox status and free radical generation in primary immune cells from children with autism. *Autism Res Treat* (2012) **2012**:986519. doi:10.1155/2012/986519
107. Sajdel-Sulkowska EM, Xu M, McGinnis W, Koibuchi N. Brain region-specific changes in oxidative stress and neurotrophin levels in autism spectrum disorders (ASD). *Cerebellum* (2011) **10**:43–8. doi:10.1007/s12311-010-0223-4
108. Adams JB, Audhya T, McDonough-Means S. Nutritional and metabolic status of children with autism vs. neuro-typical children, and the association with autism severity. *Nutr Metab* (2011) **8**:34. doi:10.1186/1743-7075-8-34
109. Nareuse H, Hayash TI, Takesada M, Nakane A, Yamazaki K, Noguchi T, et al. Therapeutic effect of tetrahydrobiopterin in infantile autism. *Proc Jpn Acad* (1987) **63**:231–3. doi:10.2183/pjab.63.231
110. Danfors T, von Knorring AL, Hartvig P, Langstrom B, Moulder R, Stromberg B, et al. Tetrahydrobiopterin in the treatment of children with autistic disorder: a double-blind placebo-controlled crossover study. *J Clin Psychopharmacol* (2005) **25**:485–9. doi:10.1097/01.jcp.0000177667.35016.e9
111. Klaiman C, Huffman L, Masaki L, Elliott GR. Tetrahydrobiopterin as a treatment for autism spectrum disorders: a double-blind, placebo-controlled trial. *J Child Adolesc Psychopharmacol* (2013) **23**:320–8. doi:10.1089/cap.2012.0127
112. Kim HW, Cho SC, Kim JW, Cho IH, Kim SA, Park M, et al. Family-based association study between NOS-I and -IIA polymorphisms and autism spectrum disorders in Korean trios. *Am J Med Genet B Neuropsychiatr Genet* (2009) **150B**:300–6. doi:10.1002/ajmg.b.30798
113. Delorme R, Betancur C, Scheid I, Anckarsater H, Chaste P, Jamain S, et al. Mutation screening of NOS1AP gene in a large sample of psychiatric patients and controls. *BMC Med Genet* (2010) **11**:108. doi:10.1186/1471-2350-11-108
114. Lakshmi Priya MD, Geetha A. A biochemical study on the level of proteins and their percentage of nitration in the hair and nail of autistic children. *Clin Chim Acta* (2011) **412**:1036–42. doi:10.1016/j.cca.2011.02.021
115. Melnyk S, Fuchs GJ, Schulz E, Lopez M, Kahler SG, Fussell JJ, et al. Metabolic imbalance associated with methylation dysregulation and oxidative damage in children with autism. *J Autism Dev Disord* (2012) **42**:367–77. doi:10.1007/s10803-011-1260-7

# 19

# Predictors of outcomes in autism early intervention: why don't we know more?

***Giacomo Vivanti*[1,2]*, *Margot Prior*[1,3], *Katrina Williams*[4] and *Cheryl Dissanayake*[1]**

[1] *Olga Tennison Autism Research Centre, School of Psychological Science, La Trobe University, Melbourne, VIC, Australia*
[2] *Victorian Autism Specific Early Learning and Care Centre, La Trobe University, Melbourne, VIC, Australia*
[3] *School of Psychological Sciences, University of Melbourne, Melbourne, VIC, Australia*
[4] *Department of Pediatrics, University of Melbourne, Melbourne, VIC, Australia*

***Edited by:***
*Roberto Canitano, University Hospital of Siena, Italy*

***Reviewed by:***
*Leslie J. Carver, University of California San Diego, USA*
*Karen M. Smith, University of Louisiana at Lafayette, USA*
*Stephanie Ameis, University of Toronto, Canada*
*Xiaoming Wang, Duke University, USA*

***Correspondence:***
*Giacomo Vivanti, Olga Tennison Autism Research Centre, School of Psychological Science, La Trobe University, Bundoora Campus, Melbourne, VIC 3086, Australia*
*e-mail: g.vivanti@latrobe.edu.au*

Response to early intervention programs in autism is variable. However, the factors associated with positive versus poor treatment outcomes remain unknown. Hence the issue of which intervention/s should be chosen for an individual child remains a common dilemma. We argue that lack of knowledge on "what works for whom and why" in autism reflects a number of issues in current approaches to outcomes research, and we provide recommendations to address these limitations. These include: a theory-driven selection of putative predictors; the inclusion of proximal measures that are directly relevant to the learning mechanisms demanded by the specific educational strategies; the consideration of family characteristics. Moreover, all data on associations between predictor and outcome variables should be reported in treatment studies.

**Keywords: autism, early intervention, outcomes, predictors, individual differences**

With increasing advances in autism research over the past decades, it has become clear that clinical heterogeneity is one of the most significant features of autism spectrum disorder (ASD) as diagnosed today. Genetic research indicates that hundreds of genes are implicated in ASD (1); neuropsychological research suggests that multiple neurocognitive mechanisms, rather than a single impairment, might underlie ASD symptoms (2); clinical research points to remarkable heterogeneity at the behavioral/phenotypic level (3, 4). Concomitantly, substantial individual differences are apparent with regard to treatment outcomes in this population (5).

On the basis of group-level data, research suggests that behavioral programs that are implemented as early as possible and in an intensive manner [often referred as early intensive behavioral interventions (EIBI)] can be efficacious in improving cognitive, adaptive, and social–communicative outcomes in young children with ASD (6, 7). However, analysis of treatment response at the individual level indicates that whilst some children show dramatic improvements, some show moderate gains, and others only show minimal or no treatment gains (8). Moreover, there is marked variation in the type and magnitude of positive outcomes seen between studies assessing effectiveness of the same intervention (5, 9–13).

Current knowledge of the factors associated with such individual differences in response to early intervention is limited. Therefore, the positive impact of these programs is hampered by lack of knowledge on the critical issue of "which children benefit from which program" (14). In the absence of this crucial information, the issue of which interventions should be chosen for a particular child is a common dilemma facing both families and clinicians. This question needs to be answered so the most effective early interventions can be provided for every child and to allow service and policy level decision making that will make best use of resources.

Recent literature indicates that choice of early intervention and education programs by families and clinicians is currently linked to factors such as regional proximity to services, anecdotal reports on effectiveness, or persuasive sales pitches/marketing, rather than based on the knowledge of which specific service is likely to result in best outcomes given the individual characteristics of the child (15, 16). This gap in knowledge creates the risk of enrolling children in programs from which they will not gain benefit, leading to a profound emotional and economic burden for affected children, their families, and the community. Given the tremendous implications of this issue at the personal, family, and societal level, in our opinion the identification of predictors of treatment outcomes should be at the top of the autism research agenda. However, advances in this area require a different lens for assessing individual differences as well as the adoption of more fine-grained research methodology, including new theoretical frameworks to analyze profiles of "responders" and "non-responders" under different types of early intervention.

In this paper, we shall argue that information about predictors of treatment response is limited because the current theoretical and methodological approaches are not adequate to address this issue. Furthermore, we will offer some directions for research, and discuss the implications for clinical practice.

## CURRENT KNOWLEDGE ON PREDICTORS OF EARLY INTERVENTION OUTCOMES

While there are a number of treatments in the field of ASD, only a small proportion of these have scientific evidence for their efficacy. EIBI programs are currently recommended as the "treatment of choice" for children diagnosed with an ASD (17, 18), with most early intervention research focused on this type of approach. EIBI is characterized by the active engagement of the child for many hours per week (usually 20+) in a planned educational intervention delivered primarily in direct 1:1 child–adult instruction, with specific goals derived from assessment results, manualized/operationalized instructional procedures, and a data collection system to facilitate progress and outcome measurement (11). Within this framework there are different programs, which vary according to the specific curriculum and teaching procedures (19–21).

A number of reviews and meta-analyses have examined group-level outcomes in response to early intervention programs (6, 10, 22), indicating that EIBI programs appear to be effective for increasing adaptive behavior and IQ in young children with ASD. Nevertheless, there are limitations to available research, including lack of randomization in most published studies, small sample sizes, and possible biases due to awareness of treatment status in parents and providers. Moreover, the definitions of EIBI vary across studies, ranging from very specific definitions (e.g., including only programs that strictly adhere to the behavioral procedures originally described by Lovaas) [e.g., Ref. (23)] to very broad ones (including programs that are implemented early and intensively but use teaching procedures that significantly depart from the work of Lovaas, such as Pivotal Response Training) (22).

Importantly, available evidence suggests that EIBI programs (and early educational programs more in general) are not equally beneficial for all treated children (8). In the following, we focus on the factors associated with individual-level variability in response to current early educational intervention approaches, including strictly defined EIBI programs based on the work of Lovaas, as well as programs that are based on behavioral techniques but are not necessarily implemented at a high level of intensity [e.g., Reciprocal Imitation Training (24)], and interventions that meet the intensity requirement but do not have an explicit behavioral orientation [e.g., the PACT program (25)].

Analysis of available evidence indicates that pre-treatment cognitive abilities (IQ) and language abilities are the most often reported correlates of gains in early intervention studies (26–33), although not all studies concur in their conclusions (34–36). Several studies also indicate pre-treatment level of adaptive behaviors as a relevant correlate of treatment gains (6, 37, 38).

Whilst there is some evidence that children who are younger and less severely affected might be more responsive to early intervention, other studies report mixed or negative findings [(31, 39–43); see also Ref. (10, 44)].

A number of studies have identified more specific abilities associated with positive treatment outcomes, including play skills (24, 45–47), interest in objects (48–50), joint attention (46, 47, 50), imitation (38), low social avoidance (51), and response to social versus non-social reinforcement (52). In addition, there have been mixed reports on family factors such as the level of maternal education (53, 54) and family stress (55, 56).

## LIMITATIONS WITH CURRENT APPROACHES TO RESEARCH ON PREDICTORS OF OUTCOME

Despite such findings on predictors, knowledge of the factors underlying positive treatment outcomes is limited and inconclusive. The major limitations to current research approaches are outlined below.

1. Variables associated with change in treated groups do not necessarily reflect actual predictors of outcomes (i.e., moderators or mediators of treatment response), as not all the observed change can be attributed to treatment (57, 58). If factors other than treatment that might contribute to change are not considered and controlled, correlates of changes within a treated group might or might not tell the full story about prediction of treatment response.
2. The selection of predictor variables is often not theory-driven (59, 60). In most papers reporting on predictors of outcomes, no rationale is provided on why specific variables are selected for analyses. It is apparent that, in most cases, the predictor variables are the measures used to characterize samples at trial commencement, with the purpose of identifying any important differences between randomized groups. Equally, the types of measures used often indicate broad constructs and thus lack the specificity required for a predictor variable. Therefore, the current findings of IQ/language variables as the most consistent predictors of response to early intervention programs tell us more about how commonly these measures are used in baseline assessments in intervention research than about their strength as predictors.
3. Analyses of specific behavioral predictors that could account for individual or subgroup differences are rarely included in research on intervention and prognosis (61). Most intervention studies focus on overall group-level outcome data, and analyses on those factors associated with identifiable subgroups of children or individual differences are either not conducted or not reported, despite the fact that treatment response is so variable in ASD. In medical research, the evaluation of intervention effectiveness often follows a progression from an initial focus on overall group-level outcomes ("does the treatment work for this condition?") to a subsequent focus on predictors of outcomes for identifiable subgroups or at an individual-level ("what are the factors associated with outcomes?"), particularly when treatment response is variable, of insufficient benefit compared to risk to warrant treatment for some, or when advances are still needed to improve outcomes. In research on autism intervention, most trials are designed to only address the question of group-level efficacy/effectiveness. However, as current research emphasizes the heterogeneity of ASD at every level of analysis, and the results of trials and meta-analyses show variable effect sizes, there is a clear need to move to the next stage of intervention research, with a focus on the specific individual predictors of treatment outcomes, and a focus on moderators and mediators of treatment response.

4. Few studies compare predictors of outcomes across different intervention programs (58). The impact of child characteristics is likely to vary according to the intervention program implemented, so that a child who is not responsive to program X (e.g., discrete trial training) might be more responsive to program Y [e.g., pivotal response training (14, 49)]. Since different programs utilize different instructional techniques (for example, different emphasis on external versus social reinforcements, different emphasis on verbal versus non-verbal instructions), it is likely that children with varying intrinsic cognitive and learning profiles will respond preferentially to different teaching approaches, just as do children who do not have ASD (60, 62, 63). However, the majority of studies on predictors of outcomes include data on response to one program only. Moreover, the inclusion of only one treatment leaves open the possibility that the change predicted by the pre-treatment factors is due to factors other than treatment (59).
5. Intervention studies recruit different samples from those that present at clinical services. Exclusion criteria in many intervention studies result in children with associated medical conditions, seizures, or a low IQs [e.g., IQ < 35 in Ref. (64)], or developmental age [e.g., <12 months in Ref. (25)] being excluded. While these exclusion criteria are set to create homogeneous samples for research purposes, they reduce generalizability to those who are seen in clinical and community-based settings, providing little information about which programs should be recommended based on different pre-treatment characteristics in the wider ASD population. Children with medical conditions, seizures, and/or severe intellectual disability make up a significant proportion of the ASD population (65, 66), and they are more likely to be referred to treatment programs compared to children with no identifiable comorbid features (67, 68). Therefore, research on their responses to different programs is crucial to inform clinical practice, so that enrollment to an intervention service is most likely to offer benefits and cause no harm.

   Current guidelines in clinical trials suggest that excluding patients with associated disorders from research should not occur when these comorbidities are common or when they affect treatment response and prognosis (69). As current research reports an increasing number of comorbid conditions associated with ASDs (66), including dysfunctions that are not diagnosable as specific disorders, the attempt to isolate "pure autism" in the ASD population by excluding "autism complicated by comorbid features" appears to be increasingly impracticable and unrealistic [see Ref. (35)].
6. Standard predictor measures currently used in research are very broad. Omnibus factors such as tested IQ, speech and language assessments, and adaptive behavior have predominated as both predictors and outcome measures in intervention research (53, 60). The use of such broad measures in intervention studies as predictors is problematic for a number of reasons. Low scores in IQ, language, and adaptive behaviors reflect a variety of distinct underlying processes, making it difficult to understand the specific mechanisms underlying the intervention response. Given that performance on IQ tests is, in itself, a measure of learning abilities (e.g., inefficient information processing), it is not surprising that children with lower IQ have more difficulties in learning from educational treatments. To avoid circular reasoning (children who have more difficulties in learning, as measured through pre-treatment IQ testing, are the ones who will have more difficulties in learning from educational treatments), research needs to focus on more proximal predictor variables. These should reflect specific and clearly defined processes that might explain difficulties in responding to educational strategies [e.g., response to social reinforcements in (52); lack of spontaneous imitation in (70)]. Moreover, broad variables such as IQ and communication scores are not robust measures in children younger than 3 years (71), and different tools used to measure IQ might provide different results depending on the instruction formats (e.g., verbal instructions versus demonstration) in the ASD population.
7. Family factors are seldom considered as predictors in outcomes studies. There is very little systematic data on how the characteristics and behaviors of parents influence children's responses to intervention (72). The motivation of parents to pursue and persist with intervention programs, which involve considerably more effort than administering medications or using complementary and alternative therapies, may be an important factor in treatment outcomes. Moreover, the parents' personal strengths (e.g., communication style, flexibility) may contribute to the developmental gains of their child. Lack of research in this area is surprising, given that (1) parents are frequently expected to engage as the main therapists for their children in many interventions, even those that are not called parent-mediated interventions, and (2) family factors have been found to impact on treatment response across a number of intervention programs for children with other conditions [see Ref. (73)]. Moreover, family factors such as higher parenting stress, negativity and depression, and low SES are ubiquitous factors in poorer outcomes across a range of child mental health interventions (74–76). The few studies that have investigated family factors in ASD indicate the relevance of parent's education, responsivity, and beliefs about the importance of child independence (77, 78). Another study (79) reported that higher distress in mothers pre-treatment was associated with lower adaptive behavior outcomes post-treatment, although the effect was not statistically significant [see also Ref. (30)]. Similarly, Osborne et al. (55) reported that high levels of parenting stress reduced the intervention gains in their children, particularly for high intensity interventions. Despite the relevance of this literature, the available evidence on family characteristics moderating treatment outcomes is limited and inconclusive.

## RECOMMENDATIONS

On the basis of the limitations in the intervention outcome literature to date, a number of recommendations are made here.

1. Selection of putative predictors should be theory-driven, and predictors should be proximal and specific rather than broad. In order to match specific learning profiles to specific teaching programs, it is important to conduct a fine-grained analysis of child characteristics. Doing so will enable us to determine not

only what the child needs to learn (which will inform treatment objectives) but also how the child learns (which will inform treatment strategies). In addition, we also need to develop a fine-grained understanding of how each treatment works; that is, what are the processes (or the active ingredients) of the intervention that interacts with the child characteristics to promote learning in that child? With time it is likely that an understanding will emerge about the role of different factors on the pathway to effective intervention, such that some will be seen as "first order" or "primary" and required for certain educational or behavioral approaches to be effective, while others will be "second or later order" indicating modification that need to be made to optimize effectiveness of intervention techniques.

The analysis of the active ingredients of treatment involves a conceptual distinction between moderators of treatment effects, and mediators through which the intervention supposedly works (80). Moderators of treatment outcomes are the pre-treatment characteristics that might determine the degree of effectiveness of treatment versus control, but do not change as a consequence of the intervention, such as chronological age, gender, or maternal education. Conversely, mediators of treatment outcomes are the factors through which a treatment exerts its effects: they are subject to change as a consequence of the treatment, and these changes, in turn, affect treatment outcomes. For example, based on the theoretical tenet and the educational strategies of the Early Start Denver Model (a program in which the therapists are instructed to follow the child's lead), it is plausible that changes in the spontaneous propensity to initiate social interactions and engage in joint activities mediate outcomes in this program (81). Similarly, it is plausible that changes in the propensity to imitate others mediate outcomes in Reciprocal Imitation Training (24), and that changes in the ability to understand and follow visually mediated task instructions would be relevant in response to the TEACCH program (82).

The study of mediators of treatment outcomes requires the knowledge of the learning processes upon which the instructional techniques of the teaching program are based, or, in other words, understanding of the active ingredients underlying treatment-related changes. Without such knowledge, selecting among the many variables that are potentially associated with response to treatment in ASD is a difficult task. Importantly, intervention programs should have manualized guidelines and fidelity procedures to ensure that the active ingredients supposedly involved in the therapy are not "diluted" when the programs are translated into community practice.

A clear definition of the processes through which the child is able to learn in response to the particular instructional techniques is therefore one starting point for defining a specific set of putative moderators and mediators. Furthermore, it is crucial to focus on proximal factors that are known to support learning, with different predictor variables reflecting distinct and defined processes, so that the specific weight of these putative predictors mediating treatment response can be measured. Processes that are known to be foundational for social learning, and might be relevant predictors of outcomes for early educational programs include: social attention [paying attention to people and their actions (83)]; social motivation [which can be operationalized in terms of social approach versus social avoidance behavior, or response to social versus non-social rewards (52, 84)]; intentional communication [using language or non-verbal communication to communicate (85)]; receptive language/communication [understanding others' communication (86)]; joint attention [both initiation and response to joint attention (87, 88)]; goal understanding (89, 90); imitation (91, 92); functional play (35, 93). All of these processes reflect different facets of social cognition that are known to support social learning, and which are associated with developmental outcomes in ASD as well as in typical development [e.g., Ref. (94, 95)]. Preliminary evidence provides encouragement on the value of these factors in predicting response to intervention [e.g., Ref. (24, 35, 38, 45, 46)]. Another factor that might be associated with outcomes is the extent of restricted/repetitive behaviors (RRBs), since engagement in inflexible routines and insistence on sameness are likely to hinder acquisition of new skills and social learning. For example, Watt et al. (96) reported that prolonged engagement with RBBs was negatively related to social competence across the crucial developmental period from 2 to 3 years. Data on the relevance of RRBs in response to treatment are scant and equivocal (52, 97, 98), so more research is needed to investigate how individual differences in the extent of RBRs affect response to intervention.

Other factors that are not specific to ASD might also be associated with treatment outcomes across intervention programs. These include attention (in particular sustained attention, e.g., the ability to be focused on a task from the beginning to the end); memory; responsivity to instrumental learning/conditioning (the ability to associate contingent rewards to own behaviors); processing speed and efficiency; generalization (the ability to use what has been learned in non-training situations). Rate of learning (e.g., number of treatment goals achieved in the first 6 months of treatment) might also be a relevant predictor of outcomes (99). Research on the predictive value of these factors in response to treatment is scant.

As standardized tests are not available for many of the processes listed above, it is necessary to develop and utilize novel, fine-grained experimental measures and observational protocols that are suitable for young children with ASD across the spectrum of severity [e.g., Ref. (35, 52)]. **Table 1** summarizes a list of the factors that have been theoretically and/or empirically linked to positive treatment outcomes (including both child and family factors, discussed in the next section), and for which psychometric development is needed to advance a methodology for identifying predictors of outcomes.

2. Family factors should be investigated in treatment studies. As family involvement is a recommended component of early intervention (100), future research should systematically investigate the family characteristics associated with responses to treatment for children with ASD. Importantly, different early intervention programs involve instructional techniques (e.g., play-based versus highly structured strategies) that may or may not fit with a family's educational practice and cultural values. Different families might also respond differently to the parent training formats used by the different programs, which

**Table 1 | Putative predictors of treatment outcomes that require standardization/psychometric development.**

| Child factors | Family factors |
|---|---|
| Functional communication (requesting, protesting) | Sociodemographic background (resource-poor versus resource-rich) |
| Social communication (sharing, commenting) | Family expectations about treatment |
| Social approach (versus avoidance) | Family sense of competence/self-efficacy |
| Joint attention | Parent/therapist alliance |
| Social understanding | Family stress and discord |
| Imitation | Father positive involvement |
| Level of RRBs | Social support |
| Functional play with objects | |
| Responsivity to reward learning | |
| Generalization | |
| Core neuropsychological functions (processing speed/efficiency, sustained attention, cognitive control, memory) | |

vary from information sessions in small groups to 1:1 sessions in which the parent is asked to implement educational strategies under a therapist's supervision. Other potential family factors mediating response to treatment are the level of parent/therapist collaboration, maintaining positive expectations for child outcomes, lack of family conflict, positive father involvement, level of social support, and level of stress in the family (14).

High levels of child behavior problems are prominent in families with children with developmental disabilities and contribute to greater stress in families than cognitive delay (101, 102). Generally, mothers of children with ASD report higher levels of distress than those of non-disabled children or those with children with other disabilities, although there is considerable variability across families (103, 104). In a recent paper, Benson (105) has shown that social network attributes, including the range and function of emotional support, are related to perceived social support, which in turn can bring about a decrease in depressed mood in mothers of children with ASD. Formal and informal social support networks can have the effect of enhancing quality of life, confidence in parenting and optimism (106) for families with children with disabilities, and might be crucial factors predicting treatment outcomes. Accurate measures that appropriately capture individual differences between families in terms of specific values, attitudes, and resources may need to be developed. Future research should investigate the role of family factors in a systematic way, selecting specific, theory-driven variables, developing novel fine-grained measures and comparing variables associated to outcomes across different programs. When examining a broad array of putative factors (e.g., family characteristics and attitudes, sociodemographic background) that may be associated with outcomes, it is important to consider that while a single factor might not be predictive of outcomes, the accumulation of multiple risks often is. Studies looking at longitudinal outcomes in at-risk populations often use cumulative risk approaches (107) in which a discreet number of risk indexes are created to capture the level of risk within a number of predefined theoretically driven domains. To illustrate, a number of studies [e.g., Ref. (108, 109)] have examined the predictive value of risk factors within the child (various child attributes), sociocultural (demographic characteristics), and parenting domains (parent beliefs/attitudes), showing that cumulative risk within each domain predicted outcomes in typically developing children. This approach can be helpful in examining whether risk factors in family related and sociodemographic domains play a role in response to treatment in the ASD population.

3. Studies on treatment efficacy/effectiveness should always report on individual differences in response to treatment as well as those factors associated with positive treatment outcomes. The analysis of individual differences (i.e., characteristics of responders and non-responders) should become a standard procedure in early intervention research [similarly to current procedures in pharmacological intervention research (110)]. Moreover, when predictor variables are measured, their association with the outcome measures should always be reported. The tendency to report on predictors of outcomes only when results indicate significant associations makes it hard to draw clear conclusions on the robustness and consistency of factors associated with treatment response. Thus, it should be mandated that all data on predictor and outcome variables are reported, as in the case of outcome measures in clinical trials (111). Reporting all available information on the association between predictors and outcomes can also be useful in studies with small sample sizes, which comprise the majority in the field of ASD, so that data from multiple small trials can be pooled for meta-analyses. While data on correlates of treatment gains *per se* do not allow for definite conclusions on predictors of treatment outcomes, this information can be critical to inform subsequent research designed to control for the predictive value of factors that appear to be relevant in relation to treatment changes.
4. Research on predictors of treatment outcomes should compare responses across different programs. As mentioned above, the analysis of correlates of gains in a treated group might not be informative on predictors of treatment outcomes, as not all observed change in a treatment study can be attributed to the treatment. Research on predictors of treatment outcomes should use designs that compare different programs, thus allowing for the analysis of the interaction between selected participant characteristics X treatment group. This approach is critical not only from a methodological point of view (distinguishing moderated treatment effects from factors that are associated with outcomes/changes in ASD more generally), but also from a clinical perspective. Different early intervention programs, while sharing many similarities, involve distinct instructional techniques that are based on different theories and which tap into different learning processes. For example, some programs involve an emphasis on teaching words/sentences that have the instrumental function of obtaining desired items, whilst in other programs language is targeted with an emphasis on its social versus instrumental function. Similarly, programs

vary across a number of teaching processes (e.g., verbal versus visually conveyed instructions, following the child's lead versus adult-directed models), reflecting different underlying theoretical frameworks. Since these different teaching practices require different learning processes on the part of the learner, it is possible that different types of learners will respond to different types of teaching procedures. Given that remarkable differences are present both in the teaching procedures of the different programs and in the social, cognitive, and learning profiles of children with ASD, it is imperative that future research compares the profiles of response to different early learning programs that use different instructional techniques. This approach would allow identification of the pre-treatment child characteristics that support learning when a specific set of teaching procedures is used. Only a few studies to date have provided information on the specificity of predictors of outcomes to one versus another treatment program [see Ref. (49, 50)].

5. Research on predictors of outcomes should involve large heterogeneous samples. It is important for studies on the predictors of response to treatment to include the full range/spectrum of children with ASD. Many children with comorbid conditions are typically excluded from research studies, such as those with severe intellectual disability and associated medical conditions or seizures. However, as discussed above, these children represent a substantial proportion of the ASD population referred to community early intervention centers. It is particularly important that research focuses on children with very low IQ to determine whether the currently available early intervention programs are appropriate for this population, and which specific factors are predictive of positive outcomes (e.g., short attention span, passivity, poor play skills). If research shows that there are child characteristics that indicate a lack of responsivity to any of the currently available early intervention programs, we need to develop novel approaches targeting the specific impairments of the "non-responders," rather than referring them routinely to programs from which they do not benefit.

## CONCLUSION

Little is known about predictors, moderators, and mediators of treatment response in children with neurodevelopmental and neuropsychiatric conditions (112, 113), and the field of ASD is no exception. With recent advances in research documenting the positive impact of early intensive behavioral programs for children with ASD, the critical issue facing researchers, clinicians, and practitioners in the field is not as much a lack of evidence-based treatments, but rather an inability to predict which treatment will work best for each child. The variability of response to EIBI and other early intervention programs is a phenomenon that very likely reflects the heterogeneity of the ASD population. While some crude prognostic variables, such as IQ level, hold some value in predicting which children will respond best to early intervention, to date, the available information on moderators and mediators of treatment response is inconclusive. In this paper, we argue that lack of knowledge on "what works for whom and why" in ASD reflects a number of methodological and theoretical issues in ASD treatment research.

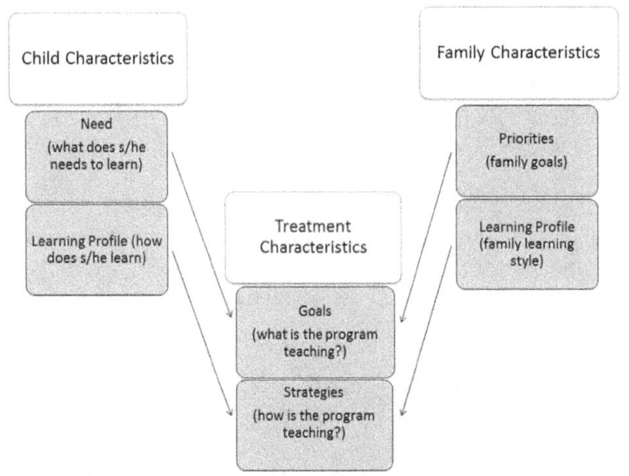


**FIGURE 1 | Treatment goals should be selected on the basis of the child's needs and family priorities.** Treatment strategies should be selected on the basis of the child learning profile and the family's learning style.

We argue that the selection of treatment objectives and treatment strategies should be informed by knowledge of: (1) child characteristics (how does the child learn best, and what does s/he needs to learn); (2) family characteristics (what are the family priorities/expectations, and what is the family learning style); (3) treatment characteristics (what are the treatment aims, and how does the treatment work). This model is illustrated in **Figure 1**. Current understanding on the interplay of these factors in determining treatment outcomes is limited, and we have offered here a number of recommendations to advance knowledge in the field. Given the complexity of the biological underpinnings of ASD, behavioral predictors might not be sufficient to predict treatment outcomes to a high degree of accuracy. Nevertheless, knowledge arising from this line of research can critically contribute to the development of decision-making guidelines in the field of ASD early intervention.

A number of questions remain, which need further critical evaluation. First, it is unclear whether predictors of intervention outcomes are specific to ASD. As reported above, a number of specific factors in the two areas of impairments that characterize ASD (social communication and repetitive behaviors domains) are likely to hinder positive responses to intervention; however, other factors that are not specific to ASD (e.g., attention span, memory) might also play an important role in predicting outcomes. For example, IQ and language abilities are associated with outcomes across a number of conditions [e.g., schizophrenia (114), depression (115), conduct disorder (116)] that are not related to ASD. Indeed, these factors might predict outcomes above and beyond receiving early intervention *per se* [see Ref. (117–119)].

It is possible that factors associated with positive responses to intervention are the same that support positive learning in children without an ASD. More research is needed, therefore, to achieve a more fine-grained understanding of mechanisms supporting early learning and cognitive development in typical development as well as atypical development (e.g., neuropsychological processes such as attention and processing speed and social processes such as social engagement, sharing of affect, and joint attention). Sophisticated research designs are also needed to identify distinctions and overlaps and the interplay between variables moderating treatment changes, those mediating outcomes, and those affecting both processes.

Given the scarcity of standardized tools to assess social and non-social factors that might be relevant for response to intervention, measurement of putative predictors of outcomes poses relevant challenges. More efforts are currently needed to develop systematic observational and experimental tasks that provide reliable measurements of such predictors.

Another critical aspect concerns the definition of positive versus nil or minimal outcomes in ASD research. Outcome measures used in treatment research might not be sufficiently sensitive to capture gains in children making very slow or very small gains. However, these small progressions might have a relevant impact on the family and child's quality of life and may be the necessary "first order" changes that are needed to allow further positive response. Thus, the operational definition of "responders" versus "non-responders" should take into account different outcome criteria besides the standard/conventional measures used in ASD research.

Moreover intervention in ASD, while promoting gains in certain areas, can also be instrumental in preventing declines or worsening in other domains. For example, there is evidence that some repetitive behaviors might increase over time in ASD (120), and it is conceivable that a treatment program could aim to prevent such increase. In this case, the absence of change in repetitive behaviors in children undergoing treatment cannot be seen as evidence of a lack of treatment response. Therefore, definitions of responders and non-responders must be conceptualized and framed on knowledge of developmental patterns in the different treatment target domains.

A related issue is the question of when do we begin to classify children as "non-responders"? If children are not showing measurable gains after 1 year, is it possible that they will start responding in the second year? Currently, our knowledge on the timing of treatment response is limited. Different studies provide information on predictors of outcomes in relation to programs that vary in duration, making it difficult to compare results and to calibrate expectations about the timing of treatment response. In order for research to inform clinical decision-making, some consensus about the timing of expected response to treatment is therefore necessary, and approaches that allow time-limited intervention with ongoing follow-up to allow future intervention planning should be developed.

A further challenge is the clinical management of "non-responders" to early intervention programs. In the best-case scenario, future research will indicate that those children who do not respond to some early intervention programs will nonetheless respond to other available programs, so that each child can be matched to the most appropriate program. However, it is possible that specific child or family factors are associated with minimal or no responses across all available treatment options. If this is the case, it will be necessary to target the specific factors that are known to limit the efficacy of the program ["treating the constraints" approach (59)], and to conduct specific research focused on these "non-responders." Until research indicates successful strategies to address the factors limiting response to treatment in this subgroup, the question is: should children who present with a "non-responder" profile be referred to programs from which they will not benefit? This raises a number of ethical issues as well as concerns with regard to cost–benefits considerations, and individual rights to access services.

Finally, the research recommendations that we have outlined, which involve a focus on individual differences in large heterogeneous samples, the measurement of a variety of theory-driven predictor variables at baseline, and the comparison of prognostic indicators across different programs, are expensive ones. To have a sufficient number of participants to identify robust profiles of responders and non-responders to available early intervention programs and to replicate findings across sites requires large-scale collaborative multisite research. Nonetheless, the practical implications of such a research program surely justify the necessary investment, especially as ASD is currently diagnosed in more than 1 in every 100 children and the problems associated with ASD have a high impact for the individual, their family, and the community.

## REFERENCES

1. Betancur C. Etiological heterogeneity in autism spectrum disorders: more than 100 genetic and genomic disorders and still counting. *Brain Res* (2011) **1380**:42–77. doi:10.1016/j.brainres.2010.11.078
2. Happe F, Ronald A, Plomin R. Time to give up on a single explanation for autism. *Nat Neurosci* (2006) **9**(10):1218–20. doi:10.1038/nn1770
3. Brock J. Commentary: complementary approaches to the developmental cognitive neuroscience of autism – reflections on Pelphrey et al. (2011). *J Child Psychol Psychiatry* (2011) **52**(6):645–6. doi:10.1111/j.1469-7610.2011.02414.x
4. Waterhouse L. *Rethinking Autism: Variation and Complexity*. London: Academic Press (2011).
5. Howlin P, Magiati I, Charman T. Systematic review of early intensive behavioral interventions for children with autism. *Am J Intellect Dev Disabil* (2009) **114**(1):23–41. doi:10.1352/2009.114:23
6. Reichow B, Barton EE, Boyd BA, Hume K. Early intensive behavioral intervention (EIBI) for young children with autism spectrum disorders (ASD). *Cochrane Database Syst Rev* (2012) **10**:CD009260. doi:10.1002/14651858.CD009260.pub2
7. Rogers S, Wallace K. Intervention for infants and toddlers with autism spectrum disorders. In: Amaral DG, Dawson G, Geschwind DH, editors. *Autism Spectrum Disorders*. New York: Oxford University Press (2011). p. 1081–94.
8. Howlin P, Charman T. Autism spectrum disorders, interventions and outcomes. In: Howlin P, Charman T, Ghaziuddin M, editors. *The SAGE Handbook of Developmental Disorders*. London: SAGE (2011). p. 309–26.
9. Eldevik S, Hastings RP, Hughes JC, Jahr E, Eikeseth S, Cross S. Meta-analysis of early intensive behavioral intervention for children with autism. *J Clin Child Adolesc Psychol* (2009) **38**(3):439–50. doi:10.1080/15374410902851739
10. Magiati I, Tay X, Howlin P. Early comprehensive behaviorally based interventions for children with autism spectrum disorders: a summary of findings from recent reviews and meta-analyses. *Neuropsychiatry* (2012) **2**:543–70. doi:10.2217/npy.12.59
11. Hepburn S. Early intensive behavioral intervention (EIBI). In: Volkmar F, editor. *Encyclopedia of Autism Spectrum Disorders*. New York: Springer (2013). p. 1028–31.
12. Fountain C, Winter A, Bearman P. Six developmental trajectories characterize children with autism. *Pediatrics* (2012) **129**:1112–20. doi:10.1542/peds.2011-1601
13. Anagnostou E, Bear M, Dawson G. Future directions in the treatment of autism spectrum disorders. In: Amaral D, Dawson G, Geschwind D, editors. *Autism Spectrum Disorders*. New York: Oxford University Press (2011). p. 1259–68.

14. Stahmer AC, Schreibman L, Cunningham AB. Toward a technology of treatment individualization for young children with autism spectrum disorders. *Brain Res* (2011) **1380**:229–39. doi:10.1016/j.brainres.2010.09.043
15. Green VA, Pituch KA, Itchon J, Choi A, O'Reilly M, Sigafoos J. Internet survey of treatments used by parents of children with autism. *Res Dev Disabil* (2006) **27**(1):70–84. doi:10.1016/j.ridd.2004.12.002
16. Levy SE, Hyman SL. Novel treatments for autistic spectrum disorders. *Ment Retard Dev Disabil Res Rev* (2005) **11**(2):131–42. doi:10.1002/mrdd.20062
17. Prior M, Roberts JMA, Rodger S, Williams K, Sutherland R. *A Review of the Research to Identify the Most Effective Models of Practice in Early Intervention of Children with Autism Spectrum Disorders.* Australian Government Department of Families, Housing, Community Services and Indigenous Affairs (2011).
18. Reichow B, Doehring P, Cicchetti DV, Volkmar FR. *Evidence-Based Practices and Treatments for Children with Autism.* New York, NY: Springer (2011).
19. Carr JE, LeBlanc LA. Autism spectrum disorders in early childhood: an overview for practicing physicians. *Prim Care* (2007) **34**:343–59. doi:10.1016/j.pop.2007.04.009
20. Grow LL, Carr JE, Kodak TM, Jostad CM, Kisamore AN. A comparison of methods for teaching receptive labeling to children with autism spectrum disorders. *J Appl Behav Anal* (2011) **44**:475–98. doi:10.1901/jaba.2011.44-475
21. Love JR, Carr JE, Almason SM, Ingeborg Pétursdóttir A. Early and intensive behavioral intervention for autism: a survey of clinical practices. *Res Autism Spectr Disord* (2009) **3**:421–8. doi:10.1016/j.rasd.2008.08.008
22. Reichow B. Overview of meta-analyses on early intensive behavioral intervention for young children with autism spectrum disorders. *J Autism Dev Disord* (2012) **42**:512–20. doi:10.1007/s10803-011-1218-9
23. Lovaas OI. *Teaching Developmentally Disabled Children: the ME Book.* Austin, TX: Pro-Ed (1981).
24. Ingersoll B. Pilot randomized controlled trial of reciprocal imitation training for teaching elicited and spontaneous imitation to children with autism. *J Autism Dev Disord* (2010) **40**(9):1154–60. doi:10.1007/s10803-010-0966-2
25. Green J, Charman T, McConachie H, Aldred C, Slonims V, Howlin P, et al. Parent-mediated communication-focused treatment in children with autism (PACT): a randomised controlled trial. *Lancet* (2010) **375**(9732):2152–60. doi:10.1016/S0140-6736(10)60587-9
26. Eldevik S, Hastings RP, Jahr E, Hughes JC. Outcomes of behavioral intervention for children with autism in mainstream pre-school settings. *J Autism Dev Disord* (2012) **42**(2):210–20. doi:10.1007/s10803-011-1234-9
27. Hayward D, Eikeseth S, Gale C, Morgan S. Assessing progress during treatment for young children with autism receiving intensive behavioural interventions. *Autism* (2009) **13**(6):613–33. doi:10.1177/1362361309340029
28. Magiati I, Moss J, Charman T, Howlin P. Patterns of change in children with Autism Spectrum Disorders who received community based comprehensive interventions in their pre-school years: a seven year follow-up study. *Res Autism Spectr Disord* (2011) **5**(3):1016–27. doi:10.1016/j.rasd.2010.11.007
29. Peters-Scheffer N, Didden R, Korzilius H, Sturmey P. A meta-analytic study on the effectiveness of comprehensive ABA-based early intervention programs for children with autism spectrum disorders. *Res Autism Spectr Disord* (2011) **5**:60–9. doi:10.1016/j.rasd.2010.03.011
30. Perry A, Cummings A, Dunn Geier J, Freeman N, Hughes S, LaRose L, et al. Effectiveness of intensive behavioural intervention in a large community based program. *Res Autism Spectr Disord* (2008) **2**:621–42. doi:10.1016/j.rasd.2008.01.002
31. Remington B, Hastings RP, Kovshoff H, degli Espinosa F, Jahr E, Brown T, et al. Early intensive behavioral intervention: outcomes for children with autism and their parents after two years. *Am J Ment Retard* (2007) **112**(6):418–38. doi:10.1352/0895-8017(2007)112[418:EIBIOF]2.0.CO;2
32. Smith IM, Koegel RL, Koegel LK, Openden DA, Fossum KL, Bryson SE. Effectiveness of a novel community-based early intervention model for children with autistic spectrum disorder. *Am J Intellect Dev Disabil* (2010) **115**(6):504–23. doi:10.1352/1944-7558-115.6.504
33. Ben-Itzchak E, Watson LR, Zachor DA. Cognitive ability is associated with different outcome trajectories in autism spectrum disorders. *J Autism Dev Disord* (2014). doi:10.1007/s10803-014-2091-0
34. Makrygianni M, Reed P. A meta-analytic review of the effectiveness of behavioural early intervention programs for children with autistic spectrum disorders. *Res Autism Spectr Disord* (2010) **4**:577–93. doi:10.1016/j.rasd.2010.01.014
35. Vivanti G, Barbaro J, Hudry K, Dissanayake C, Prior M. Intellectual development in autism spectrum disorder. *Front Hum Neurosci* (2013) **7**:354. doi:10.3389/fnhum.2013.00354
36. Zachor DA, Ben-Itzchak E, Rabinovich A, Lahat E. Change in autism core symptoms with intervention. *Res Autism Spectr Disord* (2007) **1**:304–17. doi:10.1016/j.rasd.2006.12.001
37. Eldevik S, Hastings R, Hughes J, Jahr E, Eikeseth S, Cross S. Using participant data to extend the evidence base for intensive behavioral intervention for children with autism. *Am J Intellect Dev Disabil* (2010) **115**:381–405. doi:10.1352/1944-7558-115.5.381
38. Sallows GO, Graupner TD. Intensive behavioral treatment for children with autism: four-year outcome and predictors. *Am J Ment Retard* (2005) **110**(6):417–38. doi:10.1352/0895-8017(2005)110[417:IBTFCW]2.0.CO;2
39. Flanagan HE, Perry A, Freeman NL. Effectiveness of large-scale community-based intensive behavioral intervention: a waitlist comparison study exploring outcomes and predictors. *Res Autism Spectr Disord* (2012) **6**(2):673–82. doi:10.1016/j.rasd.2011.09.011
40. Luiselli JK, Cannon BO, Ellis JT, Sisson RW. Home-based behavioral interventions for young children with autism/pervasive developmental disorder: a preliminary evaluation of outcome in relation to child age and intensity of service delivery. *Autism* (2000) **4**:426–38. doi:10.1177/1362361300004004007
41. Rogers SJ, Vismara LA. Evidence-based comprehensive treatments for early autism. *J Clin Child Adolesc Psychol* (2008) **37**(1):8–38. doi:10.1080/15374410701817808
42. Smith T, Groen AD, Wynn JW. Randomized trial of intensive early intervention for children with pervasive developmental disorder. *Am J Ment Retard* (2000) **105**:269–85. doi:10.1352/0895-8017(2000)105<0269:RTOIEI>2.0.CO;2
43. Virues-Ortega J. Applied behavior analytic intervention for autism in early childhood: meta-analysis, meta-regression and dose-response meta-analysis of multiple outcomes. *Clin Psychol Rev* (2010) **30**(4):387–99. doi:10.1016/j.cpr.2010.01.008
44. Eapen V, Crncec R, Walter A. Exploring links between genotypes, phenotypes, and clinical predictors of response to early intensive behavioral intervention in autism spectrum disorder. *Front Hum Neurosci* (2013) **7**:567. doi:10.3389/fnhum.2013.00567
45. Sherer MR, Schreibman L. Individual behavioral profiles and predictors of treatment effectiveness for children with autism. *J Consult Clin Psychol* (2005) **73**(3):525–38. doi:10.1037/0022-006X.73.3.525
46. Kasari C, Gulsrud A, Freeman S, Paparella T, Hellemann G. Longitudinal follow-up of children with autism receiving targeted interventions on joint attention and play. *J Am Acad Child Adolesc Psychiatry* (2012) **51**(5):487–95. doi:10.1016/j.jaac.2012.02.019
47. Kasari C, Paparella T, Freeman S, Jahromi LB. Language outcome in autism: randomized comparison of joint attention and play interventions. *J Consult Clin Psychol* (2008) **76**(1):125–37. doi:10.1037/0022-006X.76.1.125
48. Carter AS, Messinger DS, Stone WL, Celimli S, Nahmias AS, Yoder P. A randomized controlled trial of Hanen's 'more than words' in toddlers with early autism symptoms. *J Child Psychol Psychiatry* (2011) **52**(7):741–52. doi:10.1111/j.1469-7610.2011.02395.x
49. Schreibman L, Stahmer AC, Barlett VC, Dufek S. Brief report: toward refinement of a predictive behavioral profile for treatment outcome in children with autism. *Res Autism Spectr Disord* (2009) **3**(1):163–72. doi:10.1016/j.rasd.2008.04.008
50. Yoder P, Stone WL. A randomized comparison of the effect of two prelinguistic communication interventions on the acquisition of spoken communication in preschoolers with ASD. *J Speech Lang Hear Res* (2006) **49**(4):698–711. doi:10.1044/1092-4388(2006/051)
51. Ingersoll B, Schreibman L, Stahmer A. Brief report: differential treatment outcomes for children with autistic spectrum disorder based on level of peer social avoidance. *J Autism Dev Disord* (2001) **31**(3):343–9. doi:10.1023/A:1010703521704
52. Klintwall L, Eikeseth S. Number and controllability of reinforcers as predictors of individual outcome for children with autism receiving early and intensive behavioral intervention: a preliminary study. *Res Autism Spectr Disord* (2012) **6**:493–9. doi:10.1016/j.rasd.2011.07.009

53. Ben-Itzchak E, Zachor DA. Who benefits from early intervention in autism spectrum disorders? *Res Autism Spectr Disord* (2011) **5**:345–50. doi:10.1016/j.rasd.2010.04.018
54. Turner LM, Stone WL. Variability in outcome for children with an ASD diagnosis at age 2. *J Child Psychol Psychiatry* (2007) **48**(8):793–802. doi:10.1111/j.1469-7610.2007.01744.x
55. Osborne L, McHugh L, Saunders J, Reed P. Parenting stress reduces the effectiveness of early teaching interventions for autistic spectrum disorders. *J Autism Dev Disord* (2008) **38**:1092–103. doi:10.1007/s10803-007-0497-7
56. Rickards AL, Walstab JE, Wright-Rossi RA, Simpson J, Reddihough DS. One-year follow-up of the outcome of a randomized controlled trial of a home-based intervention program for children with autism and developmental delay and their families. *Child Care Health Dev* (2009) **35**:593–602. doi:10.1111/j.1365-2214.2009.00953.x
57. Kazdin AE. Mediators and mechanisms of change in psychotherapy research. *Annu Rev Clin Psychol* (2007) **3**:1–27. doi:10.1146/annurev.clinpsy.3.022806.091432
58. Lord C, Wagner A, Rogers S, Szatmari P, Aman M, Charman T. Challenges in evaluating psychosocial interventions for autistic spectrum disorders. *J Autism Dev Disord* (2005) **35**(6):695–708. doi:10.1007/s10803-005-0017-6
59. Yoder P, Compton D. Identifying predictors of treatment response. *Ment Retard Dev Disabil Res Rev* (2004) **10**(3):162–8. doi:10.1002/mrdd.20013
60. Trembath D, Vivanti G. Problematic but predictive: individual differences in children with autism spectrum disorders. *Int J Speech Lang Pathol* (2014) **16**:57–60. doi:10.3109/17549507.2013.859300
61. Magiati I, Tay X, Howlin P. Cognitive, language, social and behavioural outcomes in adults with autism spectrum disorders: a systematic review of longitudinal follow-up studies in adulthood. *Clin Psychol Rev* (2014) **34**(1):73–86. doi:10.1016/j.cpr.2013.11.002
62. Camarata S. Validity of early identification and early intervention in autism spectrum disorders: future directions. *Int J Speech Lang Pathol* (2014) **16**:61–9. doi:10.3109/17549507.2013.864708
63. Zachor DA, Curatolo P. Recommendations for early diagnosis and intervention in autism spectrum disorders: an Italian–Israeli consensus conference. *Eur J Paediatr Neurol* (2014) **18**(2):107–18. doi:10.1016/j.ejpn.2013.09.002
64. Dawson G, Rogers S, Munson J, Smith M, Winter J, Greenson J, et al. Randomized, controlled trial of an intervention for toddlers with autism: the early start Denver model. *Pediatrics* (2010) **125**(1):e17–23. doi:10.1542/peds.2009-0958
65. Dykens EM, Lense M. Intellectual disabilities and autism spectrum disorder: a cautionary note. In: Amaral D, Dawson G, Geschwind D, editors. *Autism Spectrum Disorders.* New York: Oxford University Press (2011). p. 261–9.
66. Gillberg C. Perspective article: autism as a medical disorder. In: Amaral DG, Dawson G, Geschwind DH, editors. *Autism Spectrum Disorders.* New York: Oxford University Press (2011). p. 611–31.
67. Dover CJ, LeCouter A. How to diagnose autism. *Arch Dis Child* (2007) **92**:540–5. doi:10.1136/adc.2005.086280
68. Matson J, Jang J. The most commonly reported behavior analytic methods in early intensive autism treatments. *Rev J Autism Dev Disord* (2014) **1**:80–6. doi:10.1007/s40489-013-0005-2
69. Cipriani A, Geddes JR. Randomised controlled trials. In: Stolerman I, editor. *Encyclopedia of Psychopharmacology.* Heidelberg: Springer-Verlag (2010). p. 1112–9.
70. Vivanti G, Dissanayake C, Zierhut C, Rogers SJ. Brief report: predictors of outcomes in the early start Denver model delivered in a group setting. *J Autism Dev Disord* (2012) **43**:1717–24. doi:10.1007/s10803-012-1705-7
71. Charman T, Taylor E, Drew A, Cockerill H, Brown JA, Baird G. Outcome at 7 years of children diagnosed with autism at age 2: predictive validity of assessments conducted at 2 and 3 years of age and pattern of symptom change over time. *J Child Psychol Psychiatry* (2005) **46**:500–13. doi:10.1111/j.1469-7610.2004.00377.x
72. Karst JS, Van Hecke AV. Parent and family impact of autism spectrum disorders: a review and proposed model for intervention evaluation. *Clin Child Fam Psychol Rev* (2012) **15**:247–77. doi:10.1007/s10567-012-0119-6
73. Singer GHS. Meta-analysis of comparative studies of depression in mothers of children with and without developmental disabilities. *Am J Ment Retard* (2006) **11**:155–69. doi:10.1352/0895-8017(2006)111[155:MOCSOD]2.0.CO;2
74. Kazdin AE, Mazurick JL. Dropping out of child psychotherapy: distinguishing early and late dropouts over the course of treatment. *J Consult Clin Psychol* (1994) **62**:1069–74. doi:10.1037/0022-006X.62.5.1069
75. Webster-Stratton C. Early intervention with videotape modeling: programs for families of young children with oppositional defiant disorder or conduct disorder. In: Hibbs ED, Jensen PS, editors. *Psychosocial Treatment Research of Child and Adolescent Disorders.* Washington, D.C: APA (1996). p. 435–74.
76. Werba BE, Eyberg SM, Boggs SR, Algina J. Predicting outcome in parent-child interaction therapy: success and attrition. *Behav Modif* (2006) **30**:618–46. doi:10.1177/0145445504272977
77. Yoder PJ, Warren SF. Maternal responsivity predicts the prelinguistic communication intervention that facilitates generalized intentional communication. *J Speech Lang Hear Res* (1998) **41**(5):1207–19.
78. Schreibman L, Koegel RL. Fostering self-management: parent-delivered pivotal response training for children with autistic disorder. In: Hibbs ED, Jensen PS, editors. *Psychosocial Treatment for Child and Adolescent Disorders: Empirically Based Strategies for Clinical Practice.* Washington, DC: American Psychological Association (1996). p. 525–52.
79. Shine R, Perry A. Brief report: the relationship between parental stress and intervention outcome of children with autism. *J Dev Disabil* (2010) **16**(2):64–6. doi:10.1007/s10803-007-0497-7
80. Scott S. Outcomes of treatment. In: Remschmidt H, Belfer M, Goodyer I, editors. *Facilitating Pathways.* Berlin: Springer (2004). p. 222–31.
81. Rogers SJ, Dawson G. *Early Start Denver Model for Young Children with Autism: Promoting Language, Learning, and Engagement.* New York: Guilford Press (2010).
82. Mesibov GBV, Schopler E. *The TEACCH Approach to Autism Spectrum Disorders.* New York: Kluwer Academic/Plenum Publishers (2005).
83. Dawson G, Bernier R. Social brain circuitry in autism. In: Coch D, Dawson G, Fischer K, editors. *Human Behavior and the Developing Brain.* New York: Guilford Press (2007). p. 28–55.
84. van Oers B. *Developmental Education for Young Children. Concept, Practice, and Implementation. International Perspectives on Early Childhood Education and Development 7.* Dordrecht: Springer (2012). p. 13–27.
85. de Haan D. Learning to communicate in young children's classrooms. In: van Oers B, editor. *Developmental Education for Young Children: Concept, Practice, Implementation.* New York: Springer (2012). p. 67–86.
86. Hart KI, Fujiki M, Brinton B, Hart CH. The relationship between social behaviour and severity of language impairment journal of speech. *Lang Hear Res* (2004) **47**(3):647. doi:10.1044/1092-4388(2004/050)
87. Bruner J. The ontogenesis of speech acts. *J Child Lang* (1975) **2**:1–19. doi:10.1017/S0305000900000866
88. Mundy P. Annotation: the neural basis of social impairments in autism: the role of the dorsal medial-frontal cortex and anterior cingulated system. *J Child Psychol Psychiatry* (2003) **44**:793–809. doi:10.1111/1469-7610.00165
89. Bandura A. *Social Learning Theory.* New York: General Learning Press (1977).
90. Csibra G, Gergely G. 'Obsessed with goals': functions and mechanisms of teleological interpretation of actions in humans. *Acta Psychol (Amst)* (2007) **124**(1):60–78. doi:10.1016/j.actpsy.2006.09.007
91. Tomasello M. *The Cultural Origins of Human Cognition.* Cambridge, MA: Harvard University Press (1999).
92. Young GS, Rogers SJ, Hutman T, Rozga A, Sigman M, Ozonoff S. Imitation from 12 to 24 months in autism and typical development: a longitudinal Rasch analysis. *Dev Psychol* (2011) **47**(6):1565–78. doi:10.1037/a0025418
93. Hernik M, Csibra G. Functional understanding facilitates learning about tools in human children. *Curr Opin Neurobiol* (2009) **19**(1):34–8. doi:10.1016/j.conb.2009.05.003
94. Zwaigenbaum L. Screening, risk, and early identification of autism spectrum disorders. In: Amaral D, Geschwind D, Dawson G, editors. *Autism Spectrum Disorders.* New York: Oxford University Press (2011). p. 75–85.
95. Poon KK, Watson LR, Baranek GT, Poe MD. To what extent do joint attention, imitation, and object play behaviors in infancy predict later communication and intellectual functioning in ASD? *J Autism Dev Disord* (2012) **42**(6):1064–74. doi:10.1007/s10803-011-1349-z
96. Watt N, Wetherby AM, Barber A, Morgan L. Repetitive and stereotyped behaviors in children with autism spectrum disorders in the second year of life. *J Autism Dev Disord* (2008) **38**(8):1518–33. doi:10.1007/s10803-007-0532-8

97. Bopp KD, Mirenda P, Zumbo BD. Behavior predictors of language development over 2 years in children with autism spectrum disorders. *J Speech Lang Hear Res* (2009) **52**(5):1106–20. doi:10.1044/1092-4388(2009/07-0262)
98. Eikeseth S, Klintwall L, Jahr E, Karlsson P. Outcome for children with autism receiving early and intensive behavioral intervention in mainstream preschool and kindergarten settings. *Res Autism Spectr Disord* (2012) **6**(2):829–35. doi:10.1007/s10803-011-1234-9
99. Levy S, Kim A, Olive M. Interventions for young children with autism: a synthesis of the literature. *Focus Autism Other Dev Disabl* (2006) **21**(1):55–62. doi:10.1177/10883576060210010701
100. Wallace KS, Rogers SJ. Intervening in infancy: implications for autism spectrum disorders. *J Child Psychol Psychiatry* (2010) **51**(12):1300–20. doi:10.1111/j.1469-7610.2010.02308.x
101. Baker B, Blacher J, Crnic K, Edelbrock C. Behavior problems and parenting stress in families of three-year-old children with and without developmental delays. *Am J Ment Retard* (2002) **107**(6):433–44. doi:10.1046/j.1365-2788.2003.00484.x
102. McStay RL, Dissanayake C, Scheeren A, Koot HM, Begeer S. Parenting stress and autism: the role of age, autism severity, quality of life and problem behaviour of children and adolescents with autism. *Autism* (2013). doi:10.1177/1362361313485163
103. Brobst J, Clopton J, Hendrick S. Parenting children with autism spectrum disorders: the couple's relationship. *Focus Autism Other Dev Disabl* (2009) **24**(1):38–49. doi:10.1177/1088357608323699
104. Giallo R, Wood C, Jellett R, Porter R. Fatigue, wellbeing and parental self-efficacy in mothers of children with an autism spectrum disorder. *Autism* (2013) **17**(4):465–80. doi:10.1177/1362361311416830
105. Benson P. Network characteristics, perceived social support, and psychological distress in mothers of children with autism spectrum disorder. *Paper Presented at the Annual Meeting of the American Sociological Association Annual Meeting.* Denver, CO: Colorado Convention Centre and Hyatt Regency (2012).
106. Minnes P, McShane J, Forkes S, Green S, Clement B, Card L. Coping resources of parents of developmentally handicapped children living in rural communities. Australia and New Zealand. *J Dev Disabil* (1989) **15**:109–18.
107. Marion SA, Schechter MT. Risk and prognosis. In: Troidl H, Spitzer W, McPeek B, Mulder D, McKneally M, Wechsler A, et al., editors. *Principles and Practice of Research.* New York: Springer (1991). p. 169–80.
108. Deater-Deckard K, Dodge KA, Bates JE, Pettit GS. Multiple risk factors in the development of externalizing behavior problems: group and individual differences. *Dev Psychopathol* (1998) **10**(3):469–93. doi:10.1017/S0954579498001709
109. Trentacosta CJ, Hyde LW, Goodlett BD, Shaw DS. Longitudinal prediction of disruptive behavior disorders in adolescent males from multiple risk domains. *Child Psychiatry Hum Dev* (2013) **44**(4):561–72. doi:10.1007/s10578-012-0349-3
110. Heimann H, Gaertner HJ. Research methodology in clinical trials of psychotropic drugs. In: Hoffmeister F, Stille G, editors. *Handbook of Experimental Pharmacology.* Berlin: Springer (1982). p. 391–407.
111. Begg C, Cho M, Eastwood S, Horton R, Moher D, Olkin I, et al. Improving the quality of reporting of randomised controlled trials. The CONSORT statement. *J Am Med Assoc* (1996) **276**:637–9. doi:10.1001/jama.1996.03540080059030
112. Fonagy P. Psychotherapy research: do we know what works for whom? *Br J Psychiatry* (2010) **197**(2):83–5. doi:10.1192/bjp.bp.110.079657
113. National Institute of Mental Health. *National Institutes of Mental Health Strategic Plan.* (2010). Available from: http://www.nimh.nih.gov/about/strategic-planning-reports/index.shtml
114. Bota RG, Munro S, Nguyen C, Preda A. Course of schizophrenia: what has been learned from longitudinal studies? In: Ritsner M, editor. *Handbook of Schizophrenia Spectrum Disorders.* (Vol. II). New York: Springer (2011). p. 281–300.
115. Treuer T, Tohen M. Predicting the course and outcome of bipolar disorder: a review. *Eur Psychiatry* (2010) **25**(6):328–33. doi:10.1016/j.eurpsy.2009.11.012
116. Lahey BB, Loeber R, Hart EL, Frick PJ, Applegate B, Zhang Q, et al. Four-year longitudinal study of conduct disorder in boys: patterns and predictors of persistence. *J Abnorm Psychol* (1995) **104**(1):83. doi:10.1037/0021-843X.104.1.83
117. Gabriels RL, Hill DE, Pierce RA, Rogers SJ, Wehner B. Predictors of treatment outcome in young children with autism: a retrospective study. *Autism* (2001) **5**(4):407–29. doi:10.1177/1362361301005004006
118. Eaves LC, Ho HH. The very early identification of autism: outcome to age 2–5. *J Autism Dev Disord* (2004) **34**(4):367–78. doi:10.1023/B:JADD.0000037414.33270.a8
119. Fernell E, Eriksson MA, Gillberg C. Early diagnosis of autism and impact on prognosis: a narrative review. *Clin Epidemiol* (2013) **5**:33. doi:10.2147/CLEP.S41714
120. Harrop C, McConachie H, Emsley R, Leadbitter K, Green J, PACT Consortium. Restricted and repetitive behaviors in autism spectrum disorders and typical development. *J Autism Dev Disord* (2014) **44**(5):1207–19. doi:10.1007/s10803-013-1986-5.

# 20

# Reducing auditory hypersensitivities in autistic spectrum disorder: preliminary findings evaluating the listening project protocol

**Stephen W. Porges[1]*, Olga V. Bazhenova[2], Elgiz Bal[2], Nancy Carlson[3], Yevgeniya Sorokin[2], Keri J. Heilman[1], Edwin H. Cook[2] and Gregory F. Lewis[1]**

[1] *Department of Psychiatry, University of North Carolina at Chapel Hill, Chapel Hill, NC, USA*
[2] *Department of Psychiatry, Institute for Juvenile Research, University of Illinois at Chicago, Chicago, IL, USA*
[3] *Department of Occupational Therapy, Elizabethtown College, Elizabethtown, PA, USA*

**Edited by:**
*Roberto Canitano, University Hospital of Siena, Italy*

**Reviewed by:**
*Hanna E. Stevens, Yale University School of Medicine, USA*
*Roberto Canitano, University Hospital of Siena, Italy*

***Correspondence:**
*Stephen W. Porges, Department of Psychiatry, University of North Carolina, 387 Medical School Wing D, Campus Box 7160, Chapel Hill, NC 27599-7160, USA*
*e-mail: stephen_porges@med.unc.edu*

Auditory hypersensitivities are a common feature of autism spectrum disorder (ASD). In the present study, the effectiveness of a novel intervention, the listening project protocol (LPP), was evaluated in two trials conducted with children diagnosed with ASD. LPP was developed to reduce auditory hypersensitivities. LPP is based on a theoretical "neural exercise" model that uses computer altered acoustic stimulation to recruit the neural regulation of middle ear muscles. Features of the intervention stimuli were informed by basic research in speech and hearing sciences that has identified the specific acoustic frequencies necessary to understand speech, which must pass through middle ear structures before being processed by other components of the auditory system. LPP was hypothesized to reduce auditory hypersensitivities by increasing the neural tone to the middle ear muscles to functionally dampen competing sounds in frequencies lower than human speech. The trials demonstrated that LPP, when contrasted to control conditions, selectively reduced auditory hypersensitivities. These findings are consistent with the polyvagal theory, which emphasizes the role of the middle ear muscles in social communication.

**Keywords: autism, auditory hypersensitivities, social engagement behaviors, listening, polyvagal theory**

## INTRODUCTION

Frequently accompanying a diagnosis of autism spectrum disorder (ASD) are speech and language delays, difficulties in extracting human voice from background sounds, auditory hypersensitivities, and a general compromise in social communication skills (1–8). In contrast to the prevalent reports of auditory processing deficits, most individuals with ASD, even those with noticeable auditory perceptual disorders, have normal hearing when tested on a standard audiogram (9).

Several mechanisms have been proposed as contributing to frequently reported deficits in auditory processing including damage or dysfunction to peripheral structures (i.e., middle ear and inner ear), neural pathways (e.g., auditory nerve), and central structures (e.g., brainstem nuclei and cortical areas) (e.g., Ref. (10–17)). A review (18) suggests that although atypical auditory processing and both hypo- and hyper-reactivity to auditory signals are frequently observed in autism, these atypical reactions cannot reliably be attributed to specific neural pathways. Thus, subjective methods remain the sole indicators of auditory hypersensitivities (19).

### PHYSIOLOGY OF THE MIDDLE EAR

Borg and Counter (20) described a role of middle ear muscles in facilitating the extraction of human speech by dampening the transmission of low frequency noise from the external environment to the inner ear. The Borg and Counter model suggests that atypical neural regulation of middle ear muscles may contribute to the frequently observed auditory hypersensitivities and auditory processing deficits in ASD. Deconstructing the path through which sound is processed illustrates the role middle ear structures have in auditory processing and how atypical neural regulation of the middle ear muscles may contribute to auditory hypersensitivities and atypical auditory processing.

Sound enters the outer ear and travels through the external auditory canal to the eardrum where it is transduced by the structures of the middle ear (i.e., small bones comprising the ossicular chain), which connects the eardrum with the cochlea. The rigidity of the ossicular chain determines the stiffness of the eardrum. The middle ear muscles, via cranial nerves, regulate the position of the ossicles and stiffen or loosen the eardrum. When the eardrum is "tightened" higher frequencies are absorbed and transmitted to the inner ear and the energy of lower frequencies is attenuated (i.e., reflected) before being encoded by the inner ear (cochlea) and transmitted via the auditory nerve (cranial nerve VIII) to the cortex. Complementing the ascending pathways are descending pathways that regulate the middle ear muscles, which functionally determine the energy (i.e., attenuate, pass, or amplify) of specific frequencies that reach the inner ear. The features describing the transformation of sound intensity from outer to inner ear defines the middle ear transfer function. If the acoustic information in the frequency band associated with speech is distorted by an atypical middle ear transfer function, the information being coded by the inner ear and subsequently being transmitted to the cortex will not contain sufficient information to enable accurate detection of speech sounds. In addition, there are descending pathways that regulate the hair cells in the cochlea to "fine tune" auditory perception, which is especially important in the development of language skills. If the acoustic information related to human speech that reaches the cortex via ascending pathways is distorted, then the descending pathways to the cochlea may also be atypical and will further distort the individual's ability to process speech and to produce language.

As proposed by Borg and Counter (20), atypical central regulation of peripheral middle ear structures may pass low frequency sounds that dominate the acoustic spectrum in our mechanized society (e.g., ventilation systems, traffic, airplanes, vacuum cleaners, and other appliances) resulting in both a hypersensitivity to sounds and distorting or "masking" the frequency components associated with human speech reaching the brain. This emphasis on the functional role of the middle ear muscles in the dampening of background noise and the extraction of voice is based on a literature documenting two points: (1) the neural regulation of the middle ear muscles modulates the transfer function of the middle ear (21, 22) and (2) the transfer function of the middle ear determines the acoustic energy from low frequencies that reach the inner ear (23). Thus, an atypical middle ear transfer function would be a potentially parsimonious explanation of both the auditory hypersensitivities and the difficulties in auditory processing frequently associated with autism.

### DESIGNING THE LISTENING PROJECT PROTOCOL

The listening project protocol (LPP) is a theoretical departure from the disciplines frequently involved in the treatment of auditory processing disorders, which emphasize the role of central structures in the processing of speech (see Ref. (18) for a review). LPP was theoretically designed to reduce auditory hypersensitivities by recruiting the anti-masking functions of the middle ear muscles to optimize the transfer function of the middle ear for the processing of human speech. LPP is based on an "exercise" model that uses computer altered acoustic stimulation to modulate the frequency band passed to the participant. The frequency characteristics of the acoustic stimulation were theoretically selected based on the documented frequency band and weights associated with the index of articulation (24) and speech intelligibility index (25). These indices emphasize the relative importance of specific frequencies in conveying the information embedded in human speech. During normal listening to human speech, via descending central mechanisms, the middle ear muscles contract and stiffen the ossicular chain. This process functionally removes most of the "masking" low frequency background sounds from the acoustic environment and allows human voice to be more effectively processed by higher brain structures. Modulation of the acoustic energy within the frequencies of human voice, similar to exaggerated vocal prosody, is hypothesized to recruit and modulate the neural regulation of the middle ear muscles and to functionally reduce auditory hypersensitivities (see Ref. (23)).

The features of the intervention including the context, the duration of stimulation, and frequency band selected were theoretically determined and based on the following neurophysiological principles: (a) the transfer function of the middle ear serves as an anti-masking mechanism to dampen low frequency sounds and to facilitate extraction of human voice from background sounds (20), (b) acoustic energy is readily transmitted across middle ear structures, regardless of the neural tone to the middle ear muscles, at a resonance frequency in children between 800 and 1200 Hz (26), (c) middle ear muscles are primarily composed of fast-twitch muscles and are vulnerable to rapid fatigue (27), and (d) the phylogenetic convergence in mammals of a brainstem area involved in the neural regulation of striated muscles of the face and head including the middle ear muscles (see (23, 28, 29)). Principles (a) and (b) were used to design the acoustic stimuli, principle (c) informed decisions related to the duration of each session, and principle (d) provided the basis for the social support provided during the intervention (i.e., the neural regulation of the middle ear muscles is optimized in a "safe" context).

LPP applies computer altered vocal music (i.e., filtered music) designed to exaggerate the features of human prosody and hypothetically to exercise the neural regulation of the middle ear muscles. By modulating the frequency band associated with human vocalizations, it was hypothesized that the ascending pathways would be providing dynamically changing information that would feedback on the descending pathways regulating the middle ear muscles. Metaphorically, the procedure could be conceptualized as a "treadmill" exercise for the middle ear muscles during which the demands to "listen" and process the acoustic features of the intervention stimuli were dynamically changing. To test the primary hypothesis that the filtered music condition would reduce hearing sensitivities in children with ASD, two trials were conducted. Trial I contrasted a filtered music group to a headphones only group and Trial II contrasted a filtered music group to an unfiltered music group.

The intervention consisted of five daily sessions of approximately 45 min during which the participant passively listened to the acoustic stimulation through headphones in a quiet room, while researchers provided social support to insure that the participants remained calm. The frequency bands were temporally modulated within each session and, independent of amplitude, the band of frequencies that were modulated progressively increased across the five sessions. Theoretically, the changing frequency bands were presented to increase the neural regulation of middle ear structures to dampen the perception of background low frequency sounds and to potentiate the extraction of human voice. Although middle ear muscle regulation could not be assessed, the Borg and Counter (20) model provided the scientific basis to hypothesize that the exercises embedded in LPP would reduce auditory hypersensitivities.

## METHODS: TRIAL I AND TRIAL II

### PARTICIPANTS

Potential participants contacted the laboratory for initial inclusion screening. Participants were informed about the research project by clinicians, parents who previously participated in our research program, and via professional presentations and/or newsletters. Individuals with a suspected diagnosis of ASD, who did not have a history of seizures, were scheduled for a diagnostic assessment that consisted of the autism diagnostic interview-revised (ADI-R) (30). The ADI-R provides a diagnostic algorithm consistent with the Diagnostic and Statistical Manual of Mental Disorders, fourth edition (DSM-IV) (31) and International Classification of Diseases, tenth edition (ICD-10) (32). Informed consent was obtained from parents. The Institutional Review Boards at the University of Maryland, the University of Illinois at Chicago, and the University of North Carolina approved the project. The protocols are excluded from the requirement to be registered (e.g., ClinicalTrials.gov), since enrollment was initiated before January 1, 2001 and data collection was completed before December 26, 2007.

Parents of 178 children contacted the laboratory to participate in the research. Based on the ADI-R criteria, 146 children met the full criteria of autism. Of the children, who did not meet full criteria, 29 exceeded the ADI-R cut off on at least the qualitative impairments in reciprocal social interaction and/or communication scales. Three children, who did not meet the cut off on either the qualitative impairments in reciprocal social interaction and/or communication scales, were excluded from participating in the research.

Based on presentation at the laboratory the first 73 children were assigned to Trial I. In Trial I, data from nine children (two in the filtered music and seven in the headphone only groups) were lost due to technical problems. In Trial I, questionnaire data were scored for 36 children in the filtered music group and 28 children in the headphones only group. Following the completion of Trial I, 102 children, who had not participated in Trial I, were enrolled in Trial II. In Trial II, due to scheduling difficulties, families of six children withdrew before participating in the trial and one family withdrew after the second day of the intervention. In Trial II, data from one child who was diagnosed with Fragile X were excluded from the data analyses. In addition, data from 12 children in the filtered music group were lost due to parents not returning the questionnaires, or returning the questionnaires late, or health issues. Data are not available for documenting the specific causes for lack of compliance. Questionnaire data in Trial II were available from 50 participants in the filtered music group and 32 participants in the unfiltered music group. Descriptive statistics of demographic features of the subjects from Trial I and Trial II with questionnaire data are reported in **Table 1**.

Trial I and Trial II included 86 participants in the filtered music condition, 32 participants in the unfiltered music condition, and 28 participants in the headphones only condition (see **Table 1**). Although mental age of the participants was not formally assessed, all participants had either speech (at least five words apart from "mama" and "dada," used spontaneously and meaningfully) or followed verbal instructions. Approximately 80% of the participants were Caucasian and the remaining 20% included children from African–American, Latino, and Asian parents.

## EXPERIMENTAL DESIGN

The intervention research was conducted as two sequential randomized controlled trials with parallel control groups. All participants were randomly assigned sequentially by presentation at the laboratory to either the filtered music group or a control condition group. No clinical or behavioral feature was used to determine group assignment. Trial I participants were randomly assigned to either a filtered music or a headphones only group, which consisted of children wearing headphones without music.

Trial I was initiated to evaluate whether the intervention had an effect beyond the contextual variables of supportive play and low intensity social interactions that characterized the experimental environment for both groups. Since data analyses of parent questionnaires indicated a treatment effect on auditory hypersensitivities, Trial II was conducted to evaluate whether the filtering of the music uniquely determined intervention effects. Trial II participants were randomly assigned to either a filtered music group or an unfiltered music group. To insure a sample size sufficient to test hypotheses related to auditory hypersensitivities, twice as many participants were assigned to the filtered music group.

Parents were not informed about their child's group assignment until the follow-up sessions were completed. Nor were parents informed about the features of the intervention (i.e., filtered music) or the control condition within each trial (i.e., headphones only in Trial I and unfiltered music in Trial II). Circumaural headphones were used, since they provide excellent sound quality, are comfortable to wear, and have excellent external noise rejection. The features of the headphone in combination with low intensity auditory stimuli precluded the parents from detecting whether their child was receiving the filtered music condition or a control condition. Based on our interactions with parents, it appeared that parents were not informed about the group assignment of their children. After the completion of the follow-up assessment sessions, the children in the unfiltered and the headphones only

**Table 1 | Demographic information for subjects with complete data by group assignment and sex.**

| | Trial I | | Trial II | |
|---|---|---|---|---|
| | **Filtered music Mean age (SD)[b]** | **Headphones only condition Mean age (SD)[b]** | **Filtered music Mean age (SD)[b]** | **Unfiltered music Mean age (SD)[b]** |
| **Met at least partial criteria on ADI-R[a]** | | | | |
| Male | 58.24 (10.14), $n=25$ | 49.46 (10.96), $n=23$ | 54.89 (14.83), $n=44$ | 56.20 (9.36), $n=27$ |
| Female[c] | 48.67 (11.99), $n=11$ | 61.00 (7.91), $n=5$ | 44 (20.66), $n=6$ | 60.33 (9.29), $n=5$ |
| **Total** | 55.37 (11.42), $n=36$ | 52.67 (11.30), $n=28$ | 53.33 (15.95), $n=50$ | 56.74 (9.25), $n=32$ |

[a] *Exceeded the ADI-R cut off on at least the qualitative impairments in reciprocal social interaction and/or communication scales.*

[b] *Mean age and standard deviation in months.*

[c] *Females in Trial I were significantly older in the headphone only group.*

conditions were given the opportunity to receive the filtered music. Since knowing group assignment might bias parental perceptions of the child's behavior, data from the children, who received the filtered music after participating in either the headphones only or unfiltered music conditions, were not included in the data analyses.

One week following the intervention, parent reports were obtained for all participants in both trials. None of the children who participated in Trial I participated in Trial II. In addition to the parent questionnaire, semi-structured play-based behavioral assessment sessions were conducted with the children and videotaped before and after the intervention.

## CONDITIONS AND PROCEDURE

Each condition (i.e., the filtered music, unfiltered music, and headphones only conditions) consisted of approximately 45 min sessions conducted during five-consecutive days. During the intervention, regardless of group assignment, each child wore headphones in the same laboratory environment. The same vocal music selections were used for both the filtered music and the unfiltered music conditions. In the filtered music condition, the vocal music was computer processed based on a proprietary algorithm developed to remove low and high frequencies and to modulate the width of the frequency band associated with human voice. The intervention stimuli were stored on compact discs and played via high quality compact disc player (Marantz CC-4000) to high quality over the ear headphones (Beyerdynamic DT831). Maximum loudness was calibrated at a peak of 75 dBC before the intervention started. During the headphones only condition, no auditory stimulation was provided through the headphones, although the context was identical to the filtered music and unfiltered music conditions. The low volume of the intervention stimuli and the use of over the ear headphones insured that the intervention stimuli could not be distinguished from the ambient background sounds in the test room by the parents.

The sessions were conducted in a research room with toys (e.g., books, doll house and accessories, parking garage and cars, pretend kitchen and accessories, stuffed animals, coloring books, and crayons). During the intervention, the children were able to freely play with the toys. One experimenter stayed in the room during the intervention to assist the child with the headphones when needed. Parents were also allowed to be in the room with their child. The experimenter and the parents were instructed to be quiet and to interact with the child only to maintain and to support a calm behavioral state. Due to the nature of the study (e.g., checking the integrity of the headphones), the experimenter who conducted the intervention session was not always blind to the child's group assignment. In Trial I, since the headphones only group received headphones without sound, the experimenter was frequently aware of the child's group assignment. However, since only the experimenter adjusted the headphones, the parents remained blind. In Trial II, since acoustic stimulation was being presented to both groups, the experimenter and the parent were unaware of the child's group assignment. Accordingly, to avoid the possibility of rating bias, the experimenter who conducted the intervention sessions did not participate in the play-based assessments during which sharing behaviors were coded.

## BEHAVIORAL ASSESSMENT

### *Parent questionnaire*

Following the intervention and the play-based assessments, parents were given a structured questionnaire developed in our laboratory, targeting specific categories of their child's developmental and behavioral problems including auditory hypersensitivities. The parents of children in all groups were instructed to complete and to return the questionnaire to the laboratory in a week. The questionnaire focused on whether the child had difficulties in a specific behavioral area and whether there were any changes in this area following participation in the research. For each behavioral category, parents were required to document changes, if any, following the intervention by providing specific examples of observed new behaviors. The structured questionnaire focused on the behavioral domains listed in **Table 2**.

**Table 2 | Behavioral domains and explanations for the structured parent questionnaire.**

| | Definitions |
|---|---|
| Hearing sensitivity | Exaggerated negative responses (e.g., crying or placing hands over the ears) to common noises (e.g., vacuum cleaner, garbage disposal, baby crying, and air conditioning) |
| Spontaneous speech | Non-prompted use of words and sentences to communicate thoughts and ideas |
| Receptive speech | Ability to understand instructions and phrases |
| Spontaneity | Non-prompted behaviors initiated by the child |
| Behavioral organization | Ability to occupy oneself (when left alone) in a productive and non-stereotypical way |
| Emotional control | Ability to calm quickly when upset, to respond to unexpected changes without getting upset, and to tolerate objections and contradictions of other people |
| Affection | Behaviors reflective of warm emotional state expressed by the child toward familiar people (e.g., hugging, kissing, and saying "I love you" to the parent) |
| Listening | Ability to focus on human speech without visual or contextual cues, to understand spoken words, and to follow verbal requests |
| Eye contact | Making and maintaining eye contact during social interactions |
| Relatedness | Non-prompted social behaviors that reflect understanding of a joint partnership in interactions and sharing the same goals during social interactions (e.g., looking at a partner, showing toys, sharing an idea or a thought, and directing emotions to the partner) |

#### *Questionnaire scoring*

Each of the 10 items representing the behavioral domains described in **Table 2** was scored as a 1, 0, or -1. A score of 1 was assigned if the parents indicated that their child had a problem in the area of interest before the participation in the project and provided an example of a new behavior that could be considered as an improvement in this area. An item received a score of 0 if the parents indicated that their child had a problem in the area of interest, but provided no example of a change. Non-specific parental responses (e.g., "somewhat better" and "a lot better") that were not supported by concrete examples of the new behaviors also were conservatively scored as 0. An item received a score of -1 if the parent indicated that the behavior became worse after participating in the research and provided an example of the new worsened behavior. If the parent did not indicate a problem in the area of interest, the item did not receive a score. Each questionnaire was scored by two researchers, at least one of whom was blind to the child's group assignment. Only when both scorers agreed that the example provided by the parent constituted a new and relevant behavior, a score of 1 was given. Scores of -1 were rare and did not occur on any of the behaviors coded in Trial I and only three times in Trial II. Thus, separate analyses for scores of -1s were not conducted.

#### *Social interaction coding scale*

Prior to and following their participation in the intervention project, all children participated in a 10-min semi-structured play-based observational assessment of social engagement skills with the social interaction coding scale (SICS) (33). The SICS provides information regarding the child's social engagement activity. Similar to the autism diagnostic observational scale (ADOS) (34) and early social communication coding scales (ESCS) (35), the SICS requires a semi-structured presentation of standard tasks. Each task provides an opportunity for social engagement by requiring the child to engage in a joint activity. In the current study, the number of spontaneous sharing behaviors was quantified.

#### *Coding social interaction coding scale*

The frequency of sharing behaviors was coded from videotapes by trained coders. Coders obtained reliability with each other on training tapes before using the scale for research (i.e., 80% agreement on individual items, mean kappa > 0.60 for three consecutive joint scoring). Each tape was coded by two trained coders independently and compared for agreement. At least one of the coders was not aware of the participant's group assignment when coding. Consensus was used to establish the final code. If raters disagreed on the same item, the code of the unbiased coder was recorded. If coders were uncertain about the final code, the opinion of the third trained coder was requested and the code that received the consensus of at least two coders was recorded. If all three coders disagreed on the final code, the behavior was not coded.

### DATA ANALYSES

Analyses of variance and non-parametric $\chi^2$ analyses were used to evaluate group differences within each trial on each of the behavioral domains. Since both analysis strategies identified the same group differences within each trial, only the analyses of variance are presented. A Bonferroni correction adjusted significance levels for multiple comparisons.

## RESULTS

### QUESTIONNAIRE DATA

#### *Global evaluation of problems*

Confirming the effectiveness of the randomization procedures, there were no group differences in the representation of the behavioral problems reported via the parental questionnaire within each trial or across trials (see **Table 3**). For example, the representation of hearing hypersensitivities across the four groups across both trials ranged from 43 to 50%. When the number of problem dimensions was summed for each participant, more than 95% of the parents reported that their child had at least one behavioral problem. The percentage of parents reporting multiple behavioral problems decreased as the number of domains increased, with approximately 80% of the parents reporting problems in at least five behavioral domains.

### TRIAL I: GLOBAL AND SPECIFIC EVALUATION OF IMPROVEMENT

To evaluate the effectiveness of the filtered music treatment, group differences were evaluated with analyses of variance for each of the 10 behavioral dimensions included in the questionnaire. As illustrated in **Figure 1**, significant improvements, relative to the headphones only group, were noted in the filtered music group in hearing sensitivity, $F(1,29) = 6.46, p = 0.017$; spontaneous speech, $F(1, 49) = 5.61$, $p = 0.022$; listening, $F(1, 52) = 8.25$, $p = 0.006$;

**Table 3 | Distribution of initial behavioral problems (%) within each trial.**[a]

| | Trial I | | Trial II | |
|---|---|---|---|---|
| | Filtered music (%) | Headphones only group (%) | Filtered music (%) | Unfiltered music (%) |
| Hearing sensitivity | 50 | 43 | 46 | 50 |
| Affect | 44 | 61 | 64 | 59 |
| Eye contact | 75 | 61 | 60 | 63 |
| Behavioral organization | 53 | 57 | 56 | 53 |
| Emotional control | 50 | 43 | 66 | 59 |
| Spontaneous speech | 75 | 82 | 82 | 78 |
| Receptive speech | 72 | 82 | 90 | 81 |
| Listening | 81 | 86 | 74 | 66 |
| Spontaneity | 69 | 71 | 44 | 44 |
| Relatedness | 83 | 82 | 64 | 66 |
| At least 1 problem | 92 | 96 | 98 | 97 |
| At least 2 problems | 92 | 93 | 98 | 94 |
| At least 3 problems | 89 | 89 | 96 | 91 |
| At least 4 problems | 83 | 79 | 94 | 88 |
| At least 5 problems | 81 | 75 | 92 | 78 |

[a]*No significant differences were found among the groups on any behavioral dimension.*

and behavioral organization, $F(1, 34) = 5.39$, $p = 0.027$. The percent of the participants improving, who had a problem within each domain, is presented in **Table 4**. At 1-week post-intervention, analysis of variance confirmed that the filtered music group exhibited significantly more improvements summed across domains than the headphones only group (i.e., 2.36 versus 0.81), $F(1, 62) = 7.76$, $p = 0.007$.

### TRIAL II: GLOBAL AND SPECIFIC EVALUATION OF IMPROVEMENT

Since the relative benefits observed during Trial I could be attributed to listening to music, independent of the computer modulation of the acoustic features, Trial II was conducted contrasting the filtered music condition to the same music in an unfiltered form. The unfiltered music condition was similar to the "structured listening" condition described by Bettison (36). As illustrated in **Figure 2**, significant improvements in the filtered music condition relative to the unfiltered music condition were observed in both hearing sensitivity, $F(1, 28) = 4.53$, $p = 0.040$, and emotional control, $F(1, 49) = 5.84$, $p = 0.019$. The percent of the participants improving, who had a problem within each domain, is presented in **Table 4**. Note that when unfiltered music is used as the control, several of the benefits of filtered music condition observed in Trial I (i.e., spontaneous speech, listening, and behavioral organization) appear to be due to listening to music (i.e., unfiltered music) and not to the algorithm used to filter the music. Consistent with this interpretation, there was no significant difference in the sum of improvements for the filtered music group (1.98) when contrasted with the unfiltered music group (1.53). These data suggest that the unique benefit of the filtered music is a significant reduction in hearing sensitivity.

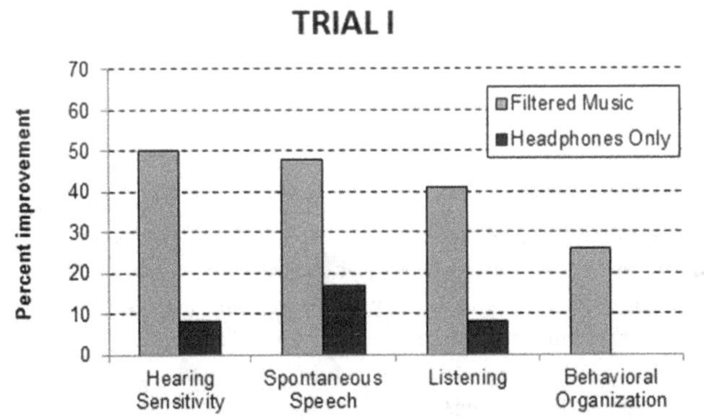


**FIGURE 1 | Behavioral improvements at the 1-week post treatment assessment in Trial I.** The data are reported as the precent of participants with a specific behavioral problem who improved.

### CONTRASTS BETWEEN TRIAL I AND TRIAL II

Analyses of variance confirmed the similarity between the filtered music condition in Trial I and Trial II. The percent of participants improving on each domain was similar for the filtered music groups within Trial I and Trial II (see **Table 4**). Similarly, the number of problem domains was similar for all groups on entry into the protocol (see **Table 3**).

### SHARING BEHAVIORS

Video data from a random subsample of children in the filtered music condition ($n = 61$) were coded. The subsample was partitioned into three groups: children who had no hearing sensitivity at the start of the study ($n = 34$), children who showed improvements on hearing sensitivity following the intervention ($n = 14$), and children who had no improvements on hearing sensitivity following the intervention ($n = 13$). A repeated measures analysis of variance identified a significant group × condition interaction, $F(2, 58) = 4.88$, $p < 0.011$. Consistent with the parental reports, only the subgroup of children with improvement on hearing sensitivity increased the amount of sharing behavior during the 10-min semi-structured play-based protocol. Descriptive statistics are reported in **Table 5**. *Post hoc* Bonferroni adjustment confirmed that only children who were reported to improve on hearing sensitivity increased the amount of sharing behavior during the 10-min

**Table 4 | Percent[a] improving who had a problem within each behavioral domain at the 1-week follow-up.**

| | Trial I | | Trial II | |
|---|---|---|---|---|
| | Filtered music | Headphones only | Filtered music | Unfiltered music |
| Hearing sensitivity | **50[b]**, $n = 18$ | 8, $n = 12$ | **43[c]**, $n = 23$ | 13, $n = 16$ |
| Affect | 19, $n = 16$ | 18, $n = 17$ | 25, $n = 32$ | 21, $n = 19$ |
| Eye contact | 41, $n = 27$ | 24, $n = 17$ | 33, $n = 30$ | 40, $n = 20$ |
| Behavioral organization | **26[b]**, $n = 19$ | 0, $n = 16$ | 29, $n = 28$ | 18, $n = 17$ |
| Emotional control | 17, $n = 18$ | 0, $n = 12$ | **24[c]**, $n = 33$ | 0, $n = 19$ |
| Spontaneous speech | **48[b]**, $n = 27$ | 17, $n = 23$ | 51, $n = 41$ | 44, $n = 25$ |
| Receptive speech | 31, $n = 26$ | 9, $n = 23$ | 9, $n = 45$ | 15, $n = 26$ |
| Listening | **41[b]**, $n = 29$ | 8, $n = 24$ | 30, $n = 37$ | 29, $n = 21$ |
| Spontaneity | 48, $n = 25$ | 20, $n = 20$ | 36, $n = 22$ | 36, $n = 14$ |
| Relatedness | 30, $n = 30$ | 13, $n = 23$ | 34, $n = 32$ | 29, $n = 21$ |

[a] *Defined by the number of individuals who improved divided by the number of individuals with problems (n) within the behavioral domain.*
[b] *Significant improvement relative to headphones only in Trial I.*
[c] *Significant improvement relative to unfiltered music in Trial II.*

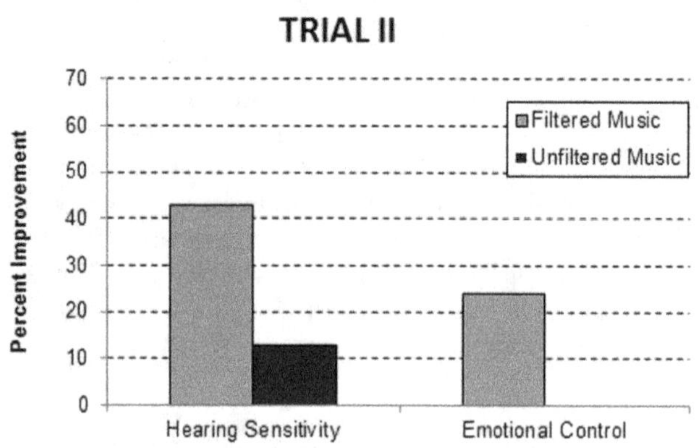


**FIGURE 2 | Behavioral improvements at the 1-week post treatment assessment in Trial II.** The data are reported as the precent of participants with a specific behavioral problem who improved.

**Table 5 | Hearing sensitivity (HS) and total number of shares (*N*, mean, and SD).**

| | *N* | Pre-intervention | | Post-intervention | |
|---|---|---|---|---|---|
| | | Mean | SD | Mean | SD |
| Children who improved on HS | 14 | 5.71 | 7.31 | 9.86 | 10.53 |
| Children who did not improve on HS | 13 | 7.46 | 7.33 | 7.62 | 6.74 |
| Children who had no HS | 34 | 5.82 | 8.50 | 6.32 | 7.97 |

semi-structured play-based protocol following the 5-day program relative to the initial assessment ($p < 0.005$).

### TREATMENT EFFECTS ON PARTICIPANTS WITHOUT HEARING SENSITIVITIES

To investigate the effects of filtered music on the participants without hearing sensitivities, analyses of variance were calculated on each behavioral domain to identify possible behavioral domains that would improve in children without auditory hypersensitivities as a function of the filtered music. These analyses did not identify any specific behavioral domain that would reliably improve in the children without auditory hypersensitivities.

## DISCUSSION

### SUMMARY OF FINDINGS AND OTHER RESEARCH EVALUATING LPP

Two randomized controlled trials were conducted to evaluate the efficacy of LPP on auditory hypersensitivities and social behavior in children with ASD. Data from both trials confirmed that LPP (i.e., filtered music) selectively reduced auditory hypersensitivities. Trial I contrasted filtered music with a headphones only condition. The results of Trial I led to a more stringent Trial II in which filtered music was contrasted with an unfiltered music condition. In both trials, the LPP selectively reduced auditory hypersensitivities. In addition, within the filtered music groups the children with auditory hypersensitivities who improved following LPP significantly increased their spontaneous sharing behaviors. These findings, consistent with the polyvagal theory, support the hypothetical basis for designing the LPP as a neural exercise of pathways involved in regulating behavioral state, listening, looking, and other social engagement behaviors such as spontaneous sharing.

The current findings are consistent with a previous study (37), evaluating LPP with a more diverse sample of ASD children. In the previous study, the effectiveness of LPP was objectively assessed by evaluating auditory processing (assumed to be a function of the transfer function of the middle ear structures) and autonomic state (assumed to mediate behavioral state regulation). The study demonstrated that LPP significantly increased vagal regulation of the heart (i.e., increased amplitude of respiratory sinus arrhythmia) and normalized auditory processing on the filtered words and competing words subtests from the SCAN test for auditory processing disorder (38, 39). Collectively, the data from the current trials and Porges et al. (37) provide convergent preliminary support that LPP enhances function of the polyvagal "social engagement system" manifested in improved auditory processing, reduced auditory hypersensitivities, increased vagal regulation of the heart, and increased spontaneous social behaviors (e.g., sharing).

### CONTRASTS WITH TRADITIONAL AUDITORY INTERVENTION THERAPIES

Since LPP delivers computer altered acoustic stimuli through headphones, it shares some of the features of auditory intervention therapies (i.e., AIT). However, although LPP is a "sound therapy," it is not a traditional clinically available AIT (e.g., Ref. (40, 41)) and differs from these procedures in method and theory. First, LPP is based on the polyvagal theory and reflects a strategic attempt to engage neural regulation of specific structures involved in the social engagement system (28). Second, LPP focuses on auditory hypersensitivities that may be expressed by individuals with and without clinical diagnoses. Third, the effectiveness of LPP can be measured through well defined behavioral and physiological features of the social engagement system. Fourth, LPP was designed with several unique features to engage and to exercise the neural regulation of the middle ear muscles, including an understanding of the transfer function of the middle ear structures and the vulnerability of the fast twitch middle ear muscles to fatigue. Fifth, the duration of LPP is shorter (i.e., less than 5 h) than most forms of AIT. Therefore, the effects of LPP described in this study should not be generalized to any other form of auditory intervention.

There are several problems related to the evaluation of traditional auditory intervention therapies. First, since the interventions have evolved from clinical observations and insights, the neurophysiological theory underlying the interventions is often not well developed or tested. Second, research has been frequently structured to ask questions of efficacy instead of developing protocols to test theoretically relevant components of the treatment in order to understand the mechanisms and to refine the methodology. Third, since auditory interventions are applied within a clinical setting, several experimental design parameters are difficult to control including (1) a constant protocol, (2) limiting concurrent treatments including medication, (3) randomization of participants into conditions, and (4) the selection of outcome variables that are theoretically relevant to the intervention model. Perhaps the greatest limiting factor is the broad range of domains that auditory interventions are proposed to improve without a description of a causal link through which the intervention would result in functional changes in behavior. Due, in part, to the above limitations, the literature documenting an efficacy for the clinically available forms of AIT has been difficult to interpret.

Some studies evaluating the effectiveness of the AIT report improvements (42, 43) and others do not (36, 44–47). However, some of the above studies that do not support unique positive effects of AIT provide documentation of positive effects. For example, Bettison (36) reports positive effects in both the experimental group (received auditory training) and the control group (listened to the same unmodified music under the same conditions). Bettison suggests, consistent with our findings, that features in the AIT shared with listening to selected unmodified music may have beneficial effects on children with autism. Moreover, as our data suggest, if participants do not have auditory hypersensitivities, then the effects of LPP may be mediated through different biobehavioral pathways with unpredictable (i.e., non-specific) positive outcomes, which are not consistent with the middle ear transfer function model. Perhaps, similar to the outcomes with children without auditory hypersensitivities in the LPP trials, observed positive effects of AIT may be recruiting pathways outside of the middle ear model via the potential therapeutic calming effects of music and social support by clinicians.

Gilmor (48) conducted a meta-analysis based on several studies conducted in the 1980s with the Tomatis method involving 231 children. Gilmor clustered the outcome measures into five behavioral domains and identified small effects for linguistic, psychomotor, personal and social adjustment, and cognitive domains. Interestingly, he found no reliable effect in the auditory domain. These findings should be cautiously interpreted because the studies were limited by small sample sizes, issues related to defining control conditions, and limited use of random assignment. Regardless of these limitations, parents and clinicians of children with ASD have reported that forms of auditory intervention therapy have been helpful.

## LIMITATIONS OF THE CURRENT STUDY

The data from the current study need to be cautiously interpreted for the reasons outlined below.

1. The major findings were dependent on the subjective reports of parents.
2. Some of the hypotheses tested were dependent on the small sizes of critical subgroups (e.g., individuals with or without auditory hypersensitivities who did or did not show improvements partitioned by the various treatment conditions).
3. The participants were receiving other treatments during the intervention and assessment period. Several participants were receiving daily interventions using behavioral approaches and other therapies, which may have enhanced or dampened the effects of the LPP.
4. Frequent contact of parents with therapists might bias parental reports and compromise the validity of the parents as objective informants. These factors could obfuscate the real effects of the intervention and inaccurately identify changes. Alternatively, features that might have improved could have been neglected. Possibly the hearing sensitivity domain on the parent questionnaire is less vulnerable to clinician–parent bias. Based on our experience, the therapists and parents appear to be less interested in this dimension, although it was the focal point of our study.
5. Improvements were observed in the groups not receiving the filtered music. Approximately 40% of the parents of children not receiving the filtered music reported improvements on at least one behavioral feature. These positive reactions might be due to non-specific features of the protocol, such as a relaxed intervention environment fostering social engagement and spontaneous play, as well as a positive "expectation" bias and the effects of familiarity with staff and context as the child progressed through the five laboratory sessions. However, the groups receiving filtered music diverged from the control groups when parents reported improvements in hearing sensitivity.
6. Standardized assessments of cognitive function and developmental landmarks were not evaluated. The lack of this information precluded confirmation of matching on these variables, although, based on the sample size, random assignment should have led to a reasonable expectation of matched samples. The randomization of participants, with regard to the evaluated parameters, was effective and there were no group differences in their representation. Standardized assessments of cognitive function and development would provide data to investigate two questions: (1) Are auditory hypersensitivities related to cognitive function and developmental landmarks? (2) Is the effectiveness of the LPP related to individual differences in cognitive function?
7. Our participants were young and on the severe end of the autism spectrum and the findings may not generalize to older or less severe ASD.
8. The studies precluded an opportunity to confirm the specific neural pathways responsible for the observed behavioral improvements. The methods employed could not confirm whether auditory hypersensitivity was due to a compromise in functional neural regulation of the middle ear muscles (as proposed by the polyvagal theory) and remediated through an exercise model.
9. The studies did not provide information necessary to distinguish among alternative pathways leading to or remediating auditory hypersensitivities, such as the potential influence of the intervention on damaged neural pathways (e.g., auditory or facial nerve), on damaged peripheral structures (e.g., middle ear and inner ear), or central structures involved in processing the acoustic signal or in cortical representation.
10. The hypothesized link between the middle ear transfer function and auditory hypersensitivities could be limited. Hypersensitivities, especially to high frequency sounds, might be due, not to the neural regulation of the middle ear muscles, but to the olivary cochlear reflexes. Tests of inner ear function and the degree of auditory hypersensitivity to high frequency sounds need to be evaluated to rule out this possibility.

11. The general improvements in behavior observed following a reduction in hearing sensitivity might not be related to the proposed integrative social engagement system. Rather, the enhanced behavior might be naturally occurring when the sounds are no longer painful and distracting.

## FUTURE DIRECTIONS

A measure of the hypothesized intervening mechanism, the middle ear transfer function, has been missing from the formal experiments evaluating effectiveness of LPP. At the time the participants were tested, no commercial clinical or research device was available to monitor the middle ear transfer function. Without a sensitive measure of the middle ear transfer function, the only method to demonstrate efficacy was to quantify physiology, auditory processing, and measures of behavior and to infer that the LPP normalized an atypical middle ear transfer function. Recently we have developed a middle ear sound absorption system (MESAS) to measure the middle ear transfer function (49). MESAS provides an objective measure of the potential mediating role that middle ear muscles play in experiencing auditory hypersensitivities (see Ref. (50)).

By providing an objective measure of the middle ear transfer function, future research with MESAS will enable a selective test of the efficacy of LPP in normalizing the middle ear transfer function. If confirmed, LPP could be applied to individuals with atypical middle ear function including rehabilitation following otitis media. In addition, MESAS will enable future research to evaluate the behavioral and psychological consequences of an atypical middle ear transfer function, provide data to validate a quantitatively scaled measure of auditory hypersensitivities independent of subjective reports, and contribute to the improvement of interventions (e.g., LPP) that may function as efficient neural exercises to normalize the middle ear transfer function.

## AUTHOR CONTRIBUTIONS

Stephen W. Porges was involved in all aspects of the research, including conception, design of the intervention stimuli, design of the protocol, analysis, interpretation, and writing the manuscript. Olga V. Bazhenova and Elgiz Bal were involved in the design, acquisition, and preliminary analyses and drafts. Nancy Carlson and Yevgeniya Sorokin were involved in acquisition of the data. Keri J. Heilman was involved in data acquisition, data analyses, and contributing to the final drafts. Edwin H. Cook was involved in developing the final draft and in interpreting the data. Gregory F. Lewis was involved in the development of the stimuli, developing the Middle Ear Sound Absorption System (MESAS), and in collecting and interpreting the preliminary data with MESAS.

## ACKNOWLEDGMENTS

Portions of this paper were presented by Stephen W. Porges at the Reiss-Davis Child Study Center and Institute, a division of Vista Del Mar Child and Family Services, on February 8, 2013 when he was awarded the Reiss-Greenberg Chair, an endowed chair of the Reiss-Davis Child Study Center. Support for the research described in this manuscript was provided, in part, by grants from the National Institute of Mental Health (MH060625), Unicorn Children's Foundation, Cure Autism Now Foundation, Nancy Lurie Marks Family Foundation, and Autism Speaks. The contents of this manuscript are solely the responsibility of the authors and do not represent the official views of NIH or other funding agencies. We would like to acknowledge the following individuals for coding, conducting intervention, interviews, and assessment sessions: Mirit Cohen, Emily Harden, Claudia Joe, Lee Anne Jones, Alexis Kramer, Jocelyn Lebow, Margro Purple, and Patricia Rao. We would like to thank Ross Apparies for his involvement in the development the stimuli used for the intervention and in the acquisition of the data. We would also like to thank the parents and children who participated in the research.

## REFERENCES

1. Coleman M, Gillberg C. *The Biology of the Autistic Syndromes.* New York: Praeger (1985).
2. Dissanayake C, Sigman M. Attachment and emotional responsiveness in children with autism. In: Masters Glidden L editor. *International Review of Research in Mental Retardation: Autism.* San Diego, CA: Academic Press (2001). p. 239–66.
3. Frith U, Baron-Cohen S. Perception in autistic children. In: Cohen DJ, Donnellan AM, Paul R, editors. *Handbook of Autism and Pervasive Developmental Disorders.* New York, NY: John Wiley & Sons (1987). p. 85–102.
4. Hayes R, Gordon A. Auditory abnormalities in autistic children. *Lancet* (1977) **2**:767. doi:10.1016/S0140-6736(77)90278-1
5. Klin A. Listening preferences in regard to speech in 4 children with developmental disabilities. *J Child Psychol Psychiatry* (1992) **33**:763–9. doi:10.1111/j.1469-7610.1992.tb00911.x
6. Lockyer L, Rutter M. A five- to-fifteen year follow-up study of infantile psychosis: III. Psychological aspects. *Br J Psychiatry* (1969) **115**:865–82. doi:10.1192/bjp.115.525.865
7. Mundy P. Joint attention and social-emotional approach behavior in children with autism. *Dev Psychopathol* (1995) **7**:63–82. doi:10.1017/S0954579400006349
8. Rosenhall U, Nordin V, Sandström M, Ahlsén G, Gillberg C. Autism and hearing loss. *J Autism Dev Disord* (1999) **29**:349–57. doi:10.1023/A:1023022709710
9. Ceponiene R, Lepistö T, Shestakova A, Vanhala A, Alku P, Näätänen R, et al. Speech-sound selective auditory impairment in autism: can perceive but do not attend. *Proc Natl Acad Sci USA* (2003) **100**:5567–72. doi:10.1073/pnas.0835631100
10. Dawson G. Cerebral lateralization in autism: clues to its role in language and affective development. In: Molfese DL, Segalowitz SJ, editors. *Brain Lateralization in Children: Developmental Implications.* New York, NY: The Guilford Press (1988). p. 437–61.
11. Gage NM, Siegel B, Roberts TPL. Cortical auditory system maturational abnormalities in children with autism disorder: an MEG investigation. *Brain Res Dev Brain Res* (2003) **144**:201–9. doi:10.1016/S0165-3806(03)00172-X
12. Gervais H, Belin P, Boddaert N, Leboyer M, Coez A, Sfaello I, et al. Abnormal cortical voice processing in autism. *Nat Neurosci* (2004) **7**:801–2. doi:10.1038/nn1291
13. Khalfa S, Bruneau N, Roge B, Georgieff N, Veuillet E, Adrien JL, et al. Increased perception of loudness in autism. *Hear Res* (2004) **198**:87–92. doi:10.1016/j.heares.2004.07.006
14. Maziade M, Merette C, Cayer M, Roy MA, Szatmari P, Cote R, et al. Prolongation of brainstem auditory-evoked responses in autistic probands and their unaffected relatives. *Arch Gen Psychiatry* (2000) **57**:1077–83. doi:10.1001/archpsyc.57.11.1077
15. Smith DE, Miller SD, Stewart M, Walter TL, McConnell JV. Conductive hearing loss in autistic, learning disabled, and normal children. *J Autism Dev Disord* (1988) **18**:53–65. doi:10.1007/BF02211818
16. Tecchio F, Benassi F, Zappasodi F, Gialloreti LE, Palermo M, Seri S, et al. Auditory sensory processing in autism: a magnetoencephalographic study. *Biol Psychiatry* (2003) **54**:647–54. doi:10.1016/S0006-3223(03)00295-6
17. Thivierge J, Bedard C, Cote R, Maziade M. Brainstem auditory evoked response and subcortical abnormalities in autism. *Am J Psychiatry* (1990) **147**:1609–13.
18. Marco JE, Hinkley LBN, Hill SS, Nagarajan SS. Sensory processing in autism: a review of neurophysiologic findings. *Pediatr Res* (2011) **69**:48–54. doi:10.1203/PDR.0b013e3182130c54

19. Khalfa S, Dubal S, Veuillet E, Perez-Diaz F, Jouvent R, Collet L. Psychometric normalization of a hyperacusis questionnaire. *ORL J Otorhinolaryngol Relat Spec* (2002) **64**:436–42. doi:10.1159/000067570
20. Borg E, Counter SA. The middle-ear muscles. *Sci Am* (1989) **261**:74–80. doi:10.1038/scientificamerican0889-74
21. Liberman CM, Guinan JJ. Feedback control of the auditory periphery: anti-masking effects of middle ear muscles vs. olivocochlear efferents. *J Commun Disord* (1998) **31**:471–83. doi:10.1016/S0021-9924(98)00019-7
22. Zwislocki JJ. Auditory system: peripheral nonlinearity and central additivity, as revealed in the human stapedius-muscle reflex. *Proc Natl Acad Sci USA* (2002) **99**:14601–6. doi:10.1073/pnas.222543199
23. Porges SW, Lewis GF. The Polyvagal hypothesis: common mechanisms mediating autonomic regulation, vocalizations and listening. In: Brudzynski SM editor. *Handbook of Mammalian Vocalization: An Integrative Neuroscience Approach.* Amsterdam: Academic Press (2009). p. 255–64.
24. Kryter KD. Methods for the calculation and use of the articulation index. *J Acoust Soc Am* (1962) **34**:1689–97. doi:10.1121/1.1909096
25. American National Standards Institute. *ANSI S3.5-1997: Methods for Calculation of the Speech Intelligibility Index.* New York, NY: Acoustical Society of America (1997).
26. Hanks WD, Rose KJ. Middle ear resonance and acoustic immittance measures in children. *J Speech Hear Res* (1993) **36**:218–22.
27. Schiaffino S, Reggiani C. Fiber types in mammalian skeletal muscles. *Physiol Rev* (2011) **91**:1447–531. doi:10.1152/physrev.00031.2010
28. Porges SW. The vagus: a mediator of behavioral and visceral features associated with autism. In: Bauman ML, Kemper TL, editors. *The Neurobiology of Autism.* Baltimore: Johns Hopkins University Press (2005). p. 65–78.
29. Porges SW. The Polyvagal perspective. *Biol Psychol* (2007) **74**:116–43. doi:10.1016/j.biopsycho.2006.06.009
30. Lord C, Rutter M, Le Couteur A. Autism diagnostic interview-revised: a revised version of a diagnostic interview for caregivers of individuals with possible pervasive developmental disorders. *J Autism Dev Disord* (1994) **24**:659–85. doi:10.1007/BF02172145
31. American Psychiatric Association. *Diagnostic and Statistical Manual of Mental Disorders.* 4th ed. Washington, DC: American Psychiatric Association (1994).
32. World Health Organization. *International Classification of Diseases.* 10th ed. Geneva: World Health Organization (1992).
33. Bazhenova OV, Sorokin Y, Bal E, Carlson N, Heilman KJ, Denver JW, et al. *The Social Interaction Coding Scale (SICS)* (unpublished).
34. Lord C, Risi S, Lambrecht L, Cook EH, Leventhal BL, DiLavore PC, et al. The autism diagnostic observation schedule – generic: a standard measure of social and communication deficits associated with the spectrum of autism. *J Autism Dev Disord* (2000) **30**(3):205–23. doi:10.1023/A:1005592401947
35. Seibert JM, Hogan AE, Mundy PC. Assessing interactional competencies: the early social-communication scales. *Infant Ment Health J* (1982) **3**:244–58. doi:10.1002/1097-0355(198224)3:4<244::AID-IMHJ2280030406>3.0.CO;2-R
36. Bettison S. The long-term effects of auditory training on children with autism. *J Autism Dev Disord* (1996) **26**:361–74. doi:10.1007/BF02172480
37. Porges SW, Macellaio M, Stanfill SD, McCue K, Lewis GF, Harden ER, et al. Respiratory sinus arrhythmia and auditory processing in autism: modifiable deficits of an integrated social engagement system? *Int J Psychophysiol* (2013) **88**:261–70. doi:10.1016/j.ijpsycho.2012.11.009
38. Keith RW. *SCAN: A Screening Test for Auditory Processing Disorders.* San Antonio: Harcourt Brace Jovanovich (1986).
39. Keith RW. *SCAN: A Screening Test for Auditory Processing Disorders in Children-Revised.* San Antonio: Harcourt Brace Jovanovich (2000).
40. Berard G. *Hearing Equals Behavior.* New Canaan, CT: Keats (1993).
41. Tomatis AA. *The Conscious Ear: My Life of Transformation Through Listening.* Barrytown, New York: Station Hill Press (1991).
42. Edelson SM, Arin D, Bauman M, Lukas SE, Rudy JH, Sholar M, et al. Auditory integration training: a double blind study of behavioral and electrophysiological effects in people with autism. *Focus Autism Other Dev Disabl* (1999) **14**:73–81. doi:10.1177/108835769901400202
43. Rimland B, Edelson SM. Brief report: a pilot study of auditory integration training in autism. *J Autism Dev Disord* (1995) **25**:61–70. doi:10.1007/BF02178168
44. Gillberg C, Johansson M, Steffenberg S, Berlin O. Auditory integration training in children with autism: brief report of an open pilot study. *Autism* (1997) **1**:97–100. doi:10.1177/1362361397011009
45. Kershner JR, Cummings RL, Clarke KA, Hadfield AJ, Kershner BA. Two-year evaluation of the Tomatis listening training program with learning disabled children. *Learn Disabil Q* (1990) **13**:43–53. doi:10.2307/1510391
46. Mudford OC, Cross BA, Breen S, Cullen C, Reeves D, Gould J, et al. Auditory integration training for children with autism: no behavioral benefits detected. *Am J Ment Retard* (2000) **105**:118–29. doi:10.1352/0895-8017(2000)105<0118:AITFCW>2.0.CO;2
47. Zollweg W, Palm D, Vance V. The efficacy of auditory integration training: a double blind study. *Am J Audiol* (1997) **6**:39.
48. Gilmor T. The efficacy of the Tomatis method for children with learning and communication disorders: a meta-analysis. *Int J Listening* (1999) **13**(12–23):doi:10.1080/10904018.1999.10499024
49. Lewis GF, Porges SW. *US Patent Application No. WO2012082721 A2.* Washington, DC: U.S. Patent and Trademark Office (2012).
50. Porges SW, Lewis GF. *US Patent Application No. 13/992,450.* Washington, DC: U.S. Patent and Trademark Office (2013).

# 21

# Potential therapeutic use of the ketogenic diet in autism spectrum disorders

***Eleonora Napoli*[1]*, Nadia Dueñas*[1] *and Cecilia Giulivi*[1,2]**

[1] *Department of Molecular Biosciences, University of California Davis, Davis, CA, USA*
[2] *Medical Investigations of Neurodevelopmental Disorders (M. I. N. D.) Institute, Sacramento, CA, USA*

***Edited by:***
*Roberto Canitano, University Hospital of Siena, Italy*

***Reviewed by:***
*Richard Eugene Frye, Children's Hospital Boston/Harvard University, USA*
*Daniel Rossignol, Rossignol Medical Center, USA*

****Correspondence:***
*Eleonora Napoli, Department of Molecular Biosciences, University of California Davis, One Shields Avenue, Davis, CA 95616, USA*
*e-mail: enapoli@ucdavis.edu*

The ketogenic diet (KGD) has been recognized as an effective treatment for individuals with glucose transporter 1 (GLUT1) and pyruvate dehydrogenase (PDH) deficiencies as well as with epilepsy. More recently, its use has been advocated in a number of neurological disorders prompting a newfound interest in its possible therapeutic use in autism spectrum disorders (ASD). One study and one case report indicated that children with ASD treated with a KGD showed decreased seizure frequencies and exhibited behavioral improvements (i.e., improved learning abilities and social skills). The KGD could benefit individuals with ASD affected with epileptic episodes as well as those with either PDH or mild respiratory chain (RC) complex deficiencies. Given that the mechanism of action of the KGD is not fully understood, caution should be exercised in ASD cases lacking a careful biochemical and metabolic characterization to avoid deleterious side effects or refractory outcomes.

**Keywords: epilepsy, autism spectrum disorders, dietary intervention, mitochondria, bioenergetics, ketogenic diet, oxidative stress**

## BIOCHEMISTRY OF THE KGD

The ketogenic diet (KGD) is a nutritional approach constituted by high-fat content with adequate protein amount for growth but insufficient levels of carbohydrates for metabolic needs (1), thus forcing the body to primarily use fat as a fuel source. The original KGD was designed as 4:1 lipid:non-lipid (carbohydrate plus protein) ratio with 80% fat, 15% protein, and 5% carbohydrate. Most of the fat is provided as long-chain triglycerides, composing ~80% of the estimated caloric dietary requirement (2). To date, several modifications to the original KGD have been introduced such as lowering the lipid:non-lipid ratio (3) and decreasing the caloric intake from fat (~60–70%) with either no restriction in calorie amount with unlimited protein and fat intake (modified Atkins diet) (4, 5), or with fat provided as triglycerides esterified with medium-chain fatty acids (FA) (to overcome deficits in carnitine metabolism; medium-chain triglyceride diet) (6).

The hormonal changes associated with a KGD include changes in circulating insulin (due to insulin reduction in response to decreasing plasma glucose) and/or leptin (7–9), thus limiting glucose utilization. Under normal conditions, FA mobilized from adipose tissue are catabolized to acetyl coenzyme A (CoA) via β-oxidation, and then oxidized to $CO_2$ and $H_2O$ in the Krebs' cycle. However, when an imbalance is created between the rate of FA mobilization and the capacity of the Krebs' cycle to process acetylCoA (e.g., low-carbohydrate and/or protein diet), the liver converts the excess of acetylCoA into ketone bodies (KB), namely acetoacetate (ACA) and D-β-hydroxybutyrate (BHB). A significant fraction of acetone (~30%), the product of the spontaneous decarboxylation of ACA, is found in urine, sweat, and breath (10, 11). KB are utilized as fuel by peripheral tissues sparing glucose and muscle wasting. They generate a comparable amount of energy to protein or carbohydrates (2.7 vs. 4 kcal/g) and, unlike FA, KB can cross the blood–brain barrier (12) constituting the main fuel sources for the brain during fasting periods (13). Most ATP from BHB is via Complex I (70–80%), with the rest via Complex II (14). The low-carbohydrate intake forces the body to sustain systemic glycemia by hepatic gluconeogenesis from non-carbohydrate precursors (e.g., lactate, glucogenic amino acids, and glycerol).

At the center of intermediary metabolism reside mitochondria. These dynamic organelles whose morphology, composition, and function adapt to changes in response to pathological and physiological signals respond to nutritional variations such as those introduced by KGD. Several reports in the literature document changes in mitochondrial number or function in a variety of biological systems, from *in vitro* to *in vivo*, when exposed to KGD or KGD-mimetics (**Table 1**).

## THERAPEUTIC USE OF THE KETOGENIC DIET IN HUMAN DISEASES

By providing alternative sources of acetylCoA, KGD is the dietary intervention for inborn genetic disorders in pyruvate dehydrogenase (PDH) and glucose transporter 1 (GLUT1) (**Table 1**), proven effective also in other metabolic conditions, including phosphofructokinase deficiency and glycogenosis type V (McArdle disease) (37). The KGD has also been investigated for the management of neurological disorders such as Alzheimer's and Parkinson's diseases (38).

Ketogenic diet has been utilized for >80 years in epilepsy treatment (39, 40) especially in children and adolescents (1, 41) with reduction in seizure frequencies (2, 42) and improvements in developmental progress (26).

Evidence supporting the use of the KGD for patients with intractable epilepsy and respiratory chain (RC) complex defects has been reported in which the majority of patients responded with decreased seizure frequencies, regardless of the RC complex defect or magnitude of deficit (27). The administration of KGD

**Table 1 | Examples extracted from the literature on effects of KGD on mitochondrial function with the potential to benefit ASD symptoms.**

| Experimental model | Diet/treatment | KGD-dependent effects | Source |
|---|---|---|---|
| **OUTCOMES RELATED TO ENERGY RESERVES AND/OR ENERGY-SENSING PATHWAYS** | | | |
| Rat hippocampus | Young rats fed KGD for 9 weeks | Increased gene expression of mt genes; 46% increase in mitochondria number with no changes in citrate synthase or any other mt enzymatic activity; [PCr]/[Cr] higher (due to lower [Cr]) | Bough et al. (15) |
| Rat hippocampus | Young rats fed KGD for 1 month | Decreased (−30%) body weight than controls; few mt genes overexpressed | Noh et al. (16) |
| Rat brain | Fed HFD for 3 weeks | [ATP]/[ADP] increased by 12%; lower [Cr] with no changes in [PCr]; lower [cAMP] and [cGMP] | DeVivo et al. (17) |
| Rat hippocampus | Slices from rat hippocampus (4–7 weeks) with BHB and ACA each at 0.5 or 1 mM | KB prevented rotenone- and 3NP-dependent decrease in ATP and decreased 3NP-dependent ROS production | Kim do et al. (18) |
| Mouse brain | Mice (8–10 weeks) treated with d-BHB or l-BHB via pumps | BHB restored NADH-supported $O_2$ consumption inhibited by $MPP^+$, partly the one inhibited by rotenone; BHB increased mtROS. 70–80% ATP from BHB produced via Complex I, the remaining via Complex II | Tieu et al. (19) |
| Rats | CR-KGD for 7 days | Body weight loss, increased brain expression of IGFR and GLUT3 | Cheng et al. (14) |
| Neuronal human SH-SY5Y cell line | FA (C8 or C10) treatment for 1–6 days | Increased citrate synthase and Complex I activities | Hughes et al. (20) |
| Rat hippocampus and liver | Rats fed with a 6:1 lipid:non-lipid KGD | Delayed occurrence of epileptic episodes via mTOR inhibition | McDaniel et al. (21) |
| **OUTCOMES RELATED TO NEUROLOGICAL SYMPTOMS/BEHAVIOR WITH RC COMPLEX AND/OR PDH DEFICIENCIES** | | | |
| Child with Leigh syndrome | KGD | Improvement of cerebral lesions by brain MRI | Wijburg et al. (22) |
| Individuals with PDH deficiency (PDHA1 an PDHX mutations) | KGD (lipid:non-lipid 3:1) | KGD improved only paroxysmal dysfunction | Barnerias et al. (23) |
| Child, idiopathic PDH deficiency | KGD for ~3 years (lipid:non-lipid 3:1 later switched to 2:1) | Seizure free; improvement in hypotonia, motor development, relationship with environment; poor weight gain, high ketonemia | Di Pisa et al. (24) |
| Children with PDHE1 mutations | KGD (varied degrees of carbohydrate restriction) | Improved longevity and mental development | Wexler et al. (25) |
| Child with PHDX | KGD (lipid:non-lipid 4:1, later switched to 3:1 plus MCT oil) | Weight gain, decreased seizure episodes, improved sociability and activity | El-Gharbawy et al. (26) |
| Children with intractable epilepsy with ETC defects | Age (mean) 45 months, KGD (4:1 lipid:non-lipid) for (mean) 18 months | Eleven of 14 patients decreased seizure frequency by 50–90%; 8 ceased or lowered antiepileptic medications; 8 showed improved cognitive and behavioral functions | Kang et al. (27) |
| **OUTCOMES RELATED TO MITOCHONDRIAL ANTIOXIDANT DEFENSES AND ROS** | | | |
| Mouse hippocampus | Young mice fed a 6:1 lipid:non-lipid KGD for 10–12 d | Decreased mtROS; increases in UCP expression | Sullivan et al. (28) |

**Table 1 | Continued**

| Experimental model | Diet/treatment | KGD-dependent effects | Source |
|---|---|---|---|
| Rat hippocampus | Adolescent rats, KGD (78% lipid, 0.76% carbs) for 1, 3 days or 1, 3 weeks | KGD-induced initial mild oxidative stress, activation of Nrf2 pathway | Milder et al. (29) |
| Rat cortex, cerebellum, and hippocampus | Adolescent rats fed with KGD or BHB for 3 weeks | Increased GPX activity and [GSH] | Ziegler et al. (30), Jarrett et al. (31) |
| Rat neocortical neurons | Neurons exposed to BHB *in vitro* | Decreased Glu-mediated excitotoxicity mtROS production via increased NADH oxidation | Maalouf et al. (32) |
| **OUTCOMES RELATED TO MITOCHONDRIA-DERIVED NEUROTRANSMITTER METABOLISM** | | | |
| Mouse forebrain | Ketotic mice fed KGD (50% lipids) for 3 days | Increased GABA and Gln production | Yudkoff et al. (33) |
| Cerebrospinal fluid | 26 children with refractory epilepsy fed KGD for 6 months | Increased [GABA], [taurine], [Ser], and [Gly]. Higher [GABA] (>50–90% seizure reduction) | Dahlin et al. (34) |
| Zebrafish with PDHE1 mutation, lower acetylcholine in inner retina | Larvae fed a mix of lauric/myristic/palmitic acid, and phosphatidyl choline | KGD rescued vision and prolong survival | Maurer et al. (35) |
| SSDAH mouse model | At PND 12 were fed KGD for 20–30 days | Increased mitochondrial number and size; increased (ATP), no changes in lifespan or neurological outcomes | Nylen et al. (36) |

*3-NP, 3-nitropropionic acid; AHA, acetoacetate; BHB, β-hydroxybutyrate; CR-KGD, calorie-restricted ketogenic diet; Cr, creatine; Gln, glutamine; Glu, glutamate; Gly, glycine; GPX, glutathione peroxidase; FA, fatty acids; HFD, high-fat diet; IGFR, insulin-like growth factor receptor; Mt, mitochondrial; MCT, medium-chain triglycerides; Nrf2, Nuclear factor-like 2; PCr, phospho-creatine; PND, post-natal day; Ser, serine.*

to epileptic patients (37, 39) has been based on the assumption that KB replace glucose as the major metabolic fuel to the brain, although the precise molecular steps still remain obscure. It has been proposed that KB metabolism is not the primary mechanism of this diet, but rather an outcome of the metabolic shifts that occur with this treatment (43) and that the anticonvulsant effects of the KGD could result from an altered gene expression profile accompanied by cellular adaptation mechanisms (15) needed to modify the brain to utilize KB over glucose over time (39).

## THERAPEUTIC USE OF KGD IN ASD

Autism spectrum disorders (ASD) include a complex neurodevelopmental condition characterized by abnormal social interaction, verbal and non-verbal communication, and limited interest in the surrounding environment associated with stereotyped and repetitive behaviors (44). Limited scientific advances have been made regarding the causes of ASD, with general agreement that both genetic and environmental factors contribute to this disorder (44–47). ASD has been associated to metabolic dysfunction (44, 48) and autism is a common trait of epilepsy-associated diseases (49), and syndromes like Landau–Kleffner, Dravet (50, 51), and Rett (52, 53). Thus, given the beneficial effects of KGD on epilepsy and increased mitochondrial function, its use has the potential to ameliorate some of the ASD-associated symptoms.

Beneficial effects of KGD in children with ASD symptoms have been reported in two independent studies (54, 55). The first study evaluated the role of KGD on 30 ASD children (54). The John Radcliffe diet (a modified medium-chain triglyceride diet with a caloric distribution of 30% in medium-chain triglyceride oil, 30% fresh cream, 11% saturated fat, 19% carbohydrates, and 10% proteins) was administered for 6 months, with intervals of 4 weeks interrupted by two diet-free weeks. Of the 30 children, 40% did not comply or did not tolerate the diet. From the rest, the two children with the milder autistic behaviors showed the most improvement (as judged by total Childhood Autism Rating Scale score, concentration and learning abilities, and social behavior and interactions), while the rest displayed mild to moderate improvements. Interestingly, the beneficial effects of KGD persisted even after termination of the trial. Six of the children enrolled in this study had a higher baseline ketonemia with no apparent PDH and/or RC deficiencies; but it is not clear if any of the other patients underwent this screening, before and/or after the administration of the diet in addition to the lack of the inclusion of a control diet before administering the KGD to the ASD group or during the trial.

The other study (55) reports the administration of a gluten-free casein-free modified KGD (1.5:1 lipid:non-lipid ratio; medium-chain and polyunsaturated FA) for 14-months to a 12-year-old child with ASD and seizures with substantial medical comorbidities associated with a family history of metabolic and immune disturbances. Due to the improvements in seizure activity, improved electroencephalogram, cognitive and social skills, language function, and complete resolution of stereotypies, anticonvulsant medication doses were reduced without worsening of seizures. Of note, the administration of the diet was accompanied by a wealth of medications, a significant weight loss, and transitioning to puberty, so it is difficult to assess the sole role of the diet with this clinical background.

In mouse models of ASD [i.e., Rett syndrome (56), BTBR model (57), and succinate semialdehyde dehydrogenase (SSADH) deficiency (36)], the use of the KGD has improved behavioral abnormalities (increased sociability and decreased self-directed repetitive behavior) and/or decreased the number of seizures, normalized ataxia, and increased lifespan of mutant mice. However, while the KGD was originally designed to be administered under controlled caloric intake (38), most of the mouse studies have been performed under *ad libitum* conditions and/or for a relatively short period [see Ref. (57)]. Moreover, a ketogenic low-carbohydrate diet does not have a significant metabolic advantage over a non-ketogenic low-carbohydrate diet as judged by equal effects in body weight reduction and decreased insulin resistance; however, the former one was associated with higher inflammatory risk and increased perception of fatigue (58).

Although the exact molecular mechanisms underlying the effect of the KGD are still under investigation, several scenarios are reported below to explore the potential therapeutic effects of the KGD in ASD.

## KGD IN PDH DEFICIENCY

Peripheral blood mononucleated cell (PBMC) from children with high severity scores for ASD has shown impaired PDH activity (44). The KGD is recommended as an alternative source of the acetylCoA in patients (37) with pathogenic mutations in PDH- or GLUT1-encoding genes (22, 25) leading to amelioration of some symptoms (59, 60) especially in those with milder phenotypes (25, 61). Thus, the use of the KGD in ASD with PDH deficiencies might prove to be beneficial.

## KGD IN β-OXIDATION DEFECTS

Some patients with ASD have been reported to have defects in fatty acid β-oxidation evidenced as long-chain acyl dehydrogenase deficiency (62) and high concentrations of short or long acyl-carnitines in plasma (63). Carnitine biosynthesis has been recently identified as a risk factor for ASD (64). Thus in these cases, it is advisable to limit the use of a high-fat diet or improve its safety by switching to short or medium-chain FA, which do not utilize the carnitine system.

## KGD IN MITOCHONDRIAL BIOGENESIS

The KGD might improve mitochondrial function by enhancing mitochondrial biogenesis in murine models (15, 65). The medium-chain triglyceride diet (6) has been shown to produce significant increases in citrate synthase and Complex I activity in SH–SY5Y neurons (20). However, the increases in mitochondrial mass would need to result in an OXPHOS outcome of $\geq$30% [30% as the limit for minor diagnostic criteria of mitochondrial RC disorder (66)] for that particular tissue, given that each tissue has a different ATP threshold (67). Otherwise the increases in mass might not be sufficient to rescue the already impaired ATP production in ASD individuals. Moreover, given the presence of mitochondrial DNA (mtDNA) deletions in PBMC from ASD (44, 68, 69), the KGD-driven mitochondrial biogenesis may result in an enrichment of defective mitochondria due to the proliferating advantage of damaged or deleted mtDNA over wild-type (70, 71). Conversely, treatment of cells containing large-scale mtDNA deletions from a patient with Kearns–Sayre syndrome with KB shifted the heteroplasmy between and within cells (72). The observation that KB can distinguish between normal and respiration-compromised cells suggests that the KB may be useful in treating patients with heteroplasmic mtDNA disorders (72).

## ROLE OF THE KGD IN RC COMPLEX DEFICITS

Children with ASD display an array of mitochondrial dysfunction (MD) of differing severity (44, 73–75). Electron transport chain (ETC) deficiencies have been reported in ASD, primarily in Complex I and IV, but also affecting others such as Complex II, III, and IV (44, 73, 74, 76). The prevalence of seizures (41%) has been observed to be significantly higher in individuals with ASD and MD than in the general ASD population (11%) (74), raising the possibility that epileptic episodes observed in ASD might have a mitochondrial origin. Indeed, epilepsy is a recurrent feature of many inherited "classic" mitochondrial disorders, like myoclonic epilepsy with ragged red fibers, mitochondrial encephalopathy with lactic acidosis, and stroke-like episodes (77), and Leigh syndrome (78). In a small study on children with ETC defects (**Table 1**), the KGD has been proven to reduce epileptic attacks, with far better prognosis among children with Complex I deficits than Complex IV (27). These results are not surprising given that KGD generates more $NADH/FADH_2$ than glucose (2 vs. 5).

## EFFECT OF KGD ON ENERGY-SENSING PATHWAYS ALTERATIONS

Recently, KGD-fed rats showed increased brain expression of insulin-like growth factor receptor (ILGFR) and neuronal GLUT3 (14). The KGD might have a beneficial effect in some ASD cases considering that IGFR is important for brain health throughout life (79–81), and that IGFR and GLUT3 have both been implicated in ASD (82, 83).

Some energy-sensing molecules and metabolism regulators (including the mammalian target of rapamycin, mTOR) have been recently indicated as possible downstream targets of KGD and may be involved in neuroprotective effects associated to the diet (84). Defects in the mTOR pathway have been linked to ASD (85–87). Failure to inhibit mTOR pathway could lead to MD due to decreased mitophagy (88) resulting in an accumulation of dysfunctional mitochondria as observed in a mouse model of ASD with phosphatase and tensin homolog on chromosome ten (*Pten*) gene haploinsuffciency (89). Indeed, inhibition of mTOR has been linked to a delay in the occurrence of the epileptic episodes (90) and KGD-fed rats showed inhibition of the activation of the mTOR pathway in brain (21), thus representing an appropriate treatment to control seizures while enhancing the clearance of defective/damaged mitochondria.

## ANTIOXIDANT AND NEUROPROTECTIVE ROLE OF THE KGD

Ketone bodies (without glucose and at concentrations 10-times higher than physiological ones) inhibit mitochondrial reactive oxygen species (ROS) production in rat neurocortical neurons by increasing NADH oxidation following glutamate (Glu) excitotoxicity (32). It has been suggested that the production of NADPH via oxidation of succinate semialdehyde (SSA) into succinate in the Glu decarboxylase (GAD)/γ-aminobutyric acid (GABA) pathway may buffer the redox changes likely to occur in stressful conditions (91–93). However, other mitochondrial NADPH sources are quantitatively more important than SSADH and fatty acid oxidation produces more mitochondrial ROS than pyruvate oxidation (94).

Thus, the use of KGD could be beneficial in ASD given that higher rates of mitochondrial ROS production and compromised cellular antioxidant status (69, 95, 96) have been reported in peripheral cells from children with ASD (44, 68, 69).

## EFFECT OF THE KGD ON GABAergic AND CHOLINERGIC SYSTEMS DISTURBANCES

The GABA shunt bypasses two steps of the tricarboxylic acid cycle – the α-ketoglutarate (KG) dehydrogenase complex and the succinylCoA synthase – for the conversion of KG into succinate (**Figure 1**). It involves three enzymes: a GAD, catalyzing the Glu decarboxylation to GABA, a GABA transaminase, converting GABA to SSA, and an SSADH, catalyzing the oxidation of SSA to succinate (97). This metabolic route (the GAD/GABA pathway) is conserved from bacteria, through yeast and plants, to vertebrates. In higher eukaryotes, SSA can be reduced to γ-hydroxybutyric acid (GHB) by an alternative reaction catalyzed by a GHB dehydrogenase (98–100). It has been proposed that KGD may limit the availability of oxaloacetate to aspartate aminotransferase, an enzyme involved in brain Glu metabolism, resulting in increased Glu or Gln availability to produce GABA (101). The increased conversion of Glu to GABA would be potentially beneficial in ASD (102–105) (**Figure 1**).

Changes in GABA neurotransmission by KGD might explain the decrease in seizure frequencies and improved behavior observed in Rett syndrome (106). Studies in patients with ASD strongly suggest a dysfunction in the GABAergic system (107–109). However, changes in other components (including Gly, taurine, and GABA) cannot be excluded (34). In the case of SSADH deficiency (SSADH), the KGD may work through restitution of GABAergic neurotransmission (36), although the use of KGD in SSADHD has been strongly argued until more research is performed to test its potential detrimental effects in humans (110). Conversely, ketotic rodents fed on KGD showed no changes

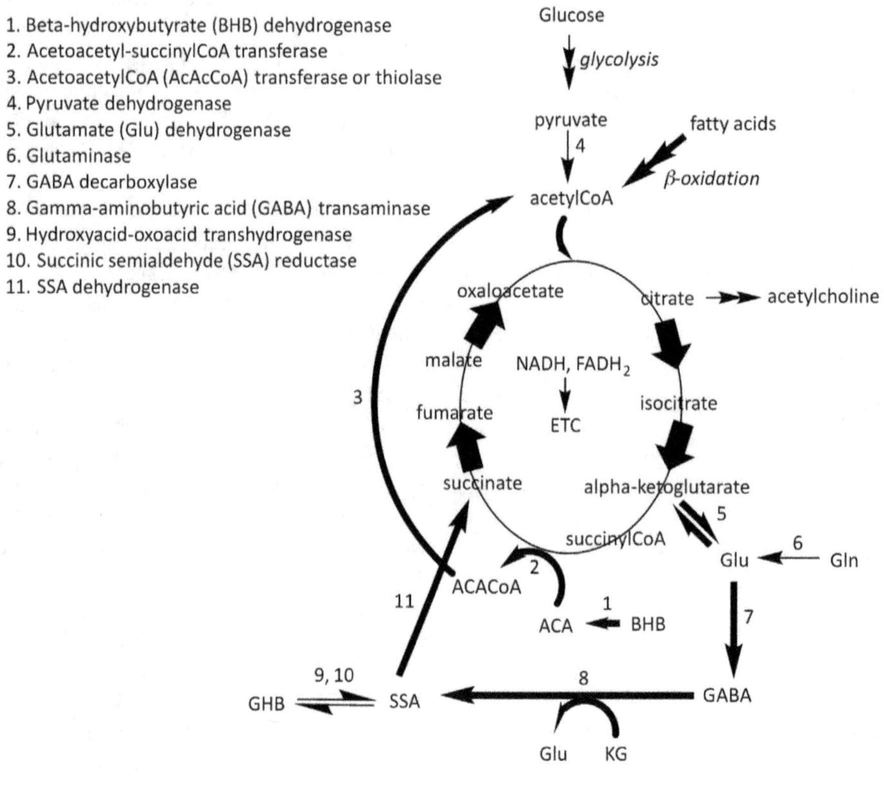


**FIGURE 1 | β-hydroxybutyrate and ACA are utilized as fuel molecules in all mitochondria-containing tissues (except liver).** BHB is oxidized to ACA by β-hydroxybutyrate dehydrogenase at the inner mitochondrial membrane (arrow 1). ACA acquires the CoA moiety from succinylCoA resulting in succinate and acetoacetylCoA (ACACoA; arrow 2). ACACoA releases acetylCoA catalyzed by ACACoA thiolase (arrow 3). AcetylCoA generated from β-oxidation of fatty acids from the diet and acetylCoA generated by the catabolism of KB is condensed into citrate in the Krebs cycle. The increased flux in the right part of this cycle, increases the concentration of α-ketoglutarate (KG) resulting in increases in the production of Glu via glutamate dehydrogenase (arrow 5) or a transaminase (not shown). Glu from these reactions in addition to that formed from the deamination of glutamine (Gln) via glutaminase (arrow 6) result in the generation of γ-aminobutyric acid (GABA). The GABA shunt bypasses two steps of the Krebs cycle – the KG dehydrogenase complex and the succinyl coenzyme A (CoA) synthase – for the conversion of KG into succinate. It involves three enzymes: a Glu decarboxylase (GAD; arrow 7), which catalyzes the decarboxylation of glutamate to GABA, a GABA transaminase (arrow 8), which converts GABA to succinate semialdehyde (SSA), and an SSA dehydrogenase (arrow 11), which catalyzes the oxidation of SSA to succinate. SSA can be reduced to γ-hydroxybutyric acid (GHB) by an alternative reaction catalyzed by either a hydroxyacid–oxoacid transhydrogenase or SSA reductase (arrows 9, 10).

in whole brain (GABA) [between brackets = concentrations; (33, 111)]; however, regional (GABA) changes cannot be ruled out (112), in addition to species-specific differences in the expression of GABA receptors subtypes (113, 114). Considering that cerebrospinal fluid from children treated with KGD showed higher (GABA) (34), it would be of interest to evaluate GABA and amino acid concentrations in different brain areas in animal models of ASD fed KGD.

Dysfunction in the cholinergic system has been observed when PDH deficits are present (115) because a block in this enzyme decreases (citrate), the precursor of acetylcholine via citrate lyase (116). Studies in humans and animal models of ASD suggested that dysfunction of the cholinergic system underlies ASD-related behavioral symptoms (117–119). Trials conducted on ASD individuals have shown beneficial effects of galantamine (an acetylcholinesterase inhibitor) in the management of aberrant behaviors in children and adolescents with ASD (120–122). Treatment of BTBR mice with the acetylcholinesterase inhibitor donepezil hydrochloride improved social preference, social interaction and decreased cognitive rigidity (123). Thus, a KGD has the potential to exhibit beneficial effects in individuals with both ASD and PDH deficiency because the metabolism of KB overcomes the decrease in (citrate) (124) and that of (acetylcholine).

## POTENTIAL SIDE EFFECTS OF KGD IN ASD

Several side effects of KGD have been reported, among them: (a) limitation in protein, carbohydrate, and other nutrients intake can result in a lack of weight gain and growth inhibition (42), which could be detrimental in ASD because of a predisposition for being underweight (125) and the presence of eating disorders (126). Thiamine, lipoic acid, and L-carnitine supplementation have been helpful in selected cases (25). (b) Dyslipidemia from KGD (127, 128) would need to be supervised in ASD patients with $\beta$-oxidation deficits, including carnitine deficiency (64, 129) and, for older patients, the additional increased risk in heart disease and atherosclerosis (130). These patients should limit their fat intake or a modified KGD possibly with carnitine and/or coenzyme Q10 supplementation (131), should be used (132). (c) KGD has an increased risk of systemic ketosis, which may result in lower affinity of hemoglobin for oxygen, resulting in severe outcomes (e.g., coma and death) especially in anemic ASD patients (133). (d) Adverse events experienced by patients with RC complex deficits and epilepsy, which could be extrapolated to those with ASD, included symptomatic persistent hypoglycemia, persistent metabolic acidosis, aspiration pneumonia, and pneumonia followed by respiratory failure (27). (e) Initial fasting and prolonged caloric restriction can cause acute metabolic decompensation in ASD patients with metabolic disorders (134). To reduce the adverse effects of fasting, some studies have omitted the initial fasting period and substituted it with a gradual increase in calories (135). (g) Other side effects include constipation, slower growth, kidney stones, and gastroesophageal reflux (136), although most of them are treatable and/or preventable.

## CONCLUDING REMARKS

More research is necessary to understand the potential therapeutic use of KGD in ASD as discussed at length for SSADHD (110). More specifically, how this diet may improve mitochondrial function in ASD and how this putative improvement derived from a better energy and/or neurotransmitter management may influence behavioral symptoms. There are concerns about utilizing KGD in patients with metabolic encephalopathies, with specific contraindications in pyruvate carboxylase deficiency, fatty acid oxidation disorders, and Krebs cycle disorders. Thus, given that the mechanism of action of KGD has not been yet fully understood, even in cases of improved behavioral symptoms, KGD in ASD might need to be prescribed on a case-by-case basis, upon careful biochemical characterization and metabolic profiling.

## AUTHOR CONTRIBUTIONS

All authors contributed to the design of the work and interpretation of the literature, drafted the work, and gave final approval of the version to be published. All authors agree to be accountable for all aspects of the work in ensuring that questions related to the accuracy or integrity of any part of the work are appropriately investigated and resolved.

## ACKNOWLEDGMENTS

This work was supported by Simons Foundation (SFARI #271406 to Cecilia Giulivi), R01-ES011269, R01-ES015359, and R01-ES020392.

## REFERENCES

1. Freeman J, Veggiotti P, Lanzi G, Tagliabue A, Perucca E. The ketogenic diet: from molecular mechanisms to clinical effects. *Epilepsy Res* (2006) **68**:145–80. doi:10.1016/j.eplepsyres.2005.10.003
2. Rogovik AL, Goldman RD. Ketogenic diet for treatment of epilepsy. *Can Fam Physician* (2010) **56**:540–2.
3. Freeman JM, Kossoff EH, Hartman AL. The ketogenic diet: one decade later. *Pediatrics* (2007) **119**:535–43. doi:10.1542/peds.2006-2447
4. Kossoff EH, Turner Z, Bluml RM, Pyzik PL, Vining EP. A randomized, crossover comparison of daily carbohydrate limits using the modified Atkins diet. *Epilepsy Behav* (2007) **10**:432–6. doi:10.1016/j.yebeh.2007.01.012
5. Weber S, Molgaard C, Taudorf K, Uldall P. Modified Atkins diet to children and adolescents with medical intractable epilepsy. *Seizure* (2009) **18**:237–40. doi:10.1016/j.seizure.2008.10.004
6. Liu YM, Wang HS. Medium-chain triglyceride ketogenic diet, an effective treatment for drug-resistant epilepsy and a comparison with other ketogenic diets. *Biomed J* (2013) **36**:9–15. doi:10.4103/2319-4170.107154
7. Sankar R, Sotero de Menezes M. Metabolic and endocrine aspects of the ketogenic diet. *Epilepsy Res* (1999) **37**:191–201. doi:10.1016/S0920-1211(99)00071-6
8. Park S, Kim Da S, Kang S, Daily JW III. A ketogenic diet impairs energy and glucose homeostasis by the attenuation of hypothalamic leptin signaling and hepatic insulin signaling in a rat model of non-obese type 2 diabetes. *Exp Biol Med (Maywood)* (2011) **236**:194–204. doi:10.1258/ebm.2010.010186
9. Ellenbroek JH, Van Dijck L, Tons HA, Rabelink TJ, Carlotti F, Ballieux BE, et al. Long-term ketogenic diet causes glucose intolerance and reduced beta- and alpha-cell mass but no weight loss in mice. *Am J Physiol Endocrinol Metab* (2014) **306**:E552–8. doi:10.1152/ajpendo.00453.2013
10. Reichard GA Jr, Haff AC, Skutches CL, Paul P, Holroyde CP, Owen OE. Plasma acetone metabolism in the fasting human. *J Clin Invest* (1979) **63**:619–26. doi:10.1172/JCI109344
11. Musa-Veloso K, Likhodii SS, Rarama E, Benoit S, Liu YM, Chartrand D, et al. Breath acetone predicts plasma ketone bodies in children with epilepsy on a ketogenic diet. *Nutrition* (2006) **22**:1–8. doi:10.1016/j.nut.2005.04.008
12. Halestrap AP. Monocarboxylic acid transport. *Compr Physiol* (2013) **3**:1611–43. doi:10.1002/cphy.c130008
13. Olpin SE. Implications of impaired ketogenesis in fatty acid oxidation disorders. *Prostaglandins Leukot Essent Fatty Acids* (2004) **70**:293–308. doi:10.1016/j.plefa.2003.06.003

14. Cheng CM, Kelley B, Wang J, Strauss D, Eagles DA, Bondy CA. A ketogenic diet increases brain insulin-like growth factor receptor and glucose transporter gene expression. *Endocrinology* (2003) **144**:2676–82. doi:10.1210/en.2002-0057
15. Bough KJ, Wetherington J, Hassel B, Pare JF, Gawryluk JW, Greene JG, et al. Mitochondrial biogenesis in the anticonvulsant mechanism of the ketogenic diet. *Ann Neurol* (2006) **60**:223–35. doi:10.1002/ana.20899
16. Noh HS, Lee HP, Kim DW, Kang SS, Cho GJ, Rho JM, et al. A cDNA microarray analysis of gene expression profiles in rat hippocampus following a ketogenic diet. *Brain Res Mol Brain Res* (2004) **129**:80–7. doi:10.1016/j.molbrainres.2004.06.020
17. DeVivo DC, Leckie MP, Ferrendelli JS, McDougal DB Jr. Chronic ketosis and cerebral metabolism. *Ann Neurol* (1978) **3**:331–7. doi:10.1002/ana.410030410
18. Kim do Y, Vallejo J, Rho JM. Ketones prevent synaptic dysfunction induced by mitochondrial respiratory complex inhibitors. *J Neurochem* (2010) **114**:130–41. doi:10.1111/j.1471-4159.2010.06728.x
19. Tieu K, Perier C, Caspersen C, Teismann P, Wu DC, Yan SD, et al. D-Beta-hydroxybutyrate rescues mitochondrial respiration and mitigates features of Parkinson disease. *J Clin Invest* (2003) **112**:892–901. doi:10.1172/JCI200318797
20. Hughes SD, Kanabus M, Anderson G, Hargreaves IP, Rutherford T, O'Donnell M, et al. The ketogenic diet component decanoic acid increases mitochondrial citrate synthase and complex I activity in neuronal cells. *J Neurochem* (2014) **129**:426–33. doi:10.1111/jnc.12646
21. McDaniel SS, Rensing NR, Thio LL, Yamada KA, Wong M. The ketogenic diet inhibits the mammalian target of rapamycin (mTOR) pathway. *Epilepsia* (2011) **52**:e7–11. doi:10.1111/j.1528-1167.2011.02981.x
22. Wijburg FA, Barth PG, Bindoff LA, Birch-Machin MA, Van Der Blij JF, Ruitenbeek W, et al. Leigh syndrome associated with a deficiency of the pyruvate dehydrogenase complex: results of treatment with a ketogenic diet. *Neuropediatrics* (1992) **23**:147–52. doi:10.1055/s-2008-1071331
23. Barnerias C, Saudubray JM, Touati G, De Lonlay P, Dulac O, Ponsot G, et al. Pyruvate dehydrogenase complex deficiency: four neurological phenotypes with differing pathogenesis. *Dev Med Child Neurol* (2010) **52**:e1–9. doi:10.1111/j.1469-8749.2009.03541.x
24. Di Pisa V, Cecconi I, Gentile V, Di Pietro E, Marchiani V, Verrotti A, et al. Case report of pyruvate dehydrogenase deficiency with unusual increase of fats during ketogenic diet treatment. *J Child Neurol* (2012) **27**:1593–6. doi:10.1177/0883073812436424
25. Wexler ID, Hemalatha SG, McConnell J, Buist NR, Dahl HH, Berry SA, et al. Outcome of pyruvate dehydrogenase deficiency treated with ketogenic diets. Studies in patients with identical mutations. *Neurology* (1997) **49**:1655–61. doi:10.1212/WNL.49.6.1655
26. El-Gharbawy AH, Boney A, Young SP, Kishnani PS. Follow-up of a child with pyruvate dehydrogenase deficiency on a less restrictive ketogenic diet. *Mol Genet Metab* (2011) **102**:214–5. doi:10.1016/j.ymgme.2010.11.001
27. Kang HC, Lee YM, Kim HD, Lee JS, Slama A. Safe and effective use of the ketogenic diet in children with epilepsy and mitochondrial respiratory chain complex defects. *Epilepsia* (2007) **48**:82–8. doi:10.1111/j.1528-1167.2006.00906.x
28. Sullivan PG, Rippy NA, Dorenbos K, Concepcion RC, Agarwal AK, Rho JM. The ketogenic diet increases mitochondrial uncoupling protein levels and activity. *Ann Neurol* (2004) **55**:576–80. doi:10.1002/ana.20062
29. Milder JB, Liang LP, Patel M. Acute oxidative stress and systemic Nrf2 activation by the ketogenic diet. *Neurobiol Dis* (2010) **40**:238–44. doi:10.1016/j.nbd.2010.05.030
30. Ziegler DR, Ribeiro LC, Hagenn M, Siqueira IR, Araujo E, Torres IL, et al. Ketogenic diet increases glutathione peroxidase activity in rat hippocampus. *Neurochem Res* (2003) **28**:1793–7. doi:10.1023/A:1026107405399
31. Jarrett SG, Milder JB, Liang LP, Patel M. The ketogenic diet increases mitochondrial glutathione levels. *J Neurochem* (2008) **106**:1044–51. doi:10.1111/j.1471-4159.2008.05460.x
32. Maalouf M, Sullivan PG, Davis L, Kim DY, Rho JM. Ketones inhibit mitochondrial production of reactive oxygen species production following glutamate excitotoxicity by increasing NADH oxidation. *Neuroscience* (2007) **145**:256–64. doi:10.1016/j.neuroscience.2006.11.065
33. Yudkoff M, Daikhin Y, Nissim I, Horyn O, Lazarow A, Luhovyy B, et al. Response of brain amino acid metabolism to ketosis. *Neurochem Int* (2005) **47**:119–28. doi:10.1016/j.neuint.2005.04.014
34. Dahlin M, Elfving A, Ungerstedt U, Åmark P. The ketogenic diet influences the levels of excitatory and inhibitory amino acids in the CSF in children with refractory epilepsy. *Epilepsy Res* (2005) **64**:115–25. doi:10.1016/j.eplepsyres.2005.03.008
35. Maurer CM, Schonthaler HB, Mueller KP, Neuhauss SC. Distinct retinal deficits in a zebrafish pyruvate dehydrogenase-deficient mutant. *J Neurosci* (2010) **30**:11962–72. doi:10.1523/JNEUROSCI.2848-10.2010
36. Nylen K, Velazquez JL, Likhodii SS, Cortez MA, Shen L, Leshchenko Y, et al. A ketogenic diet rescues the murine succinic semialdehyde dehydrogenase deficient phenotype. *Exp Neurol* (2008) **210**:449–57. doi:10.1016/j.expneurol.2007.11.015
37. Baranano KW, Hartman AL. The ketogenic diet: uses in epilepsy and other neurologic illnesses. *Curr Treat Options Neurol* (2008) **10**:410–9. doi:10.1007/s11940-008-0043-8
38. Stafstrom CE, Rho JM. The ketogenic diet as a treatment paradigm for diverse neurological disorders. *Front Pharmacol* (2012) **3**:59. doi:10.3389/fphar.2012.00059
39. Hartman AL, Gasior M, Vining EP, Rogawski MA. The neuropharmacology of the ketogenic diet. *Pediatr Neurol* (2007) **36**:281–92. doi:10.1016/j.pediatrneurol.2007.02.008
40. Kossoff EH, Wang HS. Dietary therapies for epilepsy. *Biomed J* (2013) **36**:2–8. doi:10.4103/2319-4170.107152
41. Marsh EB, Freeman JM, Kossoff EH, Vining EP, Rubenstein JE, Pyzik PL, et al. The outcome of children with intractable seizures: a 3- to 6-year follow-up of 67 children who remained on the ketogenic diet less than one year. *Epilepsia* (2006) **47**:425–30. doi:10.1111/j.1528-1167.2006.00439.x
42. Coppola G, Verrotti A, Ammendola E, Operto FF, Corte RD, Signoriello G, et al. Ketogenic diet for the treatment of catastrophic epileptic encephalopathies in childhood. *Eur J Paediatr Neurol* (2010) **14**:229–34. doi:10.1016/j.ejpn.2009.06.006
43. Bough KJ, Rho JM. Anticonvulsant mechanisms of the ketogenic diet. *Epilepsia* (2007) **48**:43–58. doi:10.1111/j.1528-1167.2007.00915.x
44. Giulivi C, Zhang YF, Omanska-Klusek A, Ross-Inta C, Wong S, Hertz-Picciotto I, et al. Mitochondrial dysfunction in autism. *JAMA* (2010) **304**:2389–96. doi:10.1001/jama.2010.1706
45. Hallmayer J, Cleveland S, Torres A, Phillips J, Cohen B, Torigoe T, et al. Genetic heritability and shared environmental factors among twin pairs with autism. *Arch Gen Psychiatry* (2011) **68**:1095–102. doi:10.1001/archgenpsychiatry.2011.76
46. Frazier TW, Thompson L, Youngstrom EA, Law P, Hardan AY, Eng C, et al. A twin study of heritable and shared environmental contributions to autism. *J Autism Dev Disord* (2014). doi:10.1007/s10803-014-2081-2
47. Holmboe K, Rijsdijk FV, Hallett V, Happe F, Plomin R, Ronald A. Strong genetic influences on the stability of autistic traits in childhood. *J Am Acad Child Adolesc Psychiatry* (2014) **53**:221–30. doi:10.1016/j.jaac.2013.11.001
48. Zecavati N, Spence SJ. Neurometabolic disorders and dysfunction in autism spectrum disorders. *Curr Neurol Neurosci Rep* (2009) **9**:129–36. doi:10.1007/s11910-009-0021-x
49. Bolton PF, Carcani-Rathwell I, Hutton J, Goode S, Howlin P, Rutter M. Epilepsy in autism: features and correlates. *Br J Psychiatry* (2011) **198**:289–94. doi:10.1192/bjp.bp.109.076877
50. Tuchman R, Cuccaro M, Alessandri M. Autism and epilepsy: historical perspective. *Brain Dev* (2010) **32**:709–18. doi:10.1016/j.braindev.2010.04.008
51. Li BM, Liu XR, Yi YH, Deng YH, Su T, Zou X, et al. Autism in Dravet syndrome: prevalence, features, and relationship to the clinical characteristics of epilepsy and mental retardation. *Epilepsy Behav* (2011) **21**:291–5. doi:10.1016/j.yebeh.2011.04.060
52. Bujas-Petkovic Z, Matijasic R, Divcic B. Rett's syndrome – differential diagnosis of autism in a case report. *Lijec Vjesn* (1989) **111**:458–60.
53. Steffenburg U, Hagberg G, Hagberg B. Epilepsy in a representative series of Rett syndrome. *Acta Paediatr* (2001) **90**:34–9. doi:10.1111/j.1651-2227.2001.tb00252.x
54. Evangeliou A, Vlachonikolis I, Mihailidou H, Spilioti M, Skarpalezou A, Makaronas N, et al. Application of a ketogenic diet in children with autistic behavior: pilot study. *J Child Neurol* (2003) **18**:113–8. doi:10.1177/08830738030180020501
55. Herbert MR, Buckley JA. Autism and dietary therapy: case report and review of the literature. *J Child Neurol* (2013) **28**:975–82. doi:10.1177/0883073813488668
56. Mantis JG, Fritz CL, Marsh J, Heinrichs SC, Seyfried TN. Improvement in motor and exploratory behavior in Rett syndrome mice with restricted

ketogenic and standard diets. *Epilepsy Behav* (2009) **15**:133–41. doi:10.1016/j.yebeh.2009.02.038

57. Ruskin DN, Svedova J, Cote JL, Sandau U, Rho JM, Kawamura M Jr, et al. Ketogenic diet improves core symptoms of autism in BTBR mice. *PLoS One* (2013) **8**:e65021. doi:10.1371/journal.pone.0065021
58. Johnston CS, Tjonn SL, Swan PD, White A, Hutchins H, Sears B. Ketogenic low-carbohydrate diets have no metabolic advantage over nonketogenic low-carbohydrate diets. *Am J Clin Nutr* (2006) **83**:1055–61. doi:10.1371/journal.pone.0065021
59. Veggiotti P, Teutonico F, Alfei E, Nardocci N, Zorzi G, Tagliabue A, et al. Glucose transporter type 1 deficiency: ketogenic diet in three patients with atypical phenotype. *Brain Dev* (2010) **32**:404–8. doi:10.1016/j.braindev.2009.04.013
60. Prasad C, Rupar T, Prasad AN. Pyruvate dehydrogenase deficiency and epilepsy. *Brain Dev* (2011) **33**:856–65. doi:10.1016/j.braindev.2011.08.003
61. Morris AA, Leonard JV. The treatment of congenital lactic acidoses. *J Inherit Metab Dis* (1996) **19**:573–80. doi:10.1007/BF01799117
62. Clark-Taylor T, Clark-Taylor BE. Is autism a disorder of fatty acid metabolism? Possible dysfunction of mitochondrial beta-oxidation by long chain acyl-CoA dehydrogenase. *Med Hypotheses* (2004) **62**:970–5. doi:10.1016/j.mehy.2004.01.011
63. Frye RE, Melnyk S, MacFabe DF. Unique acyl-carnitine profiles are potential biomarkers for acquired mitochondrial disease in autism spectrum disorder. *Transl Psychiatry* (2013) **3**:e220. doi:10.1038/tp.2012.143
64. Celestino-Soper PB, Violante S, Crawford EL, Luo R, Lionel AC, Delaby E, et al. A common X-linked inborn error of carnitine biosynthesis may be a risk factor for nondysmorphic autism. *Proc Natl Acad Sci U S A* (2012) **109**:7974–81. doi:10.1073/pnas.1120210109
65. Ahola-Erkkila S, Carroll CJ, Peltola-Mjosund K, Tulkki V, Mattila I, Seppanen-Laakso T, et al. Ketogenic diet slows down mitochondrial myopathy progression in mice. *Hum Mol Genet* (2010) **19**:1974–84. doi:10.1093/hmg/ddq076
66. Bernier FP, Boneh A, Dennett X, Chow CW, Cleary MA, Thorburn DR. Diagnostic criteria for respiratory chain disorders in adults and children. *Neurology* (2002) **59**:1406–11. doi:10.1212/01.WNL.0000033795.17156.00
67. Rossignol R, Malgat M, Mazat JP, Letellier T. Threshold effect and tissue specificity. Implication for mitochondrial cytopathies. *J Biol Chem* (1999) **274**:33426–32. doi:10.1074/jbc.274.47.33426
68. Napoli E, Wong S, Giulivi C. Evidence of reactive oxygen species-mediated damage to mitochondrial DNA in children with typical autism. *Mol Autism* (2013) **4**:2. doi:10.1186/2040-2392-4-2
69. Napoli E, Wong S, Hertz-Picciotto I, Giulivi C. Deficits in bioenergetics and impaired immune response in granulocytes from children with autism. *Pediatrics* (2014). doi:10.1542/peds.2013-1545
70. Yoneda M, Chomyn A, Martinuzzi A, Hurko O, Attardi G. Marked replicative advantage of human mtDNA carrying a point mutation that causes the MELAS encephalomyopathy. *Proc Natl Acad Sci U S A* (1992) **89**:11164–8. doi:10.1073/pnas.89.23.11164
71. Diaz F, Bayona-Bafaluy MP, Rana M, Mora M, Hao H, Moraes CT. Human mitochondrial DNA with large deletions repopulates organelles faster than full-length genomes under relaxed copy number control. *Nucleic Acids Res* (2002) **30**:4626–33. doi:10.1093/nar/gkf602
72. Santra S, Gilkerson RW, Davidson M, Schon EA. Ketogenic treatment reduces deleted mitochondrial DNAs in cultured human cells. *Ann Neurol* (2004) **56**:662–9. doi:10.1002/ana.20240
73. Weissman JR, Kelley RI, Bauman ML, Cohen BH, Murray KF, Mitchell RL, et al. Mitochondrial disease in autism spectrum disorder patients: a cohort analysis. *PLoS One* (2008) **3**:e3815. doi:10.1371/journal.pone.0003815
74. Rossignol DA, Frye RE. Mitochondrial dysfunction in autism spectrum disorders: a systematic review and meta-analysis. *Mol Psychiatry* (2012) **17**:290–314. doi:10.1038/mp.2010.136
75. Rossignol DA, Frye RE. A review of research trends in physiological abnormalities in autism spectrum disorders: immune dysregulation, inflammation, oxidative stress, mitochondrial dysfunction and environmental toxicant exposures. *Mol Psychiatry* (2012) **17**:389–401. doi:10.1038/mp.2011.165
76. Gu F, Chauhan V, Kaur K, Brown WT, Lafauci G, Wegiel J, et al. Alterations in mitochondrial DNA copy number and the activities of electron transport chain complexes and pyruvate dehydrogenase in the frontal cortex from subjects with autism. *Transl Psychiatry* (2013) **3**:e299. doi:10.1038/tp.2013.68
77. Milder J, Patel M. Modulation of oxidative stress and mitochondrial function by the ketogenic diet. *Epilepsy Res* (2012) **100**:295–303. doi:10.1016/j.eplepsyres.2011.09.021
78. Finsterer J, Zarrouk Mahjoub S. Epilepsy in mitochondrial disorders. *Seizure* (2012) **21**:316–21. doi:10.1016/j.seizure.2012.03.003
79. Werther GA, Russo V, Baker N, Butler G. The role of the insulin-like growth factor system in the developing brain. *Horm Res* (1998) **49**(Suppl 1):37–40. doi:10.1159/000053066
80. Carro E, Trejo JL, Núñez A, Torres-Aleman I. Brain repair and neuroprotection by serum insulin-like growth factor I. *Mol Neurobiol* (2003) **27**:153–62. doi:10.1385/MN:27:2:153
81. Gasparini L, Xu H. Potential roles of insulin and IGF-1 in Alzheimer's disease. *Trends Neurosci* (2003) **26**:404–6. doi:10.1016/S0166-2236(03)00163-2
82. Zhao Y, Fung C, Shin D, Shin BC, Thamotharan S, Sankar R, et al. Neuronal glucose transporter isoform 3 deficient mice demonstrate features of autism spectrum disorders. *Mol Psychiatry* (2010) **15**:286–99. doi:10.1038/mp.2009.51
83. Chen J, Alberts I, Li X. Dysregulation of the IGF-I/PI3K/AKT/mTOR signaling pathway in autism spectrum disorders. *Int J Dev Neurosci* (2014) **35C**:35–41. doi:10.1016/j.ijdevneu.2014.03.006
84. Gano L, Patel M, Rho JM. Ketogenic diets, mitochondria and neurological diseases. *J Lipid Res* (2014). doi:10.1194/jlr.R048975
85. Kelleher RJ III, Bear MF. The autistic neuron: troubled translation? *Cell* (2008) **135**:401–6. doi:10.1016/j.cell.2008.10.017
86. Sawicka K, Zukin RS. Dysregulation of mTOR signaling in neuropsychiatric disorders: therapeutic implications. *Neuropsychopharmacology* (2012) **37**:305–6. doi:10.1038/npp.2011.210
87. Gkogkas CG, Khoutorsky A, Ran I, Rampakakis E, Nevarko T, Weatherill DB, et al. Autism-related deficits via dysregulated eIF4E-dependent translational control. *Nature* (2013) **493**:371–7. doi:10.1038/nature11628
88. Gottlieb RA, Carreira RS. Autophagy in health and disease. 5. Mitophagy as a way of life. *Am J Physiol Cell Physiol* (2010) **299**:C203–10. doi:10.1152/ajpcell.00097.2010
89. Napoli E, Ross-Inta C, Wong S, Hung C, Fujisawa Y, Sakaguchi D, et al. Mitochondrial dysfunction in Pten haplo-insufficient mice with social deficits and repetitive behavior: interplay between Pten and p53. *PLoS One* (2012) **7**:e42504. doi:10.1371/journal.pone.0042504
90. Wong M. Mammalian target of rapamycin (mTOR) pathways in neurological diseases. *Biomed J* (2013) **36**:40–50. doi:10.4103/2319-4170.110365
91. Coleman ST, Fang TK, Rovinsky SA, Turano FJ, Moye-Rowley WS. Expression of a glutamate decarboxylase homologue is required for normal oxidative stress tolerance in *Saccharomyces cerevisiae*. *J Biol Chem* (2001) **276**:244–50. doi:10.1074/jbc.M007103200
92. Erasmus DJ, Van Der Merwe GK, Van Vuuren HJ. Genome-wide expression analyses: metabolic adaptation of *Saccharomyces cerevisiae* to high sugar stress. *FEMS Yeast Res* (2003) **3**:375–99. doi:10.1016/S1567-1356(02)00203-9
93. Cakir T, Patil KR, Onsan Z, Ulgen KO, Kirdar B, Nielsen J. Integration of metabolome data with metabolic networks reveals reporter reactions. *Mol Syst Biol* (2006) **2**:50. doi:10.1038/msb4100085
94. Schonfeld P, Wieckowski MR, Lebiedzinska M, Wojtczak L. Mitochondrial fatty acid oxidation and oxidative stress: lack of reverse electron transfer-associated production of reactive oxygen species. *Biochim Biophys Acta* (2010) **1797**:929–38. doi:10.1016/j.bbabio.2010.01.010
95. James SJ, Melnyk S, Fuchs G, Reid T, Jernigan S, Pavliv O, et al. Efficacy of methylcobalamin and folinic acid treatment on glutathione redox status in children with autism. *Am J Clin Nutr* (2009) **89**:425–30. doi:10.3945/ajcn.2008.26615
96. James SJ, Rose S, Melnyk S, Jernigan S, Blossom S, Pavliv O, et al. Cellular and mitochondrial glutathione redox imbalance in lymphoblastoid cells derived from children with autism. *FASEB J* (2009) **23**:2374–83. doi:10.1096/fj.08-128926
97. Ramos F, El Guezzar M, Grenson M, Wiame JM. Mutations affecting the enzymes involved in the utilization of 4-aminobutyric acid as nitrogen source by the yeast *Saccharomyces cerevisiae*. *Eur J Biochem* (1985) **149**:401–4. doi:10.1111/j.1432-1033.1985.tb08939.x
98. Andriamampandry C, Siffert JC, Schmitt M, Garnier JM, Staub A, Muller C, et al. Cloning of a rat brain succinic semialdehyde reductase involved in the synthesis of the neuromodulator gamma-hydroxybutyrate. *Biochem J* (1998) **334**(Pt 1):43–50.

99. Schaller M, Schaffhauser M, Sans N, Wermuth B. Cloning and expression of succinic semialdehyde reductase from human brain. Identity with aflatoxin B1 aldehyde reductase. *Eur J Biochem* (1999) **265**:1056–60. doi:10.1046/j.1432-1327.1999.00826.x
100. Breitkreuz KE, Allan WL, Van Cauwenberghe OR, Jakobs C, Talibi D, Andre B, et al. A novel gamma-hydroxybutyrate dehydrogenase: identification and expression of an Arabidopsis cDNA and potential role under oxygen deficiency. *J Biol Chem* (2003) **278**:41552–6. doi:10.1074/jbc.M305717200
101. Yudkoff M, Daikhin Y, Melø TM, Nissim I, Sonnewald U, Nissim I. The ketogenic diet and brain metabolism of amino acids: relationship to the anticonvulsant effect. *Annu Rev Nutr* (2007) **27**:415–30. doi:10.1146/annurev.nutr.27.061406.093722
102. Chattopadhyaya B, Cristo GD. GABAergic circuit dysfunctions in neurodevelopmental disorders. *Front Psychiatry* (2012) **3**:51. doi:10.3389/fpsyt.2012.00051
103. Han S, Tai C, Westenbroek RE, Yu FH, Cheah CS, Potter GB, et al. Autistic-like behaviour in Scn1a± mice and rescue by enhanced GABA-mediated neurotransmission. *Nature* (2012) **489**:385–90. doi:10.1038/nature11356
104. Weston MC, Chen H, Swann JW. Multiple roles for mammalian target of rapamycin signaling in both glutamatergic and GABAergic synaptic transmission. *J Neurosci* (2012) **32**:11441–52. doi:10.1523/JNEUROSCI.1283-12.2012
105. Banerjee A, Garcia-Oscos F, Roychowdhury S, Galindo LC, Hall S, Kilgard MP, et al. Impairment of cortical GABAergic synaptic transmission in an environmental rat model of autism. *Int J Neuropsychopharmacol* (2013) **16**:1309–18. doi:10.1017/S1461145712001216
106. Liebhaber GM, Riemann E, Baumeister FA. Ketogenic diet in Rett syndrome. *J Child Neurol* (2003) **18**:74–5. doi:10.1177/08830738030180011801
107. Fatemi SH, Halt AR, Stary JM, Kanodia R, Schulz SC, Realmuto GR. Glutamic acid decarboxylase 65 and 67 kDa proteins are reduced in autistic parietal and cerebellar cortices. *Biol Psychiatry* (2002) **52**:805–10. doi:10.1016/S0006-3223(02)01430-0
108. Collins AL, Ma DQ, Whitehead PL, Martin ER, Wright HH, Abramson RK, et al. Investigation of autism and GABA receptor subunit genes in multiple ethnic groups. *Neurogenetics* (2006) **7**:167–74. doi:10.1007/s10048-006-0045-1
109. Fatemi SH, Reutiman TJ, Folsom TD, Thuras PD. GABA(A) receptor downregulation in brains of subjects with autism. *J Autism Dev Disord* (2009) **39**:223–30. doi:10.1007/s10803-008-0646-7
110. Knerr I, Pearl PL. Ketogenic diet: stoking energy stores and still posing questions. *Exp Neurol* (2008) **211**:11–3. doi:10.1016/j.expneurol.2008.01.015
111. Al-Mudallal AS, Lamanna JC, Lust WD, Harik SI. Diet-induced ketosis does not cause cerebral acidosis. *Epilepsia* (1996) **37**:258–61. doi:10.1111/j.1528-1157.1996.tb00022.x
112. Nordli DR Jr, De Vivo DC. The ketogenic diet revisited: back to the future. *Epilepsia* (1997) **38**:743–9. doi:10.1111/j.1528-1157.1997.tb01460.x
113. Nguyen Q, Sapp DW, Van Ness PC, Olsen RW. Modulation of GABAA receptor binding in human brain by neuroactive steroids: species and brain regional differences. *Synapse* (1995) **19**:77–87. doi:10.1002/syn.890190203
114. Mendu SK, Bhandage A, Jin Z, Birnir B. Different subtypes of GABA-A receptors are expressed in human, mouse and rat T lymphocytes. *PLoS One* (2012) **7**:e42959. doi:10.1371/journal.pone.0042959
115. Imahori K, Uchida T. Physiology and pathology of tau protein kinases in relation to Alzheimer's disease. *J Biochem* (1997) **121**:179–88.
116. Veech RL, Chance B, Kashiwaya Y, Lardy HA, Cahill GF Jr. Ketone bodies, potential therapeutic uses. *IUBMB Life* (2001) **51**:241–7. doi:10.1080/152165401753311780
117. Kemper TL, Bauman M. Neuropathology of infantile autism. *J Neuropathol Exp Neurol* (1998) **57**:645–52. doi:10.1097/00005072-199807000-00001
118. Sokol DK, Dunn DW, Edwards-Brown M, Feinberg J. Hydrogen proton magnetic resonance spectroscopy in autism: preliminary evidence of elevated choline/creatine ratio. *J Child Neurol* (2002) **17**:245–9. doi:10.1177/088307380201700401
119. Deutsch SI, Urbano MR, Neumann SA, Burket JA, Katz E. Cholinergic abnormalities in autism: is there a rationale for selective nicotinic agonist interventions? *Clin Neuropharmacol* (2010) **33**:114–20. doi:10.1097/WNF.0b013e3181d6f7ad
120. Niederhofer H, Staffen W, Mair A. Galantamine may be effective in treating autistic disorder. *BMJ* (2002) **325**:1422. doi:10.1136/bmj.325.7377.1422/a
121. Nicolson R, Craven-Thuss B, Smith J. A prospective, open-label trial of galantamine in autistic disorder. *J Child Adolesc Psychopharmacol* (2006) **16**:621–9. doi:10.1089/cap.2006.16.621
122. Ghaleiha A, Ghyasvand M, Mohammadi MR, Farokhnia M, Yadegari N, Tabrizi M, et al. Galantamine efficacy and tolerability as an augmentative therapy in autistic children: a randomized, double-blind, placebo-controlled trial. *J Psychopharmacol* (2013) **28**:677–85. doi:10.1177/0269881113508830
123. Karvat G, Kimchi T. Acetylcholine elevation relieves cognitive rigidity and social deficiency in a mouse model of autism. *Neuropsychopharmacology* (2014) **39**:831–40. doi:10.1038/npp.2013.274
124. Sato K, Kashiwaya Y, Keon CA, Tsuchiya N, King MT, Radda GK, et al. Insulin, ketone bodies, and mitochondrial energy transduction. *FASEB J* (1995) **9**:651–8.
125. Sobanski E, Marcus A, Hennighausen K, Hebebrand J, Schmidt MH. Further evidence for a low body weight in male children and adolescents with Asperger's disorder. *Eur Child Adolesc Psychiatry* (1999) **8**:312–4. doi:10.1007/s007870050106
126. Fisman S, Steele M, Short J, Byrne T, Lavallee C. Case study: anorexia nervosa and autistic disorder in an adolescent girl. *J Am Acad Child Adolesc Psychiatry* (1996) **35**:937–40. doi:10.1097/00004583-199607000-00021
127. Kwiterovich PO Jr, Vining EPG, Pyzik P, Skolasky R Jr, Freeman JM. Effect of a high-fat ketogenic diet on plasma levels of lipids, lipoproteins, and apolipoproteins in children. *JAMA* (2003) **290**:912–20. doi:10.1001/jama.290.7.912
128. Nizamuddin J, Turner Z, Rubenstein JE, Pyzik PL, Kossoff EH. Management and risk factors for dyslipidemia with the ketogenic diet. *J Child Neurol* (2008) **23**:758–61. doi:10.1177/0883073808318061
129. Liebhaber G, Pascher B, Gempel K, Baumeister FA. Asymptomatic carnitine depletion on ketogenic diet in patients with pharmacoresistant epilepsies. *Klin Padiatr* (2006) **218**:260–3. doi:10.1055/s-2005-836811
130. Fukao T, Mitchell G, Sass JO, Hori T, Orii K, Aoyama Y. Ketone body metabolism and its defects. *J Inherit Metab Dis* (2014). doi:10.1007/s10545-014-9704-9
131. Parikh S, Saneto R, Falk MJ, Anselm I, Cohen BH, Haas R, et al. A modern approach to the treatment of mitochondrial disease. *Curr Treat Options Neurol* (2009) **11**:414–30. doi:10.1007/s11940-009-0046-0
132. Kossoff EH, Zupec-Kania BA, Rho JM. Ketogenic diets: an update for child neurologists. *J Child Neurol* (2009) **24**:979–88. doi:10.1177/0883073809337162
133. Latif A, Heinz P, Cook R. Iron deficiency in autism and Asperger syndrome. *Autism* (2002) **6**:103–14. doi:10.1177/1362361302006001008
134. Kang HC, Chung DE, Kim DW, Kim HD. Early- and late-onset complications of the ketogenic diet for intractable epilepsy. *Epilepsia* (2004) **45**:1116–23. doi:10.1111/j.0013-9580.2004.10004.x
135. Kim YM, Vaidya VV, Khusainov T, Kim HD, Kim SH, Lee EJ, et al. Various indications for a modified Atkins diet in intractable childhood epilepsy. *Brain Dev* (2012) **34**:570–5. doi:10.1016/j.braindev.2011.09.013
136. Jozwiak S, Kossoff EH, Kotulska-Jozwiak K. Dietary treatment of epilepsy: rebirth of an ancient treatment. *Neurol Neurochir Pol* (2011) **45**:370–8. doi:10.1016/S0028-3843(14)60108-0

# 22

# Repeated insulin-like growth factor 1 treatment in a patient with Rett syndrome: a single case study

**Giorgio Pini[1]*, M. Flora Scusa[1], Alberto Benincasa[1], Ilaria Bottiglioni[1], Laura Congiu[1], Cyrus Vadhatpour[2], Anna Maria Romanelli[1], Ilaria Gemo[1], Chetti Puccetti[1], Rachel McNamara[2], Seán O'Leary[2], Aiden Corvin[3], Michael Gill[3] and Daniela Tropea[1,3]***

[1] *Tuscany Rett Center, Versilia Hospital, Viareggio, Italy*
[2] *Medical School, Trinity College Dublin, Dublin, Ireland*
[3] *Department of Psychiatry, Trinity College Dublin, Dublin, Ireland*

***Edited by:***
*Roberto Canitano, University Hospital of Siena, Italy*

***Reviewed by:***
*Carlo Sala, CNR Institute of Neuroscience, Italy*
*Magdalena Romanowicz, Stanford University, USA*
*Iliyan Ivanov, Mount Sinai School of Medicine, USA*
*Arianna Maffei, State University of New York at Stony Brook, USA*

****Correspondence:***
*Giorgio Pini, Tuscany Rett Center, Versilia Hospital, Via Aurelia 335, Lido di Camaiore, ASL 12 di Viareggio, Italy*
*e-mail: g.pini@usl12.toscana.it;*
*Daniela Tropea, Department of Psychiatry, Trinity College Dublin, College Green, Dublin 2, Ireland*
*e-mail: tropead@tcd.ie*

Rett syndrome (RTT) is a devastating neurodevelopmental disorder that has no cure. Patients show regression of acquired skills, motor, and speech impairment, cardio-respiratory distress, microcephaly, and stereotyped hand movements. The majority of RTT patients display mutations in the gene that codes for the Methyl-CpG binding protein 2 (MeCP2), which is involved in the development of the central nervous system, especially synaptic and circuit maturation. Thus, agents that promote brain development and synaptic function are good candidates for ameliorating the symptoms of RTT. In particular, insulin-like growth factor 1 (IGF1) and its active peptide (1–3) IGF1 cross the Blood Brain Barrier, and therefore are ideal treatments for RTT Indeed, both (1–3) IGF1 and IGF1 treatment significantly ameliorates RTT symptoms in a mouse model of the disease In a previous study, we established that IGF1 is safe and well tolerated on Rett patients. In this open label clinical case study, we assess the safety and tolerability of IGF1 administration in two cycles of the treatment. Before and after each cycle, we monitored the clinical and blood parameters, autonomic function, and social and cognitive abilities, and we found that IGF1 was well tolerated each time and did not induce any side effect, nor it interfered with the other treatments that the patient was undergoing. We noticed a moderate improvement in the cognitive, social, and autonomic abilities of the patient after each cycle but the benefits were not retained between the two cycles, consistent with the pre-clinical observation that treatments for RTT should be administered through life. We find that repeated IGF1 treatment is safe and well tolerated in Rett patients but observed effects are not retained between cycles. These results have applications to other pathologies considering that IGF1 has been shown to be effective in other disorders of the autism spectrum.

**Keywords: Rett syndrome, insulin-like growth factor 1, social cognition, seizures, autonomic functions**

## INTRODUCTION

The clinical case study performed in this experiment depicts the efficacy and safety of insulin-like growth factor 1 (IGF1) exposure upon two cycles of treatment. The patient is a young girl with a clinical and genetic diagnosis of Rett syndrome (RTT). The study started when the patient was 5 years old. The patient received first round of treatment on the 25th of May 2010 and discontinued on the 11th of November 2010. The second round of treatment started on the 20th of November 2012 and discontinued on the 28th of February 2013.

## BACKGROUND

Rett syndrome is taxonomized as a pervasive neurodevelopmental disorder affecting mainly female children (1:10000) due to its X-linked method of inheritance (1). Methy-CpG binding protein 2 (MeCP2) dysfunction is associated with several neurodevelopmental disorders (1), and can cause a wide variety of phenotypes in females. Most males do not live past the first year due to neonatal encephalopathy and death in the classic RTT karyotype (2). The effects of MECP2 mutations lead to a loss of function or overexpression of the MeCP2 protein. If it results in a loss of function state, some examples of effects yield: classic RTT, atypical RTT, autism, and mild mental retardation (2). The majority of RTT patients (85%) have mutations in the MECP2 gene that lead to loss of MECP2 protein function. At this point of time, there is no cure to RTT syndrome, however treatment strategies are starting to emerge.

Rett syndrome is a progressive neurodevelopmental disorder that initially presents in females just past 18 months. Patients with RTT appear to have apparent normal development and milestone achievements up to the first 18 months of age (3). Early indication of neurological disease progression includes: deceleration of head growth, general growth retardation, weight loss, and weak posture via muscle hypotonia (2). Progression of RTT leads to the loss of purposeful use of their hands and the development of stereotypic hand wringing or washing movements: other hand movements are clapping, flapping, and mouthing (2). Withdrawal of social behaviors are noticeable where patients have shown symptoms such as irritability, self-abusive mannerisms, blank faces, audio hypersensitivity, reduction of eye contact, unresponsiveness to social cues, and indifference to variable environments (2). Eventual losses in motor coordination, ataxia, and gait apraxia are symptoms of motor pathway deterioration (2). Most girls eventually require wheel chair assistance during teenage years. Autonomic perturbations include hyperventilation (and other breathing abnormalities), seizures with variable severity, cardiac abnormalities, constipation, parkinsonian features, and oropharyngeal dysfunction (2). Patients may have a normal appetite but still experience weight loss and osteopenia. Structural abnormalities include scoliosis and rigidity. Behavioral complications involve teeth grinding, temper tantrums, depression, and anxiety. The condition eventually plateaus and the patient may live up to their seventh decade (2).

MeCP2 is an example of a mammalian protein that binds to methylated CpGs. For its ability to bind DNA and influence gene expression, MeCP2 is mostly believed to be a transcription factor (1), however localization of MeCP2 outside the nucleus and in the synaptic compartments (4) suggest that MeCP2 protein may have also functions directly related to synaptic activity. Inheritance of the MECP2 gene follows an X-linked dominant pattern and sporadic mutations are prevalent in 85% of classic RTT cases (2). Mutations that have been noted on the spectrum include missense, nonsense, and frame shift mutations for this protein. Mutations impacting on the nuclear localization sequence of MeCP2 or early truncating mutations have more severe phenotypes in comparison to missense mutations; while C-terminal deletions are thought to cause milder phenotypes. There is an association between the severity of the mutation and the severity of the phenotype (5). The phenotype of the female is highly variable depending on the expression levels of the unaffected copy of MECP2 on the other X chromosome.

The identification of the gene associated with Rett made possible the generation of mutant mice defective in MeCP2 functions. The mice have signs that resemble patients' symptoms and therefore constitute a valid model for the study of neurobiology of Rett and for testing candidate therapeutics. A significant discovery has emerged from two independent groups concluding that in the mouse model, the reactivation of the natural Mecp2 gene in the adult mutant mice partially reestablished normal phenotype (6,7). This finding implies that when the normal brain has impairment by a dysfunctional MeCP2, control conditions can be restored in the central nervous system. However, Zoghbi's lab has shown that drug treatment for RTT has to be administered during the whole life of the patients (8).

Neurobiological analysis shows that MeCP2 mutations produce defects in central nervous system development, specifically in the maturation of circuits and synapses (4, 9). Therefore, medical treatments focused on brain development and synaptic functioning is promising for the regression of RTT. Indeed, a research study noted that overexpression of brain-derived neurotrophic growth factor (BDNF), which is a neurotrophin that has involvement in brain development and plasticity, resulted in the neutralization of the MeCP2 deficiency (10). This allowed for the consideration of growth factors, which are centralized around their involvement of neuronal and synaptic growth, toward potential treatment options for RTT syndrome. BDNF is incapable of crossing the blood brain barrier, so it is of no use for immediate pharmacological therapy consideration. However, IGF1 and its active peptide (1–3) IGF1, are capable of crossing the blood brain barrier. This quality makes them an ideal drug for treatment in neurodevelopmental disorders like RTT. Research has shown that IGF1 peptide treatment partially restored spine density and synaptic amplitude in the mouse model (9). The treatment was started at 2 weeks of age and was noted to stabilize cortical plasticity to the wild-type level. One of the major effects noted in this study was after the treatment of IGF1; MeCP2 KO with treatment mice improved from an average of 60-day lifespan to an average of 90-day lifespan in comparison with KO without treatment mice. Not only did the KO mice with treatment have increased life span, but also improved respiratory, cardiac, and locomotor function. In the study from Tropea et al. (9) (1–3) IGF1, has already shown to ameliorate the symptoms of RTT in the mouse model of the disease. IGF1 has also been shown to be an effective therapy in MeCP2 KO mice (11). Other studies show that IGF1 is a suitable treatment for human RTT patients and that there are no known risks associated with IGF1 administration (12, 13). In our previous study, six girls with classic RTT, between 4 and 11 years of age, were administered IGF1 subcutaneously twice per day for 6 months. They were evaluated based on the effectiveness of the treatment and it was reported that IGF1 partially restored a significant amount of the symptoms of RTT. From this study, all families and caretakers noticed an improvement in cognitive abilities of the girls and their interactions with the surrounding environment. Considered McGraw's study, life-long therapy is necessary to combat RTT syndrome, like IGF1 for MeCP2 dysfunction (8).

The aim of this paper is to evaluate if repeated cycles of IGF1 is a suitable method, in respect to safety and efficacy, for a life-long treatment option in the human model. The clinical case study in this report depicts a patient receiving two cycles of IGF1 treatment and clinical parameter assessments. Also, we provide insight on how the patient responds after the treatment with two clinical evaluations after the treatment cycles. The study is an open label study, and the child displays classic RTT syndrome, where the phenotypic onset of the disease took place between the eighth and ninth month. The child started the first IGF1 cycle in May 2010, when the child was in the fifth year of age. IGF1 was administered twice daily (0.1 mg/kg) for 6 months. Two years later, another cycle of treatment was started. The dosage and routes of administration were the same, but the second cycle lasted 4 months. In between each cycle, blood parameters were monitored and autonomic responses evaluated. During both cycles, IGF1 was well tolerated in each cycle and no direct side effect was observed. IGF1 is also shown to cause no interference with the anti-epileptic medications that the patient was undergoing. Based on the conclusion of this experiment, the treatment is believed to promise a strong impact on RTT syndrome.

## SUBJECTS AND METHODS

### CLINICAL ANALYSIS

We evaluated the RTT patient's overall physical health, RTT-associated phenotypic expressions of the patient, and growth developments. We took notes, recorded in the Section "Results," during various stages of the treatment process during two cycles of IGF1 exposure. The parents kept a diary with daily annotations of glycemia levels and alterations in behavior (sleep, eating, etc.)

#### *Patient screening*

Patient was chosen based on the presentation of classic RTT syndrome and confirmed mutation in the MECP2 gene. The family gave written consent for partaking in this study before any treatment took place. The selection criteria are described in Pini et al. (12).

#### *Treatment administration*

Mecasermin–Increlex (IGF1) was subcutaneously administered twice daily (0.1 mg/kg) in two cycles: the first cycle lasted nearly 6 months, and the second cycle lasted 4 months, with a 2 years gap between the two cycles. Possible side effects include hypoglycemia (headache, dizziness, nausea, and perspiration), tonsil hypertrophia, and local irritation at the injection site. The family was thoroughly informed about the treatment process; the caretakers of the patient were trained to perform daily injections, and were provided with a kit to measure glycemic levels. Patients were observed for side effects during every visit and critical events were recorded and are in summarized in the Section "Results."

#### *Post treatment examination*

The patient was followed up twice after each cycle to evaluate general health after IGF1 exposure. Patient was physically examined based on cardio-respiratory factors, body growth parameters, and motor abilities. Critical events were recorded along with the corresponding epileptic treatment at that time. Behavioral examination along the parameters of social interaction and mood were also evaluated.

### VIDEO ANALYSIS OF COGNITIVE AND SOCIAL ABILITIES

Video analysis utilized approximately 20 h of video recordings of RTT patients and was filmed in Versilia Hospital (Italy). The RTT patient observed in this paper was an analyzed participant in this study. The investigators, analyzing the videos, were not aware that the patient had received IGF1 treatment. Observed preliminary footage from additional patients yielded the design of the scoring criteria. It was decided to score the girls on 20 features, 10 negatives, and 10 positives. The patient was scored in each feature on a scale from 1 to 5, with 1 indicating extreme RTT, 2 indicating severe RTT, 3 indicating moderate RTT, 4 indicating mild RTT, and 5 indicating absent RTT. In this way, a lower score was related to a more prevalent RTT-like behavior. The 10 negative features chosen were: hand wringing, biting, rocking, hitting, indiscriminate moaning, tongue chewing, vacant staring, bruxism, breath-holding/apnea, and Valsalva maneuver. The 10 positive features chosen were: pointing, manipulating, reaching for something, ability to mimic/imitate, indicating yes/no with head gesture, reactivity to a call, reactivity to an object, smiling in response to a stimulus, deliberate vocalization, and attention.

## RESULTS

The patient was born from the mother's first pregnancy. The mother suffers from epilepsy and was treated with anti-epileptic drugs (AEDs) since adolescence. The patient was born at week 38 of gestation by cesarean section due to an emergency response. At birth, the patient had the following dimensions: 2600 g in weight, 45.5 cm in length, and 33 cm in head circumference. The newborn received artificial feeding due to maternal agalactia. At the approximate age of 9 months, the child presented with: frequent pyloric stenosis, decreased stimulus to environment, mentally absent, and showed stereotypic hand to mouth and washing movements. The patient's motor development showed independent seat positioning acquired at 8 months with kyphosis of the bust: unimanual walking with support at 18 months with mild postural tremor. At 18 months, the patient's use of hands was discrete and she could grab objects and press buttons. The patient's language development showed production of vocalization and infrequent simple syllabic doublings (bi-bi-, ma-ma, ba-ba). The patient showed bruxism with variable power. The patient had tendency to be constipated and sphincter control was not acquired. The sleep–wake rhythm was characterized by frequent nocturnal awakening and was prescribed Niaprazine (Nopron). On the 2nd of August 2006, genetic testing for RTT indicated a mutation c. 397C > T (R133C) of exon 4 of the MECP2 gene.

The clinical case study performed in this experiment depicts the efficacy and safety of IGF1 exposure upon two cycles of treatment. Careful consideration was executed in monitoring to the effects of IGF1 in both autonomic function and blood parameters. The patient received first round of treatment on the 25th of May 2010 and discontinued on the 11th of November 2010. The second round of treatment started on the 20th of November 2012 and discontinued on the 28th of February 2013. The dosage for IGF1 was the same in both cycles: 0.1 mg/kg maintenance dosages and 0.05 mg/kg first and last weeks were adjustment dosages. Our findings are noted below during each visit with the patient during their cycles of IGF1 treatment.

### FIRST CYCLE OF IGF1 TREATMENT

The first experimentation with IGF1 started on 25th of May 2010 (first cycle), when the patients were 5 years and 8 months. We clinically assessed the patient and results were noted as follows: patient has slight ataxic ambulation, which required minimum support; slight hypotonia was noticeable and babinsky positive ROT hyper-excitability; wide-spread bouts of tremor often associated with tachypnea, and possible grasping of objects upon request. Patient demonstrated expressive language, characterized by varied and modulated vocalizations. The patient had a calm demeanor with discreet interest in external environment and surrounding people.

Second visit was on the 31st of August 2010. The patient showed good clinical health and similar ambulation as the first visit. The patient showed coastal navigation with the family. The hypotonia and wide-spread tremor was the same as first visit. The patient showed improvement in grip of objects. The patient continued to demonstrate expressive language, characterized by varied and modulated vocalizations. Communicative intentions were observed and actions were occasionally preceded by anticipatory behaviors. The demeanor remained calm.

Third visit took place on the 23th of November 2010. The patient maintained good general clinical condition and the parents reported a good clinical outcome at home. The patient was able to ambulate with unimanual support with tendency to externally rotate the march of the lower limbs, and launch of the same. The use of hands to engage in patterns of action with objects have been a new observation, such as pressing a button or lever to get a visual or sound effect. The patient demonstrates good conduct and interaction with unfamiliar people. The food and sleep–wake rhythm is regular, while obstinate constipation persists.

The patient was discontinued from IGF1 on the 27th of November 2010 and clinical assessments were continued.

The fourth visit was on the 15th of February 2011. The clinical observations were almost unchanged from the previous visit. The gait seemed to have improved, even when the child fatigued easily. There was a submission of critical events that took place. On the 8th of February 2011, at 10:40 a.m. the first epileptic crisis lasting 2–3 min was characterized by tremor, hypotonia, eyes wide and staring into space. This was followed by sleep. Secondary crisis showed facial and perioral cyanosis, tremor, and blank stares, followed by sleep. A third crisis at 6:10 p.m. noted guttural verses, staring, stiffening, and blank stares followed by sleep. A fourth crisis occurred at 7:30 p.m. where stiffening, staring, perioral cyanosis, pallor of the face, and strange vocalizations followed by sleep. Vomiting, facial and perioral cyanosis, and guttural sounds characterized the fifth crisis at 9:30 p.m. On the 9th of February 2011, the patient had a fever of 37.3°C. At 12:35 p.m., the first crisis lasted a minute and was characterized by salivation, perioral and facial cyanosis, absent eyes, and potential hypotonia causing the patient to fold on itself.

The second crisis (on February 9th) occurred at 1:38 p.m. and lasted 3 min; characterized by perioral and facial cyanosis and mouth tremors followed by sleep. The third crisis occurred at 5:27 p.m. and lasted for 2 min, characterized by an absent gaze. On the 11th of February 2011 at 10:16 a.m., the patient was noticed to have staring eyes and making guttural sob like sounds. On the 12th of February 2011 at 10:00 a.m., the patient woke up with a frightened look, began trembling with tears, and guttural vocalizations. A second crisis occurred at 3:40 p.m. characterized by neck muscle failure and appearance of sleep while sitting on the toilet, with guttural vocalizations. On the 13th of February 2011, the patient presented with a fever of 38.3°C, pharyngitis, and began Zithromax treatment.

The fifth visit took place on the 24th of May 2011. The clinical examination showed good general condition and parents reported a stable clinical experience. The child had unimanual-supported ambulation with tendency to externally rotate and launch of the lower limbs. The clinician noted a decreased resistance during walking. The patient was observed to have a discreet use of hands when she grabbed objects and pressed buttons to get a visual or sound effect. Social interaction showed observation of the environment and the maintenance of eye contact for a longer duration of time. The patient maintained a serene mood. The food and sleep–wake rhythm were regular and constipation still persisted. Critical incidents occurred almost daily and were characterized by staring, gaze deviation to the left, and clonus of the limbs. On the 13th of April 2011, the child presented a crisis with the semiotics for a 10-min period, which required Micronoan administration. The patient's anti-epileptic therapy dosage was increased: valproate 200 + 200 mg/day.

The sixth visit took place on the 21st of October 2011. The clinical examination reported a good general clinical condition. The parents informed that the child was attentive, observational of the environment, interacting with people, and mood was serene. The critical events were reported to occur on awakening and were characterized by wide-eyed, clonus of the limbs, apnea, and cyanosis of the face. The patient then took Valproate: dosage of 250 + 200 mg/day.

Upon collection of the clinical data set for the first cycle, blood test showed no morbidity related to the treatment and a noticeable improvement in bone density. Glycemic values taken during each visit all remained well within reference value (60–110 mg/dl), where the patients' average was 80 mg/dl and the range was between 75 and 86 mg/dl. The starting bone density measurement was taken on the 26th of May 2010 and a second one was taken at the end of first cycle on the 15th of February 2011. This measurement showed a BMD of 0.333 and 0.451, respectively.

Analysis of cognitive and social abilities show mixed results in positive and negative RTT features, in terms of improvement and disease progression (**Figures 1** and **2**). **Figures 1** and **2**, representing video analysis, note that the negative features (9 out of 10) increased more than positive features (5 out of 10). Hitting and breath-holding/apnea were the most improved negative features. Smiling in response to a stimulation, deliberate vocalization, and yes/no with head gesture were the most improved positive features. The patient shows an improvement in height percentile during the course of IGF1 treatment in almost immediate results, however, it returned to previous percentile among the discontinuation of the IGF1 treatment. No other significant correlations to the IGF1 treatment can be made from **Table 1**. In the ISS evaluation, we noted a starting score of 4 in autonomic function, at the first dose of the cycle; and upon the last dose, the patient reduced to a score of 3 in autonomic function. This implies that the autonomic function restored as a result of IGF1 treatment. Another improvement noted by the ISS score was in growth and development from an ISS score of 6, at first treatment, to a score of 5, at last dosage. This also implies that IGF1 treatment improved the patient's growth and development. ISS scores are shown in **Figure 3**.

#### SUMMARY OF IGF1 EFFECTS AFTER THE FIRST CYCLE OF TREATMENT

We found that IGF1 was well tolerated during the first cycle of treatment and did not show any side affect. The treatment produced an increase in height and BMI of the patient mostly during the first 3 months of treatment, and returned to baseline after the discontinuation of the drug (**Tables 1** and **4**). Significant benefits were noted as reduction of negative stereotypes, while the social and cognitive abilities did not show any significant improvement (**Figures 1** and **2**; **Table 5**). IGF1 did not show any significant effect on ISS, with the exception of the autonomic function, that appear improved also after 6 months from the last IGF1 administration (**Figure 3**; **Table 6**).

#### SECOND CYCLE OF IGF1 TREATMENT

The next cycle of IGF1 treatment started on the 20th of November 2012, when the patient was 8 years and 2 months. Since the last visit, the patient is continuing the anti-epileptic therapy: Valproate

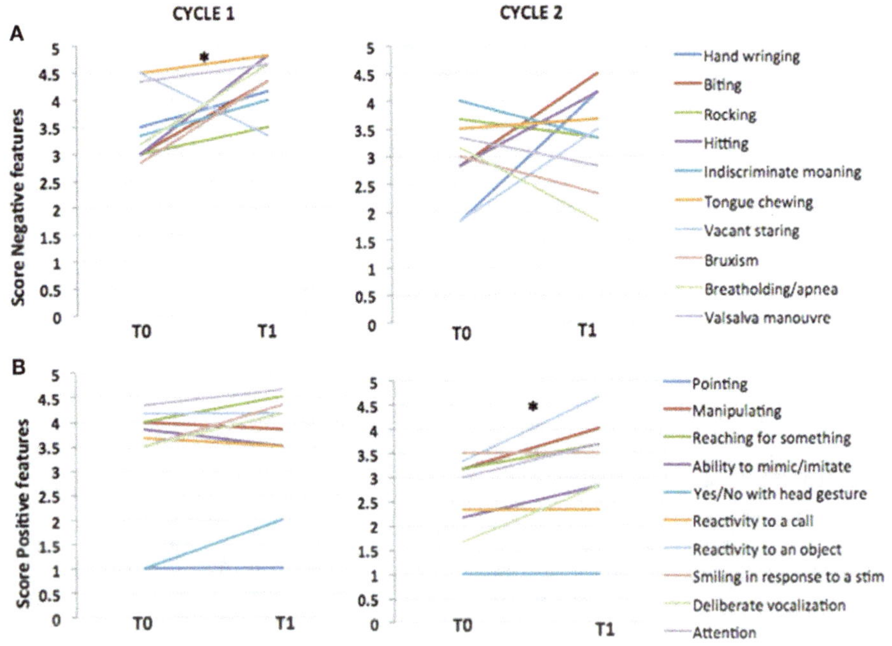


**FIGURE 1 | IGF1 treatment affects different features in different cycles.** Comparison of the scores of individual features at T0 and T1 for negative **(A)** and positive **(B)** features in cycle 1 (left) and cycle 2 (right). Paired comparison with Wilcoxon test shows that IGF1 treatment improved significantly negative features in cycle 1 (Wilcoxon test, *p*-value = 0.014), but not in cycle 2 (Wilcoxon test, *p*-value = 0.07). Viceversa, for positive features the effect was significant in cycle 2 (Wilcoxon test, *p*-value = 0.016), but not in cycle 1 (0.3).

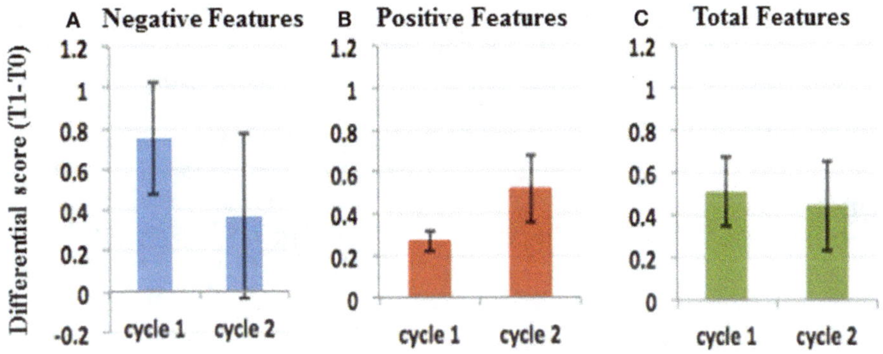


**FIGURE 2 | Effects of IGF1 treatment differ in different treatment cycles.** Plots of average (T1–T0) and SE in cycle 1 and cycle 2 for Negative features **(A)**, Positive features **(B)**, and Negative plus positive features **(C)**. The data suggest that the negative features improved more in the first cycle than in the second **(A)**. Conversely, the positive features improved more in the second cycle than the first. **(B)** Considering both positive and negative features, the effect of the treatment was comparable in both cycles **(C)**.

(250 + 200 mg/day) and Levetiracetam (300 + 300 mg/day). The clinical examination shows that health is fair and reported: patient has slight ataxic ambulation, which required minimum support; slight hypotonia was noticeable and Babinski positive ROT hyper-excitability; wide-spread bouts of tremor often associated with tachypnea; and possible grasping of objects upon request, but released after a few seconds. The patient has expressive language that is characterized by production of varied and modulated vocalizations. The mood of the patient is serene and there is a discreet interest in the environment and in surrounding people.

The second visit of the second cycle took place on the 29th of January 2013. The patient continues to have seizures three to four times a week characterized by eyes turned in backwards. The patient has an increased in dosage of Levetiracetam (350 + 350 mg/day) and maintained Valproate (250 + 200 mg/day). The parents reported an increase in bruxism with a decrease in stereotypic mannerisms. The patient showed longer attention span, improved eye contact, and smiling. The dietary intake was good and constipation improved. The clinical examination reported: patient has slight ataxic ambulation, which required minimum support; slight hypotonia was noticeable and Babinski positive ROT hyper-excitability; wide-spread bouts of tremor often associated with tachypnea; and possible grasping of objects upon request, but released after a few seconds. The patient had expressive language characterized by production of varied and modulated vocalizations. The mood of the patient was serene and there was a discreet interest in the environment and in surrounding people. We took extra note in the slight improvement of attention: specifically indicating that the patient holds her gaze for the duration of the smile and she seems more interested in the environment. Motor stereotypes decreased slightly while bruxism increased.

The third visit took place on the 3rd of December 2013. The grandfather informs about an improvement in attention span to external stimuli throughout the visual field laterally. The communication capability is improved and characterized by the improved ability to stare at an object that the patient wants to play with or a place that the patient wants to go. He also noticed an improved grip on objects. The mother reports that the patient eats less and tremors and bruxism have increased. She also states that sleep patterns are altered by presence of numerous episodes of pavor during sleep and wake states. The clinical examination reported:

**Table 1 | Growth parameters during first cycle of treatment.**

| Visit | Weight (kg) | Percentile | Height (cm) | Percentile | Head circumference | Percentile | BMI |
|---|---|---|---|---|---|---|---|
| 1 | 14.2 | 4 | 104.5 | 4 | 48 | 2 | 13 |
| 2 | 15.2 | 4 | 108 | 10 | 48 | 2 | 13.03 |
| 3 | 17 | 4 | 108.5 | 10 | 48 | 2 | 14.5 |
| 4 | 17 | 4 | 108.5 | 10 | 48.4 | 2 | 14.5 |
| 5 | 16.7 | 4 | 110.6 | 4 | 48.4 | 2 | 13.8 |

*This table compares the growth parameters of the RTT patient in the first cycle with the average child of same age. The patient remains in low percentiles, despite improvements in height during IGF1 application.*

patient has slight ataxic ambulation, which required minimum support; slight hypotonia was noticeable and Babinski positive ROT hyper-excitability; wide-spread bouts of tremor often associated with tachypnea; and possible grasping of objects upon request, but released after a few seconds. The patient has expressive language that is characterized by production of varied and modulated vocalizations. The mood of the patient is serene and there is a discreet interest in the environment and in surrounding people. The clinician took another extra note in the slight improvement of attention: specifically indicating, again, that the patient holds her gaze for the duration of the smile and she seems more interested in the environment. Motor stereotypes decreased slightly while bruxism increased.

Suspension of the second cycle of IGF1 occurred on the 28th of February 2013.

The following clinical observation was recorded on the 21st of May 2013. An anamnestic incident was recorded with a slightly increased frequency of seizures and every crisis has a longer duration of action. There is a constant intense tremor present. Parents observe the patient suffering from pharyngitis and a decrease in appetite. The clinical observation includes the patient being pale and sleepy, while being poorly responsive to environmental stimulation. They informed about two critical episodes in the morning with semiology and in few seconds durations. The gait was possible with minimal support and appeared ataxic. Slight hypotonia was noticeable and Babinski positive ROT hyper-excitability. Wide-spread bouts of tremor were noted in association with tachypnea. There was grasping of objects on presentation, but released after a few seconds. The stereotypes were unchanged.

Clinical data sets provided no insight into the second cycle of IGF1 treatment in blood work or growth parameters (**Table 2**). Glycemic values taken during each visit all remained well within reference value (60–110 mg/dl), where the patients' average was 78.2 mg/dl and the range was between 73 and 84 mg/dl. The starting bone density measurement was taken on the 20th of November 2012 and a second one was taken at the end of the second cycle on the 21st of May 2013. This measurement showed a BMD of 0.426 and 0.465, respectively.

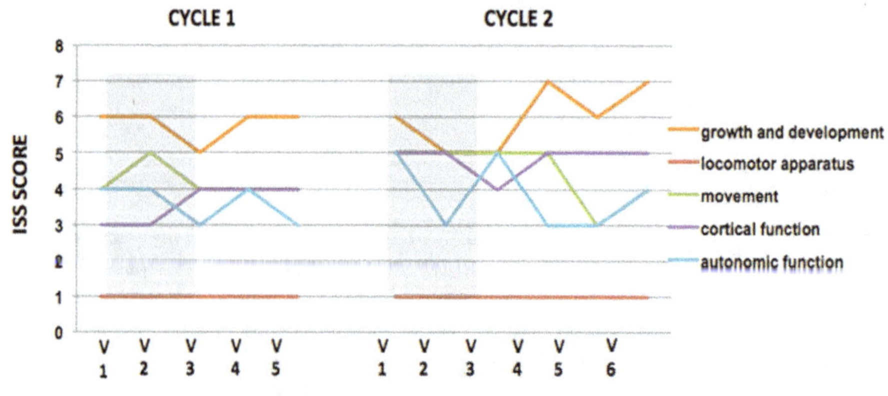


**FIGURE 3 | ISS scores plots during IGF1 cycles of treatment.** ISS scores reveal that IGF1 improves autonomic function. Plots of International Severity Scale (ISS) score at each visit during cycle 1 (left) and cycle 2 (right) of IGF1 administration. Gray rectangles show the IGF1 Administration. Higher scores represent worst performance. In both cycles, the IGF1 treatment improved the autonomic function, while the other parameters remain unchanged or worsened between the beginning and the ending of each cycle. Note that the improvement is not maintained between cycles.

**Table 2 | Growth parameters during second cycle of treatment.**

| Visit | Weight (kg) | Percentile | Height (cm) | Percentile | Head circumference | Percentile | BMI |
|---|---|---|---|---|---|---|---|
| 1 and 2 | 15 | 3 | 115 | 4 | 48 | 2 | 11.3 |
| 3 | 16 | 3 | 118.5 | 5 | 48.2 | 2 | 11.5 |
| 4 | 16.1 | 3 | 118.5 | 4 | 48.2 | 2 | 11.5 |
| 5 | 15.4 | 2 | 119.4 | 3 | 48.2 | 2 | 10.8 |

*This table shows the growth parameters during the second cycle of IGF1 treatment. There are no significant contributions to these characteristics given by the treatment. The patient maintains in low percentiles during the second IGF1 treatment cycle.*

The patient shows mixed results for positive and negative phenotypes based on the video analysis (**Figures 1** and **2**), however no adverse effects are noted in association with the second cycle of IGF1 treatment. **Figures 1** and **2**, representing video analysis, note that the negative features (4 out of 10) increased less than positive features (6 out of 10). Hand wringing and biting showed most improvement in negative features. Reactivity to an object and deliberate vocalization showed the most improvement in positive features. In the ISS evaluation: we noted a starting score of 6 in autonomic function, at the first dose of the cycle; and upon the last dose, the patient reduced to a score of 5 in autonomic function. This implies that the autonomic function restored, again, as a result of IGF1 treatment. Another consistent improvement noted by the ISS score was in growth and development from an ISS score of 6, at first treatment, to a score of 5, at last dosage. This also implies that IGF1 treatment improved the patient's growth and development. ISS scores are shown in **Figure 3**.

### SUMMARY OF IGF1 EFFECTS AFTER THE SECOND CYCLE OF TREATMENT

In the second cycle of treatment, there were no significant effects of IGF1 on the growth parameters of the patient (**Tables 1** and **4**). The scoring of the cognitive and social abilities, as well as the negative features of Rett, shows a general worsening of the conditions between the end of the first cycle and the starting of the second cycle of treatment. The second treatment with IGF1 produces a significant improvement in the scoring for the social and cognitive abilities, but no effects are visible on the negative symptoms of RTT (**Figures 1** and **2**; **Table 6**). The ISS components show a mixed effect of IGF1 on different features, with overall a long term improvement of movement and autonomic functions (**Figure 3**; **Table 5**).

### FOLLOW-UP EXAMINATIONS POST CYCLES

On September 24, 2013, the patient was 9 years old with a body mass index of 10.13 (normal values between 19 and 25 kg/m$^2$). The occipital–frontal cortex circumference was 48.2 cm and her weight was 14.6 kg. The patient's results in this report came from the evaluations of the autonomic nervous system in quiet conditions. **Table 3** depicts the cardiovascular examination that took place on this date.

The results showed normal breathing patterns for 21.2–35.9% of mixed tachypnea breath, 12.2% of deep breaths, 7.4% of breath-holding episodes, 8% of hyperpnea, and 3.8% of apnea episodes. The average heart rate recorded is about 90 beats per minute, while the mean values of CVT in relaxation amounted in about 5.6; where the registered CVT peaks results are of average and significant.

**Table 3 | Cardiovascular reflexes range during cycles.**

| Cardiovascular reflexes | Examined values | Normal values |
|---|---|---|
| Cardiac vagal tone | 5.63 | 6–19 |
| Heart rate | 90.1 beats/min | 60–140 beats/min |
| Respiratory rate | 20 breaths/min | 18–28 breaths/min |

*This table depicts that the patient falls with in the normal reference range for three out of the four cardiovascular reflexes that we observed. Cardiac vagal tone is just slightly under the reference value.*

The phenotype of the cardiopulmonary patient was classified as forced (40.2%). The general autonomic framework was that of a basal level vagal tone, which is slightly lower than normal. There were multiple types of respiratory rhythm abnormalities that were indicative of instability within the respiratory centers of the brainstem.

On 11 March 2014, a second follow-up examination was recorded. The parents noted some changes in seizure related events. Since November of 2013, the patient took Carbamazepine (25 mg in the morning and 50 mg in the evening), which was suspended while being treated with Levetiracetam. The latest crisis occurred a week before this examination where the patient had a cluster of six episodes on the same day. The patient grew agitated and had difficulty falling asleep, so Valium was given by the parents.

At this time, the patient was currently attending third grade class with support and rehabilitative physiotherapy continues 2 days a week (partially at ASL and partially privately) with swimming integrated. She was on the following AEDs: depakote (250 mg in morning and 250 mg in the evening), Carbamazepine (5 mg in morning and 50 mg in the evening), and Pepidax.

The general health conditions were satisfactory. The patient was able to autonomously maintain the sitting position with ataxia of the trunk and ambulation requires support. Tremors were noticed and the detection of bruxism. Scoliosis was absent, while there was reduced muscle tropism. The patient made little facial expression, with eye contact being only possible if the child is evoked several times; language was absent. During the visit, there were no manual stereotypes; however, the parents report it occurred when the patient was tired. The patient showed fluctuation in vigilance, and during the visit the child was alert and responsive. During neurological examinations, the child had suddenly fallen asleep for few minutes at a couple of occasions. The physician recommended that it was advisable for the patient to continue the rehabilitation treatment that was already in progress.

### COMPARISON OF IGF1 EFFECTS DURING AND AFTER THE TWO CYCLES

In order to compare the effects of IGF1 between the two cycles, we considered the relative values of each parameter (growth parameters, ISS scores, cognitive, and social abilities scores) during and after the termination of the drug administration, grouping together the effects during IGF1 administration and after the suspension of the drug (**Figure 4**). In particular, for the effects during the two cycles, was considered the differences between the last visit during treatment and the visit before treatment (**Figure 4A**). For the preservation of the effects after the cycles, we considered the difference between the values at the last visit post treatment and the values of the last visit during treatment (**Figure 4B**). We observed that the effects of the drug were comparable between the two cycles, and even with a slight positive effect during the first cycle, there were no significant differences (two tailed $t$-test, $p$-value = 0.28).

### EPILEPTIC HISTORY DURING OBSERVATION

The patient was enlisted into the study in March 2010, but because of an onset of epilepsy during this month the start treatment was postponed to May. There were two critical incidents between the months of March to May and on average the crisis occurred at a frequency of four/month. The patient then commenced the first cycle of IGF1 treatment on the 25th of May 2010. The epileptic treatment during this time was Valproate. From the time of the previous visit to the next visit on the 31st of August 2010, there were five critical episodes reported while on the Valproate therapy, on average the crisis during IGF1 administration have the same intensity and frequency than before the treatment. More frequent critical incidents occurred between the second and third visit, where the patient was on Valproate. Following this visit, there was the suspension of IGF1 on the 27th of November in 2010. On the fourth visit, 15th of February 2011, after the suspension of IGF1 administration, the crisis appeared in clusters on several occasions. At this point, the epileptic therapy was adjusted to Valproate plus Frisium (for when the patient has many crises). By the fifth visit on the 24th of May 2011, critical episodes became more frequents and occurred on almost a daily basis. The therapy was Valproate, while Frisium was suspended. Visit six, on the 21st of October 2011, indicated critical episodes occurring upon awakening. Still the patient remained on Valproate.

The second trial start date occurred on the 20th of November of 2012. Critical episodes are daily and the epileptic therapy was Valproate and Levatiracetam. The second visit showed similar critical episodes on a daily basis. Suspension of IGF1 occurred on the 28th of February 2013. The third visit took place on the 12th of March 2013, where the critical episodes remain daily. The crisis did not change with the administration of IGF1 treatment and the epileptic therapy remained on Valproate and Levatiracetam. On the 24th of September 2013, the critical episodes were reported the same on a daily basis. During this fourth visit, the patient was on the same epileptic treatment. On the 28th of October 2013, the epileptic therapy was changed: Levitiracetam was removed and Carbamazepine was added. The sixth visit, on the 3rd of November 2014, reported that Carbamazepine caused a thinning out of critical episodes, but they were clustered. The epileptic therapy was carbamazepine and valproic acid.

## DISCUSSION

The use of IGF1 represents an appealing therapy for RTT. Due to IGF1 affecting multiple symptoms of RTT in animal models, its noticeable benefits from pediatric use, and its physical properties allowing it to cross the blood brain barrier; pilot trials (12, 13), indicated that IGF1 is safe and tolerable for treatment of RTT patients.

Considering the finding that any treatment for RTT should be administered for life (8), our research addresses the issue of multiple IGF1 treatments and tolerability in children with RTT syndrome. During our first study (12), we observed the major improvements during the first weeks of IGF1 treatment, and for this reason, we decided to reduce the time of the second treatment to 20 weeks. These findings are in line with the study by Khwaja et al. (13), where the amount of IGF1 in the serum decreases during the administration period, and the authors suggest that an adjustment of the dosage and administration time could be more beneficial to the Rett patients.

Although our study is mostly oriented in confirming the safety and tolerability of IGF1 through multiple cycles, we observed an overall improvement of autonomic function during IGF1 treatment, and then a lessening of improvement upon suspension of IGF1 (**Figure 3**; **Table 5**). We recorded no hypoglycemia, which indicates that IGF1 shows good toleration in patients. This is important because it is one of the main risks associated with IGF1 treatment (13).

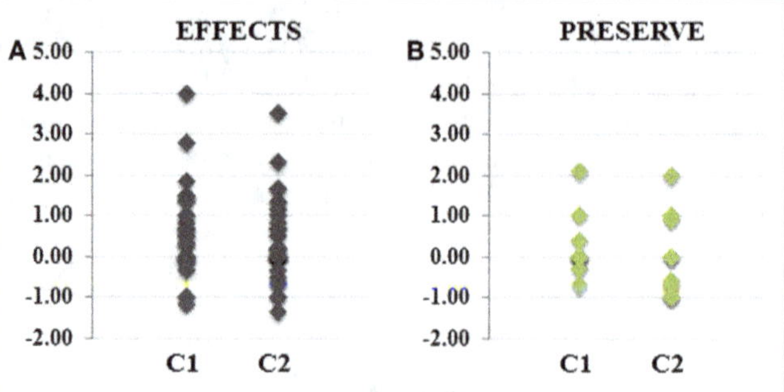


**FIGURE 4 | The effects of IGF1 treatment for each cycle are comparable.** The plots represent the differential scores of growth parameters, ISS scores and Social and cognitive scores, before and after IGF1 Administration [EFFECTS **(A)**], and in follow-up studies [PRESERVE **(B)**]. Although we observe a slightly major efficacy of IGF1 during the first cycle of treatment, the differences are limited and they are not significant.

**Table 4 | Differential scores of growth parameters during cycles.**

| Growth parameters | Cycle 1 | | Cycle 2 | |
|---|---|---|---|---|
| **Differential score** | **Effect** | **Preserve** | **Effect** | **Preserve** |
| Weight | 2.8 | −0.3 | 1 | −0.6 |
| Height | 4 | 2.1 | 3.5 | 0.9 |
| Head circumference | 0 | 0.4 | 0.2 | 0 |
| BMI | 1.5 | −0.7 | 0.2 | −0.7 |

*This table summarizes the differential scores for each component of the growth (listed on the left), considering the difference at the end versus the beginning of the treatment (effect) and the difference after 6 months from the last administration versus the scores on the day of the last administration (preserve). The original scores are those reported in **Tables 1** and **2**. The improvements are highlighted in green, and the worsenings are highlighted in red.*

In this study, similarly to what reported in the past and by other researchers (12, 13), we did not observed any specific influence of IGF1 treatment on epileptic episodes: the appearance of the epileptic crisis preceded the first cycle of IGF1 administration, and the intensity and frequency of the episodes remained on average the same before and after the treatment. The intense episodes reported between the second and third week during the first cycle of treatment, can be due to an endogeneous evolution of the crisis, as suggested also by the increased frequency after the interruption of the treatment (which required an adjustment of the therapy). Before starting the second IGF1 administration, the crisis had a daily frequency and they remained unaltered during the whole cycle of treatment. These observations are in accordance to the literature in pediatric syndromes, where IGF1 is not associated to an increase in seizures, but rather epileptic phenotype is associated to decreased IGF1 levels in the serum (14, 15). On the contrary, it is possible that the seizure medication hindered the positive effects of IGF1. It would be interesting to compare the effects of IGF1 administration in patients treated with valproate versus patients treated with alternative AEDs.

Insulin-like growth factor 1 has also been considered to be more effective when given in acute intermittent pulses, versus chronic dosing. One noted side effect from IGF1, was that long term IGF1 administration has linkage with potential puberty effects; which is already accelerated in RTT (13). Being that IGF1 has a strong feedback system, patient tolerance over cycles is worth exploring into for future studies. This implies the evaluation of lower doses in life-long treatment. An assessment of total effects on single analyzed relative parameters (ISS scores, cognitive and social abilities, and growth parameters) showed that the effects observed with the first cycle of treatment were not significantly different from those in the second cycle of treatment (**Figure 4**, two tailed $t$-test $p$-value = 0.28).

While there were some phenotypic benefits shown by the assessment of social and cognitive abilities, nine of the improvements remained after the first cycle was over, and no phenotypic improvement remained in the second trial as different phenotypes improved aside from attention. However, we observed motor control as another form of improvement. However, our research insight into motor control improvement may be a result of subjectivity further research is suggested to elucidate the validity of this potential benefit. Our analysis confirms the results of Zoghbi's team, that whatever treatment is decided for RTT syndrome patients, it must be for life (8).

The two studies of IGF1 safety and tolerability in RTT patients (12, 13), showed similar results: IGF1 did not produce hypoglycemia and it is not associated to seizures, and overall is well tolerated by patients. In addition, we observed an improvement in autonomic function, and Khwaja and colleagues concluded that motor ability showed no measurable improvement, but also found

**Table 6 | Differential scores of ISS scores during cycles.**

| ISS components | Cycle 1 | | Cycle 2 | |
|---|---|---|---|---|
| **Differential score** | **Effect** | **Preserve** | **Effect** | **Preserve** |
| Growth and development | −1 | 1 | −1 | 2 |
| Locomotor apparatus | 0 | 0 | 0 | 0 |
| Movement | 0 | 0 | 0 | −1 |
| Cortical function | 1 | 0 | −1 | 1 |
| Autonomic function | −1 | 0 | 0 | −1 |

*This table summarizes the differential scores for each component of the ISS (listed on the left), considering the difference at the end versus the beginning of the treatment (effect) and the difference after 6 months from the last administration versus the scores on the day of the last administration (preserve). The improvements are highlighted in green, and the worsenings are highlighted in red. Note that the decrease in the scoring are improvements for the ISS; on the contrary, increases in the scoring represent worsening.*

**Table 5 | Differential scores of social and cognitive abilities during cycles.**

| (T1–T0) score | Negative features | | (T1–T0) score | Positive features | |
|---|---|---|---|---|---|
| | **Cycle 1** | **Cycle 2** | | **Cycle 1** | **Cycle 2** |
| Hand wringing | 0.67 | 2.33 | Pointing | 0.00 | 0.00 |
| Biting | 1.33 | 1.67 | Manipulating | −0.17 | 0.83 |
| Rocking | 0.50 | −0.33 | Reaching for something | 0.50 | 0.50 |
| Hitting | 1.83 | 1.33 | Ability to mimic/imitate | −0.33 | 0.67 |
| Indiscriminate moaning | 0.67 | −0.67 | Yes/No with head gesture | 1.00 | 0.00 |
| Tongue chewing | 0.33 | 0.17 | Reactivity to a call | −0.17 | 0.00 |
| Vacant staring | −1.17 | 1.67 | Reactivity to an object | 0.00 | 1.33 |
| Bruxism | 1.50 | −0.67 | Smiling in response to a Stim | 0.83 | 0.00 |
| Breath-holding/apnea | 1.50 | −1.33 | Deliberate vocalization | 0.67 | 1.17 |
| Valsalva maneuver | 0.33 | −0.50 | Attention | 0.33 | 0.67 |
| Overall | 7.83 | 3.67 | Overall | 3.17 | 5.17 |

*This table summarizes the differential scores for negative and positive features of the social and cognitive abilities assessment. Each number represents the difference of the score for the specific ability at the end of the treatment (T1) versus the beginning of the treatment (T0). Improvements are therefore positive numbers and they are highlighted in green, while worsening are negative numbers and are highlighted in red.*

that respiratory complications associated with RTT syndrome showed improvement (13).

One factor to consider in our findings is the environmental surrounding that the patient experienced during and after the IGF1 treatment. The patient lived with the mother during the time of treatment. The mother suffers from anxiety and seizures, which may have limited the benefits of IGF1 treatment due to high stress levels being perceived by the patient. The consideration is due to a follow-up communication, post IGF1 second cycle treatment, where the grandparents noted an immediate amelioration of the patient's phenotypic mannerisms. The stressful environment could have caused misperception of the severity level to phenotypic hindrances, which are RTT associated.

The personal environmental surrounding, together with the onset and progression of the epileptic crisis are two of the limits of this case study for assessing the benefits of IGF1 therapy. Appropriate double blind and placebo controlled studies are necessary to define the efficacy of IGF1 treatment. However, considering the rarity of RTT (1:10,000), and the recent discovery of IGF1 as possible Rett treatment, data coming from a single case study are nonetheless useful to further develop the treatment.

Our research show that repeated treatments with IGF1 is safe and tolerable for the patient. This finding along with other findings on IGF1 treatment with RTT, should encourage further research in IGF1 treatment for additional neurodevelopmental disorders.

## CONCLUDING REMARKS

Our research shows that repeated treatments with IGF1 are safe and tolerable for the patient. We observed improved autonomic function and social and cognitive abilities in each cycle but the benefits were lost between cycles. The results in this clinical case study suggest that IGF1 is beneficial for our patient, but a larger cohort of patients and proper clinical trials are requested to establish the overall efficacy in RTT.

## ACKNOWLEDGMENTS

We thank our patient and her family for their collaboration. We thank the funding agencies: Region Tuscany, Fondazione Cassa di Risparmio di Lucca, ASL12 Viareggio, TIAMO foundation, and Marie Curie IRG (248284). We are also thankful to: Enrico Rossi, Ledo Gori, Prof. Michele Zappella, Anna Rita Bertellotti, all the doctors and operators in Versilia hospital, Fabrizio Bianchi Istituto di Fiologia Clinica, Centro Nazionale delle Ricerche Pisa.

## REFERENCES

1. Chahrour M, Zoghbi HY. The story of Rett syndrome: from clinic to neurobiology. *Neuron* (2007) **56**:422–37. doi:10.1016/j.neuron.2007.10.001
2. Percy A. Rett syndrome: a comprehensive review of the literature. *Am J Ment Retard* (1991) **96**:275–90.
3. Marschik PB, Kaufmann WE, Sigafoos J, Wolin T, Zhang D, Bartl-Pokorny KD, et al. Changing the perspective on early development of Rett syndrome. *Res Dev Disabil* (2013) **34**:1236–9. doi:10.1016/j.ridd.2013.01.014
4. Kaufmann WE, Johnston MV, Blue ME. MeCP2 expression and function during brain development: implications for Rett syndrome's pathogenesis and clinical evolution. *Brain Dev* (2005) **27**(Suppl 1):S77–87.
5. Cuddapah VA, Pillai RB, Shekar KV, Lane JB, Motil KJ, Skinner SA, et al. Methyl-CpG-binding protein 2 (MECP2) mutation type is associated with disease severity in Rett syndrome. *J Med Genet* (2014) **51**:152–8. doi:10.1136/jmedgenet-2013-102113
6. Giacometti E, Luikenhuis S, Beard C, Jaenisch R. Partial rescue of MeCP2 deficiency by postnatal activation of MeCP2. *Proc Natl Acad Sci U S A* (2007) **104**:1931–6. doi:10.1073/pnas.0610593104
7. Guy J, Gan J, Selfridge J, Cobb S, Bird A. Reversal of neurological defects in a mouse model of Rett syndrome. *Science* (2007) **315**:1143–7. doi:10.1126/science.1138389
8. McGraw CM, Samaco RC, Zoghbi HY. Adult neural function requires MeCP2. *Science* (2011) **333**:186. doi:10.1126/science.1206593
9. Tropea D, Giacometti E, Wilson NR, Beard C, McCurry C, Fu DD, et al. Partial reversal of Rett syndrome-like symptoms in MeCP2 mutant mice. *Proc Natl Acad Sci U S A* (2009) **106**:2029–34. doi:10.1073/pnas.0812394106
10. Chang Q, Khare G, Dani V, Nelson S, Jaenisch R. The disease progression of Mecp2 mutant mice is affected by the level of BDNF expression. *Neuron* (2006) **49**:341–8. doi:10.1016/j.neuron.2005.12.027
11. Castro J, Garcia R, Kwok S, Tropea D, Sur M. Functional recovery with recombinant human IGF1 treatment in a mouse model of Rett syndrome. *Society for Neuroscience Annual Meeting*, New Orleans (2012).
12. Pini G, Scusa MF, Congiu L, Benincasa A, Morescalchi P, Bottiglioni I, et al. IGF1 as a potential treatment for Rett syndrome: safety assessment in six Rett patients. *Autism Res Treat* (2012) **2012**:679801. doi:10.1155/2012/679801
13. Khwaja OS, Ho E, Barnes KV, O'Leary HM, Pereira LM, Finkelstein Y, et al. Safety, pharmacokinetics, and preliminary assessment of efficacy of mecasermin (recombinant human IGF-1) for the treatment of Rett syndrome. *Proc Natl Acad Sci U S A* (2014) **111**:4506–601. doi:10.1073/pnas.1311141111
14. Galli-Tsinopoulou A, Nousia-Arvanitakis S, Tsinopoulos I, Bechlivanides C, Shevah O, Laron Z. Lanor syndrome. First report from Greece. *Hormones (Athens)* (2003) **2**:120–4. doi:10.14310/horm.2002.1191
15. Kacinski M, Budziszewska B, Lason W, Zajac A, Skowronek-Bała B, Leskiewicz M, et al. Levels of S100 protein, neuron specific enolase, orexin A, adiponectin and insulin-like growth factor in serum of pediatric patients suffering from sleep disorders with or without epilepsy. *Pharmacol Rep* (2012) **64**:1427–33. doi:10.1016/S1734-1140(12)70940-4

# 23

# Exploring links between genotypes, phenotypes, and clinical predictors of response to early intensive behavioral intervention in autism spectrum disorder

**Valsamma Eapen[1,2]*, Rudi Črnčec[2] and Amelia Walter[1,2]**

[1] *Academic Unit of Child Psychiatry South West Sydney, South Western Sydney Local Health District, Liverpool, NSW, Australia*
[2] *School of Psychiatry, University of New South Wales, Sydney, NSW, Australia*

**Edited by:**
*Andrew Whitehouse, Telethon Institute for Child Health Research, Australia; University of Western Australia, Australia*

**Reviewed by:**
*Elisa L. Hill-Yardin, The University of Melbourne, Australia*
*Naomi E. Bishop, La Trobe University, Australia*

***Correspondence:**
*Valsamma Eapen, Academic Unit of Child Psychiatry South West Sydney, ICAMHS, Mental Health Centre L1, Locked Bag 7103, Liverpool BC, NSW 1871, Australia*
*e-mail: v.eapen@unsw.edu.au*

Autism spectrum disorder (ASD) is amongst the most familial of psychiatric disorders. Twin and family studies have demonstrated a monozygotic concordance rate of 70–90%, dizygotic concordance of around 10%, and more than a 20-fold increase in risk for first-degree relatives. Despite major advances in the genetics of autism, the relationship between different aspects of the behavioral and cognitive phenotype and their underlying genetic liability is still unclear. This is complicated by the heterogeneity of autism, which exists at both genetic and phenotypic levels. Given this heterogeneity, one method to find homogeneous entities and link these with specific genotypes would be to pursue endophenotypes. Evidence from neuroimaging, eye tracking, and electrophysiology studies supports the hypothesis that, building on genetic vulnerability, ASD emerges from a developmental cascade in which a deficit in attention to social stimuli leads to impaired interactions with primary caregivers. This results in abnormal development of the neurocircuitry responsible for social cognition, which in turn adversely affects later behavioral and functional domains dependent on these early processes, such as language development. Such a model begets a heterogeneous clinical phenotype, and is also supported by studies demonstrating better clinical outcomes with earlier treatment. Treatment response following intensive early behavioral intervention in ASD is also distinctly variable; however, relatively little is known about specific elements of the clinical phenotype that may predict response to current behavioral treatments. This paper overviews the literature regarding genotypes, phenotypes, and predictors of response to behavioral intervention in ASD and presents suggestions for future research to explore linkages between these that would enable better identification of, and increased treatment efficacy for, ASD.

**Keywords: autism spectrum disorder, genotype, phenotype, early intervention, treatment response**

## GENETIC BASIS OF AUTISM SPECTRUM DISORDER

It has been suggested that autism spectrum disorder (ASD) is one of the most familial of psychiatric disorders, with a heritability of 80%, a monozygotic concordance rate of 70–90%, dizygotic concordance of around 10%, and more than a 20-fold increase in risk for first-degree relatives (Bailey et al., 1995; O'Roak, 2008). Although there have been some significant advances in the recent past (Wang et al., 2009; Pinto et al., 2010), the rate of progress in gene discovery has been modest (Abrahams and Geschwind, 2010). Also, genomic analyses indicate extreme genetic heterogeneity and so far, over 100 genes have been reported in ASD with a conservative estimate of between 380 and 820 loci implicated (Betancur, 2011; Clarke and Eapen, in press), and with considerable overlap with other disorders such as intellectual disability, epilepsy, schizophrenia, and attention deficit hyperactivity disorder (ADHD). These findings suggest that ASD is not a single-gene disorder with Mendelian inheritance but rather a complex disorder resulting from simultaneous genetic variations in multiple genes (Dawson et al., 2002; El-Fishawy, 2010) as well as complex interactions between genetic, epigenetic, and environmental factors (Eapen, 2011).

It has been reported that some of the associated sequence variations noted in ASD are common in the general population although it is unclear as to whether the ASD phenotype results from the involvement of single genes in combination with non-genetic factors, or multiple genes through locus heterogeneity (multiple rare variations in the same gene), or multiple genes through allelic heterogeneity (variations in multiple and different genes). Furthermore, it has been proposed that multiple genes in combination with non-genetic factors may be necessary to result in the ASD phenotype or that ASD may be a collection of rare disorders, that is, a shared phenotype resulting from several different genetic defects. Thus it would seem that there are at least three major pathogenetic processes (Eapen, 2011) resulting in three different subgroups: (1) ASD-Plus group or Syndromic ASD resulting from rare single-gene disorders where ASD is a behavioral phenotype of the associated disorder; (2) Broad ASD group resulting from common variants distributed continually in

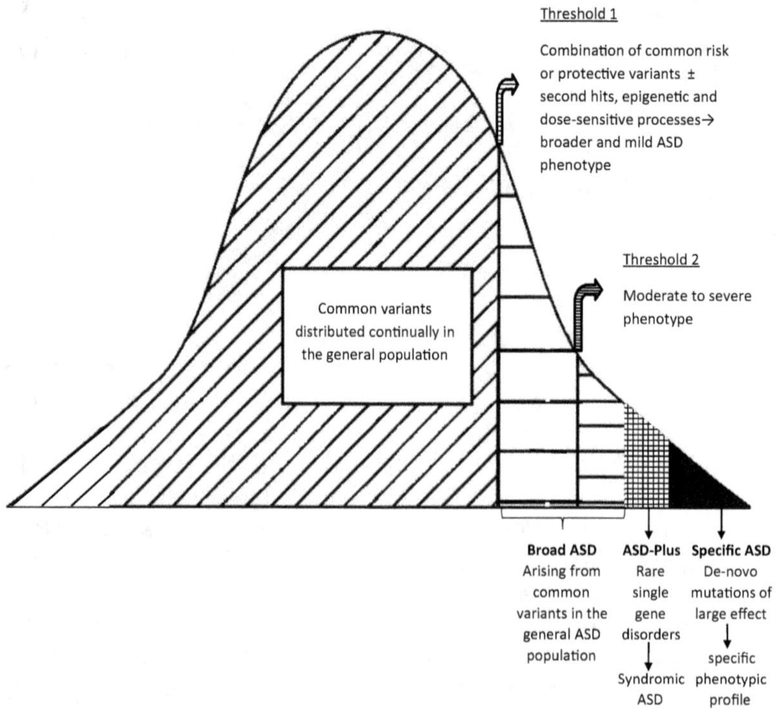


**FIGURE 1 | Genetic and phenotypic heterogeneity in ASD**. Adapted from Eapen (2011).

the general population but following a gene-environment diathesis model, when it passes the first threshold (threshold 1) due to other gene or environmental additive effects or "second hits" including epigenetic and dose-sensitive processes, it results in the broader and mild ASD phenotype which may be observed in other family members of affected individuals and when it passes a second threshold (threshold 2) it results in a moderate to severe ASD phenotype that is clinically significant; and (3) specific ASD group due to "*de novo* mutations" of large effect resulting in ASD presentations but carrying unique phenotypic profiles based on the specific site and nature of the *de novo* mutation (see **Figure 1**).

## BROAD AUTISM PHENOTYPE

The term "broad autism phenotype" (BAP) refers to the presence of subclinical levels of ASD symptoms among individuals who do not meet criteria for a diagnosis of ASD (Bolton et al., 1994; Piven and Palmer, 1999). BAP characteristics correspond to the primary features of ASD, including traits that are social, such as socially reticent or inappropriate behavior, or non-social, such as rigidity and ritualistic or repetitive behaviors (Losh et al., 2009). Twin and family studies have shown that genetic liability to autism is expressed in unaffected relatives of people with ASD through features that are milder but qualitatively similar to the defining characteristics of ASD, including social abnormalities, communication impairments, and repetitive behaviors (Bailey et al., 1998; Goussé et al., 2002; Losh et al., 2009). Previous studies suggest that around 25% of first-degree relatives of children with ASD show impairment in one of the three diagnostic domains for ASD: sociability, communication, and cognitive or behavioral flexibility (for a review, see Goussé et al., 2002). Bailey et al. (1998) conclude that the BAP features observed in relatives of individuals with ASD appear to have a genetic rather than environmental basis.

While early work on the BAP focused on examining ASD-related traits in first and second degree relatives of individuals with ASD (for a review, see Bailey et al., 1998), subsequent studies have demonstrated that the characteristics comprising the BAP exist within the general population as well (Baron-Cohen et al., 2001; Constantino and Todd, 2003, 2005). Features of ASD that have been found to be continuously distributed within the general population include restricted interests (Baron-Cohen et al., 2001), atypical visuospatial and cognitive performance (Grinter et al., 2009; Stewart et al., 2009; Richmond et al., 2013), abnormal speech perception (Stewart and Ota, 2008), reduced gaze reciprocity (Chen and Yoon, 2011), an impaired ability to recognize affect from facial expressions and body language (Ingersoll, 2010b), and reductions in social skill and social-cognitive ability (Sasson et al., 2012). These findings may be consistent with the suggestion that some of the genetic sequence variations found in ASD are common in the general population.

## HETEROGENEITY OF AUTISM

Despite major advances in the genetics of ASD, the relationship between different aspects of the behavioral and cognitive phenotype of ASD and their underlying genetic liability is still unclear (Bailey et al., 1998; Klin et al., 2002). This is complicated by the heterogeneity of ASD, which exists at both genetic and phenotypic levels (Charman et al., 2011). Further, it has been suggested that there may be gender dependent differences in the ASD phenotype

(Eapen, 2011). For example, Lai et al. (2012) observed that while performance in the social-cognitive domain was equally impaired in male and female adults with ASD, in the specific non-social-cognitive domains of attention to detail and dexterity involving executive function, there were differences based on gender. Losh et al. (2009) argue that the BAP may provide an important complementary approach for detecting the genes involved in ASD by narrowing the highly heterogeneous phenotype of an ASD diagnosis to particular features that are likely to be more conducive to genetic investigation (Wheelwright et al., 2010; Spencer et al., 2011, 2012a,b; Sucksmith et al., 2012).

Due to its heterogeneity, ASD is no longer viewed as a narrowly defined, categorical disorder, but instead as a spectrum of conditions that affect individuals differently (Wing, 1996). Some researchers have suggested that there are probably many "autisms" with different underlying biological processes and developmental pathways (Elsabbagh, 2012). The term ASD is now commonly used to describe a range of neurodevelopmental conditions that show considerable phenotypic heterogeneity at any one age and across development, and that are likely to differ in underlying etiology (Geschwind and Levitt, 2007). However, they all generally share a primary impairment in social relatedness and reciprocity, an "insistence on sameness," and impairments in the use of language for communication, which is in keeping with Kanner's (1943) description of classically "autistic" children.

It is noteworthy that genetic heterogeneity leads to clinical heterogeneity. For example, similar or identical mutations can result in very broad phenotypic variations as is evident from studies investigating endophenotypes exhibited by patients expressing mutations in the CNTNAP2 gene (Eapen, 2011). Such studies demonstrate a role for CNTNAP2 in schizophrenia, epilepsy, Tourette's syndrome, and obsessive compulsive disorder (Verkerk et al., 2003; Friedman et al., 2008). Alternatively, ASD cases resulting from different genetic lesions can have clinically distinct presentations (Bruining et al., 2010). However, such distinct phenotypic presentations are masked by the limitations of diagnostic categories. Therefore, future studies exploring risk alleles should examine homogenous and heritable endophenotypic traits rather than diagnostic groups. Thus, given the significant genotype to phenotype heterogeneity, one method to find homogeneous entities and link these with specific genotypes would be to pursue endophenotypes.

## ENDOPHENOTYPES IN ASD

Neurocognitive profiles and neurophysiological changes observed using neuroimaging, eye tracking, and electrophysiological techniques are commonly reported in individuals with ASD. Studies of head circumference and imaging studies of brain morphometry have found evidence of increased brain growth beginning within the first year of life (Courchesne et al., 2005), while functional brain imaging in older children and adults has shown abnormal patterns of interactions between brain regions, possibly related to aberrant connections being laid down during earlier stages of development (Courchesne et al., 2011). One model relating these early abnormalities in brain development to the characteristic socio-communicative impairments has hypothesized that early low-level deficits in recognition and orientation toward social stimuli lead to a lack of social engagement with primary caregivers during infancy, resulting in decreased exposure to the reciprocal social interactions critical for healthy development of brain circuits responsible for normal social behavior (Dawson, 2008).

Basic, low-level impairments of social attention and reciprocity are thought to relate to the socio-communicative impairments characteristic of ASD and are evident in children with ASD from as early as the first year of life. For example, home videos of 12-month-olds later diagnosed with ASD demonstrate reduced visual attention to people and failure to respond to vocal approaches (Werner et al., 2000; Osterling et al., 2002; Werner and Dawson, 2005), while other studies have shown poor verbal imitation (Sallows and Graupner, 2005). Prospective studies of children at high risk of ASD show similar results (Nadig et al., 2007). Young children with ASD also show a lack of joint attention and failure to coordinate attention and share their experiences with caregivers (Charman, 2003). Researchers using preferential looking techniques have identified a reduction in autistic toddlers' preference for viewing biological motion (Klin et al., 2009) and hearing the human voice (e.g., Klin, 1991; Dawson et al., 1998, 2004).

Similarly, eye gaze abnormalities have been described as indicative of later development of ASD (Bedford et al., 2012; Elsabbagh et al., 2012). Using eye tracking technology, Jones et al. (2008) found that 2-year-olds with ASD lacked the normal bias to attend to the eyes when watching videos of people, replicating earlier studies with autistic adolescents (Klin et al., 2003; see also Norbury et al., 2009) and confirming clinical reports of reduced eye contact in ASD (Zwaigenbaum et al., 2005). Psychophysical evidence suggests that differences in spatial localization between individuals with ASD and controls begins at an early cortical stage of visual processing (Latham et al., 2013). Further evidence comes from electrophysiology. Pre-school and school-aged children with ASD produce atypical cortical event-related potentials (ERPs) in response to deviations in streams of speech stimuli, despite normal responses to deviants in streams of non-speech stimuli (Kuhl et al., 2005; Lepistö et al., 2005; Ceponiene et al., 2005; Whitehouse and Bishop, 2008). Kuhl et al. (2013) compared brain responses to word stimuli between typically developing children and children with ASD, categorized into two groups according to the severity of their social symptoms. They found that the brain activity of children with ASD with less severe social symptoms resembled that of the typically developing controls, while children with ASD with more severe social symptoms showed a clearly atypical brain response. Furthermore, the ERP response among children with ASD at time 1 (when they were 2 years old) was found to predict receptive language, cognitive ability, and adaptive behaviors at two follow-up time points, when the children were 4 and 6 years old (Kuhl et al., 2013). Similarly, school-aged children are reported to show abnormal brainstem evoked responses (ABR) to trains of speech stimuli but not click sounds (Russo et al., 2009), and these abnormalities are linked to clinical assessments of language abilities.

Recognition of facial emotions has also been found to be impaired in children and adults with ASD compared to controls (Sucksmith et al., 2012; Oerlemans et al., 2013). The reduced activation in brain regions associated with facial processing in people with ASD relative to control subjects has been shown to be correlated with the clinical severity of their impairment in reciprocal social interaction (Spencer et al., 2012b). Finally, studies using electromyography (EMG) to measure facial muscle activity have shown a reduction or delay in the normal tendency to (subconsciously) mimic emotional expressions when viewing pictures of faces (McIntosh et al., 2006; Oberman et al., 2009).

Further, it is widely argued that many of the symptoms of ASD are caused by aberrant neural connectivity (e.g., Brock et al., 2002; Geschwind and Levitt, 2007), including specific findings such as reduced functional connectivity within and between "social" resting state networks in ASD (von dem Hagen et al., 2013) as well as significantly increased gray matter volume in the anterior temporal and dorsolateral prefrontal regions and significant reductions in the occipital and medial parietal regions compared with controls (Ecker et al., 2012). These findings imply that a key component of behavioral intervention may be to compensate for such early deficits and that behavioral intervention should occur as early as possible to normalize the developmental trajectory and avoid downstream effects. Thus baseline performance on neurocognitive responses to socially relevant stimuli might predict the magnitude of clinical and cognitive improvement following behavioral intervention. Recent research suggests that early behavioral intervention may be associated with normalized brain activity in young children with ASD. Previous studies have demonstrated that children receiving the Early Start Denver Model (ESDM), a behavioral intervention for children with ASD, showed gains in IQ and adaptive behavior and decreases in ASD-specific symptoms after intervention (Dawson et al., 2010; Eapen et al., 2013; Vivanti et al., 2013). In a recent study, Dawson et al. (2012) found that typically developing children and children with ASD who had been treated with the ESDM showed more cortical activation and allotted greater attentional and cognitive resources to social stimuli than to non-social stimuli, while children with ASD who had received community-based behavioral intervention showed the reverse pattern.

## BEHAVIORAL AND COGNITIVE PHENOTYPES IN ASD

There are increasing efforts to determine and refine subtypes within the ASD behavioral phenotype (e.g., Ingram et al., 2008; Munson et al., 2008a,b; Frazier et al., 2010), with contemporary studies using large samples and sophisticated statistical approaches such as taxometric and latent variable models. To date, however, few distinct behavioral subtypes have been identified, and none is yet well replicated – frustrating efforts to "carve nature at the joints." Ingram et al. (2008) provided the first taxometric analysis of ASD and sought to test putative ASD subgrouping paradigms based on seven phenotypes which vary within the ASD population: social interaction/communication, intelligence, adaptive functioning, insistence on sameness, repetitive sensory motor actions, language acquisition, and essential/complex physical phenotype. The "complex" physical phenotype was defined according to the presence of physical dysmorphology and/or microcephaly, indicating some abnormality of early morphogenesis, whereas the "essential" physical phenotype referred to the remainder of individuals with ASD without these features (Miles et al., 2005). The authors indicated that valid subgroups could be constructed using the social interaction/communication, intelligence, and essential/complex paradigms, whereas the other phenotypes were found to exhibit results consistent with a dimensional structure. Given intelligence is consistently described as one of the primary aspects of heterogeneity in ASD, Munson et al. (2008a) sought to explore whether there were distinct ASD subtypes based upon IQ. Four latent classes were ultimately identified that represented different levels of intellectual functioning as well as different patterns of relative verbal versus non-verbal abilities. Moreover, group membership was related to adaptive functioning and social impairment, above and beyond the direct relationship of verbal and non-verbal IQ (Munson et al., 2008a). In a different study, Munson et al. (2008b) reported that specific aspects of neurocognitive functioning appear to be important predictors of developmental variability during the pre-school years in children with ASD. In particular, learning of reward associations and imitation from memory and novelty preference were significantly related to Vineland socialization and communication growth rates above and beyond non-verbal problem solving ability. A review of factor analytic studies showed that, of the seven studies included, six found evidence for multiple factors underlying autistic features (Mandy and Skuse, 2008). The majority of studies reported at least one social-communication factor and all but one also reported at least one distinct non-social factor comprising repetitive interests, behaviors and activities, however, the total number of factors reported varied.

In a large scale study employing taxometric and latent variable models, Frazier et al. (2010) concluded that the available literature and study results implied a categorical model of ASD, with two to three subdimensions – social communication, repetitive/perseverative behavior, and possibly social motivation – best reflecting the structure of ASD symptoms. Related work by the same group yielded similar results and provided broad support for DSM5 ASD criteria (Frazier et al., 2012). This finding is somewhat at odds with the related body of literature that has concluded that ASDs represent the severe end of a quantitative trait or continuum of social behavior, and the differing conclusions may reflect differing theoretical and statistical approaches. It is of course also possible that both viewpoints are correct and that categorical and dimensional aspects of ASD symptoms should be considered in the conceptualization of ASD.

There is increasing momentum within the literature to conceive of the core ASD symptomatology as distinct, or "fractionable." That is, that while the core features may regularly co-occur, these features may have distinct causes at genetic, cognitive, and neural levels. In their seminal review paper, Happe et al. (2006) argue that "*it is time to give up on the search for a monolithic cause or explanation for the three core aspects of autism*" (p. 1219). This claim was based in part on Ronald and colleagues' work on a large UK general population twin sample which found that correlations between continuous measures of social, communication and repetitive behavior were lower than expected (Happe et al., 2006). Happe et al. describe several implications following from their thesis, including that at the behavioral level each aspect of the ASD behavioral triad needs to be assessed separately rather than using global rating scales. The authors also claim that "*heterogeneity in ASD, on our account, is not simply due to noise or the complex unfolding of development, but is an unavoidable consequence of variation along at least three largely independent (although of course interacting) dimensions of impairment*" (p. 1220).

A large number of studies have also explored the ASD cognitive phenotype and a number of cognitive models of ASD have been proposed over time. These include the theory of mind account (Baron-Cohen et al., 1985); the executive dysfunction account (Ozonoff et al., 1991); the weak central coherence account (Happe and Frith, 2006); the enhanced perceptual functioning account (Mottron et al., 2006); the theory of reduced generalization and enhanced discrimination ability (Plaisted, 2001); and the empathizing – systematizing theory (Baron-Cohen, 2010; Grove et al., 2013). Each of these cognitive characteristics has been successfully linked to specific aspects of the ASD behavioral phenotype (Taylor et al., 2012) although none would appear to provide a parsimonious account of features observed in ASD. Charman et al. (2011) provide an excellent review of studies in this area and also a compelling account of the potential benefits of articulating ASD cognitive phenotypes with respect to advancing both treatment and genetic research. Charman also highlights the challenges involved in conducting high quality research in this area from statistical and methodological perspectives.

## VARIABILITY IN AND PREDICTORS OF RESPONSE TO BEHAVIORAL TREATMENT IN ASD

The heterogeneity of ASD may also underlie the variability in response to treatment that is observed among individuals with ASD. Meta-analyses conducted in recent years have tended to conclude that Early Intensive Behavioral Intervention (EIBI), incorporating the principles of applied behavior analysis (ABA), is the treatment of choice for young children with ASD (Vismara and Rogers, 2010; Reichow, 2012), and that superior outcomes are associated with entry into EIBI at the earliest possible age (Granpeesheh et al., 2009; Wallace and Rogers, 2010). Despite the efficacy of EIBI for some children, there is tremendous variation in treatment response in ASD, with other children who receive EIBI failing to have a dramatic response (Dawson et al., 2002). A systematic review of controlled studies of EIBI showed that, while EIBI resulted in improved outcomes for children with ASD compared to comparison groups at a group level, there was marked variability in outcome at an individual level (Howlin et al., 2009). This differential response to treatment is common across all of the evidence-based approaches for treatment of ASD, with up to 50% of children showing substantial positive gains, and the other 50% making variable progress, some with extremely limited skills development (Stahmer et al., 2011).

Therefore, research aimed at methods of individualizing treatment is important. Such research requires an understanding of the pre-treatment characteristics associated with differential response to treatment, including child and family variables, and how specific behavioral intervention techniques address each of these characteristics (Stahmer et al., 2011). The goal of this line of research is to allow treatments to be tailored to individual children and thereby increase the overall rate of positive outcomes for children with ASD (Stahmer et al., 2011). In a recent systematic review of EIBI for ASD, however, Warren et al. (2011) concluded that the ability to predict children's response to treatment and outcome was very limited and warranted further investigation. The genetic and phenotypic heterogeneity inherent in ASD may also imply that no single EIBI can be universally effective and that, in a sense, many nuanced treatment approaches may ultimately be required for the many autisms in existence.

Nonetheless, available evidence indicates that a number of pre-treatment factors may be associated with response to treatment across various EIBI models. These include overall IQ (McEachin et al., 1993; Harris and Handleman, 2000; Eldevik et al., 2006; Magiati et al., 2007; Remington et al., 2007; Perry et al., 2011), language and communication abilities (Sallows and Graupner, 2005; Eldevik et al., 2006; Eikeseth et al., 2007; Magiati et al., 2007; Remington et al., 2007), adaptive skills (Remington et al., 2007; Makrygianni and Reed, 2010; Flanagan et al., 2012), imitation (Sallows and Graupner, 2005; Vivanti et al., 2013), play skills (Kasari et al., 2008, 2012; Ingersoll, 2010a), joint attention (Yoder and Stone, 2006; Kasari et al., 2008), interest in objects (Yoder and Stone, 2006; Schreibman et al., 2009; Carter et al., 2011), functional use of objects (Vivanti et al., 2013), symptom severity (Smith et al., 2000; Sallows and Graupner, 2005; Remington et al., 2007; Vivanti et al., 2013), and younger age (Harris and Handleman, 2000; Perry et al., 2011). Some studies, however, have failed to find relationships between these factors and treatment response. For example, Eldevik et al. (2006) found that age at intake was not a predictor of children's response to a low-intensity behavioral treatment, while Sallows and Graupner (2005) found that initial IQ did not predict children's response to an intensive behavioral intervention. Furthermore, the direction of relationships between these pre-treatment factors and intervention response is sometimes inconsistent. For example, Remington et al. (2007) found that higher ASD symptom scores at intake were associated with improved EIBI outcomes, while Smith et al. (2000) found that children with milder symptoms (i.e., a diagnosis of Pervasive Developmental Disorder-NOS) tended to have a better response to EIBI than children with more severe symptoms (i.e., a diagnosis of ASD).

## INCREASING TREATMENT EFFICACY FOR ASD BY IDENTIFYING INDIVIDUAL DIFFERENCES

Given the heterogeneity of ASD, it is likely that a personalized medicine approach, considering individual differences in etiologic and phenotypic characteristics, would result in increased treatment efficacy (Perrin et al., 2012). Georgiades et al. (2013) suggest that, rather than conducting studies that compare individuals with a diagnosis of ASD with typically developing individuals, future research should focus on understanding the meaning of individual and subgroup differences within the autism spectrum on treatment outcomes. The identification of such differences, and an understanding of how these might impact on response to treatment, has implications for the ability to individually tailor treatment programs and thereby improve their effectiveness.

As an example, this type of approach has been found to be useful in explaining differences in presentation and treatment response in children with diagnoses of oppositional defiant disorder and conduct disorder. There is increasing support for the subtyping of childhood conduct problems based on whether children exhibit high versus low levels of callous-unemotional (CU) traits, such as a lack of guilt and empathy (Hawes et al., 2013). Research suggests that the conduct problems of children with high levels of CU traits are more severe and less responsive to established psychological interventions than those of children without CU traits (Hawes and Dadds, 2005; Waschbusch et al., 2007). This has allowed research into interventions that may contribute to reductions in the CU traits of young children (Hawes and Dadds, 2007; McDonald et al., 2011). Furthermore, articulating these phenotypic differences has contributed to a better understanding of the etiology of conduct disorder (e.g., Viding et al., 2007).

One method to potentially identify subgroups among children with ASD would be to investigate phenotypic characteristics that may predict response to treatment, which has important implications for guiding choice of treatment. Furthermore, using a longitudinal design, it would be beneficial to compare the developmental trajectory of young children with ASD receiving a standardized treatment with those in "waitlist" conditions as well as with healthy control groups. This would provide a significant contribution to the sparse body of knowledge about developmental changes in brain function during this period of development. Even more importantly, determining which characteristics correspond with observable changes in the treatment group would allow us to identify specific individual characteristics and relevant biomarkers sensitive to behavioral intervention, with implications for assessing response to intervention in clinical and research settings (see **Figure 2**). This would also reveal whether and which variations in the baseline measures of brain function predict response to treatment. Given the significant investment represented by EIBI programs, their overall utility could be greatly enhanced by determining whether there are measurable characteristics at baseline capable of predicting response. Finally, if such phenotypic

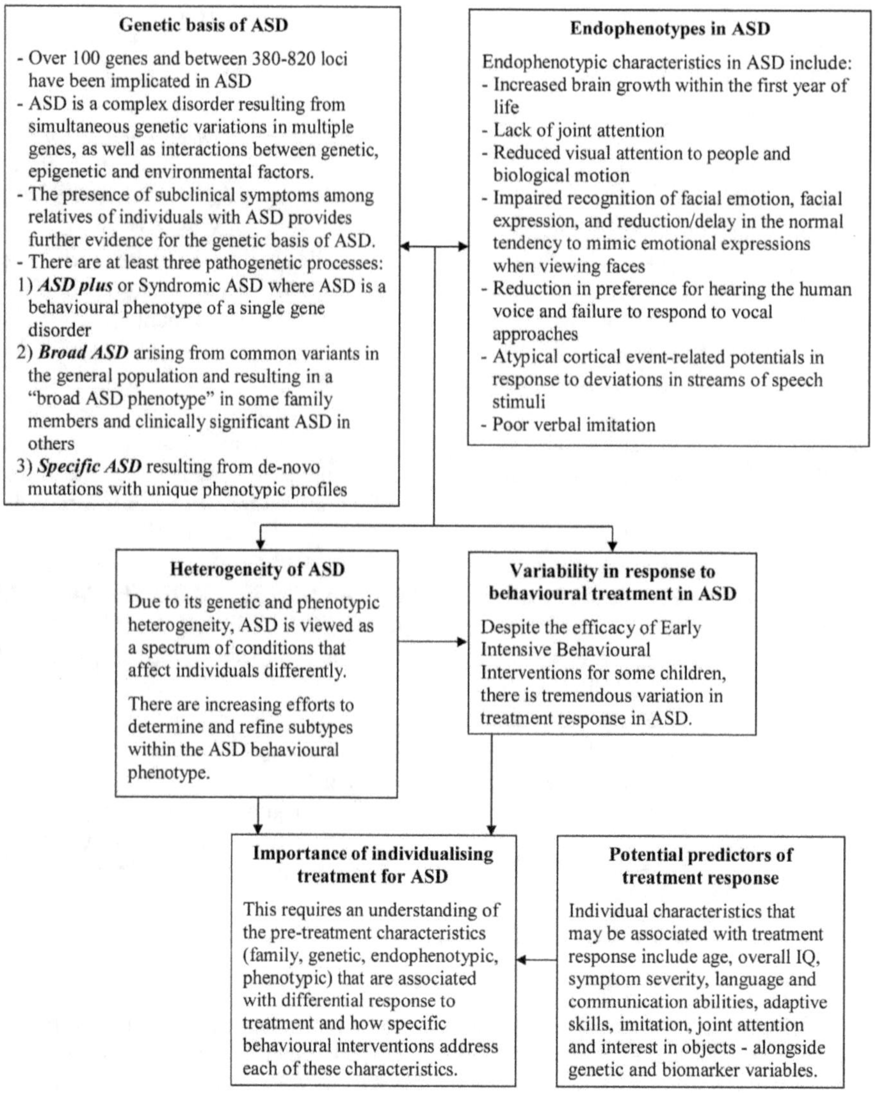


**FIGURE 2 | Summary of key points and links between genotypes, endophenotypes, and clinical predictors of response to behavioral intervention in ASD.**

predictors were established, this could further our understanding of the genetic basis of ASD, by allowing future research to attempt to link these predictors to specific underlying genetic causes. The task ahead is certainly great, but also tantalizing with respect to the potential refinements in our understanding and also benefits to affected individuals that are possible.

## REFERENCES


1. Abrahams, B. S., and Geschwind, D. H. (2010). Connecting genes to brain in the autism spectrum disorders. *Arch. Neurol.* 67, 395. doi:10.1001/ archneurol.2010.47
2. Bailey, A., Le Couteur, A., Gottes- man, I., Bolton, P., Simonoff, E., Yuzda, E., et al. (1995). Autism as a strongly genetic disorder: evi- dence from a British twin study. *Psy- chol. Med.* 25, 63–77. doi:10.1017/ S0033291700028099
3. Bailey, A., Palferman, S., Heavey, L., and Le Couteur, A. (1998). Autism: the phenotype in relatives. *J. Autism Dev. Disord.* 28, 369–392. doi:10.1023/A: 1026048320785
4. Baron-Cohen, S. (2010). "Empathizing, systemizing and the extreme male brain theory of autism," in *Progress in Brain Research: Sex Differences in the Human Brain, Their Under- pinnings and Implications*, ed. I. Savic (Cambridge: Academic Press), 167–176.
5. Baron-Cohen, S., Leslie, A. M., and Frith, U. (1985). Does the autistic child have a "theory of mind"? *Cog- nition* 21, 37–46. doi:10.1016/0010-0277(85)90022-8
6. Baron-Cohen, S., Wheelwright, S., Skin- ner, R., Martin, J., and Clubley, E. (2001). The autism-spectrum quo- tient (AQ): evidence from Asperger syndrome/high-functioning autism, males and females, scientists and mathematicians. *J. Autism Dev. Disord.* 31, 5–17. doi:10.1023/A: 1005653411471
7. Bedford, R., Elsabbagh, M., Gliga, T., Pickles, A., Senju, A., Charman, T., et al. (2012). Precursors to social and communication difficulties in infants at-risk for autism: gaze following and attentional engage- ment. *J. Autism Dev. Disord.* 42, 2208–2218. doi:10.1007/s10803- 012-1450-y
8. Betancur, C. (2011). Etiological hetero- geneity in autism spectrum disorders: more than 100 genetic and genomic disorders and still count- ing. *Brain Res.* 1380, 42–77. doi:10. 1016/j.brainres.2010.11.078
9. Bolton, P., MacDonald, H., Pickles, A., Rios, P., Goode, S., Crowson, M., et al. (1994). A case-control family his- tory study of autism. *J. Child Psychol. Psychiatry* 35, 877–900. doi:10.1111/ j.1469-7610.1994.tb02300.x
10. Brock, J., Brown, C. C., Boucher, J., and Rippon, G. (2002). The temporal binding deficit hypothesis of autism.*Dev. Psychopathol.* 14, 209–224. doi: 10.1017/S0954579402002018
11. Bruining, H., de Sonneville, L., Swaab, H., de Jonge, M., Kas, M., van Engeland, H., et al. (2010). Dis- secting the clinical heterogeneity of autism spectrum disorders through defined genotypes. *PLoS ONE* 5:e10887. doi:10.1371/journal.pone. 0010887
12. Carter, A. S., Messinger, D. S., Stone, W. L., Celimli, S., Nahmias, A. S., and Yoder, P. (2011). A randomized con- trolled trial of Hanen's 'More Than Words' in toddlers with early autism symptoms. *J. Child Psychol. Psychiatry* 52, 741–752. doi:10.1111/j.1469- 7610.2011.02395.x
13. Ceponiene, R., Alku, P., Westerfield, M., Torki, M., and Townsend, J. (2005). ERPs differentiate syllable and nonphonetic sound processing in children and adults. *Psychophys- iology* 42, 391–406. doi:10.1111/j.1469-8986.2005.00305.x
14. Charman, T. (2003). Why is joint atten- tion a pivotal skill in autism? *Philos. Trans. R. Soc. Lond. B Biol. Sci.* 358, 315–324. doi:10.1098/rstb.2002.1199
15. Charman, T., Jones, C., Pickles, A., Simonoff, E., Baird, G., and Happé, F. (2011). Defining the cognitive phe- notype of autism. *Brain Res.* 1380, 10–21. doi:10.1016/j.brainres.2010. 10.075
16. Chen, F. S., and Yoon, J. M. (2011). Brief report: broader autism phenotype predicts spontaneous reciprocity of direct gaze. *J. Autism Dev. Disord.* 41, 1131–1134. doi:10.1007/s10803-010-1136-2
17. Clarke, R., and Eapen, V. (in press). Balance within the neurexin trans- synaptic connexus functions as a gate-keeper of behavioural control. *Front. Psychiatry* Constantino, J. N., and Todd, R. D. (2003). Autistic traits in the gen- eral population: a twin study. *Arch. Gen. Psychiatry* 60, 524. doi:10.1001/ archpsyc.60.5.524
18. Constantino, J. N., and Todd, R. D. (2005). Intergenerational transmis- sion of subthreshold autistic traits in the general population. *Biol. Psy- chiatry* 57, 655–660. doi:10.1016/j. biopsych.2004.12.014
19. Courchesne, E., Campbell, K., and Solso, S. (2011). Brain growth across the life span in autism: age-specific changes in anatomical pathology. *Brain Res.* 1380, 138–145. doi:10. 1016/j.brainres.2010.09.101
20. Courchesne, E., Redcay, E., Morgan, J. T., and Kennedy, D. P. (2005). Autism at the beginning: microstructural and growth abnormalities under- lying the cognitive and behavioral phenotype of autism. *Dev. Psy- chopathol.* 17, 577–597. doi:10.1017/ S0954579405050285
21. Dawson, G. (2008). Early behavioral intervention, brain plasticity, and the prevention of autism spectrum disorder. *Dev. Psychopathol.* 20, 775. doi:10.1017/S0954579408000370
22. Dawson, G., Jones, E., Merkle, K., Ven-ema, K., Lowy, R., Faja, S., et al. (2012). Early behavioral interven- tion is associated with normalized brain activity in young children with autism. *J. Am. Acad. Child Ado- lesc. Psychiatry* 51, 1150–1159. doi: 10.1016/j.jaac.2012.08.018
23. Dawson, G., Meltzoff, A. N., Osterling, J., Rinaldi, J., and Brown, E. (1998). Children with autism fail to orient to naturally occurring social stimuli. *J. Autism Dev. Disord.* 28, 479–485. doi:10.1023/A:1026043926488
24. Dawson, G., Rogers, S., Munson, J., Smith, M., Winter, J., Greenson, J., et al. (2010). Randomized, controlled trial of an intervention for toddlers with autism: the Early Start Den- ver Model. *Pediatrics* 125, e17–e23. doi:10.1542/ peds.2009-0958
25. Dawson, G., Toth, K., Abbott, R., Oster- ling, J., Munson, J., Estes, A., et al. (2004). Early social attention impairments in autism: social ori- enting, joint attention, and attention to distress. *Dev. Psychol.* 40, 271–282. doi:10.1037/0012-1649.40.2.271
26. Dawson, G., Webb, S., Schellenberg, G. D., Dager, S., Friedman, S., Aylward, E., et al. (2002). Defining the broader phenotype of autism: genetic, brain, and behavioral perspectives. *Dev. Psychopathol.* 14, 581–611. doi:10. 1017/ S0954579402003103
27. Eapen, V. (2011). Genetic basis of autism: is there a way forward? *Curr. Opin. Psychiatry* 24, 226. doi:10. 1097/YCO.0b013e328345927e
28. Eapen, V., Crncec, R., and Walter, A. (2013). Clinical outcomes of an early intervention program for preschool children with Autism Spectrum Disorder in a community group set- ting. *BMCPediatr.* 13:3. doi:10.1186/ 1471-2431-13-3
29. Ecker, C., Suckling, J., Deoni, S. C., Lombardo, M. V., Bullmore, E. T., Baron-Cohen, S., et al. (2012). Brain anatomy and its relationship to behavior in adults with autism spectrum disorder: a multicenter magnetic resonance imaging study. *Arch. Gen. Psychiatry* 69, 195. doi:10. 1001/archgenpsychiatry.2011.1251
30. Eikeseth, S., Smith, T., Jahr, E., and Elde- vik, S. (2007). Outcome for children with autism who began inten- sive behavioral treatment between ages 4 and 7 a comparison controlled study. *Behav. Modif.* 31, 264–278. doi:10.1177/0145445506291396
31. Eldevik, S., Eikeseth, S., Jahr, E., and Smith, T. (2006). Effects of low- intensity behavioral treatment for children with autism and mental retardation. *J. Autism Dev. Disord.* 36, 211–224. doi:10.1007/s10803-005-0058-x
32. El-Fishawy, P. (2010). The genetics of autism: key issues, recent findings and clinical implications. *Psychiatr. Clin. North Am.* 33, 83. doi:10.1016/ j.psc.2009.12.002
33. Elsabbagh, M. (2012). The emerg- ing autistic brain: processes of risk and resilience. *Neuropsychiatry* 2, 181–183. doi:10.2217/npy.12.29
34. Elsabbagh, M., Mercure, E., Hudry, K., Chandler, S., Pasco, G., Charman, T., et al. (2012). Infant neural sen- sitivity to dynamic eye gaze is asso- ciated with later emerging autism. *Curr. Biol.* 22, 338–342. doi:10.1016/ j.cub.2011.12.056
35. Flanagan, H. E., Perry, A., and Free- man, N. L. (2012). Effectiveness of large-scale community-based inten- sive behavioral Intervention: a wait- list comparison study exploring out- comes and predictors. *Res. Autism Spectr. Disord.* 6, 673–682. doi:10. 1016/j.rasd.2011.09.011
36. Frazier, T. W., Youngstrom, E. A., Sin- clair, L., Kubu, C. S., Law, P., Rezai, A., et al. (2010). Autism spectrum disorders as a qualitatively distinct category from typical behavior in a large, clinically ascertained sam- ple. *Assessment* 17, 308–320. doi:10. 1177/1073191109356534
37. Frazier, T. W., Youngstrom, E. A., Speer, L., Embacher, R., Law, P., Constantino, J., et al. (2012). Valida- tion of proposed DSM-5 criteria for autism spectrum disorder. *J. Am. Acad. Child Adolesc. Psychiatry* 51, e23. doi:10.1016/j.jaac.2011.09.021
38. Friedman, J. I., Vrijenhoek, T., Markx, S., Janssen, I. M., van der Vliet, W. A., Faas, B. H., et al. (2008). CNTNAP2 gene dosage variation is associated with schizophrenia and epilepsy. *Mol. Psychiatry* 13, 261–266. doi:10. 1038/ sj.mp.4002049

39. Georgiades, S., Szatmari, P., and Boyle, M. (2013). Importance of studying heterogeneity in autism. *Neuropsy- chiatry* 3, 123–125. doi:10.2217/npy. 13.8
40. Geschwind, D. H., and Levitt, P. (2007). Autism spectrum disorders: devel- opmental disconnection syndromes. *Curr. Opin. Neurobiol.* 17, 103–111. doi:10.1016/j.conb.2007.01.009
41. Goussé, V., Plumet, M.-H., Chabane, N., Mouren-Siméoni, M.-C., Ferradian, N., and Leboyer, M. (2002). Fringe phenotypes in autism: a review of clinical, biochemical and cognitive studies. *Eur. Psychiatry* 17, 120–128. doi:10.1016/S0924- 9338(02)00640-5
42. Granpeesheh, D., Tarbox, J., and Dixon, D. R. (2009). Applied behavior ana- lytic interventions for children with autism: a description and review of treatment research. *Ann. Clin. Psy- chiatry* 21, 162–173.
43. Grinter, E. J., Van Beek, P. L., Maybery, M. T., and Badcock, D. R. (2009). Brief report: visuospatial analysis and self-rated autistic-like traits. *J. Autism Dev. Disord.* 39, 670–677. doi:10.1007/s10803-008-0658-3
44. Grove, R., Baillie, A., Allison, C., Baron- Cohen, S., and Hoekstra, R. A. (2013). Empathizing, systemizing, and autistic traits: latent struc- ture in individuals with autism, their parents, and general popula- tion controls. *J. Abnorm. Psychol.* 122, 600–609. doi:10.1037/a0031919
45. Happe, F., and Frith, U. (2006). The weak coherence account: detail-focused cognitive style in autism spectrum disorders. *J. Autism Dev. Disord.* 36, 5–25. doi:10.1007/s10803-005-0039-0
46. Happe, F., Ronald, A., and Plomin, R. (2006). Time to give up on a single explanation for autism. *Nat. Neurosci.* 9, 1218–1220. doi:10.1038/ nn1770
47. Harris, S. L., and Handleman, J. S. (2000). Age and IQ at intake as predictors of placement for young children with autism: a four-to six- year follow-up. *J. Autism Dev. Dis- ord.* 30, 137–142. doi:10.1023/A: 1005459606120
48. Hawes, D. J., and Dadds, M. R. (2005). The treatment of conduct problems in children with callous- unemotional traits. *J. Consult. Clin. Psychol.* 73, 737–741. doi:10.1037/ 0022-006X.73.4.737
49. Hawes, D. J., and Dadds, M. R. (2007). Stability and malleability of callous-unemotional traits during treatment for childhood conduct problems. *J. Clin. Child Adolesc. Psychol.* 36, 347–355.
50. Hawes, D. J., Dadds, M. R., Brennan, J., Rhodes, T., and Cauchi, A. (2013). Revisiting the treatment of conduct problems in children with cal- lous- unemotional traits. *Aust. N. Z. J. Psychiatry* 47, 646–653. doi:10.1177/ 0004867413484092
51. Howlin, P., Magiati, I., and Charman, T. (2009). Systematic review of early intensive behavioral interventions for children with autism. *Am. J. Intel- lect. Dev. Disabil.* 114, 23–41. doi:10. 1352/2009.114:23
52. Ingersoll, B. (2010a). Brief report: pilot randomized controlled trial of reciprocal imitation training for teaching elicited and sponta- neous imitation to children with autism. *J. Autism Dev. Disord.* 40, 1154–1160. doi:10.1007/ s10803- 010-0966-2
53. Ingersoll, B. (2010b). Broader autism phenotype and nonverbal sensitiv- ity: evidence for an association in the general population. *J. Autism Dev. Disord.* 40, 590–598. doi:10.1007/ s10803-009-0907-0
54. Ingram, D. G., Takahashi, T. N., and Miles, J. H. (2008). Defining autism subgroups: a taxometric solution. *J. Autism Dev. Disord.* 38, 950–960. doi:10.1007/s10803-007-0469-y
55. Jones, W., Carr, K., and Klin, A. (2008). Absence of preferential looking to the eyes of approaching adults pre- dicts level of social disability in 2- year-old toddlers with autism spec- trum disorder. *Arch. Gen. Psychia- try* 65, 946. doi:10.1001/archpsyc.65. 8.946
56. Kanner, L. (1943). Autistic disturbances of affective contact. *Nerv. Child* 2, 217–250.
57. Kasari, C., Gulsrud, A., Freeman, S., Paparella, T., and Hellemann, G. (2012). Longitudinal follow-up of children with autism receiving tar- geted interventions on joint atten- tion and play. *J. Am. Acad. Child Ado- lesc. Psychiatry* 51, 487–495. doi:10. 1016/j.jaac.2012.02.019
58. Kasari, C., Paparella, T., Freeman, S., and Jahromi, L. B. (2008). Language outcome in autism: random- ized comparison of joint attention and play interventions. *J. Consult. Clin. Psychol.* 76, 125. doi:10.1037/ 0022-006X.76.1.125
59. Klin, A. (1991). Young autistic chil- dren's listening preferences in regard to speech: a possible characteriza- tion of the symptom of social with- drawal. *J. Autism Dev. Disord.* 21, 29–42. doi:10.1007/BF02206995
60. Klin, A., Jones, W., Schultz, R., and Volk- mar, F. (2003). The enactive mind, or from actions to cognition: lessons from autism. *Philos. Trans. R. Soc. Lond. B Biol. Sci.* 358, 345–360. doi: 10.1098/rstb.2002.1202
61. Klin, A., Jones, W., Schultz, R., Volk- mar, F., and Cohen, D. (2002). Defining and quantifying the social phe- notype in autism. *Am. J. Psychiatry* 159, 895–908. doi:10.1176/appi.ajp. 159.6.895
62. Klin, A., Lin, D. J., Gorrindo, P., Ramsay, G., and Jones, W. (2009). Two-year-olds with autism orient to non-social contingencies rather than biologi- cal motion. *Nature* 459, 257–261. doi:10.1038/nature07868
63. Kuhl, P. K., Coffey-Corina, S., Padden, D., and Dawson, G. (2005). Links between social and linguistic pro- cessing of speech in preschool chil- dren with autism: behavioral and electrophysiological measures. *Dev. Sci.* 8, F1–F12. doi:10.1111/j.1467- 7687.2004.00384.x
64. Kuhl, P. K., Coffey-Corina, S., Padden, D., Munson, J., Estes, A., and Dawson, G. (2013). Brain responses to words in 2-year-olds with autism predict developmental outcomes at age 6. *PLoS ONE* 8:e64967. doi:10. 1371/journal. pone.0064967
65. Lai, M. C., Lombardo, M. V., Ruigrok, A. N., Chakrabarti, B., Wheelwright, S. J., Auyeung, B., et al. (2012). Cog- nition in males and females with autism: similarities and differences. *PLoS ONE* 7:e47198. doi:10.1371/ journal. pone.0047198
66. Latham, K., Chung, S. T., Allen, P. M., Tavassoli, T., and Baron-Cohen, S. (2013). Spatial localisation in autism: evidence for differences in early cortical visual processing. *Mol. Autism* 4, doi:10.1186/2040-2392-4- 4
67. Lepistö, T., Kujala, T., Vanhala, R., Alku, P., Huotilainen, M., and Näätänen, R. (2005). The discrimination of and orienting to speech and non-speech sounds in children with autism. *Brain Res.* 1066, 147–157. doi:10. 1016/j. brainres.2005.10.052
68. Losh, M., Adolphs, R., Poe, M. D., Cou-ture, S., Penn, D., Baranek, G. T., et al. (2009). Neuropsychological pro- file of autism and the broad autism phenotype. *Arch. Gen. Psychiatry* 66, 518. doi:10.1001/archgenpsychiatry. 2009.34
69. Magiati, I., Charman, T., and Howlin, P. (2007). A two-year prospec- tive follow-up study of community- based early intensive behavioural intervention and specialist nursery provision for children with autism spectrum disorders. *J. Child Psychol. Psychiatry* 48, 803–812. doi:10.1111/ j.1469-7610.2007.01756.x
70. Makrygianni, M. K., and Reed, P. (2010). A meta-analytic review of the effectiveness of behavioural early intervention programs for chil- dren with Autistic Spectrum Disor- ders. *Res. Autism Spectr. Disord.* 4, 577–593.
71. Mandy, W. P., and Skuse, D. H. (2008). Research review: what is the association between the social- communication element of autism and repetitive interests, behaviours and activities? *J. Child Psychol. Psy- chiatry* 49, 795–808. doi:10.1111/j. 1469-7610.2008.01911.x
72. McDonald, R., Dodson, M. C., Rosen- field, D., and Jouriles, E. N. (2011). Effects of a parenting interven- tion on features of psychopathy in children. *J. Abnorm. Child Psychol.* 39, 1013–1023. doi:10.1007/s10802- 011-9512-8
73. McEachin, J. J., Smith, T., and Lovaas, O. (1993). Long-term outcome for chil- dren with autism who received early intensive behavioral treatment. *Am. J. Ment. Retard.* 97, 359–359.
74. McIntosh, D. N., Reichmann-Decker, A., Winkielman, P., and Wilbarger, J. L. (2006). When the social mir- ror breaks: deficits in automatic, but not voluntary, mimicry of emotional facial expressions in autism. *Dev. Sci.* 9, 295–302. doi:10.1111/j.1467- 7687.2006.00492.x
75. Miles, J. H., Takahashi, T. N., Bagby, S., Sahota, P. K., Vaslow, D. F.,Wang, C. H., et al. (2005). Essen- tial versus complex autism: defini- tion of fundamental prognostic sub- types. *Am. J. Med. Genet. A* 135, 171–180.
76. Mottron, L., Dawson, M., Soulieres, I., Hubert, B., and Burack, J. (2006). Enhanced perceptual functioning in autism: an update, and eight principles of autistic perception. *J. Autism Dev. Disord.* 36, 27–43. doi:10.1007/ s10803-005-0040-7
77. Munson, J., Dawson, G., Sterling, L., Beauchaine, T., Zhou, A., Elizabeth, K., et al. (2008a). Evidence for latent classes of IQ in young children with autism spectrum disorder. *Am. J. Ment. Retard.* 113, 439–452. doi:10. 1352/2008.113:439-452
78. Munson, J., Faja, S., Meltzoff, A., Abbott, R., and Dawson, G. (2008b). Neurocognitive predictors of social and communicative developmental tra- jectories in preschoolers with autism spectrum disorders. *J. Int. Neuropsy- chol. Soc.* 14, 956–966. doi:10.1017/ S1355617708081393
79. Nadig, A. S., Ozonoff, S., Young, G. S., Rozga, A., Sigman, M., and Rogers, S. J. (2007). A prospective study of response to name in infants at risk for autism. *Arch. Pediatr. Adolesc. Med.* 161, 378.
80. Norbury, C. F., Brock, J., Cragg, L., Einav, S., Griffiths, H., and Nation, (2009). Eye-movement patterns are associated with communicative competence in autistic spectrum dis- orders. *J. Child Psychol. Psychia- try* 50, 834–842. doi:10.1111/j.1469- 7610.2009.02073.x
81. Oberman, L. M., Winkielman, P., and Ramachandran, V. S. (2009). Slow echo: facial EMG evidence for the delay of spontaneous, but not voluntary, emotional mimicry in children with autism spectrum disorders. *Dev. Sci.* 12, 510–520. doi:10.1111/j.1467-7687. 2008.00796.x

82. Oerlemans, A., Meer, J. J., Steijn, D., Ruiter, S., Bruijn, Y. E., Sonneville, J., et al. (2013). Recognition of facial emotion and affective prosody in children with ASD (+ADHD) and their unaffected siblings. *Eur. Child Adolesc. Psychiatry* 1–15. doi: 10.1007/s00787-013-0446-2
83. O'Roak, B. J. (2008). Autism genetics: strategies, challenges, and opportunities. *Autism Res.* 1, 4–17. doi:10. 1002/aur.3
84. Osterling, J. A., Dawson, G., and Mun- son, J. A. (2002). Early recog- nition of 1-year-old infants with autism spectrum disorder ver- sus mental retardation. *Dev. Psy- chopathol.* 14, 239–251. doi:10.1017/ S0954579402002031
85. Ozonoff, S., Pennington, B. F., and Rogers, S. J. (1991). Executive func- tion deficits in high-functioning autistic individuals: relationship to theory of mind. *J. Child Psychol. Psy- chiatry* 32, 1081–1105. doi:10.1111/ j.1469-7610.1991.tb00351.x
86. Perrin, J. M., Coury, D. L., Jones, N., and Lajonchere, C. (2012). The autism treatment network and autism inter- vention research network on physical health: future directions. *Pedi- atrics* 130, S198–S201. doi:10.1542/ peds.2012-0900S
87. Perry, A., Cummings, A., Geier, J. D., Freeman, N. L., Hughes, S., Managhan, T., et al. (2011). Predictors of outcome for children receiv- ing intensive behavioral interven- tion in a large, community-based program. *Res. Autism Spectr. Disord.* 5, 592–603. doi:10.1016/j.rasd.2010. 07.003
88. Pinto, D., Pagnamenta, A. T., Klei, L., Anney, R., Merico, D., Regan, R., et al. (2010). Functional impact of global rare copy number varia- tion in autism spectrum disorders. *Nature* 466, 368–372. doi:10.1038/ nature09146
89. Piven, J., and Palmer, P. (1999). Psy- chiatric disorder and the broad autism phenotype: evidence from a family study of multiple-incidence autism families. *Am. J. Psychiatry* 156, 557–563.
90. Plaisted, K. C. (2001). "Reduced gen- eralisation in autism: an alternative to weak central coherence," in *The Development of Autism: Perspectives from Theory and Research*, eds J. A. Burack, T. Charman, N. Yirmiya, and P. R. Zelazo (Nahwah, NJ: Erlbaum), 149–169.
91. Reichow, B. (2012). Overview of meta- analyses on early intensive behavioral intervention for young chil- dren with autism spectrum disor- ders. *J. Autism Dev. Disord.* 42, 512–520. doi:10.1007/s10803-011-1218-9
92. Remington, B., Hastings, R. P., Kovshoff, H., degli Espinosa, F., Jahr, E., Brown, T., et al. (2007). Early intensive behavioral inter- vention: outcomes for children with autism and their parents after two years. *Am. J. Ment. Retard.* 112, 418–438. doi:10.1352/0895-8017(2007)112[418:EIBIOF]2.0. CO;2
93. Richmond, L. L., Thorpe, M., Berry- hill, M. E., Klugman, J., and Olson, I. R. (2013). Individual differences in autistic trait load in the general population pre- dict visual working memory per- formance. *Q. J. Exp. Psychol.* 66, 1182–1195. doi:10.1080/17470218. 2012.734831
94. Russo, N., Nicol, T., Trommer, B., Zecker, S., and Kraus, N. (2009). Brainstem transcription of speech is disrupted in children with autism spectrum disorders. *Dev. Sci.* 12, 557–567. doi:10.1111/j.1467-7687. 2008.00790.x
95. Sallows, G. O., and Graupner, T. D. (2005). Intensive behavioral treat- ment for children with autism: four- year outcome and predictors. *Am. J. Ment. Retard.* 110, 417–438.
96. Sasson, N. J., Nowlin, R. B., and Pinkham, A. E. (2012). Social cognition, social skill, and the broad autism phenotype. *Autism.* doi: 10.1177/1362361312455704. [Epub ahead of print].
97. Schreibman, L., Stahmer, A. C., Bar- lett, V. C., and Dufek, S. (2009). Brief report: toward refinement of a predictive behavioral profile for treatment outcome in children with autism. *Res. Autism Spectr. Disord.* 3, 163–172. doi:10.1016/j.rasd.2008. 04.008
98. Smith, T., Groen, A. D., and Wynn, J. W. (2000). Randomized trial of intensive early intervention for children with pervasive developmental disorder. *Am. J. Ment. Retard.* 105, 269–285. doi:10.1352/0895-8017(2000) 105<0269:RTOIEI>2.0.CO;2
99. Spencer, M., Chura, L., Holt, R., Suck- ling, J., Calder, A., Bullmore, E., et al. (2012a). Failure to deactivate the default mode network indicates a possible endophenotype of autism. *Mol. Autism* 3, 1–9. doi:10.1186/2040-2392-3-15
100. Spencer, M., Holt, R., Chura, L., Calder, A., Suckling, J., Bullmore, E., et al. (2012b). Atypical activation dur- ing the Embedded Figures Task as a functional magnetic resonance imaging endophenotype of autism. *Brain* 135, 3469–3480. doi:10.1093/brain/aws229
101. Spencer, M., Holt, R., Chura, L., Suck- ling, J., Calder, A., Bullmore, E., et al. (2011). A novel functional brain imaging endophenotype of autism: the neural response to facial expres- sion of emotion. *Transl. Psychiatry* 1, e19. doi:10.1038/tp.2011.18
102. Stahmer, A. C., Schreibman, L., and Cunningham, A. B. (2011). Toward a technology of treatment individ- ualization for young children with autism spectrum disorders. *Brain Res.* 1380, 229–239. doi:10.1016/j. brainres.2010.09.043
103. Stewart, M. E., and Ota, M. (2008). Lexical effects on speech per- ception in individuals with "autistic" traits. *Cognition* 109, 157–162. doi:10.1016/j. cognition. 2008.07.010
104. Stewart, M. E., Watson, J., Allcock, A.- J., and Yaqoob, T. (2009). Autistic traits predict performance on the block design. *Autism* 13, 133–142. doi:10.1177/1362361308098515
105. Sucksmith, E., Allison, C., Baron- Cohen, S., Chakrabarti, B., and Hoekstra, R. (2012). Empathy and emotion recognition in people with autism, first-degree relatives, and controls. *Neuropsycholo- gia* 51, 98–105. doi:10.1016/j. neuropsychologia.2012.11.013 Taylor, L. J., Maybery, M. T., and White-house, A. J. (2012). Do children with specific language impairment have a cognitive profile reminiscent of autism? A review of the liter- ature. *J. Autism Dev. Disord.* 42, 2067–2083. doi:10.1007/s10803-012-1456-5
106. Verkerk, A. J., Mathews, C. A., Joosse, M., Eussen, B. H., Heutink, P., Oostra, B. A., et al. (2003). CNT-NAP2 is disrupted in a family with Gilles de la Tourette syn- drome and obsessive compulsive disorder. *Genomics* 82, 1–9. doi:10. 1016/S0888-7543(03)00097-1
107. Viding, E., Frick, P. J., and Plomin, R. (2007). Aetiology of the relationship between callous–unemotional traits and conduct problems in childhood. *Br. J. Psychiatry Suppl.* 190, s33–s38. doi:10.1192/bjp.190.5.s33
108. Vismara, L. A., and Rogers, S. J. (2010). Behavioral treatments in autism spectrum disorder: what do we know? *Annu. Rev. Clin. Psychol.* 6, 447–468. doi:10.1146/annurev. clinpsy.121208.131151
109. Vivanti, G., Dissanayake, C., Zierhut, C., and Rogers, S. J. (2013). Brief report: predictors of outcomes in the early start Denver model delivered in a group setting. *J. Autism Dev. Disord.* 43, 1717–1724. doi:10.1007/s10803-012-1705-7
110. von dem Hagen, E. A., Stoyanova, R. S., Baron-Cohen, S., and Calder, A. J. (2013). Reduced functional con- nectivity within and between 'social' resting state networks in Autism Spectrum Conditions. *Soc. Cogn. Affect. Neurosci.* 8, 694–701. doi:10. 1093/scan/nss053
111. Wallace, K. S., and Rogers, S. J. (2010). Intervening in infancy: implications for autism spectrum disor- ders. *J. Child Psychol. Psychiatry* 51, 1300–1320. doi:10.1111/j.1469-7610.2010.02308.x
112. Wang, K., Zhang, H., Ma, D., Bucan, M., Glessner, J. T., Abrahams, B. S., et al. (2009). Common genetic vari- ants on 5p14. 1 associate with autism spectrum disorders. *Nature* 459, 528–533. doi:10.1038/nature07999
113. Warren, Z., McPheeters, M. L., Sathe, N., Foss-Feig, J. H., Glasser, A., and Veenstra-VanderWeele, J. (2011). A systematic review of early intensive intervention for autism spectrum disorders. *Pediatrics* 127, e1303–e1311. doi:10.1542/peds.2011-0426
114. Waschbusch, D. A., Carrey, N. J., Willoughby, M. T., King, S., and Andrade, B. F. (2007). Effects of methylphenidate and behavior modification on the social and aca- demic behavior of children with dis- ruptive behavior disorders: the mod- erating role of callous/unemotional traits. *J. Clin. Child Adolesc. Psychol.* 36, 629–644.
115. Werner, E., and Dawson, G. (2005). Val- idation of the phenomenon of autis- tic regression using home video- tapes. *Arch. Gen. Psychiatry* 62, 889. doi:10.1001/archpsyc.62.8.889
116. Werner, E., Dawson, G., Osterling, J., and Dinno, N. (2000). Brief report: recognition of autism spec- trum disorder before one year of age: a retrospective study based on home videotapes. *J. Autism Dev. Disord.* 30, 157–162. doi:10.1023/A: 1005463707029
117. Wheelwright, S., Auyeung, B., Allison, C., and Baron-Cohen, S. (2010). Research defining the broader, medium and narrow autism phe- notype among parents using the Autism Spectrum Quotient (AQ). *Mol. Autism* 1:10. doi:10.1186/2040- 2392-1-10
118. Whitehouse, A. J., and Bishop, D. V. (2008). Do children with autism 'switch off' to speech sounds? An investigation using event-related potentials. *Dev. Sci.* 11, 516–524. doi: 10.1111/j.1467-7687.2008.00697.x
119. Wing, L. (1996). *The Autistic Spectrum: A Guide for Parents and Professionals.* London: Constable.
120. Yoder, P., and Stone, W. L. (2006). Randomized comparison of two communication interventions for preschoolers with autism spectrum disorders. *J. Consult. Clin. Psychol.* 74, 426. doi:10.1037/0022-006X.74. 3.426
121. Zwaigenbaum, L., Bryson, S., Rogers, T., Roberts, W., Brian, J., and Szatmari, P. (2005). Behavioral manifestations of autism in the first year of life. *Int. J. Dev. Neurosci.* 23, 143–152. doi:10.1016/j.ijdevneu.2004.05.001

# 24

# Genome-wide association study of autistic-like traits in a general population study of young adults

**_Rachel Maree Jones[1†], Gemma Cadby[1†], Phillip E. Melton[1], Lawrence J. Abraham[1,2], Andrew J. Whitehouse[3] and Eric K. Moses[1]*_**

[1] *Centre for Genetic Origins of Health and Disease, University of Western Australia, Perth, WA, Australia*
[2] *School of Chemistry and Biochemistry, University of Western Australia, Perth, WA, Australia*
[3] *Telethon Institute for Child Health Research, Perth, WA, Australia*

***Edited by:***
*Charles Claudianos, University of Queensland, Australia*

***Reviewed by:***
*Raymond Allan Clarke, Ingham Institute University of Western Sydney, Australia*
*Irina Voineagu, The University of New South Wales, Australia*

****Correspondence:***
*Eric K. Moses, Centre for Genetic Origins of Health and Disease, University of Western Australia, 35 Stirling Highway, Crawley, Perth, WA 6009, Australia*
*e-mail: eric.moses@uwa.edu.au*

*[†] Rachel Maree Jones and Gemma Cadby have contributed equally to this work.*

**Lay abstract:** It has been proposed that autistic-like traits in the general population lie on a continuum, with clinical Autism Spectrum Disorder (ASD), representing the extreme end of this distribution. The current study undertook a genome-wide association (GWA) scan of 965 young Western Australian adults to identify novel risk variants associated with autistic-like traits. No associations reached genome-wide significance; however, a review of nominally associated single nucleotide polymorphisms (SNPs) indicated two positional candidate loci that have been previously implicated in autistic-like trait etiology.

**Scientific abstract:** Research has proposed that autistic-like traits in the general population lie on a continuum, with clinical ASD representing the extreme end of this distribution. Inherent in this proposal is that biological mechanisms associated with clinical ASD may also underpin variation in autistic-like traits within the general population. A GWA study using 2,462,046 SNPs was undertaken for ASD in 965 individuals from the Western Australian Pregnancy Cohort (Raine) Study. No SNP associations reached genome-wide significance ($p < 5.0 \times 10^{-8}$). However, investigations into nominal observed SNP associations ($p < 1.0 \times 10^{-5}$) add support to two positional candidate genes previously implicated in ASD etiology, PRKCB1, and CBLN1. The rs198198 SNP ($p = 9.587 \times 10^{-6}$), is located within an intron of the protein kinase C, beta 1 (PRKCB1) gene on chromosome 16p11. The PRKCB1 gene has been previously reported in linkage and association studies for ASD, and its mRNA expression has been shown to be significantly down regulated in ASD cases compared with controls. The rs16946931 SNP ($p = 1.78 \times 10^{-6}$) is located in a region flanking the Cerebellin 1 (CBLN1) gene on chromosome 16q12.1. The CBLN1 gene is involved with synaptogenesis and is part of a gene family previously implicated in ASD. This GWA study is only the second to examine SNPs associated with autistic-like traits in the general population, and provides evidence to support roles for the PRKCB1 and CBLN1 genes in risk of clinical ASD.

**Keywords: autistic-like traits, genome-wide association, PRKCB1, autism spectrum disorder, autism spectrum quotient, CBLN1**

## INTRODUCTION

Autism Spectrum Disorders (ASD) represent a group of neurodevelopmental conditions characterized by impairments in social interaction and communication, and repetitive interests and behaviors. A recent review estimated the median global prevalence of ASD at 62 cases per 10,000 children (Elsabbagh et al., 2012). The overall heritability of ASD is estimated at 90%, which is amongst the highest for any neuropsychiatric disorder (Hollander et al., 2003; Skuse et al., 2005). Evidence suggests that ASD have a complex inheritance where different, likely overlapping, groups of genetic variants may cause susceptibility to disease (Veenstra-VanderWeele et al., 2004). Increasing numbers of epidemiological and genetic studies have deepened the understanding of genetic contribution to ASD, and show that a variety of genetic mechanisms may be involved in the etiology (Li et al., 2012).

Autistic-like traits are sub-threshold deficits in socialization, communication, and restricted interests that do not meet formal criteria for ASD (Constantino and Todd, 2003). Several authors have suggested that ASD can be conceptualized as the conditions arising in individuals found at the extreme end of a normal distribution of autistic-like traits (Gillberg, 1992; Constantino and Todd, 2003; Ronald et al., 2005). Population-based studies have supported this by finding that, in addition to individuals with ASD, many others exhibit sub-threshold autistic or autistic-like traits (Constantino and Todd, 2003; Posserud et al., 2006; Lundström et al., 2012). Sub-threshold autistic-like traits have been examined in general population twin studies, with heritability estimates ranging from 36 to 87% in these studies (Ronald and Hoekstra, 2011).

With the discovery of common genetic variants associated with ASD, the question is raised whether common risk loci also contribute to variation in phenotypes such as autistic-like traits (St Pourcain et al., 2010). One methodological approach that is gaining influence in ASD research is the examination of the quantitative distribution of autistic-like traits in the broader community, rather than a dichotomy of ASD cases and controls. Many authors have postulated that common genetic variants that are present in a significant proportion of the general population may play a role in the etiology of ASD (Campbell et al., 2006; Alarcón et al., 2008; Chakrabarti et al., 2009; Wang et al., 2009; Anney et al., 2010; Ronald et al., 2010). Further to this, it is thought that understanding the etiology of individual differences in autistic-like traits in the general population will help in understanding the causes of ASD (Ronald and Hoekstra, 2011).

The aim of the current study was to use genome-wide association (GWA) methods to search for novel risk variants associated with autistic-like traits in a Western Australian population sample.

## MATERIALS AND METHODS

### ETHICS STATEMENT

Participant recruitment of the study families were approved by the Human Ethics Committee at King Edward Memorial Hospital. The 20 year follow-up ethics approval was received from the Human Research Ethics Committee at the University of Western Australia. Participants provided written informed consent for data collection of autistic-like trait outcomes at approximately 20 years of age.

### GWA STUDY SAMPLE POPULATION

Data were obtained from the Western Australian Pregnancy Cohort (Raine) Study based at the Telethon Institute for Child Health Research. The Raine Study is a longitudinal investigation of pregnant women and their offspring, who were recruited from King Edward Memorial Hospital, Perth, Western Australia or nearby private practices between 1989 and 1991 (Newnham et al., 1993). From the 2,900 pregnancies recruited into the Raine Study, 2,868 live-born children have been followed since the commencement of the study. The final sample consisted of 965 individuals from the Raine study with both genotype and outcome measures.

### MEASURE OF AUTISTIC-LIKE TRAITS

At the 20 year follow-up, Raine Study participants who did not have a diagnosis of intellectual disability or ASD were asked to complete the Autism Spectrum Quotient (AQ) (Baron-Cohen et al., 2001). The AQ is a self-report questionnaire that provides a quantitative measure of autistic-like traits in the general population (Baron-Cohen et al., 2001). Individuals are provided with 50 statements and asked to indicate on a 4-point scale how well that statement applies to them (strongly agree, agree, disagree, strongly disagree). The items were scored on a scale ranging from 1 to 4, based on previous research that this scoring method retains more information about responses than the dichotomous scoring first proposed for this instrument (Baron-Cohen et al., 2001; Austin, 2005; Stewart and Austin, 2009; Russell-Smith et al., 2011). Scores on each item are summed to provide a Total AQ, with higher scores indicating greater autistic-like traits. The Total AQ is known to have good test-retest reliability ($r = 0.7$), and validation studies have found that scores in the general population follow a normal quantitative distribution (Baron-Cohen et al., 2001; Whitehouse et al., 2011). Factor analyses of the AQ in several countries have consistently identified three clear factors, relating to social ability, attention to detail/patterns, and the understanding of others. In the current study, we divided items into the subscales identified in a study of Western Australian adults (Russell-Smith et al., 2011), who were highly similar to the sample under investigation here: Social Skills, Details/Patterns, and Communication/Mindreading. There is minimal difference between the items pertaining to these subscales, and those reported in other factor analyses. For the current data set, internal reliability for the scales ranged from moderate (Communication/Mindreading: $\alpha = 0.63$) to good (Details/Patterns: $\alpha = 0.78$) and excellent (Social Skills: $\alpha = 0.85$). In this study, Total AQ scores and the scores of the three subscales were used as four outcome measures.

### GWA STUDY GENOTYPING

In the Raine Study, DNA was collected using standardized procedures from 74% of adolescents who attended the 14 year follow-up, and a further 5% at the 16 year follow-up. Of the 1,593 offspring for whom genome-wide data were available, 99 individuals were excluded for the following reasons: 16 had low genotyping success (>3% missing); 3 had excessive heterozygosity, 68 were in high identical-by-descent with another Raine Study participant (related), 7 whose sex was ambiguous, and 5 individuals had mislabeled samples. There were 1,494 individuals whose DNA sample passed quality control criteria and were eligible for the genetic analyses (768 males, 726 females), see **Figure 1**.

Genome-wide data were generated using an Illumina Human 660W Quad array at the Center for Applied Genomics (Toronto,

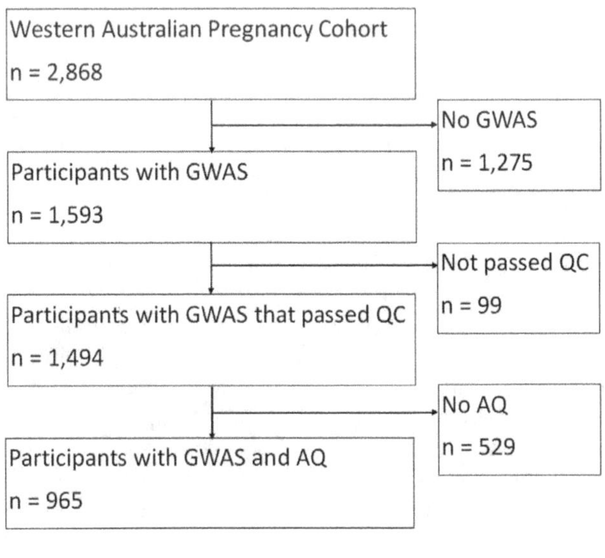


**FIGURE 1 | Flow chart of study sample selection.**

ON, Canada). The 660W Quad Array includes 657,366 genetic variants including ~560,000 single nucleotide polymorphisms (SNPs) and ~95,000 copy number variants. SNPs were excluded based on the Wellcome Trust Case Control Consortium thresholds:

HWE $p$-value must be $>5.7 \times 10^{-7}$ (919 markers excluded)
Call rate must be >0.95 (95%) (97,718 markers excluded)
MAF must be >0.01 (1%) (119,246 markers excluded – includes copy number variants)
A/T and G/C SNPs were removed due to possible strand ambiguity.

In total, 535,632 SNPs passed genotype quality control before genotype imputation. Imputation was performed using MACH (Li and Abecasis, 2006) software on the 22 autosomes. Once the data were cleaned, a two-step process was carried out using the CEU samples from HapMap phase2 build 36 release 22 as a reference panel. This imputation process imputed both individual genotypes for SNPs that were typed but not called for a particular individual, and SNPs that were not typed in all individuals. After imputation, genotype information was available for 2,543,887 SNPs.

## DATA ANALYSIS

### *Power calculations*

Power calculations were performed using the statistical software package Quanto (Gauderman, 2002) for a sample size of 965 and MAF ranging from 0 to 0.5. The means and standard deviations for Total AQ and each subscale were used for the power calculations. Power was calculated to detect a minimum change of one unit assuming an additive genetic model. An alpha level of $1.0 \times 10^{-8}$ was used for the GWA studies.

### *Methods for genome-wide association*

Allelic dosage scores generated from MACH were used in analyses. The GWA studies were run adjusting for both age and sex. To account for potential population substructure, first and second principal components were also included in the multivariate GWA model. According to the Eigenvectors the first principal component accounted for 6.5% of variation, and the second component accounted for 2.3% of variation. Analysis was run using the ProbABEL package (Aulchenko et al., 2010). The combined results and SNP details file were then filtered to remove SNPs with MAF <1% and an imputation quality value of <0.3 (suggesting poor imputation quality).

A quantile–quantile (Q–Q) plot depicting –log10 transformations of the observed $p$-values as a function of the expected $p$-values was generated using "*qqunif*" function of the R Genetic Analysis Package (GAP) (R Development Core Team, 2008). The genomic inflation factor, $\lambda$, was calculated from the observed $p$-values. A Manhattan plot displaying a –log10 transformation of the observed $p$-values was generated using "*mhtplot*" function of the R GAP (R Development Core Team, 2008).

Genome-wide significance of results was defined as a $p$-value $\leq 5.0 \times 10^{-8}$ (Panagiotou and Ioannidis, 2011). Tables of SNPs were generated, based on a $p$-value $< 1.0 \times 10^{-5}$, which has been used by the National Human Genome Research Institute for the identification and archiving of suggestive associations (National Human Genome Research Institute, 2012). Information regarding genes and function for SNPs included in these tables were sourced from SNP Annotation and Proxy Search (SNAP, 2008). Genes and/or regions that appeared in the generated tables were searched using the Simon's Foundation Autism Research Initiative (SFARI) database (Simons Foundation Autism Research Initiative, 2012) for any previous associations with ASD and biological plausibility. LocusZoom (Pruim et al., 2010) was used to generate a regional association plot for loci of interest (±400 kb) based on hg18 genome build and HapMap Phase II CEU133 as the linkage disequilibrium (LD) population.

# RESULTS

## POWER CALCULATIONS

Total AQ, Social Skills, and Details/Patterns did not reach sufficient power (>80%) to detect a change by one unit. Communication/Mindreading reached sufficient power at 47% MAF.

## NORMAL DISTRIBUTION OF SCORES

Autism Spectrum Quotient scores have been described in previous literature to provide a quantitative measurement of autistic-like traits in the general population (Baron-Cohen et al., 2001). Histograms and Q–Q plots indicate that the scores of the total AQ and each subscale were normally distributed. The histograms and Q–Q plots can be found in Figures S1–S4 in Supplementary Material.

## DESCRIPTIVE STATISTICS

Characteristics of the current study sample can be found in **Table 1**. About 51.3% of the sample were female and the mean age at AQ completion was 19.68 (SD = 0.70). Mean total AQ score was 103.2 (SD = 12.60).

## GENOME-WIDE ASSOCIATION RESULTS

After filtering for effect allele frequencies ≤1 and ≥99% and imputation quality $R$ squared values <0.3, 2,462,046 successfully genotyped or imputed SNPs remained for analysis. No SNP associations in any outcome reached genome-wide significance, defined as $p$-value $< 5.0 \times 10^{-8}$ (Panagiotou and Ioannidis, 2011). Putative associations, defined as $p < 1.0 \times 10^{-5}$, were examined with respect to candidate genes in the SFARI Gene database. None of the genes that were putatively associated with Total AQ, Details/Patterns and Communication/Mindreading were found to be represented in this gene database. One putative gene association found in the Social Skills GWA results was found to be reported in the SFARI Gene database, prompting further investigation.

### *Social skills genome-wide association results*

In the set of 965 Raine Study participants for Social Skills scores, the observed distribution of $p$-values for the SNPs exhibited minimal deviation from the expected distribution (see **Figure 2**) indicating minimal test statistic bias or underlying population structure ($\lambda = 0.994$). The Manhattan plot –log10 transformation of observed $p$-values across the genome are displayed in **Figure 3**.

**Table 2** displays association results for Social Skills, selected on a $p$-value below $1.0 \times 10^{-5}$. None of these associations reached genome-wide significance. However, the rs198198

**Table 1 | Characteristics of Raine study participants with AQ and GWA data available.**

| Continuous | *n* | Mean (SD) |
|---|---|---|
| Maternal age at conception | 965 | 28.66 (5.65) |
| Paternal age at conception | 646 | 31.68 (6.18) |
| Maternal BMI at conception | 956 | 22.25 (4.00) |
| Paternal BMI at conception | 827 | 24.44 (3.28) |
| Age at AQ completion | 965 | 19.68 (0.70) |
| Total AQ score | 965 | 103.2 (12.60) |
| **Categorical** | ***n*** | ***n* (%)** |
| Season of birth | 965 | |
| Summer | | 301 (31.2) |
| Autumn | | 222 (23.0) |
| Winter | | 196 (20.3) |
| Spring | | 246 (25.5) |
| Sex | 965 | |
| Male | | 470 (48.7) |
| Female | | 495 (51.3) |
| Gestational age | 955 | |
| <32 weeks | | 13 (1.4) |
| 32–37 weeks | | 157 (16.4) |
| 38–40 weeks | | 624 (65.3) |
| >40 weeks | | 161 (16.9) |
| Family income | 937 | |
| Income < \$24 k | | 293 (31.3) |
| Income > \$24 k | | 644 (68.7) |
| Maternal education | 956 | |
| Secondary school not completed | | 501 (52.4) |
| Secondary school completed | | 455 (47.6) |

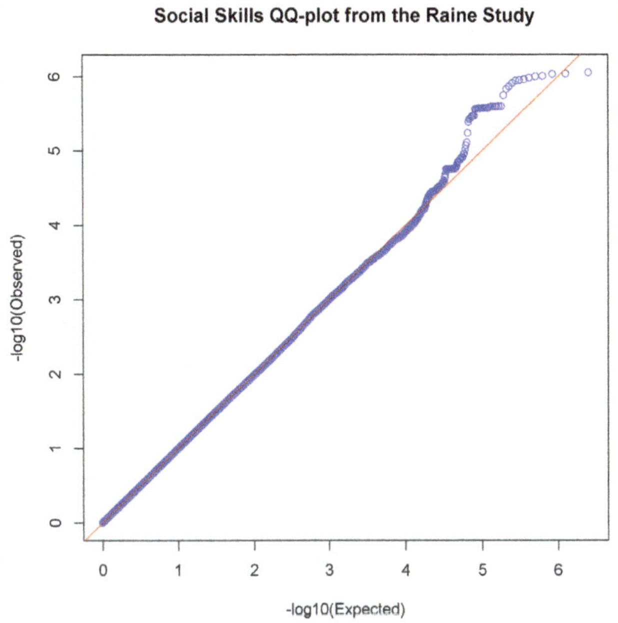


**FIGURE 2 | Quantile–Quantile Plot of association results for social skills.** Q–Q plots compare the observed *p*-values [−log10(Observed)] to expected *p*-values. [−log10(Expected)] on the logarithmic scale under the null hypothesis of no significant association.

SNP ($p$-value $= 9.587 \times 10^{-6}$, effect size $= -1.411$) is located within the *protein kinase C, beta 1* (*PRKCB1*) gene that has been previously reported to be associated with ASD. Exploratory analysis of data revealed a nominal association of rs198198 with Total AQ score ($p$-value $= 0.002$), but no association with Details/Patterns ($p$-value $= 0.434$) or Communication/Mindreading ($p$-value $= 0.202$). In addition, the rs16946931 SNP ($p = 1.78 \times 10^{-6}$, effect size $= 1.681$) is located in a region flanking the *Cerebellin 1* (*CBLN1*), a gene previously implicated in ASD. This SNP was nominally associated with the Total AQ score ($p$-value $= 4.27 \times 10^{-4}$), but no association with Details/Patterns ($p$-value $= 0.472$), or Communication/Mindreading ($p$-value $= 0.138$). When association analysis was done conditional on rs16946931 for Social Skills, $p$-values for the 20 additional *CBLN1* SNPs became insignificant ($p$-value $> 0.05$), demonstrating that high LD between these SNPs was responsible for their inclusion in the model.

**Figures 4** and **5** show regional association plots of SNPs rs198198 and rs16946931, respectively.

## BIOINFORMATIC EVALUATION

All SNPs with $p$-value below $1.0 \times 10^{-5}$ were evaluated for possible functional potential. As all SNPs were in non-coding regions they were assessed for regulatory potential using available ENCODE data through Regulome DB (Boyle et al., 2012) and the UCSC Genome (2012) browser. No SNP was shown to be part of a transcription factor binding site or be located in a region of the genome likely to have regulatory potential except the nominally associated SNP rs198198 located within an intron of *PRKCB1*. The major allele (T) was found to be embedded within a near-consensus CCAAT/enhancer binding protein (C/EBP) gamma binding site whereas the minor allele (A) is predicted to ablate C/EBP gamma binding. Further evidence for function comes from ENCODE ChIP-seq data indicating that rs198198 is located in a region subject to histone H3K9 modification.

## DISCUSSION

In this paper we report only the second contemporary GWAS for autistic-like traits in the broader community and the first to use a quantitative distribution measured by the AQ. Although we did not find any SNP associations reaching genome-wide significance (defined as $p$-value $< 5.0 \times 10^{-8}$) this GWAS has provided some evidence to support the further investigation of two previously identified candidate genes, namely *PRKCB1* and *CBLN1*.

## *PRKCB1* GENE

Protein kinase C enzymes play an important role in signal transduction, regulation of gene expression, and control of cell division and differentiation (Lintas et al., 2009; NCBI, 2012). The alternative splicing of *PRKCB1* generates two mRNA isoforms named PRKCB1-1 and PRKCB1-2, coding for two isoenzymes βI and βII. These mRNA isoforms are expressed in a variety of tissues within the central nervous system, including the hippocampus, striatum,

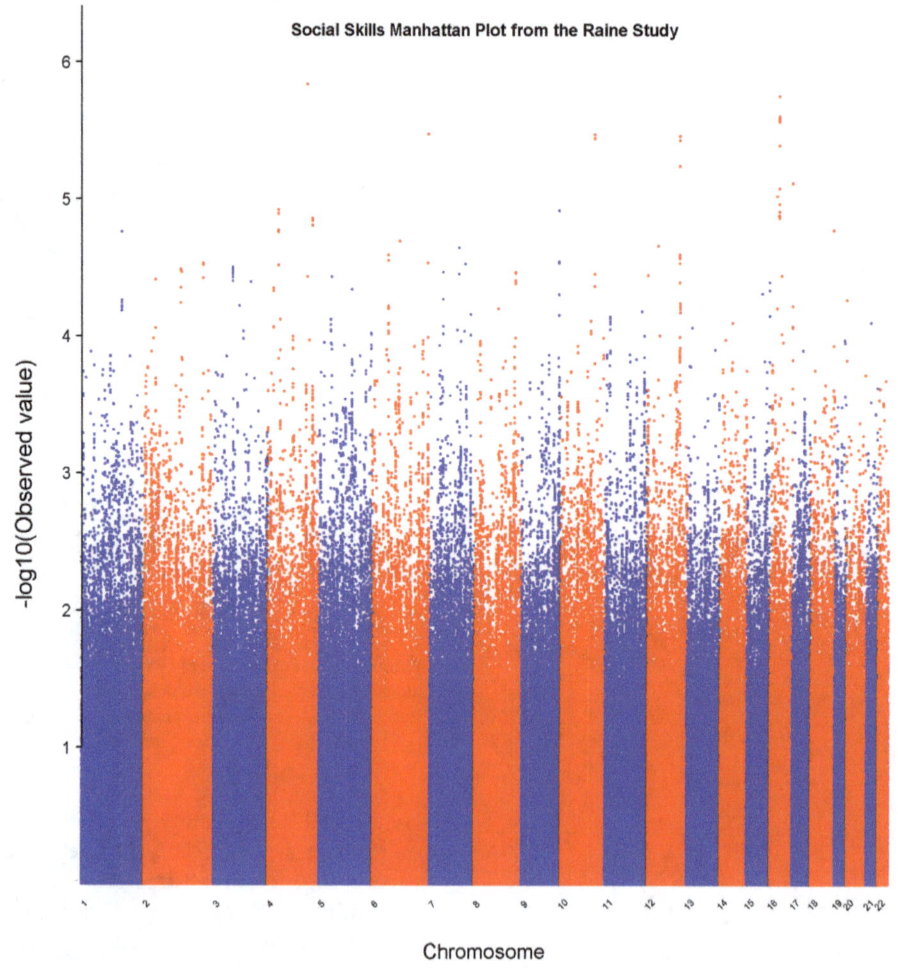


**FIGURE 3 | Manhattan plot for social skills.** Statistical significance of each SNP on the −log10 scale as a function of the chromosome position.

suprachiasmatic nucleus, and cerebellar granule cells (Lintas et al., 2009).

Several previous genetic studies have supported a role for *PRKCB1* in ASD. A genome-wide linkage scan of 116 families from the Autism Genetic Resource Exchange cohort (Philippi et al., 2005) applied direct physical identity-by-descent mapping using a strict ASD phenotype. Their results demonstrated linkage to a region on chromosome 16p ($p$-value = 0.0027). Subsequent high-resolution SNP genotyping and analysis of this region showed that haplotypes in the *PRKCB1* gene were strongly associated with ASD (Philippi et al., 2005), a finding that was independently confirmed in two other family studies (Philippi et al., 2005) (Lintas et al., 2009) but not in a study on 171 Irish ASD trios (Yang et al., 2007). These haplotypes were not significantly associated with ASD in the current study (results not shown).

These genetic association studies have been supported by a study of PRKCB1 gene expression in post mortem brain tissue from 11 autistic patients and controls (Lintas et al., 2009). The superior temporal gyrus (BA 41/42) region was chosen for study because of a known role in processing socially relevant information and well documented structural and functional abnormalities seen in ASD (Zilbovicius et al., 2006). A significant down regulation of PRKCB1 gene expression was found to be associated with ASD (Lintas et al., 2009) providing additional strong evidence in support of a role for the *PRKCB1* gene in the etiology of ASD.

### *CBLN1* GENE

The *CBLN1* gene encodes the cerebellum-specific precursor protein, precerebellin and is involved along with *Cerebellin 2* (*CBLN2*) in encoding ligands for the neurexin-neuroligin trans-synaptic complex (NTSC) (Clarke et al., 2012; Cristino et al., 2013). *CBLN1* belongs to the CBLN subfamily of the C1q/tumor necrosis factor superfamily, which plays a role in intercellular signaling, neuronal cell adhesion, brain development, and formation of synapses (Clarke et al., 2012). In a mouse study, Uemura et al. (2010) found that post-synaptic GluRδ2/GRID2 (a member of the δ-type glutamate receptor) interacts with pre-synaptic neurexins through *CBLN1* to mediate parallel fiber-Purkinje cell synaptic formation in the cerebellum. A recent study has identified rare copy number variants in NTSC gene family members and proposed

**Table 2 | Association results for social skills (*p*-value $< 1.0 \times 10^{-5}$).**

| Chr | SNP | Position | Imputation | Function | Gene | Alleles | $R^2$ | Effect size | SE | *p*-Value |
|---|---|---|---|---|---|---|---|---|---|---|
| 4 | rs11947645 | 151321122 | imp | Intronic | *DCLK2* | A/G | 0.859 | 5.329 | 1.100 | 1.47E-06 |
| 16 | rs16946931 | 47700007 | imp | Intergenic | *N4BP1/CBLN1* | C/T | 0.973 | 1.681 | 0.350 | 1.78E-06 |
| 16 | rs7499215 | 47680431 | gen | Intergenic | *N4BP1/CBLN1* | G/T | 1 | −1.639 | 0.346 | 2.51E-06 |
| 16 | rs11860027 | 47679816 | imp | Intergenic | *N4BP1/CBLN1* | C/T | 1 | −1.639 | 0.346 | 2.52E-06 |
| 16 | rs16946881 | 47677288 | imp | Intergenic | *N4BP1/CBLN1* | C/T | 0.999 | −1.639 | 0.346 | 2.53E-06 |
| 16 | rs16946880 | 47676950 | imp | Intergenic | *N4BP1/CBLN1* | C/T | 0.999 | −1.639 | 0.346 | 2.53E-06 |
| 16 | rs16946876 | 47675600 | imp | Intergenic | *N4BP1/CBLN1* | C/T | 0.998 | 1.638 | 0.346 | 2.54E-06 |
| 16 | rs9635530 | 47674912 | imp | Intergenic | *N4BP1/CBLN1* | A/C | 0.998 | −1.638 | 0.346 | 2.54E-06 |
| 16 | rs2883805 | 47693566 | imp | Intergenic | *N4BP1/CBLN1* | G/T | 0.995 | −1.640 | 0.347 | 2.59E-06 |
| 16 | rs4785161 | 47686589 | imp | Intergenic | *N4BP1/CBLN1* | A/C | 0.997 | 1.636 | 0.346 | 2.66E-06 |
| 16 | rs753858 | 47685051 | imp | Intergenic | *N4BP1/CBLN1* | C/T | 0.998 | 1.635 | 0.346 | 2.66E-06 |
| 16 | rs11859884 | 47670664 | imp | Intergenic | *N4BP1/CBLN1* | A/G | 0.995 | −1.633 | 0.346 | 2.67E-06 |
| 16 | rs1861572 | 47684489 | imp | Intergenic | *N4BP1/CBLN1* | A/T | 0.999 | 1.635 | 0.346 | 2.67E-06 |
| 16 | rs1009302 | 47670836 | imp | Intergenic | *N4BP1/CBLN1* | C/T | 0.995 | −1.633 | 0.346 | 2.68E-06 |
| 16 | rs1009301 | 47670978 | imp | Intergenic | *N4BP1/CBLN1* | G/T | 0.995 | 1.633 | 0.346 | 2.68E-06 |
| 16 | rs1345404 | 47681670 | imp | Intergenic | *N4BP1/CBLN1* | A/G | 1 | −1.633 | 0.346 | 2.69E-06 |
| 16 | rs1345406 | 47681539 | gen | Intergenic | *N4BP1/CBLN1* | A/C | 1 | −1.633 | 0.346 | 2.69E-06 |
| 16 | rs1345405 | 47681629 | gen | Intergenic | *N4BP1/CBLN1* | A/G | 1 | −1.633 | 0.346 | 2.69E-06 |
| 16 | rs1420612 | 47672854 | imp | Intergenic | *N4BP1/CBLN1* | G/T | 0.996 | −1.631 | 0.346 | 2.72E-06 |
| 16 | rs10521175 | 47673463 | imp | Intergenic | *N4BP1/CBLN1* | A/C | 0.997 | 1.629 | 0.345 | 2.75E-06 |
| 6 | rs11575088 | 167477024 | imp | Intergenic | *CCR6/GPR31* | A/C | 0.998 | 1.620 | 0.347 | 3.40E-06 |
| 6 | rs11575089 | 167477189 | gen | Intergenic | *CCR6/GPR31* | A/G | 0.999 | 1.620 | 0.347 | 3.41E-06 |
| 10 | rs927821 | 104197789 | gen | Intergenic | *MIR146B/LOC100505761* | A/C | 0.985 | 1.7024 | 0.365 | 3.44E-06 |
| 12 | rs10444533 | 105753835 | gen | Intronic | *RIC8B* | C/T | 0.996 | 1.458 | 0.313 | 3.54E-06 |
| 10 | rs7086205 | 104192719 | gen | Intergenic | *MIR146B/LOC100505761* | C/T | 0.998 | −1.688 | 0.362 | 3.67E-06 |
| 12 | rs10778511 | 105749461 | imp | Intronic | *RIC8B* | A/T | 0.993 | 1.454 | 0.313 | 3.80E-06 |
| 16 | rs1362594 | 47682845 | imp | Intergenic | *N4BP1/CBLN1* | C/G | 0.943 | −1.648 | 0.356 | 4.09E-06 |
| 12 | rs4964491 | 105746645 | imp | Intronic | *RIC8B* | A/G | 0.985 | −1.429 | 0.314 | 5.79E-06 |
| 16 | rs533581 | 87494938 | imp | Intronic | *CBFA2T3* | C/T | 0.859 | 1.363 | 0.303 | 7.75E-06 |
| 16 | rs4785276 | 47678880 | imp | Intergenic | *N4BP1/CBLN1* | A/G | 0.974 | −1.529 | 0.341 | 8.46E-06 |
| 16 | rs198198 | 24035898 | imp | Intronic | *PRKCB1* | A/T | 0.777 | −1.411 | 0.317 | 9.59E-06 |

*Position: base pair. Imputation: imputed (imp) or genotyped (gen). Gene: for intergenic SNPs, 5′/3′ flanking genes listed. Alleles: effect allele/non-effect allele. $R^2$: imputation quality from MACH. Effect size: regression coefficient. SE, Standard Error.*

their potential biological function with ASD and Tourette syndrome (TS) (Clarke et al., 2012) and mutations in these and other synaptic genes are common in ASD (Arons et al., 2012; Clarke et al., 2012). Therefore, it is plausible that long-range genetic variants affecting *CBLN1* expression may be associated with ASD traits.

While no previous genetic linkage or association studies have detected significant associations between *CBLN1* and ASD, *CBLN2* (belonging to the same CBLN subfamily) on Chromosome 18q has been deleted in TS and is located near two TS translocation breakpoints (Clarke et al., 2012). There is evidence to suggest an overlap between TS and ASD from epidemiological perspectives, with an increased prevalence of TS among autistic patients of 6.5% (Baron-Cohen et al., 1999), compared to between 2 and 3% in the general population (Mason et al., 1998). Common susceptibility genes (Sundaram et al., 2010; Fernandez et al., 2012) have also been reported between ASD and TS.

This study was conducted on a well characterized, population-based cohort of adolescents and ASD measurements were collected without ascertainment for autism risk. Despite this study's small sample size ($n = 965$), we were independently able to identify two regions on chromosome 16 that have been previously implicated in the etiology of ASD. While no variants in these regions reached genome-wide significance, they do demonstrate suggestive evidence for association and provide good candidates for future follow-up studies. The difference in observed signal between the two regions is due to high LD around the *CBLN1* SNP, rs16946931, which disappears with conditional association analysis. The lack of replication for the previously identified *PRKCB1* haplotype is potentially due to different underlying LD structure between populations, as the previous study focused on families (Philippi et al., 2005) whereas our study is composed of unrelated individuals. These observed associations are either intergenic or intronic variants suggesting that they are tagging nearby rare variants that may be causal. In most GWAS, the SNPs showing

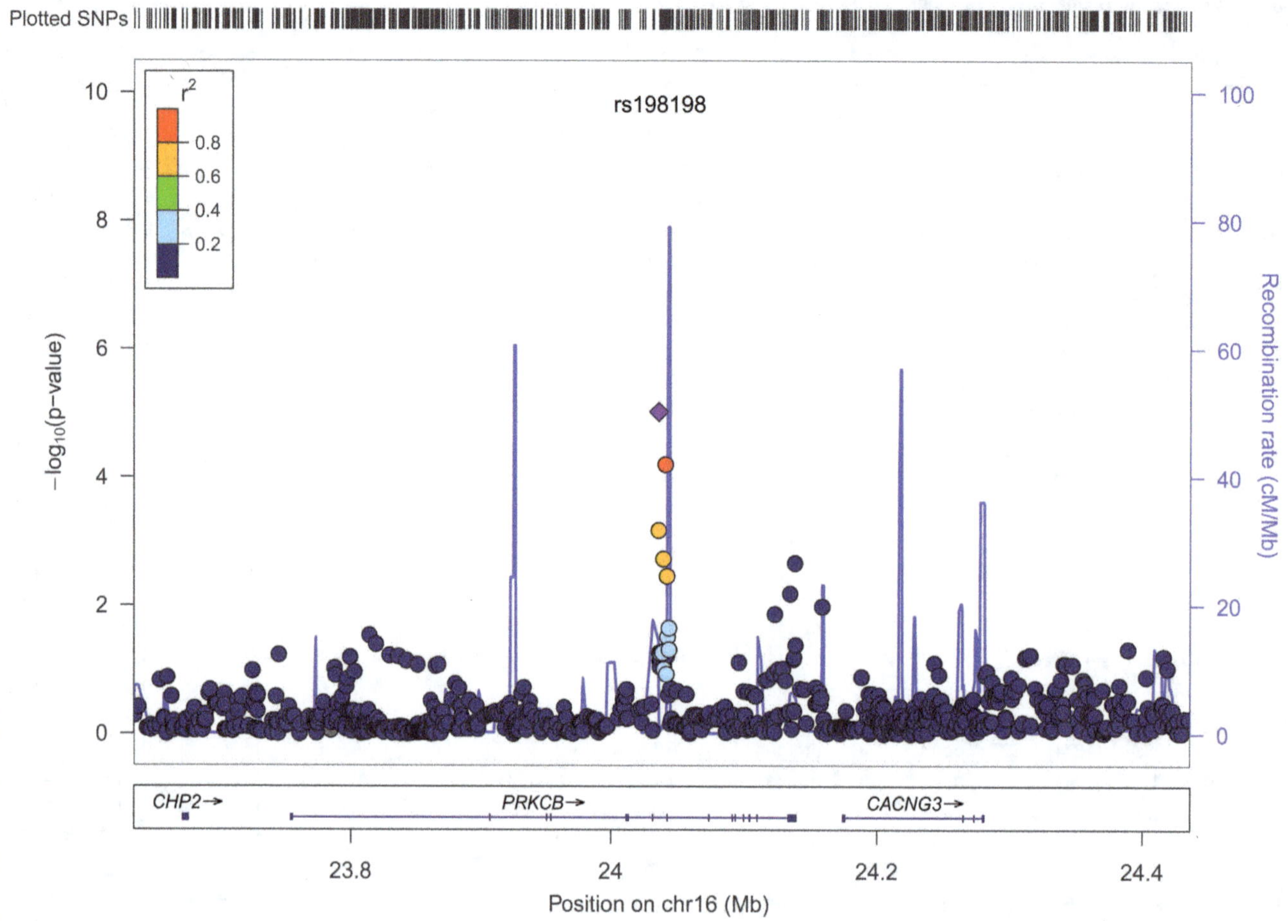


**FIGURE 4 | Regional association plot of SNP rs198198 (±400 kb).** Statistical significance of each SNP on the –log10 scale as a function of the chromosome position. The top SNP is shown as the purple diamond; the correlations ($r^2$) of each of the surrounding SNPs to the top SNP are shown in the indicated colors. Recombination rate is shown in pale blue.

evidence of association are not usually the actual causal variants at play but rather are in LD with such variants. The failure to replicate the previously reported haplotype associations with ASD and PRKCB1 and any specific SNP associations in both PRKCB1 and CBLN1 does not invalidate the findings in this study. Over the last 5 years, considerable attention has been paid to the potential reasons why true associations may not replicate across independent data sets and genetic heterogeneity, environmental interactions, age-dependent effects, epistasis, and inadequate statistical power have all been cited as possible explanations (Chanock et al., 2007; Shriner et al., 2007; Williams et al., 2007; Greene et al., 2009).

The identification and characterization of the causal variants at play in common complex human traits/diseases is presenting to be a great challenge in human genetics, in particular as a large proportion are not in coding regions directly altering protein structure/function but rather are in non-coding regions (i.e., intronic and intergenic regions) having a likely regulatory function, such as may be the case for the *PRKCB1* intronic rs198198 SNP identified in this study. The further characterization of this and other genetic variation within the *PRKCB1* and *CBLN1* gene regions is beyond the scope of this study possibly requiring exhaustive DNA sequencing to identify all variants within the regions of association followed by a variety of detailed molecular biological analyses, like those we have recently described (Karimi et al., 2009; Kaskow et al., 2013).

## ACKNOWLEDGMENTS

Grant sponsor: National Health and Medical Research Council; Grant number: 572613.

## SUPPLEMENTARY MATERIAL

**Figure S1 | Histogram and Quantile–Quantile Plot of Total AQ Scores.** Histograms depict the frequency of the Total AQ observations. Q–Q plots compare the quantiles from the current study (sample quantiles) to the quantiles from a Normal distribution (theoretical quantiles).

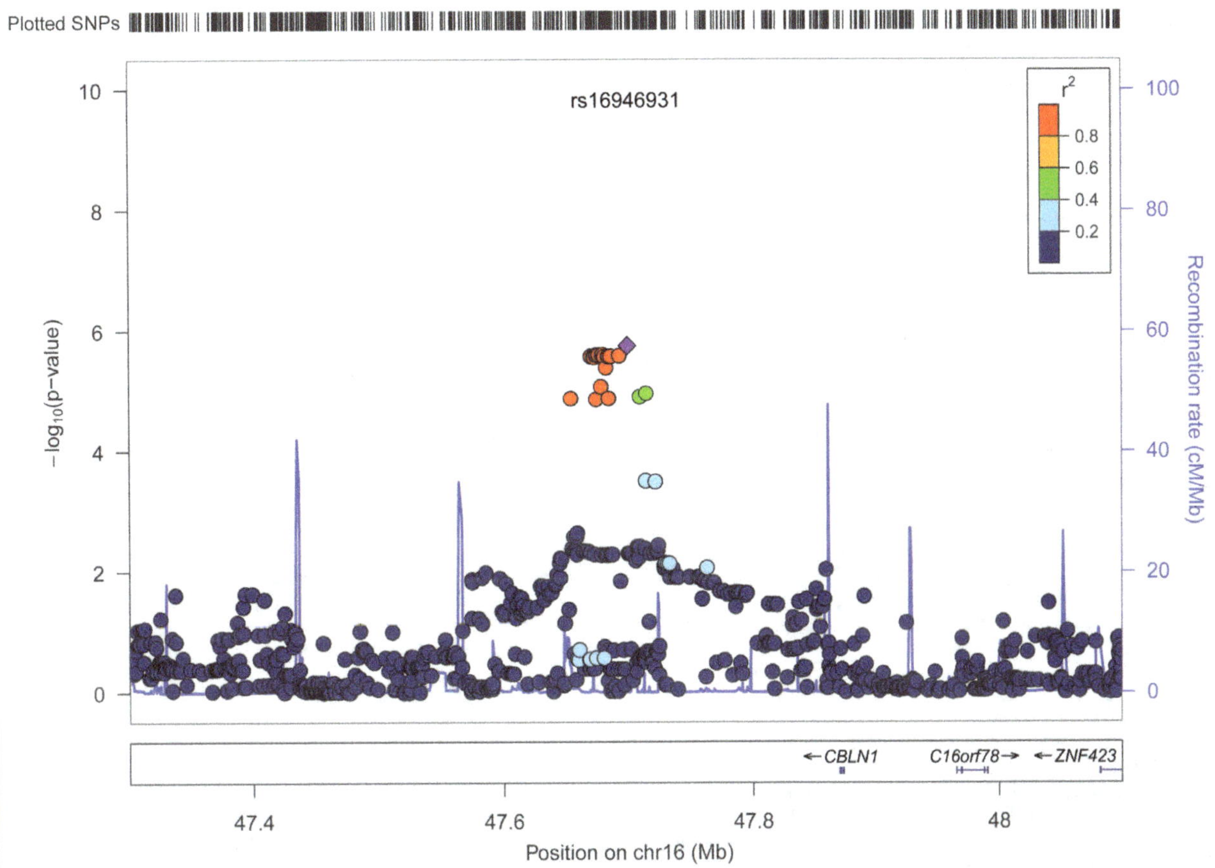


**FIGURE 5 | Regional association plot of SNP rs16946931 (±400 kb).** Statistical significance of each SNP on the –log10 scale as a function of the chromosome position. The top SNP is shown as the purple diamond; the correlations ($r^2$) of each of the surrounding SNPs to the top SNP are shown in the indicated colors. Recombination rate is shown in pale blue.

**Figure S2 | Histogram and Quantile–Quantile Plot of Social Skills Scores**. Histogram depicts the frequency of the Social Skills observations. Q–Q plots compare the quantiles from the current study (sample quantiles) to the quantiles from a Normal distribution (theoretical quantiles).

**Figure S3 | Histogram and Quantile–Quantile Plot of Details/Patterns Scores**. Histogram depicts the frequency of the Details/Patterns observations. Q–Q plots compare the quantiles from the current study (sample quantiles) to the quantiles from a Normal distribution (theoretical quantiles).

**Figure S4 | Histogram and Quantile–Quantile Plot of Communication/Mindreading Scores**. Histogram depicts the frequency of the Communication/Mindreading observations. Q–Q plots compare the quantiles from the current study (sample quantiles) to the quantiles from a Normal distribution (theoretical quantiles).

## REFERENCES


1. Alarcón, M., Abrahams, B. S., Stone, J. L., Duvall, J. A., Perederiy, J. V., Bomar, J. M., et al. (2008). Linkage, association, and gene- expression analyses identify CNT- NAP2 as an autism-susceptibility gene. *Am. J. Hum. Genet.* 82, 150–159. doi:10.1016/j.ajhg.2007. 09.005
2. Anney, R., Klei, L., Pinto, D., Regan, R., Conroy, J., Magalhaes, T. R., et al. (2010). A genome-wide scan for common alleles affecting risk for autism. *Hum. Mol. Genet.* 19, 4072–4082. doi:10.1093/hmg/ ddq307
3. Arons, M. H., Thynne, C. J., Grabrucker, A. M., Li, D., Schoen, M., Cheyne, J. E., et al. (2012). Autism-associated mutations in ProSAP2/Shank3 impair synaptic transmission and neurexin-neuroligin-mediated transsynaptic signaling. *J. Neurosci.* 32, 14966–14978. doi:10.1523/ JNEUROSCI.2215-12.2012
4. Aulchenko, Y. S., Struchalin, M. V., and van Duijn, C. M. (2010). ProbABEL package for genome-wide association analysis of imputed data. *BMC Bioinformatics* 11:134. doi:10. 1186/1471-2105-11-134
5. Austin, E. J. (2005). Personality cor- relates of the broader autism phenotype as assessed by the Autism Spectrum Quotient (AQ). *Pers. Individ. Dif.* 38, 451–460. doi:10.1016/j.paid.2004. 04.022
6. Baron-Cohen, S., Scahill, V. L., Iza- guirre, J., Hornsey, H., and Robert- son, M. M. (1999). The prevalence of Gilles de la Tourette syndrome in children and adolescents with autism: a large scale study. *Psychol. Med.* 29, 1151–1159. doi:10.1017/ S003329179900896X
7. Baron-Cohen, S., Wheelwright, S., Skinner, R., Martin, J., and Clubley, E. (2001). The autism- spectrum quotient (AQ): evidence from Asperger syndrome/high- functioning autism, males and females, scientists and mathemati- cians. *J. Autism Dev. Disord.* 31, 5–17. doi:10.1023/A: 1005653411471
8. Boyle, A. P., Hong, E. L., Hariha-ran, M., Cheng, Y., Schaub, M. A., Kasowski, M., et al. (2012). Annota- tion of functional variation in per- sonal genomes using RegulomeDB. *Genome Res.* 22, 1790–1797. doi:10. 1101/gr.137323.112
9. Campbell, D. B., Sutcliffe, J. S., Ebert, P. J., Militerni, R., Bravaccio, C., Trillo, S., et al. (2006). A genetic variant that disrupts MET transcription is associated with autism. *Proc. Natl. Acad. Sci. U.S.A.* 103, 16834–16839. doi:10.1073/ pnas.0605296103
10. Chakrabarti, B., Dudbridge, F., Kent, L., Wheelwright, S., Hill-Cawthorne, G., Allison, C., et al. (2009). Genes related to sex steroids, neural growth, and social-emotional behavior are associated with autis- tic traits, empathy, and Asperger syn- drome. *Autism Res.* 2, 157–177. doi: 10.1002/aur.80

11. Chanock, S., Manolio, T., Boehnke, M., Boerwinkle, E., Hunter, D., Thomas, G., et al. (2007). Repli- cating genotype-phenotype associa- tions. *Nature* 447, 655–660. doi:10. 1038/447655a
12. Clarke, R. A., Lee, S., and Eapen, V. (2012). Pathogenetic model for Tourette syndrome delineates over- lap with related neurodevelopmen- tal disorders including Autism. *Transl. Psychiatry* 2, e158. doi:10. 1038/tp.2012.75
13. Constantino, J., and Todd, R. (2003). Autistic traits in the general pop- ulation: a twin study. *Arch. Gen. Psychiatry* 60, 524–530. doi:10.1001/ archpsyc.60.5.524
14. Cristino, A. S., Williams, S. M., Hawi, Z., An, J. Y., Bellgrove, M. A., Schwartz, C. E., et al. (2013). Neurodevel- opmental and neuropsychiatric dis- orders represent an interconnected molecular system. *Mol. Psychiatry* doi:10.1038/ mp.2013.16
15. Elsabbagh, M., Divan, G., Koh, Y.-J., Kim, Y. S., Kauchali, S., Marcín, C., et al. (2012). Global prevalence of autism and other pervasive devel- opmental disorders. *Autism Res.* 5, 160–179. doi:10.1002/aur.239
16. Fernandez, T. V., Sanders, S. J., Yurkiewicz, I. R., Ercan-Sencicek, A. G., Kim, Y. S., Fishman, D. O., et al. (2012). Rare copy number vari- ants in Tourette syndrome disrupt genes in histaminergic pathways and overlap with autism. *Biol. Psychiatry* 71, 392–402. doi:10.1016/j.biopsych. 2011.09.034
17. Gauderman, W. J. (2002). Sample size requirements for association stud- ies of gene–gene interactions. *Am. J. Epidemiol.* 155, 478–484. doi:10. 1093/ aje/155.5.478
18. Gillberg, C. L. (1992). The Emanuel Miller Memorial Lecture 1991. Au- tism and autistic-like condi- tions: subclasses among disorders of empathy. *J. Child Psychol. Psychia- try* 33, 813–842. doi:10.1111/j.1469- 7610.1992. tb01959.x
19. Greene, C. S., Penrod, N. M., Williams, S. M., and Moore, J. H. (2009). Fail- ure to replicate a genetic association may provide important clues about genetic architecture. *PLoS ONE* 4:e5639. doi:10.1371/journal.pone. 0005639
20. Hollander, E., King, A., Delaney, K., Smith, C. J., and Silverman, J. M. (2003). Obsessive-compulsive behaviors in parents of multiplex autism families. *Psychiatry Res.* 117, 11–16. doi:10.1016/S0165-1781(02) 00304-9
21. Karimi, M., Goldie, L. C., Cruickshank, M. N., Moses, E. K., and Abraham, L. J. (2009). A critical assessment of the factors affecting reporter gene assays for promoter SNP function: a reassessment of −308 TNF poly- morphism function using a novel integrated reporter system. *Eur. J. Hum. Genet.* 17, 1454–1462. doi:10. 1038/ejhg.2009.80
22. Kaskow, B. J., Diepeveen, L. A., Proffitt, J. M., Rea, A. J., Ulgiati, D., Blangero, J., et al. (2013). Molecular prioritisa- tion strategies to identify functional genetic variants in the cardiovas- cular disease-associated expression QTL Vanin-1. *Eur. J. Hum. Genet.* doi:10.1038/ejhg.2013.208
23. Li, X., Zou, H., and Brown, W. T. (2012). Genes associated with autism spec- trum disorder. *Brain Res. Bull.* 88, 543–552. doi:10.1016/j.brainresbull. 2012.05.017
24. Li, Y., and Abecasis, G. (2006). Mach 1.0: rapid haplotype reconstruction and missing genotype inference. *Am. J. Hum. Genet.* 79, 2290.
25. Lintas, C., Sacco, R., Garbett, K., Mir- nics, K., Militerni, R., Bravaccio, C., et al. (2009). Involvement of the PRKCB1 gene in autistic disorder: significant genetic association and reduced neocortical gene expression. *Mol. Psychia- try* 14, 705–718. doi:10. 1038/mp.2008.21
26. Lundström, S., Chang, Z., Råstam, M., Gillberg, C., Larsson, H., Anck- arsäter, H., et al. (2012). Autism spectrum disorders and autistic like traits: similar etiology in the extreme end and the normal variation. *Arch. Gen. Psychiatry* 69, 46–52. doi:10.1001/archgenpsychiatry.2011.144
27. Mason, A., Banerjee, S., Eapen, V., Zeitlin, H., and Robertson, M. M. (1998). The prevalence of Tourette syndrome in a mainstream school population. *Dev. Med. Child Neurol.* 40, 292–296.
28. National Human Genome Research Institute. (2012). *A Catalog of Ge- nome-Wide Association Studies [Online]*. Bethesda, MD. Avail- able at: http://www.genome.gov/ 26525384 (accessed 2012).
29. NCBI. (2012). *PRKCB Protein Kinase C, Beta [Online]*. Bethesda: National Center for Biotechnology Information.
30. Newnham, J. P., Evans, S. F., Michael, C. A., Stanley, F. J., and Lan- dau, L. I. (1993). Effects of fre- quent ultrasound during pregnancy: a randomised controlled trial. *Lancet* 342, 887–891. doi:10.1016/0140- 6736(93)91944-H
31. Panagiotou, O. A., and Ioannidis, J. P. A. (2011). What should the ge- nome-wide significance threshold be? Empirical replication of border- line genetic associations. *Int. J. Epi- demiol.* 41, 273–286. doi:10.1093/ije/ dyr178
32. Philippi, A., Roschmann, E., Tores, G., Lindenbaum, P., Benajou, A., Ger- main-Leclerc, L., et al. (2005). Haplotypes in the gene encoding protein ki- nase c-beta (PRKCB1) on chromosome 16 are associated with autism. *Mol. Psychiatry* 10, 950–960. doi:10.1038/sj.mp. 4001704
33. Posserud, M.-B., Lundervold, A. J., and Gillberg, C. (2006). Autistic features in a total population of 7–9-year- old children assessed by the ASSQ (Au- tism Spectrum Screening Ques- tionnaire). *J. Child Psychol. Psychia- try* 47, 167–175. doi:10.1111/j.1469- 7610.2005.01462.x
34. Pruim, R. J., Welch, R. P., Sanna, S., Teslovich, T. M., Chines, P. S., Gliedt, T. P., et al. (2010). LocusZoom: regional visualization of genome- wide association scan results. *Bioin- formatics* 26, 2336–2337. doi:10. 1093/bioinformatics/ btq419
35. R Development Core Team. (2008). *R: A Language and Environment for Sta- tistical Computing*. Vienna: R Foun- dation for Statistical Computing.
36. Ronald, A., Butcher, L. M., Docherty, S., Davis, O. S. P., Schalkwyk, L. C., Craig, I. W., et al. (2010). A genome-wide association study of social and non-social autistic-like traits in the general population using pooled DNA, 500 K SNP microar- rays and both community and diag- nosed autism replication samples. *Behav. Genet.* 40, 31–45. doi:10. 1007/s10519-009-9308-6
37. Ronald, A., Happé, F., and Plomin, R. (2005). The genetic relation- ship between individual differences in social and nonsocial behaviours characteristic of autism. *Dev. Sci.* 8, 444–458. doi:10.1111/j.1467-7687. 2005.00433.x
38. Ronald, A., and Hoekstra, R. A. (2011). Autism spectrum disorders and autistic traits: a decade of new twin studies. *Am. J. Med. Genet. B Neu- ropsychiatr. Genet.* 156, 255–274. doi:10.1002/ajmg.b.31159
39. Russell-Smith, S. N., Maybery, M. T., and Bayliss, D. M. (2011). Rela- tionships between autistic-like and schizotypy traits: an analysis using the Autism Spectrum Quotient and Oxford-Liverpool Inventory of Feel- ings and Experiences. *Pers. Individ. Dif.* 51, 128–132. doi:10.1016/j.paid. 2011.03.027
40. Shriner, D., Vaughan, L. K., Padilla, M. A., and Tiwari, H. K. (2007). Problems with genome-wide association studies. *Science* 316, 1840–1842. doi:10.1126/science. 316.5833.1840c
41. Simons Foundation Autism Research Initiative. (2012). *SFARI Gene: A Modular Database for Autism Research [Online]*. New York. Avail- able at: https://gene.sfari.org/autdb/ Welcome.do (accessed June 4, 2012).
42. Skuse, D. H., Mandy, W. P. L., and Scour- field, J. (2005). Measuring autis- tic traits: heritability, reliability and validity of the Social and Communi- cation Disorders Checklist. *Br. J. Psy- chiatry* 187, 568–572. doi:10.1192/ bjp.187.6.568
43. SNAP. (2008). *SNP Annotation and Proxy Search [Online]*. Cambridge. Available at: http://www.broadinstitute.org/ mpg/snap/ldsearch.php (accessed 2012).
44. St Pourcain, B., Wang, K., Glessner, J., Golding, J., Steer, C., Ring, S., et al. (2010). Association between a high- risk autism locus on 5p14 and social communication spectrum pheno- types in the general population. *Am. J. Psychiatry* 167, 1364–1372. doi:10. 1176/appi.ajp.2010.09121789
45. Stewart, M. E., and Austin, E. J. (2009). The structure of the Autism- Spectrum Quotient (AQ): evidence from a student sample in Scotland. *Pers. Individ. Dif.* 47, 224–228. doi: 10.1016/j.paid.2009.03.004
46. Sundaram, S. K., Huq, A. M., Wilson, B. J., and Chugani, H. T. (2010). Tourette syndrome is associated with recurrent exonic copy number vari- ants. *Neurology* 74, 1583–1590. doi: 10.1212/WNL.0b013e3181e0f147
47. UCSC Genome. (2012). *Bioinformatics, [Online]*. Santa Cruz. Available at: http://genome.ucsc.edu/ [accessed 2012].
48. Uemura, T., Lee, S. J., Yasumura, M., Takeuchi, T., Yoshida, T., Ra, M., et al. (2010). Trans-synaptic inter- action of GluRdelta2 and Neurexin through Cbln1 mediates synapse formation in the cerebellum. *Cell* 141, 1068–1079. doi:10.1016/j.cell. 2010.04.035
49. Veenstra-VanderWeele, J., Christian, S. L., and Cook, E. H. (2004). Autism as a paradigmatic com- plex genetic disorder. *Annu. Rev. Genomics Hum. Genet.* 5, 379–405. doi:10.1146/annurev.genom.5. 061903.180050
50. Wang, K., Zhang, H., Ma, D., Bucan, M., Glessner, J. T., Abrahams, B. S., et al. (2009). Common genetic variants on 5p14.1 associate with autism spectrum dis- orders. *Nature* 459, 528–533. doi:10.1038/nature07999
51. Whitehouse, A. J. O., Hickey, M., and Ronald, A. (2011). Are autistic traits in the general population sta- ble across development? *PLoS ONE* 6:e23029. doi:10.1371/journal.pone. 0023029
52. Williams, S. M., Canter, J. A., Crawford, D. C., Moore, J. H., Ritchie, M. D., and Haines, J. L. (2007). Problems with genome-wide association stud- ies. *Science* 316, 1840–1842. doi:10. 1126/science.316.5833.1840c
53. Yang, M. S., Cochrane, L., Conroy, J., Hawi, Z., Fitzgerald, M., Gallagher, L., et al. (2007). Protein kinase C- beta 1 gene variants are not associ- ated with autism in the Irish popula- tion. *Psychiatr. Genet.* 17, 39–41. doi: 10.1097/ YPG.0b013e3280115428
54. Zilbovicius, M., Meresse, I., Chabane, N., Brunelle, F., Samson, Y., and Boddaert, N. (2006). Autism, the superior temporal sulcus and social perception. *Trends Neurosci.* 29, 359–366. doi:10.1016/j.tins.2006.06. 004

# 25

# Reducing maladaptive behaviors in preschool-aged children with autism spectrum disorder using the Early Start Denver Model

***Elizabeth Fulton*[1,2]*, Valsamma Eapen*[2,3]***, ***Rudi Črnčec*[2]*, Amelia Walter*[2,3] *and Sally Rogers*[4]**

[1] *KU Marcia Burgess Autism Specific Early Learning and Care Centre (ASELCC), Liverpool, NSW, Australia*
[2] *Academic Unit of Child Psychiatry, School of Psychiatry, University of New South Wales, Sydney, NSW, Australia*
[3] *Infant, Child and Adolescent Mental Health (ICAMHS), South Western Sydney Local Health District, Liverpool, NSW, Australia*
[4] *School of Psychiatry and Behavioral Sciences, University of California Davis Medical Center MIND Institute, Davis, CA, USA*

***Edited by:***
*Roberto Canitano, University Hospital of Siena, Italy*

***Reviewed by:***
*Stephanie Ameis, University of Toronto, Canada*
*Jean Marc Guilé, Université Picardie Jules Verne, France*

****Correspondence:***
*Valsamma Eapen, Academic Unit of Child Psychiatry, Infant, Child and Adolescent Mental Health (ICAMHS), Mental Health Centre L1, Locked Bag 7103, Liverpool, NSW 1871, Australia*
*e-mail: v.eapen@unsw.edu.au*

The presence of maladaptive behaviors in young people with autism spectrum disorder (ASD) can significantly limit engagement in treatment programs, as well as compromise future educational and vocational opportunities. This study aimed to explore whether the Early Start Denver Model (ESDM) treatment approach reduced maladaptive behaviors in preschool-aged children with ASD in a community-based long day care setting. The level of maladaptive behavior of 38 children with ASD was rated using an observation-based measure on three occasions during the intervention: on entry, 12 weeks post-entry, and on exit (post-intervention) over an average treatment duration of 11.8 months. Significant reductions were found in children's maladaptive behaviors over the course of the intervention, with 68% of children showing a treatment response by 12 weeks and 79% on exit. This change was accompanied by improvement in children's overall developmental level as assessed by the Mullen scales of early learning, but not by significant changes on the Vineland Adaptive Behavior Scales-II or Social Communication Questionnaire. Replication with a larger sample, control conditions, and additional measures of maladaptive behavior is necessary in order to determine the specific factors underlying these improvements; however, the findings of the present study suggest that the ESDM program may be effective in improving not only core developmental domains, but also decreasing maladaptive behaviors in preschool-aged children with ASD.

**Keywords: autism spectrum disorder, Early Start Denver Model, maladaptive behavior, early intervention, efficacy**

## INTRODUCTION

Autism spectrum disorder (ASD) is a life-long neurodevelopmental disorder characterized by impairments in social interaction and communication, and restricted, repetitive patterns of behavior, activities, or interests (1). The prevalence of ASD appears to be rising worldwide (2), with ASD estimated to affect around 1 in every 88 persons (3).

Autism spectrum disorder is recognized as a major public health concern because of its early onset, life-long persistence, and high levels of associated impairment (4). This impairment is attributable not only to the core symptoms of ASD, but also to the range of co-existing conditions that individuals with ASD often experience, including emotional and behavioral problems, sleep, feeding and eating problems, sensory sensitivities, learning and intellectual disabilities, as well as co-morbid health and mental health diagnoses (5). These co-existing conditions can be of equal or greater concern for parents and teachers of children with ASD than the core features of ASD, and have a significant impact on behavior management, learning acquisition, and the development of social relationships (6).

Problem behaviors (or maladaptive behaviors as they are referred to in this paper), characterized by disruptive, destructive, aggressive, or significantly repetitive behaviors, are prevalent in young children with ASD (7). For example, Dominick et al. (7) found that 32.7% of children with ASD displayed aggressive behaviors including hitting, kicking, biting, and pinching others. More than three-quarters of these children showed aggressive behaviors both at home and outside the home, and aggression was directed toward more than one person in 92% of cases. Self-injurious behavior, including head banging, hitting oneself, and biting oneself, was present in almost one-third of children with ASD (7). Furthermore, 70.9% of children with ASD had experienced a period of severe temper tantrums and, for 60% of these children, tantrums occurred on a daily basis and were a constant (rather than episodic) problem during the period in which they were present (7).

Several authors have noted a strong negative relationship between the ability to communicate and the prevalence of maladaptive behavior in young children with ASD (8). Self-injurious behaviors among children with ASD have also been linked to their receptive and/or expressive communication deficits (9). It follows that when treatment programs focus on developing the young child's communication skills to the extent that they can serve as effective replacement behaviors, a reduction in the maladaptive behavior may result (10).

Maladaptive behaviors are particularly problematic in group settings, such as early intervention services, childcare services, and preschools, as they can be disruptive to the learning program and pose significant challenges to the children with ASD themselves, their peers, and staff. For these reasons, maladaptive behaviors are amongst the most commonly identified barriers to the inclusion of children with ASD in group settings (11).

Further, once maladaptive behaviors become an established part of a child's behavioral repertoire, they are unlikely to decrease and, according to Berg et al. (12), will typically remain or worsen without intervention. If left untreated, these behaviors can significantly reduce a child's social and educational opportunities by limiting their access to available treatments, learning activities, interactions with others, community experiences and, in particular, their ability to transition to, and participate in, school programs (13). In addition to having a negative impact on children with ASD themselves, a number of studies have shown that parents' level of psychological distress is associated with the severity of their child's maladaptive behaviors as well as their ASD symptoms (14–20).

Therefore, early interventions for young children with ASD should incorporate the management of maladaptive behaviors (21). Given the relationship between maladaptive behaviors and deficits in communication and social skills, it is important that intervention approaches target these core deficits. Myers and Johnson (22) argue that the primary goals of intervention for children with ASD should be to maximize the child's functional independence and quality of life by reducing the core symptoms of ASD; facilitate development and learning; promote socialization; reduce maladaptive behaviors; educate and support families. They suggest that, in addition to targeting communication and social skills, contemporary comprehensive intervention approaches for ASD should target a reduction in disruptive or maladaptive behavior by using empirically supported strategies, including functional behavior assessment (FBA). FBA is "the process of determining the intent an inappropriate behavior serves for obtaining a desired outcome and replacing that behavior with a more appropriate one that accomplishes the same goal" [Ref. (23), 136 p.].

The general importance of early intervention for ASD is widely recognized, and is supported by studies showing better outcomes with earlier treatment (24, 25). Early intervention for ASD, especially that commencing before the age of 3 years, results in significantly improved outcomes relative to intervention commencing later in life (26–28). Early intervention in the first years of life offers the best potential for children as brain plasticity is greatest during this period, enabling the establishment and reorganization of neuronal networks in response to environmental stimulation (26).

A review of research conducted by Prior et al. (29) to identify the most effective models of early intervention for children with ASD classifies approaches into three main categories.

Each target maladaptive behaviors differently:

- Biologically based interventions, including medication, have been used to treat the co-morbid symptoms of ASD such as anxiety and hyperactive behavior with varying degrees of effectiveness.
- Psychodynamic interventions target the emotional component of behavior only. However, because ASD is considered a neurodevelopmental, rather than emotional, disorder, there is little empirical evidence demonstrating their effectiveness.
- Educational interventions including behavioral interventions such as applied behavior analysis (ABA); the Lovaas program; Pivotal Response Training; developmental and relationship-based interventions including ESDM; communication-focused interventions and sensory–motor interventions tend to have a positive treatment response. Each of these approaches uses different mechanisms to target maladaptive behaviors, and some advocate for the use of FBA as part of this process. These interventions usually approach behavior modification directly, focusing on the behavior itself.

Programs such as the Early Start Denver Model (ESDM) focus on building communication skills, especially by following the child's lead and increasing the reinforcement value of social interaction, thereby teaching children adaptive ways of getting their needs met (30). Given that the ESDM is designed to enhance the social attention and communicative abilities of young children with ASD, with particular focus on the critical skills of social attention, affect sharing, imitation, and joint attention, it is conceivable that a significant reduction in maladaptive behavior may result.

Several meta-analyses conducted in recent years have tended to conclude that early intensive behavioral intervention (EIBI), generally defined as intervention that is delivered at an intensity of 15–20 h/week, incorporating the principles of ABA, is the treatment of choice for young children with ASD [cf. (8, 31)]. The literature indicates that superior outcomes are associated with entry into EIBI at the earliest possible age (32, 33).

The only comprehensive EIBI program available for children aged <30 months that has been empirically evaluated is the ESDM (27). The ESDM is specifically designed for children aged 12–60 months and is a manualized, comprehensive intervention that integrates ABA into a developmental and relationship-based approach (30). The ESDM is an intensive and comprehensive early intervention model that aims to reduce the severity of ASD symptoms and accelerate children's development in all areas, with particular emphasis in the cognitive, social–emotional, and language domains.

The ESDM draws from teaching practices developed in the original Denver Model such as relationship-based aspects of the therapist's work with the child, using play as a foundation for learning, and using communication intervention principles from the field of communication science (30). Positive behavior approaches focus on replacement of unwanted behaviors with more conventional behaviors and FBA is used when behaviors are more challenging.

The first and only randomized controlled trial of the ESDM demonstrated that, compared with children receiving community intervention, children receiving the ESDM showed significant gains in visual processing and improvements in language abilities, with subsequent gains in IQ and adaptive behaviors (27). In that study, children received 20 h/week of one-to-one ESDM intervention in a University clinic setting. There was also a separate parent training module. Two further studies (34, 35) have investigated the efficacy of delivery of the ESDM in group settings. Both studies reported significant developmental gains following the intervention and Eapen et al. (34) also found a significant decrease in autism-specific symptoms.

While Dawson et al. (27) and Eapen et al. (34) investigated the impact of the ESDM on children's adaptive behavior, no studies of the ESDM to date have focused on the effect of the ESDM on children's maladaptive behaviors. Given the adverse effect that maladaptive behaviors have on children with ASD, as well as their parents, it is important to investigate the impact of interventions on these behaviors. This was the primary aim of the present study.

## MATERIALS AND METHODS

The study was approved by the local institutional and University ethics committees and all families recruited to the study provided informed consent to participate.

### STUDY DESIGN AND PARTICIPANTS

A pre–post study of children treated with ESDM was conducted. Note that clinical outcomes, but not ESDM clinician behavioral ratings data, for a portion of the cohort have been described previously in Eapen et al. (34). Participants were 38 children attending an Autism Specific Early Learning and Care Centre (ASELCC) in metropolitan Sydney, Australia. The center is one of the six ASELCCs established by the Australian Government within the setting of a long day child care center for children aged 2–6 years. All children had a DSM-IV-TR diagnosis of Autistic Disorder, made by a community-based physician, with the exception of one child who had a diagnosis of pervasive developmental disorder not otherwise specified. These children would all have met criteria for a DSM-5 diagnosis of ASD. Exclusion criteria included neurological (e.g., uncontrolled epilepsy) disorders, and significant vision, hearing, motor, or physical impairment.

The average age of children at the time of study commencement was 52.2 months (SD 5.4, range: 38.8–63.7 months), and 35 (92%) were male. English was the primary language spoken at home in 82% of families, although 60% of families reported a cultural background other than Australian.

None of the participants were receiving an EIBI outside of the ESDM intervention offered as part of this program. No families withdrew from the study during the course of the intervention; however, there were instances of missing data due to families not completing measures within the necessary timeframes.

### INTERVENTION

The study employed the ESDM curriculum and teaching principles within a group setting. Other than accommodations to allow translation to the group context, which are described in Eapen et al. (34), no modifications were made to the ESDM curriculum.

Rogers and Dawson (30) outline a specific teaching approach in the ESDM that was followed in this study. ESDM teaching principles are embedded in play and in natural daily routines within elaborated joint activity routines that address multiple objectives across multiple developmental domains. The main focus is on teaching imitation; developing awareness of social interactions and reciprocity; teaching the power of communication; teaching more flexible, conventional, and creative play skills; making the social world as understandable as the world of objects. Rogers and Dawson (30) contend that just as typically developing children spend their waking hours engaged in the social milieu and learning from it, children with ASD need to be drawn into a carefully prepared and planned social milieu that they can understand, predict, and participate in.

Whilst a primary focus on maladaptive behaviors is not central to the ESDM curriculum, the general approach in this model for children whose level of maladaptive behavior has not improved after 3 weeks of intervention follows the principles of positive behavior supports (36, 37). This is a method of applying the principles of ABA that focus on the use of reinforcement strategies to teach children adaptive and conventional behaviors for meeting their needs and expressing their feelings, as well as promoting independent functioning (30). There were only two children in the current sample whose behavior had not improved after 3 weeks of intervention. For these children, FBA was conducted by the Behavior Analyst on the Intervention team. This process determined the functions of the child's behavior and the consequence that was reinforcing the behavior. This is based on the premise that the behavior is in the child's current repertoire because it leads to a rewarding consequence; therefore the effects of a range of consequences must be tested to determine how the behavior is being reinforced or maintained. The FBA also enabled the Behavior Analyst to identify replacement behaviors that would serve a similar function for the child, but were more conventional behaviors for the child to learn. The ESDM then identifies the skills that can be converted into objectives and targeted in the child's individualized program, so that he/she can quickly learn, master, and generalize the new adaptive behaviors to become part of their behavioral repertoire.

During their attendance at the center, participants received an hour of intensive individualized ESDM therapy each week, in addition to an hour of intensive small group ESDM therapy daily, and ESDM-driven learning experiences throughout the day. Each child also received between 15 and 20 h/week of group ESDM intervention. The one-to-one sessions were conducted by the child's key worker, who carried a caseload of five-to-six children across the period of the intervention. Each child had an individualized treatment plan that incorporated a range of objectives dependent on the child's level of functioning. These objectives were developed from the child's initial assessment using the ESDM curriculum checklist, which includes a list of skills spanning receptive communication; expressive communication; social skills; joint attention behaviors; fine motor; gross motor; imitation; cognition; play skills; behavior; and personal independence (eating, dressing, grooming, and chores).

All interventions were delivered by therapists with tertiary-level qualifications who were trained to certification in the ESDM by an accredited trainer. In order to be certified in direct delivery of this model, therapists were required to achieve: (1) a fidelity rate of 80% or more with the ESDM trainer on each of the 13 ESDM teaching principles across multiple children and sessions, and (2) to achieve the same level of concordance on the individualized written treatment plans they had developed and data they collated on each child. That is, 80% or more concordance was required in both the clinical delivery and data recording aspects of the ESDM, including on the ESDM behavior checklist, which formed a key measure in this study. There were six key workers, each trained in this way, involved in the study. Therapists also continued to receive clinical supervision in their delivery of the ESDM by an Accredited Trainer.

## MEASURES

Pre- and post-measures included the (1) ESDM behavior rating as well as the (2) Vineland Adaptive Behavior Scales, second edition (Parent Form) [VABS-II; (38)]; (3) Social Communication Questionnaire [SCQ; (39)]; and (4) Mullen Scales of Early Learning [MSEL; (40)]. The ESDM behavior rating was also completed 12 weeks after entry to the program.

The rating of children's maladaptive behavior was completed during the child's individual 1 h ESDM session using the ESDM Behavior Coding system. The coding system allows therapists to quantify the child's behavior for each 15-min period, as well as for the hourly session as a whole. The rating for the session as a whole was used in this study. This rating measured the level of maladaptive behavior that was typically present over the hour rather than the best or worst behavior observed during the session.

The Behavior Coding system designed by Rogers and Dawson (30) for measurement of maladaptive behaviors is described below:

1. *Severe problem behaviors* including aggression, self-injurious behavior, frequent and intense tantrums;
2. *Mild problem behaviors* including non-compliance, some tantrums, but able to participate to some extent;
3. *Some problem behaviors* including fussy, whining, some non-compliance, but able to participate in most of the activity;
4. *No problem behavior* but difficulty staying on task;
5. *Compliant* on task, working at ability level;
6. *Above average* performance for that child; pleasant, excited about the activity.

Rating of behavior codes was completed by each child's key worker who conducted their individual ESDM therapy and was responsible for collecting their data within the group program also. These data were then discussed and peer reviewed in daily Key Worker meetings. Discrepancies were discussed with the ESDM trainer. Senior ESDM trainers working in the UC Davis MIND Institute were available to discuss significant discrepancies; however this was not required for any behavioral ratings. All child data, including the behavior codes, were reviewed on a quarterly basis by the ESDM trainer, including through the use of videos of therapy sessions or live viewing (from the observation room) of therapy sessions to ensure ongoing fidelity.

A pre-intervention behavior score was coded on entry to the program (in the therapy session following the initial assessment), a second behavior score was coded after the first 12 weeks of intervention, and a post-intervention behavior score was coded before the child exited the program.

Parents of participating children completed two measures. The VABS-II (38) assesses parents' perceptions of their child's everyday adaptive functioning in the domains of Communication (including expressive and receptive language), Daily Living Skills, Socialization, and Motor Skills. For each domain, including an overall Adaptive Behavior Composite, a norm-referenced standardized score with a mean of 100 and SD of 15 is calculated. *V*-scale scores with a mean of 15 and a SD of 3 and age-equivalent scores are calculated for each sub-domain, including Internalizing Behavior, Externalizing Behavior, and the Maladaptive Behavior Index. The VABS-II has well-established strong psychometric properties (38). The SCQ (39) is a 40-item measure of autism-specific symptoms where scores of 15 or more indicate probable ASD. The SCQ has robust psychometric properties (41–43). These measures were administered at two time points (on entry to and exit from the program). Parents also completed a demographic questionnaire at the start of the study.

In addition, children were assessed at entry to and exit from the program using the MSEL (40), a widely used, standardized measure of early development for children aged from birth to 68 months, yielding standardized *T* Scores and age-equivalent scores on the following subscales: Visual Reception, Fine Motor, Receptive Language, Expressive Language, and Gross Motor. The Gross Motor subscale was not administered in this study. Given the majority of children in the current sample did not receive MSEL subscale raw scores that were high enough for calculation of a meaningful *T* score (i.e., they were performing at a level $<0.1$ percentile), standardized developmental quotients (DQs) were calculated for each subscale of the MSEL by dividing each child's age-equivalent score by their chronological age at the time of testing and multiplying by 100, as is common practice. In this regard, a child who was aged 48 months, but who had an age-equivalent score of 24 months, would receive a DQ of $(24/48) \times 100 = 50$. An overall DQ was also calculated for each child by taking the average of the child's DQs for the four completed subscales in order to provide an estimate of overall intellectual ability. Note that the sum of the *T* scores for these four subscales (i.e., Visual Reception, Fine Motor, Receptive Language, and Expressive Language) is used to calculate the Early Learning Composite Score of the MSEL. It should also be noted that the DQs calculated in this study are not equivalent to *T* scores or the Early Learning Composite Score of the MSEL, but represent an attempt by the study team to standardize scores for the purpose of making comparisons over time.

## STATISTICAL ANALYSIS

Paired samples *t*-tests were conducted to compare children's scores pre- and post-intervention on the aggregate measures of clinician ESDM child behavior ratings; Vineland Adaptive Behavior Composite score; Vineland Maladaptive Behavior Index Score; SCQ total score; and overall MSEL DQ. Cohen's *d* effect sizes were also reported. It is widely accepted that Cohen's *d* values of 0.2–0.49 denote small-sized effects; 0.5–0.79 denote medium-sized effects; and $>0.8$ denote large effect sizes. To explore change, pre- and post-intervention in the subscales of measures used, a series of repeated measures MANOVA analyses were conducted using the Pillai's Trace criterion. The aggregate scores noted above were not included in these MANOVA analyses as these scores were not independent of the subscale scores. Partial eta values were reported as a measure of effect size for MANOVA analyses. Correlations were also computed to investigate relationships between children's behavior and baseline demographic and clinical variables. Analyses were conducted using SPSS statistical software. Alpha was set at 0.05 for the majority comparisons, following recommendations by

Saville (44) who argues for this per-comparison level rather than a family wise approach when conducting research in novel areas. An exception to this was in the instance where multivariate effects detected in the MANOVA analyses were further explored using paired samples $t$-tests. In those cases, a Bonferroni correction was applied.

## RESULTS

The average time between pre- and post-intervention assessment was 11.8 months (SD 5.8). As shown in **Table 1**, a significant reduction in clinician-rated ESDM behavior rating was found, $t(37) = -16.6$, $p < 0.001$. The size of this effect was Cohen's $d = -3.7$, which is large. There was also a significant increase to children's overall MSEL DQ, $t(17) = -5.0$, $p < 0.001$, $d = -0.41$, which approaches a medium-sized effect. There was, however, no significant change in children's VABS-II Adaptive Behavior Composite, VABS-II Maladaptive Behavior Index, or SCQ total scores.

To explore changes in core subscales of the VABS-II, a repeated measures MANOVA was performed with VABS-II standard domain scores as the dependent variables (Communication; Socialization; Daily Living Skills; and Motor Skills). The within-subjects independent variable was time, with two levels (pre-intervention and post-intervention). There was no significant multivariate effect of time $F(1, 11) = 0.18$, $p < 0.05$ or VABS-II subscale scores $F(3, 9) = 2.8$ $p > 0.05$, nor a domain scores by time interaction. With respect to the VABS-II Maladaptive Behavior subscales, a repeated measures MANOVA was performed with Internalizing Behavior and Externalizing Behavior as the dependent variables and time as the within-subjects independent variable. The multivariate effect of time $F(1, 13) = 0.67$, $p < 0.001$ and the time by VABS-II Maladaptive Behavior subscale score interaction $F(1, 13) = 0.18$, $p > 0.05$ were not statistically significant. However, the multivariate effect for subscale scores was significant $F(1, 13) = 23.1$, $p < 0.001$, $\eta_p^2 = 0.64$. When explored further using paired sample $t$-tests with an adjusted alpha rate of

**Table 1 | Pre- to post-intervention scores in a cohort of preschoolers treated with group ESDM.**

| | Pre-intervention | | Post-intervention | | $t$[a] | df | $p$ | Cohen's $d$[h] |
|---|---|---|---|---|---|---|---|---|
| | Mean | SD | Mean | SD | | | | |
| ESDM behavior rating | 1.8 | 1.0 | 5.1 | 0.8 | −16.6 | 37 | <0.001** | −3.67 |
| **VINELAND ADAPTIVE BEHAVIOR SCALES-II STANDARD DOMAIN SCORES** | | | | | | | | |
| Communication[b] | 62.4 | 15.2 | 64.8 | 19.7 | | | | −0.14 |
| Socialization[b] | 66.8 | 14.2 | 63.7 | 13.6 | | | | 0.22 |
| Daily Living Skills[b] | 62.1 | 14.7 | 62.2 | 16.6 | | | | −0.01 |
| Motor Skills[b] | 69.4 | 20.7 | 65.3 | 23.2 | | | | 0.19 |
| Adaptive Behavior Composite[b] | 62.2 | 14.8 | 62.5 | 14.7 | −0.2 | 12 | 0.84 | −0.02 |
| **VINELAND ADAPTIVE BEHAVIOR SCALES-II MALADAPTIVE BEHAVIOR** | | | | | | | | |
| Internalizing Behavior[c] | 19.4 | 1.8 | 18.9 | 4.0 | 0.5 | 13 | 0.60 | 0.17 |
| Externalizing Behavior[c] | 16.0 | 2.2 | 15.1 | 3.0 | 1.0 | 13 | 0.34 | 0.35 |
| Maladaptive Behavior Index[c] | 18.8 | 1.4 | 18.8 | 1.8 | 0.0 | 13 | 1.0 | 0.00 |
| SCQ total score[d] | 18.3 | 6.3 | 17.0 | 7.3 | 1.0 | 13 | 0.34 | 0.19 |
| **MULLEN SCALES OF EARLY LEARNING** | | | | | | | | |
| Visual Reception DQ[e] | 37.2 | 19.9 | 48.3 | 27.3 | −2.7 | 19 | 0.013[g],* | −0.47 |
| Fine Motor DQ[e] | 46.3 | 24.3 | 50.6 | 21.2 | −1.4 | 21 | 0.17[g] | −0.19 |
| Receptive Language DQ[e] | 30.4 | 22.3 | 39.7 | 24.4 | −3.5 | 17 | 0.003[g],** | −0.40 |
| Expressive Language DQ[e] | 33.4 | 18.4 | 40.7 | 20.0 | −4.5 | 20 | <0.001[g],** | −0.38 |
| Overall MSEL DQ[f] | 37.9 | 19.8 | 46.5 | 22.2 | −5.0 | 17 | <0.001[g],** | −0.41 |

**p < 0.05, **p < 0.01, SCQ, Social Communication Questionnaire.*

*For the SCQ total score, lower scores are indicative of fewer ASD symptoms. Similarly, for VABS-II Maladaptive Behavior subscales (Internalizing Behavior, Externalizing Behavior, and Maladaptive Behavior Index), lower scores denote fewer symptoms. For all other measures, higher scores are indicative of better functioning.*

*[a] Paired samples t-tests were conducted a priori for aggregate scores of ESDM behavior rating, VABS-II Adaptive Behavior Composite, VABS-II Maladaptive Behavior Index, SCQ total and overall MSEL DQ. In other instances, paired samples t-tests were conducted only following significant results in multivariate repeated measures MANOVA analyses.*

*[b] Standard score (mean: 100, SD: 15).*

*[c] V-scale score (mean: 15, SD: 3).*

*[d] Range = 0–40. Scores of 15 or more denote probable ASD.*

*[e] DQ (developmental quotient) = (age-equivalent score/chronological age) × 100.*

*[f] Overall MSEL DQ = (Visual Reception DQ + Fine Motor DQ + Receptive Language DQ + Expressive Language DQ)/4.*

*[g] Bonferroni adjusted $\alpha = 0.013$.*

*[h] Following the recommendations of Dunlap et al. (45), Cohen's d scores were calculated using the pooled standard deviation score uncorrected for the correlation between pre-post scores.*

0.05/2 = 0.025 neither of the Internalizing or Externalizing scores changed significantly over time, however effect sizes were non-trivial (see **Table 1**). In the case of the MSEL, a repeated measures MANOVA was performed with Visual Reception DQ, Fine Motor DQ, Receptive Language DQ, and Expressive Language DQ as the dependent variables and time as the within-subjects independent variable. The multivariate effects of MSEL subscale scores $F(3, 15) = 6.5$, $p = 0.005$, $\eta_p^2 = 0.57$ and time $F(1, 17) = 24.69$, $p < 0.001$, $\eta_p^2 = 0.59$ were significant; however, the subscale scores by time interaction were not. When explored further using paired sample $t$-tests with an adjusted alpha rate of 0.05/4 = 0.013, the Visual Reception DQ, Receptive Language DQ, and Expressive Language DQ all showed significant improvement from pre- to post-intervention with effect sizes approaching medium size (see **Table 1**).

To further explore the speed with which improvement in the level of maladaptive behaviors occurred, *post hoc* analyses were conducted using ESDM clinician-rated behavior checklist data obtained at entry, 12 weeks post-entry, and exit from the ESDM program. It emerged that, at entry to the program, only one of the 38 children had a behavior score of 5 or 6 (indicating compliant or above average behavior). This number increased to 26 of 38 children (68%) after 12 weeks of intervention, and to 30 of 38 children (79%) by the end of the intervention.

A related analysis involved examining the number of participants whose scores improved by three points or more on the six point scale (taken to denote a conservative estimate of meaningful change) at the different time points. One participant had an entry score that would preclude improvement by three points; hence subsequent analyses were conducted on the remaining 37 children. After 12 weeks of intervention, 25/37 children (68%) had improved by three or more points (rapid responder sub-group), whereas 32% of children had not responded in this way (non-responder sub-group). By program exit, the non-responder group had dropped to 24% of the sample.

A series of independent samples $t$-tests were conducted to examine whether the rapid responder sub-group differed from the 12-week non-responder sub-group according to baseline variables. Given the relatively small sample size in these analyses, MANOVAs were not performed and Cohen's $d$ effect sizes were also inspected for cases where the effect size was of medium size or larger (Cohen's $d > 0.50$). Analysis revealed that the SCQ score for the rapid responder sub-group (mean = 16.1) was lower than that of the non-responder sub-group (mean = 21.5) at a level that approached significance $t(27) = 1.86$, $p = 0.07$, Cohen's $d = 0.77$, that is, the rapid responder group tended to have lower baseline ASD symptoms than the non-responder group. Other areas where the difference between rapid responder and non-responder groups was above Cohen's $d = 0.5$ at baseline were VABS-II Communication, Daily Living Skills, and Motor Skills Standard Scores. In all instances, the rapid responder group performed better than the non-responder group at baseline.

Correlations between baseline clinical variables and pre- and post-intervention behavior ratings as well as change in behavior ratings are presented in **Table 2**. As shown in **Table 2**, clinician-rated behavior at entry was not significantly related to any baseline clinical variables, including DQs, autism severity, or adaptive behavior (all $ps > 0.05$).

**Table 2 | Correlations between clinician-rated behavior scores and baseline clinical variables.**

| | Entry behavior | Exit behavior | Change in behavior |
|---|---|---|---|
| Entry behavior rating | – | – | – |
| Exit behavior rating | 0.14 | – | – |
| Change in behavior rating | −0.72** | 0.59** | – |
| VABS-II Communication | 0.22 | 0.26 | −0.04 |
| VABS-II Socialization | 0.22 | 0.14 | −0.12 |
| VABS-II Daily Living Skills | 0.25 | 0.42* | −0.02 |
| VABS-II Motor Skills | 0.12 | 0.36 | 0.10 |
| VABS-II ABC | −0.23 | 0.31 | −0.02 |
| VABS-II Internalizing | −0.17 | −0.09 | 0.08 |
| VABS-II Externalizing | −0.05 | 0.37* | 0.28 |
| VABS-II Maladaptive | −0.13 | 0.02 | 0.10 |
| SCQ total | 0.08 | −0.20 | −0.20 |
| SCQ Communication | 0.16 | −0.18 | −0.26 |
| SCQ Restricted Social Interaction | −0.13 | −0.24 | −0.06 |
| SCQ Repetitive Behavior | 0.13 | −0.09 | −0.17 |
| VRDQ | 0.07 | 0.37 | 0.18 |
| FMDQ | 0.17 | 0.55** | 0.21 |
| RLDQ | 0.26 | 0.48* | 0.10 |
| ELDQ | 0.32 | 0.46* | 0.02 |
| Overall DQ | 0.23 | 0.53** | 0.16 |

*$^*p < 0.05$, $^{**}p < 0.01$, VABS-II, Vineland Adaptive Behavior Scales-II; ABC, Adaptive Behavior Composite; SCQ, Social Communication Questionnaire; VRDQ, Visual Reception DQ Score; FMDQ, Fine Motor DQ Score; RLDQ, Receptive Language DQ Score; ELDQ, Expressive Language DQ Score.*

Clinician-rated behavior at exit was shown to be significantly and positively correlated with Fine Motor, Receptive Language, Expressive Language, and overall DQs at entry ($r = 0.46$–$0.55$, $ps < 0.05$). Clinician-rated behavior at exit was also positively correlated with baseline daily living skills ($r = 0.42$, $p < 0.05$), that is, the better a child's daily living skills at entry, the better their clinician-rated behavior at exit. Finally, clinician-rated behavior at exit was found to be positively correlated with baseline externalizing behavior, as measured by standardized VABS-II scores ($r = 0.37$, $p < 0.05$), suggesting that the more problematic a child's externalizing behavior at entry, the better their clinician-rated behavior at exit.

Change in clinician-rated behavior was not found to be significantly associated with any baseline variables (all $ps > 0.05$).

## DISCUSSION

Children with ASD frequently engage in maladaptive behaviors such as aggression, self-injurious behavior, and stereotyped behaviors (7). These behaviors are problematic in group settings, as they disrupt the learning program and place children at increased risk for social exclusion, making it very difficult for them to transition to and access mainstream education settings (13). These behaviors also correlate positively with levels of stress in caregivers (17).

While the genesis of these maladaptive behaviors is thought principally to reside in communication and social skills difficulties, there is some uncertainty in the literature as to whether maladaptive behaviors are best managed via direct behavioral intervention; via treatments targeted primarily at improving pro-social and communicative skills; or via a combination approach. This study sought to examine the behavioral benefits to maladaptive behaviors of the ESDM, an early intervention focused predominantly on improving communication and pro-social skills, within natural daily play and care routines.

Several key findings were obtained. Principally, the level of maladaptive behaviors in the cohort of children studied, as assessed by clinician rating, reduced substantially following the 11-month ESDM intervention period. Moreover, for 68% of the children studied, substantial positive change was observed within the first 12 weeks of intervention. This group, who we have described as "rapid responders" tended to have less severe ASD symptoms at baseline and had a higher level of communication, daily living, and motor skills at baseline compared with children whose level of maladaptive behavior did not respond quickly to the ESDM. The behavior rating obtained at entry was not associated with any of the other baseline variables, which together with the finding that only 1 out of the 38 participants had ratings of good behavior at baseline, suggests that maladaptive behaviors occurred relatively uniformly within the sample. Across the whole sample, the degree of change in behavior rating from pre- to post-intervention was not associated with any baseline variables. However, clinician-rated behavior at exit was shown to be significantly and positively correlated with Fine Motor, Receptive Language, Expressive Language, and overall DQs; daily living skills; higher level of externalizing behavior at entry. In general terms, we would contend therefore that while maladaptive behaviors appear to have been ubiquitous in our cohort, children with relatively better adaptive functioning and fewer ASD symptoms at baseline seemed more likely to show rapid and subsequent improvement in their level of maladaptive behaviors. Overall, however, more than three-quarters of participants showed improvements (of three points on the six point scale) in maladaptive behaviors by the end of the intervention. Given the negative consequences of maladaptive behavior on children's learning (6), the ESDM's ability to bring about reductions in maladaptive behaviors – early in the intervention for around 3/4 of participants – may have allowed children to access and gain from the intervention program more effectively.

Significant improvements were also found following ESDM intervention in MSEL Visual Reception, Receptive Language, Expressive Language, and overall DQs. This is consistent with previous research (27, 34, 35). It is possible that, by promoting child development across domains, particularly receptive and expressive communication, and by using appropriate behavior management strategies, the ESDM resulted in an increase in conventional behaviors and a reduction of maladaptive behaviors. This is consistent with research showing a strong relationship between communication skills and the presence of maladaptive behavior in young children with ASD (8), and provides support for the suggestion by Myers and Johnson (22) that contemporary comprehensive intervention approaches for ASD should target communication and social skills in addition to disruptive or maladaptive behavior.

Furthermore, a child who is highly motivated is also more likely to learn at a faster rate (8). The ESDM works to increase child motivation by incorporating components such as child choice, turn taking, reinforcing attempts, and interspersing maintenance with acquisition tasks (30). The ESDM therapist is also highly trained in managing child attention; delivering clear antecedent, behavior, consequence sequences; modulating child arousal; creating interesting routines; building dyadic engagement though joint activity routines; responding with sensitivity to all child communicative attempts. The teaching principle that targets modulation of child arousal equips ESDM therapists to recognize and respond immediately to changes in child arousal levels and modulate these in the moment, potentially preventing maladaptive behaviors from developing in the first place.

Despite improvements in clinician-rated behavior and developmental skills, maladaptive behavior ratings on the VABS-II did not show improvement from pre- to post-intervention. It is interesting to observe that the externalizing behavior score on the VABS-II did show the largest Cohen's *d* effect size change of any VABS-II score ($d = 0.35$), but this was not statistically significant. One possible explanation for this finding is offered by Weiss et al. (46), who question the validity of the Maladaptive Behavior domain of the VABS-II in assessing levels of maladaptive behavior among children with ASD. It is also important to note that normative data on the VABS are only available for much older children than those in the current sample, and is not available for those with ASD. It is also possible that, while children's behavior during ESDM therapy sessions improved, this improvement did not generalize to the home environment and therefore no changes were found in parent-reported maladaptive behavior. Mastering the teaching principles of the ESDM equips adults to engage, modulate, and motivate the child into an optimal state for learning, hence promoting pro-social behavior. It is possible that the optimal behavior elicited during ESDM sessions was not replicated in other settings as parents or other caregivers were not similarly equipped with the skill set to elicit these pro-social behaviors. This suggestion highlights the potential importance of training parents and other professionals, such as those in school settings, in the ESDM model in order to provide the child adequate opportunities to generalize their newly acquired skills, and ideally of future research to explore the relative outcome for children in groups where parents had, or had not received intervention. We note that there was no specific parent training component to the ESDM intervention applied in this study; however, optional parent education evenings were offered at the center. Similarly, no significant improvements were found in the VABS-II standard domain scores or on the SCQ. This could again be attributable to these measures being parent reports, and skills not generalizing to the home setting; however, the lack of change observed in the current study on the SCQ is inconsistent with findings of significant improvement on this measure by Eapen et al. (34).

Findings of reduced clinician-rated maladaptive behavior and accelerated developmental rates in the present study are promising; however, due to the design of the current study, it is not possible to make conclusions about the mechanisms behind these improvements. That is, it is not possible to determine whether the reduction in maladaptive behavior observed in the present study was a consequence of the ESDM's focus on social attention, affect sharing, imitation, and joint attention, or whether it was due to the use of behavioral techniques that are not specific to the ESDM, such as FBA and positive behavior supports, which have previously been shown to be effective in managing behavior within the framework of multiple treatment approaches. While ABA principles, FBA, and positive behavior supports are integral components of the ESDM, it is important to note that their specific implementation was only required for 2 of the 38 children in the present study whose behavior had not significantly improved after 3 weeks of intervention. It is therefore unlikely that the improvements in maladaptive behavior observed in the present study were directly and solely attributable to these behavioral strategies. Nonetheless, it is necessary to replicate the present study using a larger cohort and control conditions (both a different treatment condition and a non-treatment condition) in order to establish whether the reductions in maladaptive behavior occurring during ESDM intervention are significantly different to reductions that may occur in the context of a different treatment program or by maturation alone.

Regardless of the exact mechanisms behind the improvements in maladaptive behavior in the present study, our findings suggest that the ESDM program may be an effective tool in improving not only core developmental domains, but also decreasing maladaptive behaviors in preschool-aged children. This finding is important, given previous research demonstrating the negative impact of maladaptive behaviors and developmental delays on the child's learning acquisition and the development of social relationships (6). The relatively quick reduction in maladaptive behaviors observed in the present study (68% of children showed a significant decrease in maladaptive behavior by 12 weeks) may allow children to more effectively participate in and benefit from learning opportunities, including the intervention itself, and may be a key factor in the developmental gains observed in the present study and previous research (27, 34, 35). It is hypothesized that these developmental gains, particularly in the areas of receptive and expressive communication, may then provide children with adaptive means of getting their needs met, thereby further reducing maladaptive behaviors.

## LIMITATIONS

This pilot study was limited by the use of a clinician-rated behavior score as the main dependent variable, particularly given that there were no blind raters on any measures. The fact that significant improvements were found in this rating over the course of the intervention, despite no change in VABS-II Internalizing, Externalizing, or Overall Maladaptive Behavior, raises questions over the reliability and validity of the ESDM clinician-rated behavior score. However, as noted previously, the validity of the VABS-II in assessing levels of maladaptive behavior among children with ASD has been questioned (46). Furthermore, the achievement of inter-rater reliability is fundamental to becoming certified as an ESDM therapist, with a requirement of initial and ongoing consistency of ratings with peers and the ESDM trainer. The fact that 32% of children did not show a change of three or more points in clinician-rated behavior over the first 12 weeks of the intervention is also an argument against rater bias.

A further limitation of the present study was the lack of a control group, which makes it difficult to determine whether the observed behavioral and developmental improvements were the effect of maturation or the intervention. Literature suggests, however, that maladaptive behaviors, once they become part of a child's behavioral repertoire, will typically remain or worsen without intervention (12). Moreover, the size of the improvement in maladaptive behaviors observed was large $d = 3.67$, which suggests that maturation alone is unlikely to be the causative factor. Similarly, the common course among children with severe ASD presentations without intervention is for IQ to remain the same or regress (47). The children in the current study had relatively severe presentations, including MSEL DQs <47 and VABS-II adaptive behavior scores within the range of 62–70 at baseline. Therefore, it appears that the behavioral and developmental improvements observed from pre- to post-intervention in this study are unlikely to arise as a result of maturation. The uncontrolled design of the present study also means that it is not possible to determine whether the observed reductions in maladaptive behavior were the result of ESDM-specific principles or to behavioral techniques that are not specific to the ESDM. Therefore, replication of the present study using a larger cohort and control conditions is necessary. Follow-up studies are also required to determine whether the behavioral and developmental improvements observed in the present study are maintained, which has the potential to foster ongoing educational opportunities and improve quality of life for children with ASD and their families.

Since maladaptive and challenging behaviors often pose a barrier to inclusion and community participation with significant consequences on social and educational opportunities, harm or injury to self or others, and family distress, it is critical to address these behaviors in the comprehensive management of children with ASD. The findings of the present study are promising, suggesting that the ESDM delivered in a community setting with relatively minimal one-to-one intensive therapy has the potential to reduce children's maladaptive behaviors which, in turn, may increase their capacity to participate in intervention and educational programs and make gains in other developmental domains.

## ACKNOWLEDGMENTS

KU Marcia Burgess ASELCC in Liverpool, NSW, Australia, was established by KU Children's Services with the University of New South Wales (UNSW) as research partner through Australian Government funding. The authors would like to thank the staff and families who participated in the project and in particular Kate Piromalli and Tara Shine who assisted in collecting the data and Dr. Roger Blackmore for his assistance with reliability checks and peer support. Dr. Laurie Vismara and Dr. Cynthia Zierhut of the MIND Institute UC Davis provided assistance with ESDM training and peer support. We would also like to acknowledge the research funding from the Australian Government and the support provided by the management of KU Children's Services in conducting this research, especially the six Key Workers and the Manager, Anne Lawrence.

## REFERENCES

1. APA. *Diagnostic and Statistical Manual of Mental Disorders – Fifth Edition (DSM-5)*. Washington, DC: American Psychiatric Publishing (2013).

2. Elsabbagh M, Divan G, Koh YJ, Kim YS, Kauchali S, Marcin C, et al. Global prevalence of autism and other pervasive developmental disorders. *Autism Res* (2012) **5**(3):160–79. doi:10.1002/aur.239
3. Centers for Disease Control and Prevention. Prevalence of autism spectrum disorders – autism and developmental disabilities monitoring network, 14 sites, United States, 2008. *MMWR Surveill Summ* (2012) **61**(3):1–19.
4. Simonoff E, Pickles A, Charman T, Chandler S, Loucas T, Baird G. Psychiatric disorders in children with autism spectrum disorders: prevalence, comorbidity, and associated factors in a population-derived sample. *J Am Acad Child Adolesc Psychiatry* (2008) **47**(8):921–9. doi:10.1097/CHI.0b013e318179964f
5. Maskey M, Warnell F, Parr JR, Le Couteur A, McConachie H. Emotional and behavioural problems in children with autism spectrum disorder. *J Autism Dev Disord* (2012) **43**(4):851–9. doi:10.1007/s10803-012-1622-9
6. Pearson DA, Loveland KA, Lachar D, Lane DM, Reddoch SL, Mansour R, et al. A comparison of behavioral and emotional functioning in children and adolescents with autistic disorder and PDD-NOS. *Child Neuropsychol* (2006) **12**(4–5):321–33. doi:10.1080/09297040600646847
7. Dominick KC, Davis NO, Lainhart J, Tager-Flusberg H, Folstein S. Atypical behaviors in children with autism and children with a history of language impairment. *Res Dev Disabil* (2007) **28**(2):145–62. doi:10.1016/j.ridd.2006.02.003
8. Vismara LA, Rogers SJ. Behavioral treatments in autism spectrum disorder: what do we know? *Annu Rev Clin Psychol* (2010) **6**:447–68. doi:10.1146/annurev.clinpsy.121208.131151
9. McClintock K, Hall S, Oliver C. Risk markers associated with challenging behaviours in people with intellectual disabilities: a meta-analytic study. *J Intellect Disabil Res* (2003) **47**(6):405–16. doi:10.1046/j.1365-2788.2003.00517.x
10. Durand VM, Carr EG. Functional communication training to reduce challenging behavior: maintenance and application in new settings. *J Appl Behav Anal* (1991) **24**(2):251–64. doi:10.1901/jaba.1991.24-251
11. Grace R, Llewellyn G, Wedgwood N, Fenech M, McConnell D. Far from ideal everyday experiences of mothers and early childhood professionals negotiating an inclusive early childhood experience in the Australian context. *Topics Early Child Spec Educ* (2008) **28**(1):18–30. doi:10.1177/0271121407313525
12. Berg WK, Peck S, Wacker DP, Harding J, McComas J, Richman D, et al. The effects of presession exposure to attention on the results of assessments of attention as a reinforcer. *J Appl Behav Anal* (2000) **33**(4):463–77. doi:10.1901/jaba.2000.33-463
13. Horner RH, Carr EG, Strain PS, Todd AW, Reed HK. Problem behavior interventions for young children with autism: a research synthesis. *J Autism Dev Disord* (2002) **32**(5):423–46. doi:10.1023/A:1020593922901
14. Allik H, Larsson J-O, Smedje H. Health-related quality of life in parents of school-age children with Asperger syndrome or high-functioning autism. *Health Qual Life Outcomes* (2006) **4**(1):1–8. doi:10.1186/1477-7525-4-1
15. Bromley J, Hare DJ, Davison K, Emerson E. Mothers supporting children with autistic spectrum disorders social support, mental health status and satisfaction with services. *Autism* (2004) **8**(4):409–23. doi:10.1177/1362361304047224
16. Davis NO, Carter AS. Parenting stress in mothers and fathers of toddlers with autism spectrum disorders: associations with child characteristics. *J Autism Dev Disord* (2008) **38**(7):1278–91. doi:10.1007/s10803-007-0512-z
17. Hastings RP, Kovshoff H, Ward NJ, Degli Espinosa F, Brown T, Remington B. Systems analysis of stress and positive perceptions in mothers and fathers of pre-school children with autism. *J Autism Dev Disord* (2005) **35**(5):635–44. doi:10.1007/s10803-005-0007-8
18. Konstantareas MM, Papageorgiou V. Effects of temperament, symptom severity and level of functioning on maternal stress in Greek children and youth with ASD. *Autism* (2006) **10**(6):593–607. doi:10.1177/1362361306068511
19. Stuart M, McGrew JH. Caregiver burden after receiving a diagnosis of an autism spectrum disorder. *Res Autism Spectr Disord* (2009) **3**(1):86–97. doi:10.1016/j.rasd.2008.04.006
20. Tomanik S, Harris GE, Hawkins J. The relationship between behaviours exhibited by children with autism and maternal stress. *J Intellect Dev Disabil* (2004) **29**(1):16–26. doi:10.1080/13668250410001662892
21. Koegel LK, Koegel RL, Dunlap G. *Positive Behavioral Support*. Baltimore, MD: Paul H Brookes (1996).
22. Myers SM, Johnson CP. Management of children with autism spectrum disorders. *Pediatrics* (2007) **120**(5):1162–82. doi:10.1542/peds.2007-2362
23. Maag JW. Managing resistance. *Interv Sch Clin* (2000) **35**(3):131–40. doi:10.1177/105345120003500301
24. Makrygianni MK, Reed P. A meta-analytic review of the effectiveness of behavioural early intervention programs for children with autistic spectrum disorders. *Res Autism Spectr Disord* (2010) **4**(4):577–93. doi:10.1016/j.rasd.2010.01.014
25. Perry A, Cummings A, Geier JD, Freeman NL, Hughes S, Managhan T, et al. Predictors of outcome for children receiving intensive behavioral intervention in a large, community-based program. *Res Autism Spectr Disord* (2011) **5**(1):592–603. doi:10.1016/j.rasd.2010.07.003
26. Dawson G. Early behavioral intervention, brain plasticity, and the prevention of autism spectrum disorder. *Dev Psychopathol* (2008) **20**(3):775–803. doi:10.1017/S0954579408000370
27. Dawson G, Rogers S, Munson J, Smith M, Winter J, Greenson J, et al. Randomized, controlled trial of an intervention for toddlers with autism: the Early Start Denver Model. *Pediatrics* (2010) **125**:e17–23. doi:10.1542/peds.2009-0958
28. Seida JK, Ospina MB, Karkhaneh M, Hartling L, Smith V, Clark B. Systematic reviews of psychosocial interventions for autism: an umbrella review. *Dev Med Child Neurol* (2009) **51**(2):95–104. doi:10.1111/j.1469-8749.2008.03211.x
29. Prior M, Roberts J, Rodger S, Williams K, Sutherland R. *A Review of the Research to Identify the Most Effective Models of Practice in Early Intervention of Children with Autism Spectrum Disorders*. Australian Government Department of Families, Housing, Community Services and Indigenous Affairs (2011).
30. Rogers SJ, Dawson G. *Early Start Denver Model for Young Children with Autism: Promoting Language, Learning, and Engagement*. New York: The Guilford Press (2010).
31. Reichow B. Overview of meta-analyses on early intensive behavioral intervention for young children with autism spectrum disorders. *J Autism Dev Disord* (2012) **42**(4):512–20. doi:10.1007/s10803-011-1218-9
32. Granpeesheh D, Tarbox J, Dixon DR. Applied behavior analytic interventions for children with autism: a description and review of treatment research. *Ann Clin Psychiatry* (2009) **21**(3):162–73.
33. Wallace KS, Rogers SJ. Intervening in infancy: implications for autism spectrum disorders. *J Child Psychol Psychiatry* (2010) **51**(12):1300–20. doi:10.1111/j.1469-7610.2010.02308.x
34. Eapen V, Črnčec R, Walter A. Clinical outcomes of an early intervention program for preschool children with autism spectrum disorder in a community group setting. *BMC Pediatr* (2013) **13**(1):3. doi:10.1186/1471-2431-13-3
35. Vivanti G, Dissanayake C, Zierhut C, Rogers SJ, Victorian ASELCC Team. Brief report: predictors of outcomes in the Early Start Denver Model delivered in a group setting. *J Autism Dev Disord* (2013) **43**(7):1717–24. doi:10.1007/s10803-012-1705-7
36. Carr EG, Dunlap G, Horner RH, Koegel RL, Turnbull AP, Sailor W, et al. Positive behavior support evolution of an applied science. *J Posit Behav Interv* (2002) **4**(1):4–16. doi:10.1177/109830070200400102
37. Duda MA, Dunlap G, Fox L, Lentini R, Clarke S. An experimental evaluation of positive behavior support in a community preschool program. *Topics Early Child Spec Educ* (2004) **24**(3):143–55. doi:10.1177/02711214040240030201
38. Sparrow S, Cicchetti D, Balla D. *Vineland Adaptive Behavior Scales: (Vineland II), Survey Interview Form/Caregiver Rating Form*. Livonia, MN: Pearson Assessments (2005).
39. Rutter M, Bailey A, Lord C. *The Social Communication Questionnaire: Manual*. Los Angeles, CA: Western Psychological Services (2003).
40. Mullen EM. *Mullen Scales of Early Learning*. San Antonio, TX: Pearson (1995).
41. Chandler S, Charman T, Baird G, Simonoff E, Loucas T, Meldrum D, et al. Validation of the social communication questionnaire in a population cohort of children with autism spectrum disorders. *J Am Acad Child Adolesc Psychiatry* (2007) **46**(10):1324–32. doi:10.1097/chi.0b013e31812f7d8d
42. Skuse DH, Mandy WP, Scourfield J. Measuring autistic traits: heritability, reliability and validity of the social and communication disorders checklist. *Br J Psychiatry* (2005) **187**(6):568–72. doi:10.1192/bjp.187.6.568
43. Snow AV, Lecavalier L. Sensitivity and specificity of the modified checklist for autism in toddlers and the social communication questionnaire in preschoolers suspected of having pervasive developmental disorders. *Autism* (2008) **12**(6):627–44. doi:10.1177/1362361308097116

44. Saville DJ. Multiple comparison procedures: the practical solution. *Am Stat* (1990) **44**(2):174–80. doi:10.1080/00031305.1990.10475712
45. Dunlap WP, Cortina JM, Vaslow JB, Burke MJ. Meta-analysis of experiments with matched groups or repeated measures designs. *Psychol Methods* (1996) **1**:170–7. doi:10.1037/1082-989X.1.2.170
46. Weiss O, Perry A, Wells K. Brief report: maladaptive behaviour in autism. *J Dev Disab* (2010) **16**(2):69–71.
47. Begovac I, Begovac B, Majic G, Vidovic V. Longitudinal studies of IQ stability in children with childhood autism – literature survey. *Psychiatr Danub* (2009) **21**(3):310–9.

# Permissions

All chapters in this book were first published in NTPASD, by Frontiers; hereby published with permission under the Creative Commons Attribution License or equivalent. Every chapter published in this book has been scrutinized by our experts. Their significance has been extensively debated. The topics covered herein carry significant findings which will fuel the growth of the discipline. They may even be implemented as practical applications or may be referred to as a beginning point for another development.

The contributors of this book come from diverse backgrounds, making this book a truly international effort. This book will bring forth new frontiers with its revolutionizing research information and detailed analysis of the nascent developments around the world.

We would like to thank all the contributing authors for lending their expertise to make the book truly unique.

They have played a crucial role in the development of this book. Without their invaluable contributions this book wouldn't have been possible. They have made vital efforts to compile up to date information on the varied aspects of this subject to make this book a valuable addition to the collection of many professionals and students.

This book was conceptualized with the vision of imparting up-to-date information and advanced data in this field. To ensure the same, a matchless editorial board was set up. Every individual on the board went through rigorous rounds of assessment to prove their worth. After which they invested a large part of their time researching and compiling the most relevant data for our readers.

The editorial board has been involved in producing this book since its inception. They have spent rigorous hours researching and exploring the diverse topics which have resulted in the successful publishing of this book. They have passed on their knowledge of decades through this book. To expedite this challenging task, the publisher supported the team at every step. A small team of assistant editors was also appointed to further simplify the editing procedure and attain best results for the readers.

Apart from the editorial board, the designing team has also invested a significant amount of their time in understanding the subject and creating the most relevant covers. They scrutinized every image to scout for the most suitable representation of the subject and create an appropriate cover for the book.

The publishing team has been an ardent support to the editorial, designing and production team. Their endless efforts to recruit the best for this project, has resulted in the accomplishment of this book. They are a veteran in the field of academics and their pool of knowledge is as vast as their experience in printing. Their expertise and guidance has proved useful at every step. Their uncompromising quality standards have made this book an exceptional effort. Their encouragement from time to time has been an inspiration for everyone.

The publisher and the editorial board hope that this book will prove to be a valuable piece of knowledge for researchers, students, practitioners and scholars across the globe.

# List of Contributors

**Giada Cellot**
Department of Neuroscience, Scuola Internazionale Superiore di Studi Avanzati, Trieste, Italy

**Enrico Cherubini**
Department of Neuroscience, Scuola Internazionale Superiore di Studi Avanzati, Trieste, Italy
European Brain Research Institute, Rome, Italy

**Silvia Giovedí and Anna Corradi**
Department of Experimental Medicine, University of Genova, Genova, Italy

**Anna Fassio and Fabio Benfenati**
Department of Experimental Medicine, University of Genova, Genova, Italy
Department of Neuroscience and Brain Technologies, Fondazione Istituto Italiano di Tecnologia, Genova, Italy

**Giovanni Provenzano, Elena Clementi, Sacha Genovesi and Paola Sgadò**
Laboratory of Molecular Neuropathology, Centre for Integrative Biology (CIBIO), University of Trento, Trento, Italy

**Manuela Scali and Prem PrakashTripathi**
Neuroscience Institute, National Research Council (CNR), Pisa, Italy
Laboratory of Neurobiology, Scuola Normale Superiore, Pisa, Italy

**Yuri Bozzi**
Laboratory of Molecular Neuropathology, Centre for Integrative Biology (CIBIO), University of Trento, Trento, Italy
Neuroscience Institute, National Research Council (CNR), Pisa, Italy

**Valentina Gigliucci**
Institute of Neuroscience, National Research Council, Milan, Italy

**Marianna Leonzino, Marta Busnelli and Bice Chini**
Institute of Neuroscience, National Research Council, Milan, Italy
Dipartimento di Biotecnologie e Medicina Traslazionale, Università degli Studi di Milano, Milan, Italy

**Alessandra Luchetti and Viola Stella Palladino**
Institute of Cellular Biology and Neurobiology, National Research Council, Rome, Italy

**Francesca R. D'Amato**
Institute of Cellular Biology and Neurobiology, National Research Council, Rome, Italy
IRCCS Santa Lucia Foundation, Rome, Italy

**Andrew Argyropoulos and Krista L. Gilby**
Department of Medicine, The University of Melbourne, Parkville, VIC, Australia

**Elisa L. Hill-Yardin**
Department of Physiology, The University of Melbourne, Parkville, VIC, Australia

**Lisa M. Unwin and Andrew J. O. Whitehouse**
School of Psychology, The University ofWestern Australia, Perth,WA, Australia
Telethon Institute for Child Health Research, Centre for Child Health Research, The University ofWestern Australia, Perth,WA, Australia

**MurrayT. Maybery**
School of Psychology, The University ofWestern Australia, Perth,WA, Australia

**John A.Wray**
Child and Adolescent Health Service, State Child Development Centre, Princess Margaret Hospital for Children, Perth,WA, Australia

**Lucia Billeci and Giovanni Pioggia**
Institute of Clinical Physiology, National Council of Research (CNR), Pisa, Italy

**Federico Sicca, Giulia Campatelli, Sara Calderoni and Fabio Apicella**
IRCCS Stella Maris Foundation, Pisa, Italy

**Koushik Maharatna**
Electronics and Computer Science, Faculty of Physical and Applied Sciences, University of Southampton, Southampton, United Kingdom

**Antonio Narzisi and Filippo Muratori**
IRCCS Stella Maris Foundation, Pisa, Italy
Department of Developmental Medicine, University of Pisa, Pisa, Italy

**Rhoshel K. Lenroot and Pui KaYeung**
School of Psychiatry, University of New SouthWales, Sydney, NSW, Australia
Neuroscience Research Australia, Sydney, NSW, Australia

**IrinaVoineagu**
School of Biotechnology and Biomolecular Sciences, University of New SouthWales, Sydney, NSW, Australia

**Valsamma Eapen**
Department of Infant, Child and Adolescent Psychiatry, Academic Unit of Child Psychiatry, University of New SouthWales, SouthWest Sydney, Sydney, NSW, Australia

**Blythe A. Corbett, Lydia R. Qualls and Stéphanie-M. Fecteau**
Department of Psychiatry, Vanderbilt University, Nashville, TN, USA
Vanderbilt Kennedy Center, Nashville, TN, USA

**BlytheValencia**
Vanderbilt Child Studies, Nashville, TN, USA

**Deanna M. Swain**
Virginia Polytechnic Institute and State University, Blacksburg, VA, USA

**Caterina Michetti**
Neurotoxicology and Neuroendocrinology Section, Department of Cell Biology and Neuroscience, Istituto Superiore di Sanità, Rome, Italy
Department of Physiology and Pharmacology "V. Erspamer", Sapienza University of Rome, Rome, Italy

**Emilia Romano**
Behavioural Neuroscience Section, Department of Cell Biology and Neuroscience, Istituto Superiore di Sanità, Rome, Italy
Bambino Gesù Children's Hospital, Istituto Di Ricovero e Cura a Carattere Scientifico, Rome, Italy

**Luisa Altabella**
Molecular and Cellular Imaging Section, Department of Cell Biology and Neuroscience, Istituto Superiore di Sanità, Rome, Italy

**Angela Caruso**
Neurotoxicology and Neuroendocrinology Section, Department of Cell Biology and Neuroscience, Istituto Superiore di Sanità, Rome, Italy
Department of Psychology, School of Behavioural Neuroscience, Sapienza University of Rome, Rome, Italy

**Paolo Castelluccio and Maria Luisa Scattoni**
Neurotoxicology and Neuroendocrinology Section, Department of Cell Biology and Neuroscience, Istituto Superiore di Sanità, Rome, Italy

**Gaurav Bedse and Silvana Gaetani**
Department of Physiology and Pharmacology "V. Erspamer", Sapienza University of Rome, Rome, Italy

**Rossella Canese**
Molecular and Cellular Imaging Section, Department of Cell Biology and Neuroscience, Istituto Superiore di Sanità, Rome, Italy

**Giovanni Laviola**
Behavioural Neuroscience Section, Department of Cell Biology and Neuroscience, Istituto Superiore di Sanità, Rome, Italy

**GiacomoVivanti**
Olga Tennison Autism Research Centre, School of Psychological Science, La Trobe University, Melbourne, VIC, Australia
Victorian Autism Specific Early Learning and Care Centre, La Trobe University, Melbourne, VIC, Australia

**Josephine Barbaro, Kristelle Hudry and Cheryl Dissanayake**
Olga Tennison Autism Research Centre, School of Psychological Science, La Trobe University, Melbourne, VIC, Australia

**Roberto Canitano**
Division of Child Neuropsychiatry, University Hospital of Siena, Siena, Italy

**SylvieTordjman and Solenn Kermarrec**
Laboratoire Psychologie de la Perception, Université Paris Descartes, CNRS, UMR 8158, Paris, France
Pôle Hospitalo-Universitaire de Psychiatrie de l'Enfant et de l'Adolescent (PHUPEA), Centre Hospitalier Guillaume Régnier, Université de Rennes 1, Rennes, France

**Katherine S. Davlantis and Geraldine Dawson**
Department of Psychiatry and Behavioral Sciences, Duke University School of Medicine, Durham, NC, USA

**Nicolas Georgieff and Marie-Maude Geoffray**
Department of Child and Adolescent Psychiatry, Centre Hospitalier Le Vinatier, Lyon, France

**Mario Speranza**
Department of Child and Adolescent Psychiatry, Centre Hospitalier de Versailles, Université de Versailles Saint-Quentin-en-Yvelines, Le Chensay, France

**George M. Anderson**
Child Study Center, Yale University School of Medicine, New Haven, CT, USA

**Jean Xavier and David Cohen**
Department of Child and Adolescent Psychiatry, Assistance Publique – Hôpitaux de Paris, Groupe Hospitalier Pitié-Salpêtrière, CNRS FRE 2987, University Pierre and Marie Curie, Paris, France

**Michel Botbol**
Laboratoire Psychologie de la Perception, Université Paris Descartes, CNRS, UMR 8158, Paris, France
Service Hospitalo-Universitaire de Psychiatrie de l'Enfant et de l'Adolescent, CHU de Brest, Université de Bretagne Occidentale, Brest, France

**Cécile Oriol**
Pôle Hospitalo-Universitaire de Psychiatrie de l'Enfant et de l'Adolescent (PHUPEA), Centre Hospitalier Guillaume Régnier, Université de Rennes 1, Rennes, France

**Eric Bellissant**
Clinical Investigation Center, INSERM CIC 0203, University Hospital, Rennes 1 University, Rennes, France
Department of Clinical Pharmacology, University Hospital, Rennes 1 University, Rennes, Franc

**JulieVernay-Leconte**
Pôle Hospitalo-Universitaire de Psychiatrie Adulte (PHUPA), Centre Hospitalier Guillaume Régnier, Université de Rennes 1, Rennes, France

**Claire Fougerou, Anne Hespel and AudeTavenard**
Clinical Investigation Center, INSERM CIC 0203, University Hospital, Rennes 1 University, Rennes, France
Department of Clinical Pharmacology, University Hospital, Rennes 1 University, Rennes, France

**Nathalie Coulon and Olivier Bonnot**
Laboratoire Psychologie de la Perception, Université Paris Descartes, CNRS, UMR 8158, Paris, France

**Molly Losh and Abigail L. Hogan-Brown**
Roxelyn and Richard Pepper Department of Communication Sciences and Disorders, Northwestern University, Evanston, IL, USA

**Gary E. Martin and Jessica Klusek**
Frank Porter Graham Child Development Institute, University of North Carolina at Chapel Hill, Chapel Hill, NC, USA
Division of Speech and Hearing Sciences, Department of Allied Health Sciences, University of North Carolina at Chapel Hill, Chapel Hill, NC, USA

**John Sideris**
Frank Porter Graham Child Development Institute, University of North Carolina at Chapel Hill, Chapel Hill, NC, USA

**Claire Amiet**
IntegraGen, Evry, France
Department of Child and Adolescent Psychiatry, AP-HP, Groupe Hospitalier Pitié-Salpêtrière, Université Pierre et Marie Curie, Paris, France

**Jerôme Carayol**
IntegraGen, Evry, France

**Elizabeth Couchon**
IntegraGen Inc., Cambridge, MA, USA

**Kelly Carr**
University of Notre Dame, South Bend, IN, USA

**Daniel A. Rossignol**
Rossignol Medical Center, Irvine, CA, USA

**Richard E. Frye**
Arkansas Children's Hospital Research Institute, University of Arkansas for Medical Sciences, Little Rock, AR, USA

**Margot Prior**
Olga Tennison Autism Research Centre, School of Psychological Science, La Trobe University, Melbourne, VIC, Australia
School of Psychological Sciences, University of Melbourne, Melbourne, VIC, Australia

**Katrina Williams**
Department of Pediatrics, University of Melbourne, Melbourne, VIC, Australia

**StephenW. Porges, Keri J. Heilman and Gregory F. Lewis**
Department of Psychiatry, University of North Carolina at Chapel Hill, Chapel Hill, NC, USA

**OlgaV. Bazhenova, Elgiz Bal, Yevgeniya Sorokin and Edwin H. Cook**
Department of Psychiatry, Institute for Juvenile Research, University of Illinois at Chicago, Chicago, IL, USA

**Nancy Carlson**
Department of Occupational Therapy, Elizabethtown College, Elizabethtown, PA, USA

**Eleonora Napoli and Nadia Dueñas**
Department of Molecular Biosciences, University of California Davis, Davis, CA, USA

**Cecilia Giulivi**
Department of Molecular Biosciences, University of California Davis, Davis, CA, USA
Medical Investigations of Neurodevelopmental Disorders (M. I. N. D.) Institute, Sacramento, CA, USA

**Giorgio Pini, M. Flora Scusa, Alberto Benincasa, Ilaria Bottiglioni, Laura Congiu, Anna Maria Romanelli, Ilaria Gemo and Chetti Puccetti**
Tuscany Rett Center, Versilia Hospital, Viareggio, Italy

**CyrusVadhatpour, Rachel McNamara and Seán O'Leary**
Medical School, Trinity College Dublin, Dublin, Ireland

**Aiden Corvin and Michael Gill**
Department of Psychiatry, Trinity College Dublin, Dublin, Ireland

**DanielaTropea**
Tuscany Rett Center, Versilia Hospital, Viareggio, Italy
Department of Psychiatry, Trinity College Dublin, Dub-lin, Ireland

**Valsamma Eapen and AmeliaWalter**
Academic Unit of Child Psychiatry SouthWest Sydney, SouthWestern Sydney Local Health District, Liverpool, NSW, Australia
School of Psychiatry, University of New SouthWales, Sydney, NSW, Australia

**Rudi Črnčec**
School of Psychiatry, University of New SouthWales, Sydney, NSW, Australia

**Rachel Maree Jones, Gemma Cadby, Phillip E. Melton and Eric K. Moses**
Centre for Genetic Origins of Health and Disease, University ofWestern Australia, Perth,WA, Australia

**Lawrence J. Abraham**
Centre for Genetic Origins of Health and Disease, University ofWestern Australia, Perth,WA, Australia
School of Chemistry and Biochemistry, University ofWestern Australia, Perth,WA, Australia

**Andrew J. Whitehouse**
Telethon Institute for Child Health Research, Perth,WA, Australia

**Elizabeth Fulton**
KU Marcia Burgess Autism Specific Early Learning and Care Centre (ASELCC), Liverpool, NSW, Australia
Academic Unit of Child Psychiatry, School of Psychiatry, University of New SouthWales, Sydney, NSW, Australia

**Sally Rogers**
School of Psychiatry and Behavioral Sciences, University of California Davis Medical Center MIND Institute, Davis, CA, USA

# Index

## O



## P



## Q



## R



## S



## T



## U

www.ingramcontent.com/pod-product-compliance
Lightning Source LLC
LaVergne TN
LVHW080928210926
848485LV00004B/753
* 9 7 8 1 6 3 9 8 7 0 6 6 0 *